DIRTY OLD TANK GIRL

Martin Dayglo McMahon

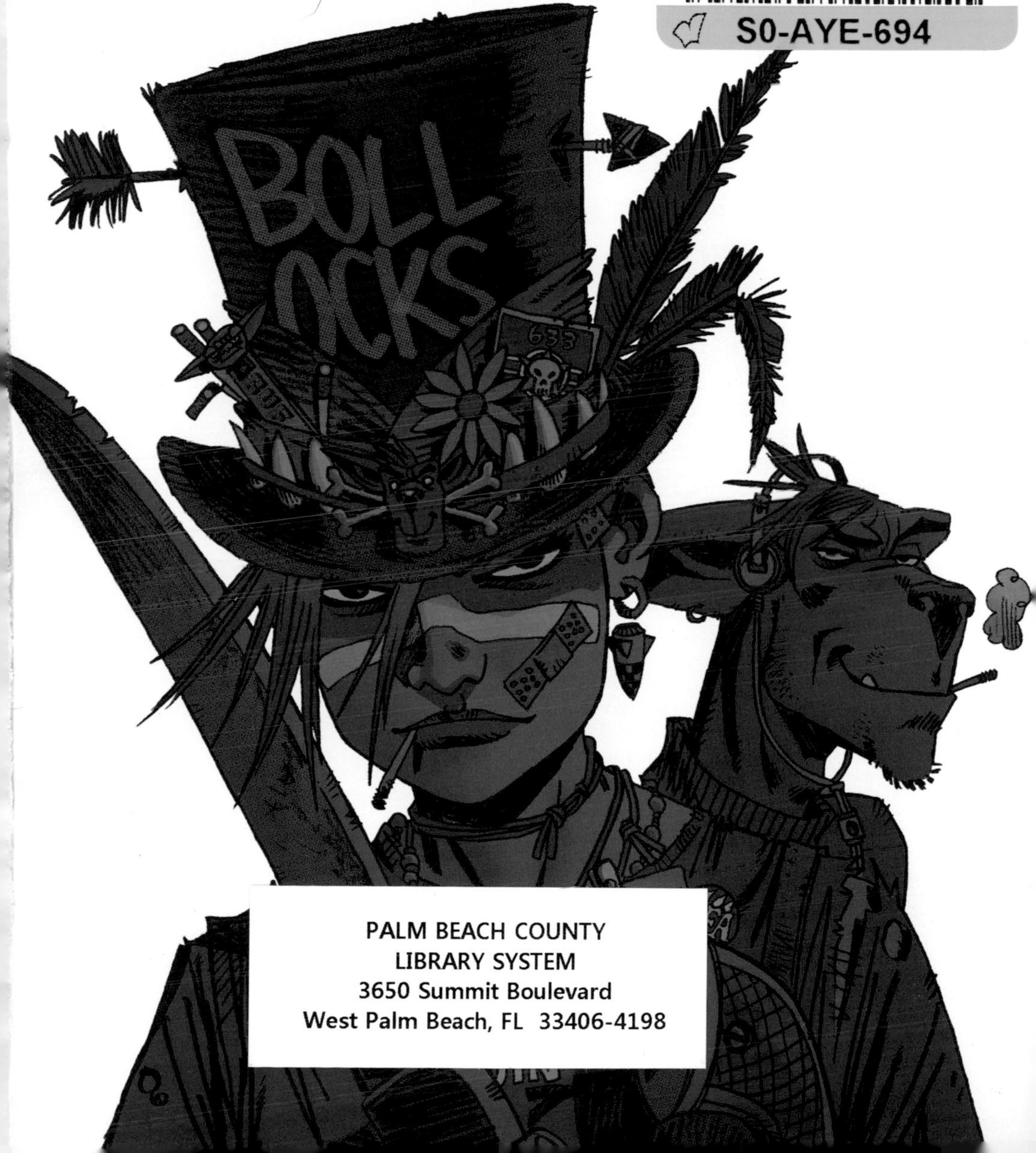
BOLL
OCKS

DIRTY OLD
TANK GIRL

WRITTEN BY
ALAN MARTIN

'SKIDMARKS'
DRAWN BY
RUFUS DAYGLO

COLOURED BY
CHRISTIAN KRANK

LETTERED BY
SIMON BOWLAND

'CARIOCA'
DRAWN BY
MICK MCMAHON

LETTERED BY
JIMMY BETANCOURT
COMICRAFT

FRONT COVER BY
BRETT PARSON

TITAN COMICS

SENIOR DESIGNER
ANDREW LEUNG

DESIGNER
DONNA ASKEM

MANAGING & LAUNCH EDITOR **ANDREW JAMES**	ART DIRECTOR **OZ BROWNE**	PUBLICIST **IMOGEN HARRIS**	PUBLISHING MANAGER **DARRYL TOTHILL**
DEPUTY EDITOR **JONATHAN STEVENSON**	SENIOR SALES MANAGER **STEVE TOTHILL**	ADS & MARKETING ASSISTANT **BELLA HOY**	PUBLISHING DIRECTOR **CHRIS TEATHER**
SENIOR PRODUCTION CONTROLLER **JACKIE FLOOK**	MARKETING ASSISTANT **CHARLIE RASPIN**	DIRECT SALES & MARKETING MANAGER **RICKY CLAYDON**	OPERATIONS DIRECTOR **LEIGH BAULCH**
PRODUCTION CONTROLLER **PETER JAMES**	BRAND MANAGER **CHRIS THOMPSON**	ADVERTISING MANAGER **MICHELLE FAIRLAMB**	EXECUTIVE DIRECTOR **VIVIAN CHEUNG**
PRODUCTION ASSISTANT **RHIANNON ROY**	PRESS OFFICER **WILL O'MULLANE**	HEAD OF RIGHTS **JENNY BOYCE**	PUBLISHER **NICK LANDAU**

TANK GIRL: DIRTY OLD TANK GIRL OMNIBUS
ISBN: 9781785869822

PUBLISHED BY TITAN COMICS,
A DIVISION OF TITAN PUBLISHING GROUP, LTD.
144 SOUTHWARK STREET, LONDON, SE1 0UP

A CIP CATALOGUE FOR THIS TITLE IS AVAILABLE FROM THE BRITISH LIBRARY

First edition March 2019

10 9 8 7 6 5 4 3 2 1

WWW.TITAN-COMICS.COM
BECOME A FAN ON FACEBOOK.COM/COMICSTITAN | FOLLOW US ON TWITTER @COMICSTITAN
VISIT THE OFFICIAL TANK GIRL WEBSITE AT WWW.TANK-GIRL.COM

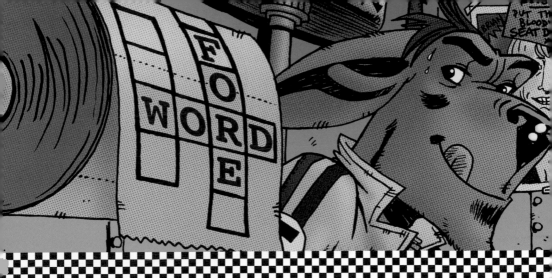

Hello friends, welcome to our new, shiny, rule-breaking, celebrity-filled, stupid, and somewhat unsavoury graphic novel. The message that comes at the end of the Skidmarks strip lays out everything we want to say on how we feel about the story, so, rather than repeat myself here, I thought I'd take this opportunity to tell you a little tale…

It was a lovely early summer morning. I was 16, just about to finish my final year at **Durrington High School** in **Worthing**. I'd been out late drinking the night before, watching a school band called **Toy Factory** playing in the upstairs room of the Montague pub in town, and was now en route to the home of my friend **Philip** (**Bond**, later a fellow **Deadline** artist) on my jet-black, home-assembled bicycle with **ridiculously long cow-horn handlebars**. We were planning a rehearsal of our own band **The University Smalls**. Cycling rapidly along the flat road, I fell asleep for a few seconds. I awoke to find myself flying over the roof of a stationary, parked **Triumph Herald**. I hit the rear end of the car with my shoulder and rolled onto the road behind. Quickly dusting myself down and looking around to see if anyone had spotted the incident, I walked around to the front of the car to find my bike wheel completely buckled, rendering it unrideable. I pushed the bike into a large bush and continued my journey on foot. That was the last I ever saw of it, but since that day I have been on a desperate search to find another set of similarly huge cow-horn handlebars. They made for such an easy ride and were very responsive to the smallest twitch of the wrist.

I'm not 100% sure why that story is relevant here, but take my advice and try not to fall asleep whilst cycling – you may lose your favourite handlebars forever.

Peace and Love

Alan C. Martin
The Maltings Stage Door Bar
Berwick upon Tweed
April 2010

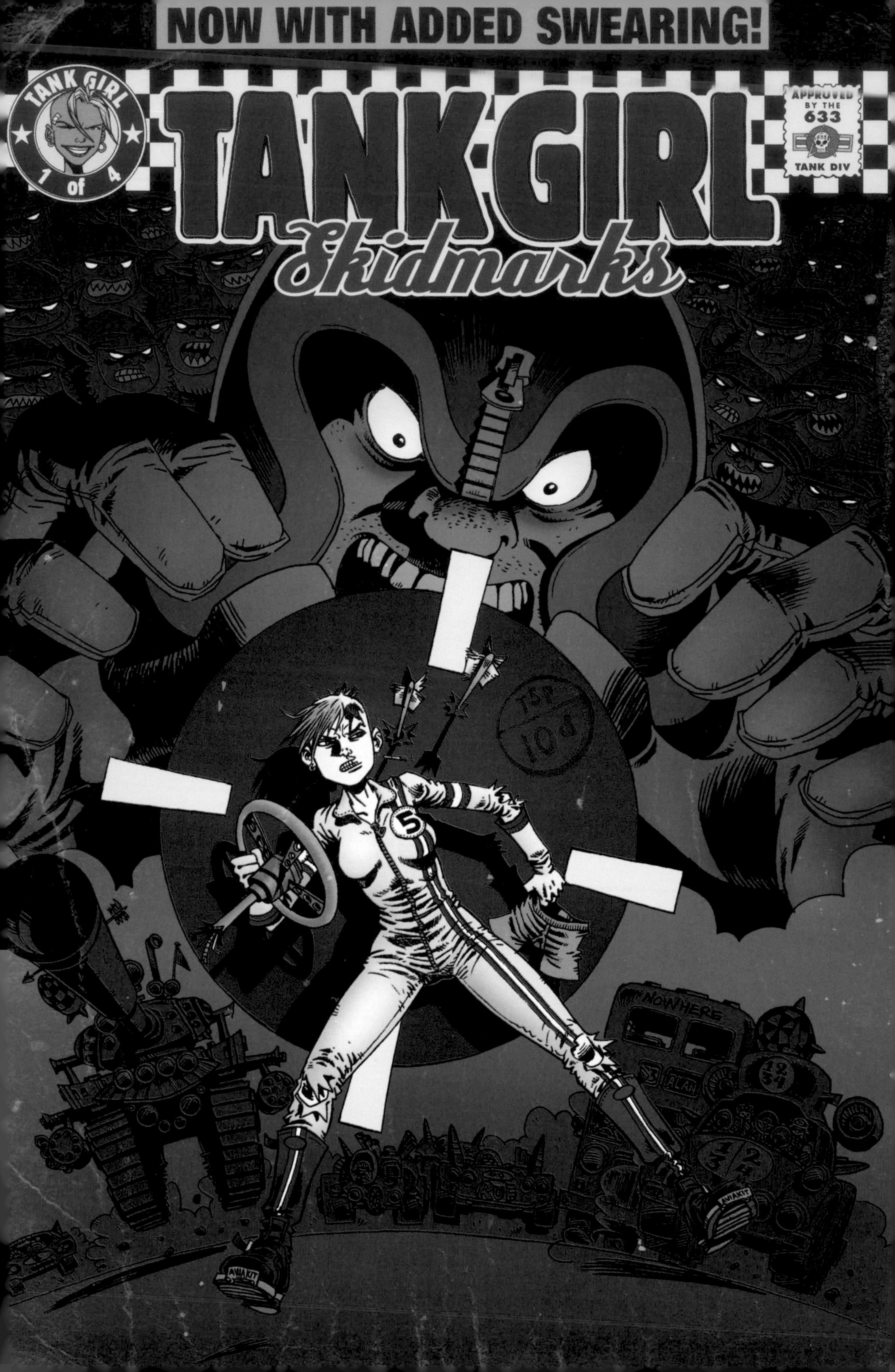
NOW WITH ADDED SWEARING!
TANK GIRL
1 of 4
APPROVED BY THE 633
TANK DIV
TANK GIRL
Skidmarks
5
NOWHERE

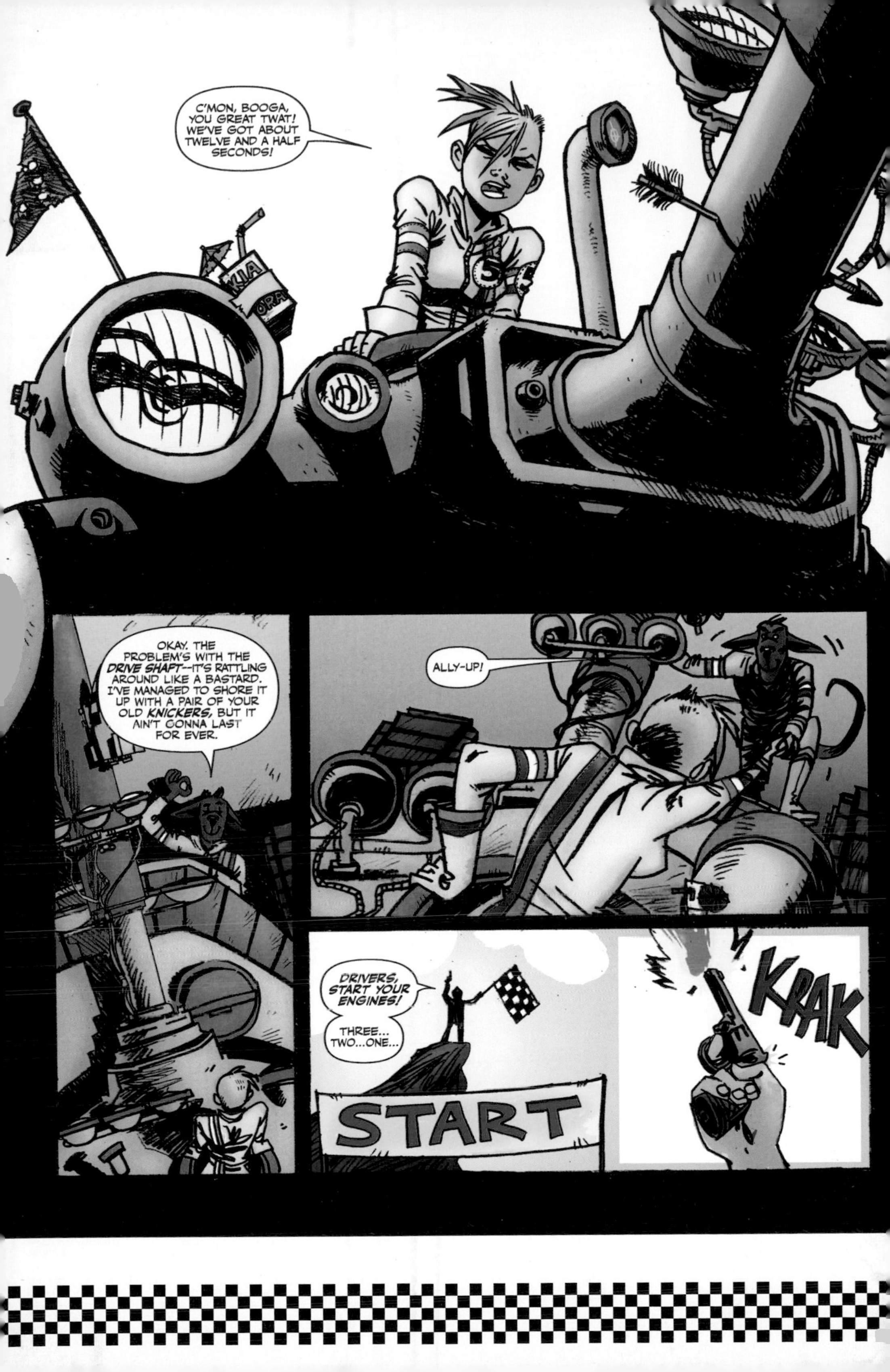

C'MON, BOOGA, YOU GREAT TWAT! WE'VE GOT ABOUT TWELVE AND A HALF SECONDS!
OKAY. THE PROBLEM'S WITH THE DRIVE SHAFT--IT'S RATTLING AROUND LIKE A BASTARD. I'VE MANAGED TO SHORE IT UP WITH A PAIR OF YOUR OLD KNICKERS, BUT IT AIN'T GONNA LAST FOR EVER.
ALLY-UP!
DRIVERS, START YOUR ENGINES!
THREE... TWO...ONE...
START
KRAK

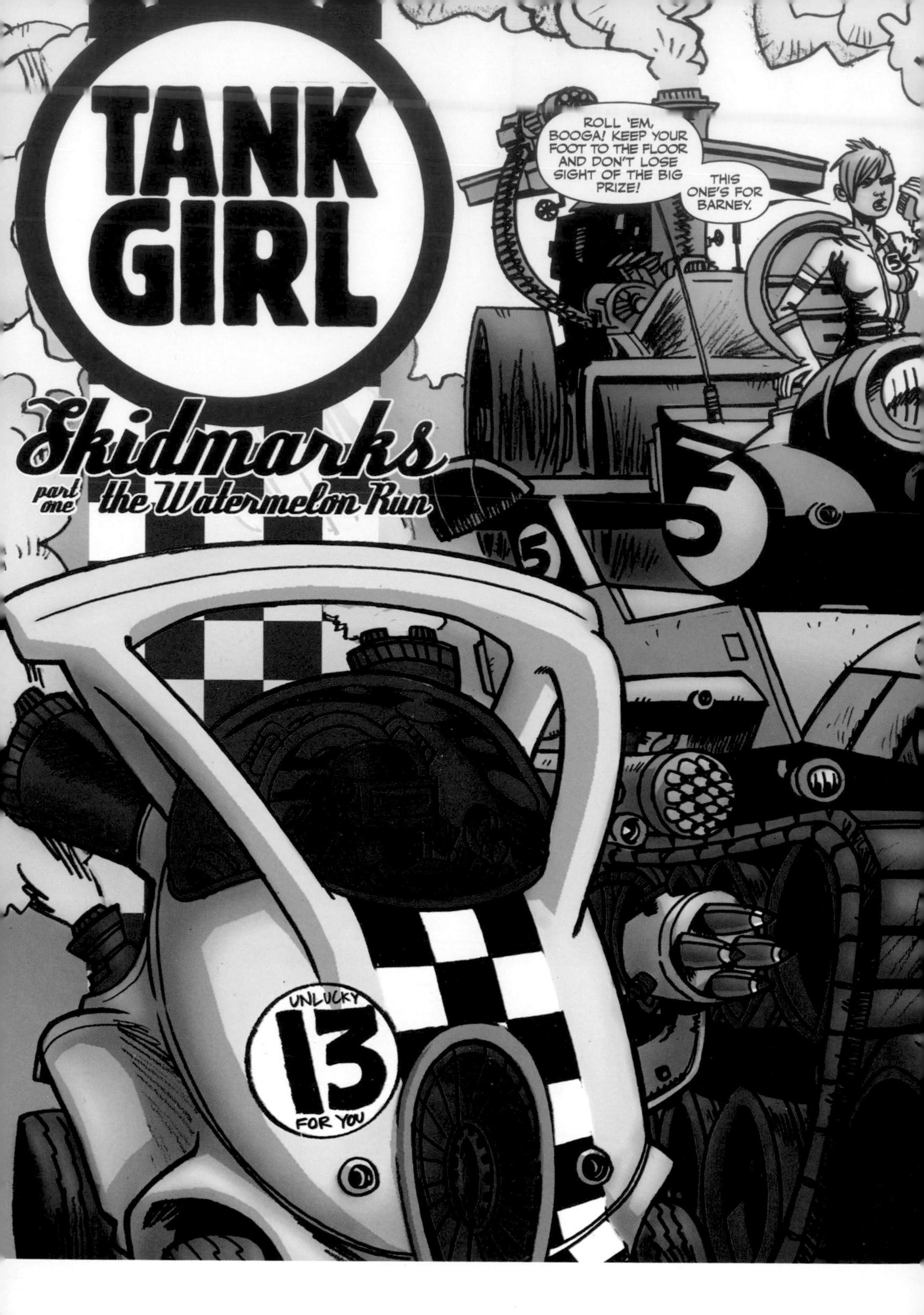
TANK GIRL
Skidmarks
part one the Watermelon Run
ROLL 'EM, BOOGA! KEEP YOUR FOOT TO THE FLOOR AND DON'T LOSE SIGHT OF THE BIG PRIZE!
THIS ONE'S FOR BARNEY.
UNLUCKY 13 FOR YOU

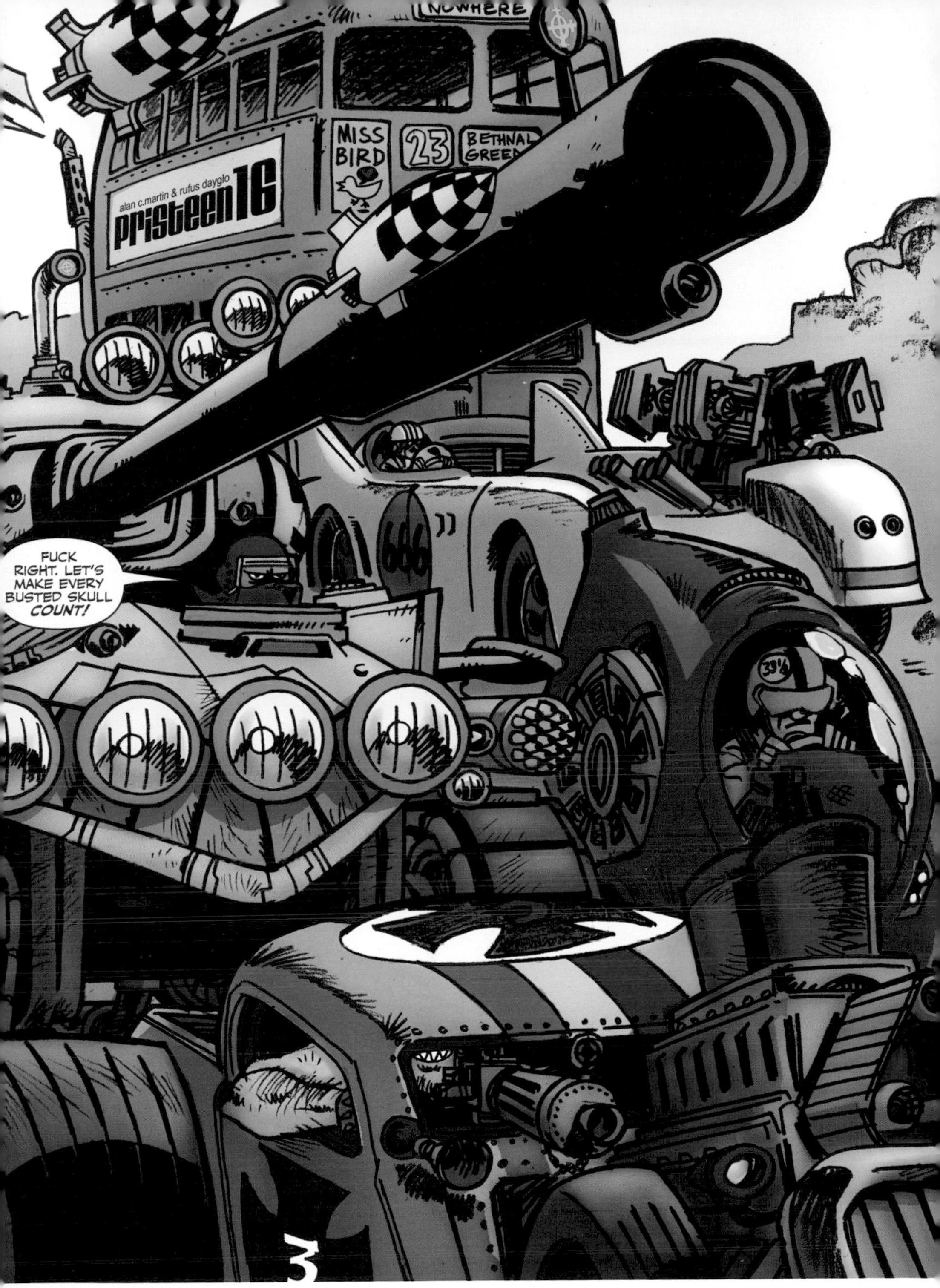
NOWHERE
MISS BIRD
23
BETHNAL
alan c.martin & rufus dayglo
pristeen 16
666
FUCK RIGHT. LET'S MAKE EVERY BUSTED SKULL *COUNT!*
3

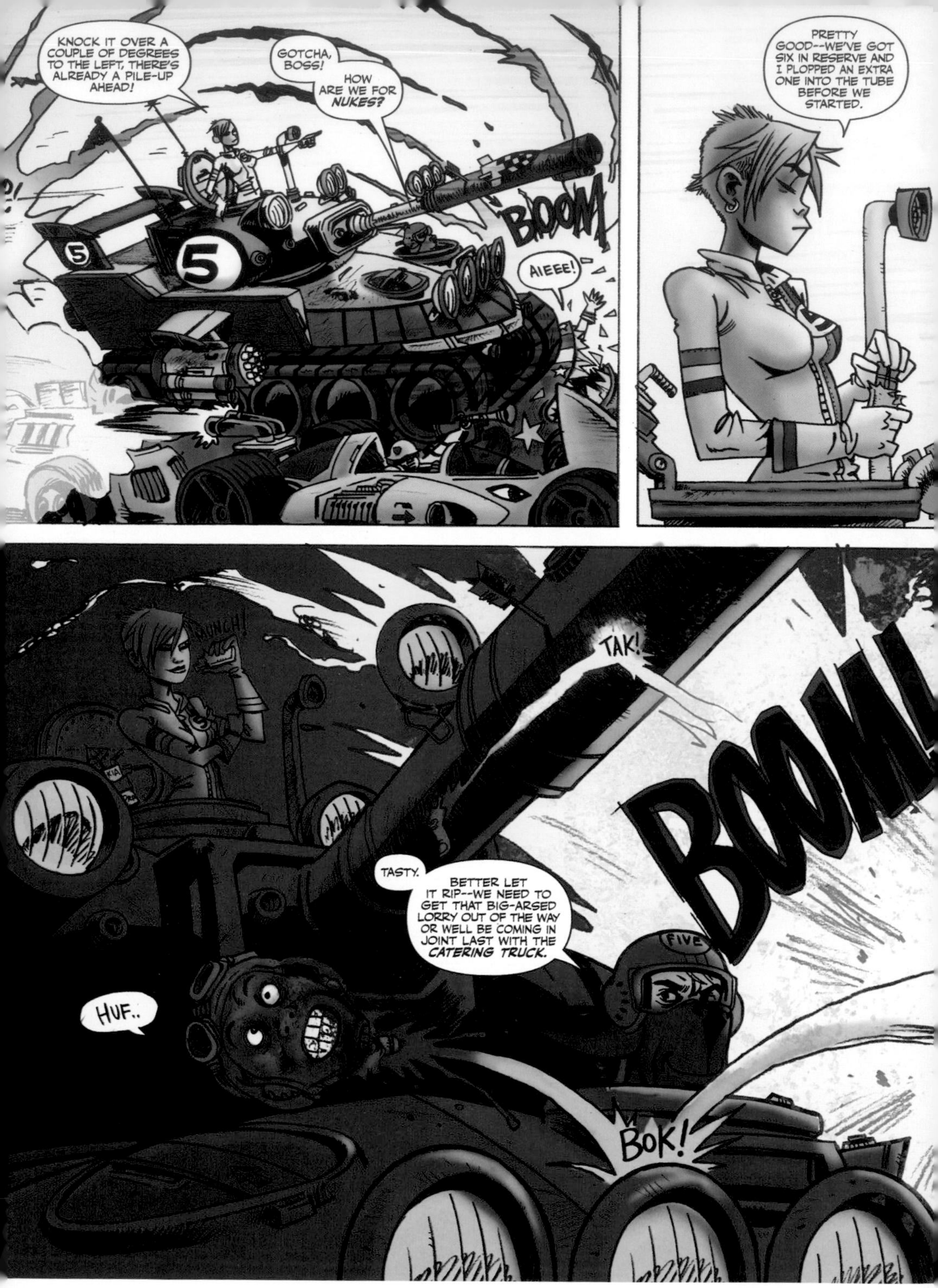
KNOCK IT OVER A COUPLE OF DEGREES TO THE LEFT, THERE'S ALREADY A PILE-UP AHEAD!
GOTCHA, BOSS!
HOW ARE WE FOR NUKES?
BOOM
AIEEE!
PRETTY GOOD--WE'VE GOT SIX IN RESERVE AND I PLOPPED AN EXTRA ONE INTO THE TUBE BEFORE WE STARTED.
TAK!
BOOM!
TASTY.
BETTER LET IT RIP--WE NEED TO GET THAT BIG-ARSED LORRY OUT OF THE WAY OR WELL BE COMING IN JOINT LAST WITH THE CATERING TRUCK.
FIVE
HUF..
BOK!

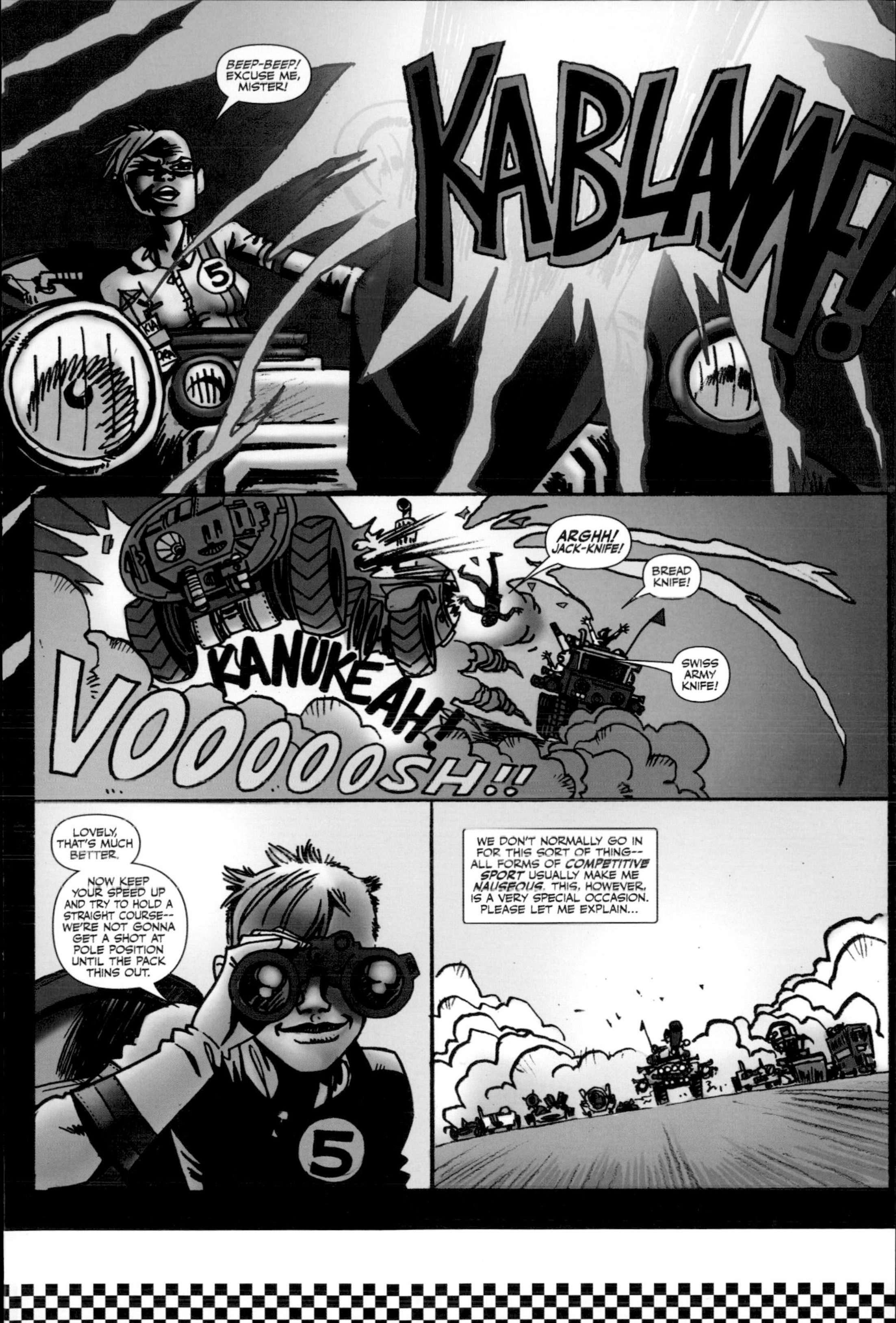
BEEP-BEEP! EXCUSE ME, MISTER!
KABLAMM!
ARGHH! JACK-KNIFE!
BREAD KNIFE!
SWISS ARMY KNIFE!
KANUKEAH!
VOOOOOOSH!!
LOVELY, THAT'S MUCH BETTER.
NOW KEEP YOUR SPEED UP AND TRY TO HOLD A STRAIGHT COURSE-- WE'RE NOT GONNA GET A SHOT AT POLE POSITION UNTIL THE PACK THINS OUT.
WE DON'T NORMALLY GO IN FOR THIS SORT OF THING-- ALL FORMS OF COMPETITIVE SPORT USUALLY MAKE ME NAUSEOUS. THIS, HOWEVER, IS A VERY SPECIAL OCCASION. PLEASE LET ME EXPLAIN...

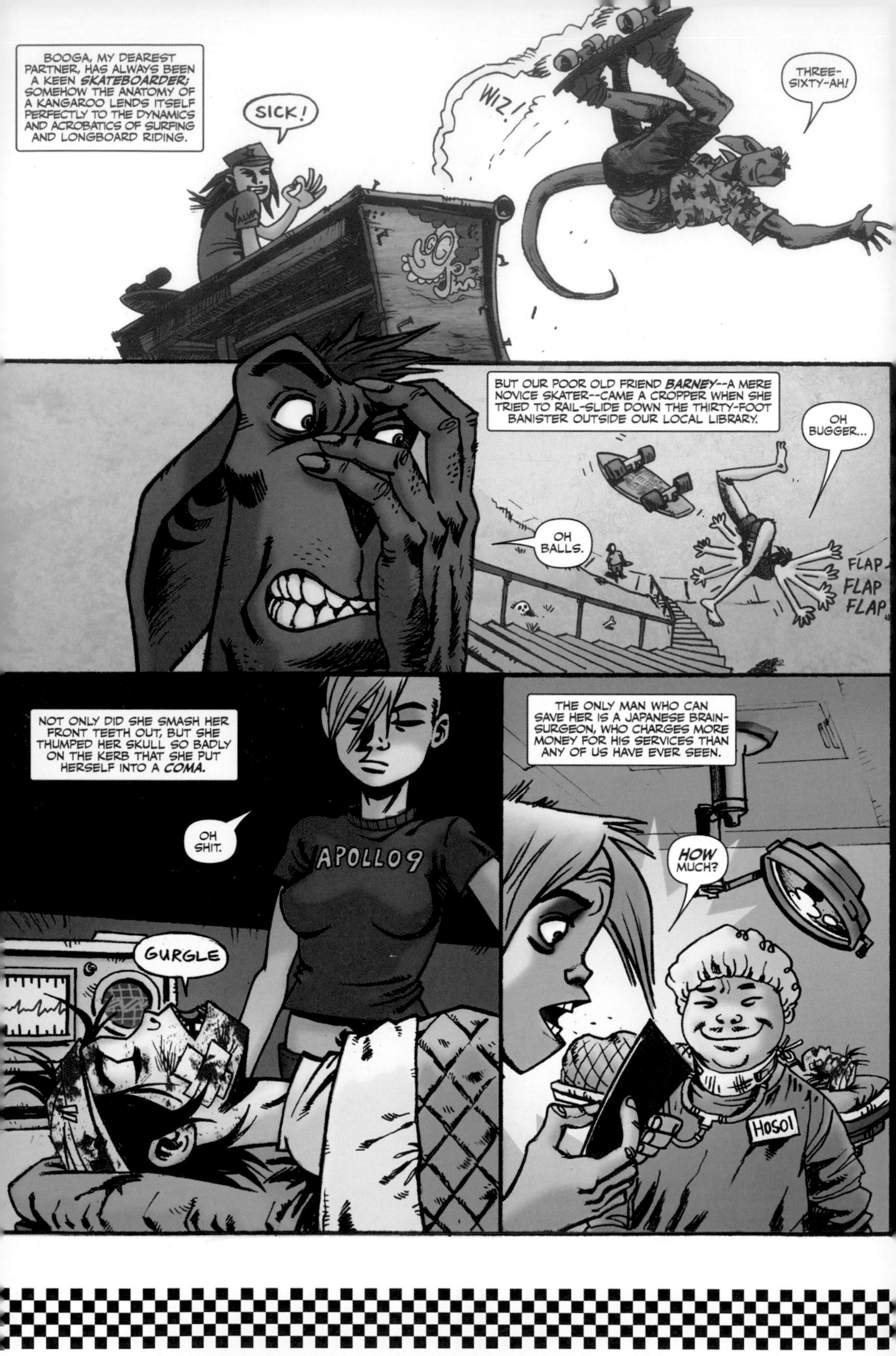
BOOGA, MY DEAREST PARTNER, HAS ALWAYS BEEN A KEEN SKATEBOARDER; SOMEHOW THE ANATOMY OF A KANGAROO LENDS ITSELF PERFECTLY TO THE DYNAMICS AND ACROBATICS OF SURFING AND LONGBOARD RIDING.
SICK!
WIZ!
THREE-SIXTY-AH!
BUT OUR POOR OLD FRIEND BARNEY--A MERE NOVICE SKATER--CAME A CROPPER WHEN SHE TRIED TO RAIL-SLIDE DOWN THE THIRTY-FOOT BANISTER OUTSIDE OUR LOCAL LIBRARY.
OH BUGGER...
OH BALLS.
FLAP FLAP FLAP
NOT ONLY DID SHE SMASH HER FRONT TEETH OUT, BUT SHE THUMPED HER SKULL SO BADLY ON THE KERB THAT SHE PUT HERSELF INTO A COMA.
OH SHIT.
APOLLO 9
GURGLE
THE ONLY MAN WHO CAN SAVE HER IS A JAPANESE BRAIN-SURGEON, WHO CHARGES MORE MONEY FOR HIS SERVICES THAN ANY OF US HAVE EVER SEEN.
HOW MUCH?
HOSOI

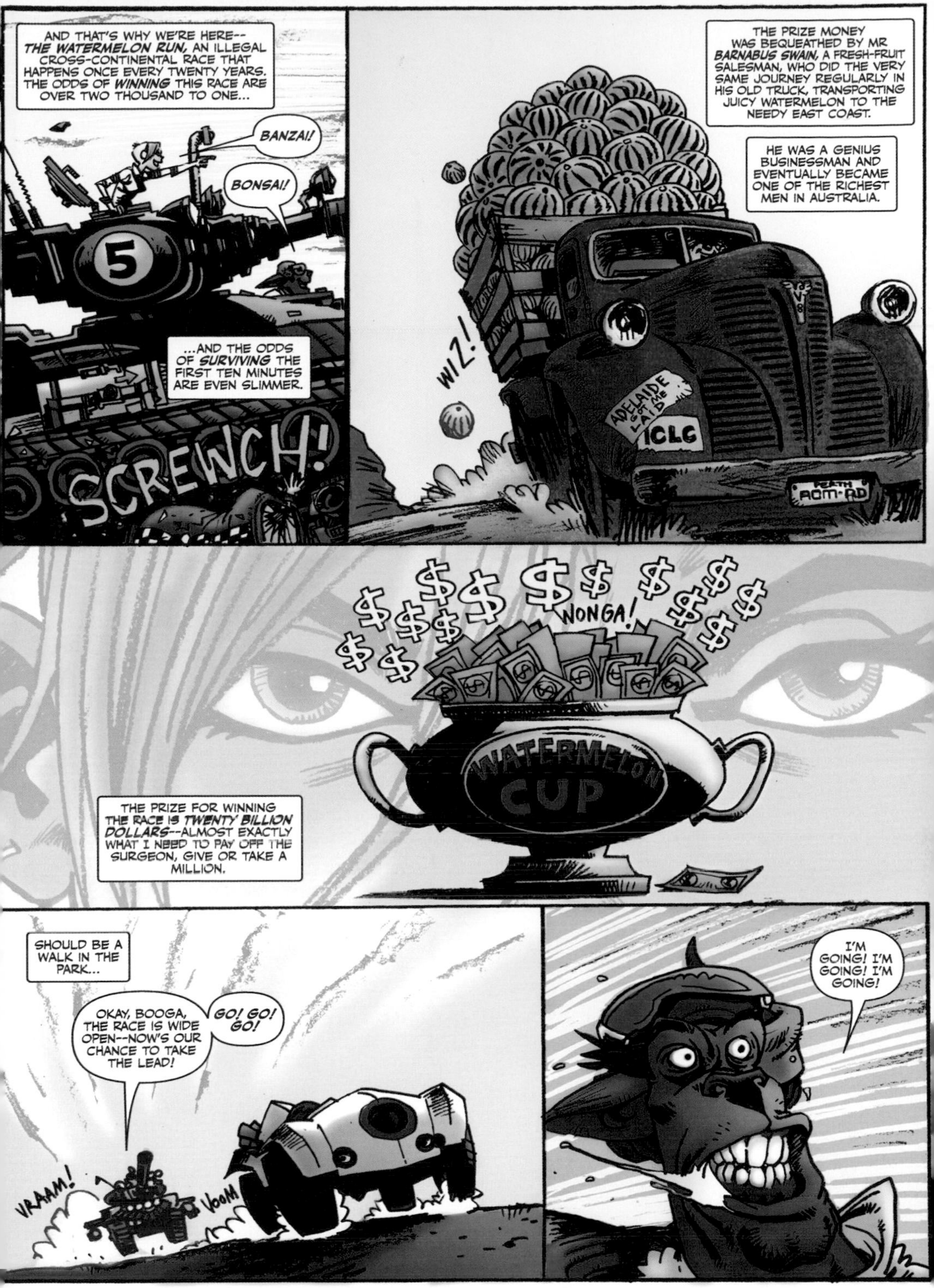
AND THAT'S WHY WE'RE HERE--*THE WATERMELON RUN,* AN ILLEGAL CROSS-CONTINENTAL RACE THAT HAPPENS ONCE EVERY TWENTY YEARS. THE ODDS OF *WINNING* THIS RACE ARE OVER TWO THOUSAND TO ONE...
BANZAI!
BONSAI!
5
...AND THE ODDS OF *SURVIVING* THE FIRST TEN MINUTES ARE EVEN SLIMMER.
SCREWCH!
THE PRIZE MONEY WAS BEQUEATHED BY MR *BARNABUS SWAIN,* A FRESH-FRUIT SALESMAN, WHO DID THE VERY SAME JOURNEY REGULARLY IN HIS OLD TRUCK, TRANSPORTING JUICY WATERMELON TO THE NEEDY EAST COAST.
HE WAS A GENIUS BUSINESSMAN AND EVENTUALLY BECAME ONE OF THE RICHEST MEN IN AUSTRALIA.
WIZ!
ADELAIDE GOT ME LAID
ICLG
PERTH AOM-AD
NONGA!
WATERMELON CUP
THE PRIZE FOR WINNING THE RACE IS *TWENTY BILLION DOLLARS*--ALMOST EXACTLY WHAT I NEED TO PAY OFF THE SURGEON, GIVE OR TAKE A MILLION.
SHOULD BE A WALK IN THE PARK...
OKAY, BOOGA, THE RACE IS WIDE OPEN--NOW'S OUR CHANCE TO TAKE THE LEAD!
GO! GO! GO!
VRAAM!
VOOM
I'M GOING! I'M GOING! I'M GOING!

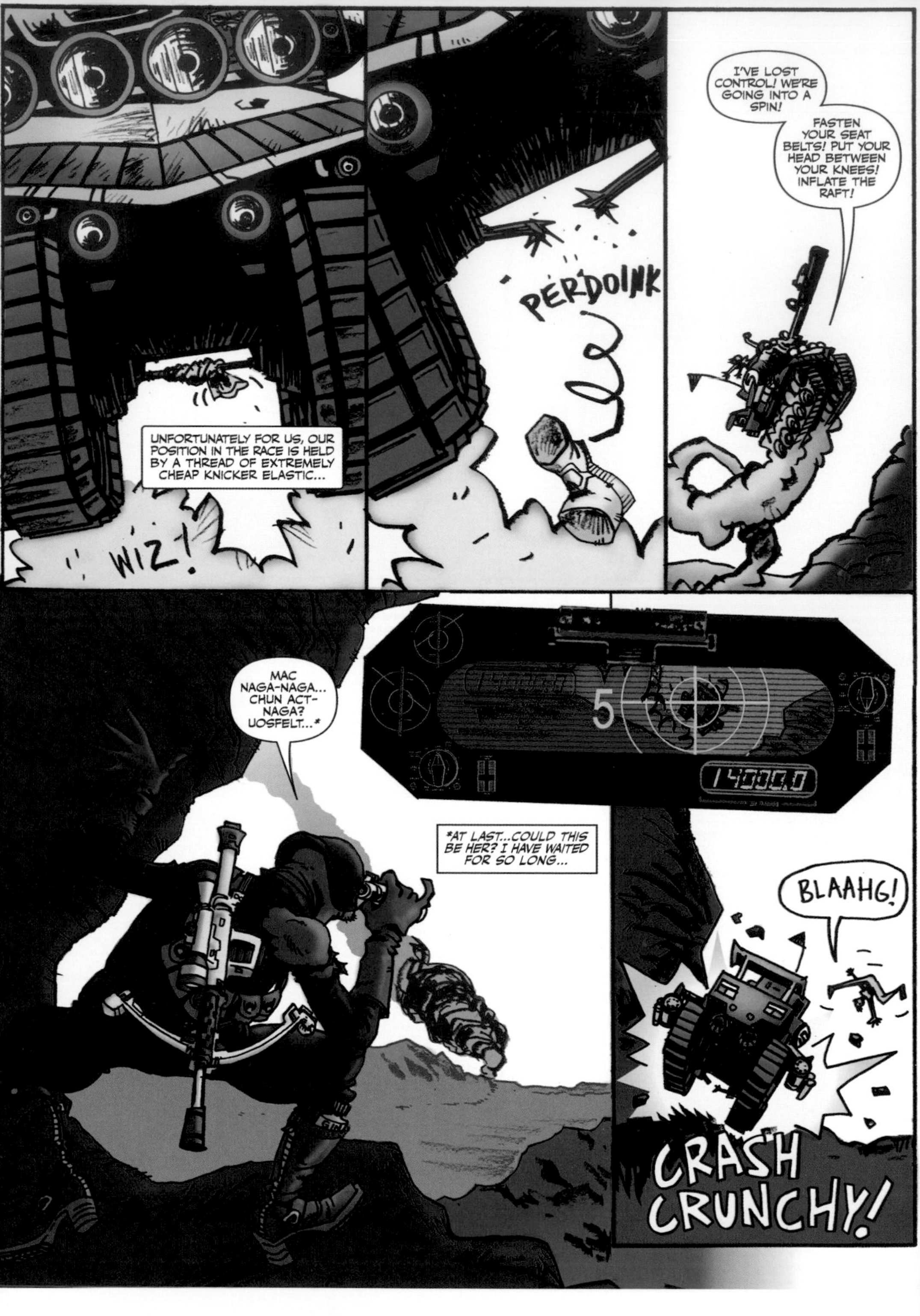
UNFORTUNATELY FOR US, OUR POSITION IN THE RACE IS HELD BY A THREAD OF EXTREMELY CHEAP KNICKER ELASTIC...
WIZ!
PERDOINK
I'VE LOST CONTROL! WE'RE GOING INTO A SPIN!
FASTEN YOUR SEAT BELTS! PUT YOUR HEAD BETWEEN YOUR KNEES! INFLATE THE RAFT!
MAC NAGA-NAGA... CHUN ACT-NAGA? UOSFELT...*
5
14000.0
*AT LAST...COULD THIS BE HER? I HAVE WAITED FOR SO LONG...
BLAAHG!
CRASH CRUNCHY!

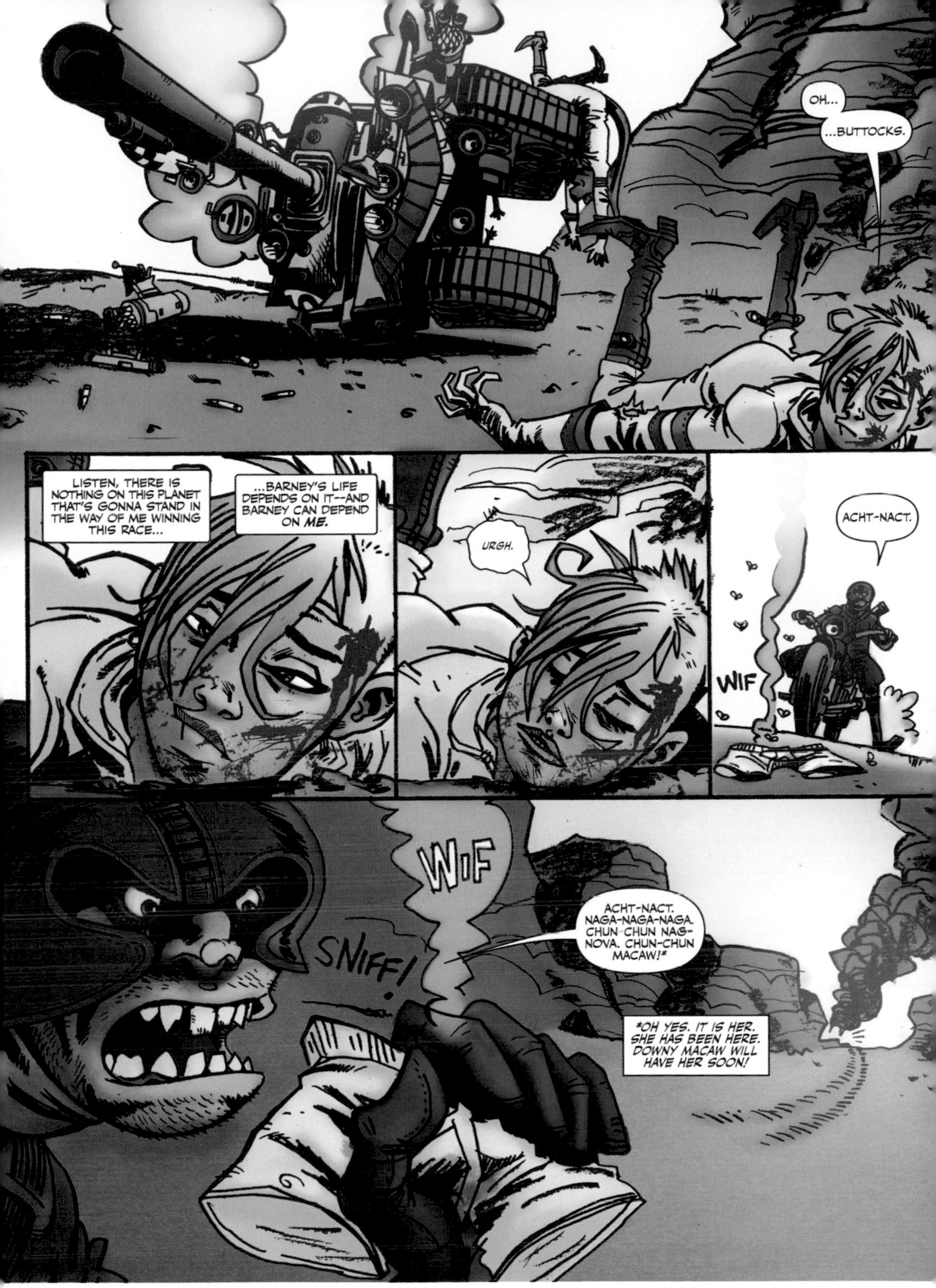
OH...
...BUTTOCKS.
LISTEN, THERE IS NOTHING ON THIS PLANET THAT'S GONNA STAND IN THE WAY OF ME WINNING THIS RACE...
...BARNEY'S LIFE DEPENDS ON IT--AND BARNEY CAN DEPEND ON ME.
URGH.
ACHT-NACT.
WIF
WIF
SNIFF!
ACHT-NACT. NAGA-NAGA-NAGA. CHUN CHUN NAG-NOVA. CHUN-CHUN MACAW!*
*OH YES. IT IS HER. SHE HAS BEEN HERE. DOWNY MACAW WILL HAVE HER SOON!

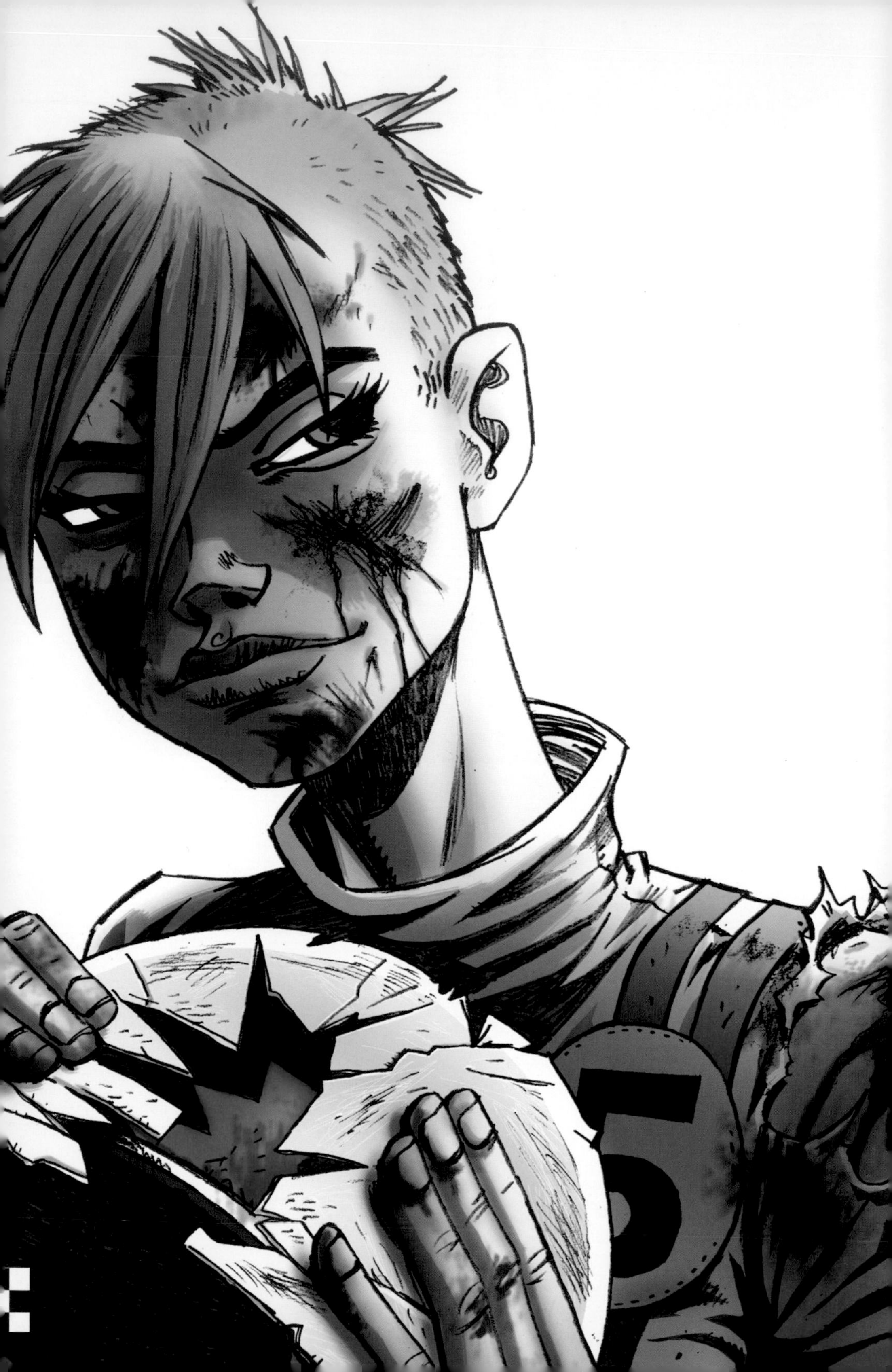

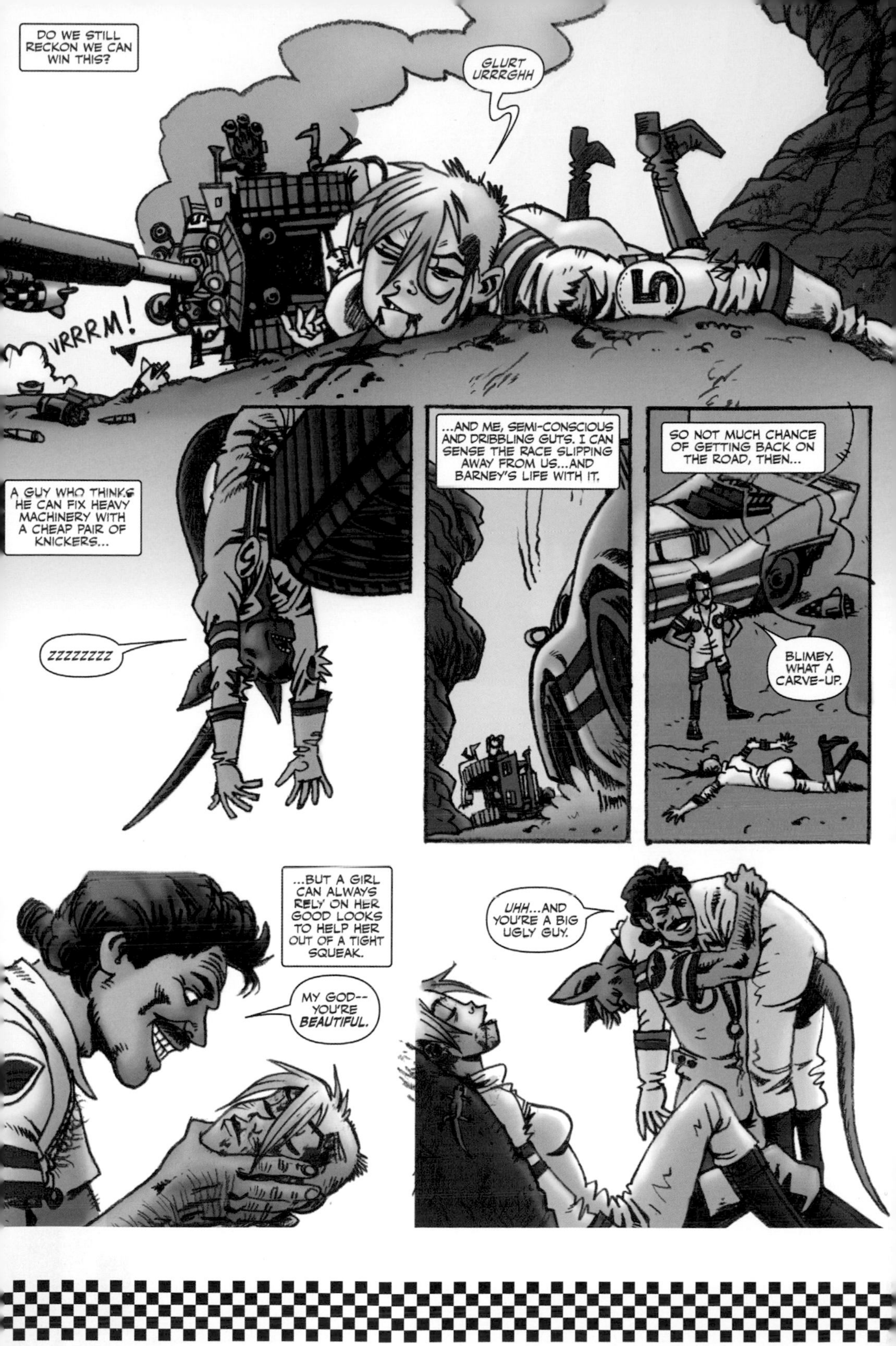
DO WE STILL RECKON WE CAN WIN THIS?
GLURT URRRGHH
VRRRM!
A GUY WHO THINKS HE CAN FIX HEAVY MACHINERY WITH A CHEAP PAIR OF KNICKERS...
ZZZZZZZZ
...AND ME, SEMI-CONSCIOUS AND DRIBBLING GUTS. I CAN SENSE THE RACE SLIPPING AWAY FROM US...AND BARNEY'S LIFE WITH IT.
SO NOT MUCH CHANCE OF GETTING BACK ON THE ROAD, THEN...
BLIMEY. WHAT A CARVE-UP.
...BUT A GIRL CAN ALWAYS RELY ON HER GOOD LOOKS TO HELP HER OUT OF A TIGHT SQUEAK.
MY GOD-- YOU'RE BEAUTIFUL.
UHH...AND YOU'RE A BIG UGLY GUY.

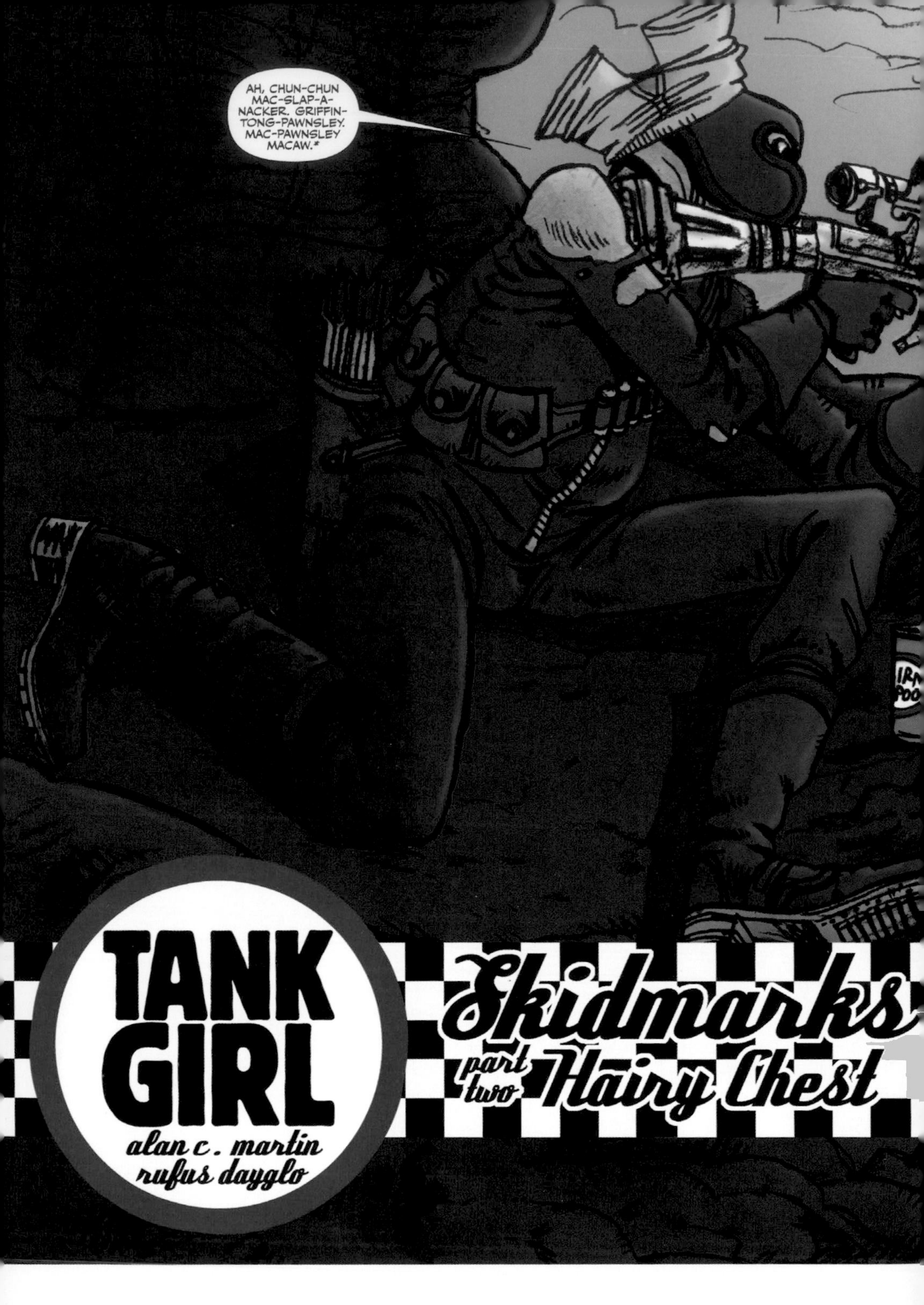
AH, CHUN-CHUN MAC-SLAP-A-NACKER. GRIFFIN-TONG-PAWNSLEY. MAC-PAWNSLEY MACAW.*
TANK GIRL
alan c. martin
rufus dayglo
Skidmarks
part two Hairy Chest

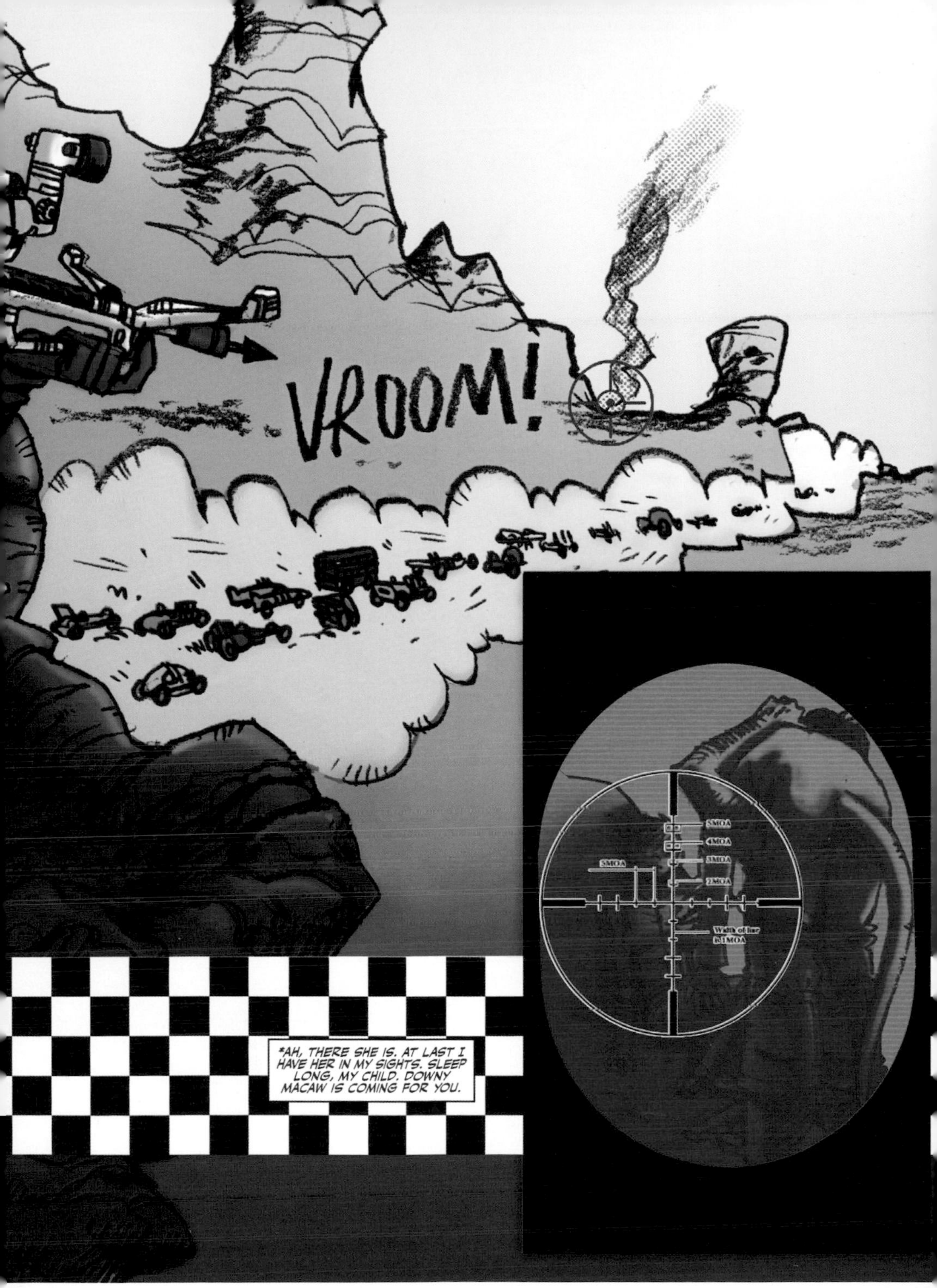
VROOM!
5MOA
4MOA
3MOA
2MOA
*AH, THERE SHE IS. AT LAST I HAVE HER IN MY SIGHTS. SLEEP LONG, MY CHILD. DOWNY MACAW IS COMING FOR YOU.

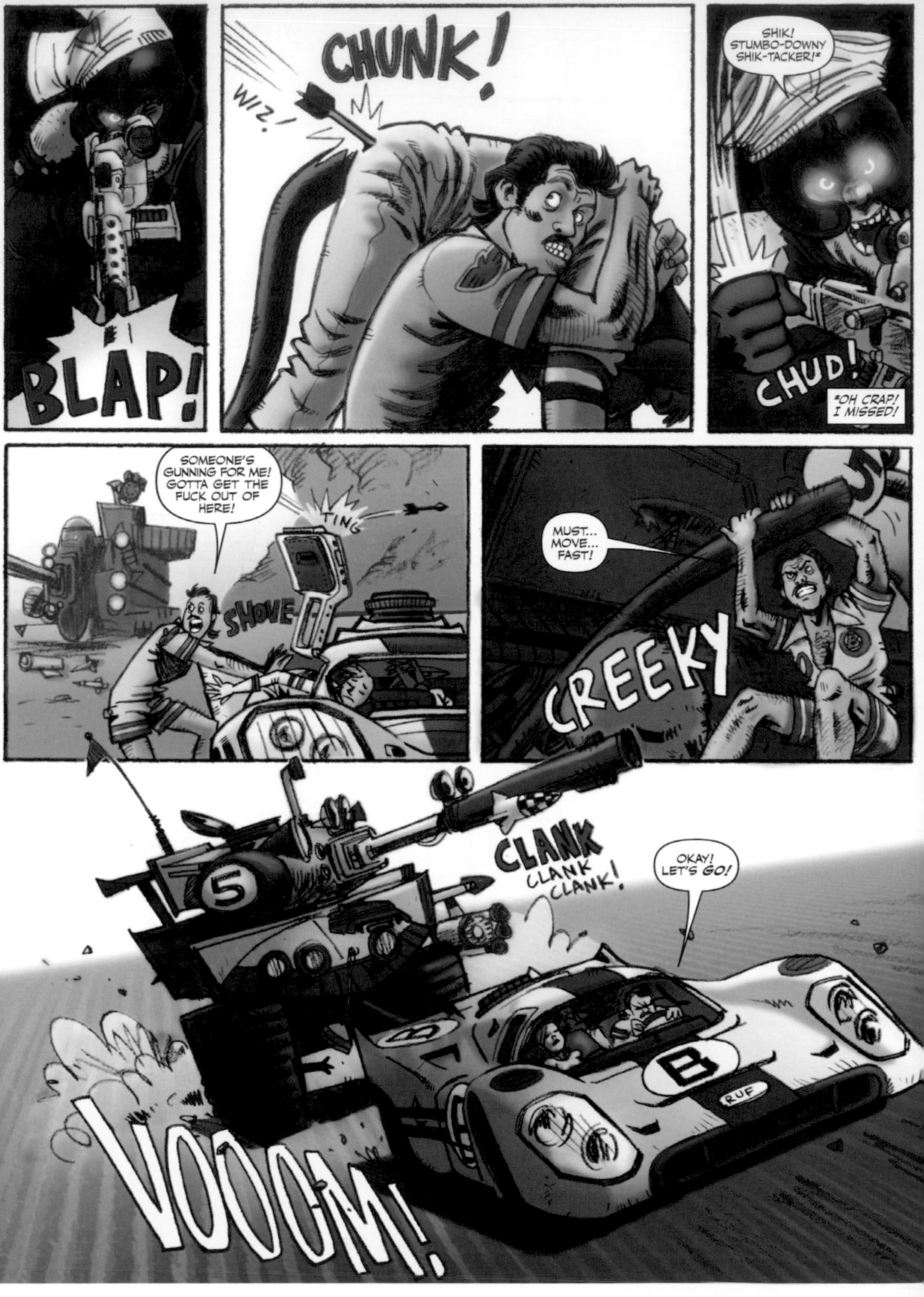
BLAP!
WIZ!
CHUNK!
SHIK! STUMBO-DOWNY SHIK-TACKER!*
CHUD!
*OH CRAP! I MISSED!
SOMEONE'S GUNNING FOR ME! GOTTA GET THE FUCK OUT OF HERE!
TING
SHOVE
MUST... MOVE... FAST!
CREEKY
CLANK
CLANK
CLANK!
OKAY! LET'S GO!
RUF
VOOOM!

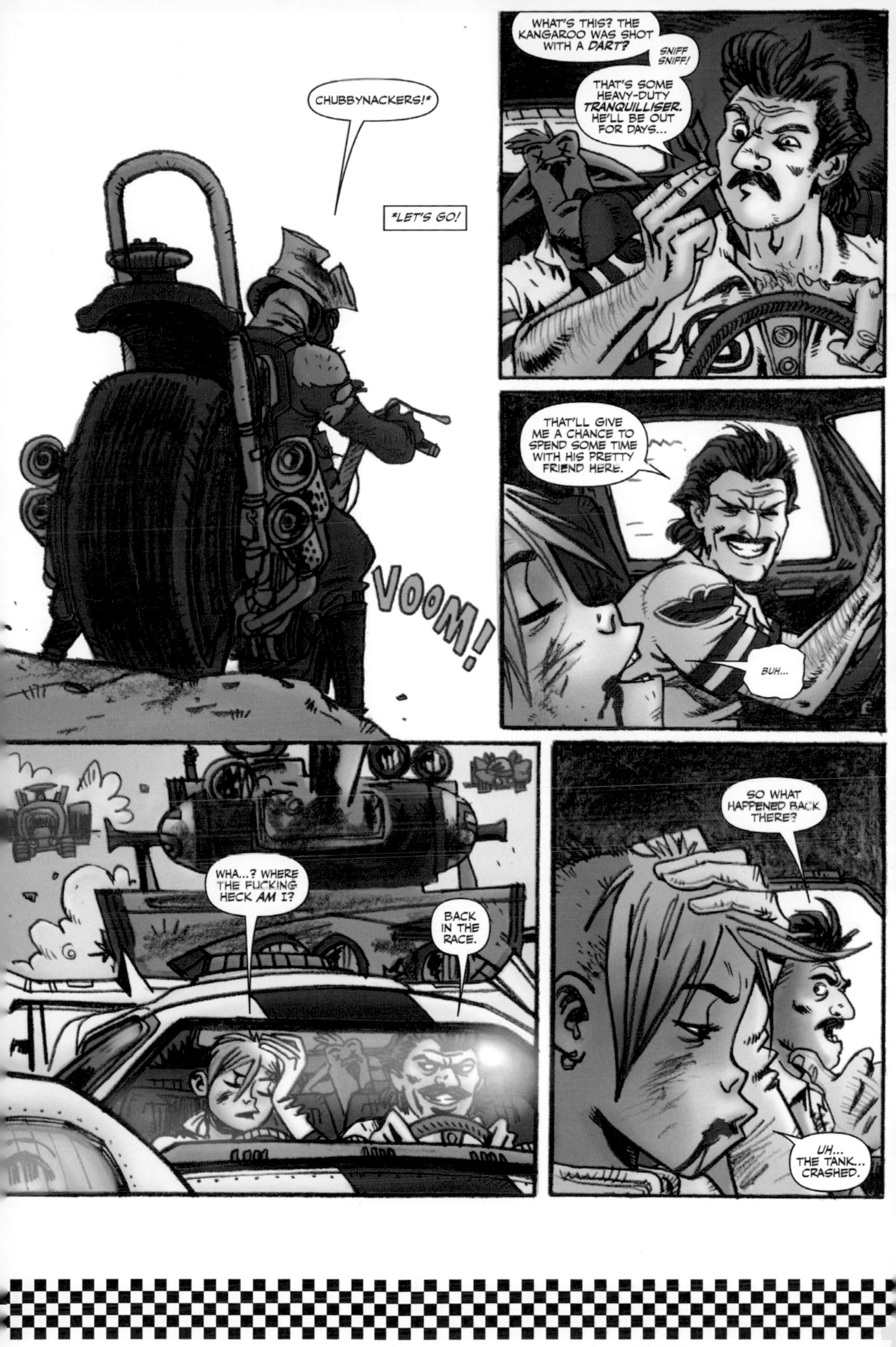

CHUBBYNACKERS!*
*LET'S GO!
VOOM!
WHAT'S THIS? THE KANGAROO WAS SHOT WITH A DART?
SNIFF SNIFF!
THAT'S SOME HEAVY-DUTY TRANQUILLISER. HE'LL BE OUT FOR DAYS...
THAT'LL GIVE ME A CHANCE TO SPEND SOME TIME WITH HIS PRETTY FRIEND HERE.
BUH...
WHA...? WHERE THE FUCKING HECK AM I?
BACK IN THE RACE.
SO WHAT HAPPENED BACK THERE?
UH... THE TANK... CRASHED.

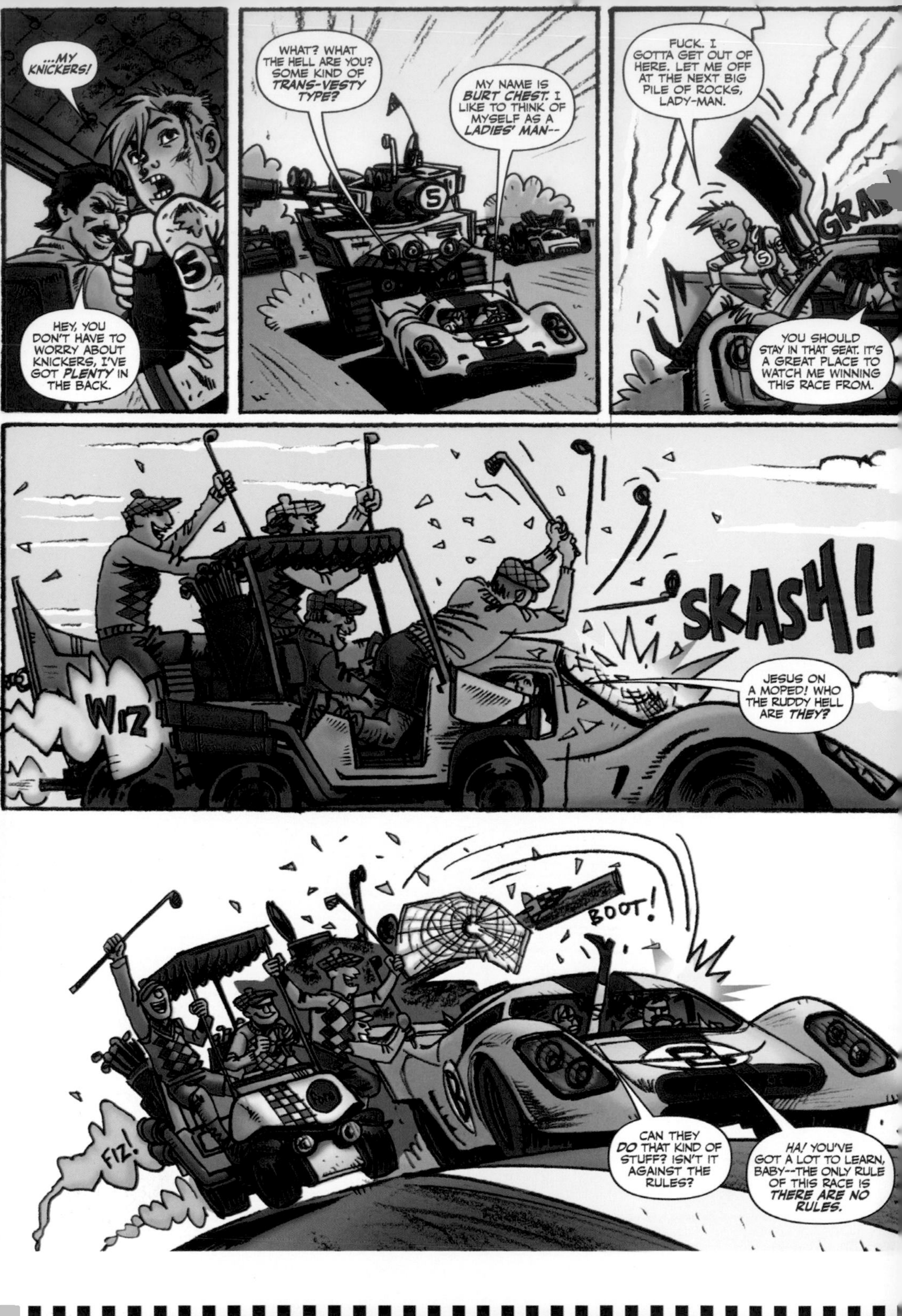
...MY KNICKERS!
HEY, YOU DON'T HAVE TO WORRY ABOUT KNICKERS, I'VE GOT *PLENTY* IN THE BACK.
WHAT? WHAT THE HELL ARE YOU? SOME KIND OF *TRANS-VESTY TYPE?*
MY NAME IS *BURT CHEST.* I LIKE TO THINK OF MYSELF AS A *LADIES' MAN--*
FUCK. I GOTTA GET OUT OF HERE. LET ME OFF AT THE NEXT BIG PILE OF ROCKS, LADY-MAN.
GRAB
YOU SHOULD STAY IN THAT SEAT. IT'S A GREAT PLACE TO WATCH ME WINNING THIS RACE FROM.
SKASH!
WIZ
JESUS ON A MOPED! WHO THE RUDDY HELL ARE *THEY?*
BOOT!
FIZ!
CAN THEY *DO* THAT KIND OF STUFF? ISN'T IT AGAINST THE RULES?
HA! YOU'VE GOT A LOT TO LEARN, BABY--THE ONLY RULE OF THIS RACE IS ***THERE ARE NO RULES.***

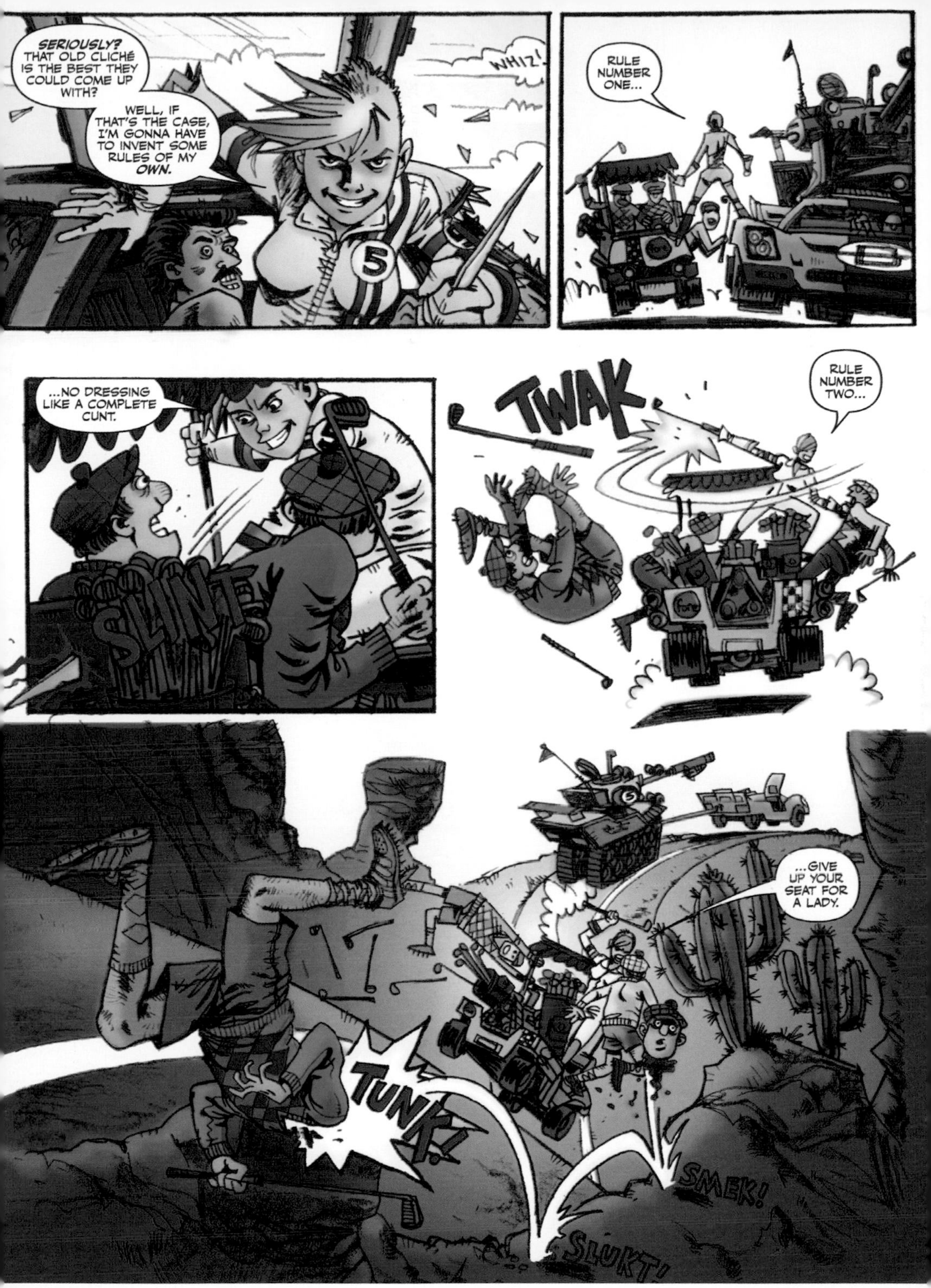

SERIOUSLY? THAT OLD CLICHÉ IS THE BEST THEY COULD COME UP WITH?
WHIZ!
WELL, IF THAT'S THE CASE, I'M GONNA HAVE TO INVENT SOME RULES OF MY OWN.
RULE NUMBER ONE...
...NO DRESSING LIKE A COMPLETE CUNT.
SLINT
TWAK
RULE NUMBER TWO...
...GIVE UP YOUR SEAT FOR A LADY.
TUNK!
SMEK!
SLUKT!

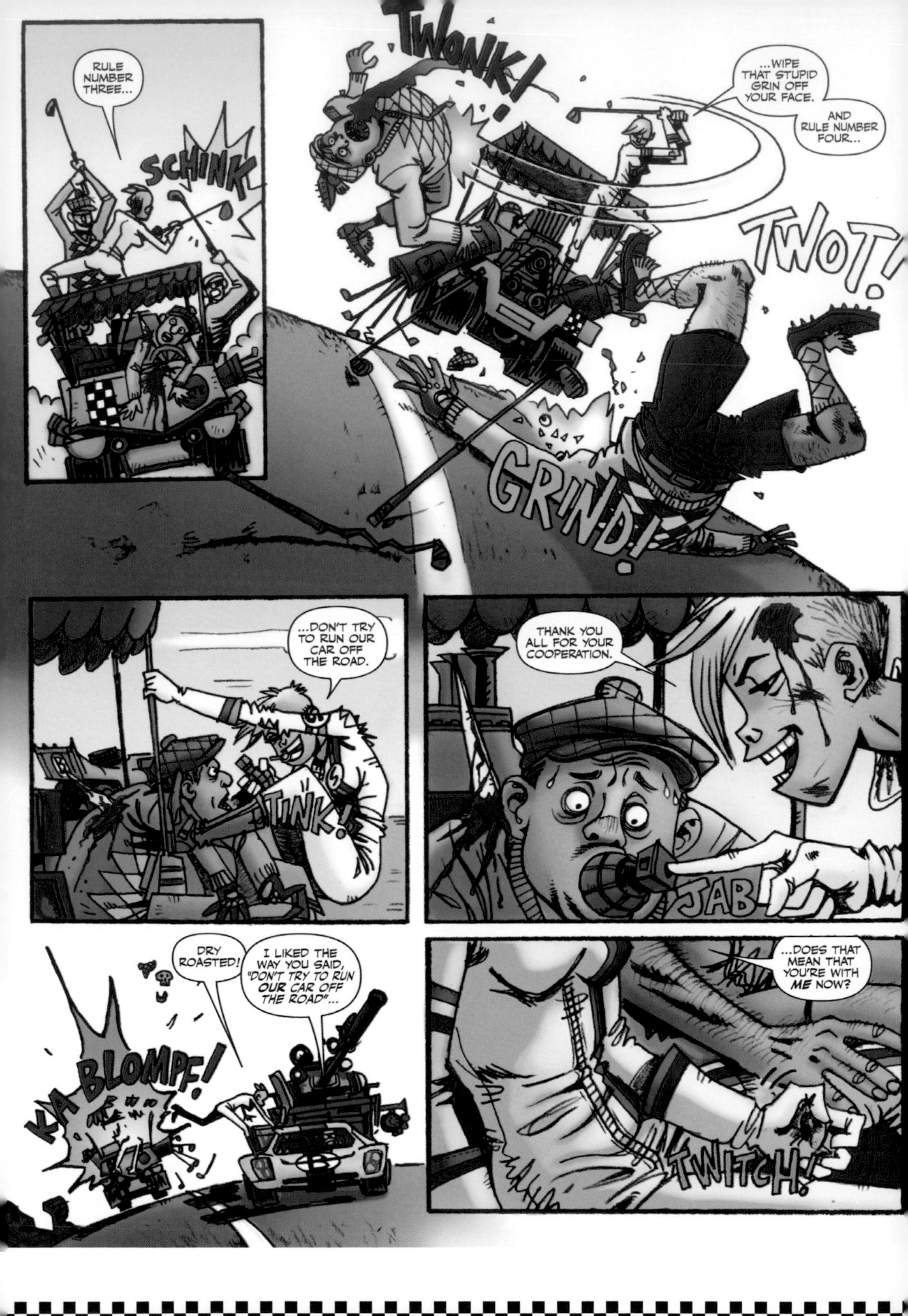

RULE NUMBER THREE...
SCHINK
TWONK!
...WIPE THAT STUPID GRIN OFF YOUR FACE.
AND RULE NUMBER FOUR...
TWOT!
GRIND!
...DON'T TRY TO RUN OUR CAR OFF THE ROAD.
TINK!
THANK YOU ALL FOR YOUR COOPERATION.
JAB
DRY ROASTED!
I LIKED THE WAY YOU SAID, "DON'T TRY TO RUN OUR CAR OFF THE ROAD"...
KA BLOMPF!
...DOES THAT MEAN THAT YOU'RE WITH ME NOW?
TWITCH!

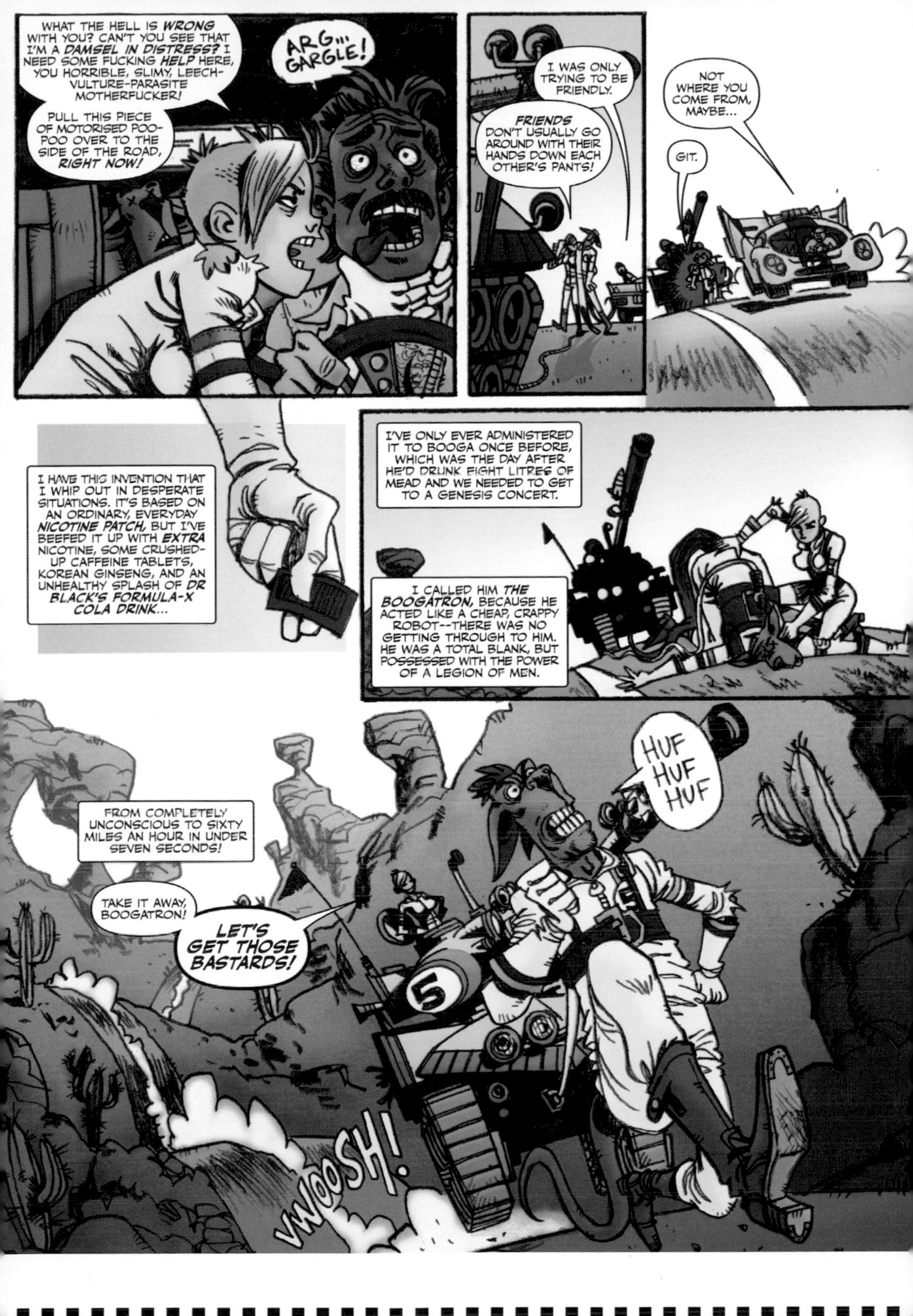
WHAT THE HELL IS *WRONG* WITH YOU? CAN'T YOU SEE THAT I'M A *DAMSEL IN DISTRESS?* I NEED SOME FUCKING *HELP* HERE, YOU HORRIBLE, SLIMY, LEECH-VULTURE-PARASITE MOTHERFUCKER!
ARG... GARGLE!
PULL THIS PIECE OF MOTORISED POO-POO OVER TO THE SIDE OF THE ROAD, *RIGHT NOW!*
I WAS ONLY TRYING TO BE FRIENDLY.
FRIENDS DON'T USUALLY GO AROUND WITH THEIR HANDS DOWN EACH OTHER'S PANTS!
NOT WHERE YOU COME FROM, MAYBE...
GIT.
I HAVE THIS INVENTION THAT I WHIP OUT IN DESPERATE SITUATIONS. IT'S BASED ON AN ORDINARY, EVERYDAY *NICOTINE PATCH,* BUT I'VE BEEFED IT UP WITH *EXTRA* NICOTINE, SOME CRUSHED-UP CAFFEINE TABLETS, KOREAN GINSENG, AND AN UNHEALTHY SPLASH OF *DR BLACK'S FORMULA-X COLA DRINK*...
I'VE ONLY EVER ADMINISTERED IT TO BOOGA ONCE BEFORE, WHICH WAS THE DAY AFTER HE'D DRUNK EIGHT LITRES OF MEAD AND WE NEEDED TO GET TO A GENESIS CONCERT.
I CALLED HIM *THE BOOGATRON,* BECAUSE HE ACTED LIKE A CHEAP, CRAPPY ROBOT--THERE WAS NO GETTING THROUGH TO HIM. HE WAS A TOTAL BLANK, BUT POSSESSED WITH THE POWER OF A LEGION OF MEN.
FROM COMPLETELY UNCONSCIOUS TO SIXTY MILES AN HOUR IN UNDER SEVEN SECONDS!
HUF HUF HUF
TAKE IT AWAY, BOOGATRON!
LET'S GET THOSE BASTARDS!
VWOOSH!

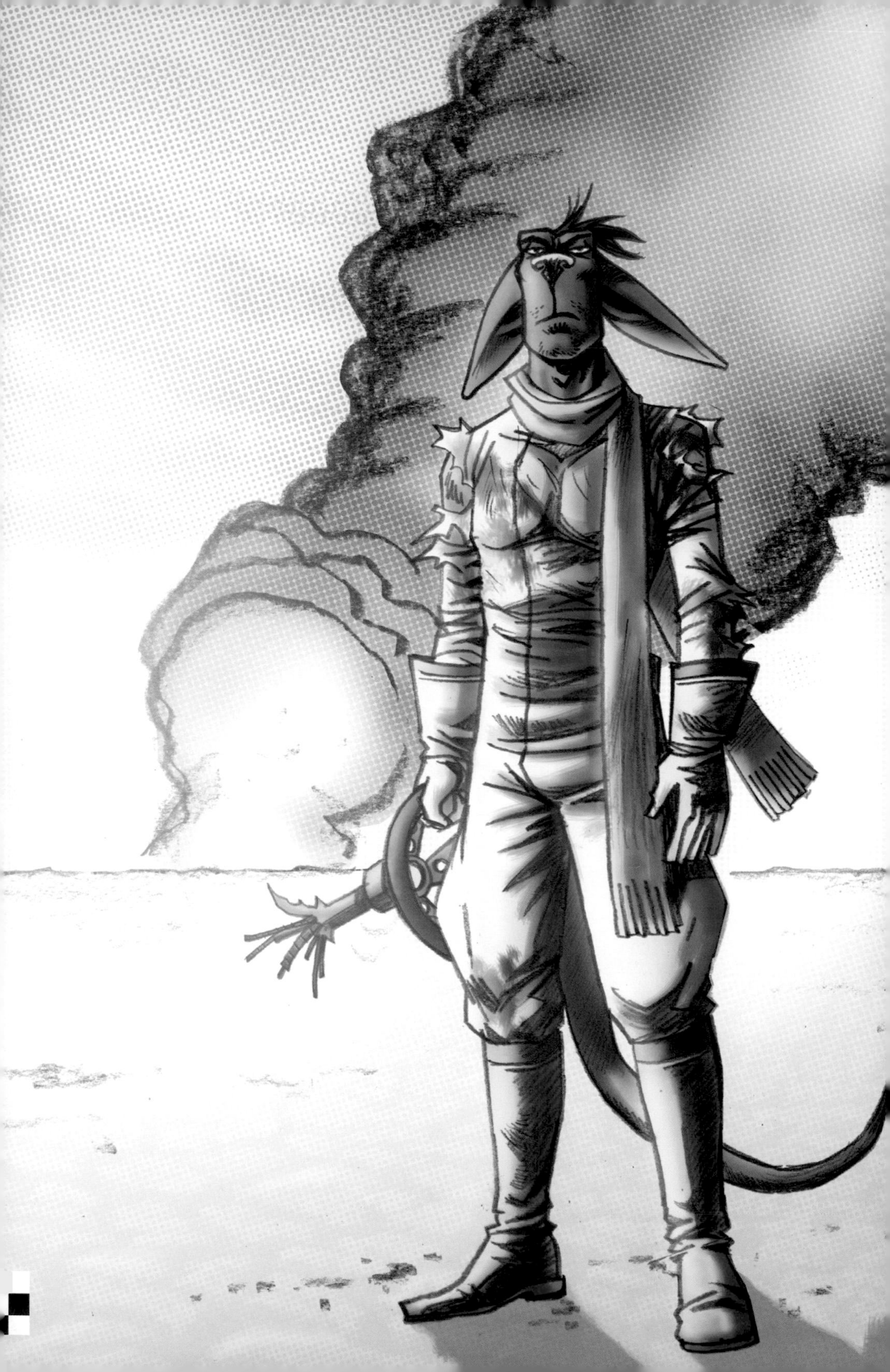

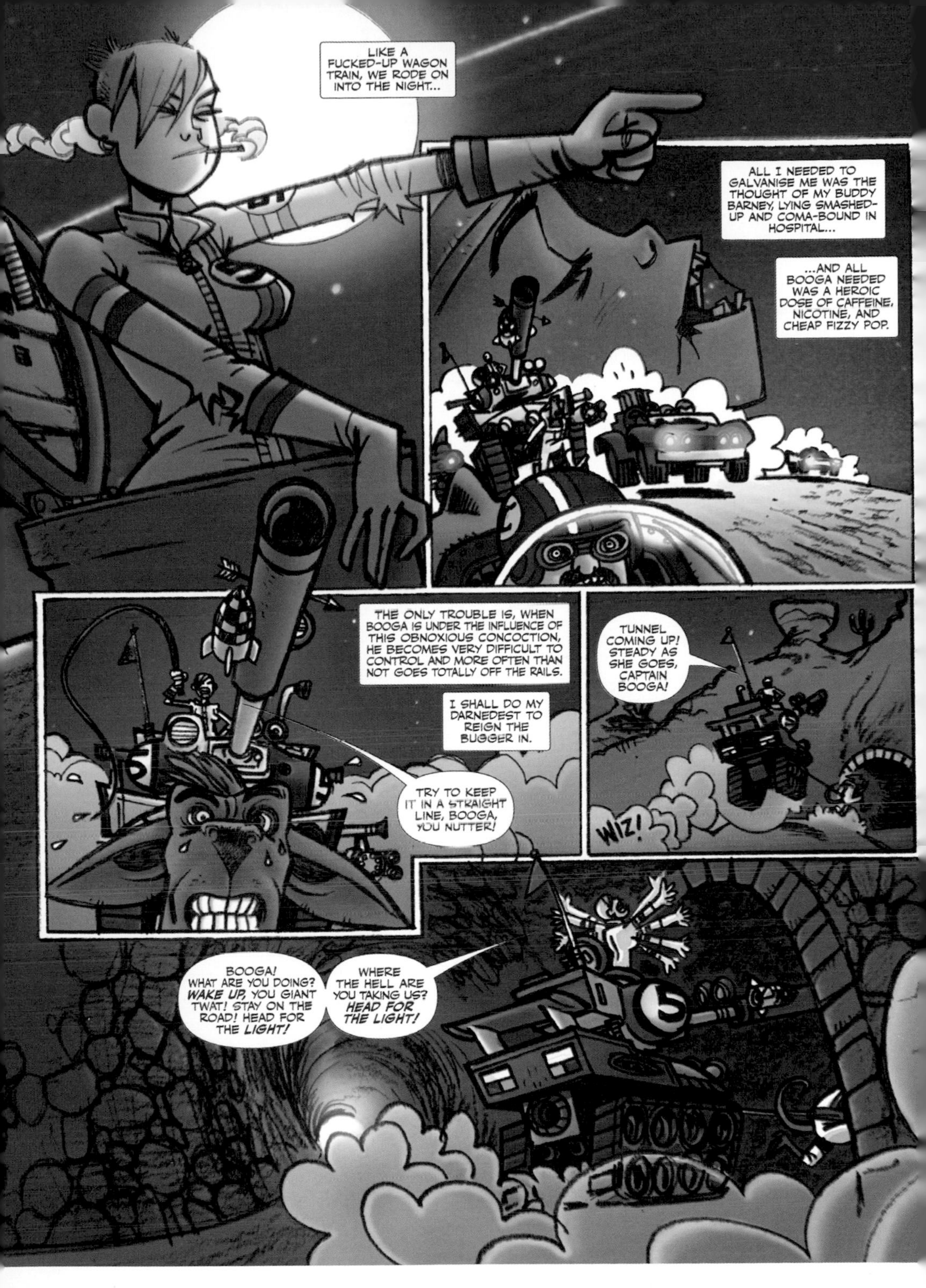

LIKE A FUCKED-UP WAGON TRAIN, WE RODE ON INTO THE NIGHT...
ALL I NEEDED TO GALVANISE ME WAS THE THOUGHT OF MY BUDDY BARNEY, LYING SMASHED-UP AND COMA-BOUND IN HOSPITAL...
...AND ALL BOOGA NEEDED WAS A HEROIC DOSE OF CAFFEINE, NICOTINE, AND CHEAP FIZZY POP.
THE ONLY TROUBLE IS, WHEN BOOGA IS UNDER THE INFLUENCE OF THIS OBNOXIOUS CONCOCTION, HE BECOMES VERY DIFFICULT TO CONTROL AND MORE OFTEN THAN NOT GOES TOTALLY OFF THE RAILS.
I SHALL DO MY DARNEDEST TO REIGN THE BUGGER IN.
TRY TO KEEP IT IN A STRAIGHT LINE, BOOGA, YOU NUTTER!
TUNNEL COMING UP! STEADY AS SHE GOES, CAPTAIN BOOGA!
WIZ!
BOOGA! WHAT ARE YOU DOING? WAKE UP, YOU GIANT TWAT! STAY ON THE ROAD! HEAD FOR THE LIGHT!
WHERE THE HELL ARE YOU TAKING US? HEAD FOR THE LIGHT!

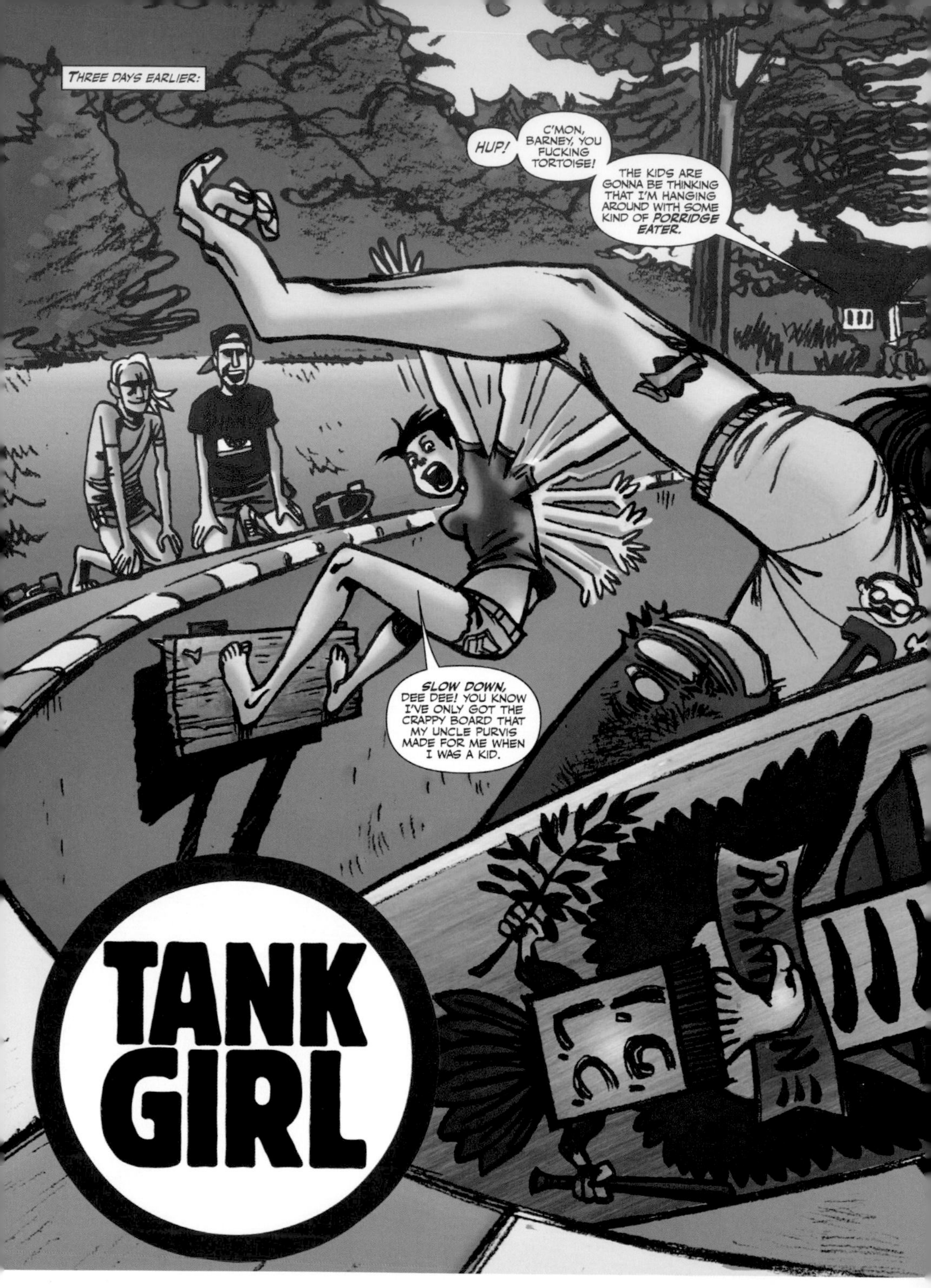
THREE DAYS EARLIER:
HUP!
C'MON, BARNEY, YOU FUCKING TORTOISE!
THE KIDS ARE GONNA BE THINKING THAT I'M HANGING AROUND WITH SOME KIND OF PORRIDGE EATER.
SLOW DOWN, DEE DEE! YOU KNOW I'VE ONLY GOT THE CRAPPY BOARD THAT MY UNCLE PURVIS MADE FOR ME WHEN I WAS A KID.
TANK GIRL

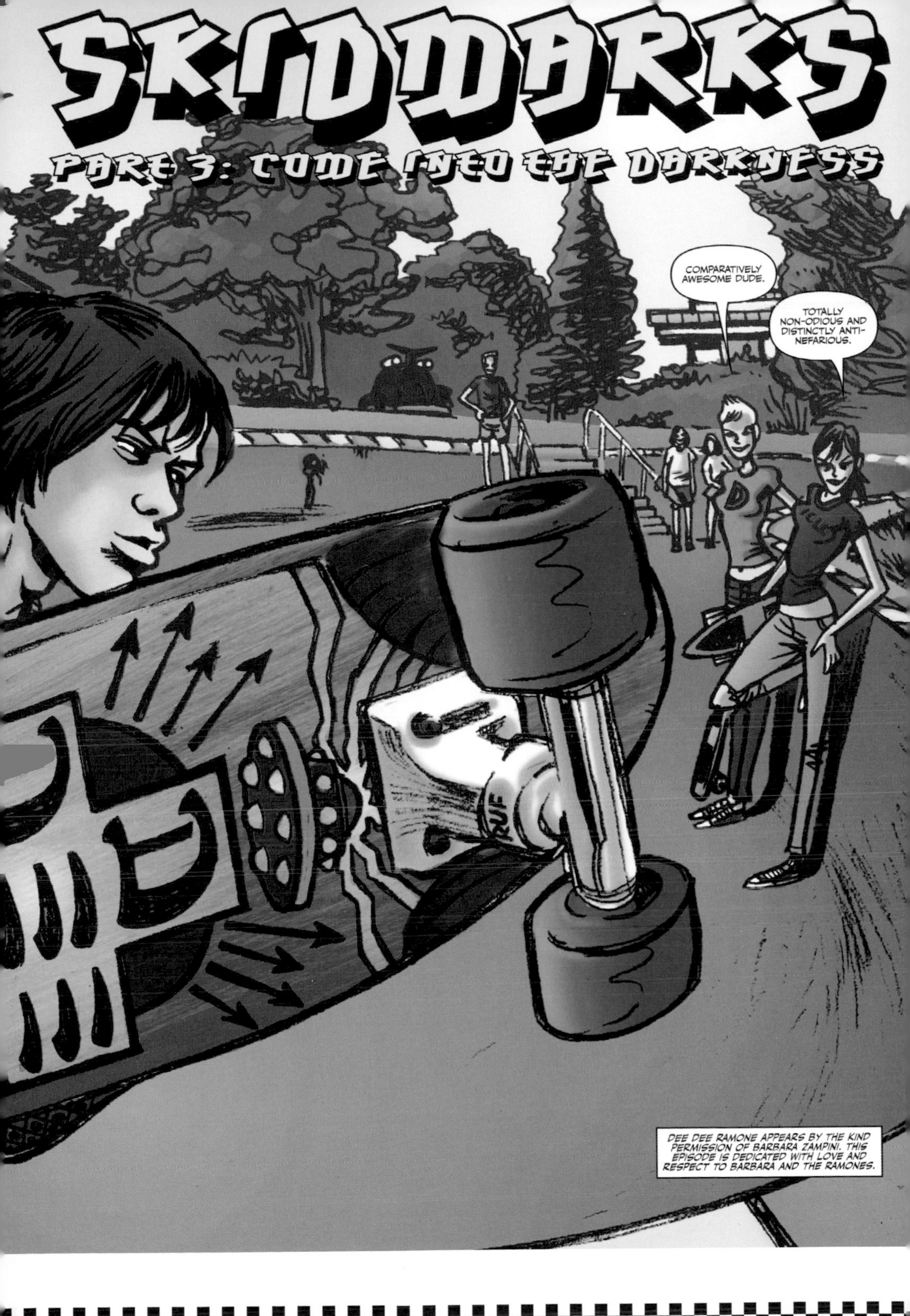
SKIDMARKS
PART 3: COME INTO THE DARKNESS
COMPARATIVELY AWESOME DUDE.
TOTALLY NON-ODIOUS AND DISTINCTLY ANTI-NEFARIOUS.
DEE DEE RAMONE APPEARS BY THE KIND PERMISSION OF BARBARA ZAMPINI. THIS EPISODE IS DEDICATED WITH LOVE AND RESPECT TO BARBARA AND THE RAMONES.

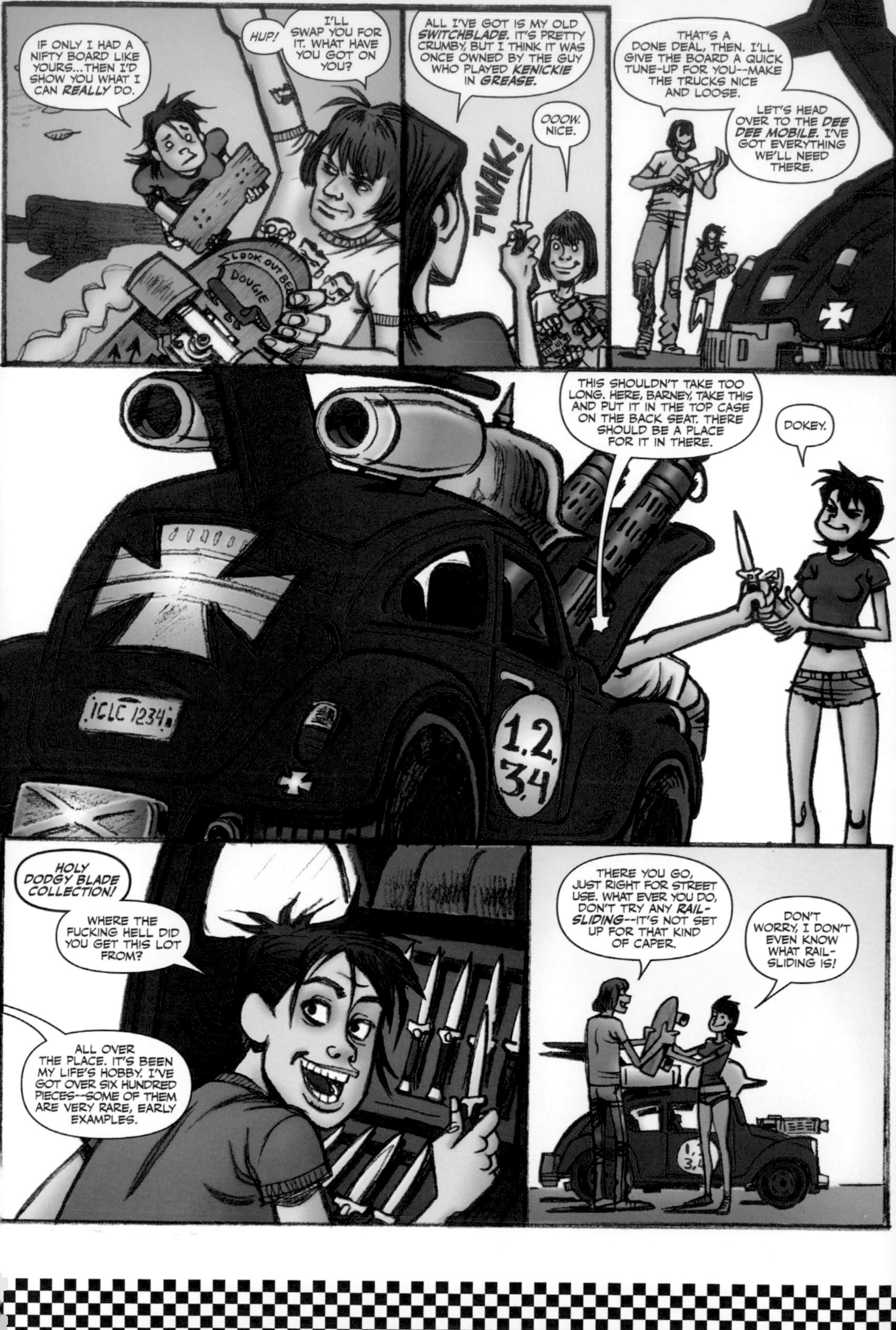
IF ONLY I HAD A NIFTY BOARD LIKE YOURS...THEN I'D SHOW YOU WHAT I CAN REALLY DO.
HUP!
I'LL SWAP YOU FOR IT. WHAT HAVE YOU GOT ON YOU?
LOOK OUT BE
DOUGIE
ALL I'VE GOT IS MY OLD SWITCHBLADE. IT'S PRETTY CRUMBY, BUT I THINK IT WAS ONCE OWNED BY THE GUY WHO PLAYED KENICKIE IN GREASE.
TWAK!
OOOW. NICE.
THAT'S A DONE DEAL, THEN. I'LL GIVE THE BOARD A QUICK TUNE-UP FOR YOU--MAKE THE TRUCKS NICE AND LOOSE.
LET'S HEAD OVER TO THE DEE DEE MOBILE. I'VE GOT EVERYTHING WE'LL NEED THERE.
THIS SHOULDN'T TAKE TOO LONG. HERE, BARNEY, TAKE THIS AND PUT IT IN THE TOP CASE ON THE BACK SEAT. THERE SHOULD BE A PLACE FOR IT IN THERE.
DOKEY.
ICLC 1234
1,2, 3,4
HOLY DODGY BLADE COLLECTION!
WHERE THE FUCKING HELL DID YOU GET THIS LOT FROM?
ALL OVER THE PLACE. IT'S BEEN MY LIFE'S HOBBY. I'VE GOT OVER SIX HUNDRED PIECES--SOME OF THEM ARE VERY RARE, EARLY EXAMPLES.
THERE YOU GO, JUST RIGHT FOR STREET USE. WHAT EVER YOU DO, DON'T TRY ANY RAIL-SLIDING--IT'S NOT SET UP FOR THAT KIND OF CAPER.
DON'T WORRY, I DON'T EVEN KNOW WHAT RAIL-SLIDING IS!

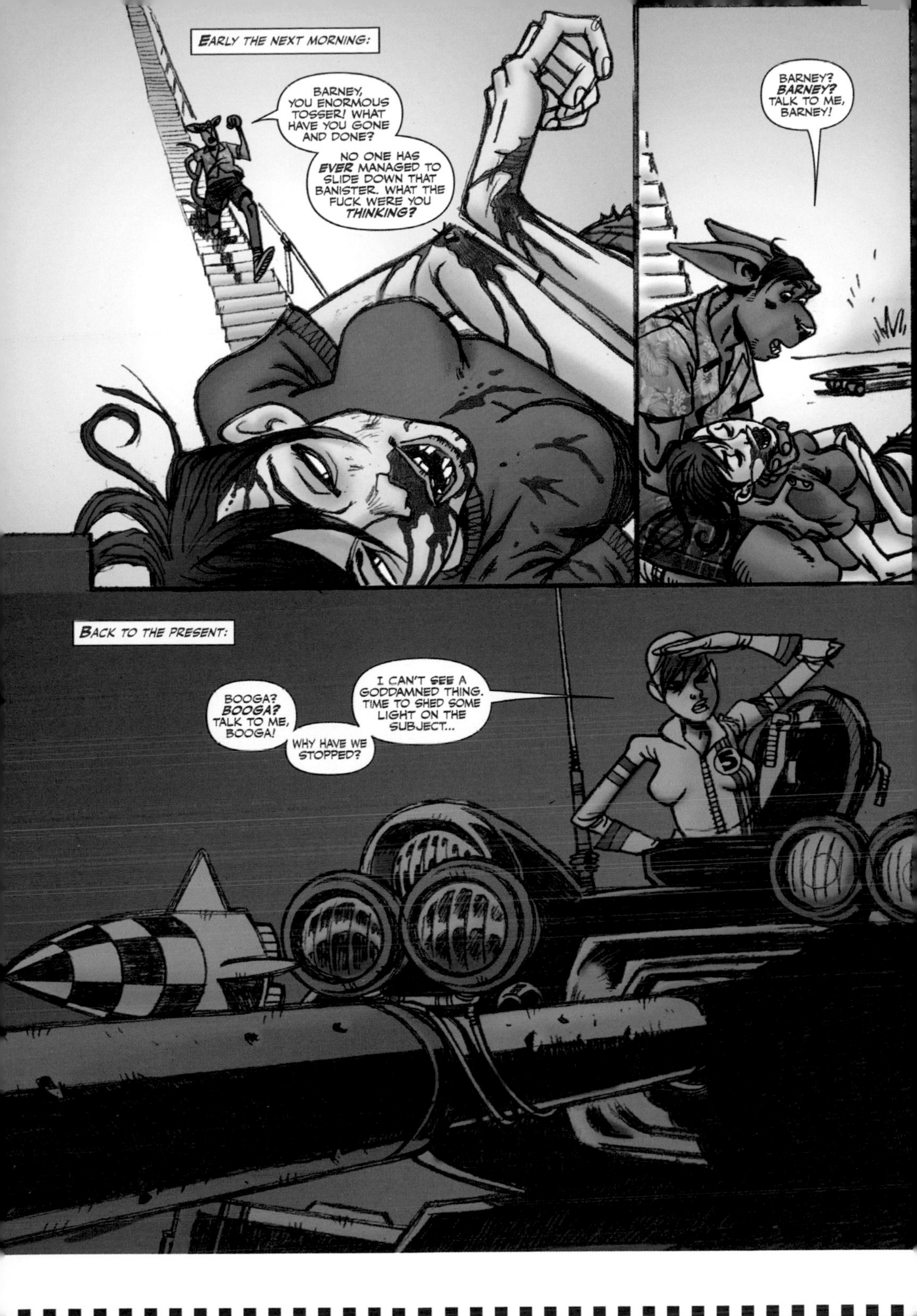
EARLY THE NEXT MORNING:
BARNEY, YOU ENORMOUS TOSSER! WHAT HAVE YOU GONE AND DONE?
NO ONE HAS **EVER** MANAGED TO SLIDE DOWN THAT BANISTER. WHAT THE FUCK WERE YOU ***THINKING?***
BARNEY? ***BARNEY?*** TALK TO ME, BARNEY!
BACK TO THE PRESENT:
BOOGA? ***BOOGA?*** TALK TO ME, BOOGA!
WHY HAVE WE STOPPED?
I CAN'T SEE A GODDAMNED THING. TIME TO SHED SOME LIGHT ON THE SUBJECT...

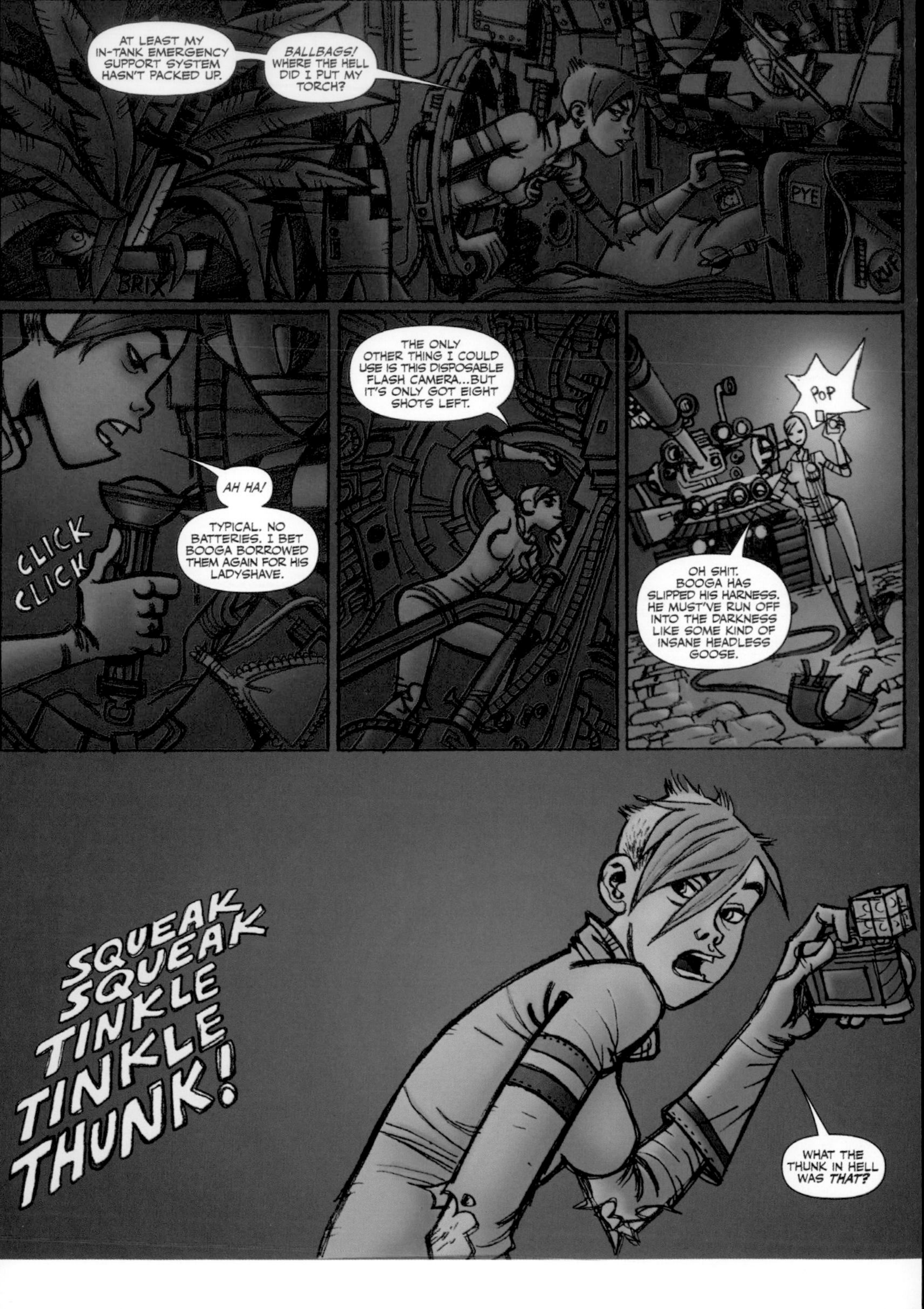
AT LEAST MY IN-TANK EMERGENCY SUPPORT SYSTEM HASN'T PACKED UP.
BALLBAGS! WHERE THE HELL DID I PUT MY TORCH?
PYE
BRIX
AH HA!
CLICK CLICK
TYPICAL. NO BATTERIES. I BET BOOGA BORROWED THEM AGAIN FOR HIS LADYSHAVE.
THE ONLY OTHER THING I COULD USE IS THIS DISPOSABLE FLASH CAMERA...BUT IT'S ONLY GOT EIGHT SHOTS LEFT.
POP
OH SHIT. BOOGA HAS SLIPPED HIS HARNESS. HE MUST'VE RUN OFF INTO THE DARKNESS LIKE SOME KIND OF INSANE HEADLESS GOOSE.
SQUEAK SQUEAK TINKLE TINKLE THUNK!
WHAT THE THUNK IN HELL WAS THAT?

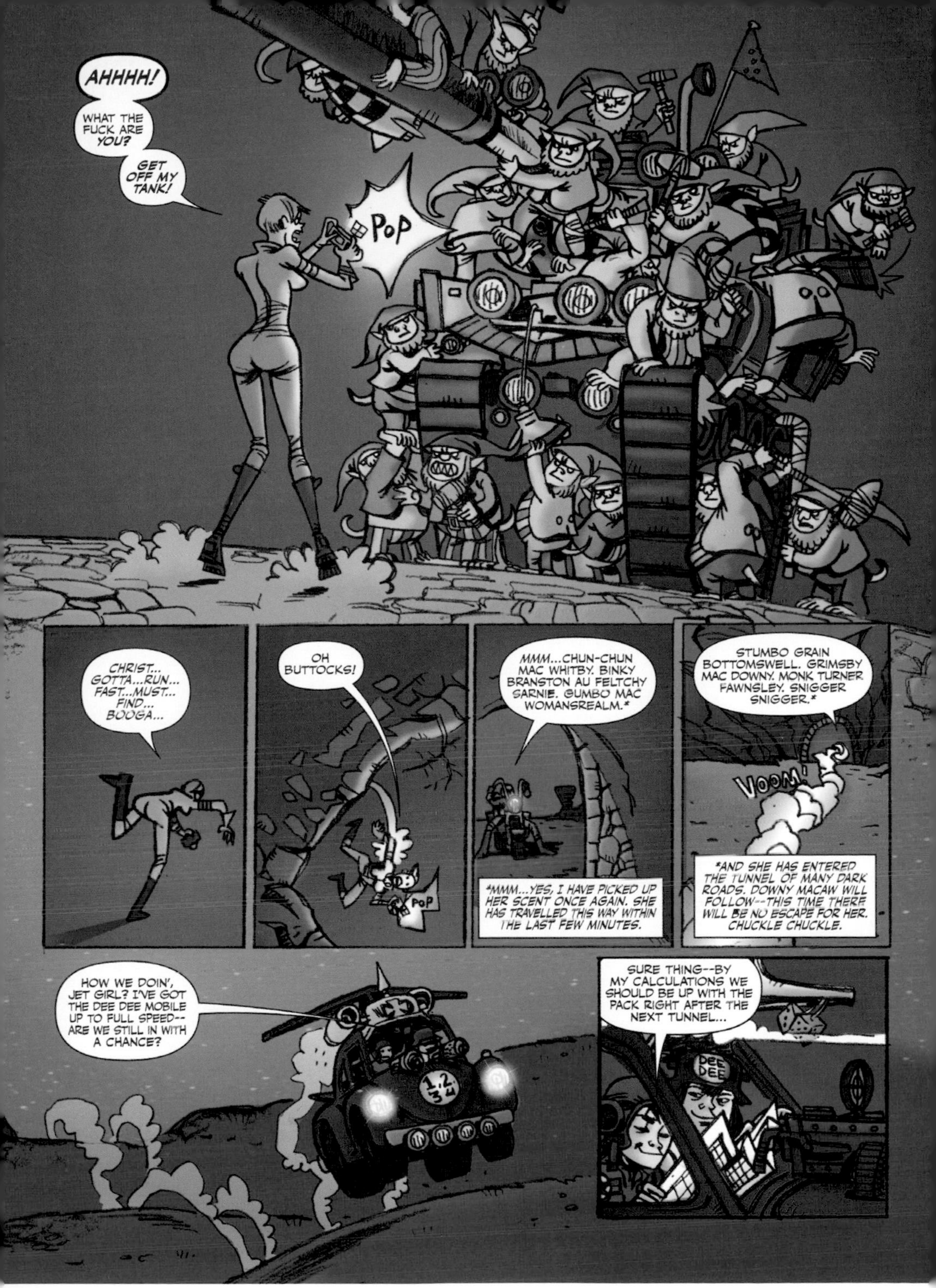
AHHHH!
WHAT THE FUCK ARE YOU?
GET OFF MY TANK!
POP
CHRIST... GOTTA...RUN... FAST...MUST... FIND... BOOGA...
OH BUTTOCKS!
POP
MMM...CHUN-CHUN MAC WHITBY. BINKY BRANSTON AU FELTCHY SARNIE. GUMBO MAC WOMANSREALM.*
*MMM...YES, I HAVE PICKED UP HER SCENT ONCE AGAIN. SHE HAS TRAVELLED THIS WAY WITHIN THE LAST FEW MINUTES.
STUMBO GRAIN BOTTOMSWELL. GRIMSBY MAC DOWNY. MONK TURNER FAWNSLEY. SNIGGER SNIGGER.*
VOOM!
*AND SHE HAS ENTERED THE TUNNEL OF MANY DARK ROADS. DOWNY MACAW WILL FOLLOW--THIS TIME THERE WILL BE NO ESCAPE FOR HER. CHUCKLE CHUCKLE.
HOW WE DOIN', JET GIRL? I'VE GOT THE DEE DEE MOBILE UP TO FULL SPEED--ARE WE STILL IN WITH A CHANCE?
SURE THING--BY MY CALCULATIONS WE SHOULD BE UP WITH THE PACK RIGHT AFTER THE NEXT TUNNEL...

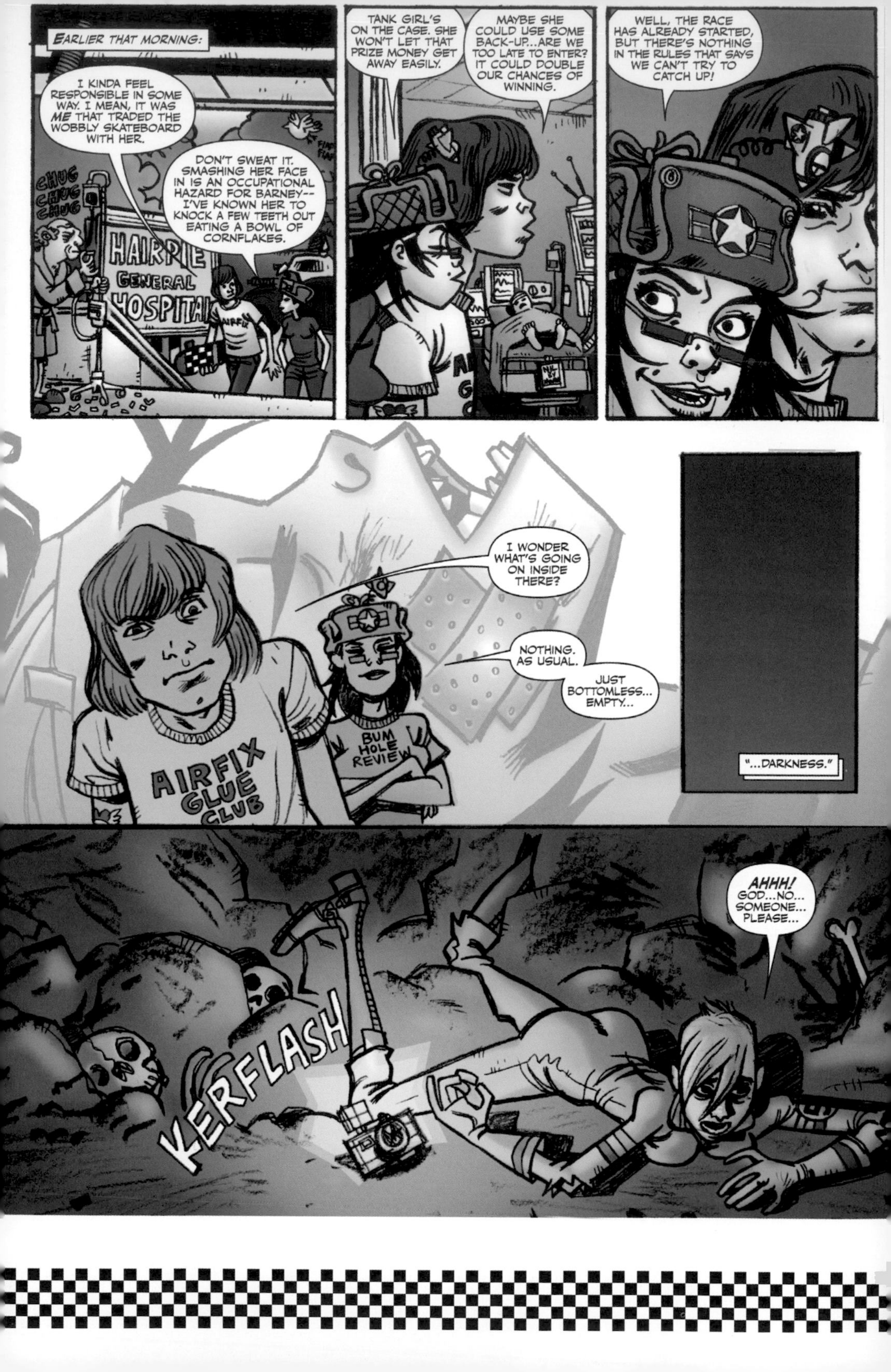
EARLIER THAT MORNING:
I KINDA FEEL RESPONSIBLE IN SOME WAY. I MEAN, IT WAS ME THAT TRADED THE WOBBLY SKATEBOARD WITH HER.
DON'T SWEAT IT. SMASHING HER FACE IN IS AN OCCUPATIONAL HAZARD FOR BARNEY-- I'VE KNOWN HER TO KNOCK A FEW TEETH OUT EATING A BOWL OF CORNFLAKES.
CHUG CHUG CHUG
HAIRPIE GENERAL HOSPITAL
AIRFIX
TANK GIRL'S ON THE CASE. SHE WON'T LET THAT PRIZE MONEY GET AWAY EASILY.
MAYBE SHE COULD USE SOME BACK-UP...ARE WE TOO LATE TO ENTER? IT COULD DOUBLE OUR CHANCES OF WINNING.
WELL, THE RACE HAS ALREADY STARTED, BUT THERE'S NOTHING IN THE RULES THAT SAYS WE CAN'T TRY TO CATCH UP!
I WONDER WHAT'S GOING ON INSIDE THERE?
NOTHING. AS USUAL.
JUST BOTTOMLESS... EMPTY...
"...DARKNESS."
AIRFIX GLUE CLUB
BUM HOLE REVIEW
AHHH! GOD...NO... SOMEONE... PLEASE...
KERFLASH

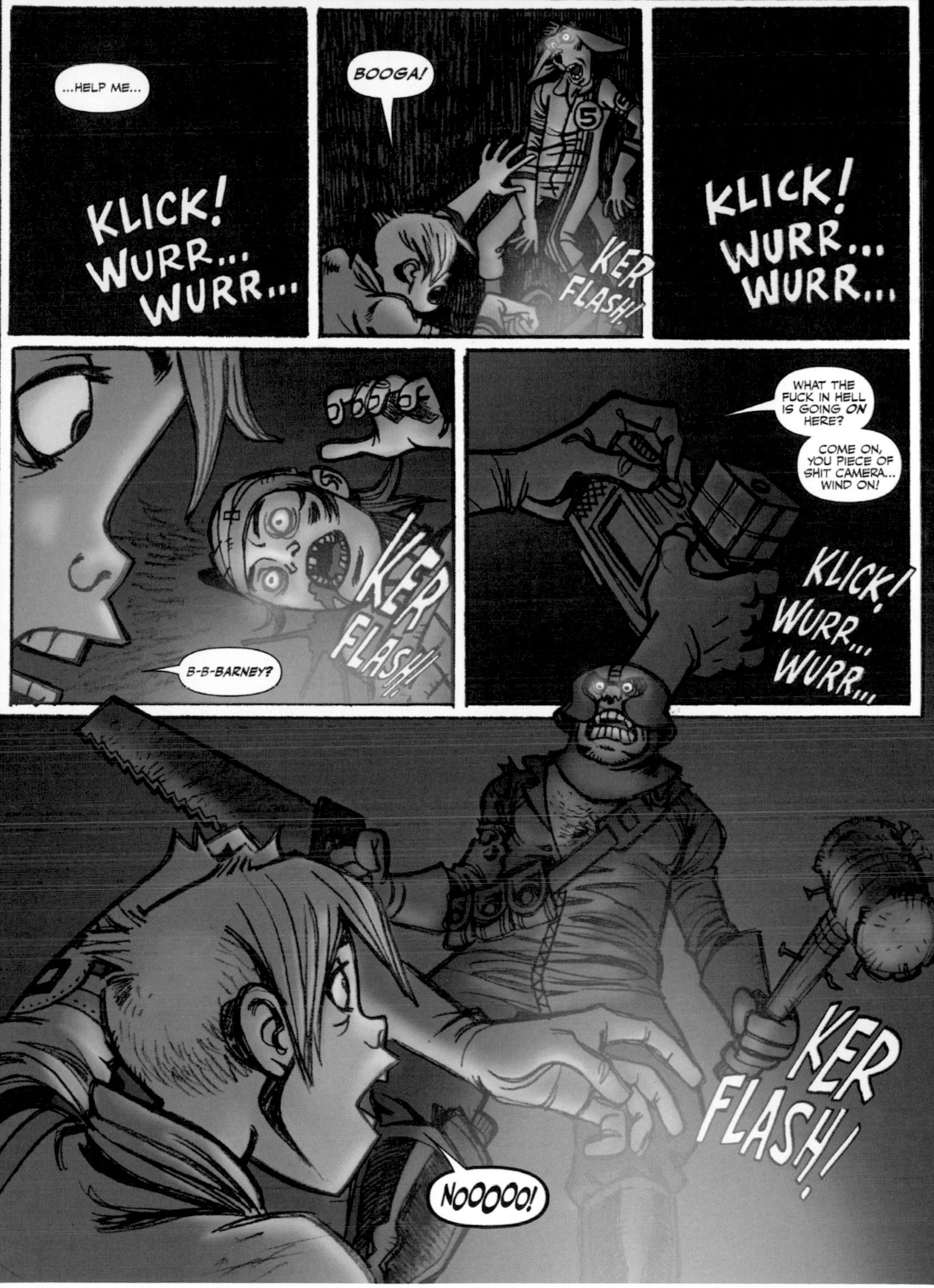

...HELP ME...
KLICK! WURR... WURR...
BOOGA!
KER FLASH!
KLICK! WURR... WURR...
KER FLASH!!
B-B-BARNEY?
WHAT THE FUCK IN HELL IS GOING ON HERE?
COME ON, YOU PIECE OF SHIT CAMERA... WIND ON!
KLICK! WURR... WURR...
KER FLASH!
NOOOOO!

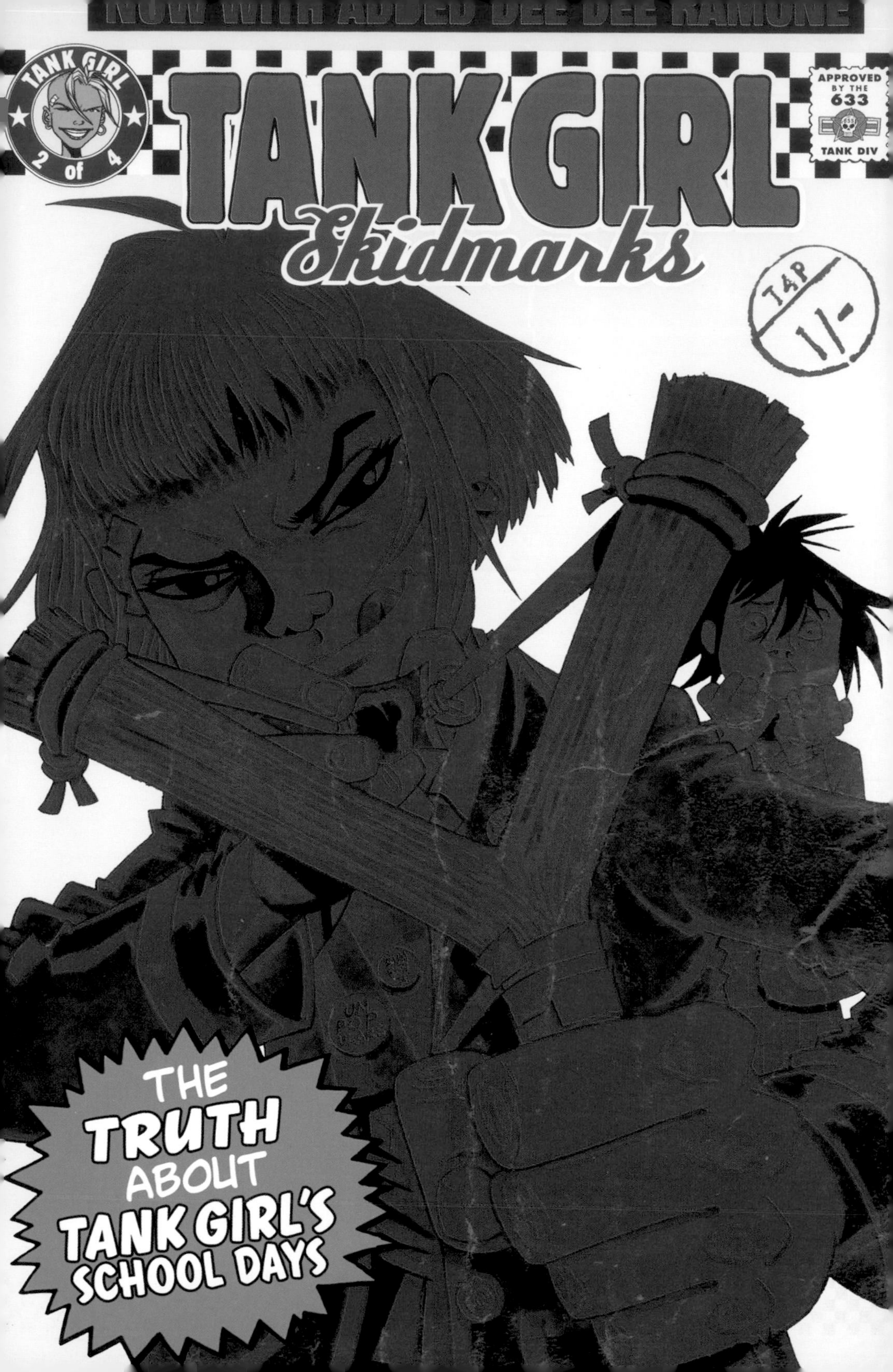

NOW WITH ADDED DEE DEE RAMONE
TANK GIRL 2 of 4
TANK GIRL
Skidmarks
APPROVED BY THE 633
TANK DIV
T4P
1/-
THE TRUTH ABOUT TANK GIRL'S SCHOOL DAYS

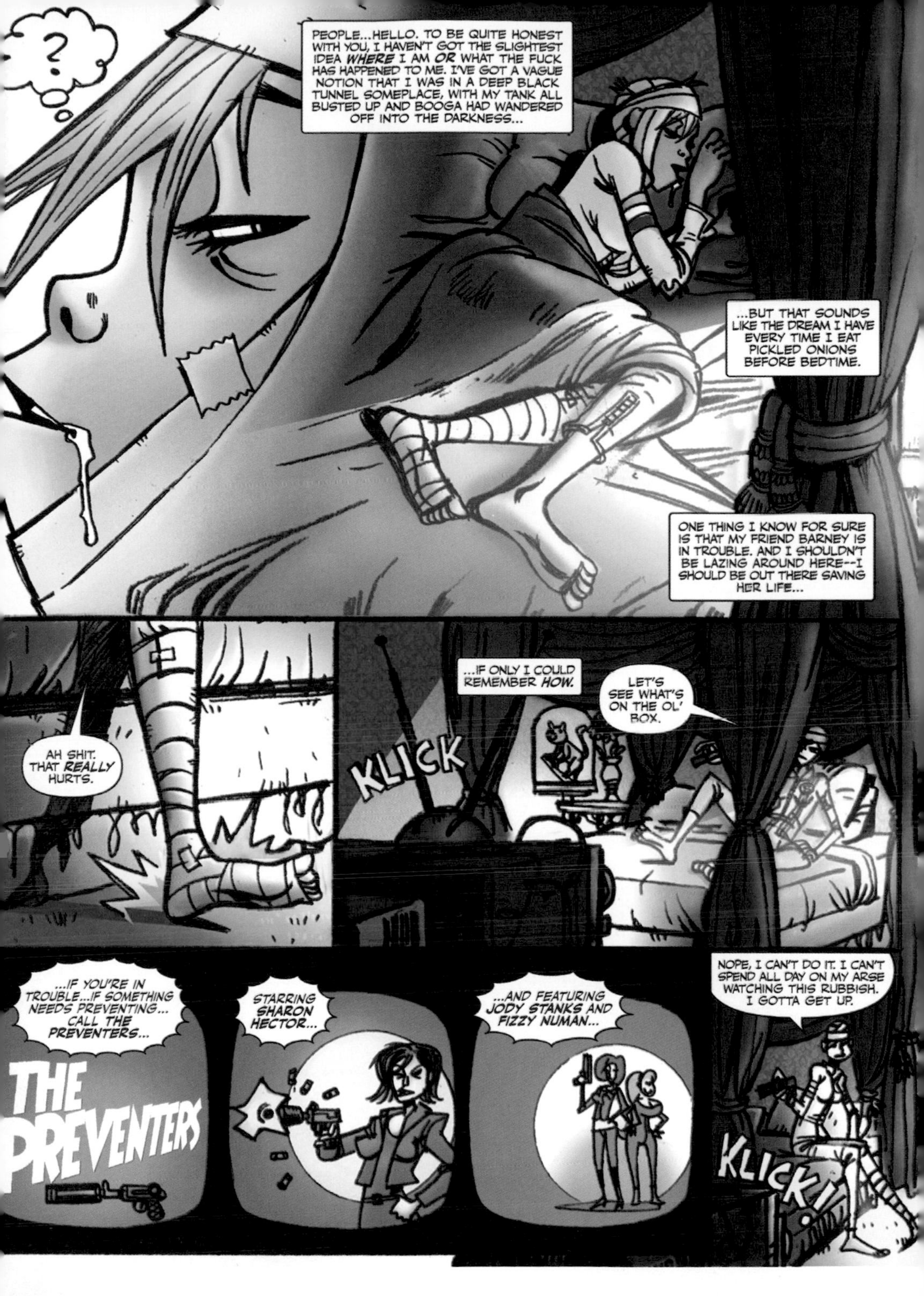
?
PEOPLE...HELLO. TO BE QUITE HONEST WITH YOU, I HAVEN'T GOT THE SLIGHTEST IDEA WHERE I AM OR WHAT THE FUCK HAS HAPPENED TO ME. I'VE GOT A VAGUE NOTION THAT I WAS IN A DEEP BLACK TUNNEL SOMEPLACE, WITH MY TANK ALL BUSTED UP AND BOOGA HAD WANDERED OFF INTO THE DARKNESS...
...BUT THAT SOUNDS LIKE THE DREAM I HAVE EVERY TIME I EAT PICKLED ONIONS BEFORE BEDTIME.
ONE THING I KNOW FOR SURE IS THAT MY FRIEND BARNEY IS IN TROUBLE. AND I SHOULDN'T BE LAZING AROUND HERE--I SHOULD BE OUT THERE SAVING HER LIFE...
AH SHIT. THAT REALLY HURTS.
...IF ONLY I COULD REMEMBER HOW.
LET'S SEE WHAT'S ON THE OL' BOX.
KLICK
...IF YOU'RE IN TROUBLE...IF SOMETHING NEEDS PREVENTING... CALL THE PREVENTERS...
THE PREVENTERS
STARRING SHARON HECTOR...
...AND FEATURING JODY STANKS AND FIZZY NUMAN...
NOPE, I CAN'T DO IT. I CAN'T SPEND ALL DAY ON MY ARSE WATCHING THIS RUBBISH. I GOTTA GET UP.
KLICK!

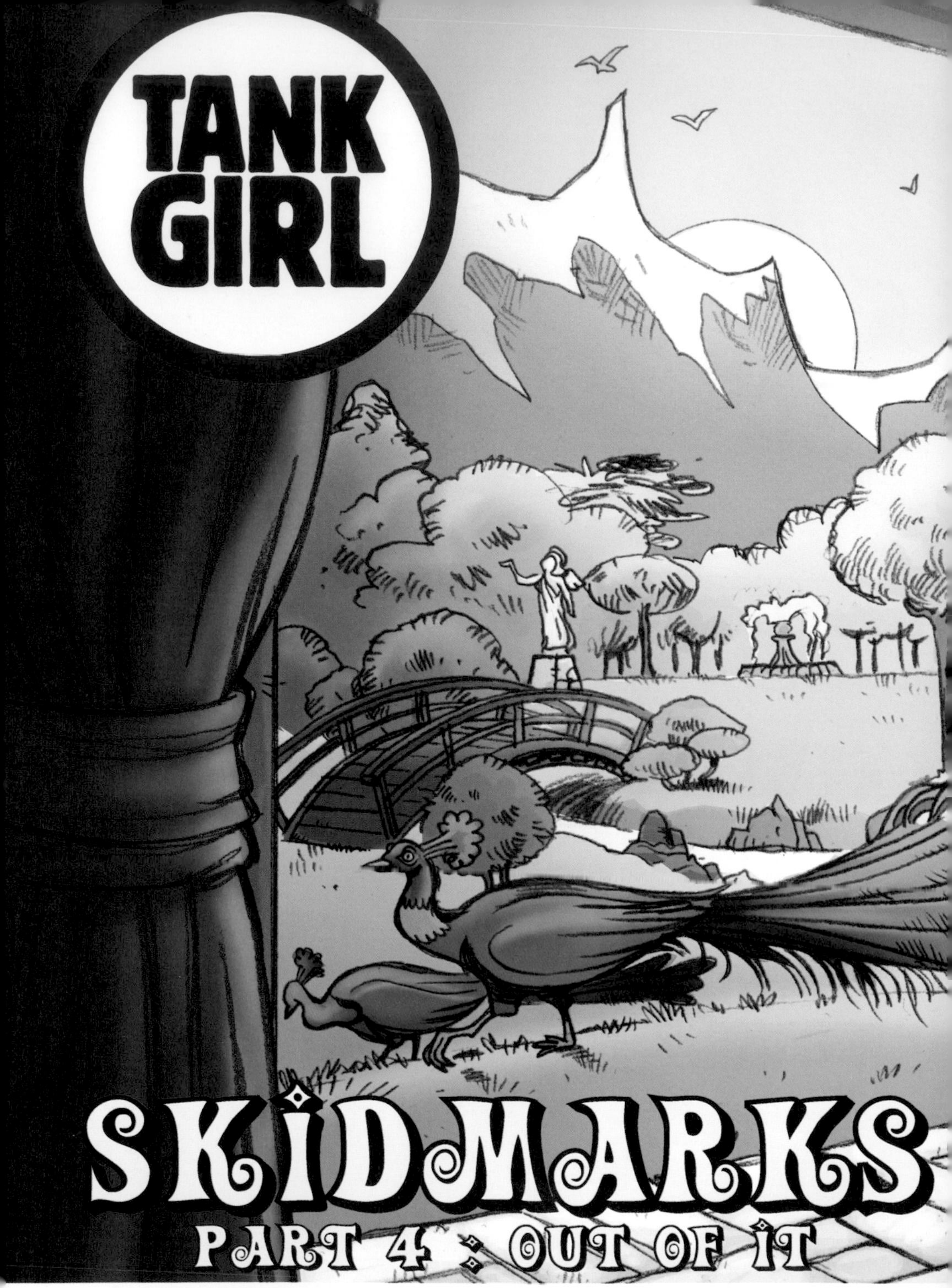
TANK GIRL
SKIDMARKS
PART 4 : OUT OF IT

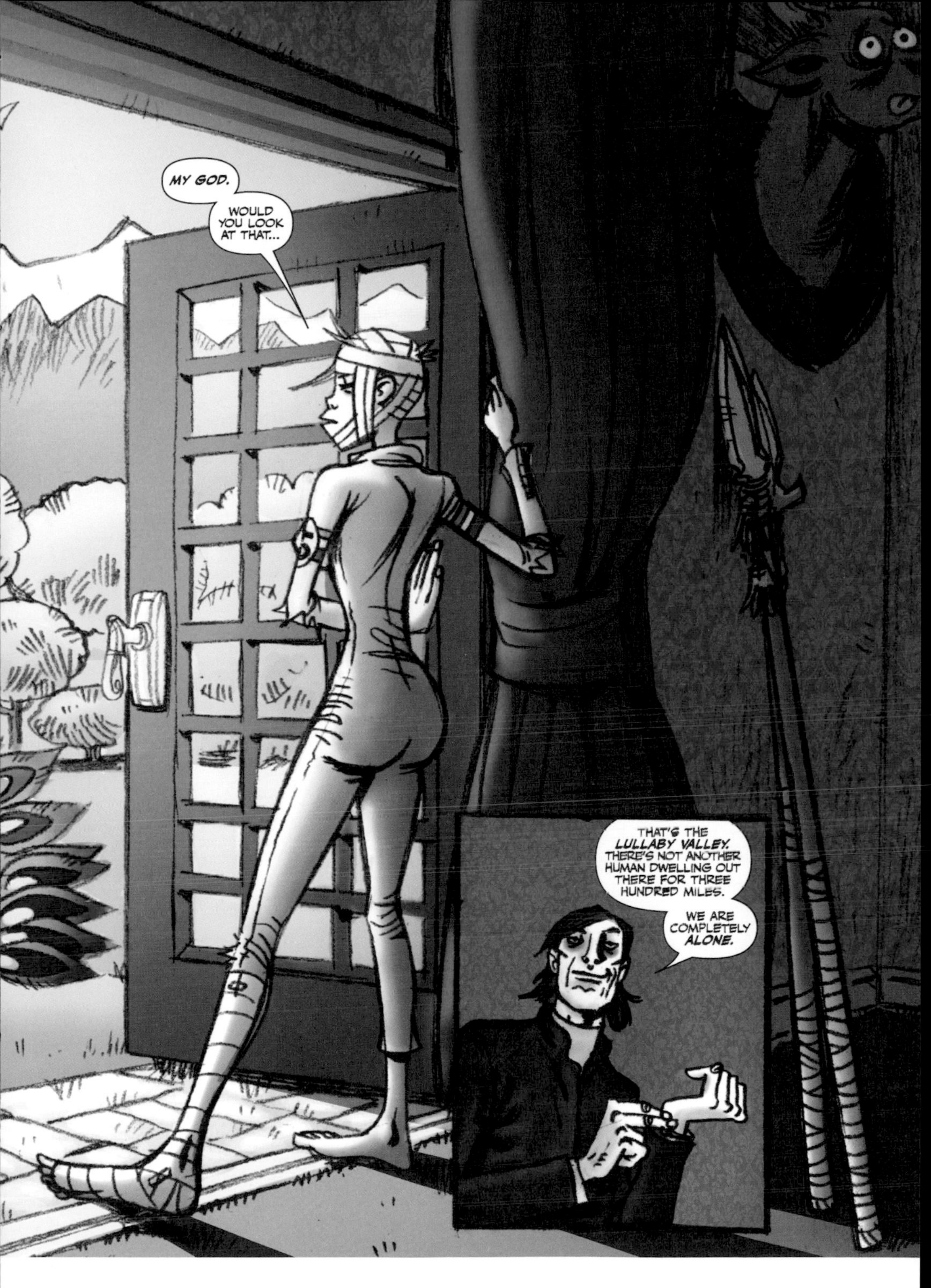
MY GOD.
WOULD YOU LOOK AT THAT...
THAT'S THE LULLABY VALLEY. THERE'S NOT ANOTHER HUMAN DWELLING OUT THERE FOR THREE HUNDRED MILES.
WE ARE COMPLETELY ALONE.

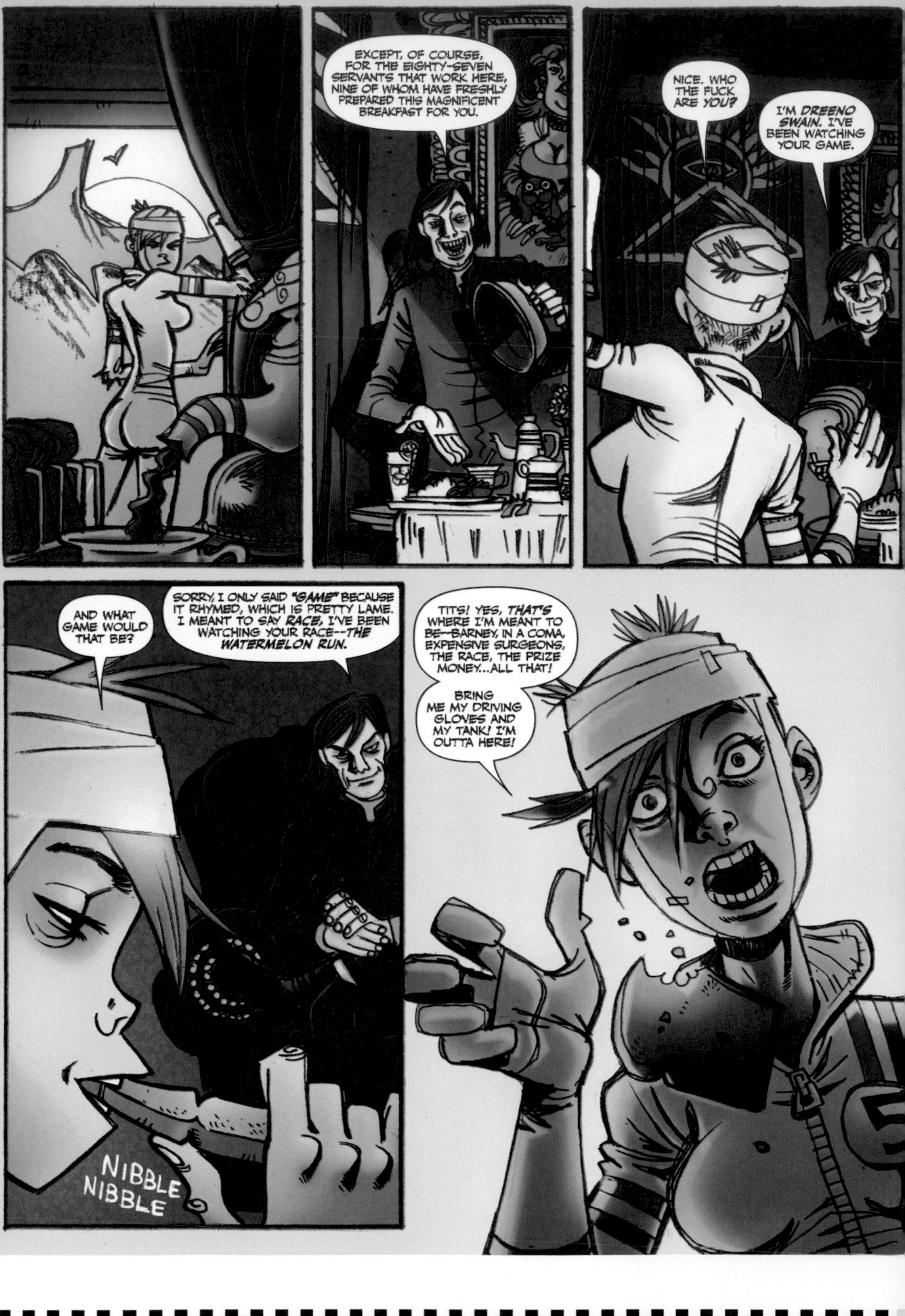
EXCEPT, OF COURSE, FOR THE EIGHTY-SEVEN SERVANTS THAT WORK HERE, NINE OF WHOM HAVE FRESHLY PREPARED THIS MAGNIFICENT BREAKFAST FOR YOU.
NICE. WHO THE FUCK ARE YOU?
I'M DREENO SWAIN. I'VE BEEN WATCHING YOUR GAME.
AND WHAT GAME WOULD THAT BE?
SORRY, I ONLY SAID "GAME" BECAUSE IT RHYMED, WHICH IS PRETTY LAME. I MEANT TO SAY RACE, I'VE BEEN WATCHING YOUR RACE--THE WATERMELON RUN.
NIBBLE NIBBLE
TITS! YES, THAT'S WHERE I'M MEANT TO BE--BARNEY, IN A COMA, EXPENSIVE SURGEONS, THE RACE, THE PRIZE MONEY...ALL THAT!
BRING ME MY DRIVING GLOVES AND MY TANK! I'M OUTTA HERE!

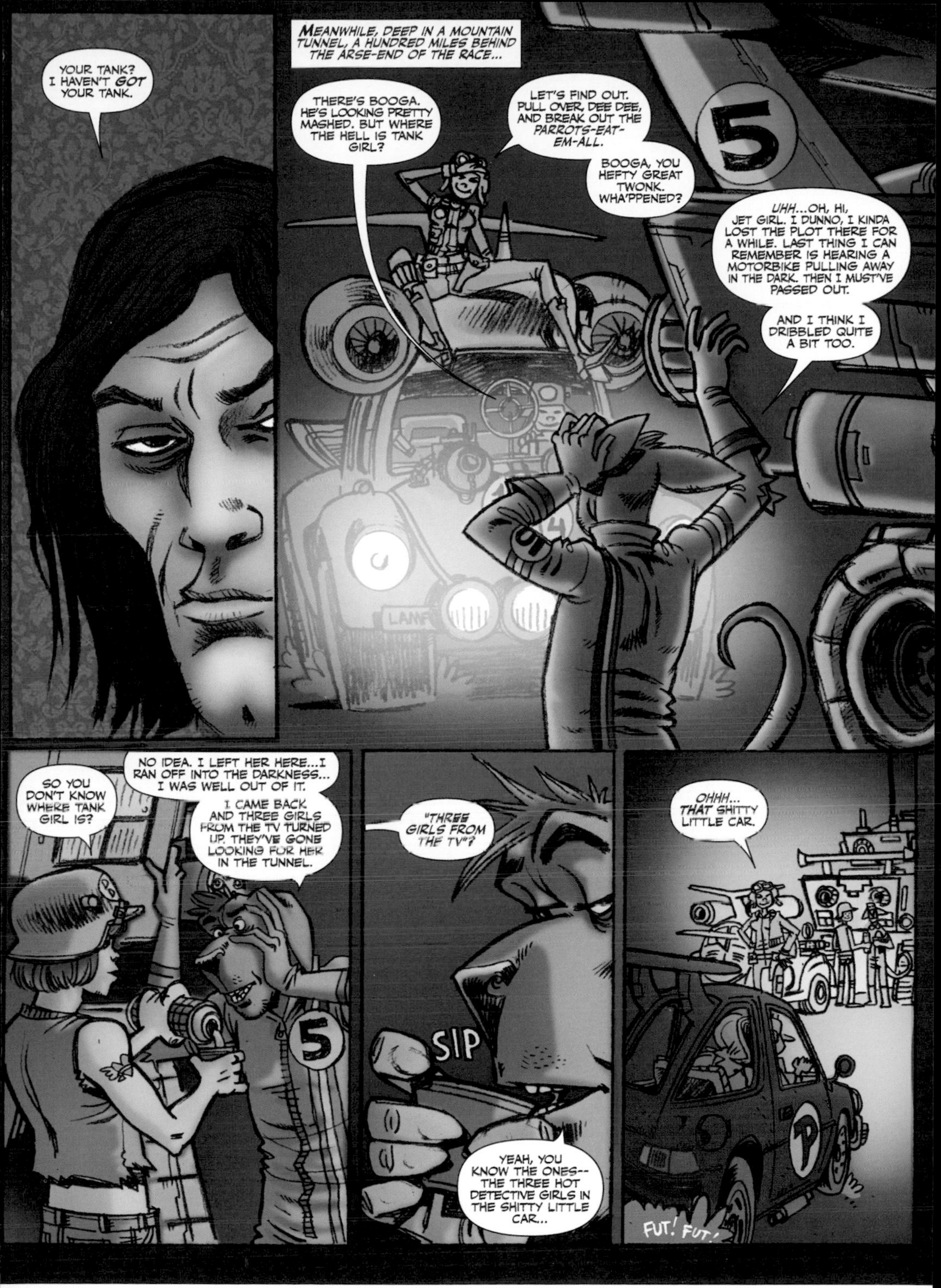
YOUR TANK? I HAVEN'T GOT YOUR TANK.
MEANWHILE, DEEP IN A MOUNTAIN TUNNEL, A HUNDRED MILES BEHIND THE ARSE-END OF THE RACE...
THERE'S BOOGA. HE'S LOOKING PRETTY MASHED. BUT WHERE THE HELL IS TANK GIRL?
LET'S FIND OUT. PULL OVER, DEE DEE, AND BREAK OUT THE PARROTS-EAT-EM-ALL.
BOOGA, YOU HEFTY GREAT TWONK. WHA'PPENED?
5
UHH...OH, HI, JET GIRL. I DUNNO, I KINDA LOST THE PLOT THERE FOR A WHILE. LAST THING I CAN REMEMBER IS HEARING A MOTORBIKE PULLING AWAY IN THE DARK. THEN I MUST'VE PASSED OUT.
AND I THINK I DRIBBLED QUITE A BIT TOO.
LAMP
SO YOU DON'T KNOW WHERE TANK GIRL IS?
NO IDEA. I LEFT HER HERE...I RAN OFF INTO THE DARKNESS... I WAS WELL OUT OF IT.
I CAME BACK AND THREE GIRLS FROM THE TV TURNED UP. THEY'VE GONE LOOKING FOR HER IN THE TUNNEL.
5
"THREE GIRLS FROM THE TV"?
SIP
YEAH, YOU KNOW THE ONES-- THE THREE HOT DETECTIVE GIRLS IN THE SHITTY LITTLE CAR...
OHHH... THAT SHITTY LITTLE CAR.
FUT! FUT!

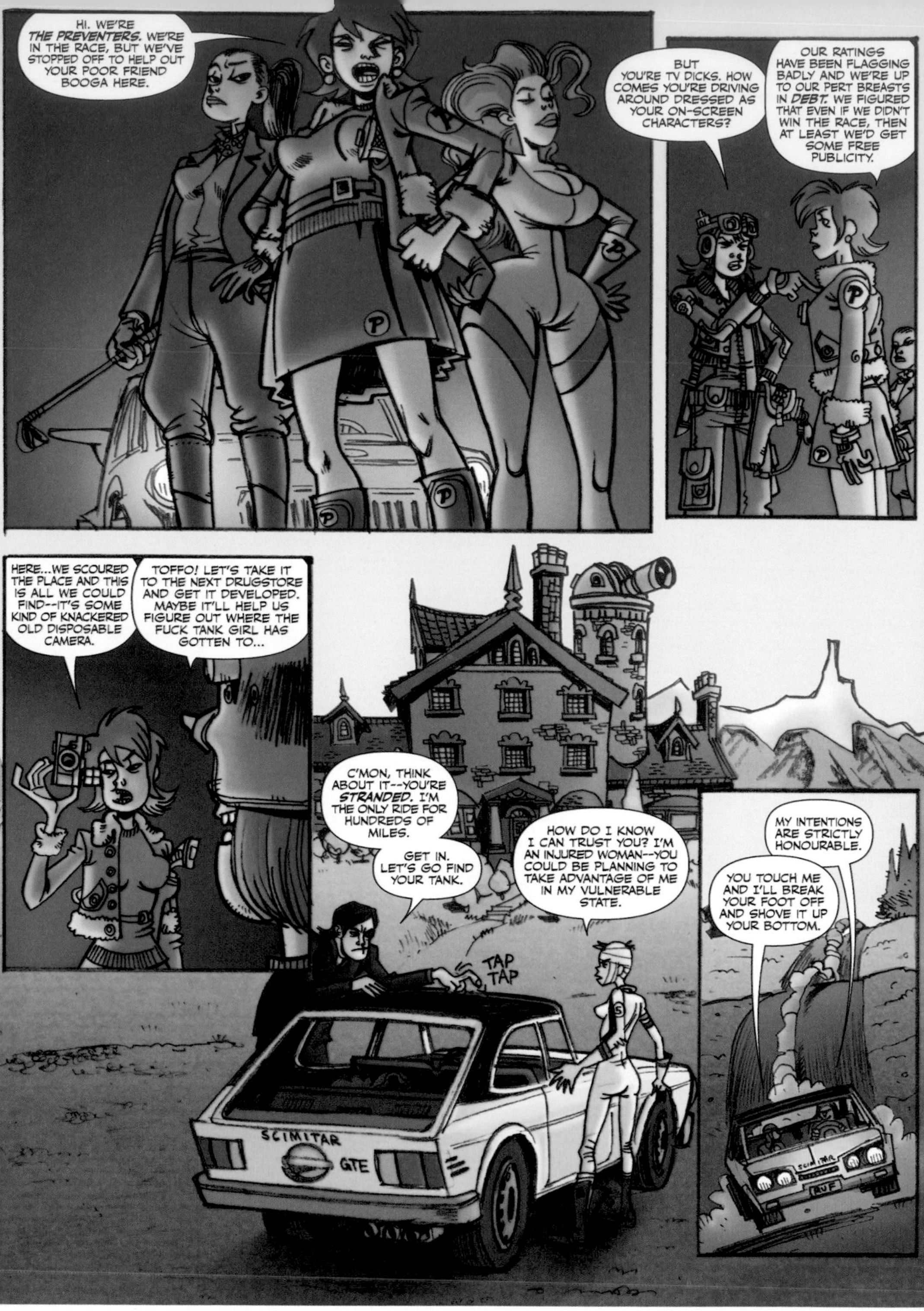
HI. WE'RE THE PREVENTERS. WE'RE IN THE RACE, BUT WE'VE STOPPED OFF TO HELP OUT YOUR POOR FRIEND BOOGA HERE.
BUT YOU'RE TV DICKS. HOW COMES YOU'RE DRIVING AROUND DRESSED AS YOUR ON-SCREEN CHARACTERS?
OUR RATINGS HAVE BEEN FLAGGING BADLY AND WE'RE UP TO OUR PERT BREASTS IN DEBT. WE FIGURED THAT EVEN IF WE DIDN'T WIN THE RACE, THEN AT LEAST WE'D GET SOME FREE PUBLICITY.
HERE...WE SCOURED THE PLACE AND THIS IS ALL WE COULD FIND--IT'S SOME KIND OF KNACKERED OLD DISPOSABLE CAMERA.
TOFFO! LET'S TAKE IT TO THE NEXT DRUGSTORE AND GET IT DEVELOPED. MAYBE IT'LL HELP US FIGURE OUT WHERE THE FUCK TANK GIRL HAS GOTTEN TO...
C'MON, THINK ABOUT IT--YOU'RE STRANDED. I'M THE ONLY RIDE FOR HUNDREDS OF MILES.
GET IN. LET'S GO FIND YOUR TANK.
HOW DO I KNOW I CAN TRUST YOU? I'M AN INJURED WOMAN--YOU COULD BE PLANNING TO TAKE ADVANTAGE OF ME IN MY VULNERABLE STATE.
TAP TAP
SCIMITAR
GTE
MY INTENTIONS ARE STRICTLY HONOURABLE.
YOU TOUCH ME AND I'LL BREAK YOUR FOOT OFF AND SHOVE IT UP YOUR BOTTOM.

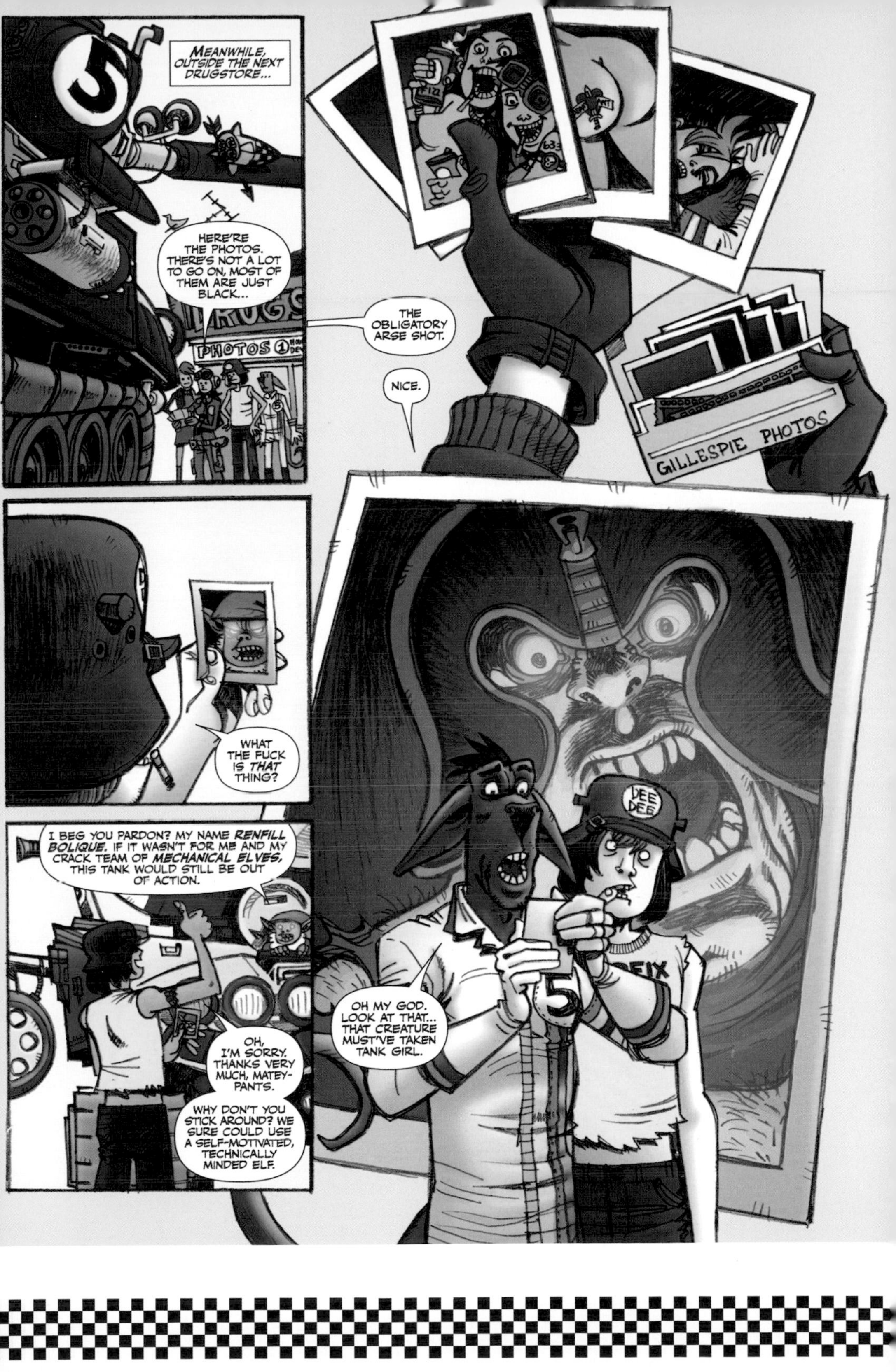
MEANWHILE, OUTSIDE THE NEXT DRUGSTORE...
DRUGS
PHOTOS 1
HERE'RE THE PHOTOS. THERE'S NOT A LOT TO GO ON, MOST OF THEM ARE JUST BLACK...
THE OBLIGATORY ARSE SHOT.
NICE.
GILLESPIE PHOTOS
WHAT THE FUCK IS *THAT* THING?
OH MY GOD. LOOK AT THAT... THAT CREATURE MUST'VE TAKEN TANK GIRL.
DEE DEE
I BEG YOU PARDON? MY NAME *RENFILL BOLIQUE*. IF IT WASN'T FOR ME AND MY CRACK TEAM OF *MECHANICAL ELVES*, THIS TANK WOULD STILL BE OUT OF ACTION.
OH, I'M SORRY. THANKS VERY MUCH, MATEY-PANTS.
WHY DON'T YOU STICK AROUND? WE SURE COULD USE A SELF-MOTIVATED, TECHNICALLY MINDED ELF.

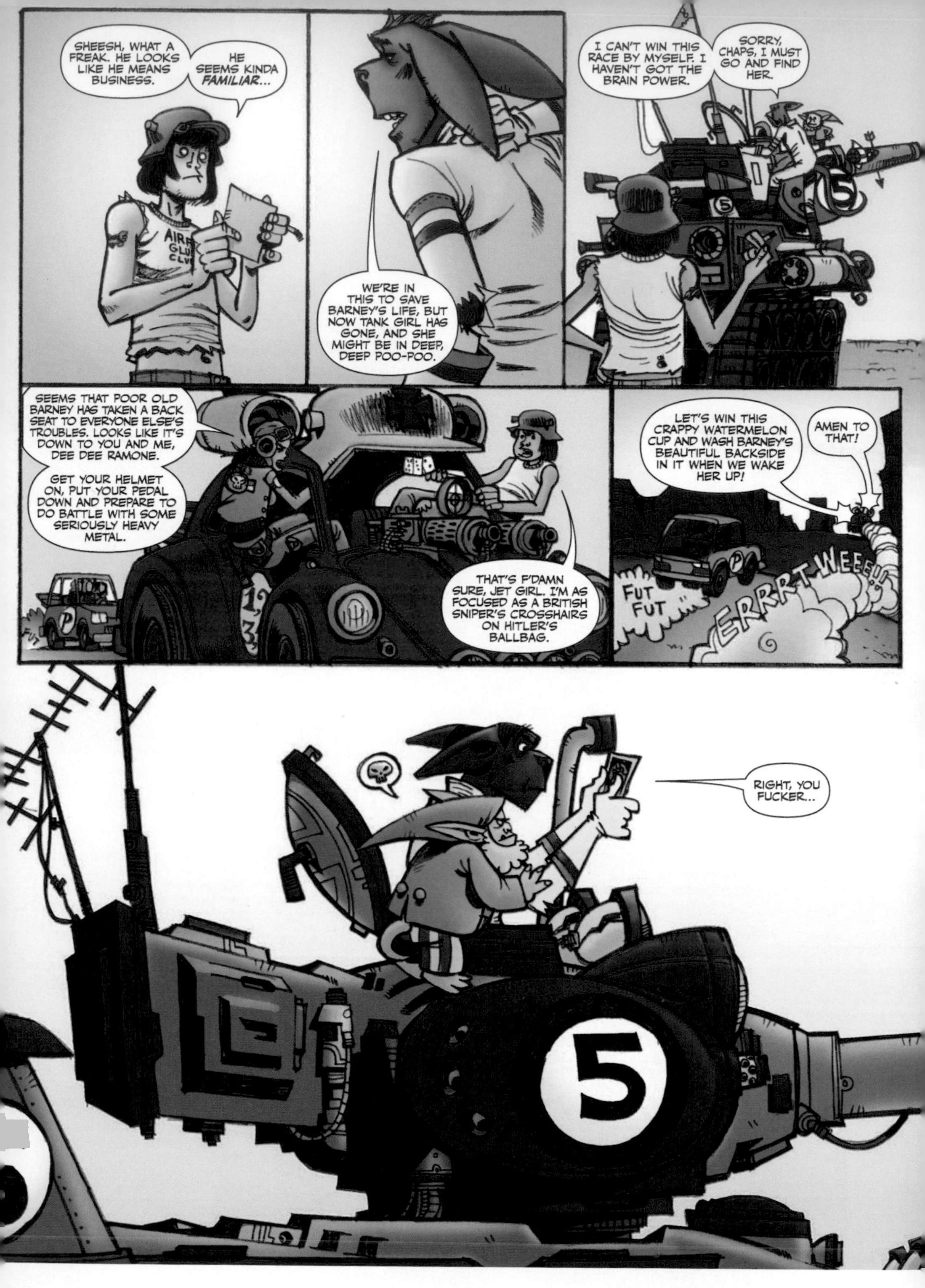
SHEESH, WHAT A FREAK. HE LOOKS LIKE HE MEANS BUSINESS.
HE SEEMS KINDA *FAMILIAR*...
WE'RE IN THIS TO SAVE BARNEY'S LIFE, BUT NOW TANK GIRL HAS GONE, AND SHE MIGHT BE IN DEEP, DEEP POO-POO.
I CAN'T WIN THIS RACE BY MYSELF. I HAVEN'T GOT THE BRAIN POWER.
SORRY, CHAPS, I MUST GO AND FIND HER.
SEEMS THAT POOR OLD BARNEY HAS TAKEN A BACK SEAT TO EVERYONE ELSE'S TROUBLES. LOOKS LIKE IT'S DOWN TO YOU AND ME, DEE DEE RAMONE.
GET YOUR HELMET ON, PUT YOUR PEDAL DOWN AND PREPARE TO DO BATTLE WITH SOME SERIOUSLY HEAVY METAL.
THAT'S F'DAMN SURE, JET GIRL. I'M AS FOCUSED AS A BRITISH SNIPER'S CROSSHAIRS ON HITLER'S BALLBAG.
LET'S WIN THIS CRAPPY WATERMELON CUP AND WASH BARNEY'S BEAUTIFUL BACKSIDE IN IT WHEN WE WAKE HER UP!
AMEN TO THAT!
FUT FUT
ERRRTWEEE!!
RIGHT, YOU FUCKER...
5

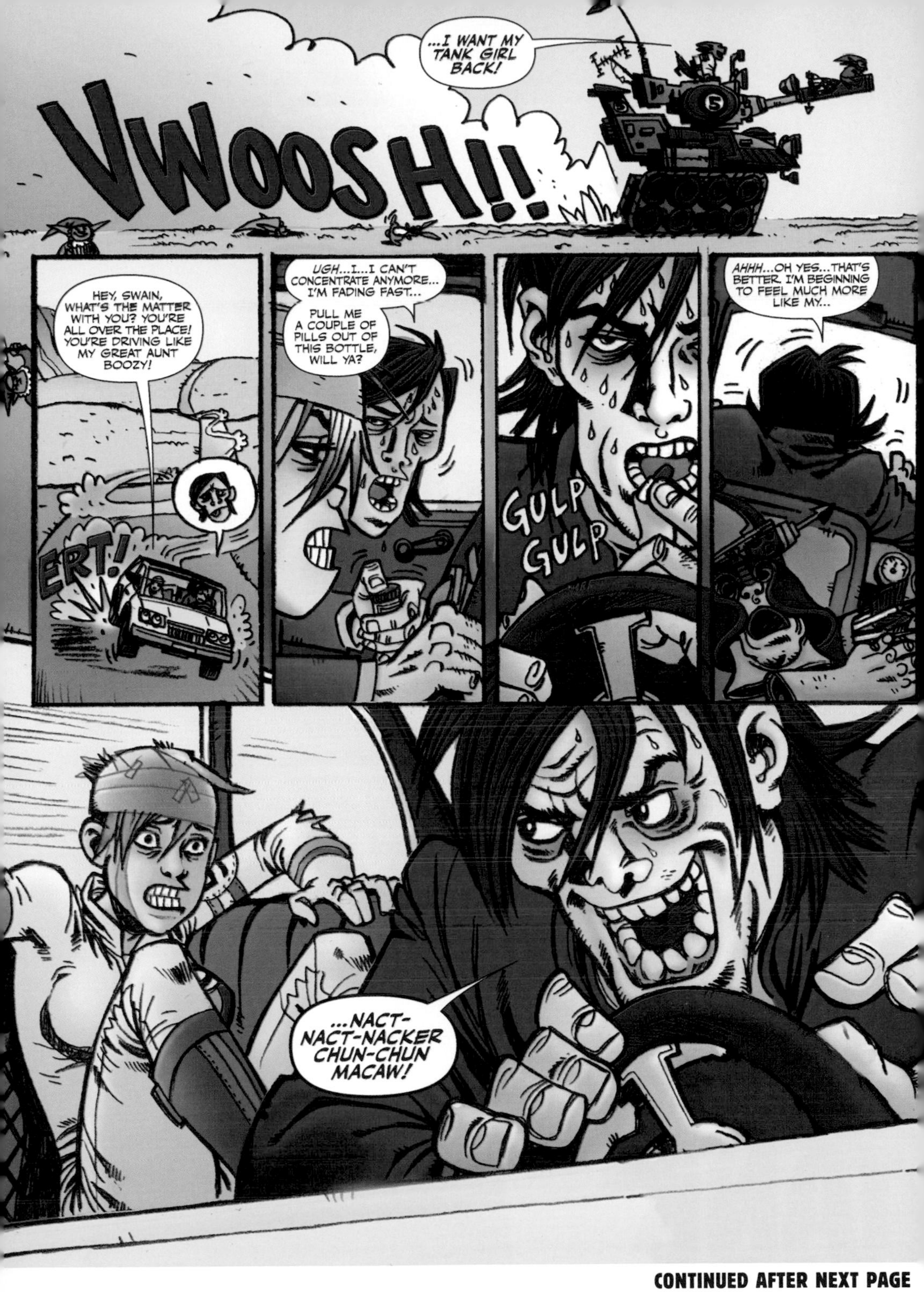

...I WANT MY TANK GIRL BACK!
VWOOSH!!
HEY, SWAIN, WHAT'S THE MATTER WITH YOU? YOU'RE ALL OVER THE PLACE! YOU'RE DRIVING LIKE MY GREAT AUNT BOOZY!
ERT!
UGH...I...I CAN'T CONCENTRATE ANYMORE... I'M FADING FAST...
PULL ME A COUPLE OF PILLS OUT OF THIS BOTTLE, WILL YA?
GULP GULP
AHHH...OH YES...THAT'S BETTER. I'M BEGINNING TO FEEL MUCH MORE LIKE MY...
...NACT-NACT-NACKER CHUN-CHUN MACAW!

CONTINUED AFTER NEXT PAGE

DEAR SANTA, YOU BASTARD.

HOW COMES TANK GIRL GOT A TOMMY ATOMSMASHER SPACE PILOT POPGUN AND ALL I GOT WAS A POXY BOW AND ARROW (WHICH I HAVE BUST ALREADY)?

BELIEVE ME WHEN I SAY THAT THE SECURITY OF YOUR REINDEER HAS BEEN SEVERELY COMPROMISED.

P.S. I HAVE BEEN A GOOD BOY SO FAR THIS YEAR...

BOOGA XX

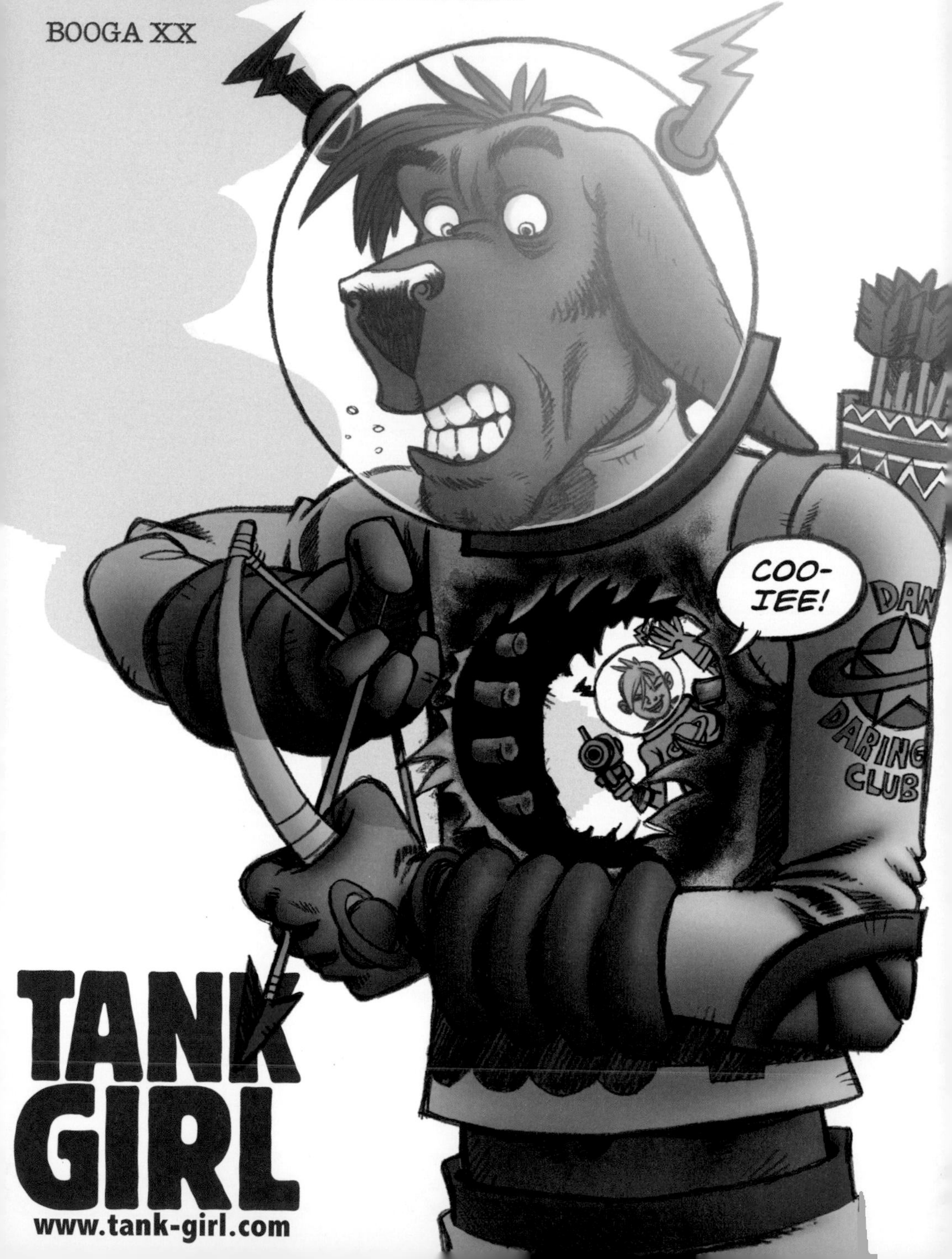
COO-IEE!
DARING CLUB

TANK GIRL

www.tank-girl.com

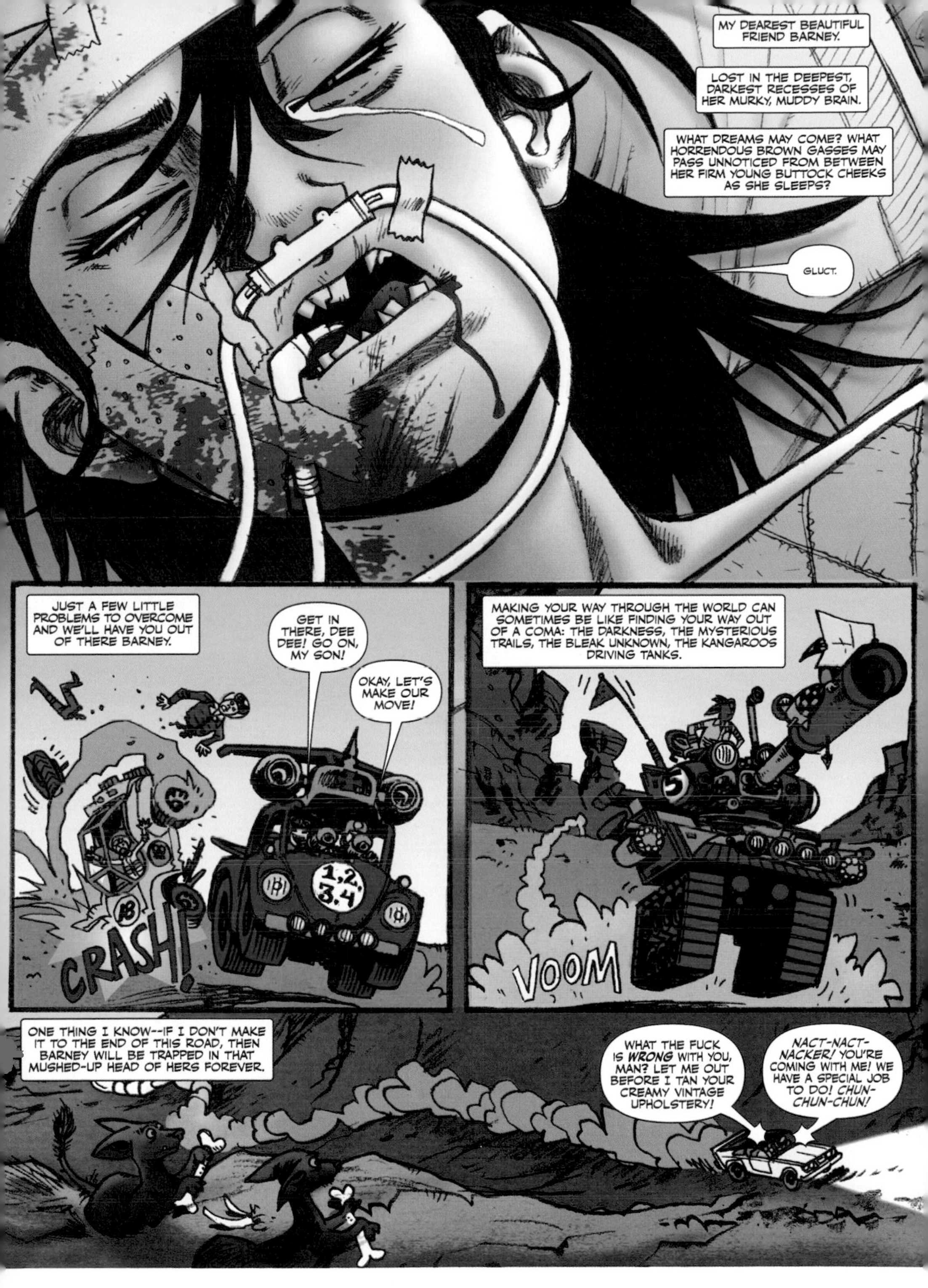
MY DEAREST BEAUTIFUL FRIEND BARNEY.
LOST IN THE DEEPEST, DARKEST RECESSES OF HER MURKY, MUDDY BRAIN.
WHAT DREAMS MAY COME? WHAT HORRENDOUS BROWN GASSES MAY PASS UNNOTICED FROM BETWEEN HER FIRM YOUNG BUTTOCK CHEEKS AS SHE SLEEPS?
GLUCT.
JUST A FEW LITTLE PROBLEMS TO OVERCOME AND WE'LL HAVE YOU OUT OF THERE BARNEY.
GET IN THERE, DEE DEE! GO ON, MY SON!
OKAY, LET'S MAKE OUR MOVE!
1,2, 3,4
CRASH!
MAKING YOUR WAY THROUGH THE WORLD CAN SOMETIMES BE LIKE FINDING YOUR WAY OUT OF A COMA: THE DARKNESS, THE MYSTERIOUS TRAILS, THE BLEAK UNKNOWN, THE KANGAROOS DRIVING TANKS.
VOOM
ONE THING I KNOW--IF I DON'T MAKE IT TO THE END OF THIS ROAD, THEN BARNEY WILL BE TRAPPED IN THAT MUSHED-UP HEAD OF HERS FOREVER.
WHAT THE FUCK IS WRONG WITH YOU, MAN? LET ME OUT BEFORE I TAN YOUR CREAMY VINTAGE UPHOLSTERY!
NACT-NACT-NACKER! YOU'RE COMING WITH ME! WE HAVE A SPECIAL JOB TO DO! CHUN-CHUN-CHUN!

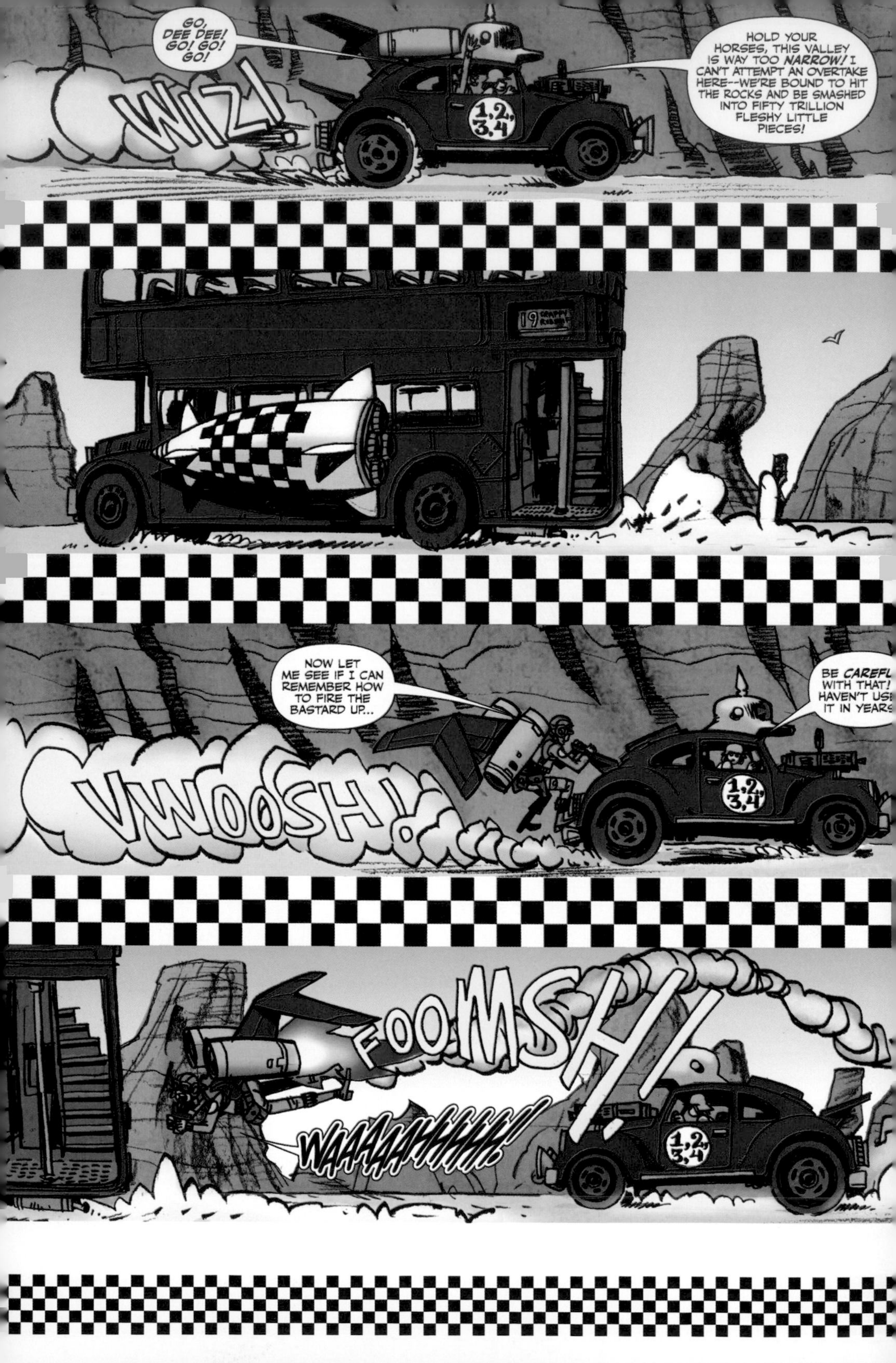
GO, DEE DEE! GO! GO! GO!
WIZZ!
HOLD YOUR HORSES, THIS VALLEY IS WAY TOO *NARROW!* I CAN'T ATTEMPT AN OVERTAKE HERE--WE'RE BOUND TO HIT THE ROCKS AND BE SMASHED INTO FIFTY TRILLION FLESHY LITTLE PIECES!
19
NOW LET ME SEE IF I CAN REMEMBER HOW TO FIRE THE BASTARD UP...
BE *CAREFU* WITH THAT! HAVEN'T USE IT IN YEARS
VWOOSH!
FOOMSH!
WAAAAAHHHH!

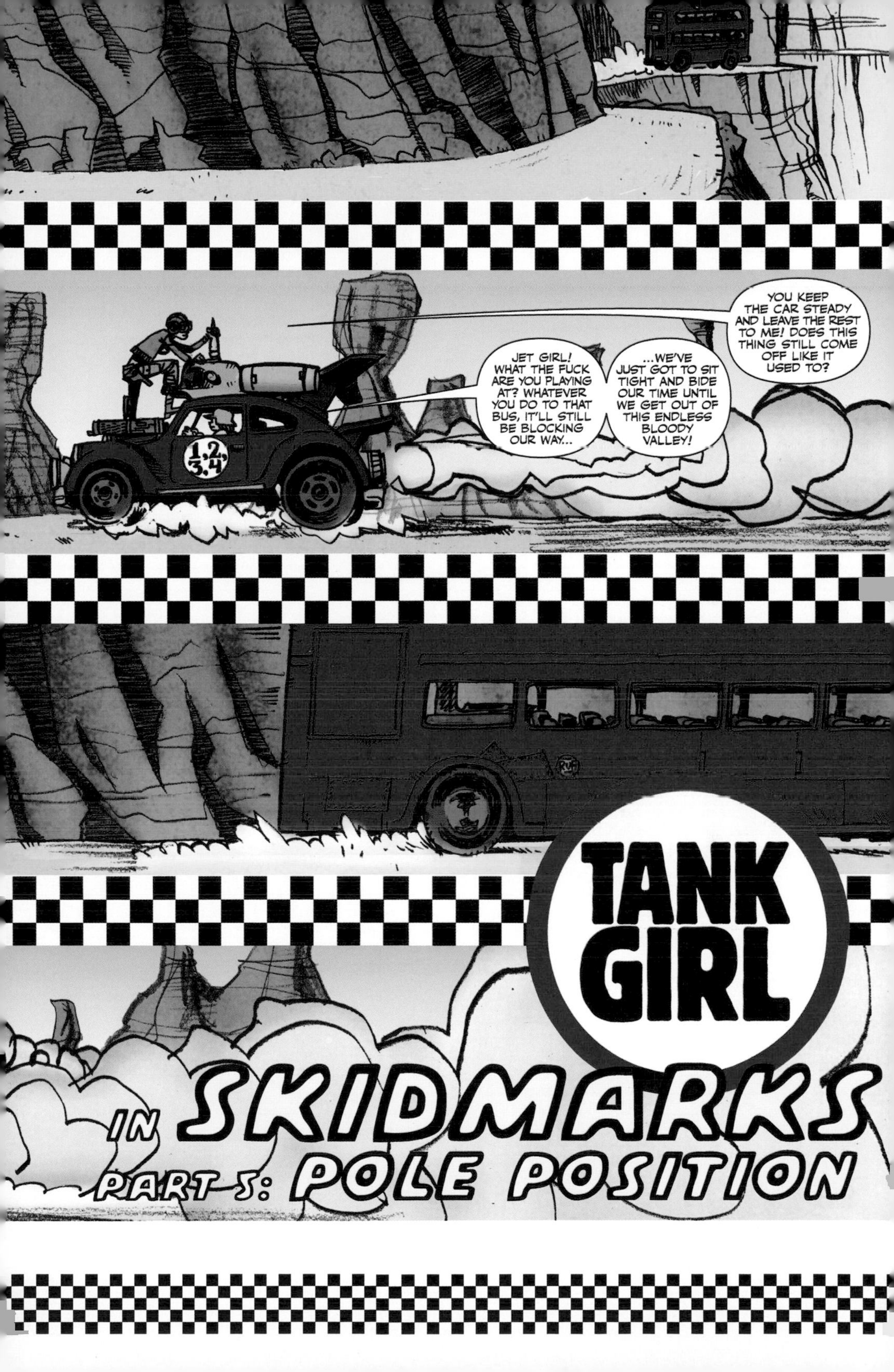
YOU KEEP THE CAR STEADY AND LEAVE THE REST TO ME! DOES THIS THING STILL COME OFF LIKE IT USED TO?
JET GIRL! WHAT THE FUCK ARE YOU PLAYING AT? WHATEVER YOU DO TO THAT BUS, IT'LL STILL BE BLOCKING OUR WAY...
...WE'VE JUST GOT TO SIT TIGHT AND BIDE OUR TIME UNTIL WE GET OUT OF THIS ENDLESS BLOODY VALLEY!
1,2,3,4
TANK GIRL
IN SKIDMARKS
PART 5: POLE POSITION

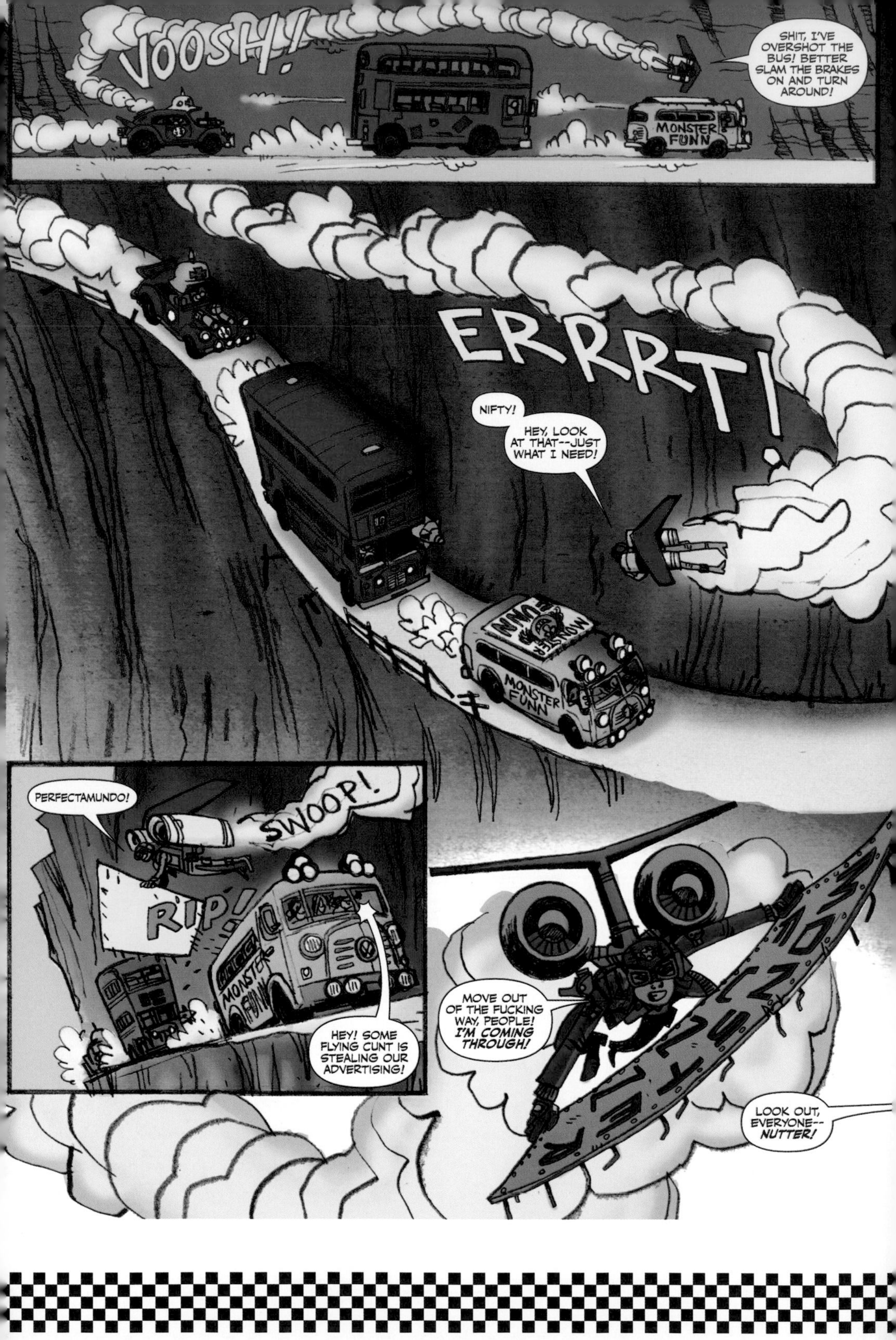
VOOSH!
SHIT, I'VE OVERSHOT THE BUS! BETTER SLAM THE BRAKES ON AND TURN AROUND!
MONSTER FUNN
ERRRT!
NIFTY!
HEY, LOOK AT THAT--JUST WHAT I NEED!
MONSTER FUNN
PERFECTAMUNDO!
SWOOP!
RIP!
HEY! SOME FLYING CUNT IS STEALING OUR ADVERTISING!
MOVE OUT OF THE FUCKING WAY, PEOPLE! *I'M COMING THROUGH!*
LOOK OUT, EVERYONE-- *NUTTER!*

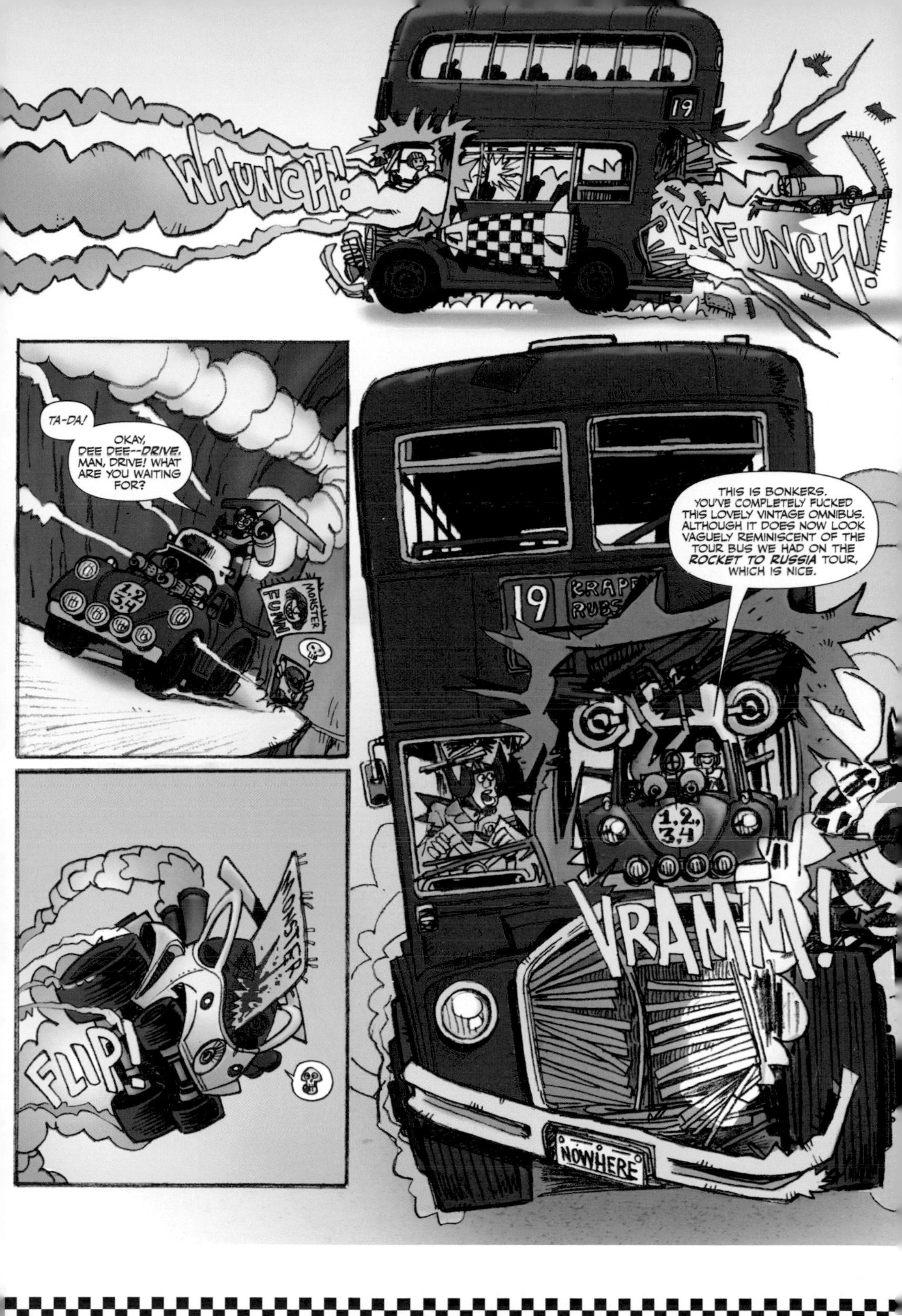
WHUNCH!
19
KAFUNCH!
TA-DA!
OKAY, DEE DEE--DRIVE, MAN, DRIVE! WHAT ARE YOU WAITING FOR?
1,2, 3,4
MONSTER FUN
THIS IS BONKERS. YOU'VE COMPLETELY FUCKED THIS LOVELY VINTAGE OMNIBUS. ALTHOUGH IT DOES NOW LOOK VAGUELY REMINISCENT OF THE TOUR BUS WE HAD ON THE ROCKET TO RUSSIA TOUR, WHICH IS NICE.
19
1,2, 3,4
VRAMM!
NOWHERE
MONSTER
FLIP!

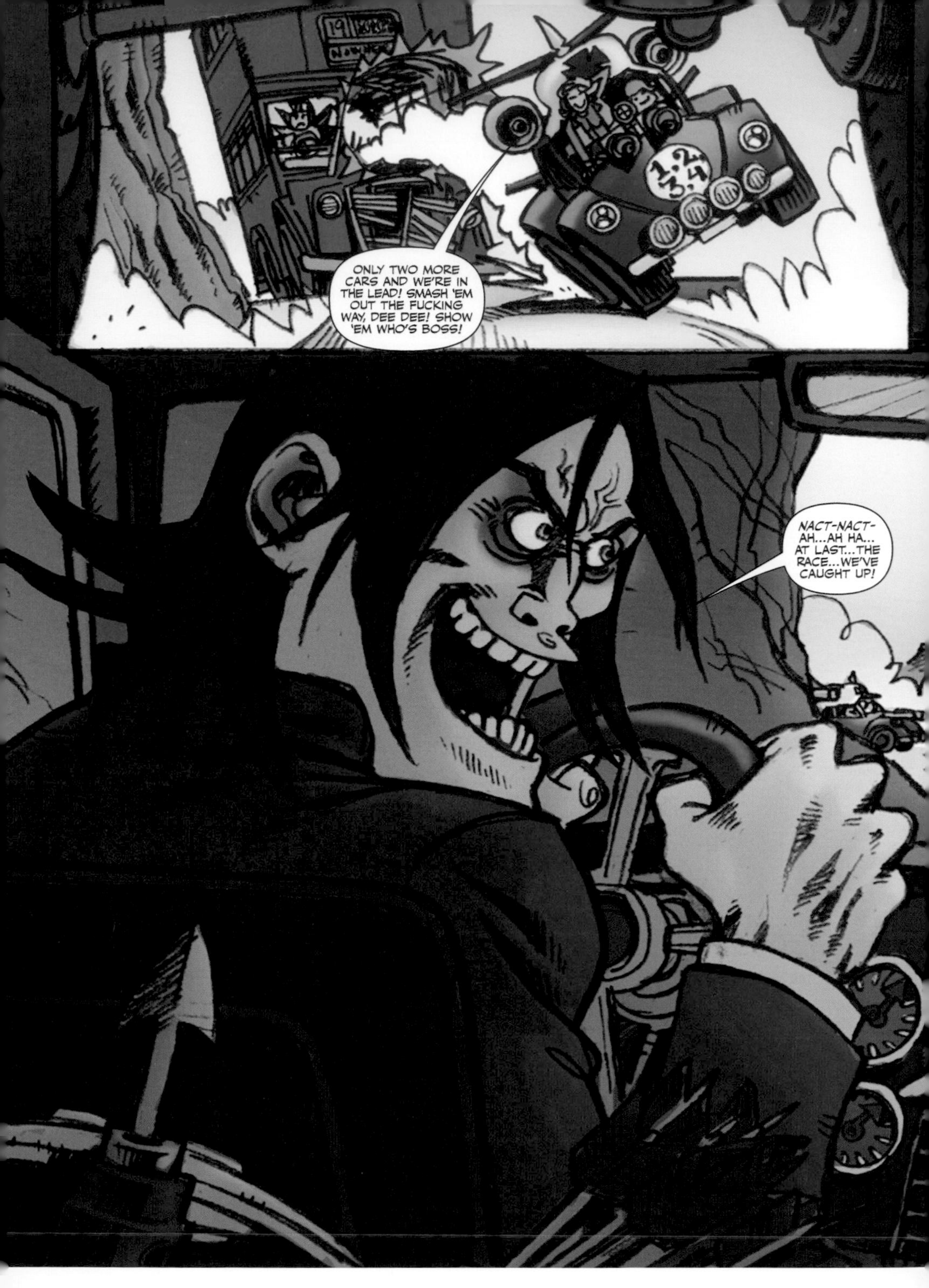
ONLY TWO MORE CARS AND WE'RE IN THE LEAD! SMASH 'EM OUT THE FUCKING WAY, DEE DEE! SHOW 'EM WHO'S BOSS!
NACT-NACT-AH...AH HA... AT LAST...THE RACE...WE'VE CAUGHT UP!

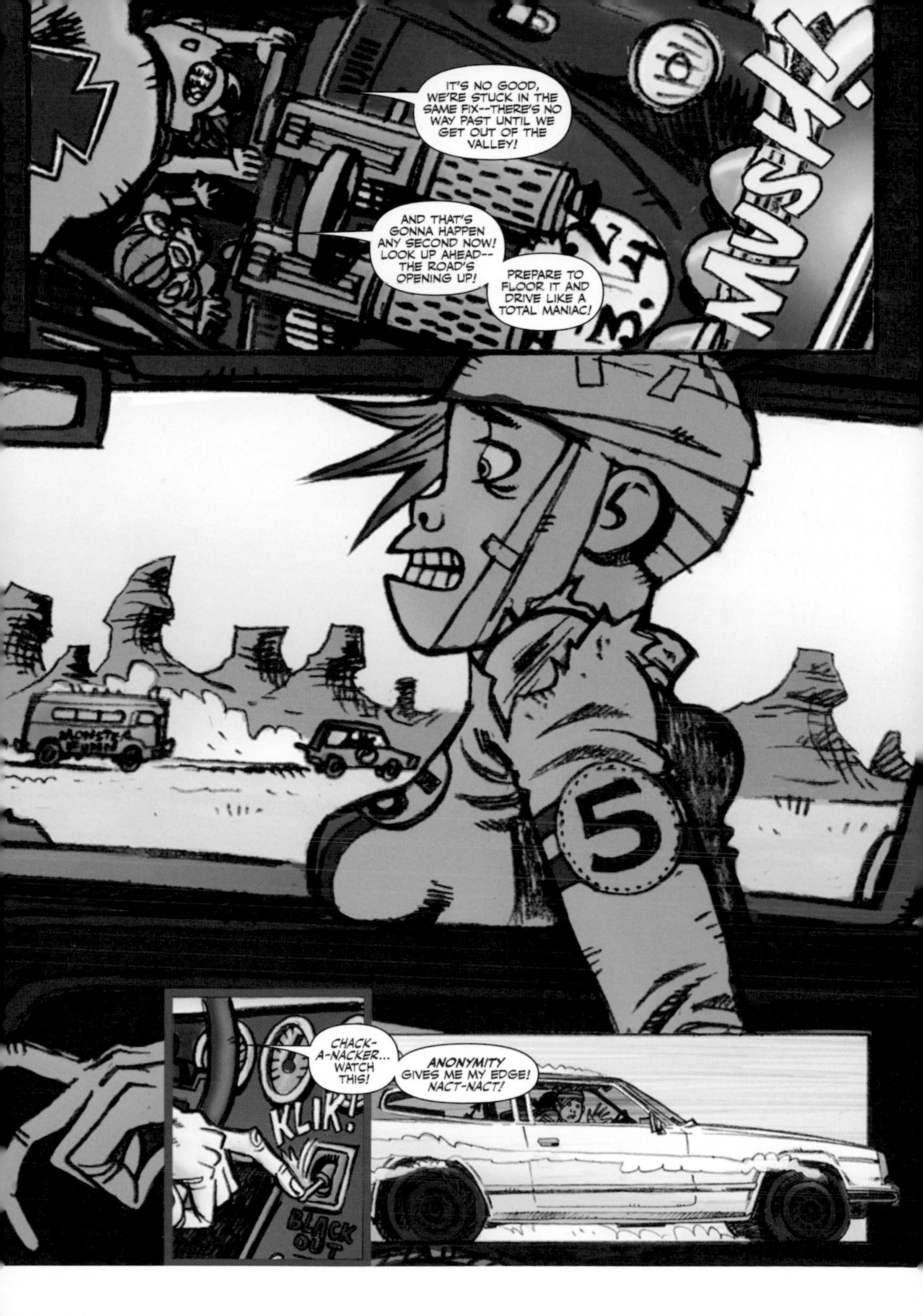
IT'S NO GOOD, WE'RE STUCK IN THE SAME FIX--THERE'S NO WAY PAST UNTIL WE GET OUT OF THE VALLEY!
MUSH!
AND THAT'S GONNA HAPPEN ANY SECOND NOW! LOOK UP AHEAD-- THE ROAD'S OPENING UP!
PREPARE TO FLOOR IT AND DRIVE LIKE A TOTAL MANIAC!
CHACK-A-NACKER... WATCH THIS!
ANONYMITY GIVES ME MY EDGE! NACT-NACT!
KLIK!
BLACK OUT

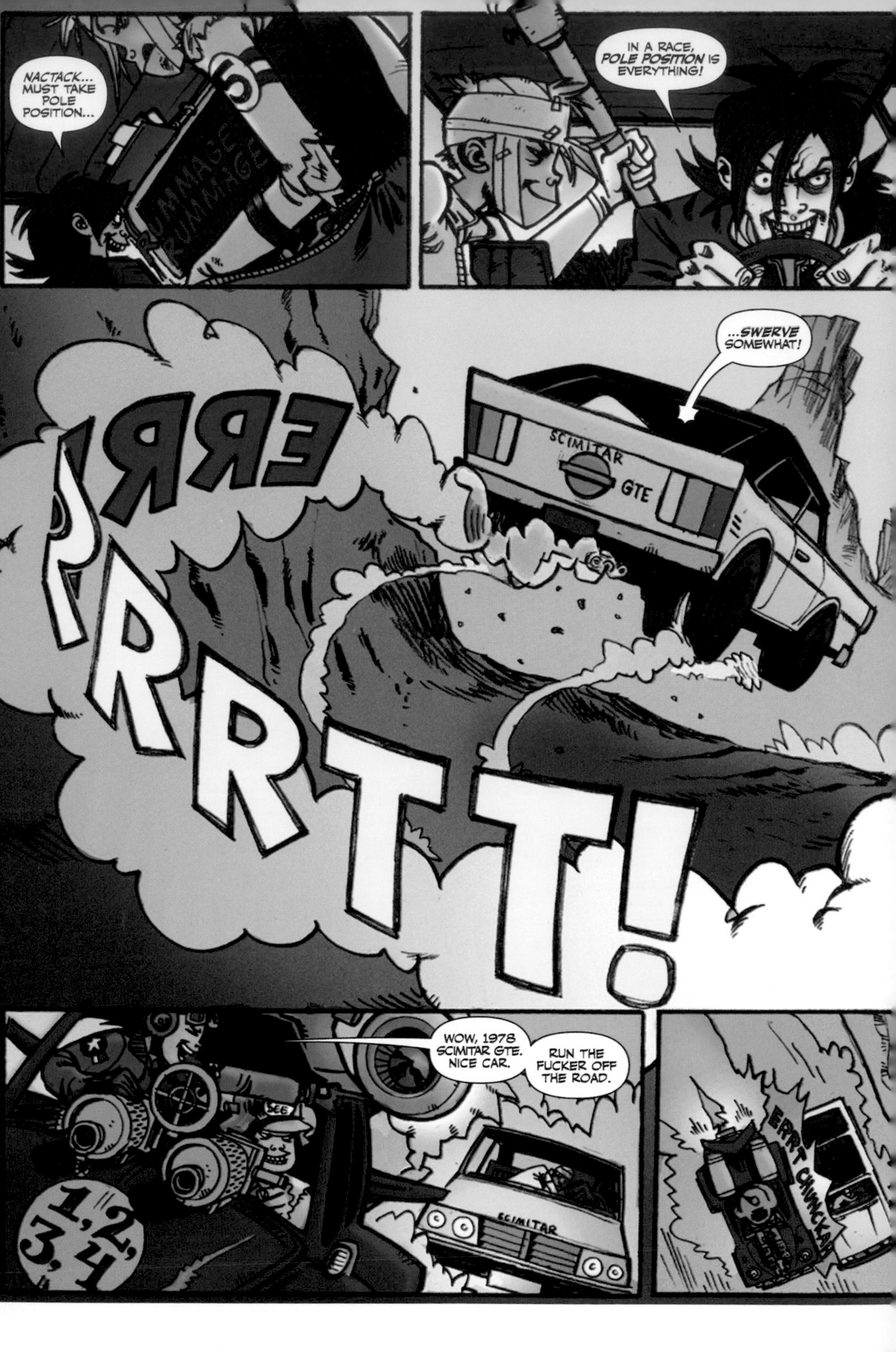
NACTACK... MUST TAKE POLE POSITION...
RUMMAGE RUMMAGE
IN A RACE, *POLE POSITION* IS EVERYTHING!
...*SWERVE* SOMEWHAT!
SCIMITAR GTE
ERRRRRTT!
WOW, 1978 SCIMITAR GTE. NICE CAR.
RUN THE FUCKER OFF THE ROAD.
1,2,3,4
SCIMITAR
ERRT CHUNCKA

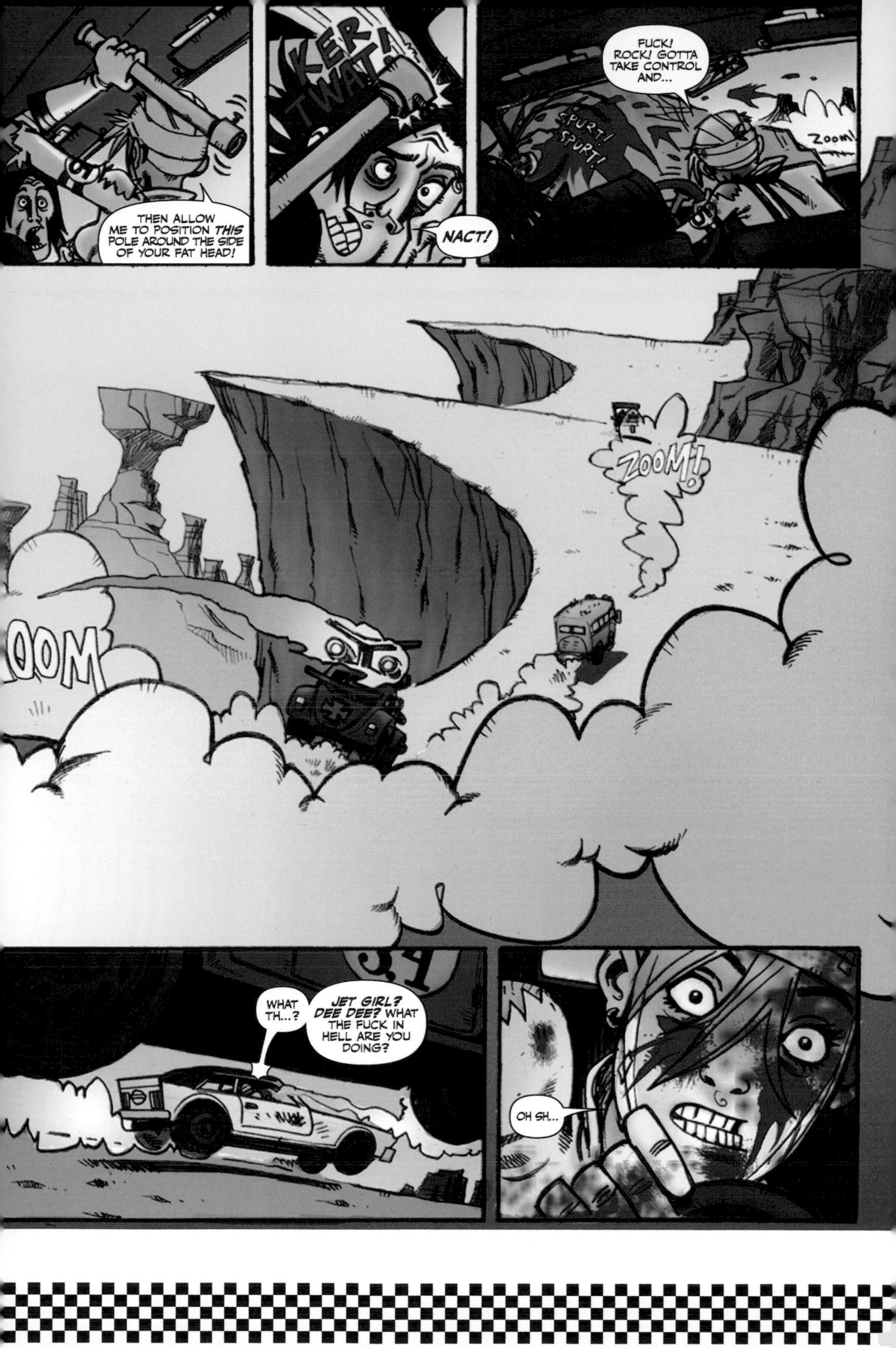
THEN ALLOW ME TO POSITION THIS POLE AROUND THE SIDE OF YOUR FAT HEAD!
KER TWAT!
NACT!
FUCK! ROCK! GOTTA TAKE CONTROL AND...
SPURT! SPURT!
ZOOM!
ZOOM!
OOM
WHAT TH...?
JET GIRL? DEE DEE? WHAT THE FUCK IN HELL ARE YOU DOING?
OH SH...

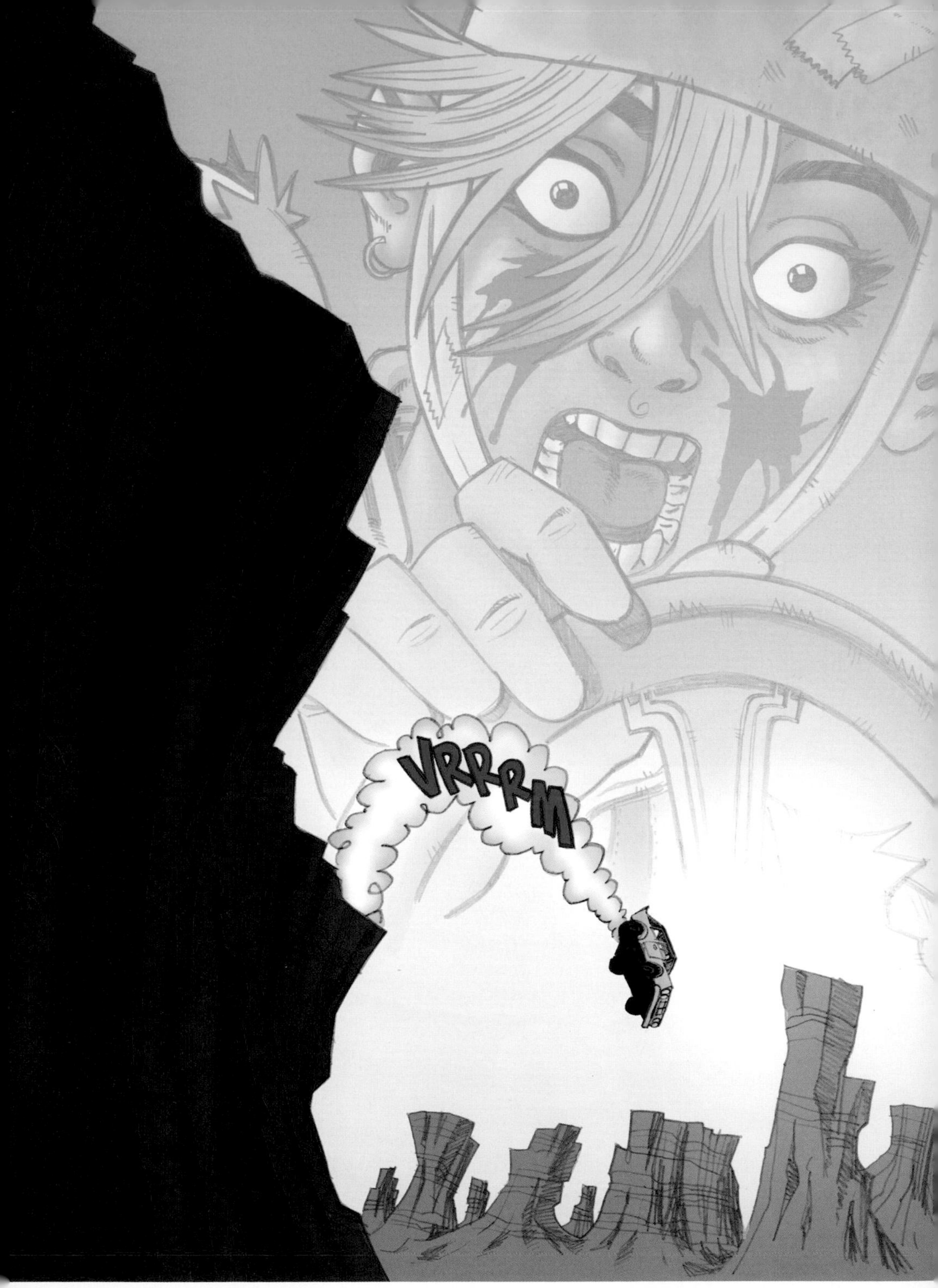
VRRRM

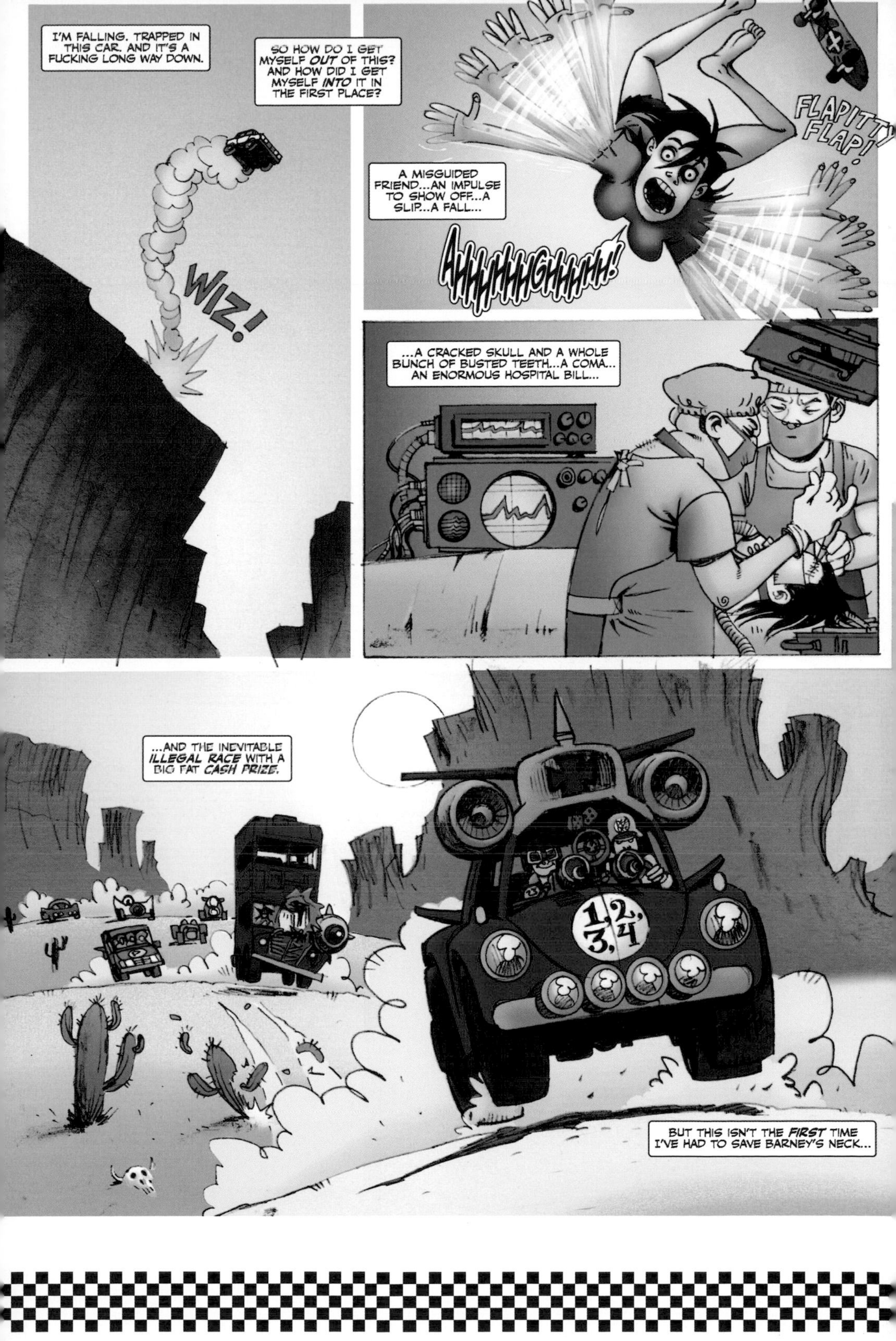

I'M FALLING. TRAPPED IN THIS CAR. AND IT'S A FUCKING LONG WAY DOWN.
SO HOW DO I GET MYSELF OUT OF THIS? AND HOW DID I GET MYSELF INTO IT IN THE FIRST PLACE?
WIZ!
FLAPITTY FLAP!
A MISGUIDED FRIEND...AN IMPULSE TO SHOW OFF...A SLIP...A FALL...
AHHHHHHGHHHHH!
...A CRACKED SKULL AND A WHOLE BUNCH OF BUSTED TEETH...A COMA... AN ENORMOUS HOSPITAL BILL...
...AND THE INEVITABLE ILLEGAL RACE WITH A BIG FAT CASH PRIZE.
1,2, 3,4
BUT THIS ISN'T THE FIRST TIME I'VE HAD TO SAVE BARNEY'S NECK...

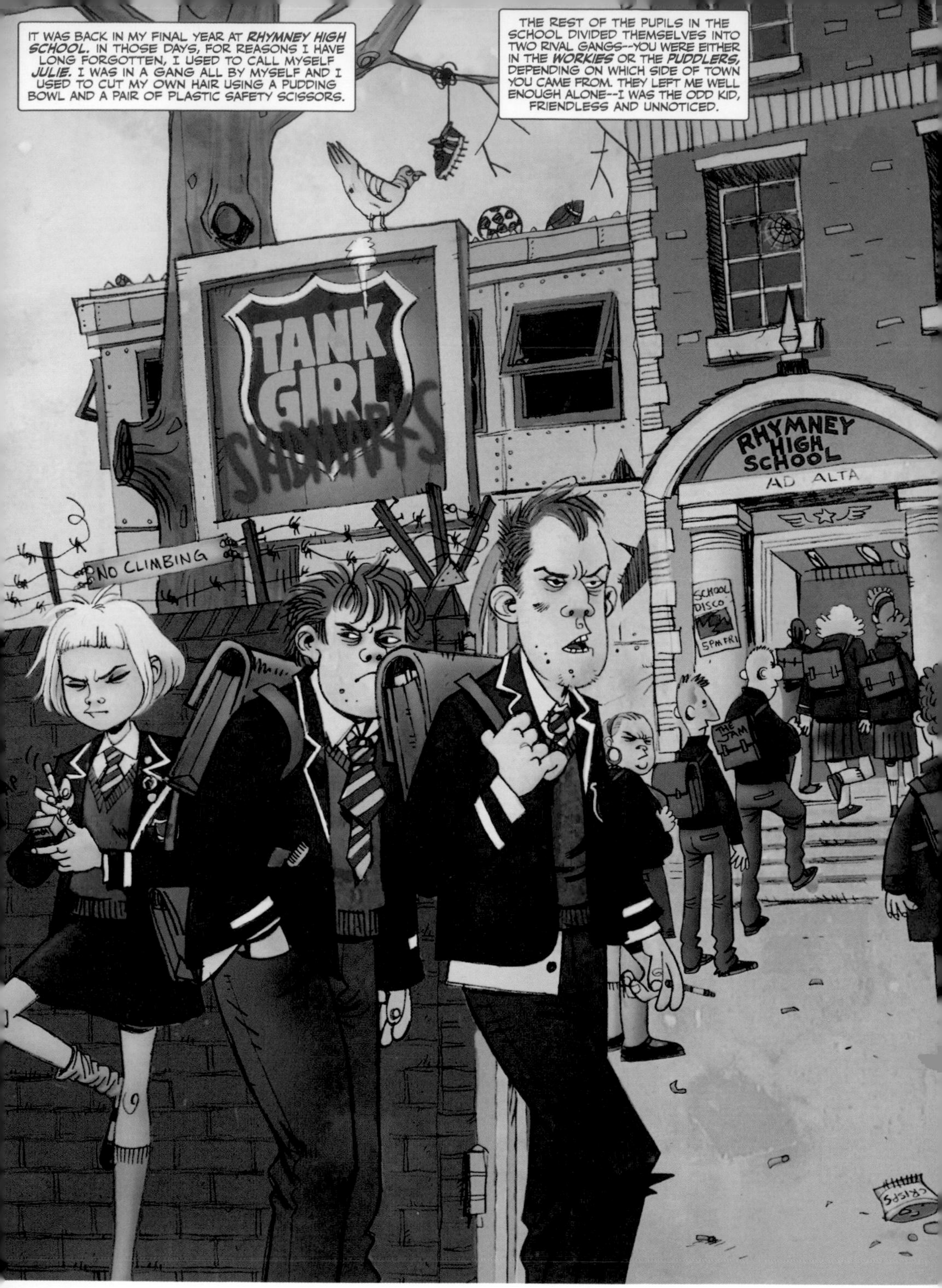
IT WAS BACK IN MY FINAL YEAR AT *RHYMNEY HIGH SCHOOL*. IN THOSE DAYS, FOR REASONS I HAVE LONG FORGOTTEN, I USED TO CALL MYSELF *JULIE*. I WAS IN A GANG ALL BY MYSELF AND I USED TO CUT MY OWN HAIR USING A PUDDING BOWL AND A PAIR OF PLASTIC SAFETY SCISSORS.
THE REST OF THE PUPILS IN THE SCHOOL DIVIDED THEMSELVES INTO TWO RIVAL GANGS--YOU WERE EITHER IN THE *WORKIES* OR THE *PUDDLERS*, DEPENDING ON WHICH SIDE OF TOWN YOU CAME FROM. THEY LEFT ME WELL ENOUGH ALONE--I WAS THE ODD KID, FRIENDLESS AND UNNOTICED.
TANK GIRL
RHYMNEY HIGH SCHOOL
AD ALTA
NO CLIMBING
SCHOOL DISCO
5PM FRI
THE JAM
CRISPS

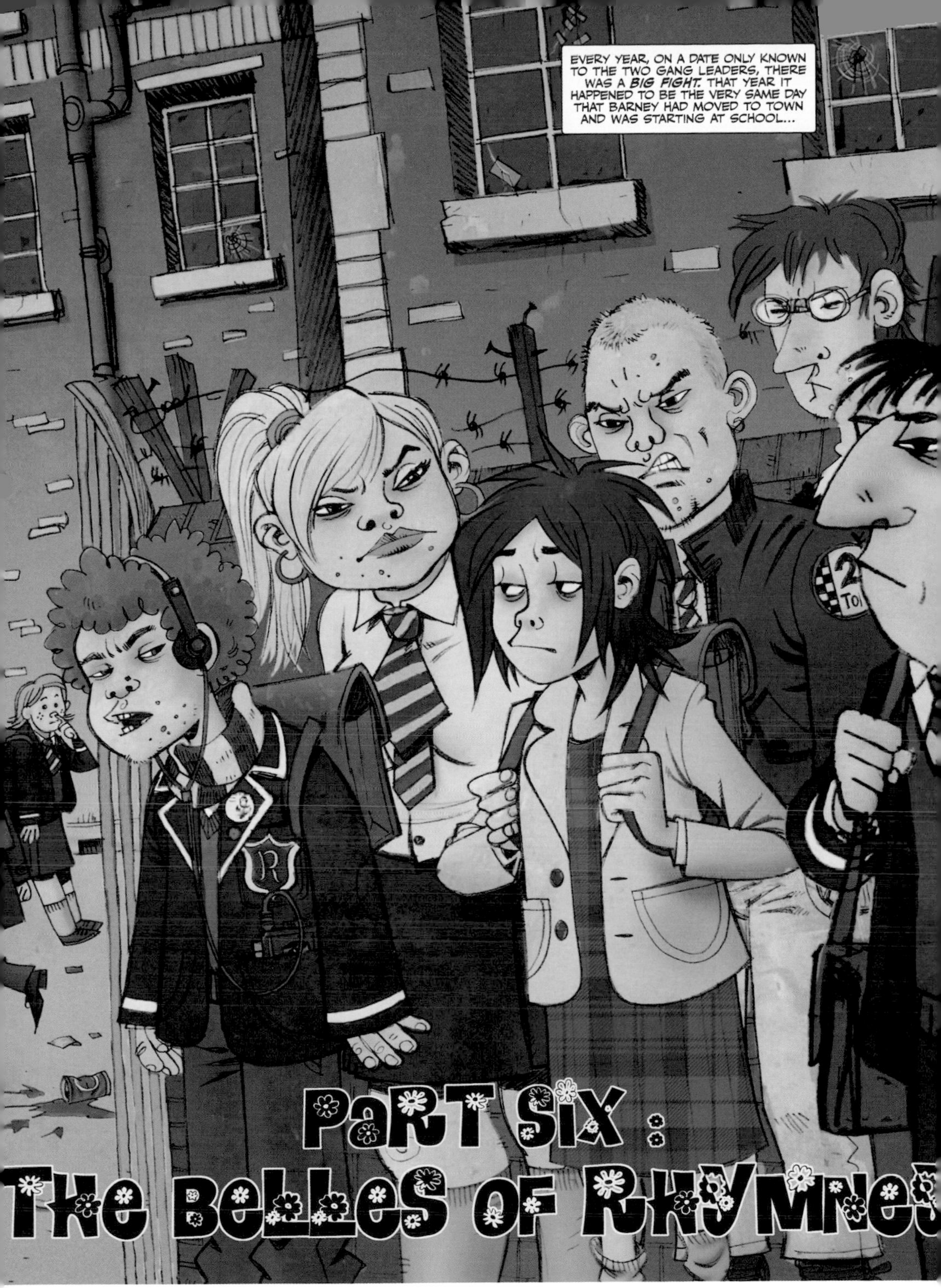
EVERY YEAR, ON A DATE ONLY KNOWN TO THE TWO GANG LEADERS, THERE WAS A BIG FIGHT. THAT YEAR IT HAPPENED TO BE THE VERY SAME DAY THAT BARNEY HAD MOVED TO TOWN AND WAS STARTING AT SCHOOL...
PART SIX :
THE BELLES OF RHYMNEY

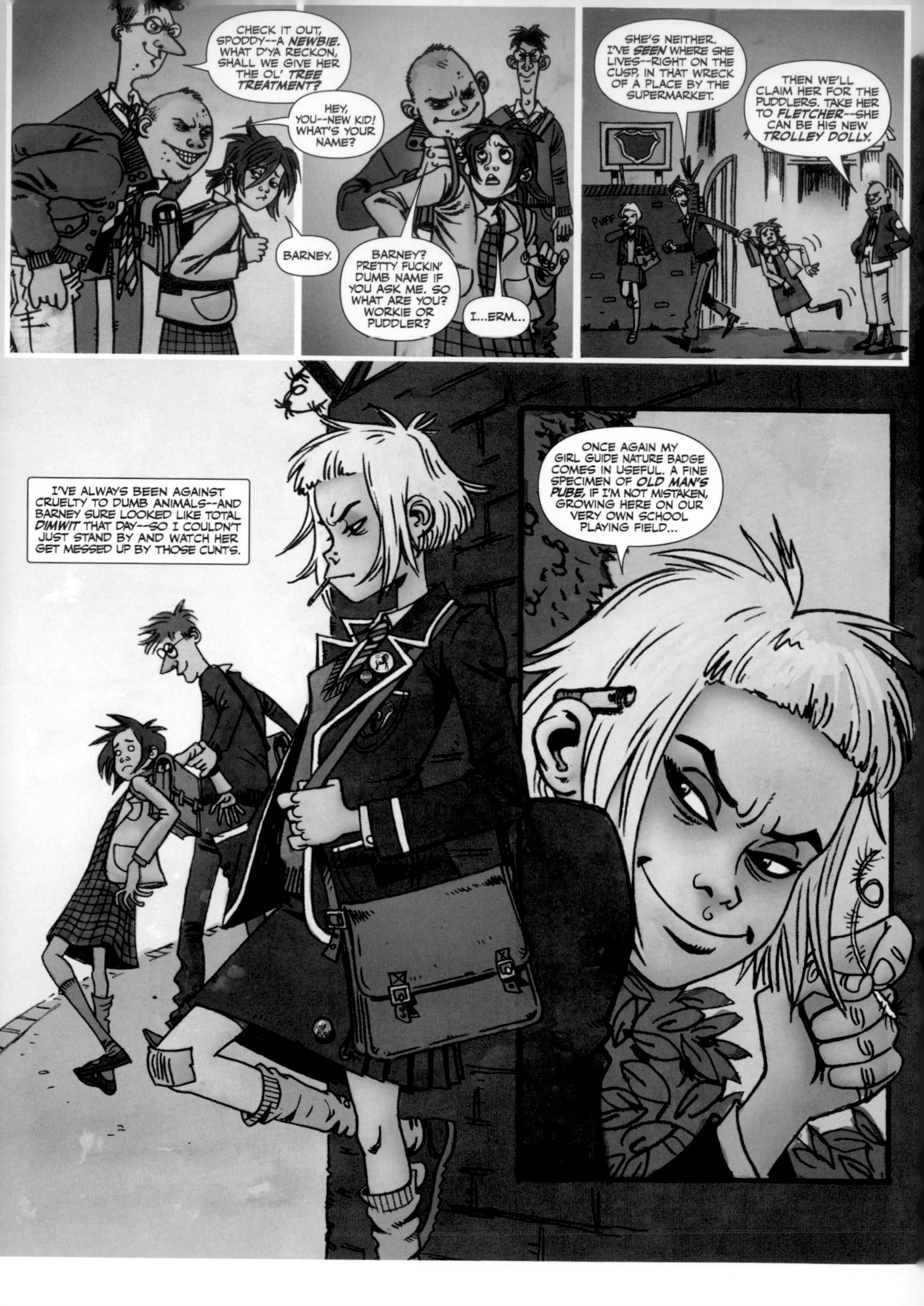

CHECK IT OUT, SPODDY--A NEWBIE. WHAT D'YA RECKON, SHALL WE GIVE HER THE OL' TREE TREATMENT?
HEY, YOU--NEW KID! WHAT'S YOUR NAME?
BARNEY.
BARNEY? PRETTY FUCKIN' DUMB NAME IF YOU ASK ME. SO WHAT ARE YOU? WORKIE OR PUDDLER?
I...ERM...
SHE'S NEITHER. I'VE SEEN WHERE SHE LIVES--RIGHT ON THE CUSP, IN THAT WRECK OF A PLACE BY THE SUPERMARKET.
THEN WE'LL CLAIM HER FOR THE PUDDLERS. TAKE HER TO FLETCHER--SHE CAN BE HIS NEW TROLLEY DOLLY.
PUFF
I'VE ALWAYS BEEN AGAINST CRUELTY TO DUMB ANIMALS--AND BARNEY SURE LOOKED LIKE TOTAL DIMWIT THAT DAY--SO I COULDN'T JUST STAND BY AND WATCH HER GET MESSED UP BY THOSE CUNTS.
ONCE AGAIN MY GIRL GUIDE NATURE BADGE COMES IN USEFUL. A FINE SPECIMEN OF OLD MAN'S PUBE, IF I'M NOT MISTAKEN, GROWING HERE ON OUR VERY OWN SCHOOL PLAYING FIELD...

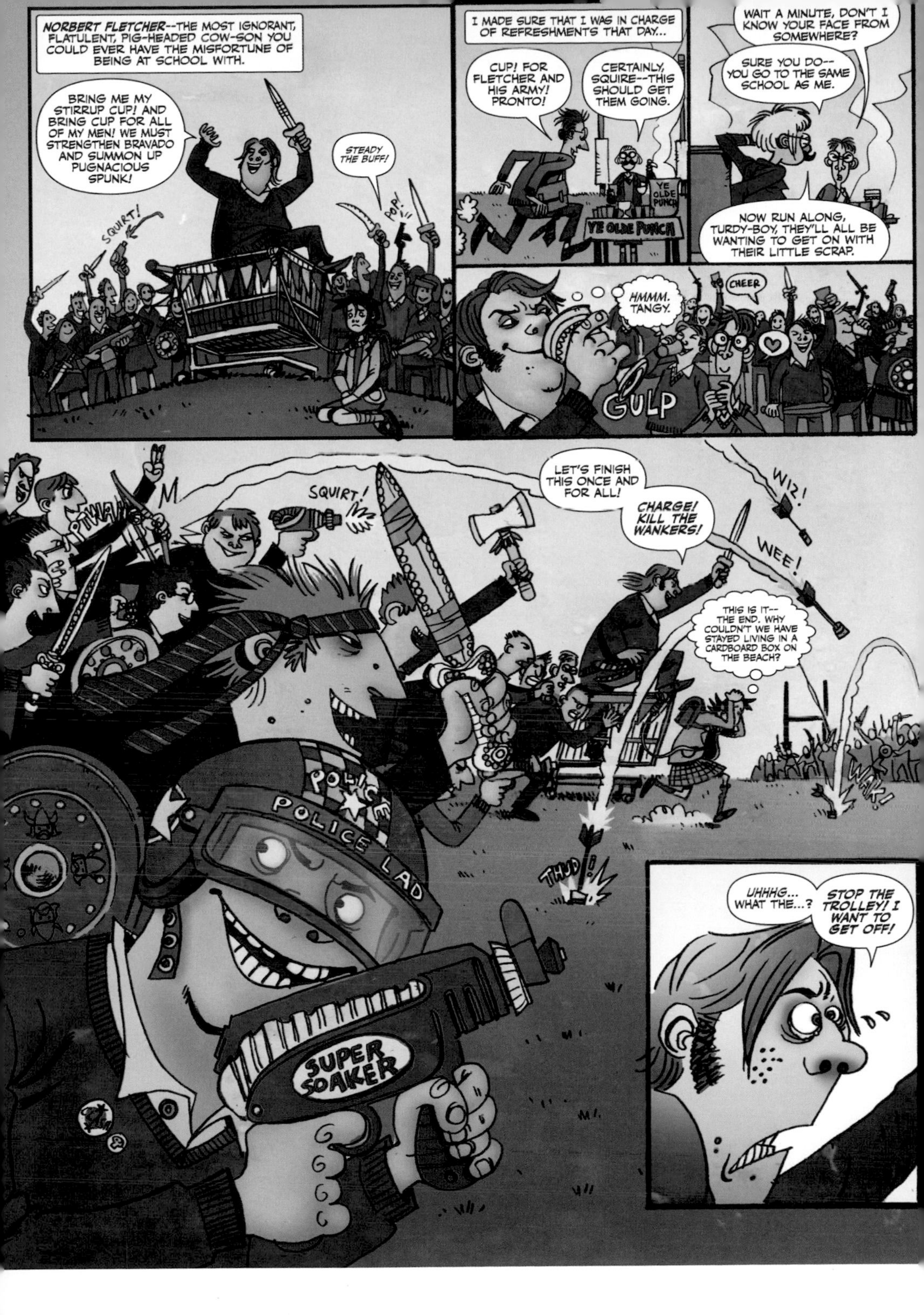
NORBERT FLETCHER--THE MOST IGNORANT, FLATULENT, PIG-HEADED COW-SON YOU COULD EVER HAVE THE MISFORTUNE OF BEING AT SCHOOL WITH.
BRING ME MY STIRRUP CUP! AND BRING CUP FOR ALL OF MY MEN! WE MUST STRENGTHEN BRAVADO AND SUMMON UP PUGNACIOUS SPUNK!
STEADY THE BUFF!
SQUIRT!
POP!
I MADE SURE THAT I WAS IN CHARGE OF REFRESHMENTS THAT DAY...
CUP! FOR FLETCHER AND HIS ARMY! PRONTO!
CERTAINLY, SQUIRE--THIS SHOULD GET THEM GOING.
YE OLDE PUNCH
YE OLDE PUNCH
WAIT A MINUTE, DON'T I KNOW YOUR FACE FROM SOMEWHERE?
SURE YOU DO-- YOU GO TO THE SAME SCHOOL AS ME.
NOW RUN ALONG, TURDY-BOY, THEY'LL ALL BE WANTING TO GET ON WITH THEIR LITTLE SCRAP.
HMMM. TANGY.
CHEER
GULP
LET'S FINISH THIS ONCE AND FOR ALL!
CHARGE! KILL THE WANKERS!
SQUIRT!
WIZ!
WEE!
THIS IS IT-- THE END. WHY COULDN'T WE HAVE STAYED LIVING IN A CARDBOARD BOX ON THE BEACH?
POLICE
POLICE LAD
THUD!
SUPER SOAKER
UHHHG... WHAT THE...?
STOP THE TROLLEY! I WANT TO GET OFF!

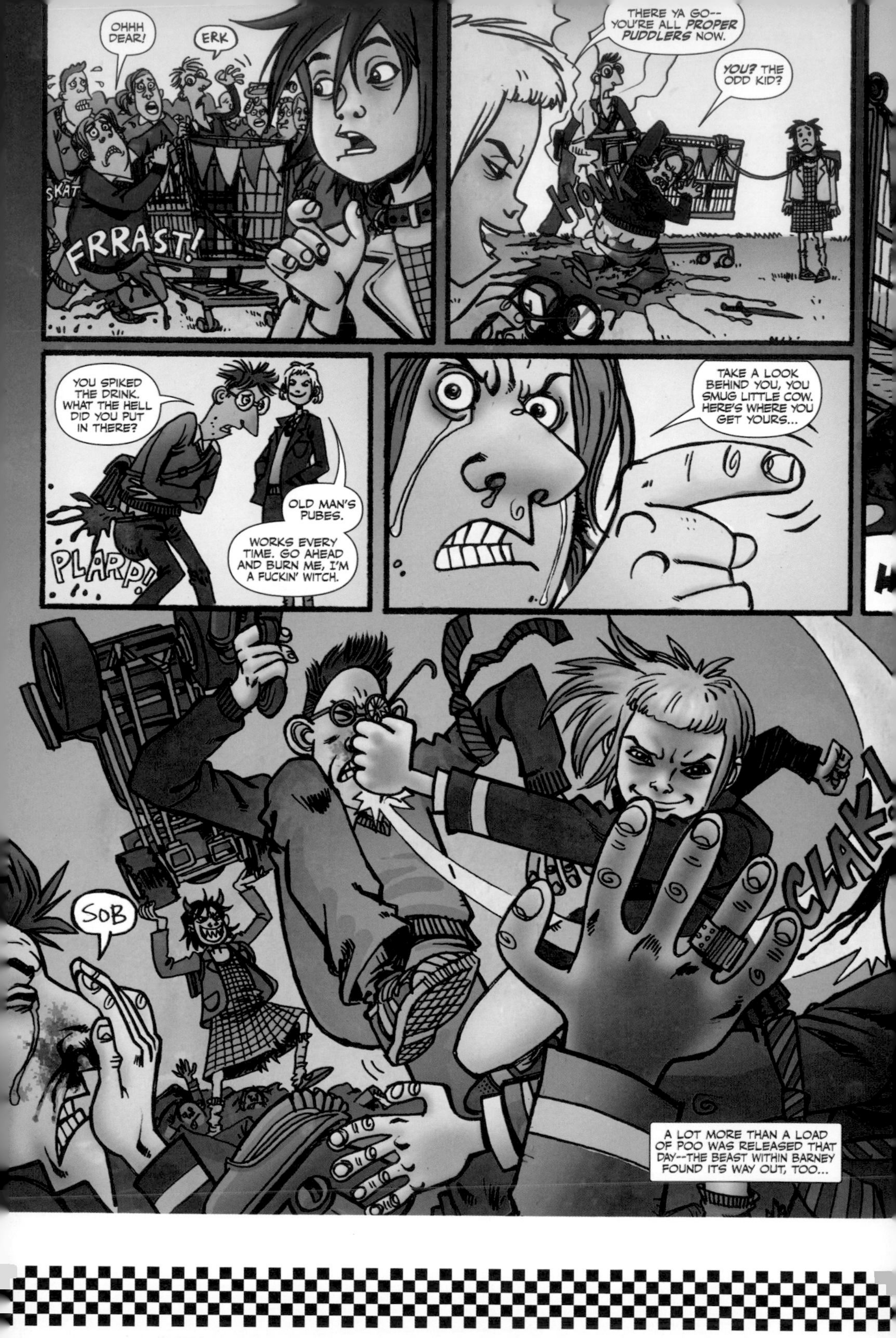
OHHH DEAR!
ERK
SKAT
FRRAST!
THERE YA GO-- YOU'RE ALL *PROPER PUDDLERS* NOW.
YOU? THE ODD KID?
HONK
YOU SPIKED THE DRINK. WHAT THE HELL DID YOU PUT IN THERE?
OLD MAN'S PUBES.
WORKS EVERY TIME. GO AHEAD AND BURN ME, I'M A FUCKIN' WITCH.
PLARP!
TAKE A LOOK BEHIND YOU, YOU SMUG LITTLE COW. HERE'S WHERE YOU GET YOURS...
SOB
CLAK!
A LOT MORE THAN A LOAD OF POO WAS RELEASED THAT DAY--THE BEAST WITHIN BARNEY FOUND ITS WAY OUT, TOO...

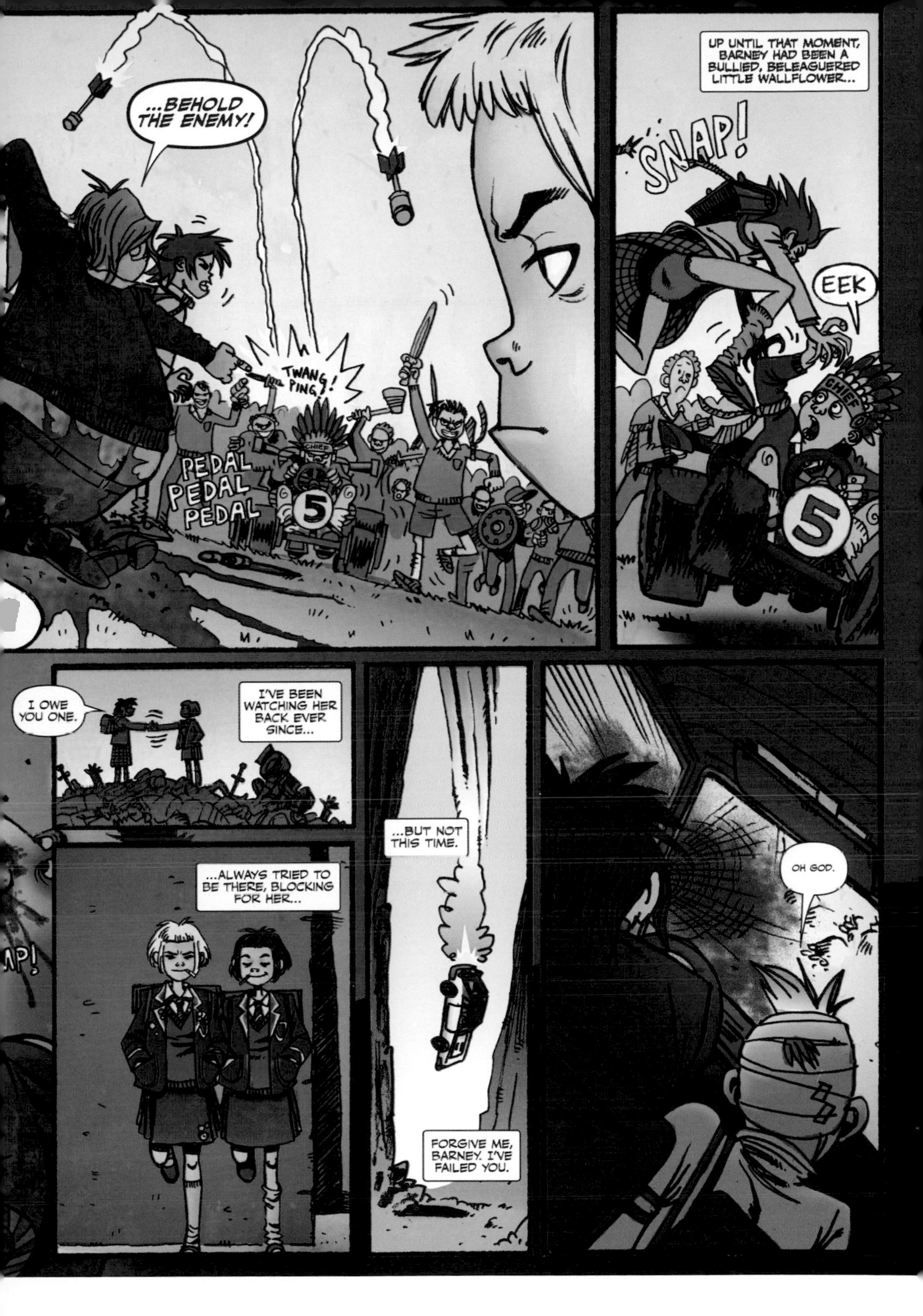
...BEHOLD THE ENEMY!
TWANG PING!
PEDAL PEDAL PEDAL
5
CHIEF
UP UNTIL THAT MOMENT, BARNEY HAD BEEN A BULLIED, BELEAGUERED LITTLE WALLFLOWER...
SNAP!
EEK
CHIEF
5
I OWE YOU ONE.
I'VE BEEN WATCHING HER BACK EVER SINCE...
...ALWAYS TRIED TO BE THERE, BLOCKING FOR HER...
...BUT NOT THIS TIME.
FORGIVE ME, BARNEY. I'VE FAILED YOU.
OH GOD.

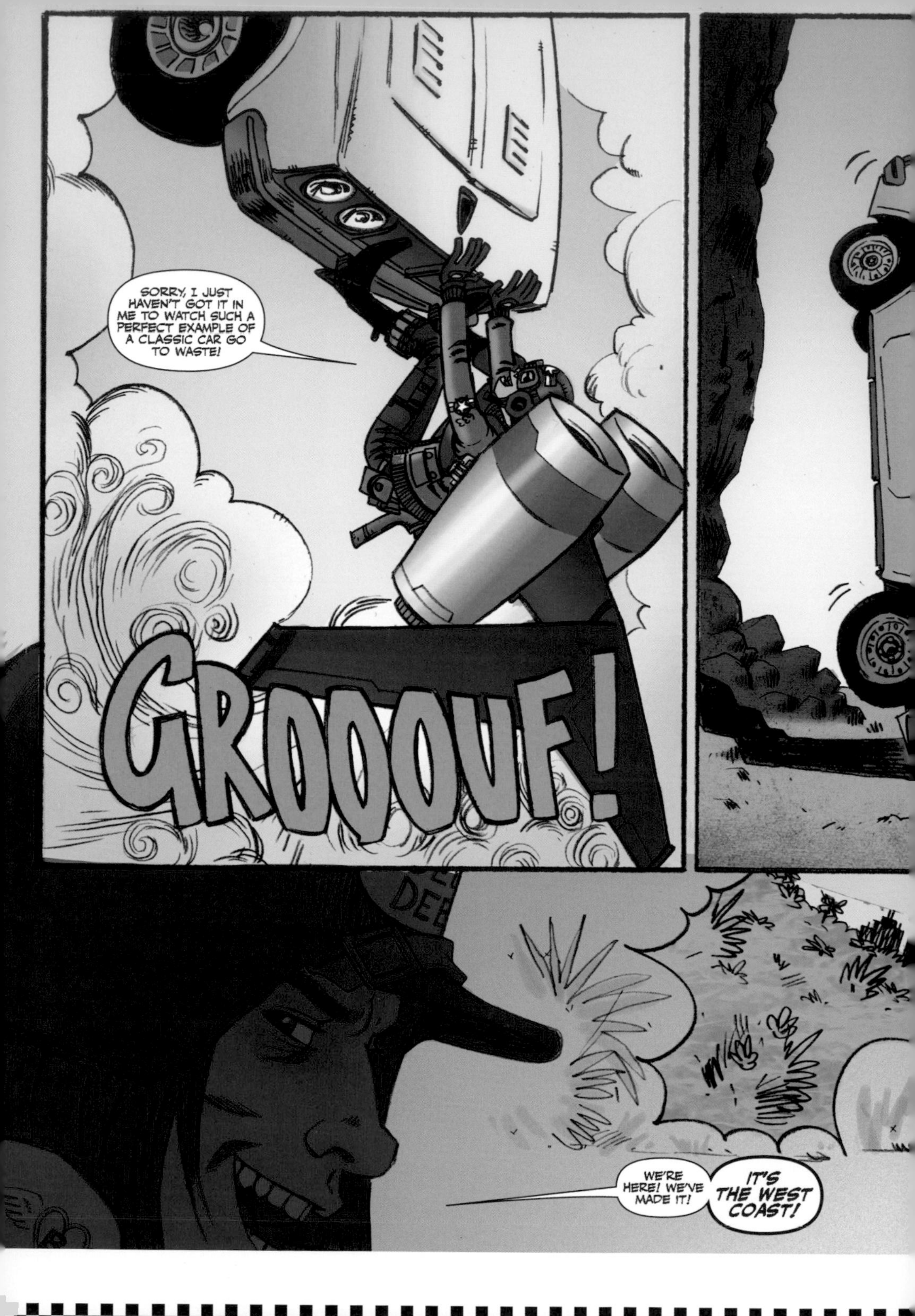
SORRY, I JUST HAVEN'T GOT IT IN ME TO WATCH SUCH A PERFECT EXAMPLE OF A CLASSIC CAR GO TO WASTE!
GROOOUF!
WE'RE HERE! WE'VE MADE IT!
IT'S THE WEST COAST!

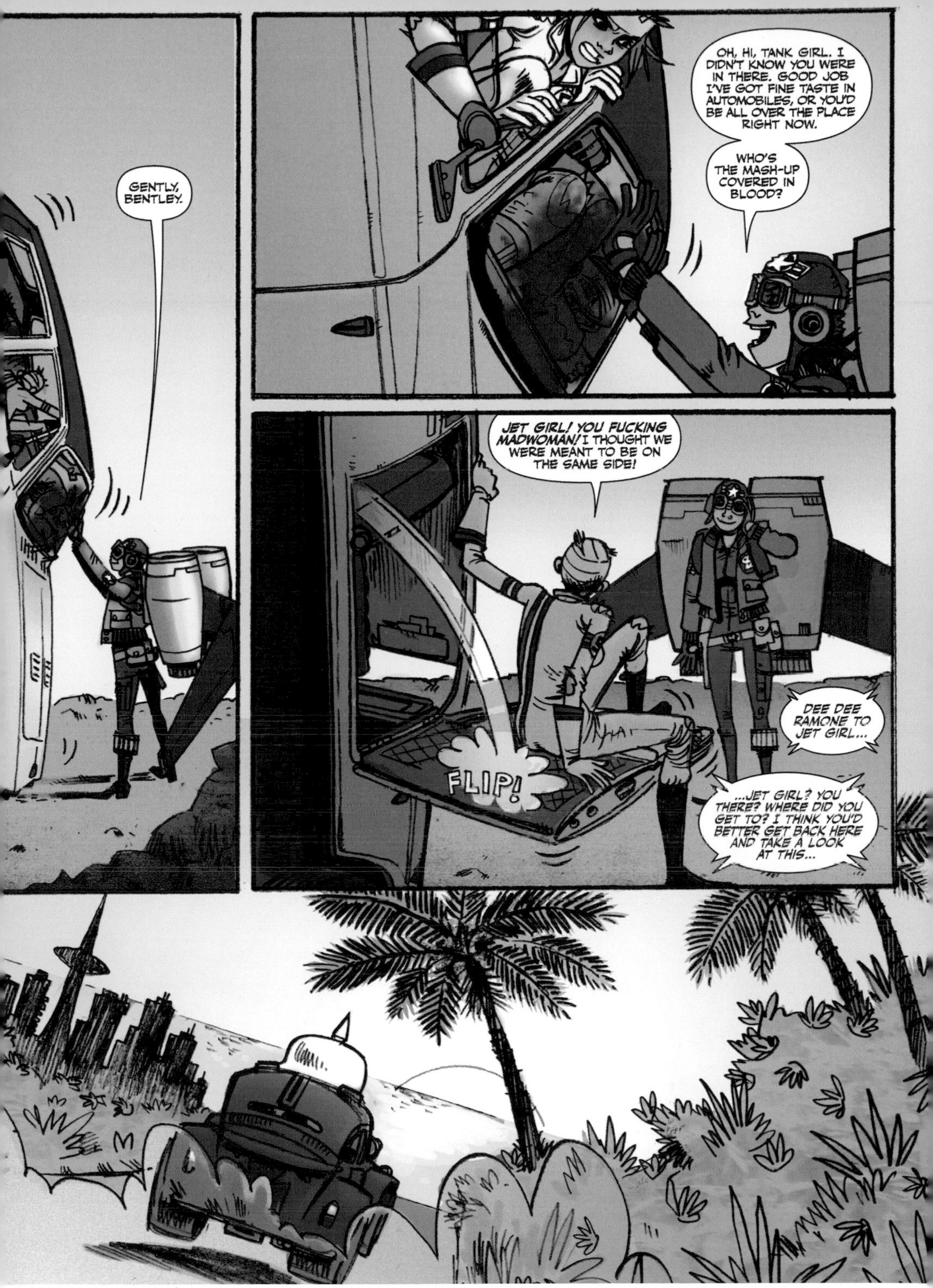
GENTLY, BENTLEY.
OH, HI, TANK GIRL. I DIDN'T KNOW YOU WERE IN THERE. GOOD JOB I'VE GOT FINE TASTE IN AUTOMOBILES, OR YOU'D BE ALL OVER THE PLACE RIGHT NOW.
WHO'S THE MASH-UP COVERED IN BLOOD?
JET GIRL! YOU FUCKING MADWOMAN! I THOUGHT WE WERE MEANT TO BE ON THE SAME SIDE!
FLIP!
DEE DEE RAMONE TO JET GIRL...
...JET GIRL? YOU THERE? WHERE DID YOU GET TO? I THINK YOU'D BETTER GET BACK HERE AND TAKE A LOOK AT THIS...

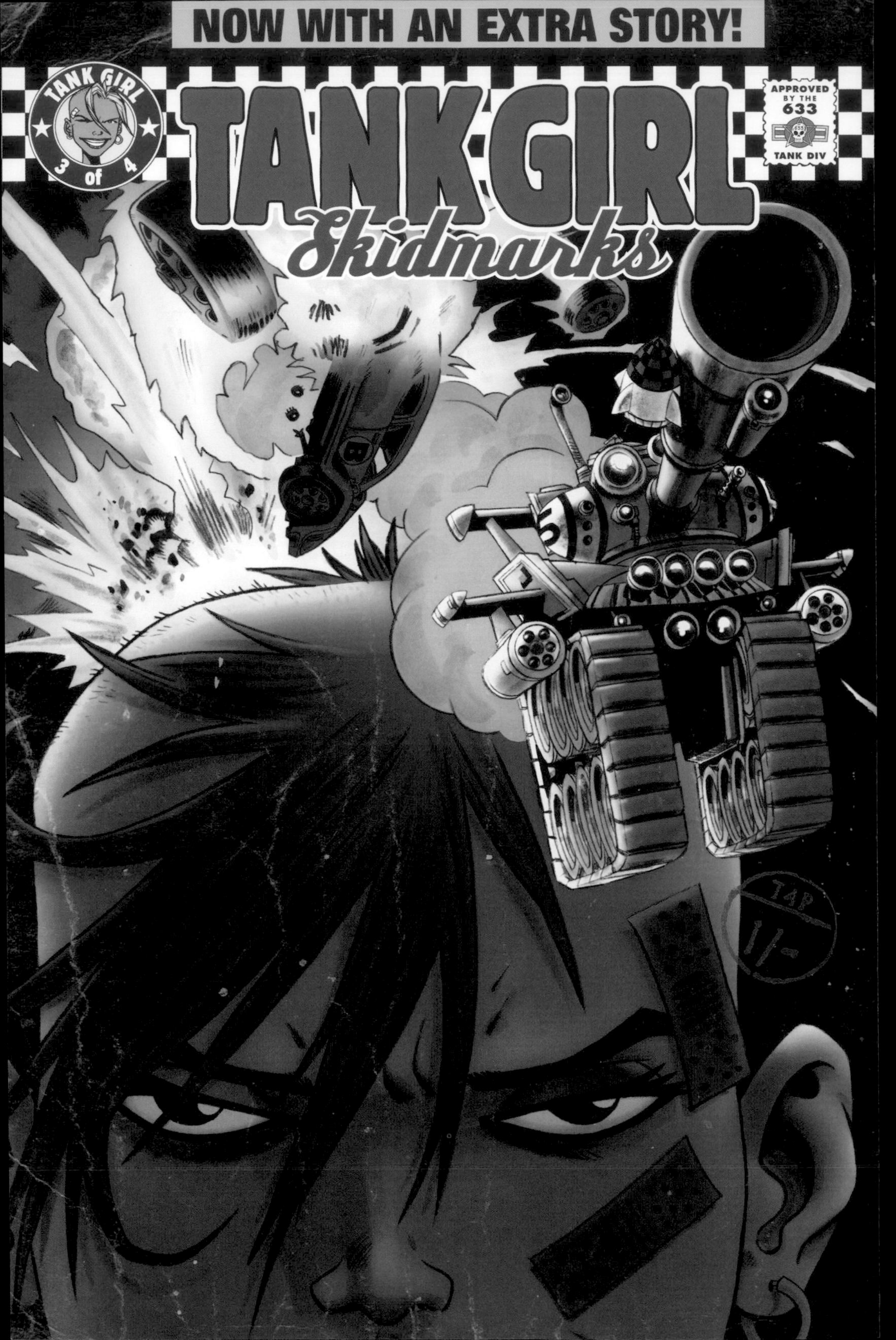
NOW WITH AN EXTRA STORY!
TANK GIRL
3 of 4
TANK GIRL
Skidmarks
APPROVED BY THE 633
TANK DIV

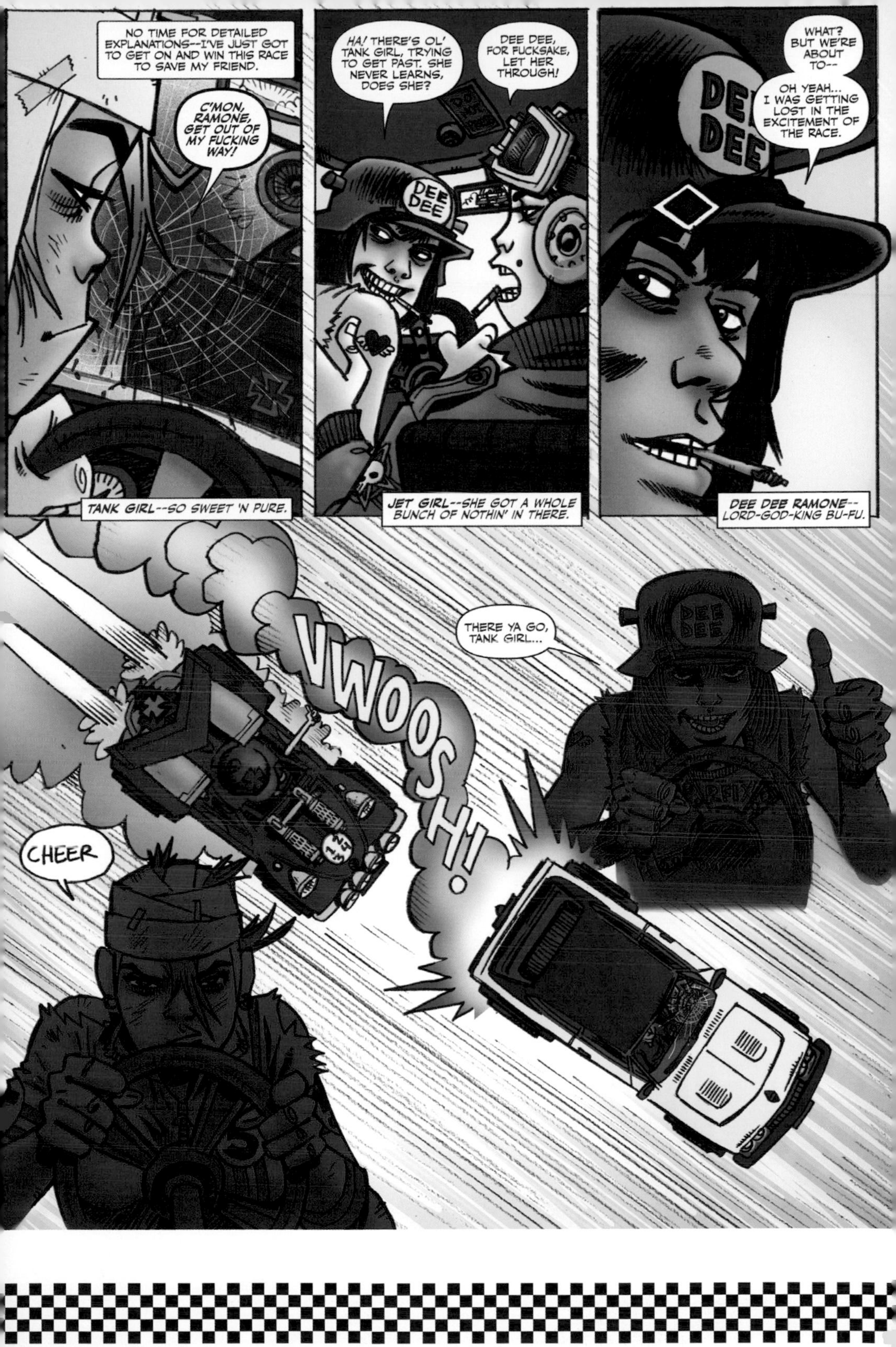

NO TIME FOR DETAILED EXPLANATIONS--I'VE JUST GOT TO GET ON AND WIN THIS RACE TO SAVE MY FRIEND.
C'MON, RAMONE, GET OUT OF MY FUCKING WAY!
TANK GIRL--SO SWEET 'N PURE.
HA! THERE'S OL' TANK GIRL, TRYING TO GET PAST. SHE NEVER LEARNS, DOES SHE?
DEE DEE, FOR FUCKSAKE, LET HER THROUGH!
DEE DEE
JET GIRL--SHE GOT A WHOLE BUNCH OF NOTHIN' IN THERE.
WHAT? BUT WE'RE ABOUT TO--
OH YEAH... I WAS GETTING LOST IN THE EXCITEMENT OF THE RACE.
DEE DEE
DEE DEE RAMONE--LORD-GOD-KING BU-FU.
THERE YA GO, TANK GIRL...
DEE DEE
VWOOSH!
CHEER

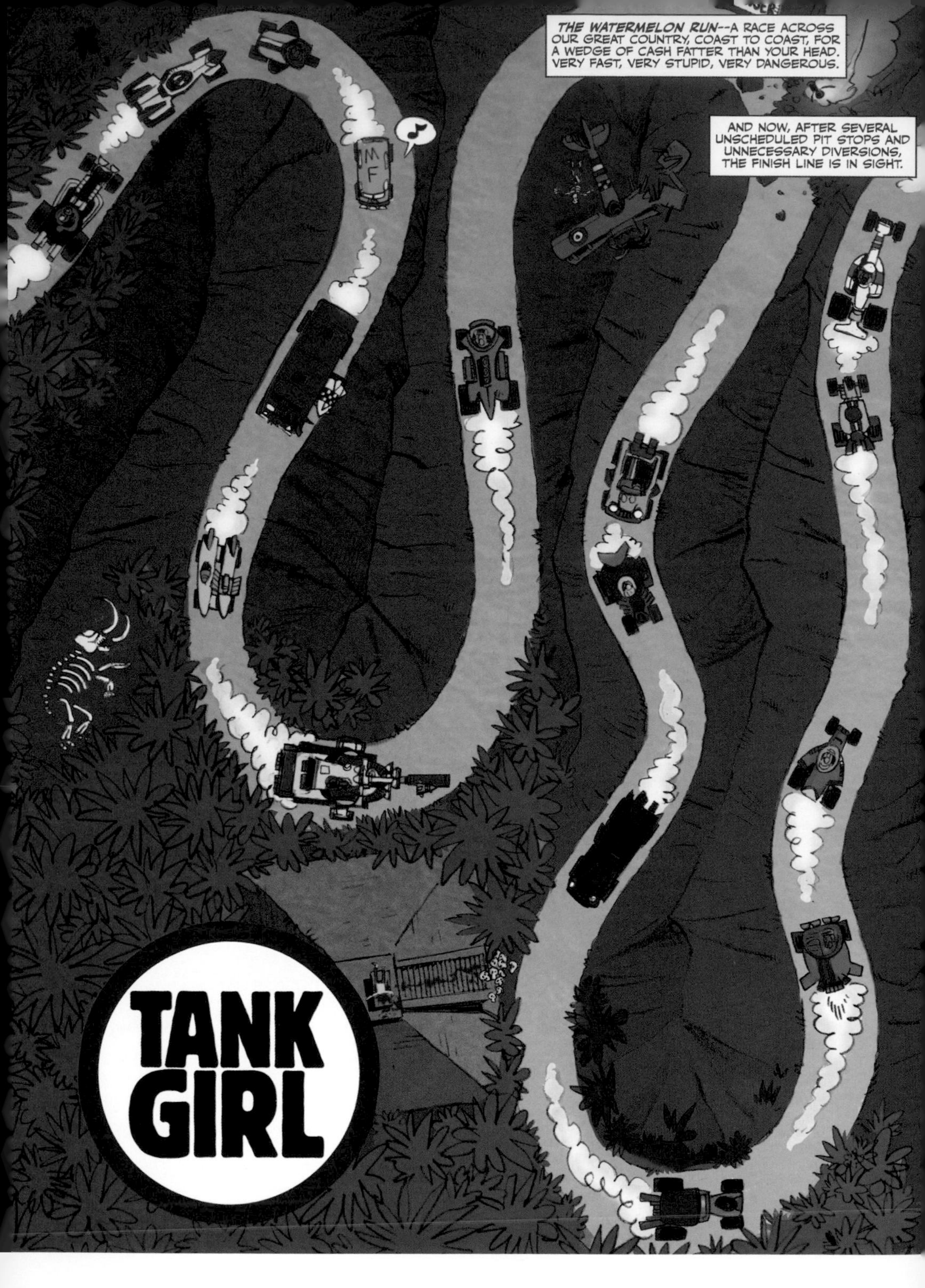
THE WATERMELON RUN--A RACE ACROSS OUR GREAT COUNTRY, COAST TO COAST, FOR A WEDGE OF CASH FATTER THAN YOUR HEAD. VERY FAST, VERY STUPID, VERY DANGEROUS.
AND NOW, AFTER SEVERAL UNSCHEDULED PIT STOPS AND UNNECESSARY DIVERSIONS, THE FINISH LINE IS IN SIGHT.
TANK GIRL

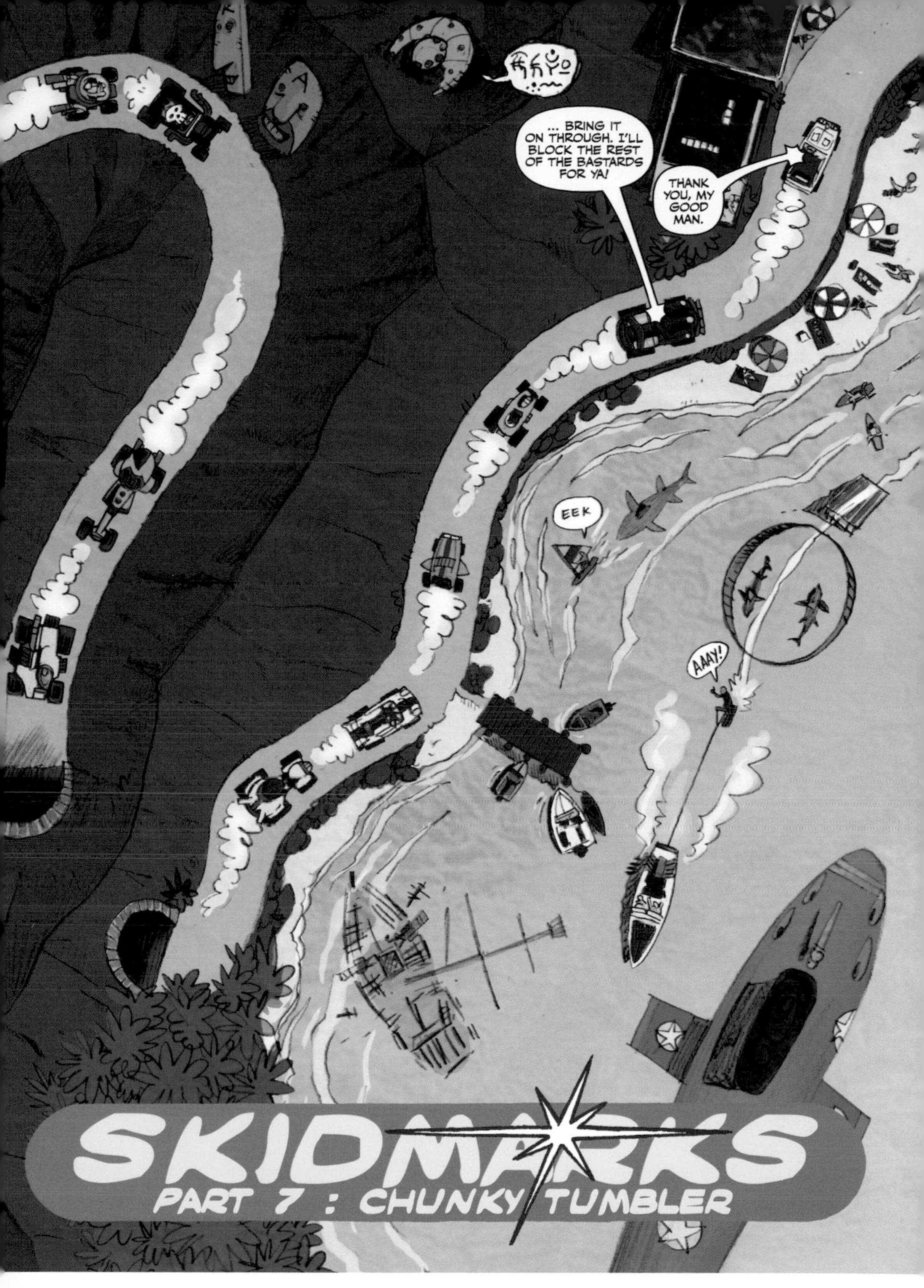

... BRING IT ON THROUGH. I'LL BLOCK THE REST OF THE BASTARDS FOR YA!
THANK YOU, MY GOOD MAN.
EEK
AAAY!
SKIDMARKS
PART 7 : CHUNKY TUMBLER

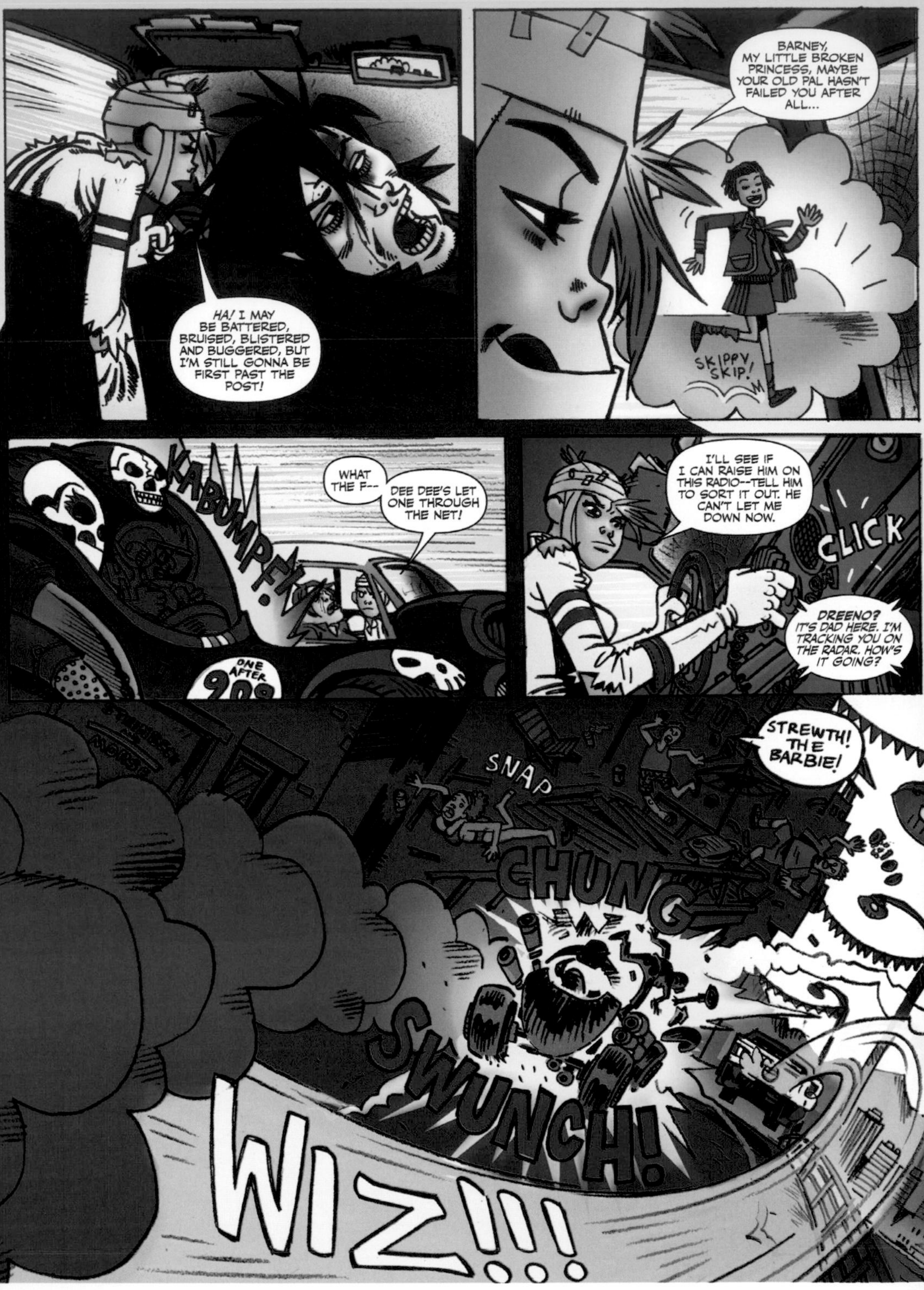
HA! I MAY BE BATTERED, BRUISED, BLISTERED AND BUGGERED, BUT I'M STILL GONNA BE FIRST PAST THE POST!
BARNEY, MY LITTLE BROKEN PRINCESS, MAYBE YOUR OLD PAL HASN'T FAILED YOU AFTER ALL...
SKIPPY SKIP!
KABUMPF!
WHAT THE F--
DEE DEE'S LET ONE THROUGH THE NET!
ONE AFTER 909
I'LL SEE IF I CAN RAISE HIM ON THIS RADIO--TELL HIM TO SORT IT OUT. HE CAN'T LET ME DOWN NOW.
CLICK
DREENO? IT'S DAD HERE. I'M TRACKING YOU ON THE RADAR. HOW'S IT GOING?
STREWTH! THE BARBIE!
SNAP
CHUNG
SWUNCH!
WIZ!!!

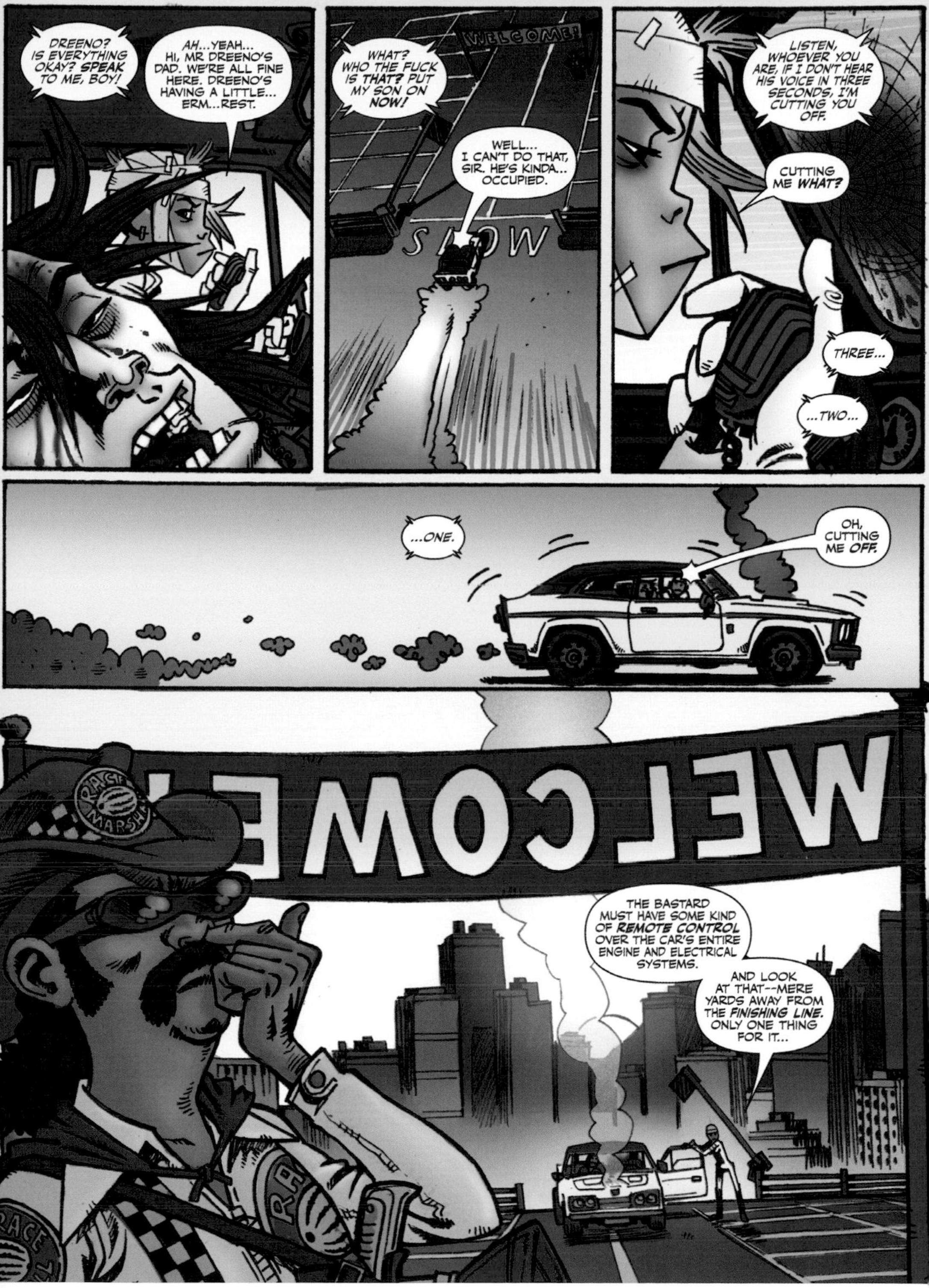
DREENO? IS EVERYTHING OKAY? SPEAK TO ME, BOY!
AH...YEAH... HI, MR DREENO'S DAD. WE'RE ALL FINE HERE. DREENO'S HAVING A LITTLE... ERM...REST.
WHAT? WHO THE FUCK IS THAT? PUT MY SON ON NOW!
WELL... I CAN'T DO THAT, SIR. HE'S KINDA... OCCUPIED.
LISTEN, WHOEVER YOU ARE, IF I DON'T HEAR HIS VOICE IN THREE SECONDS, I'M CUTTING YOU OFF.
CUTTING ME WHAT?
THREE...
...TWO...
...ONE.
OH, CUTTING ME OFF.
THE BASTARD MUST HAVE SOME KIND OF REMOTE CONTROL OVER THE CAR'S ENTIRE ENGINE AND ELECTRICAL SYSTEMS.
AND LOOK AT THAT--MERE YARDS AWAY FROM THE FINISHING LINE. ONLY ONE THING FOR IT...

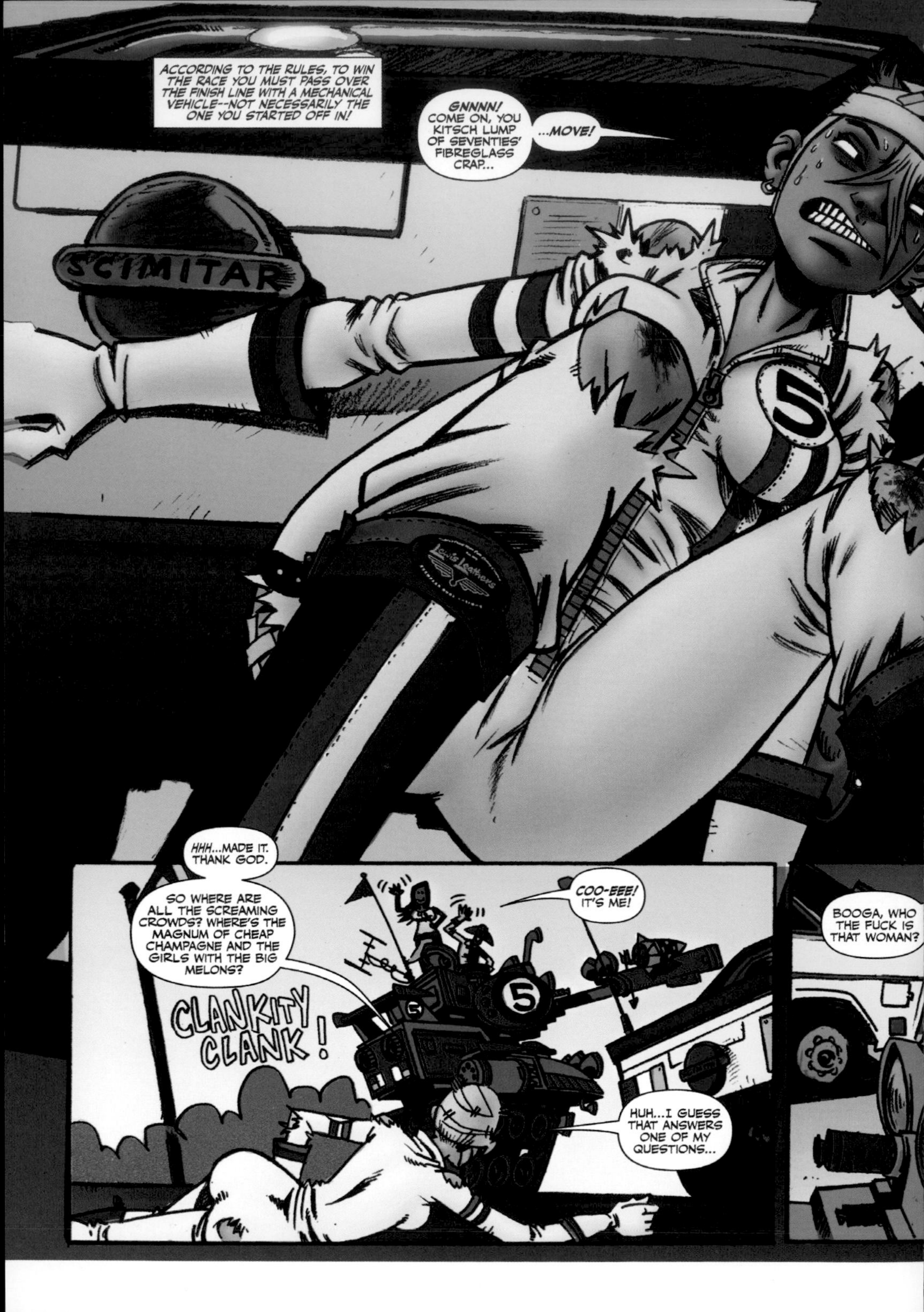
ACCORDING TO THE RULES, TO WIN THE RACE YOU MUST PASS OVER THE FINISH LINE WITH A MECHANICAL VEHICLE--NOT NECESSARILY THE ONE YOU STARTED OFF IN!
GNNNN! COME ON, YOU KITSCH LUMP OF SEVENTIES' FIBREGLASS CRAP...
...MOVE!
SCIMITAR
HHH...MADE IT. THANK GOD.
SO WHERE ARE ALL THE SCREAMING CROWDS? WHERE'S THE MAGNUM OF CHEAP CHAMPAGNE AND THE GIRLS WITH THE BIG MELONS?
COO-EEE! IT'S ME!
CLANKITY CLANK!
HUH...I GUESS THAT ANSWERS ONE OF MY QUESTIONS...
BOOGA, WHO THE FUCK IS THAT WOMAN?

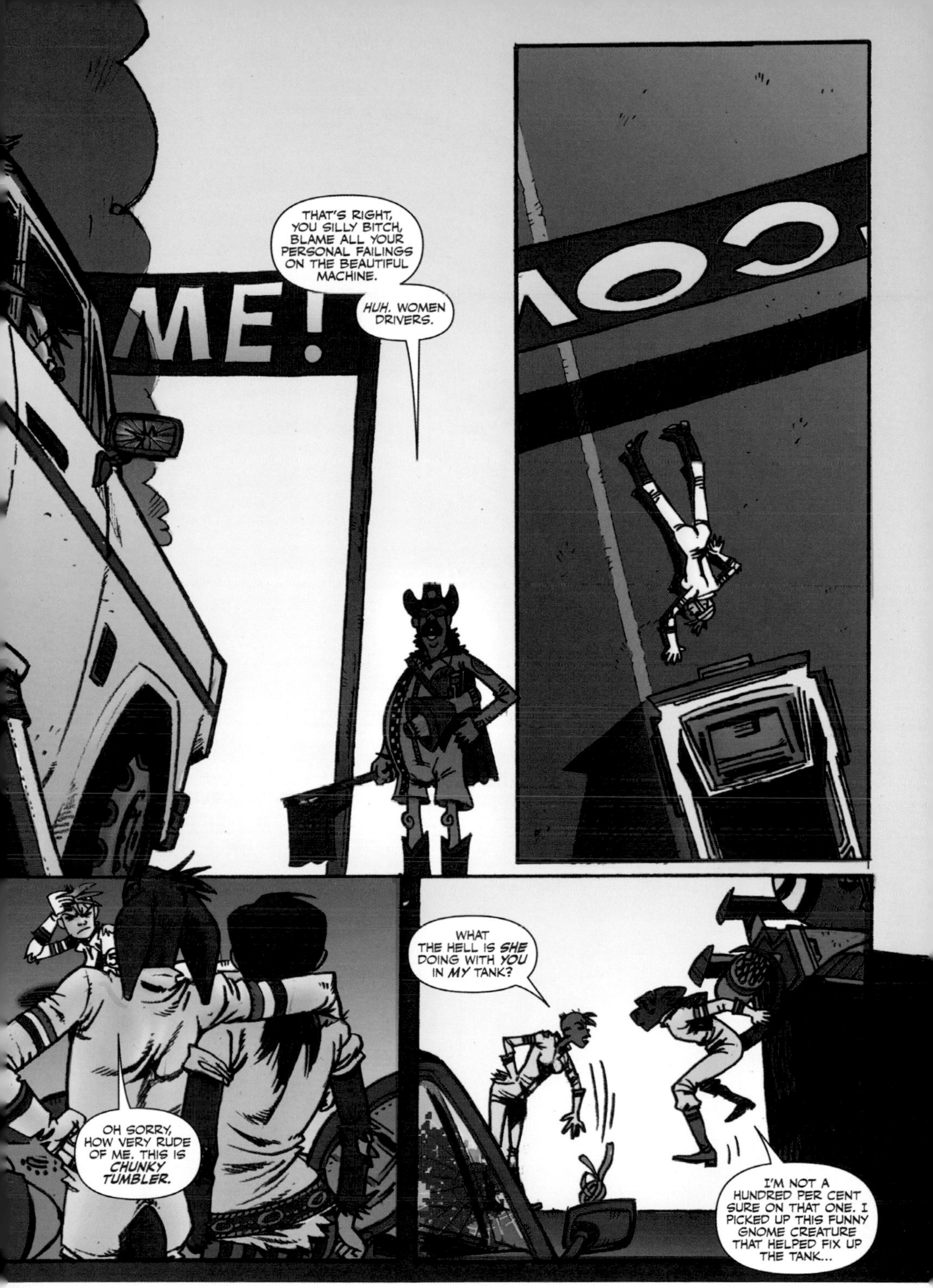
ME!
THAT'S RIGHT, YOU SILLY BITCH, BLAME ALL YOUR PERSONAL FAILINGS ON THE BEAUTIFUL MACHINE.
HUH. WOMEN DRIVERS.
OH SORRY, HOW VERY RUDE OF ME. THIS IS CHUNKY TUMBLER.
WHAT THE HELL IS SHE DOING WITH YOU IN MY TANK?
I'M NOT A HUNDRED PER CENT SURE ON THAT ONE. I PICKED UP THIS FUNNY GNOME CREATURE THAT HELPED FIX UP THE TANK...

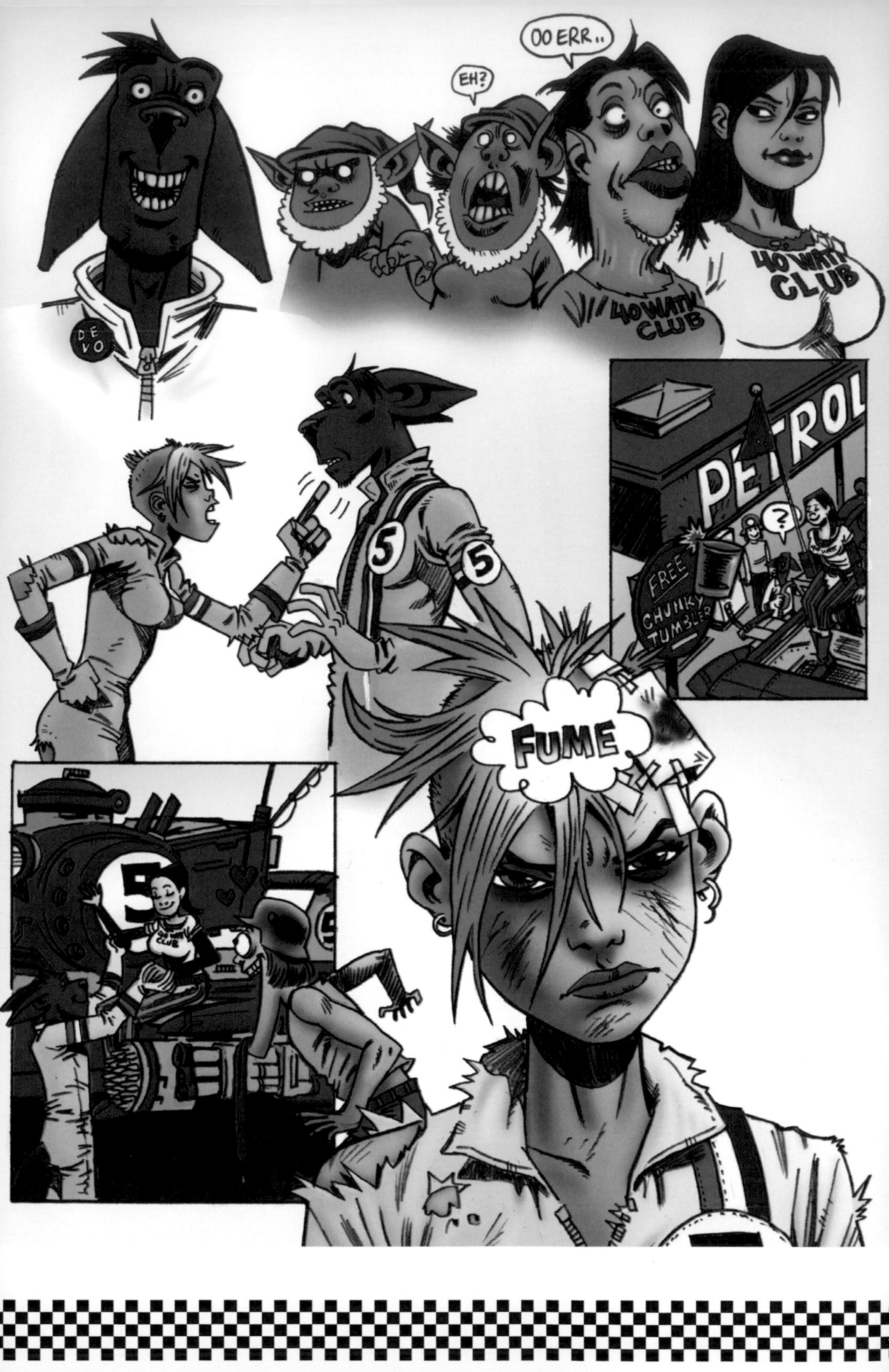
DE VO
EH?
OO ERR..
40 WATT CLUB
40 WATT CLUB
5
5
PETROL
?
40 WATT
FREE CHUNKY TUMBLER
FUME
5
40 WATT CLUB
5

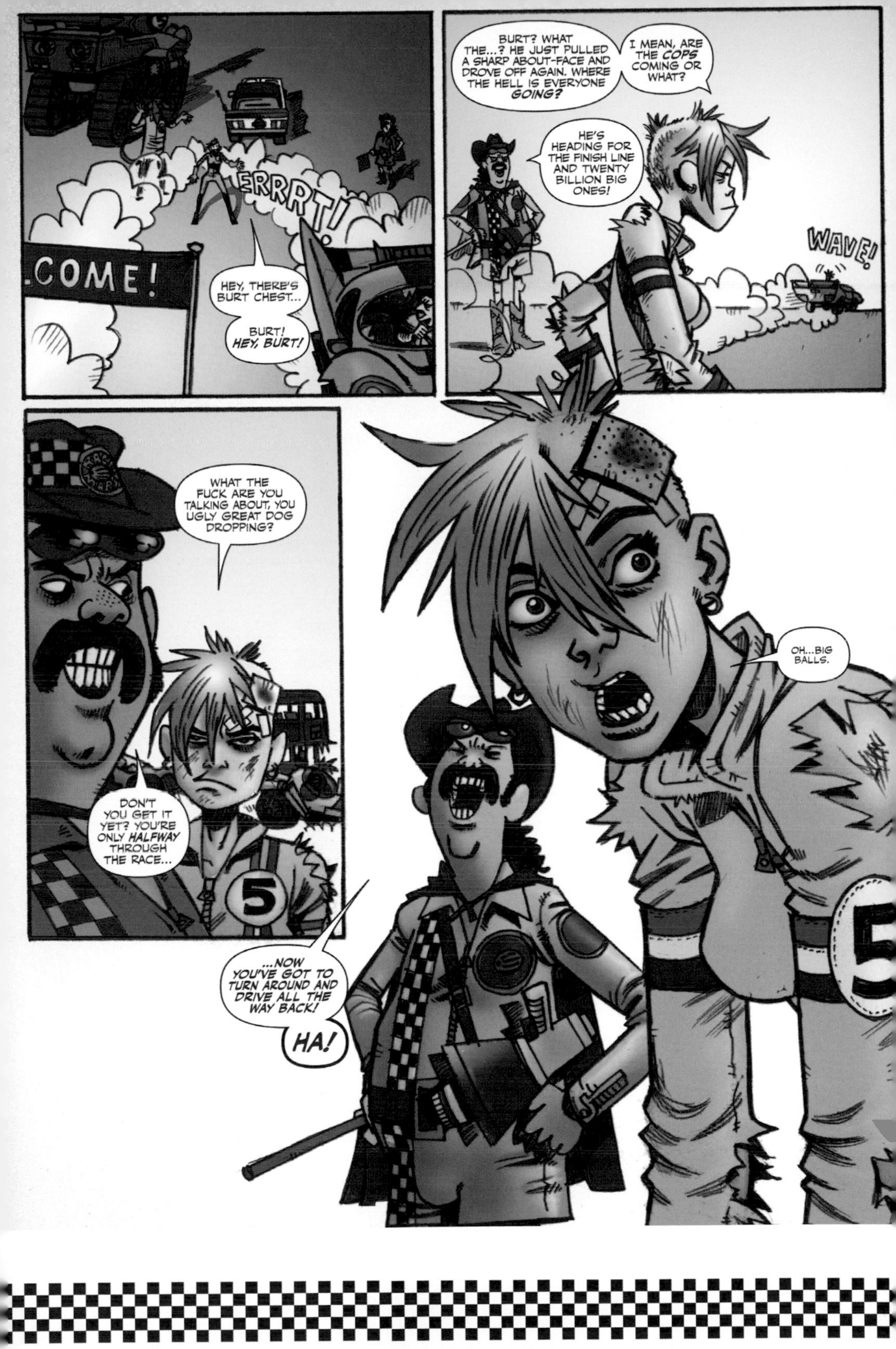
ERRRT!
HEY, THERE'S BURT CHEST...
BURT! HEY, BURT!
.COME!
BURT? WHAT THE...? HE JUST PULLED A SHARP ABOUT-FACE AND DROVE OFF AGAIN. WHERE THE HELL IS EVERYONE GOING?
I MEAN, ARE THE COPS COMING OR WHAT?
HE'S HEADING FOR THE FINISH LINE AND TWENTY BILLION BIG ONES!
WAVE!
WHAT THE FUCK ARE YOU TALKING ABOUT, YOU UGLY GREAT DOG DROPPING?
DON'T YOU GET IT YET? YOU'RE ONLY HALFWAY THROUGH THE RACE...
...NOW YOU'VE GOT TO TURN AROUND AND DRIVE ALL THE WAY BACK!
HA!
OH...BIG BALLS.

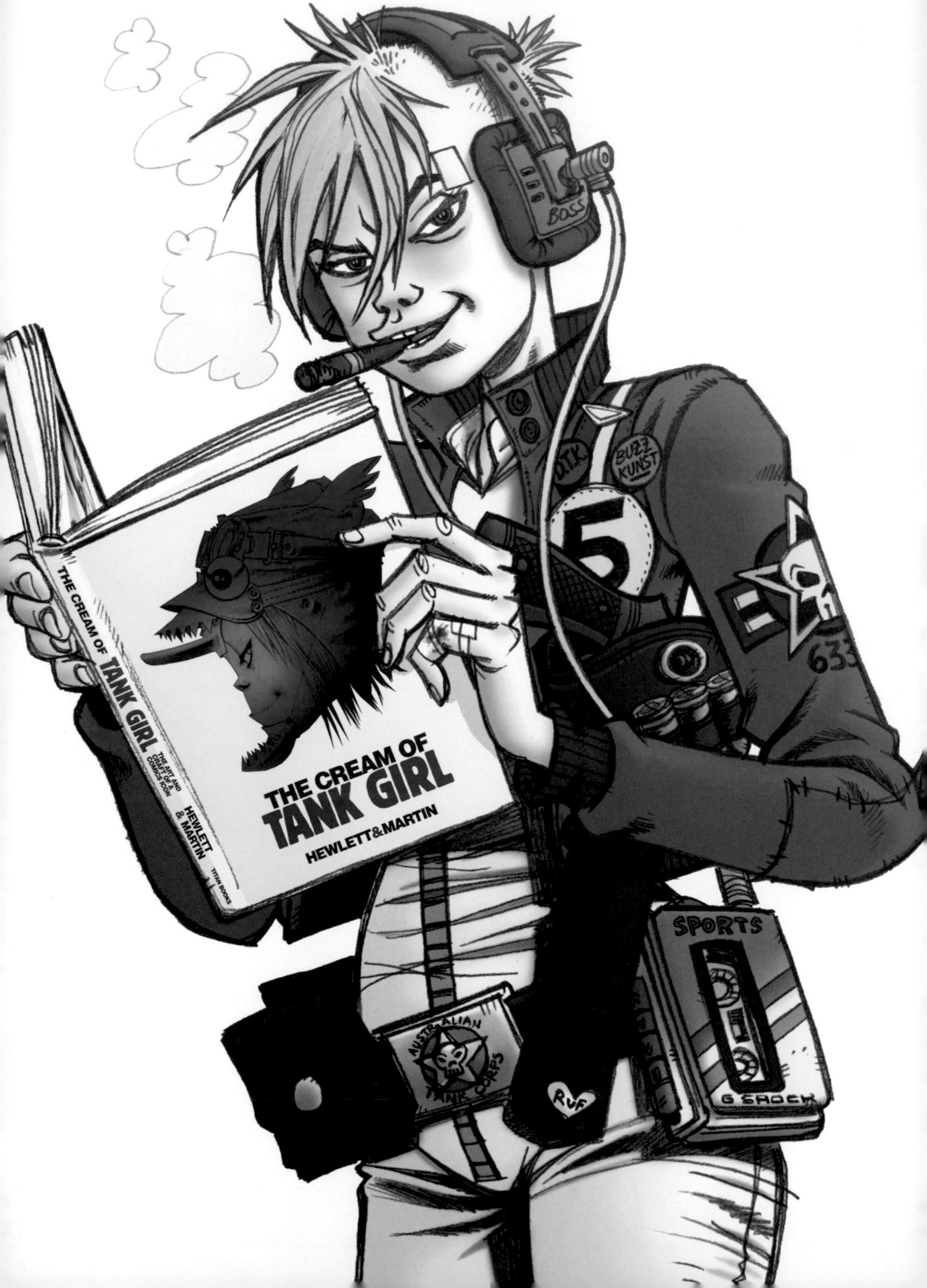
BOSS
O.T.K.
BUZZ KUNST
5
633
THE CREAM OF TANK GIRL
THE ART AND CRAFT OF A COMICS ICON
HEWLETT & MARTIN
TITAN BOOKS
THE CREAM OF
TANK GIRL
HEWLETT&MARTIN
SPORTS
G SHOCK
AUSTRALIAN TANK CORPS
RUF

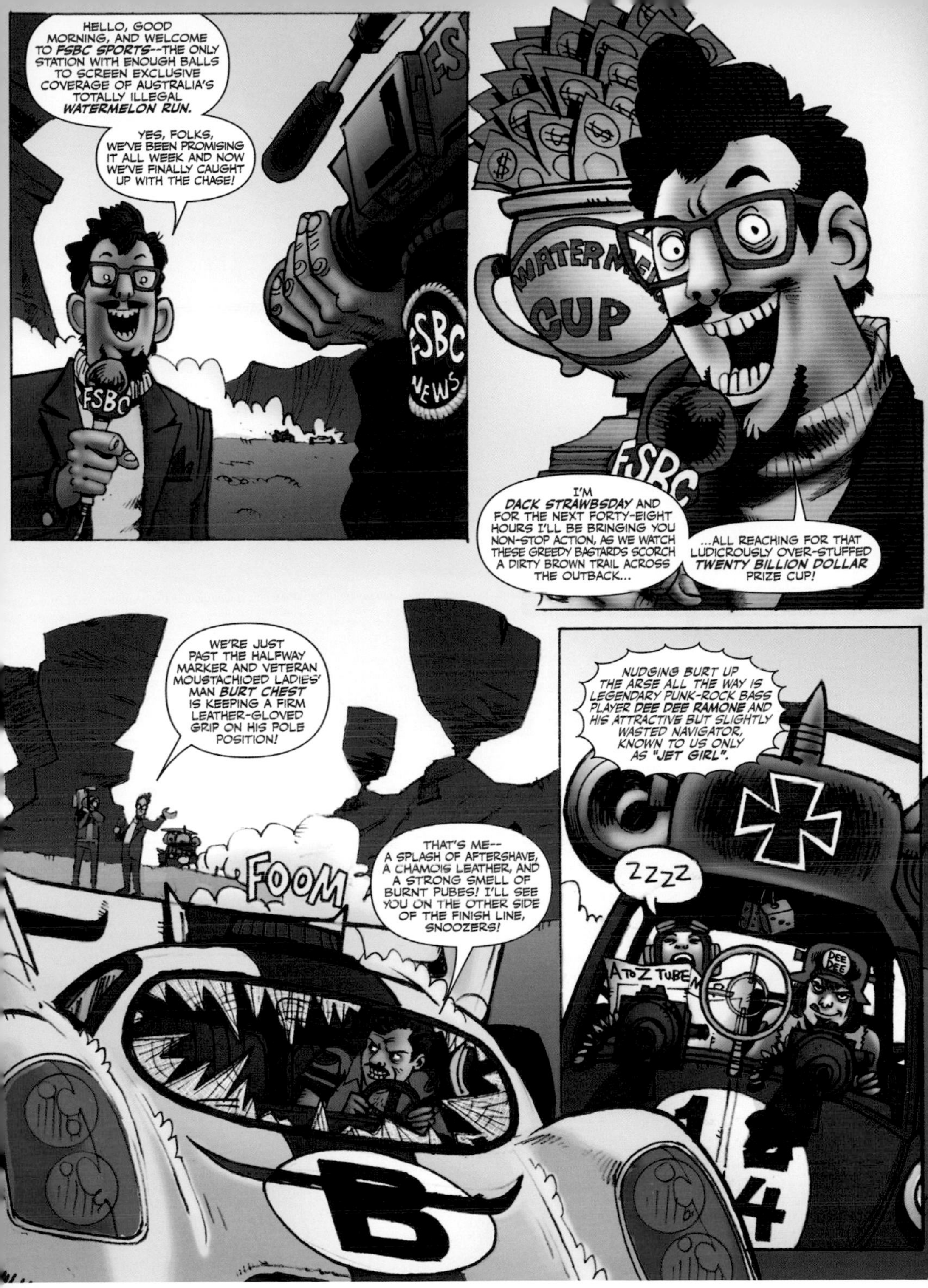
HELLO, GOOD MORNING, AND WELCOME TO FSBC SPORTS--THE ONLY STATION WITH ENOUGH BALLS TO SCREEN EXCLUSIVE COVERAGE OF AUSTRALIA'S TOTALLY ILLEGAL WATERMELON RUN.
YES, FOLKS, WE'VE BEEN PROMISING IT ALL WEEK AND NOW WE'VE FINALLY CAUGHT UP WITH THE CHASE!
FSBC
FSBC NEWS
CUP
FSBC
I'M DACK STRAWBSDAY AND FOR THE NEXT FORTY-EIGHT HOURS I'LL BE BRINGING YOU NON-STOP ACTION, AS WE WATCH THESE GREEDY BASTARDS SCORCH A DIRTY BROWN TRAIL ACROSS THE OUTBACK...
...ALL REACHING FOR THAT LUDICROUSLY OVER-STUFFED TWENTY BILLION DOLLAR PRIZE CUP!
WE'RE JUST PAST THE HALFWAY MARKER AND VETERAN MOUSTACHIOED LADIES' MAN BURT CHEST IS KEEPING A FIRM LEATHER-GLOVED GRIP ON HIS POLE POSITION!
FOOM
THAT'S ME-- A SPLASH OF AFTERSHAVE, A CHAMOIS LEATHER, AND A STRONG SMELL OF BURNT PUBES! I'LL SEE YOU ON THE OTHER SIDE OF THE FINISH LINE, SNOOZERS!
NUDGING BURT UP THE ARSE ALL THE WAY IS LEGENDARY PUNK-ROCK BASS PLAYER DEE DEE RAMONE AND HIS ATTRACTIVE BUT SLIGHTLY WASTED NAVIGATOR, KNOWN TO US ONLY AS "JET GIRL".
ZZZZ
DEE DEE
A TO Z TUBE
B
14

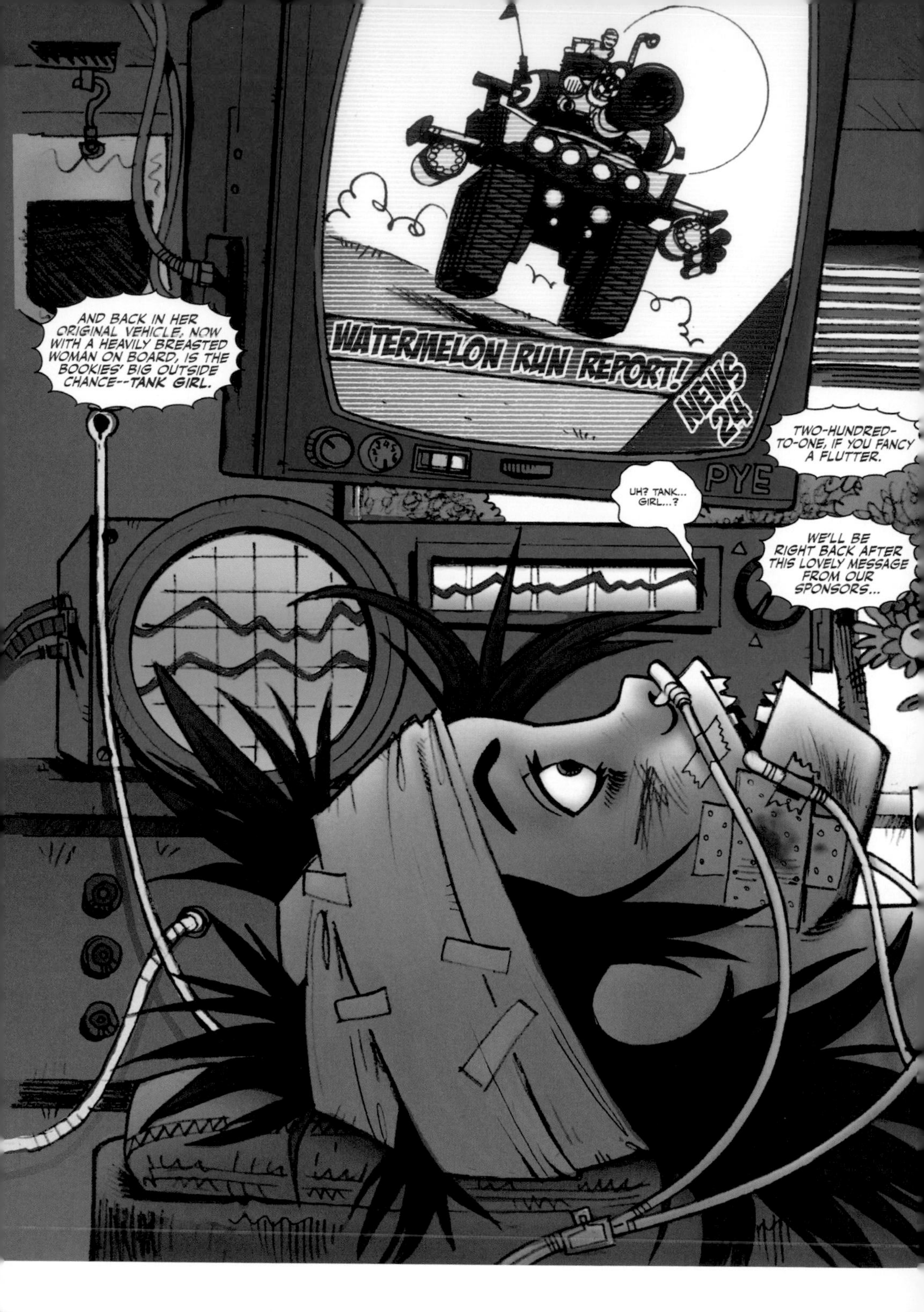
WATERMELON RUN REPORT!
NEWS 24
PYE
AND BACK IN HER ORIGINAL VEHICLE, NOW WITH A HEAVILY BREASTED WOMAN ON BOARD, IS THE BOOKIES' BIG OUTSIDE CHANCE--TANK GIRL.
TWO-HUNDRED-TO-ONE, IF YOU FANCY A FLUTTER.
UH? TANK... GIRL...?
WE'LL BE RIGHT BACK AFTER THIS LOVELY MESSAGE FROM OUR SPONSORS...

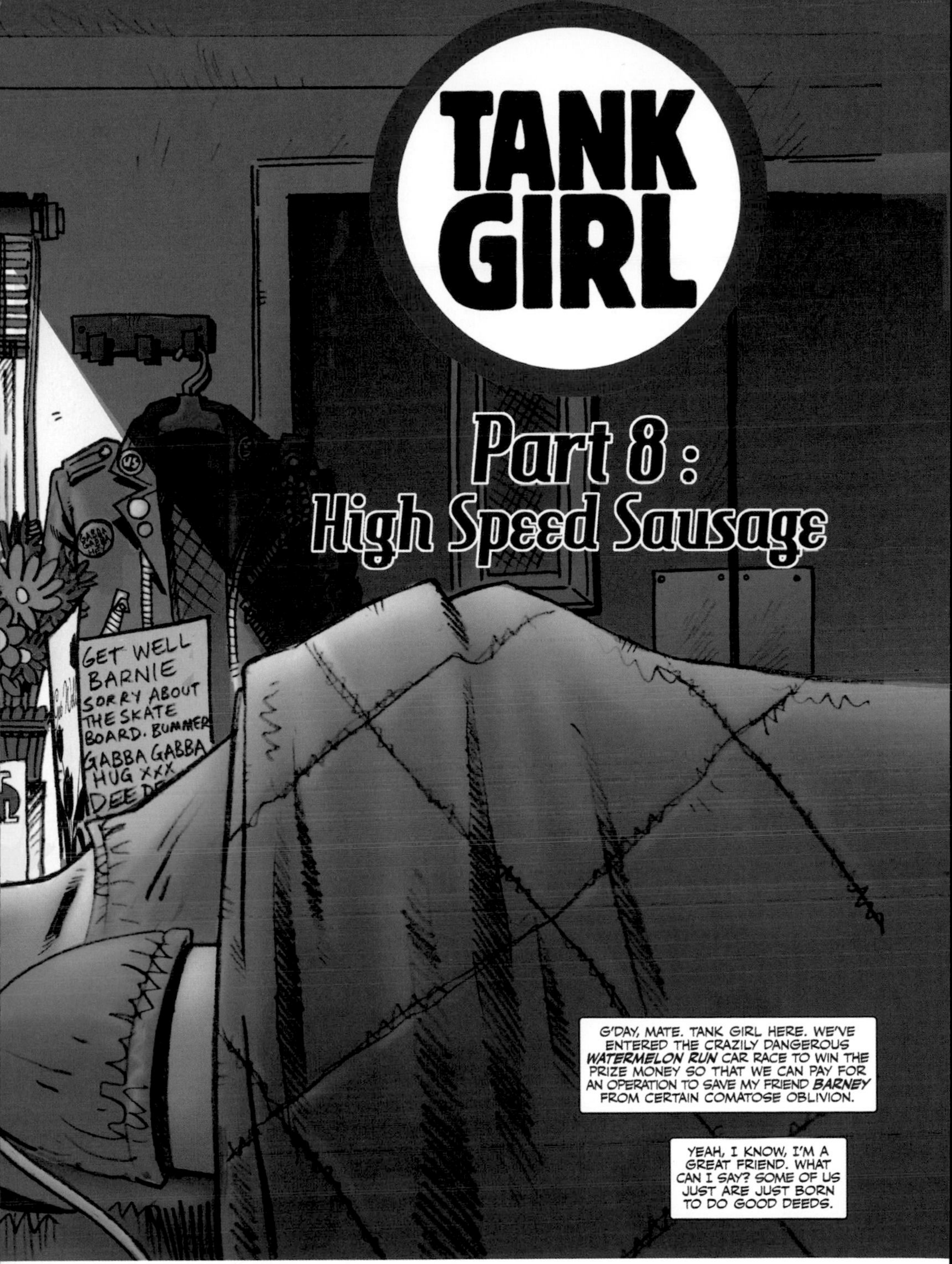
TANK GIRL
Part 8 : High Speed Sausage
GET WELL BARNIE SORRY ABOUT THE SKATE BOARD. BUMMER GABBA GABBA HUG XXX DEE DEE
G'DAY, MATE. TANK GIRL HERE. WE'VE ENTERED THE CRAZILY DANGEROUS WATERMELON RUN CAR RACE TO WIN THE PRIZE MONEY SO THAT WE CAN PAY FOR AN OPERATION TO SAVE MY FRIEND BARNEY FROM CERTAIN COMATOSE OBLIVION.
YEAH, I KNOW, I'M A GREAT FRIEND. WHAT CAN I SAY? SOME OF US JUST ARE JUST BORN TO DO GOOD DEEDS.

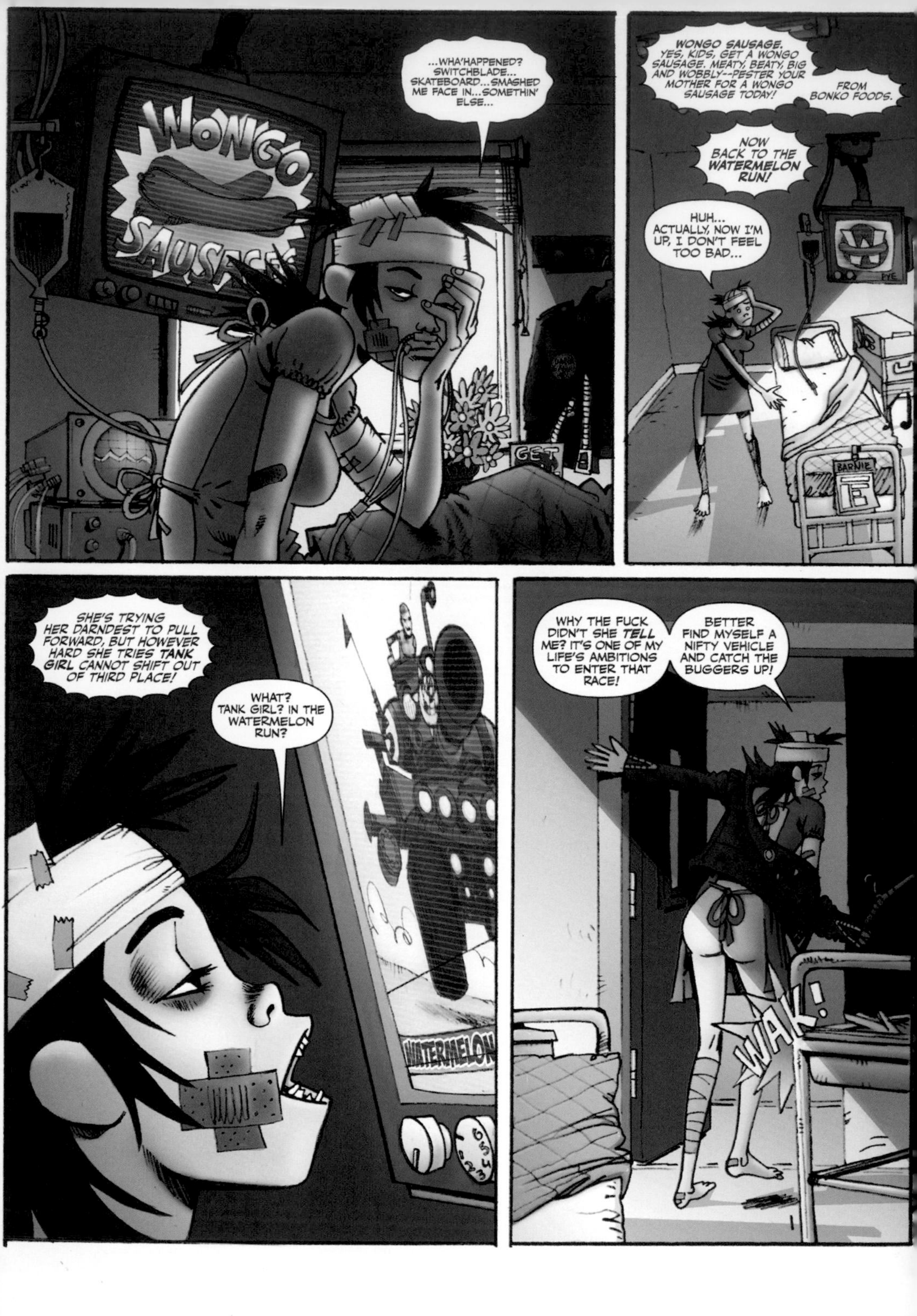

WONGO SAUSAGE
...WHA'HAPPENED? SWITCHBLADE... SKATEBOARD...SMASHED ME FACE IN...SOMETHIN' ELSE...
GET
WONGO SAUSAGE. YES, KIDS, GET A WONGO SAUSAGE. MEATY, BEATY, BIG AND WOBBLY--PESTER YOUR MOTHER FOR A WONGO SAUSAGE TODAY!
FROM BONKO FOODS.
NOW BACK TO THE WATERMELON RUN!
HUH... ACTUALLY, NOW I'M UP, I DON'T FEEL TOO BAD...
PYE
BARNIE
SHE'S TRYING HER DARNDEST TO PULL FORWARD, BUT HOWEVER HARD SHE TRIES TANK GIRL CANNOT SHIFT OUT OF THIRD PLACE!
WHAT? TANK GIRL? IN THE WATERMELON RUN?
WATERMELON
WHY THE FUCK DIDN'T SHE TELL ME? IT'S ONE OF MY LIFE'S AMBITIONS TO ENTER THAT RACE!
BETTER FIND MYSELF A NIFTY VEHICLE AND CATCH THE BUGGERS UP!
WAK!

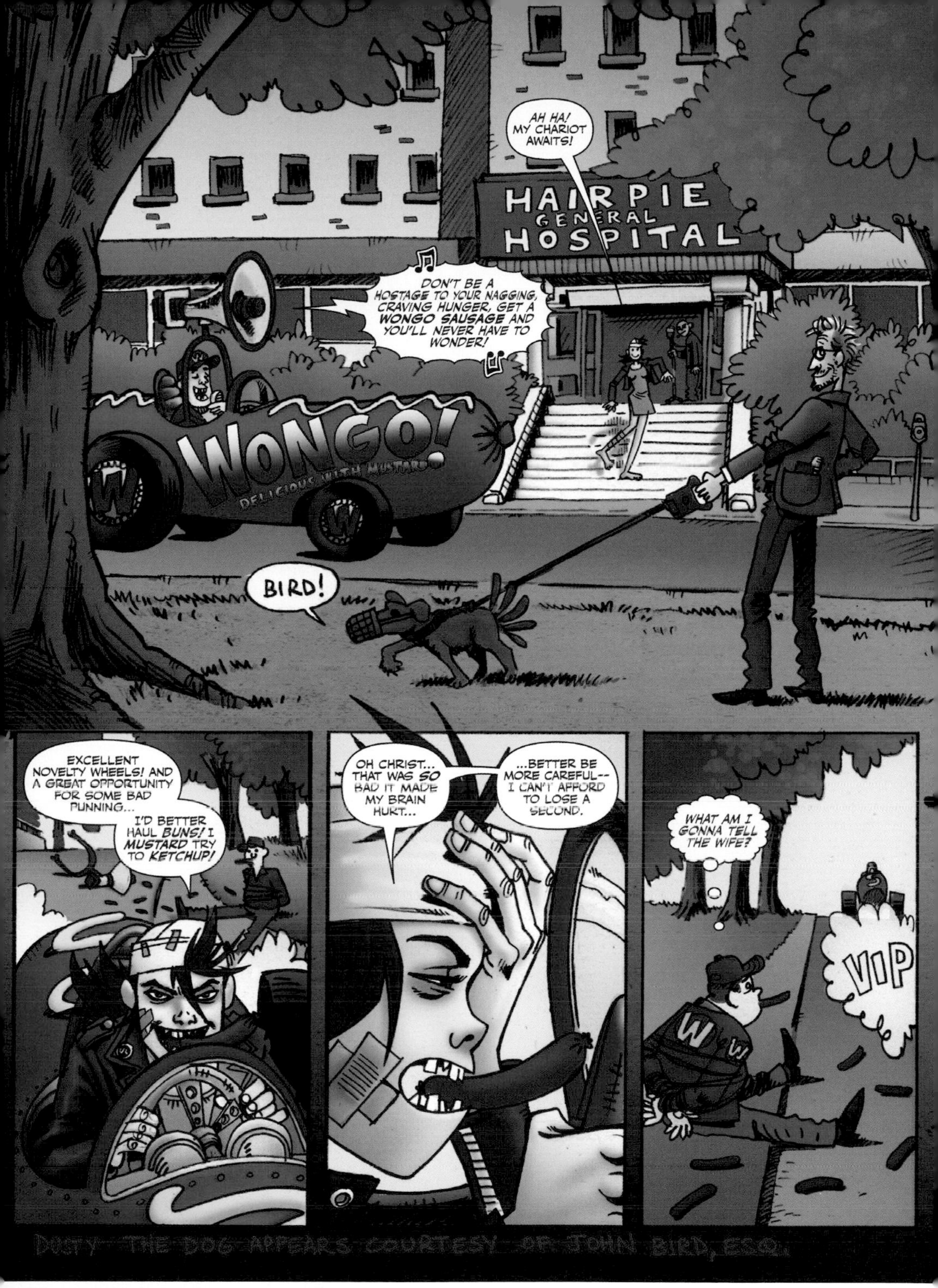
AH HA! MY CHARIOT AWAITS!
HAIRPIE GENERAL HOSPITAL
DON'T BE A HOSTAGE TO YOUR NAGGING, CRAVING HUNGER, GET A WONGO SAUSAGE AND YOU'LL NEVER HAVE TO WONDER!
WONGO!
DELICIOUS WITH MUSTARD
BIRD!
EXCELLENT NOVELTY WHEELS! AND A GREAT OPPORTUNITY FOR SOME BAD PUNNING...
I'D BETTER HAUL BUNS! I MUSTARD TRY TO KETCHUP!
OH CHRIST... THAT WAS SO BAD IT MADE MY BRAIN HURT...
...BETTER BE MORE CAREFUL-- I CAN'T AFFORD TO LOSE A SECOND.
WHAT AM I GONNA TELL THE WIFE?
VIP

DUSTY THE DOG APPEARS COURTESY OF JOHN BIRD, ESQ.

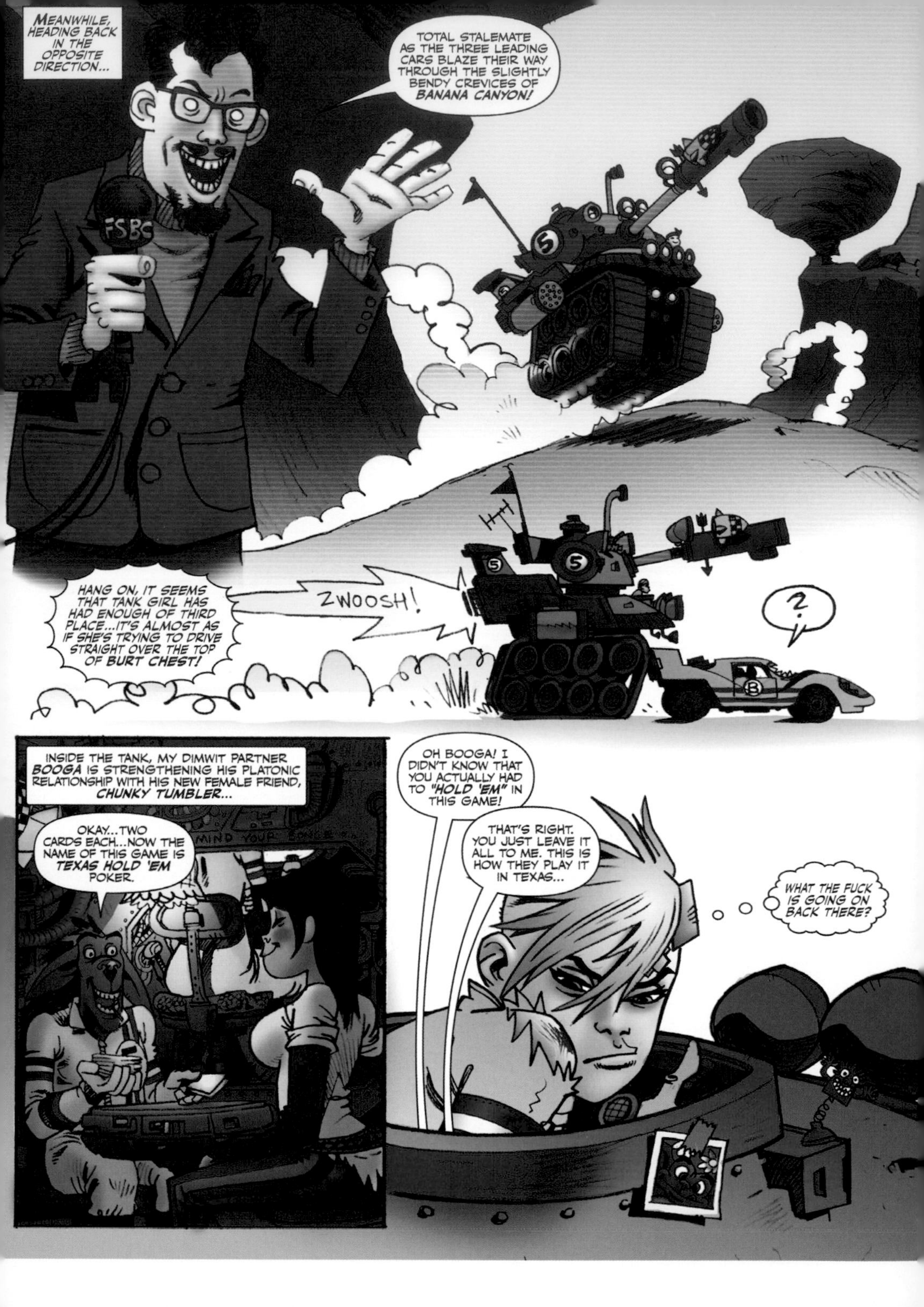
MEANWHILE, HEADING BACK IN THE OPPOSITE DIRECTION...
TOTAL STALEMATE AS THE THREE LEADING CARS BLAZE THEIR WAY THROUGH THE SLIGHTLY BENDY CREVICES OF BANANA CANYON!
FSBC
HANG ON, IT SEEMS THAT TANK GIRL HAS HAD ENOUGH OF THIRD PLACE...IT'S ALMOST AS IF SHE'S TRYING TO DRIVE STRAIGHT OVER THE TOP OF BURT CHEST!
ZWOOSH!
?
INSIDE THE TANK, MY DIMWIT PARTNER BOOGA IS STRENGTHENING HIS PLATONIC RELATIONSHIP WITH HIS NEW FEMALE FRIEND, CHUNKY TUMBLER...
OKAY...TWO CARDS EACH...NOW THE NAME OF THIS GAME IS TEXAS HOLD 'EM POKER.
OH BOOGA! I DIDN'T KNOW THAT YOU ACTUALLY HAD TO "HOLD 'EM" IN THIS GAME!
THAT'S RIGHT. YOU JUST LEAVE IT ALL TO ME. THIS IS HOW THEY PLAY IT IN TEXAS...
WHAT THE FUCK IS GOING ON BACK THERE?

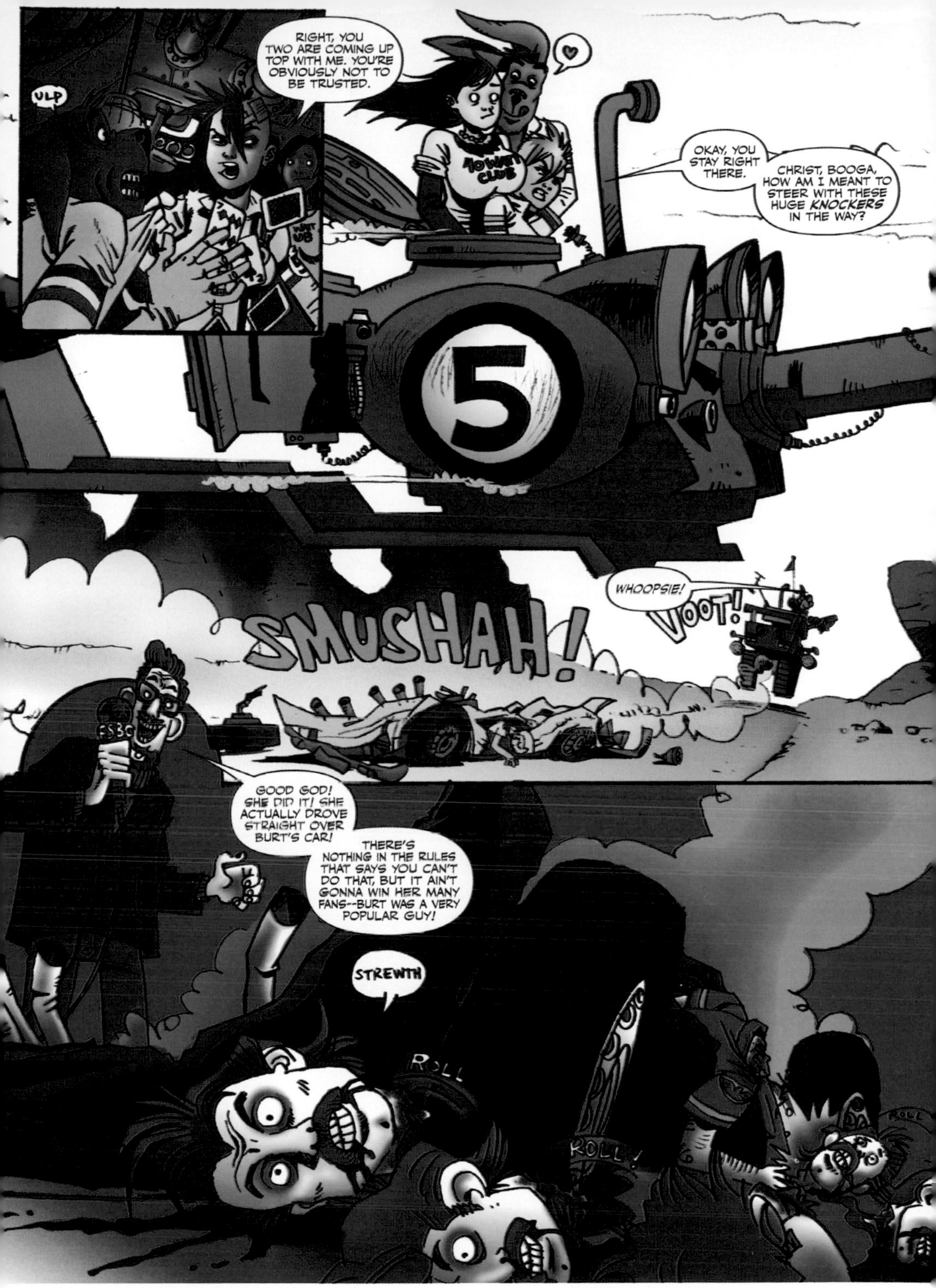
ULP
RIGHT, YOU TWO ARE COMING UP TOP WITH ME. YOU'RE OBVIOUSLY NOT TO BE TRUSTED.
OKAY, YOU STAY RIGHT THERE.
CHRIST, BOOGA, HOW AM I MEANT TO STEER WITH THESE HUGE *KNOCKERS* IN THE WAY?
SMUSHAH!
WHOOPSIE!
VOOT!
GOOD GOD! SHE DID IT! SHE ACTUALLY DROVE STRAIGHT OVER BURT'S CAR!
THERE'S NOTHING IN THE RULES THAT SAYS YOU CAN'T DO THAT, BUT IT AIN'T GONNA WIN HER MANY FANS--BURT WAS A VERY POPULAR GUY!
STREWTH

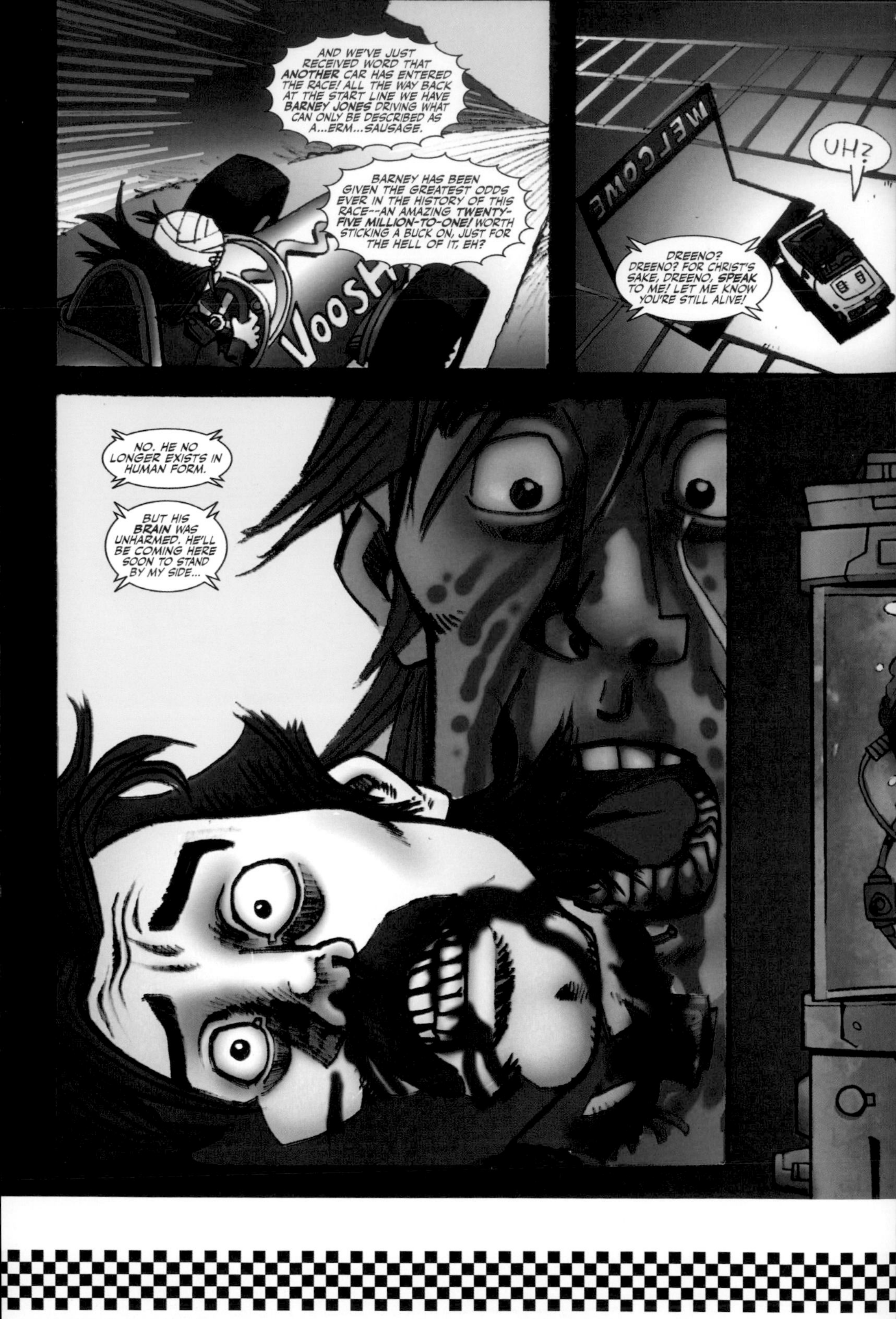
AND WE'VE JUST RECEIVED WORD THAT **ANOTHER** CAR HAS ENTERED THE RACE! ALL THE WAY BACK AT THE START LINE WE HAVE **BARNEY JONES** DRIVING WHAT CAN ONLY BE DESCRIBED AS A...ERM...SAUSAGE.
BARNEY HAS BEEN GIVEN THE GREATEST ODDS EVER IN THE HISTORY OF THIS RACE--AN AMAZING **TWENTY-FIVE MILLION-TO-ONE!** WORTH STICKING A BUCK ON, JUST FOR THE HELL OF IT, EH?
Voosh
WELCOME
UH?
DREENO? DREENO? FOR CHRIST'S SAKE, DREENO, **SPEAK** TO ME! LET ME KNOW YOU'RE STILL ALIVE!
NO. HE NO LONGER EXISTS IN HUMAN FORM.
BUT HIS **BRAIN** WAS UNHARMED. HE'LL BE COMING HERE SOON TO STAND BY MY SIDE...

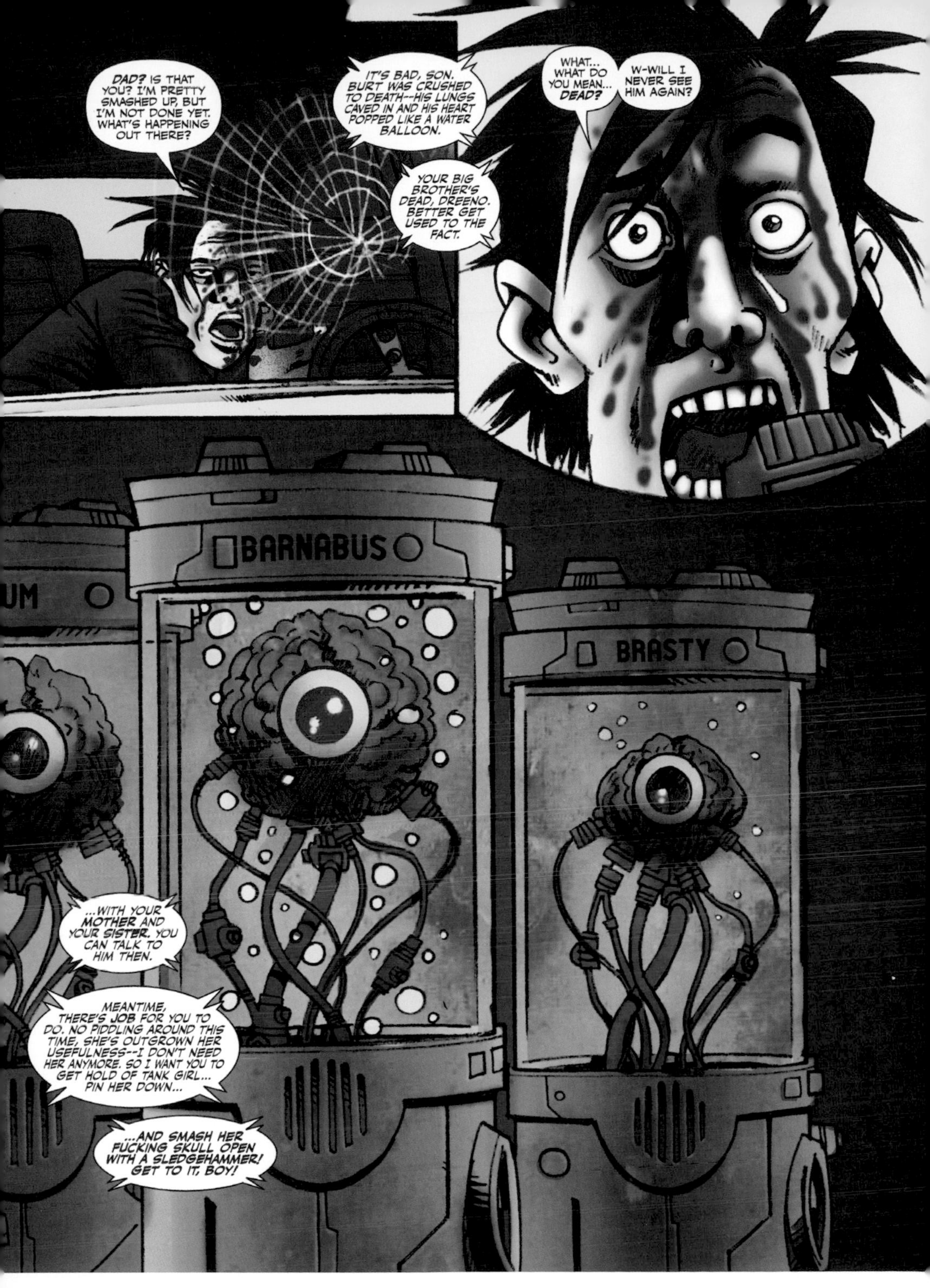
DAD? IS THAT YOU? I'M PRETTY SMASHED UP, BUT I'M NOT DONE YET. WHAT'S HAPPENING OUT THERE?
IT'S BAD, SON. BURT WAS CRUSHED TO DEATH--HIS LUNGS CAVED IN AND HIS HEART POPPED LIKE A WATER BALLOON.
YOUR BIG BROTHER'S DEAD, DREENO. BETTER GET USED TO THE FACT.
WHAT... WHAT DO YOU MEAN... DEAD?
W-WILL I NEVER SEE HIM AGAIN?
UM
BARNABUS
BRASTY
...WITH YOUR MOTHER AND YOUR SISTER. YOU CAN TALK TO HIM THEN.
MEANTIME, THERE'S JOB FOR YOU TO DO. NO PIDDLING AROUND THIS TIME, SHE'S OUTGROWN HER USEFULNESS--I DON'T NEED HER ANYMORE. SO I WANT YOU TO GET HOLD OF TANK GIRL... PIN HER DOWN...
...AND SMASH HER FUCKING SKULL OPEN WITH A SLEDGEHAMMER! GET TO IT, BOY!

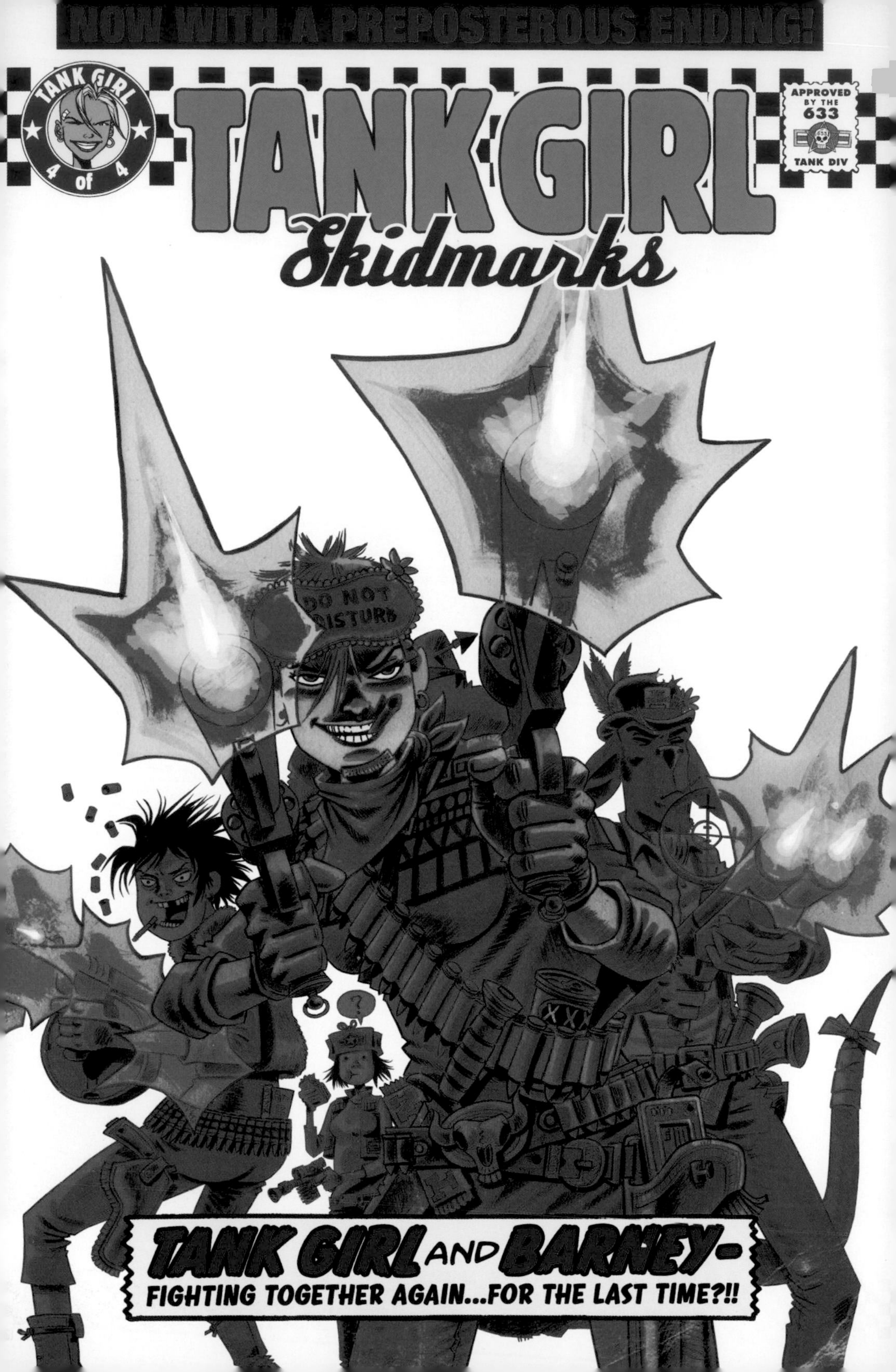
NOW WITH A PREPOSTEROUS ENDING!
TANK GIRL
4 of 4
TANK GIRL
Skidmarks
APPROVED BY THE 633
TANK DIV
DO NOT DISTURB
?
XXX
TANK GIRL AND BARNEY-
FIGHTING TOGETHER AGAIN...FOR THE LAST TIME?!!

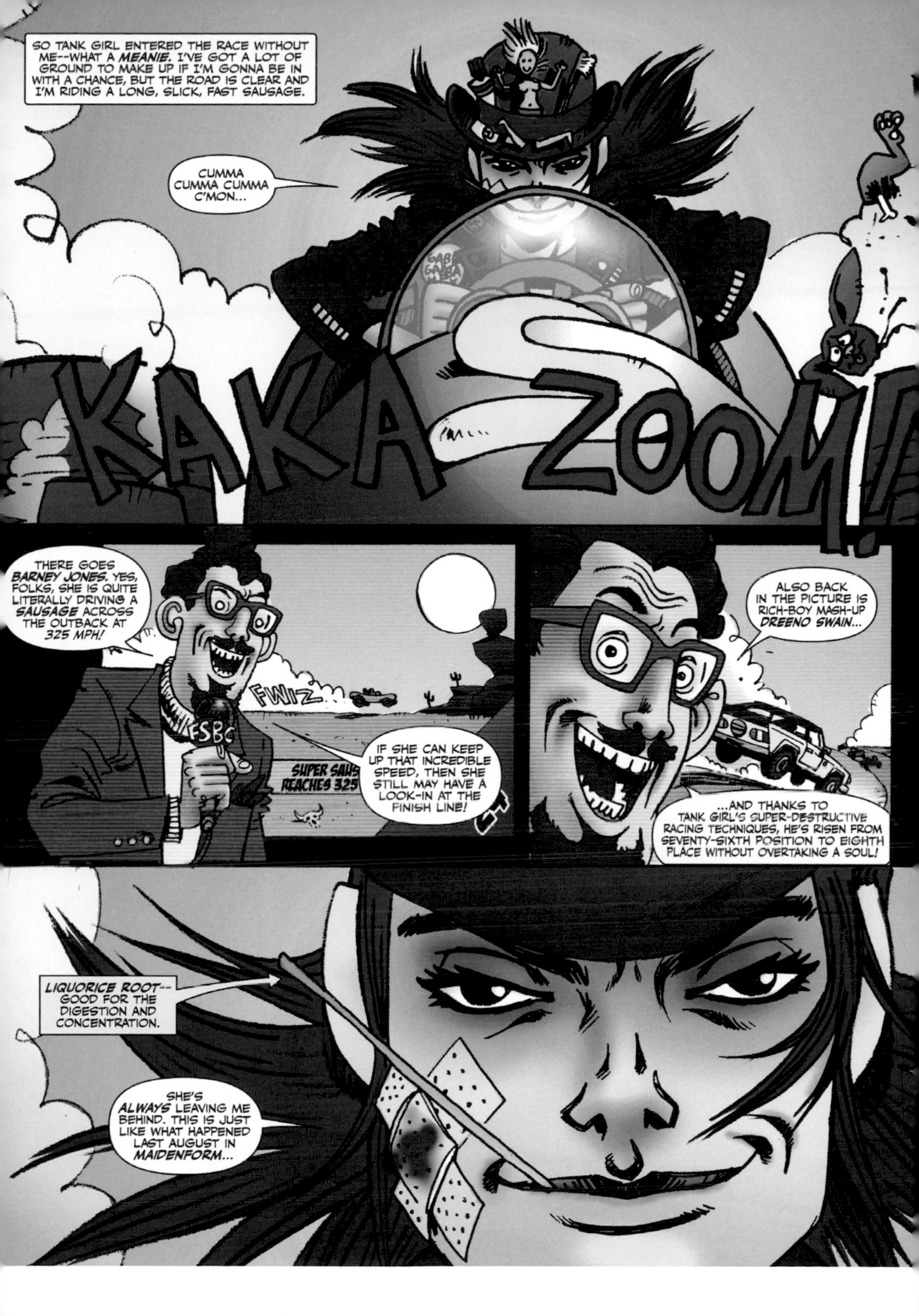
SO TANK GIRL ENTERED THE RACE WITHOUT ME--WHAT A MEANIE. I'VE GOT A LOT OF GROUND TO MAKE UP IF I'M GONNA BE IN WITH A CHANCE, BUT THE ROAD IS CLEAR AND I'M RIDING A LONG, SLICK, FAST SAUSAGE.
CUMMA CUMMA CUMMA C'MON...
KAKA ZOOM!!
THERE GOES BARNEY JONES. YES, FOLKS, SHE IS QUITE LITERALLY DRIVING A SAUSAGE ACROSS THE OUTBACK AT 325 MPH!
FWIZ
FSBC
SUPER SAUS REACHES 325
IF SHE CAN KEEP UP THAT INCREDIBLE SPEED, THEN SHE STILL MAY HAVE A LOOK-IN AT THE FINISH LINE!
ALSO BACK IN THE PICTURE IS RICH-BOY MASH-UP DREENO SWAIN...
...AND THANKS TO TANK GIRL'S SUPER-DESTRUCTIVE RACING TECHNIQUES, HE'S RISEN FROM SEVENTY-SIXTH POSITION TO EIGHTH PLACE WITHOUT OVERTAKING A SOUL!
LIQUORICE ROOT-- GOOD FOR THE DIGESTION AND CONCENTRATION.
SHE'S ALWAYS LEAVING ME BEHIND. THIS IS JUST LIKE WHAT HAPPENED LAST AUGUST IN MAIDENFORM...

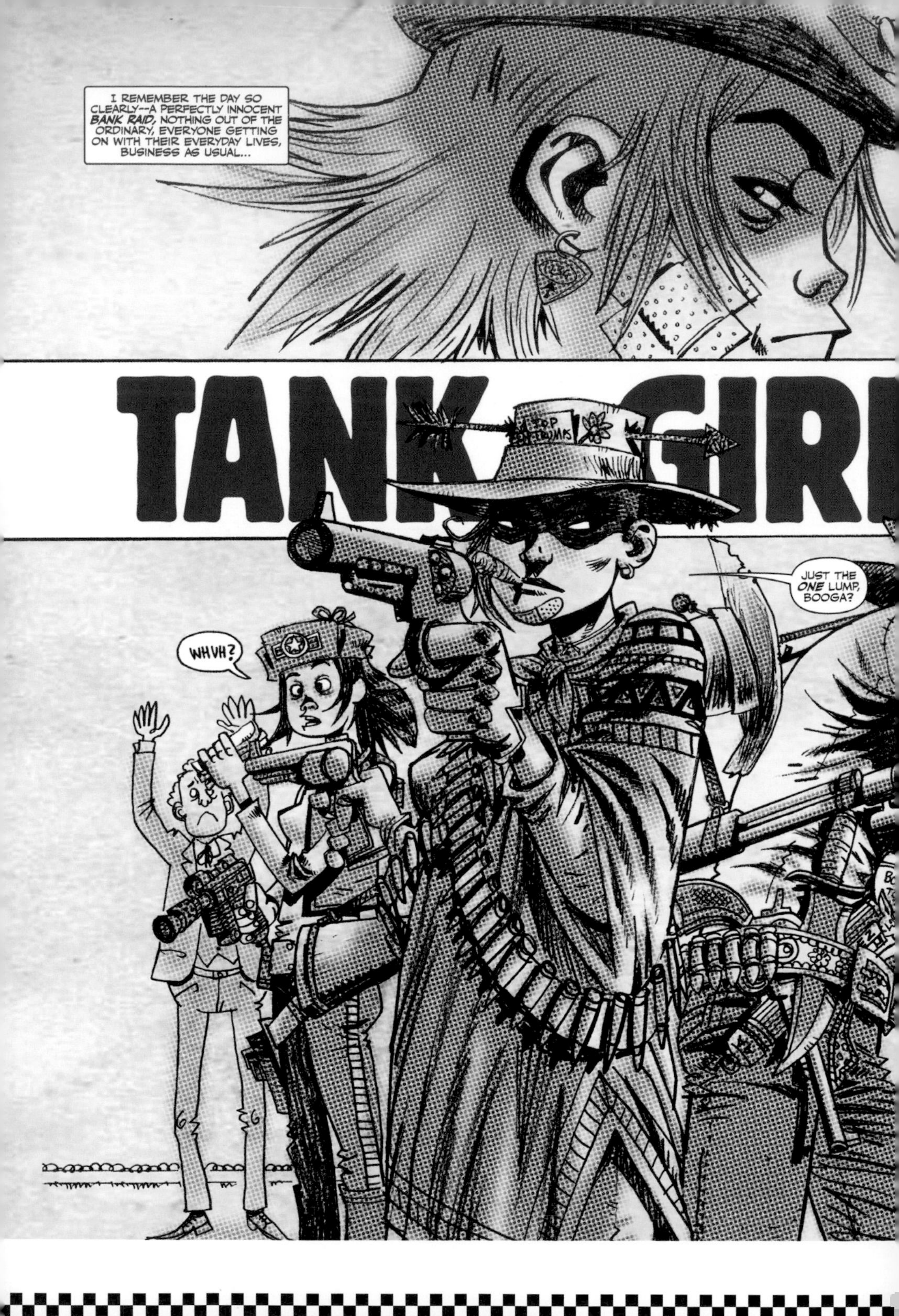
I REMEMBER THE DAY SO CLEARLY--A PERFECTLY INNOCENT BANK RAID, NOTHING OUT OF THE ORDINARY, EVERYONE GETTING ON WITH THEIR EVERYDAY LIVES, BUSINESS AS USUAL...
TANK GIRL
TOP TRUMPS
JUST THE ONE LUMP, BOOGA?
WHUH?

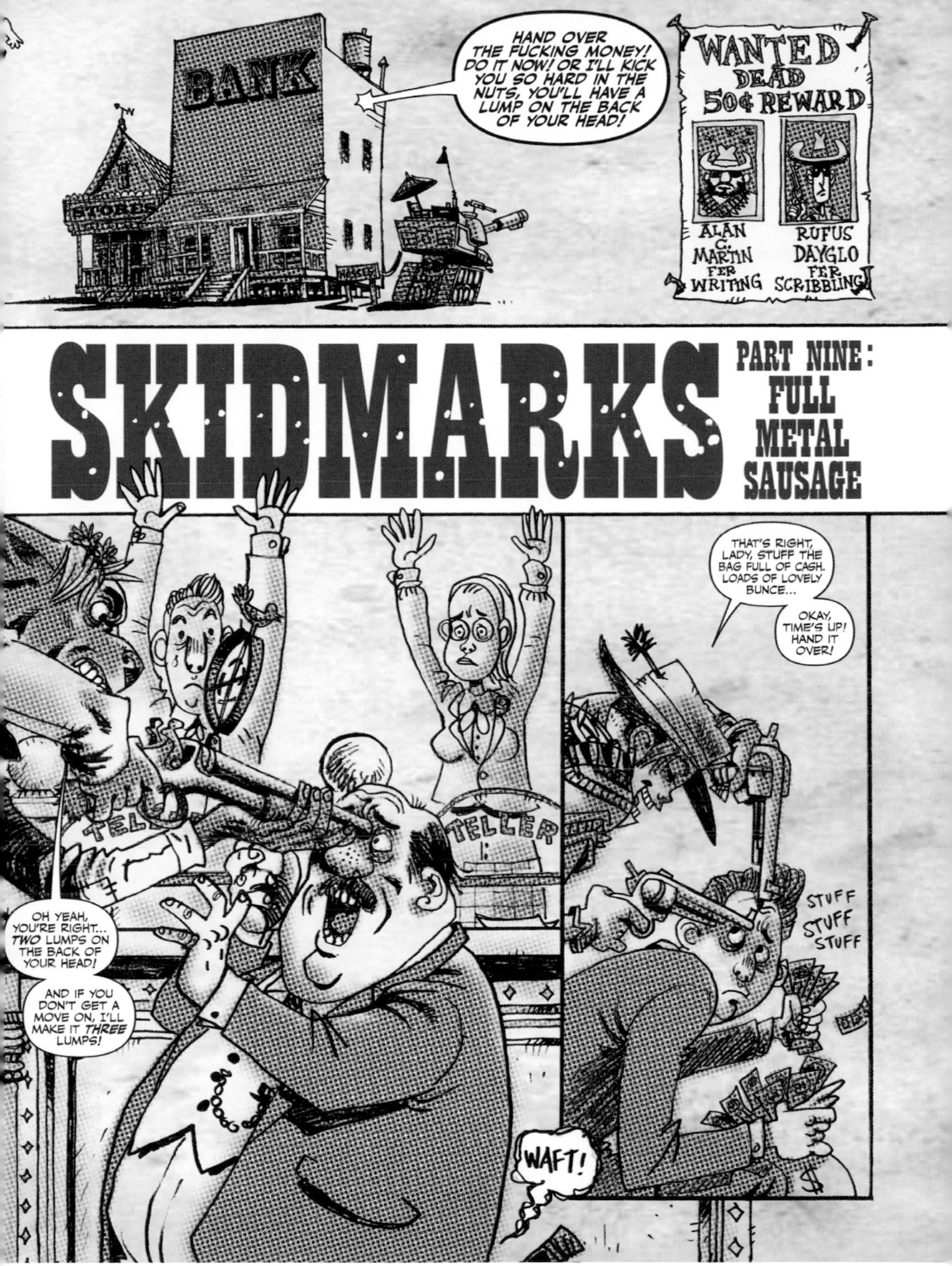
HAND OVER THE FUCKING MONEY! DO IT NOW! OR I'LL KICK YOU SO HARD IN THE NUTS, YOU'LL HAVE A LUMP ON THE BACK OF YOUR HEAD!
BANK
STORES
WANTED DEAD 50¢ REWARD
ALAN C. MARTIN FER WRITING
RUFUS DAYGLO FER SCRIBBLING
SKIDMARKS
PART NINE: FULL METAL SAUSAGE
TELLER
OH YEAH, YOU'RE RIGHT... TWO LUMPS ON THE BACK OF YOUR HEAD!
AND IF YOU DON'T GET A MOVE ON, I'LL MAKE IT THREE LUMPS!
WAFT!
THAT'S RIGHT, LADY, STUFF THE BAG FULL OF CASH. LOADS OF LOVELY BUNCE...
OKAY, TIME'S UP! HAND IT OVER!
STUFF STUFF STUFF

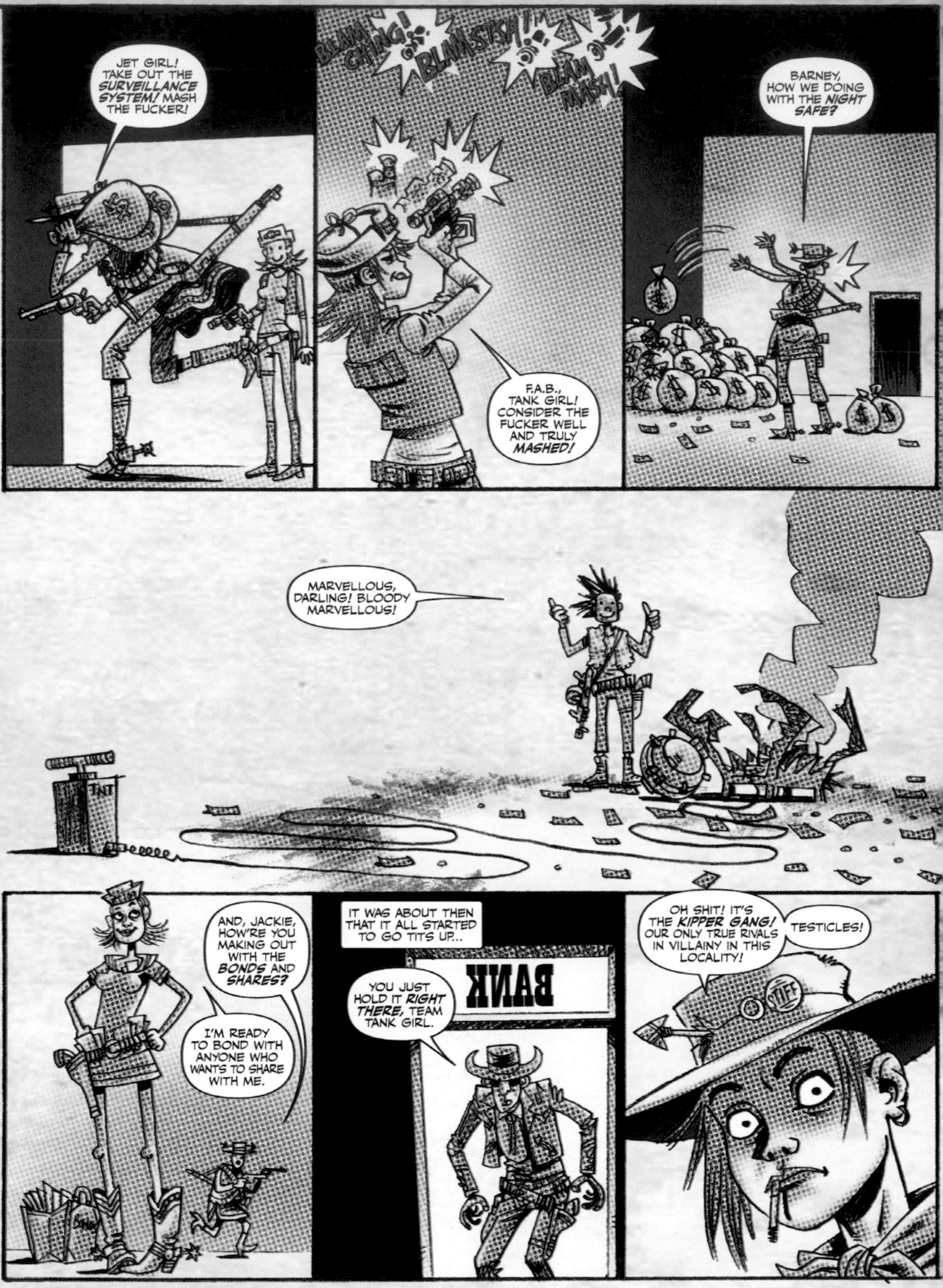
JET GIRL! TAKE OUT THE SURVEILLANCE SYSTEM! MASH THE FUCKER!
BLAM CHING!
BLAM STSH!
BLAM MASH!
F.A.B., TANK GIRL! CONSIDER THE FUCKER WELL AND TRULY MASHED!
BARNEY, HOW WE DOING WITH THE NIGHT SAFE?
MARVELLOUS, DARLING! BLOODY MARVELLOUS!
TNT
AND, JACKIE, HOW'RE YOU MAKING OUT WITH THE BONDS AND SHARES?
I'M READY TO BOND WITH ANYONE WHO WANTS TO SHARE WITH ME.
IT WAS ABOUT THEN THAT IT ALL STARTED TO GO TITS UP...
BANK
YOU JUST HOLD IT RIGHT THERE, TEAM TANK GIRL.
OH SHIT! IT'S THE KIPPER GANG! OUR ONLY TRUE RIVALS IN VILLAINY IN THIS LOCALITY!
TESTICLES!
STIFF

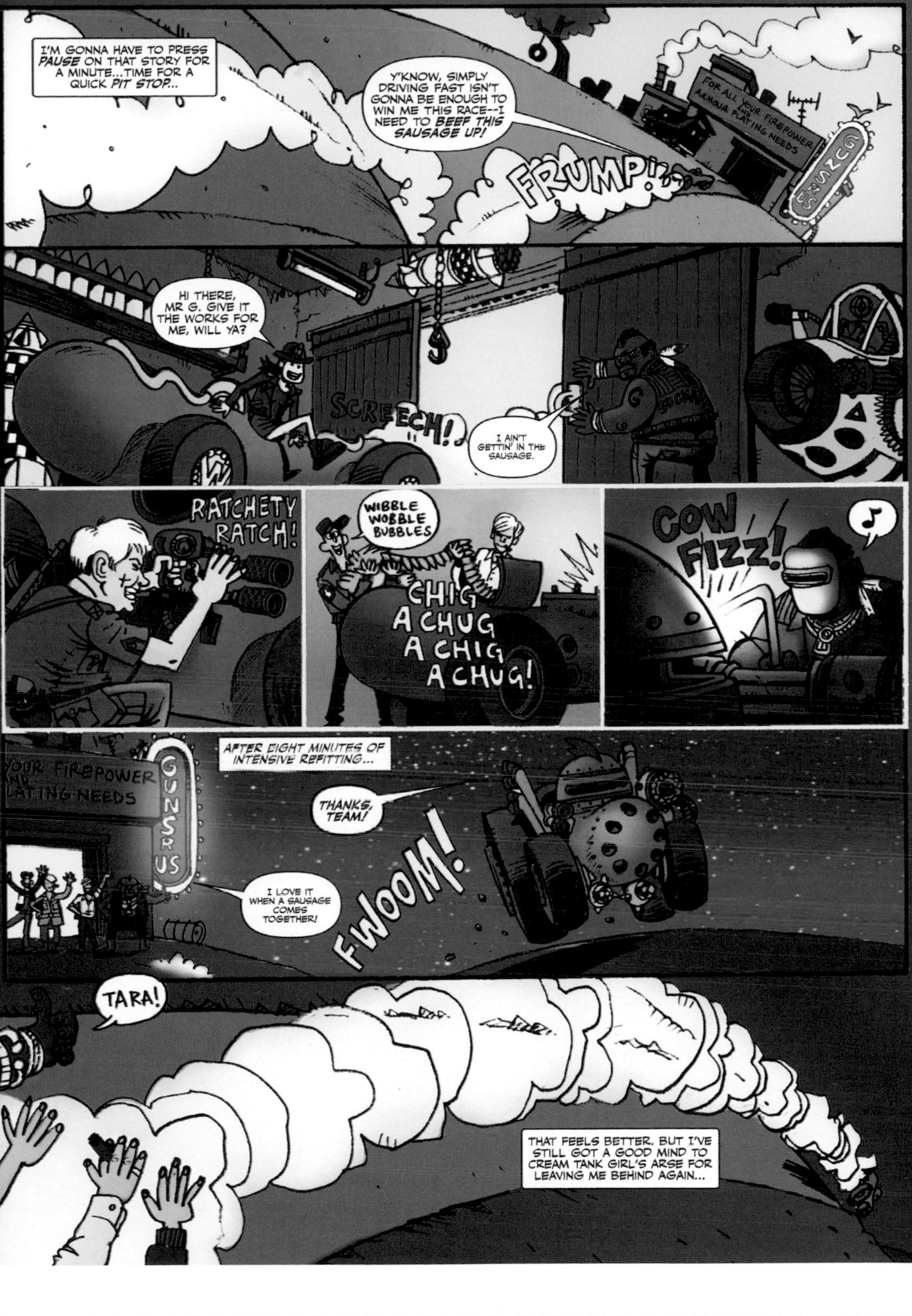
I'M GONNA HAVE TO PRESS *PAUSE* ON THAT STORY FOR A MINUTE...TIME FOR A QUICK *PIT STOP*...
Y'KNOW, SIMPLY DRIVING FAST ISN'T GONNA BE ENOUGH TO WIN ME THIS RACE--I NEED TO ***BEEF THIS SAUSAGE UP!***
FOR ALL YOUR FIREPOWER AND ARMOUR PLATING NEEDS
GUNS R US
FRUMP!
HI THERE, MR G. GIVE IT THE WORKS FOR ME, WILL YA?
SCREECH!
I AIN'T GETTIN' IN THE SAUSAGE.
RATCHETY RATCH!
WIBBLE WOBBLE BUBBLES
CHIG A CHUG A CHIG A CHUG!
COW FIZZ!
♪
AFTER EIGHT MINUTES OF INTENSIVE REFITTING...
YOUR FIREPOWER AND PLATING NEEDS
GUNS R US
THANKS, TEAM!
I LOVE IT WHEN A SAUSAGE COMES TOGETHER!
FWOOM!
TARA!
THAT FEELS BETTER. BUT I'VE STILL GOT A GOOD MIND TO CREAM TANK GIRL'S ARSE FOR LEAVING ME BEHIND AGAIN...

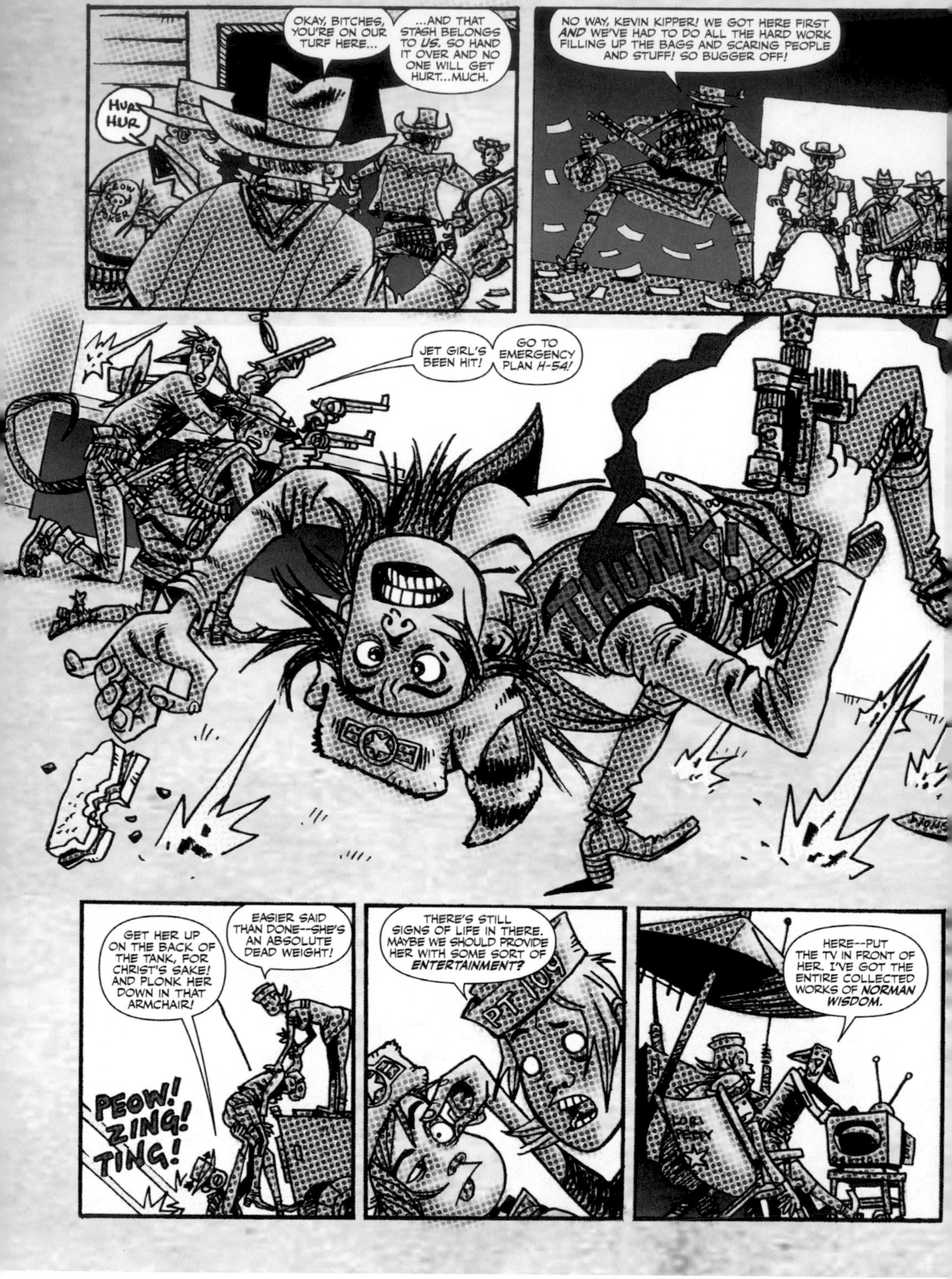
OKAY, BITCHES, YOU'RE ON OUR TURF HERE...
...AND THAT STASH BELONGS TO *US.* SO HAND IT OVER AND NO ONE WILL GET HURT...MUCH.
HUR HUR
NO WAY, KEVIN KIPPER! WE GOT HERE FIRST *AND* WE'VE HAD TO DO ALL THE HARD WORK FILLING UP THE BAGS AND SCARING PEOPLE AND STUFF! SO BUGGER OFF!
JET GIRL'S BEEN HIT!
GO TO EMERGENCY PLAN *H-54!*
THUNK!
GET HER UP ON THE BACK OF THE TANK, FOR CHRIST'S SAKE! AND PLONK HER DOWN IN THAT ARMCHAIR!
EASIER SAID THAN DONE--SHE'S AN ABSOLUTE DEAD WEIGHT!
PEOW! ZING! TING!
THERE'S STILL SIGNS OF LIFE IN THERE. MAYBE WE SHOULD PROVIDE HER WITH SOME SORT OF *ENTERTAINMENT?*
PT 109
HERE--PUT THE TV IN FRONT OF HER. I'VE GOT THE ENTIRE COLLECTED WORKS OF *NORMAN WISDOM.*

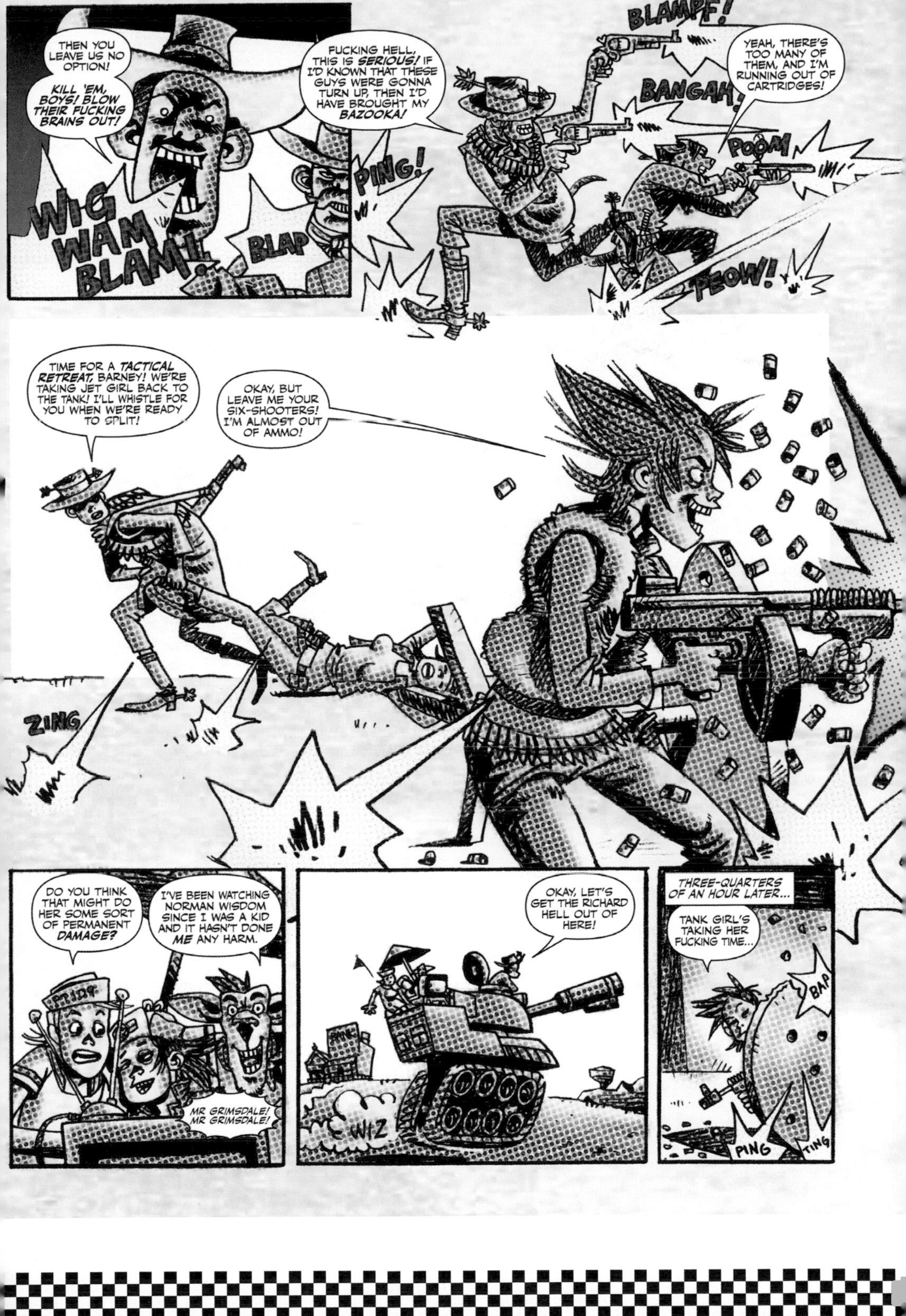
THEN YOU LEAVE US NO OPTION!
KILL 'EM, BOYS! BLOW THEIR FUCKING BRAINS OUT!
WIG WAM BLAM!
BLAP
PING!
FUCKING HELL, THIS IS SERIOUS! IF I'D KNOWN THAT THESE GUYS WERE GONNA TURN UP, THEN I'D HAVE BROUGHT MY BAZOOKA!
BLAMPF!
BANGAH!
YEAH, THERE'S TOO MANY OF THEM, AND I'M RUNNING OUT OF CARTRIDGES!
POOM
PEOW!
TIME FOR A TACTICAL RETREAT, BARNEY! WE'RE TAKING JET GIRL BACK TO THE TANK! I'LL WHISTLE FOR YOU WHEN WE'RE READY TO SPLIT!
OKAY, BUT LEAVE ME YOUR SIX-SHOOTERS! I'M ALMOST OUT OF AMMO!
ZING
DO YOU THINK THAT MIGHT DO HER SOME SORT OF PERMANENT DAMAGE?
I'VE BEEN WATCHING NORMAN WISDOM SINCE I WAS A KID AND IT HASN'T DONE ME ANY HARM.
MR GRIMSDALE! MR GRIMSDALE!
OKAY, LET'S GET THE RICHARD HELL OUT OF HERE!
WIZ
THREE-QUARTERS OF AN HOUR LATER...
TANK GIRL'S TAKING HER FUCKING TIME...
BAP
PING
TING

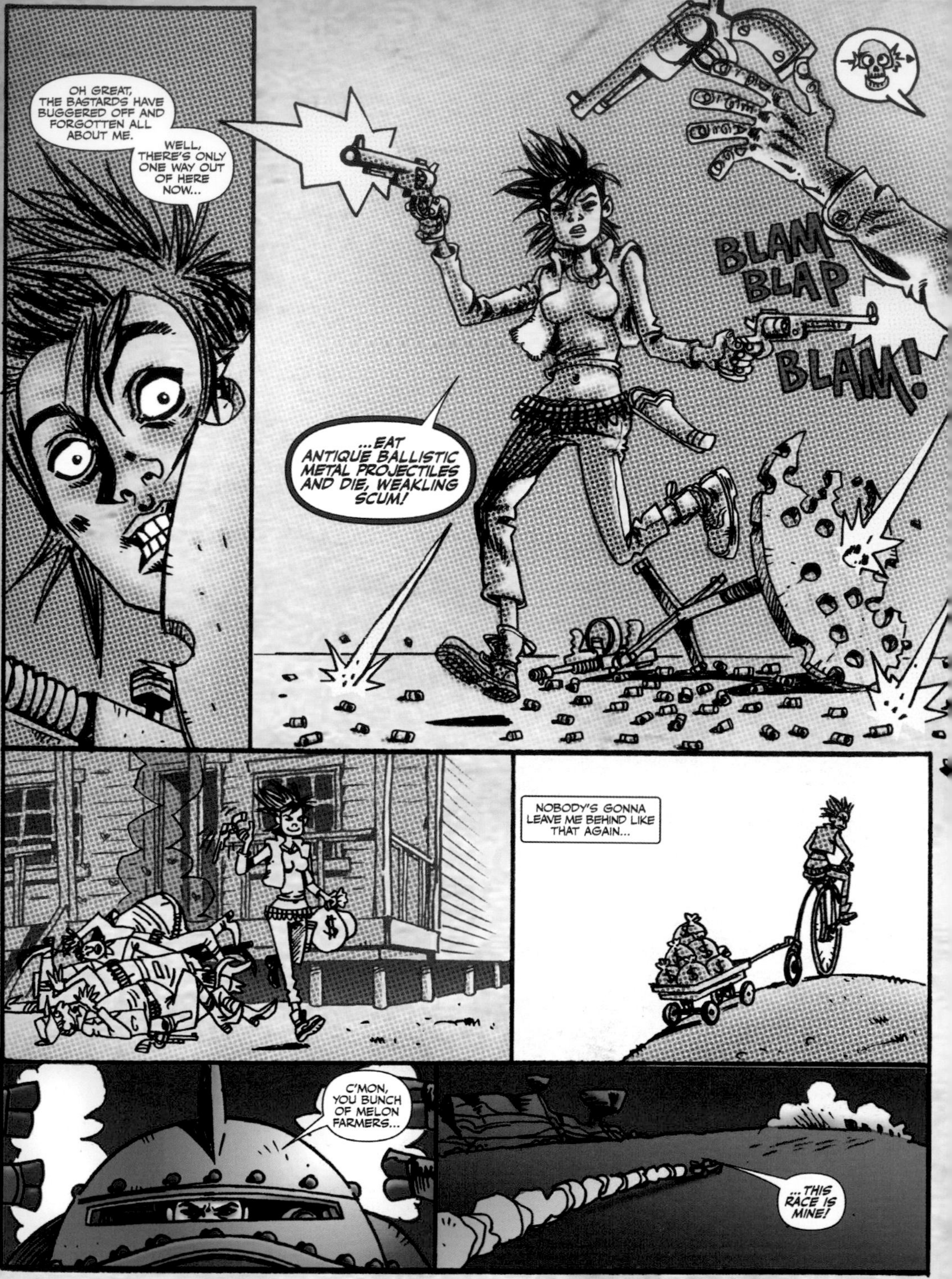
OH GREAT, THE BASTARDS HAVE BUGGERED OFF AND FORGOTTEN ALL ABOUT ME.
WELL, THERE'S ONLY ONE WAY OUT OF HERE NOW...
...EAT ANTIQUE BALLISTIC METAL PROJECTILES AND DIE, WEAKLING SCUM!
BLAM
BLAP
BLAM!
NOBODY'S GONNA LEAVE ME BEHIND LIKE THAT AGAIN...
C'MON, YOU BUNCH OF MELON FARMERS...
...THIS RACE IS MINE!

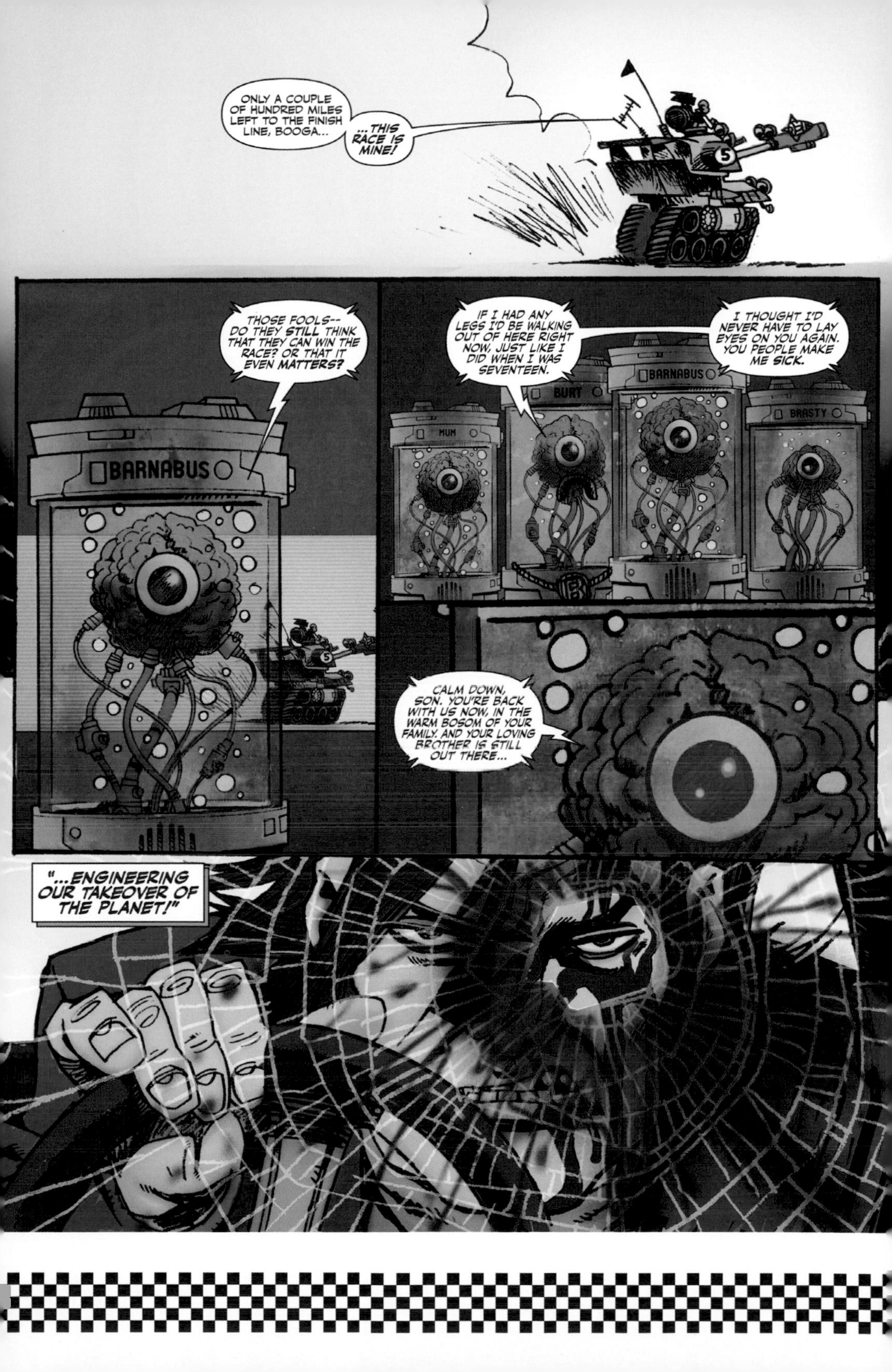
ONLY A COUPLE OF HUNDRED MILES LEFT TO THE FINISH LINE, BOOGA...
...THIS RACE IS MINE!
THOSE FOOLS-- DO THEY STILL THINK THAT THEY CAN WIN THE RACE? OR THAT IT EVEN MATTERS?
BARNABUS
IF I HAD ANY LEGS I'D BE WALKING OUT OF HERE RIGHT NOW, JUST LIKE I DID WHEN I WAS SEVENTEEN.
I THOUGHT I'D NEVER HAVE TO LAY EYES ON YOU AGAIN. YOU PEOPLE MAKE ME SICK.
MUM
BURT
BARNABUS
BRASTY
CALM DOWN, SON. YOU'RE BACK WITH US NOW, IN THE WARM BOSOM OF YOUR FAMILY. AND YOUR LOVING BROTHER IS STILL OUT THERE...
"...ENGINEERING OUR TAKEOVER OF THE PLANET!"

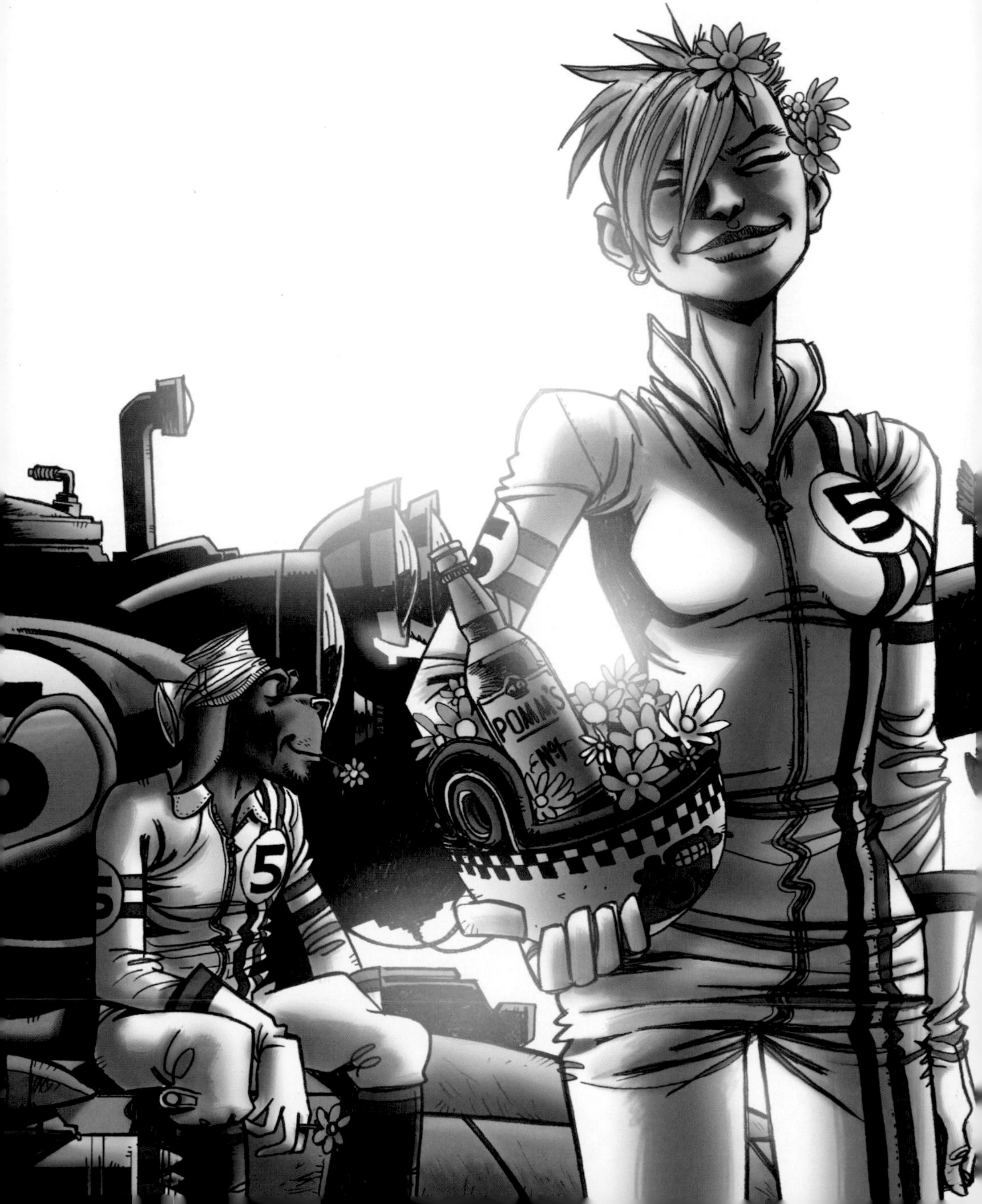
POMM'S
Nº1

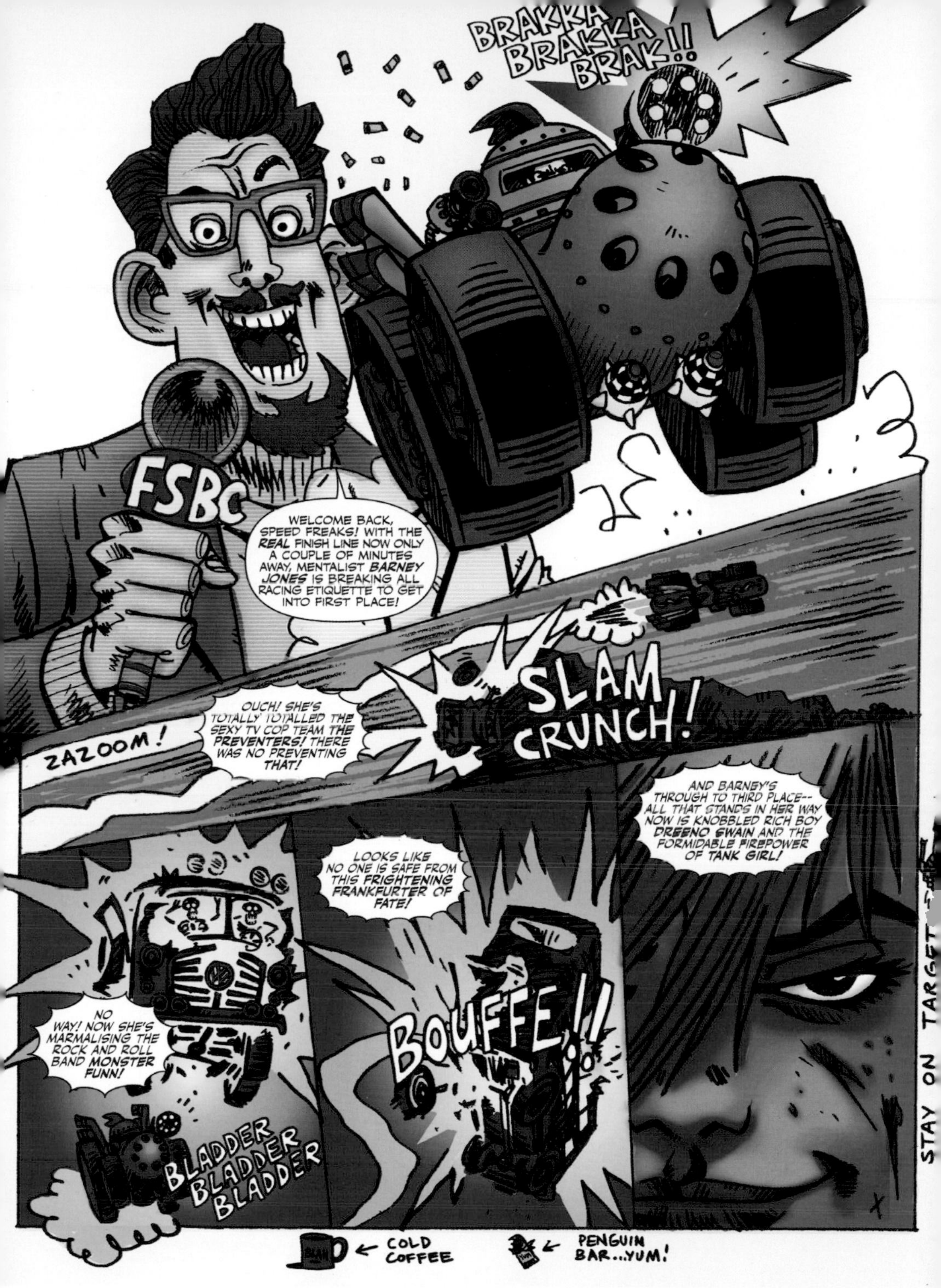
BRAKKA BRAKKA BRAK!!
FSBC
WELCOME BACK, SPEED FREAKS! WITH THE REAL FINISH LINE NOW ONLY A COUPLE OF MINUTES AWAY, MENTALIST BARNEY JONES IS BREAKING ALL RACING ETIQUETTE TO GET INTO FIRST PLACE!
SLAM CRUNCH!
ZAZOOM!
OUCH! SHE'S TOTALLY TOTALLED THE SEXY TV COP TEAM THE PREVENTERS! THERE WAS NO PREVENTING THAT!
NO WAY! NOW SHE'S MARMALISING THE ROCK AND ROLL BAND MONSTER FUNN!
BLADDER BLADDER BLADDER
LOOKS LIKE NO ONE IS SAFE FROM THIS FRIGHTENING FRANKFURTER OF FATE!
BOUFFE!!
AND BARNEY'S THROUGH TO THIRD PLACE-- ALL THAT STANDS IN HER WAY NOW IS KNOBBLED RICH BOY DREENO SWAIN AND THE FORMIDABLE FIREPOWER OF TANK GIRL!
STAY ON TARGET
COLD COFFEE
PENGUIN BAR...YUM!

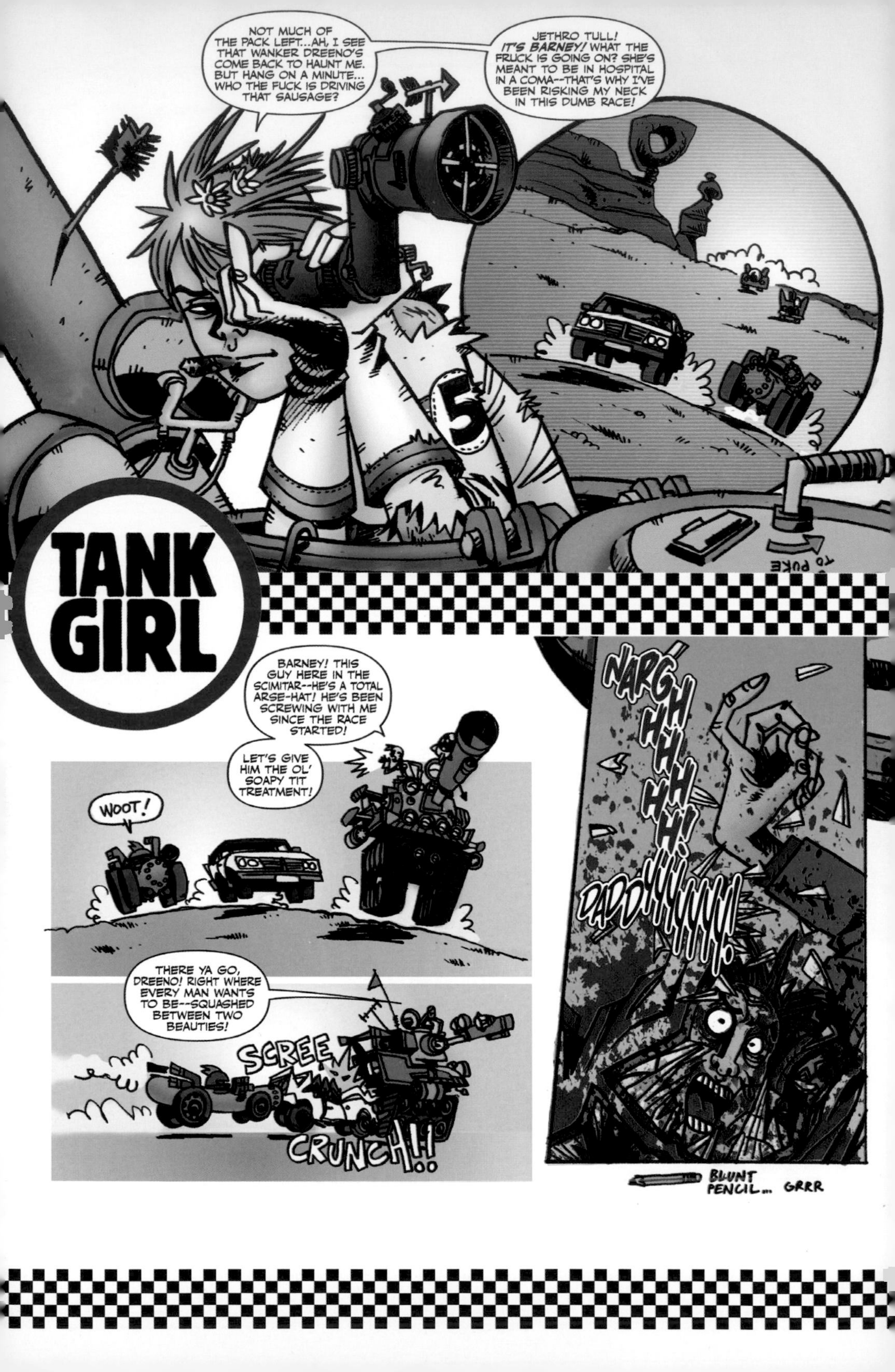
NOT MUCH OF THE PACK LEFT...AH, I SEE THAT WANKER DREENO'S COME BACK TO HAUNT ME. BUT HANG ON A MINUTE... WHO THE FUCK IS DRIVING THAT SAUSAGE?
JETHRO TULL! *IT'S BARNEY!* WHAT THE FRUCK IS GOING ON? SHE'S MEANT TO BE IN HOSPITAL IN A COMA--THAT'S WHY I'VE BEEN RISKING MY NECK IN THIS DUMB RACE!
TO PUKE
TANK GIRL
BARNEY! THIS GUY HERE IN THE SCIMITAR--HE'S A TOTAL ARSE-HAT! HE'S BEEN SCREWING WITH ME SINCE THE RACE STARTED!
LET'S GIVE HIM THE OL' SOAPY TIT TREATMENT!
WOOT!
THERE YA GO, DREENO! RIGHT WHERE EVERY MAN WANTS TO BE--SQUASHED BETWEEN TWO BEAUTIES!
SCREE
CRUNCH!!!
NARGHHHHHHHH!
DADDYYYYYY!
BLUNT PENCIL... GRRR

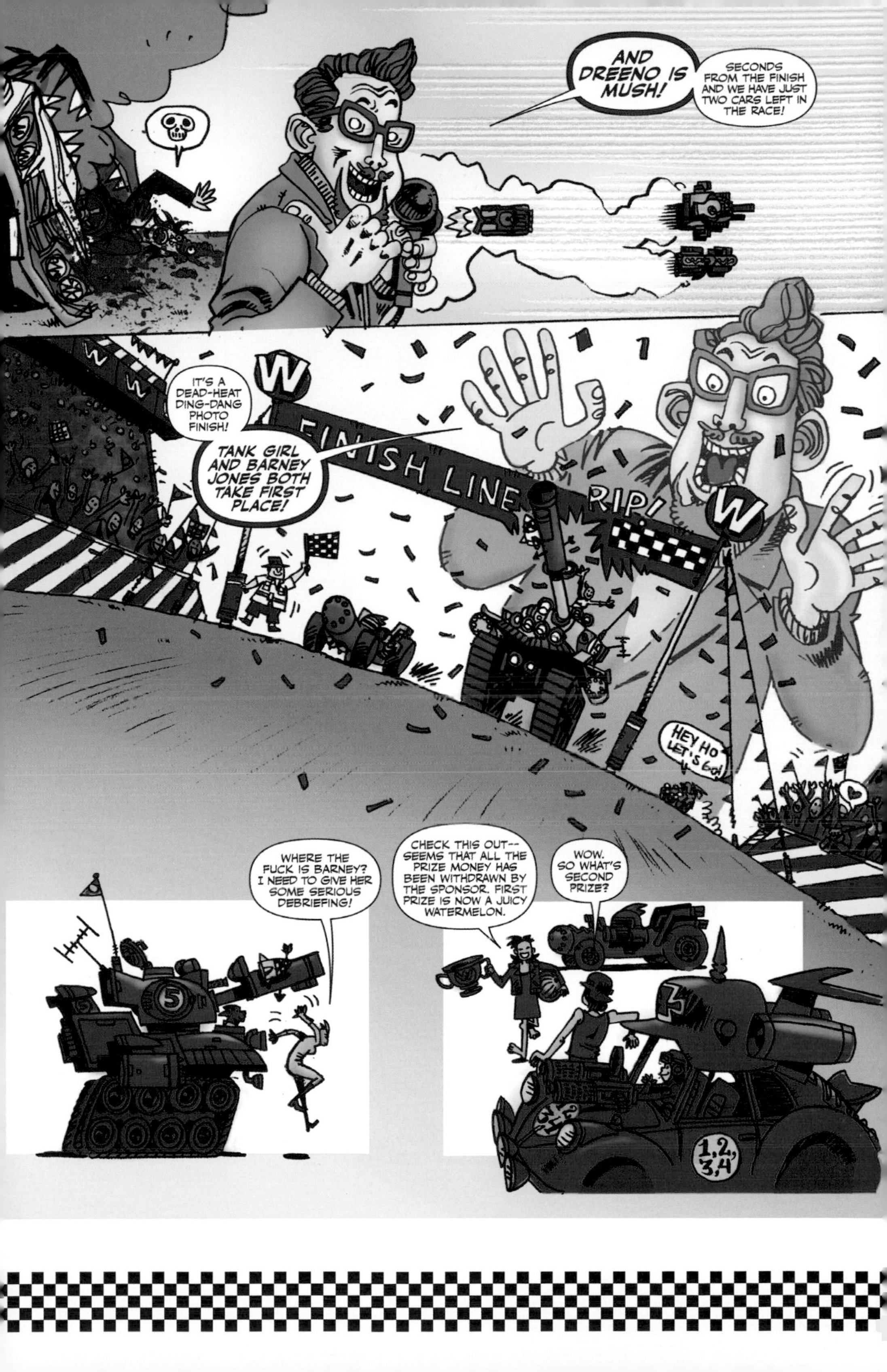
AND DREENO IS MUSH!
SECONDS FROM THE FINISH AND WE HAVE JUST TWO CARS LEFT IN THE RACE!
IT'S A DEAD-HEAT DING-DANG PHOTO FINISH!
TANK GIRL AND BARNEY JONES BOTH TAKE FIRST PLACE!
FINISH LINE
RIP!
HEY HO LET'S GO!
WHERE THE FUCK IS BARNEY? I NEED TO GIVE HER SOME SERIOUS DEBRIEFING!
CHECK THIS OUT-- SEEMS THAT ALL THE PRIZE MONEY HAS BEEN WITHDRAWN BY THE SPONSOR. FIRST PRIZE IS NOW A JUICY WATERMELON.
WOW. SO WHAT'S SECOND PRIZE?
1,2, 3,4

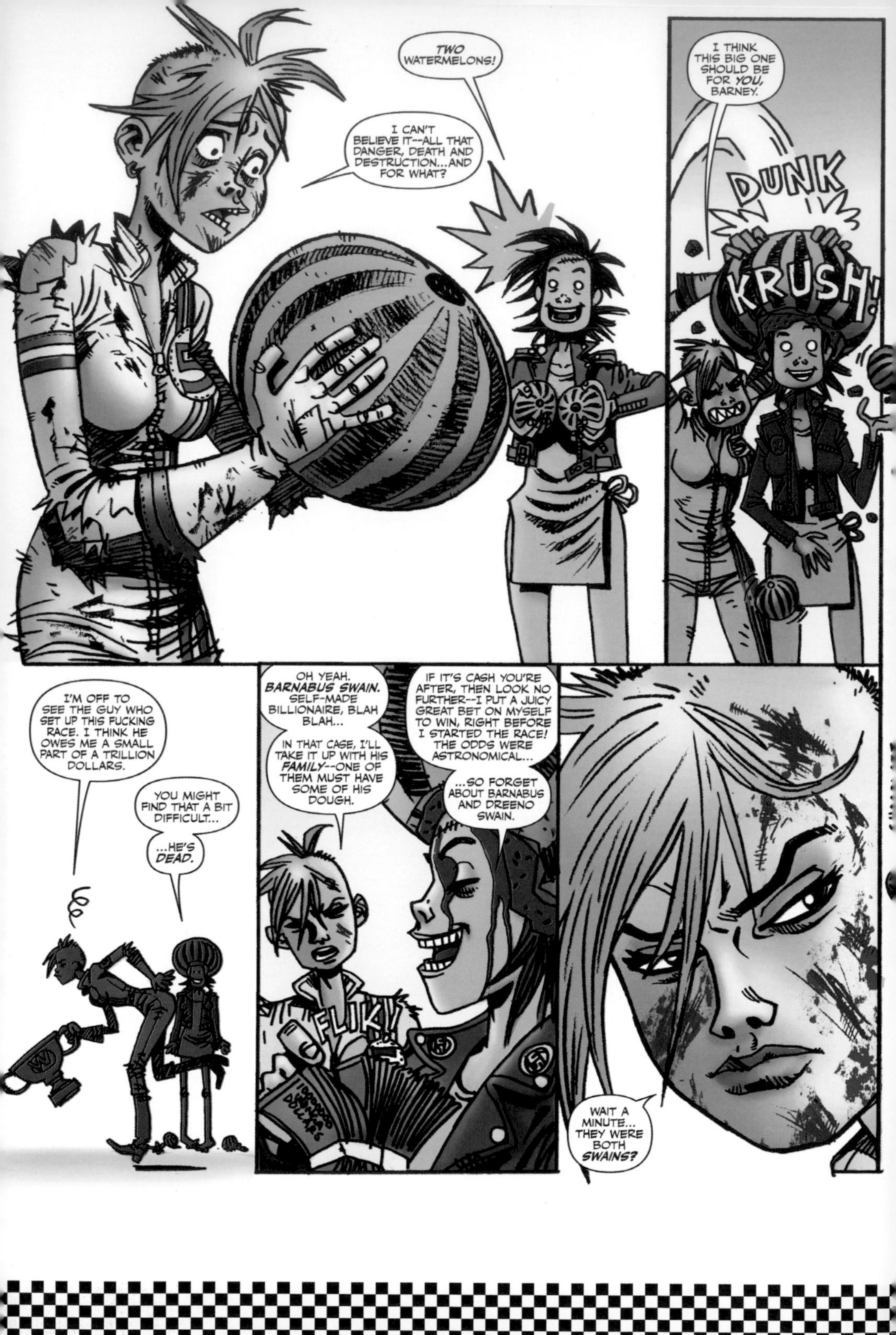
TWO WATERMELONS!
I CAN'T BELIEVE IT--ALL THAT DANGER, DEATH AND DESTRUCTION...AND FOR WHAT?
I THINK THIS BIG ONE SHOULD BE FOR YOU, BARNEY.
DUNK
KRUSH!
I'M OFF TO SEE THE GUY WHO SET UP THIS FUCKING RACE. I THINK HE OWES ME A SMALL PART OF A TRILLION DOLLARS.
YOU MIGHT FIND THAT A BIT DIFFICULT...
...HE'S DEAD.
OH YEAH. BARNABUS SWAIN. SELF-MADE BILLIONAIRE, BLAH BLAH...
IN THAT CASE, I'LL TAKE IT UP WITH HIS FAMILY--ONE OF THEM MUST HAVE SOME OF HIS DOUGH.
IF IT'S CASH YOU'RE AFTER, THEN LOOK NO FURTHER--I PUT A JUICY GREAT BET ON MYSELF TO WIN, RIGHT BEFORE I STARTED THE RACE! THE ODDS WERE ASTRONOMICAL...
...SO FORGET ABOUT BARNABUS AND DREENO SWAIN.
FLIK!
WAIT A MINUTE... THEY WERE BOTH SWAINS?

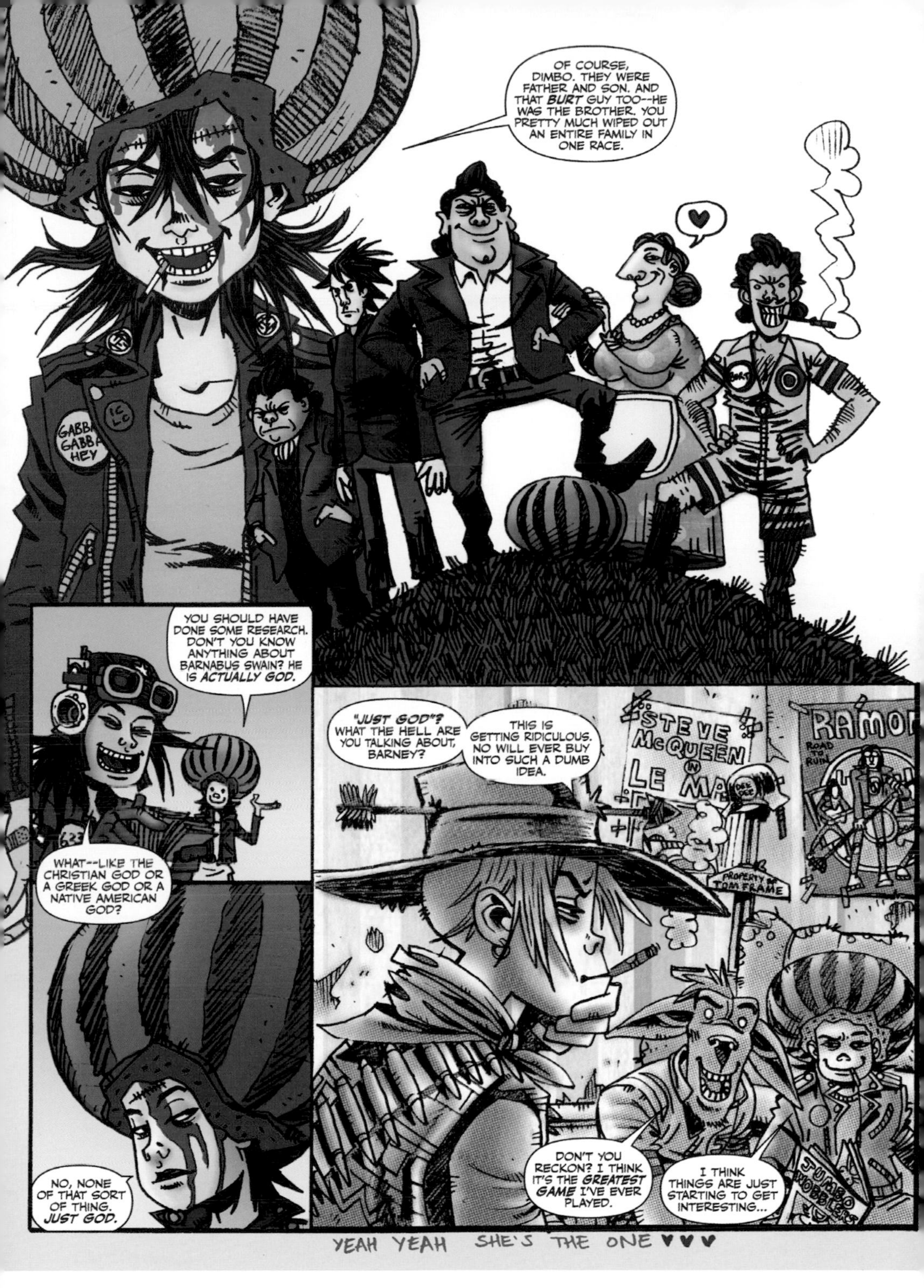
OF COURSE, DIMBO. THEY WERE FATHER AND SON. AND THAT *BURT* GUY TOO--HE WAS THE BROTHER. YOU PRETTY MUCH WIPED OUT AN ENTIRE FAMILY IN ONE RACE.
GABBA GABBA HEY
BURT
YOU SHOULD HAVE DONE SOME RESEARCH. DON'T YOU KNOW ANYTHING ABOUT BARNABUS SWAIN? HE IS *ACTUALLY GOD.*
WHAT--LIKE THE CHRISTIAN GOD OR A GREEK GOD OR A NATIVE AMERICAN GOD?
NO, NONE OF THAT SORT OF THING. *JUST GOD.*
"JUST GOD"? WHAT THE HELL ARE YOU TALKING ABOUT, BARNEY?
THIS IS GETTING RIDICULOUS. NO WILL EVER BUY INTO SUCH A DUMB IDEA.
STEVE McQUEEN IN LE MA
RAMO
ROAD TO RUIN
PROPERTY OF TOM FRAME
DON'T YOU RECKON? I THINK IT'S THE *GREATEST GAME* I'VE EVER PLAYED.
I THINK THINGS ARE JUST STARTING TO GET INTERESTING...
JUMBO WOBBLERS

YEAH YEAH SHE'S THE ONE ♥♥♥

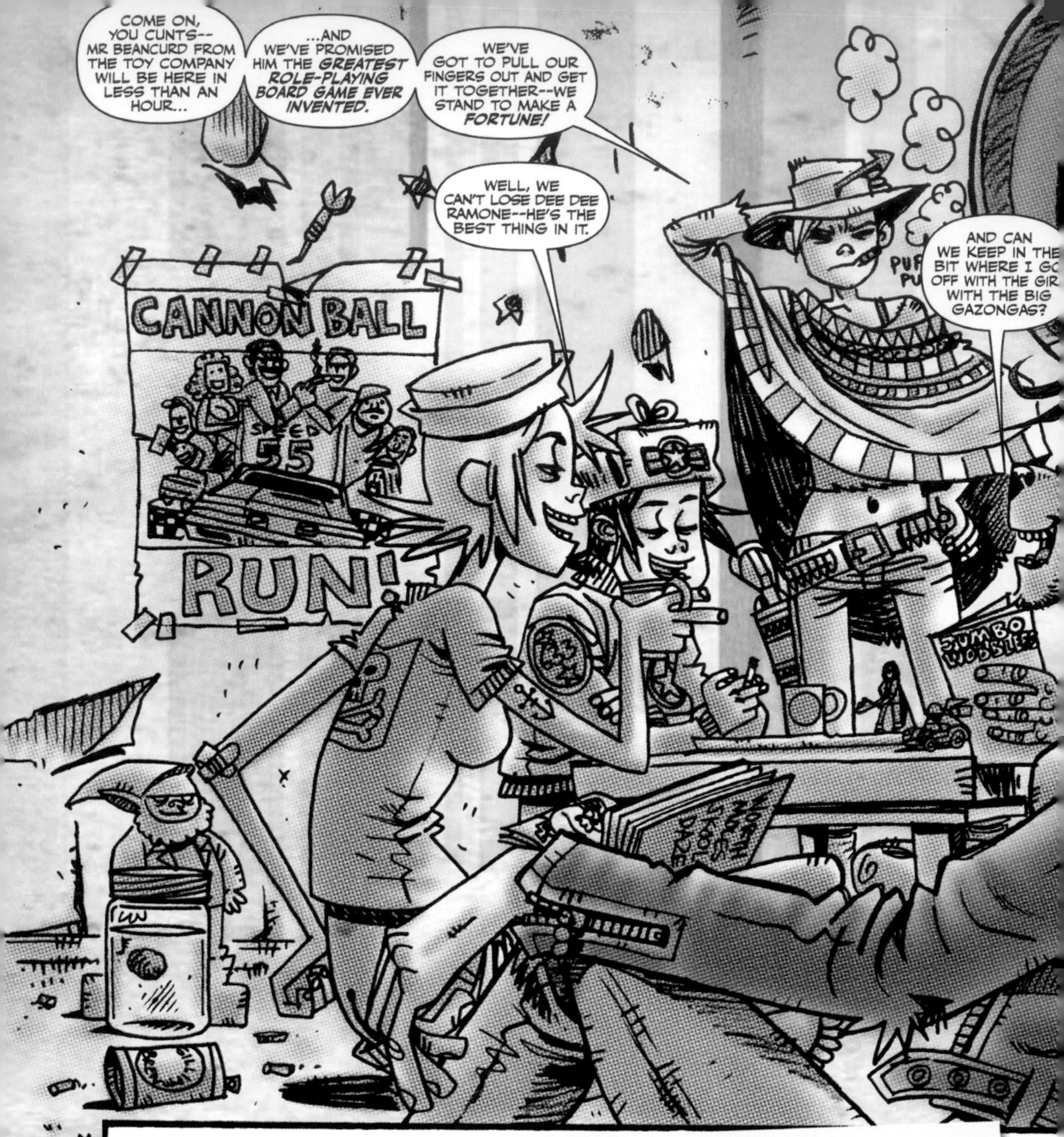
COME ON, YOU CUNTS-- MR BEANCURD FROM THE TOY COMPANY WILL BE HERE IN LESS THAN AN HOUR...
...AND WE'VE PROMISED HIM THE *GREATEST ROLE-PLAYING BOARD GAME EVER INVENTED.*
WE'VE GOT TO PULL OUR FINGERS OUT AND GET IT TOGETHER--WE STAND TO MAKE A *FORTUNE!*
WELL, WE CAN'T LOSE DEE DEE RAMONE--HE'S THE BEST THING IN IT.
AND CAN WE KEEP IN THE BIT WHERE I GO OFF WITH THE GIR WITH THE BIG GAZONGAS?
CANNON BALL RUN!
SPEED 55

FRIENDS, ROMULANS, CRUNCHYMEN - IF YOU HAVE REACHED THIS POINT IN THE STORY THEN YOU ARE PROBABLY THINKING ONE OF THREE THINGS:

1. THAT WAS TOTAL SHITE
2. THAT WAS PARTIAL SHITE WITH A FEW FUNNY BITS AND SOME NICE DRAWING
3. I LIKED IT BUT I DIDN'T LIKE IT. IT WAS GOOD BUT IT WAS SHIT. I AM ENLIGHTENED BUT CONFUSED.

HOPEFULLY MOST OF YOU WILL FALL INTO THE FINAL CATEGORY, AND, FOR THOSE OF YOU THAT DO, WE FEEL YOU ARE OWED SOME KIND OF EXPLANATION.

THE COOL-CRAP-CONTINUUM

AT THE DAWN OF THE FINAL DECADE OF THE 20th CENTURY, AFTER SEVERAL YEARS OF EXPERIMENTATION, A SMALL GROUP OF US LIVING IN WORTHING, SUSSEX CAME UP WITH THIS STARTLING REVELATION: NOTHING WAS ACTUALLY COOL OR CRAP, AND, AT THE SAME TIME, EVERYTHING WAS COOL AND CRAP.
ROUND ABOUT THAT TIME WE COINED THE IMMORTAL PHRASE "SO GOOD IT'S SHIT".
ALLOCATING COOL AND CRAP QUALITIES TO ANY THING, ANIMATE OR INANIMATE, CAN ONLY EVER BE A SUBJECTIVE PERSPECTIVE. OUR PERSONAL TASTES ARE ALL AT THE WHIM OF EXPERIENCE, PEER PRESSURE, INGRAINED IDEOLOGY, AND IMMEDIATE LOCAL CULTURE.
THEREFORE ONE MAN'S COOL IS ANOTHER MAN'S CRAP.
WITH THIS IN MIND WE SET TO WORK CONSTRUCTING SKIDMARKS, ALWAYS KEEPING OURSELVES IN CHECK THAT ITS CONTENTS WERE NEITHER TOO COOL, NOR TOO CRAP.
WE HOPE THAT THIS BOOK GOES SOME WAY TO HELP FREE IMPRISONED SOULS FROM THE BONDAGE OF CULTURAL AND IDEOLOGICAL ENTRAPMENT.
IN MAKING CRUMBY COMICS OUR ONLY WISH IS THE SALVATION OF THIS PLANET AND ITS INHABITANTS.

WE THANK YOU.
TEAM TANK GIRL.

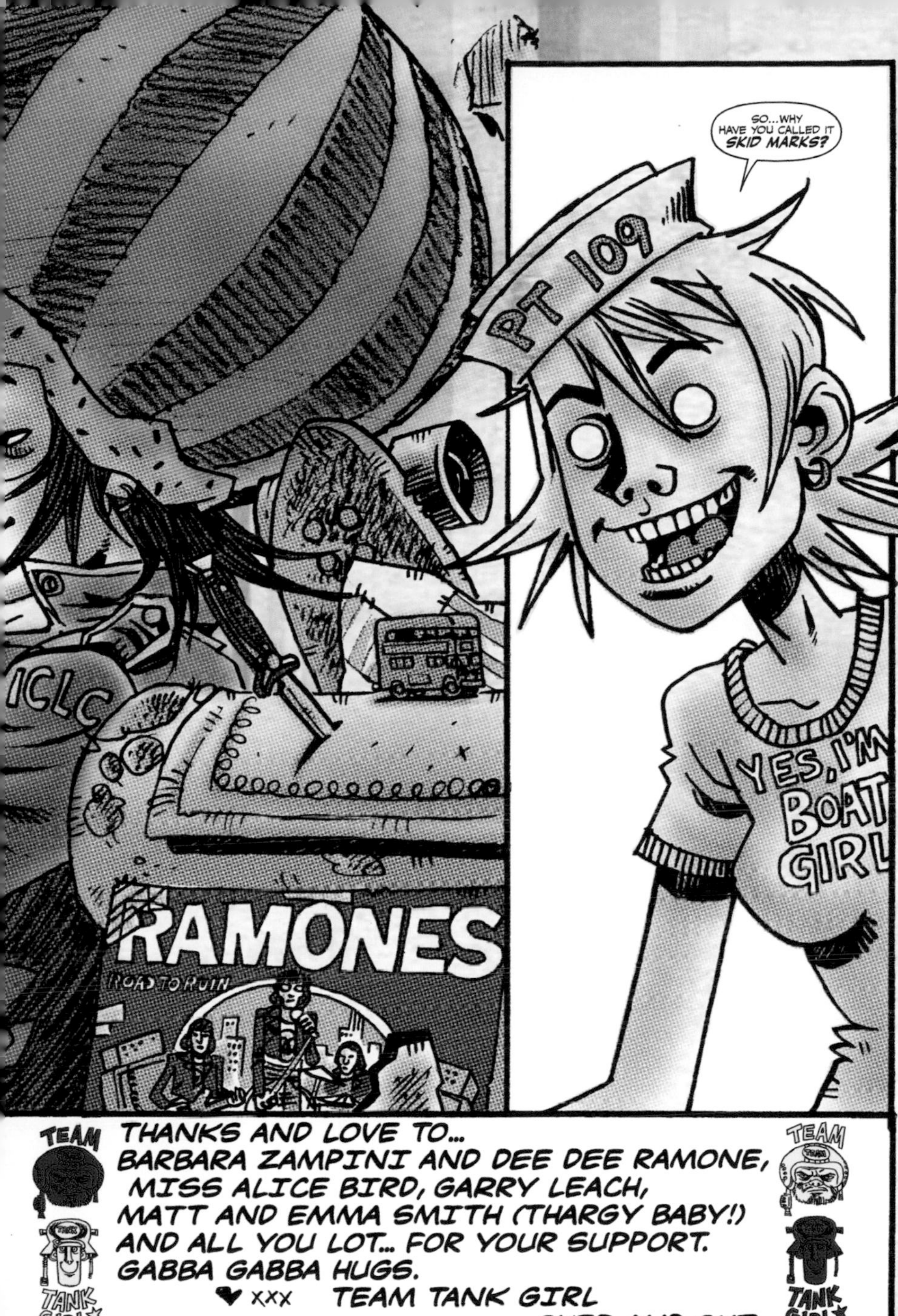
SO...WHY HAVE YOU CALLED IT SKID MARKS?
PT 109
ICLC
YES, I'M BOAT GIRL
RAMONES
ROAD TO RUIN

THANKS AND LOVE TO...
BARBARA ZAMPINI AND DEE DEE RAMONE,
MISS ALICE BIRD, GARRY LEACH,
MATT AND EMMA SMITH (THARGY BABY!)
AND ALL YOU LOT... FOR YOUR SUPPORT.
GABBA GABBA HUGS.
♥ xxx TEAM TANK GIRL
OVER AND OUT.

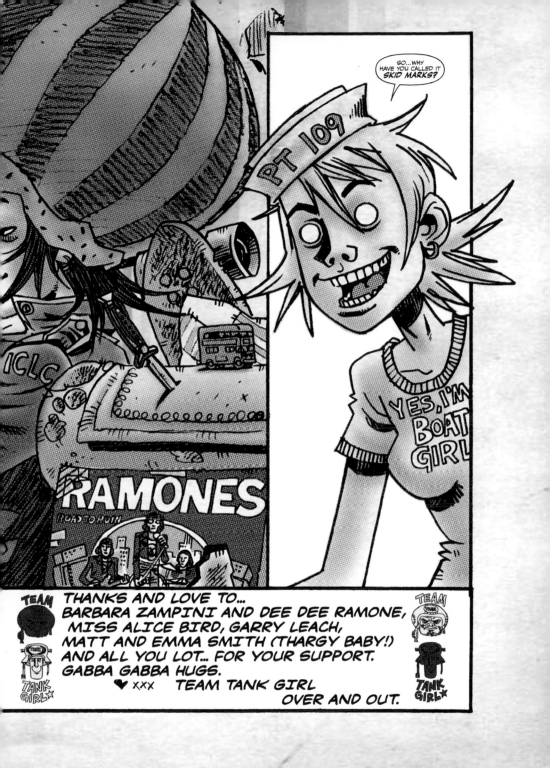

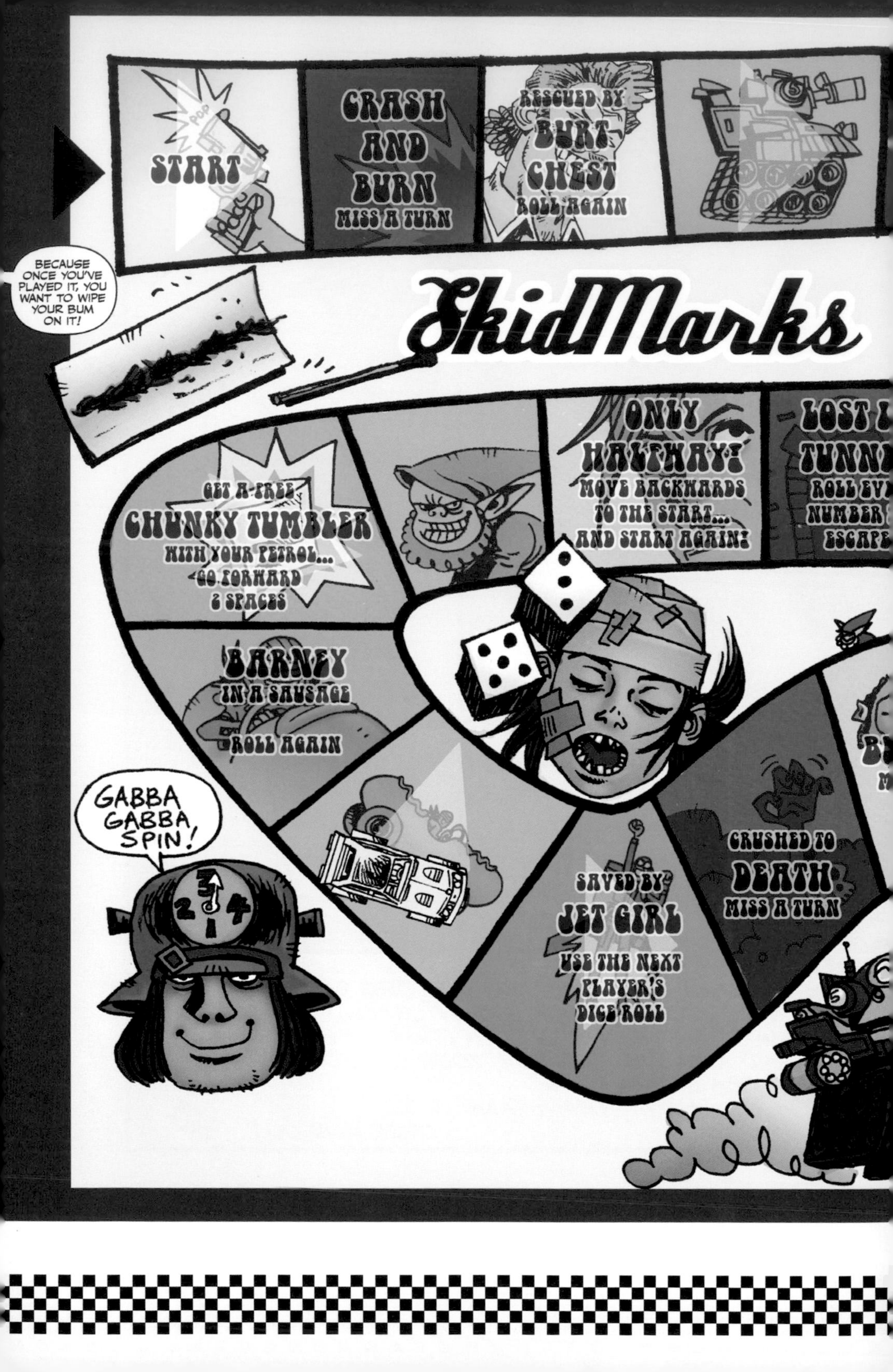

START
POP
CRASH AND BURN MISS A TURN
RESCUED BY BURT CHEST ROLL AGAIN
BECAUSE ONCE YOU'VE PLAYED IT, YOU WANT TO WIPE YOUR BUM ON IT!
SkidMarks
GET A FREE CHUNKY TUMBLER WITH YOUR PETROL... GO FORWARD 2 SPACES
ONLY HALFWAY! MOVE BACKWARDS TO THE START... AND START AGAIN!
BARNEY IN A SAUSAGE ROLL AGAIN
GABBA GABBA SPIN!
CRUSHED TO DEATH MISS A TURN
SAVED BY JET GIRL USE THE NEXT PLAYER'S DICE ROLL

D BY THE
ATRON
...

ROLL AN ODD
NUMBER TO GO
THROUGH THE
TUNNEL

HELPED BY SEXY
T.V. COP TEAM
MOVE FORWARD 4 SPACES

The Game

WAKE UP IN
DREENO'S HOUSE
MISS A TURN

RIDE IN
DREENO'S
CAR
ROLL AGAIN...
BUT MOVE
BACKWARDS

...TLY
...
...HEST
...HEAD
...ES

TANK GIRL

BLOWN
OFF THE
ROAD
GO BACK TO
START

WATERMELON CUP

END

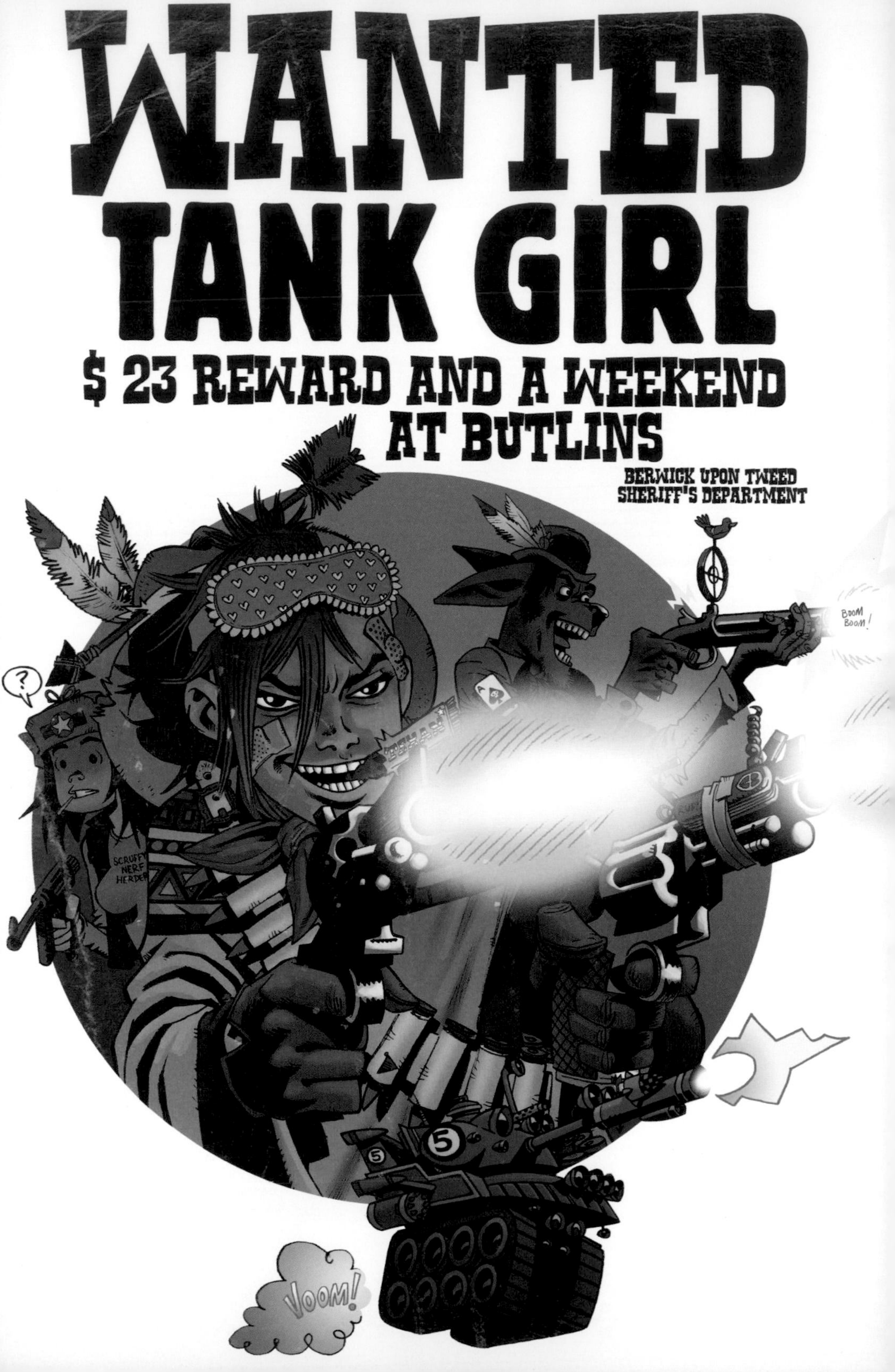
WANTED
TANK GIRL
$ 23 REWARD AND A WEEKEND AT BUTLINS
BERWICK UPON TWEED SHERIFF'S DEPARTMENT
?
SCRUFFY NERF HERDER
BOOM BOOM!
VOOM!

McMAHON & MARTIN

TANK GIRL

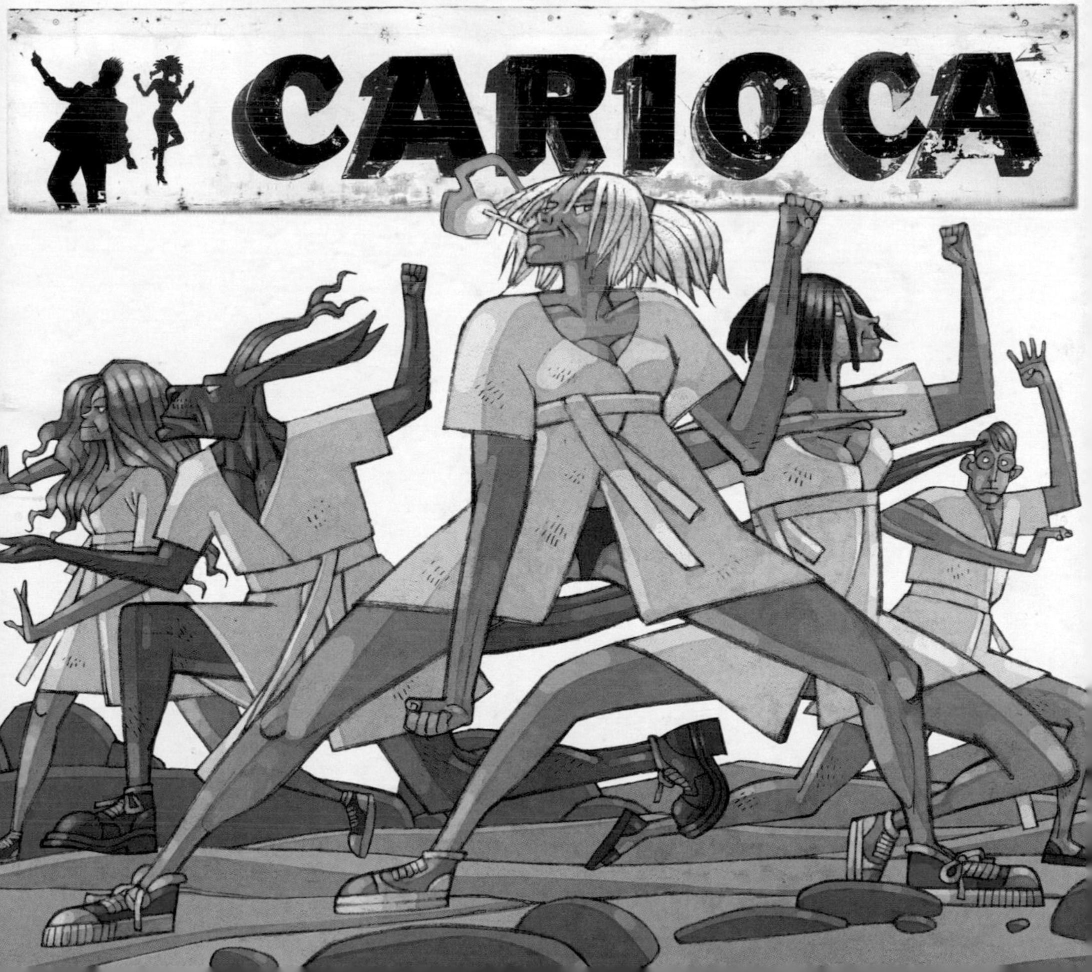
CARIOCA

McMAHON & MARTIN

TANK GIRL

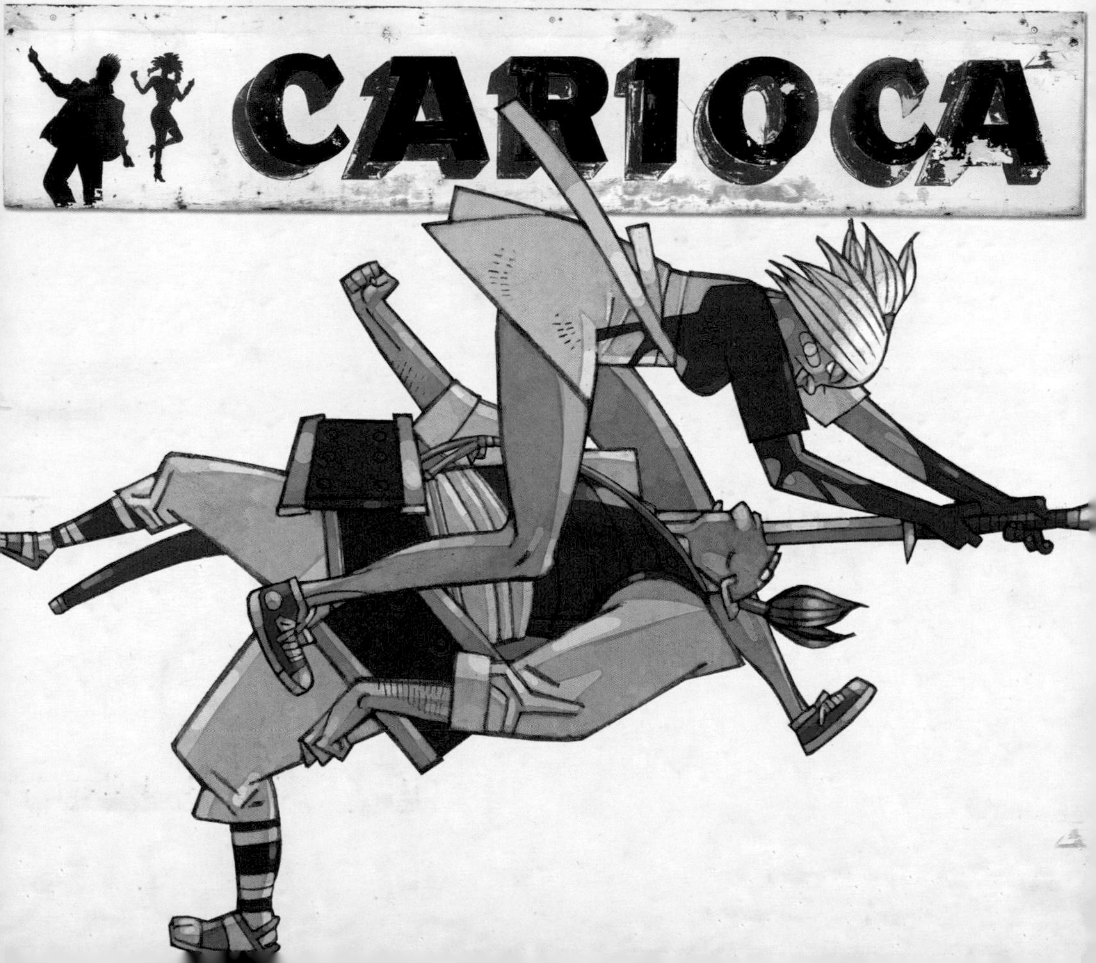
CARIOCA

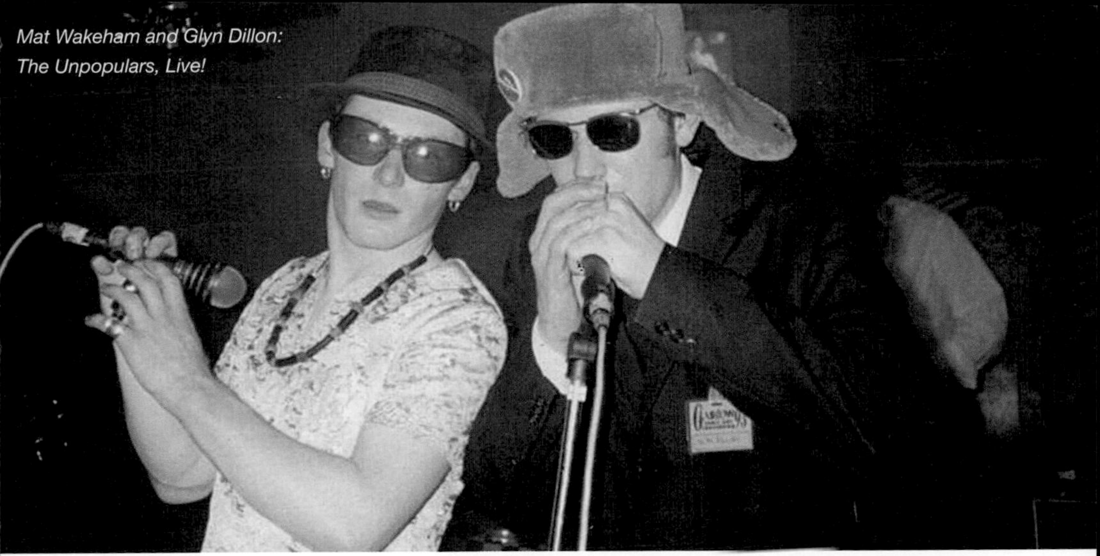

Mat Wakeham and Glyn Dillon:
The Unpopulars, Live!

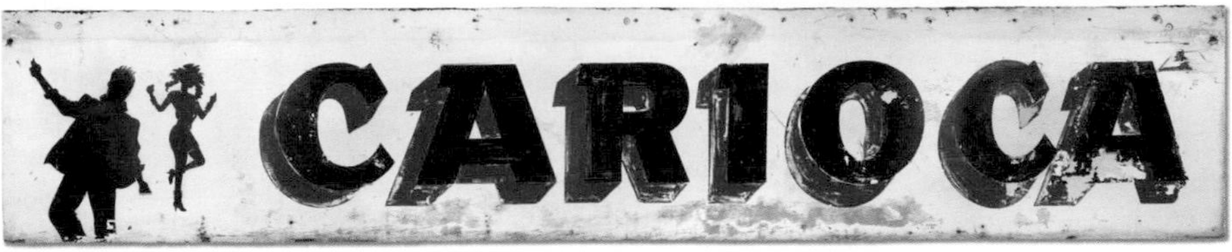
CARIOCA

Hell City

The Carioca Club stood on the corner of Friswell Road and Rowlands Road in my hometown of Worthing, Sussex. It has since been demolished, but, for a large part of my teens, and on into my twenties, it was the only place worth hanging out at in the whole town.

My first experience of the club came before I'd left school, at the beginning of the eighties, when, on weekday nights, it played host to a string of youthful bands from my high school (Durrington High) and my brother's school (Tarring High). Many friends were in these bands, some of whom have gone on to fame and fortune elsewhere, but there has never been a list of them, let alone a tribute, so I'm gonna make one now. It was a seminal, post-punk scene, everything was homemade and cobbled together, it was a safe, fun, creative, and virtually ego-free zone. Here are some of the bands that I remember:

The Rotten Bananas	*Toy Factory*	*The Electric Sideshow*
The Earnest Boys	*Knotted Beard*	*Standard Issue*

My own band, The University Smalls, never made it onto the stage during this golden era; we were always hampered by a lack of equipment, a lack of songs, and a lack of balls.

This period soon dissolved as everyone progressed on to further education and real jobs, but I stuck around and frequented the club's indie night, 'The Magic Roundabout'.

After I met up with *Tank Girl* co-creator Jamie Hewlett at art college, The Carioca became the default hang-out for our gang. When college finished, I found myself DJing there at our own indie night, 'Hell City'.

My final dalliance with the club was in the nineties, paying guitar live on the stage in art-destructo band The Unpopulars, with *Deadline* collaborators Glyn Dillon, Mat Wakeham and Ashley Whiting.

After that I left town, and the place got pulled down, but the name of the club has always remained a watchword for the inimitable brand of independent, scummy, crazy, puke-stained, drunken creativity we experienced there.

The initial inspiration for this book came from a desire to attack bogus figures of authority; those otherwise powerless people who may have you by the balls because it's part of your job to be subservient, or those who hold you by financial strings – in fact, anyone who abuses a position of power.

I wrote this story to remind myself that I have the ability to destroy these creeps, and that I can retreat to a place inside me where my powers can be replenished (a bit like Superman's Fortress Of Solitude!). Then I can come out, all guns blazing, and wielding my sword of ultimate justice.

Charlie Happy represents every twisted cunt that has taken advantage of their position over me; from school teachers to shitty job bosses and onwards.

This book is pure self-indulgence on my part (as is this introduction!), but I hope you find something of worth in my ranting rambling story.

It's turned out very different from how I first envisaged it – starting as a short strip, then mutating into an epic as it was commissioned as a six-part (?!) story. The style and pace is like no other *Tank Girl* story to date.

I'd like to thank the very brilliant Mike McMahon for his patience and hard work as he ploughed on through the artwork. A tough hill to climb, but he did it with dazzling, groundbreaking and consistent results.

Finally,
To all the power abusers of the world –

This one's for you
You spineless fucking bastards
You can't touch me
I've got my Carioca

Hang tough,

Alan C. Martin
The ruins of the Carioca Club
Worthing
June 2012

Dancing on the stage of the Carioca.

Hell City in full swing. Jamie Hewlett is far right in the white jeans.

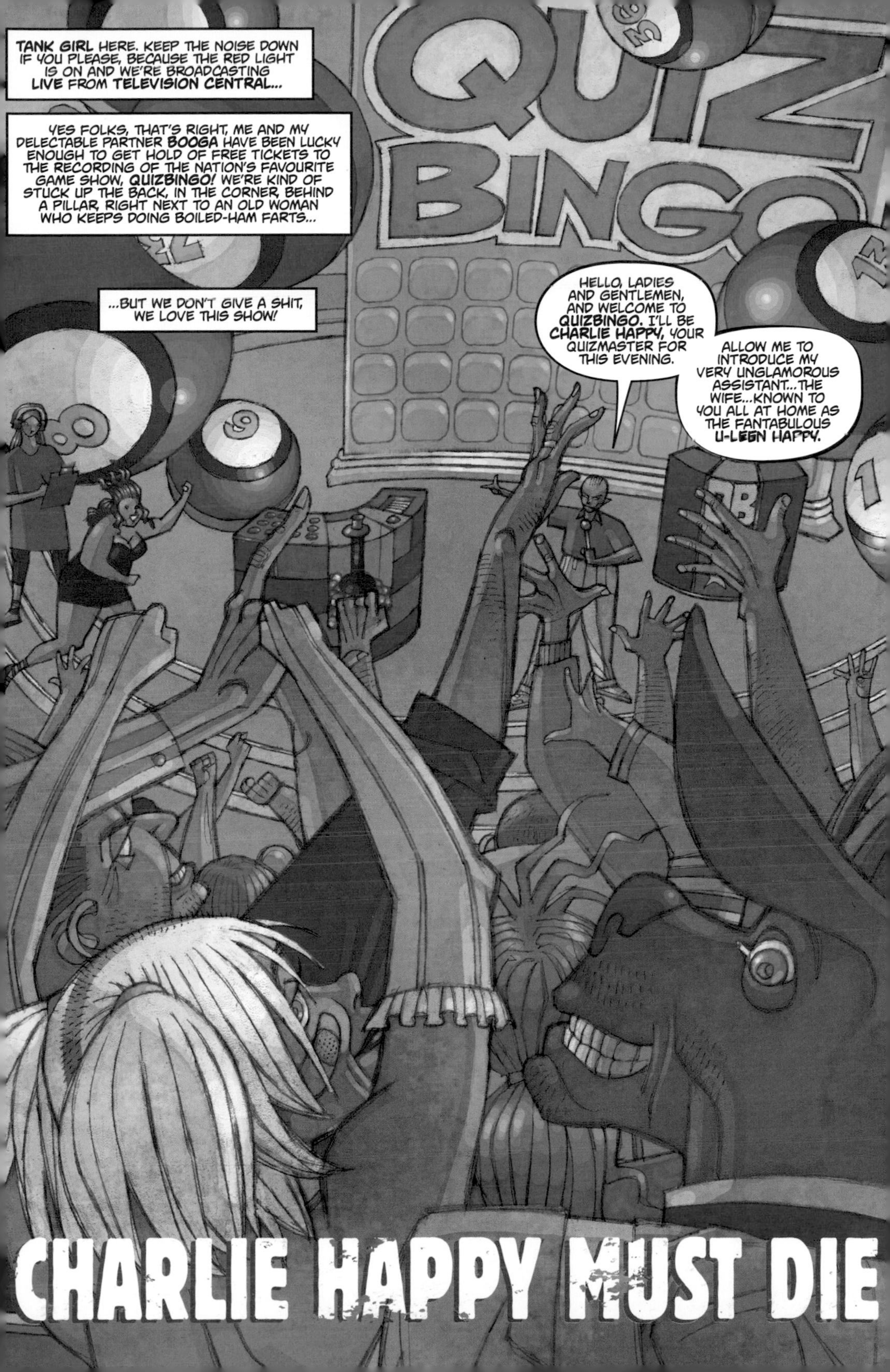
TANK GIRL HERE. KEEP THE NOISE DOWN IF YOU PLEASE, BECAUSE THE RED LIGHT IS ON AND WE'RE BROADCASTING LIVE FROM TELEVISION CENTRAL...
YES FOLKS, THAT'S RIGHT, ME AND MY DELECTABLE PARTNER BOOGA HAVE BEEN LUCKY ENOUGH TO GET HOLD OF FREE TICKETS TO THE RECORDING OF THE NATION'S FAVOURITE GAME SHOW, QUIZBINGO! WE'RE KIND OF STUCK UP THE BACK, IN THE CORNER, BEHIND A PILLAR, RIGHT NEXT TO AN OLD WOMAN WHO KEEPS DOING BOILED-HAM FARTS...
...BUT WE DON'T GIVE A SHIT, WE LOVE THIS SHOW!
QUIZ BINGO
HELLO, LADIES AND GENTLEMEN, AND WELCOME TO QUIZBINGO. I'LL BE CHARLIE HAPPY, YOUR QUIZMASTER FOR THIS EVENING.
ALLOW ME TO INTRODUCE MY VERY UNGLAMOROUS ASSISTANT...THE WIFE...KNOWN TO YOU ALL AT HOME AS THE FANTABULOUS U-LEGN HAPPY.
CHARLIE HAPPY MUST DIE

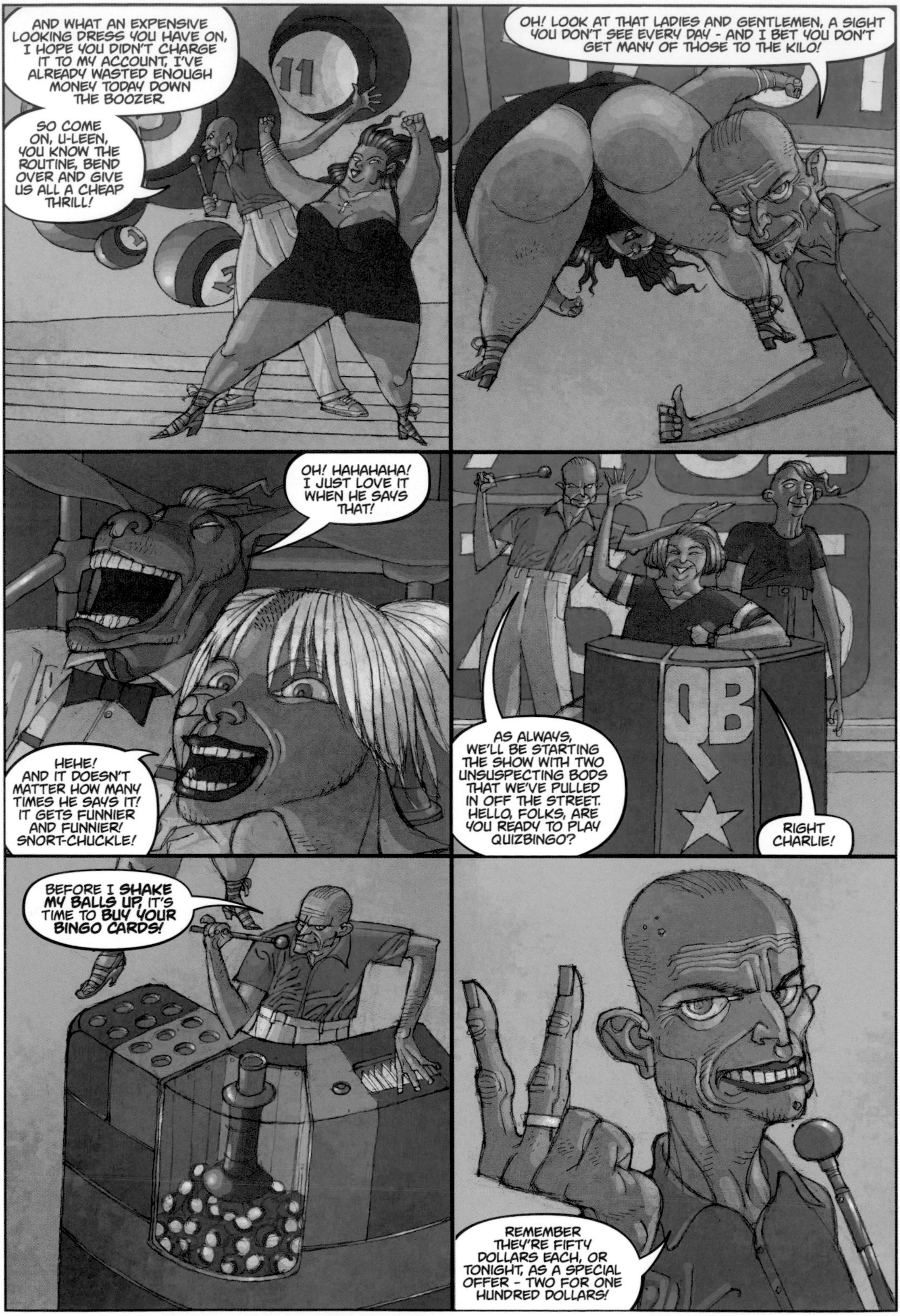
AND WHAT AN EXPENSIVE LOOKING DRESS YOU HAVE ON, I HOPE YOU DIDN'T CHARGE IT TO MY ACCOUNT, I'VE ALREADY WASTED ENOUGH MONEY TODAY DOWN THE BOOZER.
SO COME ON, U-LEEN, YOU KNOW THE ROUTINE, BEND OVER AND GIVE US ALL A CHEAP THRILL!
11
OH! LOOK AT THAT LADIES AND GENTLEMEN, A SIGHT YOU DON'T SEE EVERY DAY - AND I BET YOU DON'T GET MANY OF THOSE TO THE KILO!
OH! HAHAHAHA! I JUST LOVE IT WHEN HE SAYS THAT!
HEHE! AND IT DOESN'T MATTER HOW MANY TIMES HE SAYS IT! IT GETS FUNNIER AND FUNNIER! SNORT-CHUCKLE!
AS ALWAYS, WE'LL BE STARTING THE SHOW WITH TWO UNSUSPECTING BODS THAT WE'VE PULLED IN OFF THE STREET. HELLO, FOLKS, ARE YOU READY TO PLAY QUIZBINGO?
QB
RIGHT CHARLIE!
BEFORE I **SHAKE MY BALLS UP**, IT'S TIME TO **BUY YOUR BINGO CARDS!**
REMEMBER THEY'RE FIFTY DOLLARS EACH, OR TONIGHT, AS A SPECIAL OFFER - TWO FOR ONE HUNDRED DOLLARS!

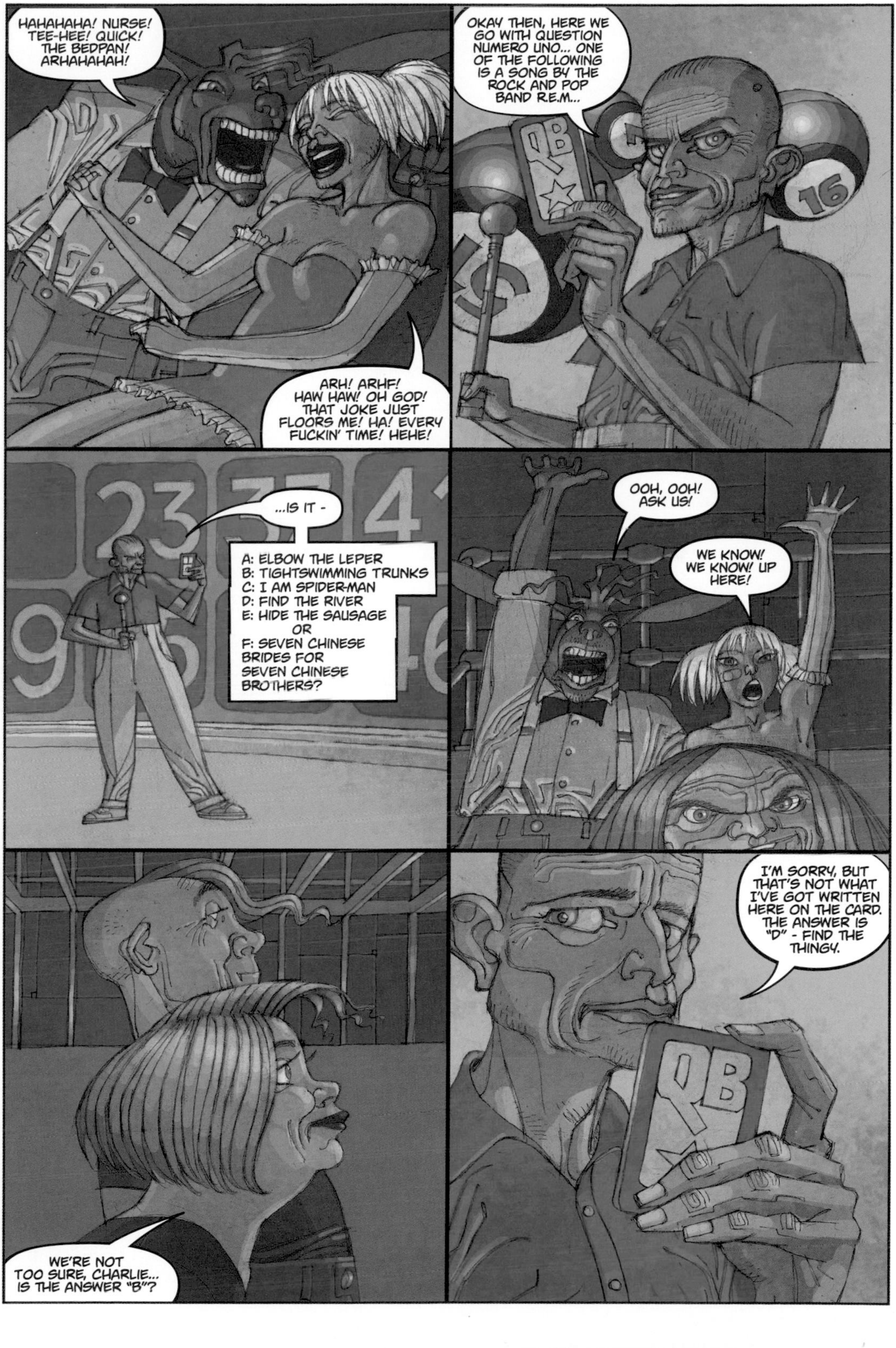
HAHAHAHA! NURSE! TEE-HEE! QUICK! THE BEDPAN! ARHAHAHAH!
ARH! ARHF! HAW HAW! OH GOD! THAT JOKE JUST FLOORS ME! HA! EVERY FUCKIN' TIME! HEHE!
OKAY THEN, HERE WE GO WITH QUESTION NUMERO UNO... ONE OF THE FOLLOWING IS A SONG BY THE ROCK AND POP BAND R.E.M...
QB
16
23
41
...IS IT -
A: ELBOW THE LEPER
B: TIGHTSWIMMING TRUNKS
C: I AM SPIDER-MAN
D: FIND THE RIVER
E: HIDE THE SAUSAGE
OR
F: SEVEN CHINESE BRIDES FOR SEVEN CHINESE BROTHERS?
OOH, OOH! ASK US!
WE KNOW! WE KNOW! UP HERE!
WE'RE NOT TOO SURE, CHARLIE... IS THE ANSWER "B"?
I'M SORRY, BUT THAT'S NOT WHAT I'VE GOT WRITTEN HERE ON THE CARD. THE ANSWER IS "D" - FIND THE THINGY.
QB

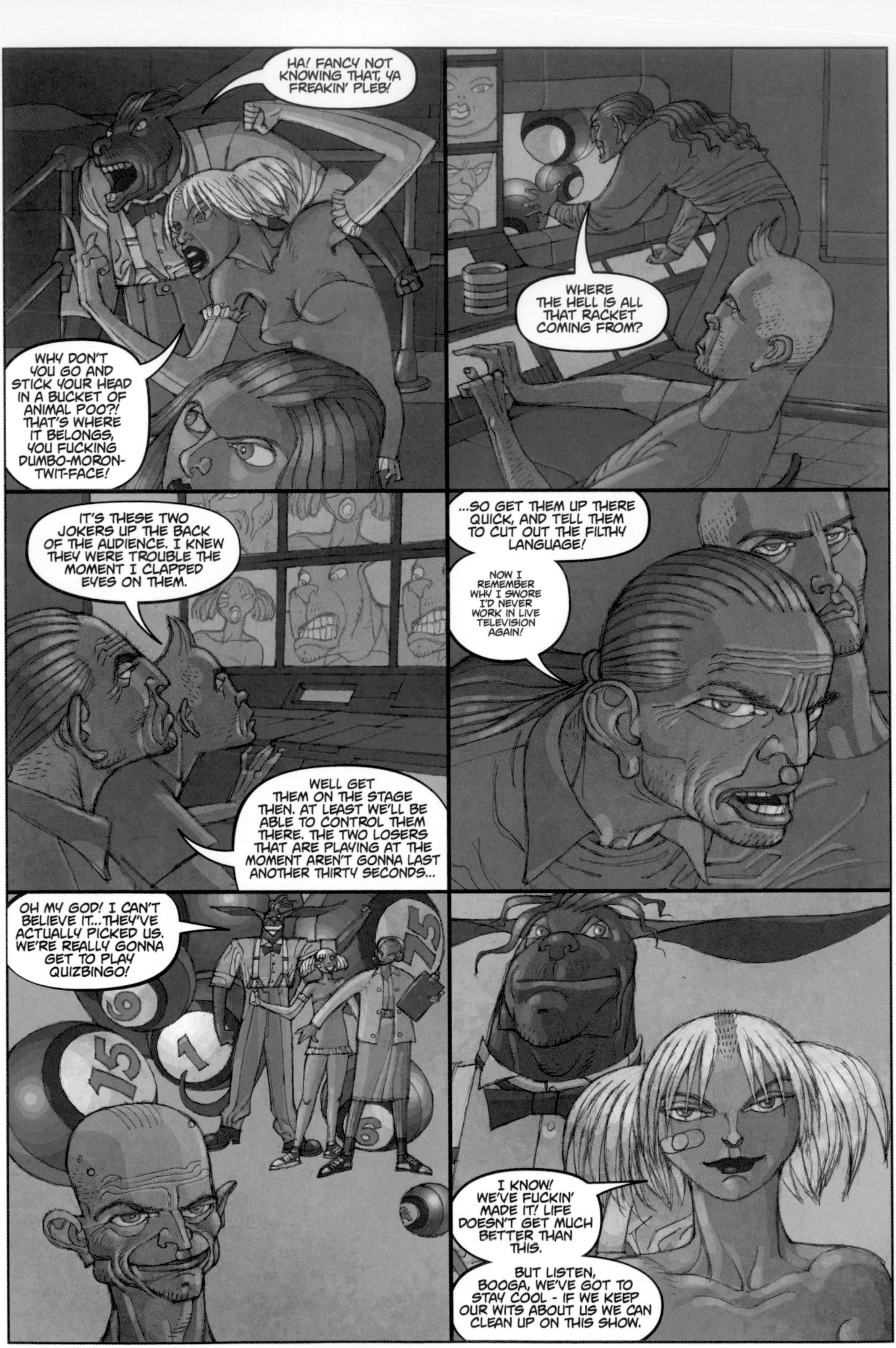
HA! FANCY NOT KNOWING THAT, YA FREAKIN' PLEB!
WHY DON'T YOU GO AND STICK YOUR HEAD IN A BUCKET OF ANIMAL POO?! THAT'S WHERE IT BELONGS, YOU FUCKING DUMBO-MORON-TWIT-FACE!
WHERE THE HELL IS ALL THAT RACKET COMING FROM?
IT'S THESE TWO JOKERS UP THE BACK OF THE AUDIENCE. I KNEW THEY WERE TROUBLE THE MOMENT I CLAPPED EYES ON THEM.
WELL GET THEM ON THE STAGE THEN. AT LEAST WE'LL BE ABLE TO CONTROL THEM THERE. THE TWO LOSERS THAT ARE PLAYING AT THE MOMENT AREN'T GONNA LAST ANOTHER THIRTY SECONDS...
...SO GET THEM UP THERE QUICK, AND TELL THEM TO CUT OUT THE FILTHY LANGUAGE!
NOW I REMEMBER WHY I SWORE I'D NEVER WORK IN LIVE TELEVISION AGAIN!
OH MY GOD! I CAN'T BELIEVE IT...THEY'VE ACTUALLY PICKED US. WE'RE REALLY GONNA GET TO PLAY QUIZBINGO!
I KNOW! WE'VE FUCKIN' MADE IT! LIFE DOESN'T GET MUCH BETTER THAN THIS.
BUT LISTEN, BOOGA, WE'VE GOT TO STAY COOL - IF WE KEEP OUR WITS ABOUT US WE CAN CLEAN UP ON THIS SHOW.

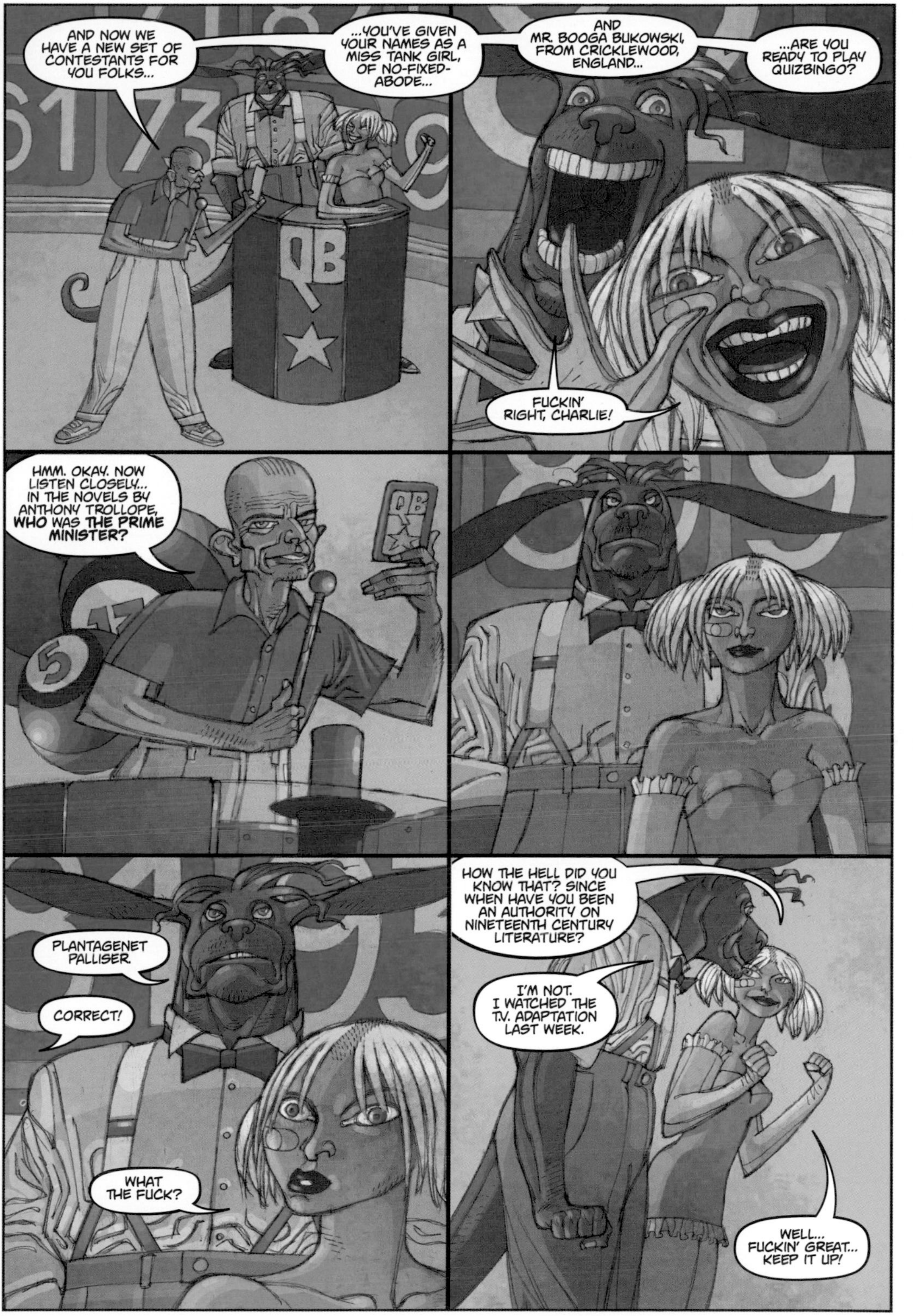
AND NOW WE HAVE A NEW SET OF CONTESTANTS FOR YOU FOLKS...
...YOU'VE GIVEN YOUR NAMES AS A MISS TANK GIRL, OF NO-FIXED-ABODE...
AND MR. BOOGA BUKOWSKI, FROM CRICKLEWOOD, ENGLAND...
...ARE YOU READY TO PLAY QUIZBINGO?
QB
FUCKIN' RIGHT, CHARLIE!
HMM. OKAY. NOW LISTEN CLOSELY... IN THE NOVELS BY ANTHONY TROLLOPE, WHO WAS THE PRIME MINISTER?
PLANTAGENET PALLISER.
CORRECT!
WHAT THE FUCK?
HOW THE HELL DID YOU KNOW THAT? SINCE WHEN HAVE YOU BEEN AN AUTHORITY ON NINETEENTH CENTURY LITERATURE?
I'M NOT. I WATCHED THE T.V. ADAPTATION LAST WEEK.
WELL... FUCKIN' GREAT... KEEP IT UP!

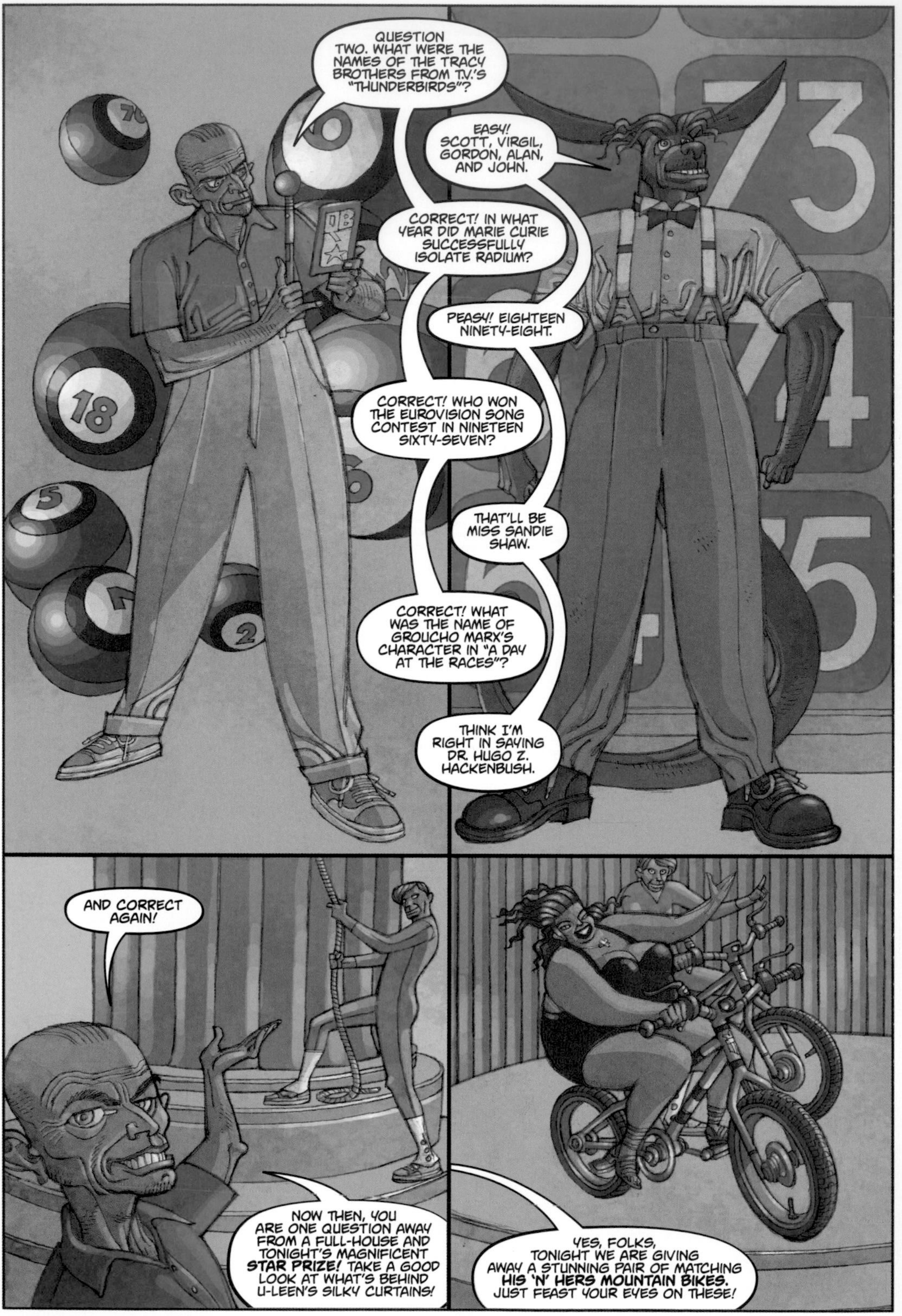
QUESTION TWO. WHAT WERE THE NAMES OF THE TRACY BROTHERS FROM T.V.'S "THUNDERBIRDS"?
EASY! SCOTT, VIRGIL, GORDON, ALAN, AND JOHN.
CORRECT! IN WHAT YEAR DID MARIE CURIE SUCCESSFULLY ISOLATE RADIUM?
PEASY! EIGHTEEN NINETY-EIGHT.
CORRECT! WHO WON THE EUROVISION SONG CONTEST IN NINETEEN SIXTY-SEVEN?
THAT'LL BE MISS SANDIE SHAW.
CORRECT! WHAT WAS THE NAME OF GROUCHO MARX'S CHARACTER IN "A DAY AT THE RACES"?
THINK I'M RIGHT IN SAYING DR. HUGO Z. HACKENBUSH.
AND CORRECT AGAIN!
NOW THEN, YOU ARE ONE QUESTION AWAY FROM A FULL-HOUSE AND TONIGHT'S MAGNIFICENT **STAR PRIZE!** TAKE A GOOD LOOK AT WHAT'S BEHIND U-LEEN'S SILKY CURTAINS!
YES, FOLKS, TONIGHT WE ARE GIVING AWAY A STUNNING PAIR OF MATCHING **HIS 'N' HERS MOUNTAIN BIKES.** JUST FEAST YOUR EYES ON THESE!

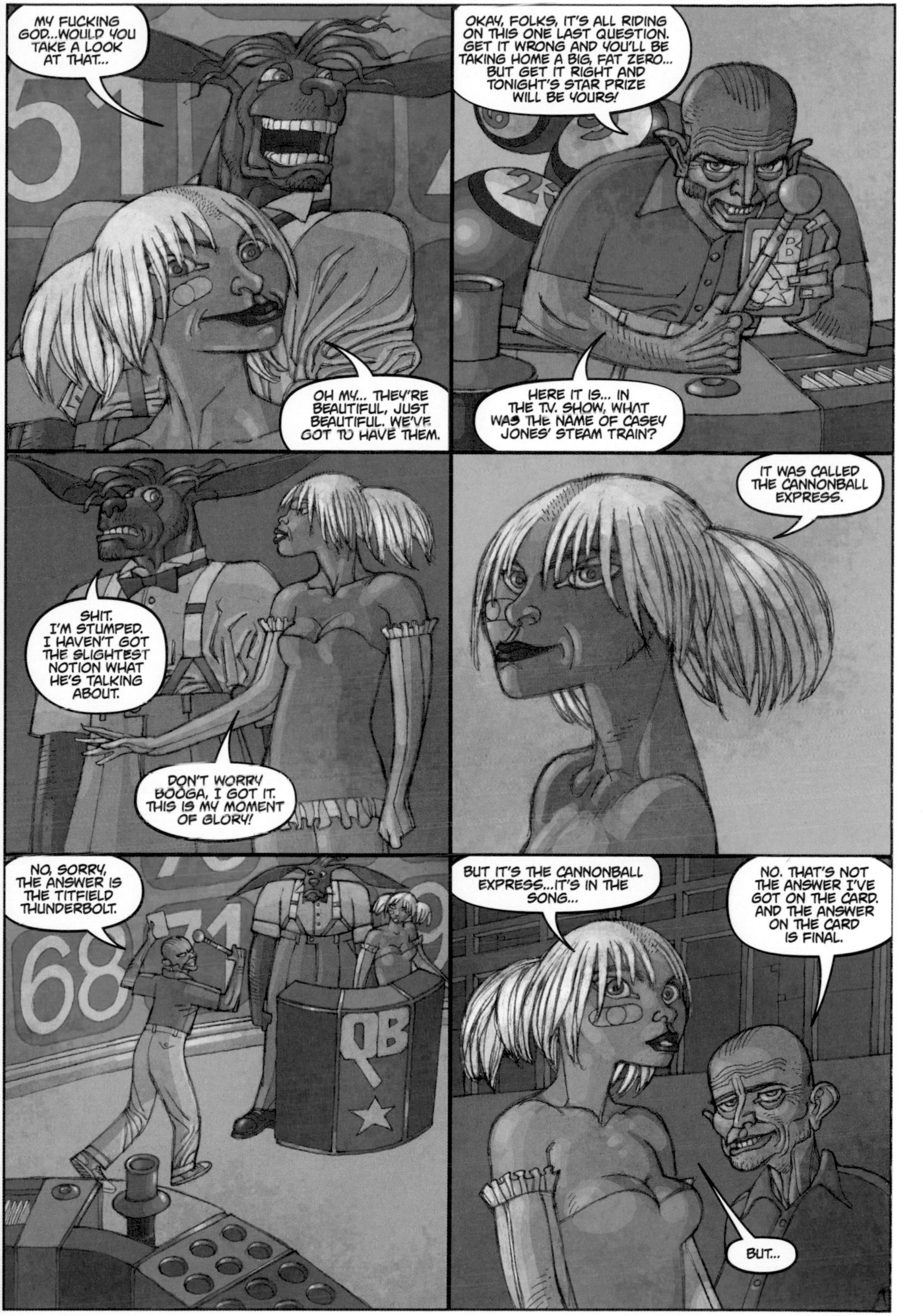
MY FUCKING GOD...WOULD YOU TAKE A LOOK AT THAT...
OH MY... THEY'RE BEAUTIFUL, JUST BEAUTIFUL. WE'VE GOT TO HAVE THEM.
OKAY, FOLKS, IT'S ALL RIDING ON THIS ONE LAST QUESTION. GET IT WRONG AND YOU'LL BE TAKING HOME A BIG, FAT ZERO... BUT GET IT RIGHT AND TONIGHT'S STAR PRIZE WILL BE YOURS!
HERE IT IS... IN THE T.V. SHOW, WHAT WAS THE NAME OF CASEY JONES' STEAM TRAIN?
SHIT. I'M STUMPED. I HAVEN'T GOT THE SLIGHTEST NOTION WHAT HE'S TALKING ABOUT.
DON'T WORRY BOOGA, I GOT IT. THIS IS MY MOMENT OF GLORY!
IT WAS CALLED THE CANNONBALL EXPRESS.
NO, SORRY, THE ANSWER IS THE TITFIELD THUNDERBOLT.
QB
BUT IT'S THE CANNONBALL EXPRESS...IT'S IN THE SONG...
NO. THAT'S NOT THE ANSWER I'VE GOT ON THE CARD. AND THE ANSWER ON THE CARD IS FINAL.
BUT...

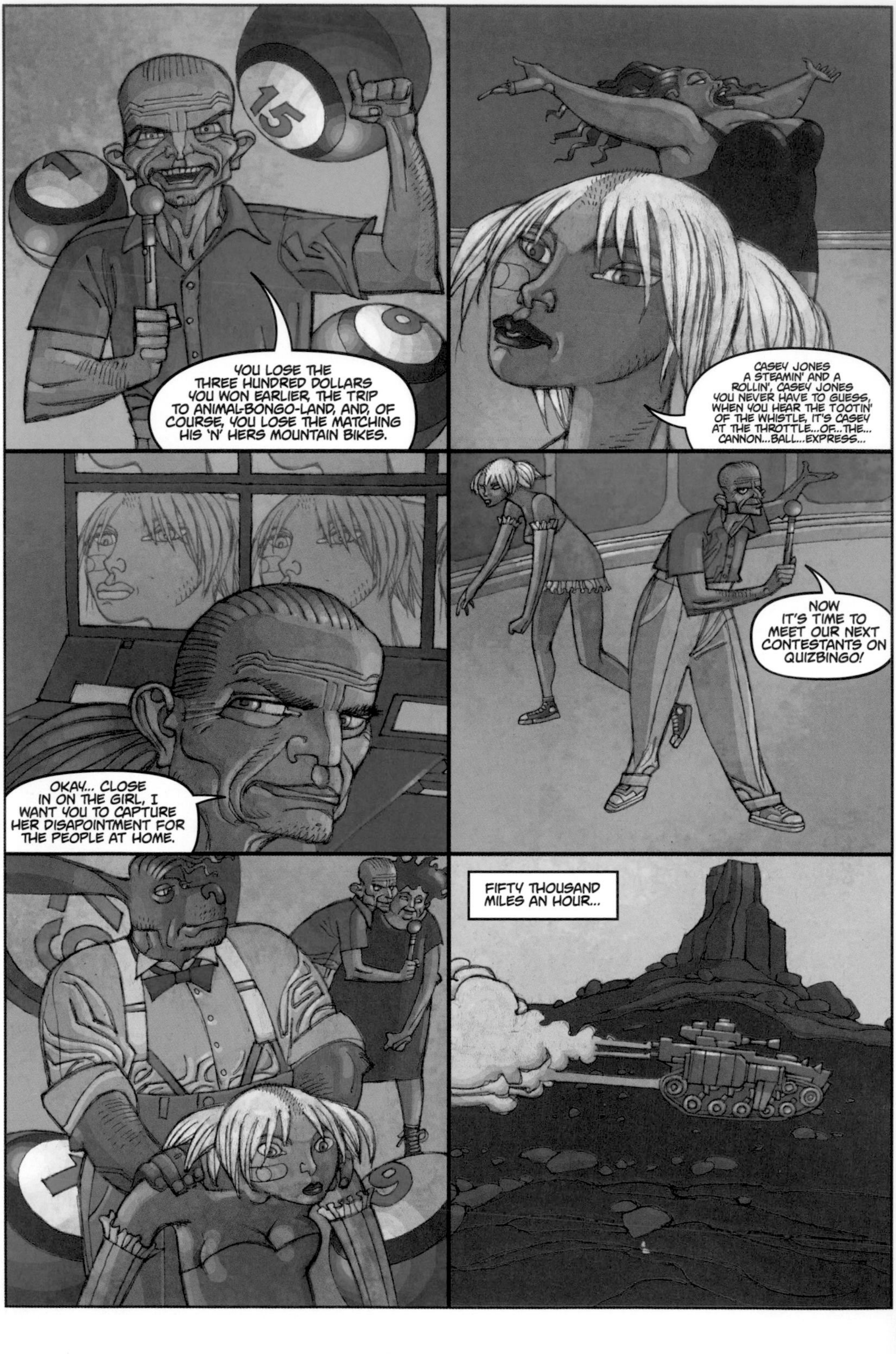

YOU LOSE THE THREE HUNDRED DOLLARS YOU WON EARLIER, THE TRIP TO ANIMAL-BONGO-LAND, AND, OF COURSE, YOU LOSE THE MATCHING HIS 'N' HERS MOUNTAIN BIKES.
CASEY JONES A STEAMIN' AND A ROLLIN', CASEY JONES YOU NEVER HAVE TO GUESS, WHEN YOU HEAR THE TOOTIN' OF THE WHISTLE, IT'S CASEY AT THE THROTTLE...OF...THE... CANNON...BALL...EXPRESS...
OKAY... CLOSE IN ON THE GIRL, I WANT YOU TO CAPTURE HER DISAPOINTMENT FOR THE PEOPLE AT HOME.
NOW IT'S TIME TO MEET OUR NEXT CONTESTANTS ON QUIZBINGO!
FIFTY THOUSAND MILES AN HOUR...

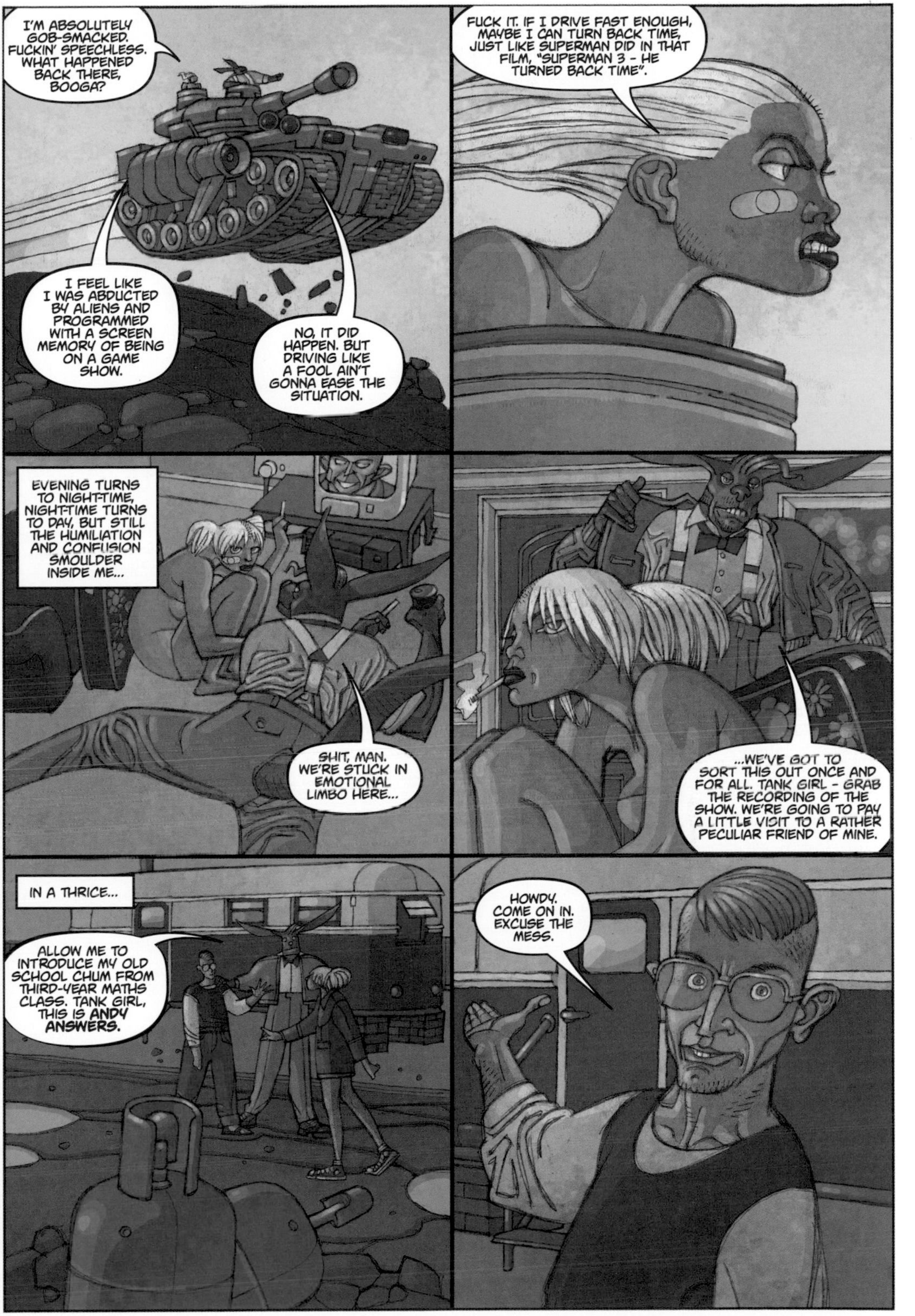
I'M ABSOLUTELY GOB-SMACKED. FUCKIN' SPEECHLESS. WHAT HAPPENED BACK THERE, BOOGA?
I FEEL LIKE I WAS ABDUCTED BY ALIENS AND PROGRAMMED WITH A SCREEN MEMORY OF BEING ON A GAME SHOW.
NO, IT DID HAPPEN. BUT DRIVING LIKE A FOOL AIN'T GONNA EASE THE SITUATION.
FUCK IT. IF I DRIVE FAST ENOUGH, MAYBE I CAN TURN BACK TIME, JUST LIKE SUPERMAN DID IN THAT FILM, "SUPERMAN 3 - HE TURNED BACK TIME".
EVENING TURNS TO NIGHT-TIME, NIGHT-TIME TURNS TO DAY, BUT STILL THE HUMILIATION AND CONFUSION SMOULDER INSIDE ME...
SHIT, MAN. WE'RE STUCK IN EMOTIONAL LIMBO HERE...
...WE'VE GOT TO SORT THIS OUT ONCE AND FOR ALL. TANK GIRL - GRAB THE RECORDING OF THE SHOW. WE'RE GOING TO PAY A LITTLE VISIT TO A RATHER PECULIAR FRIEND OF MINE.
IN A THRICE...
ALLOW ME TO INTRODUCE MY OLD SCHOOL CHUM FROM THIRD-YEAR MATHS CLASS. TANK GIRL, THIS IS ANDY ANSWERS.
HOWDY. COME ON IN. EXCUSE THE MESS.

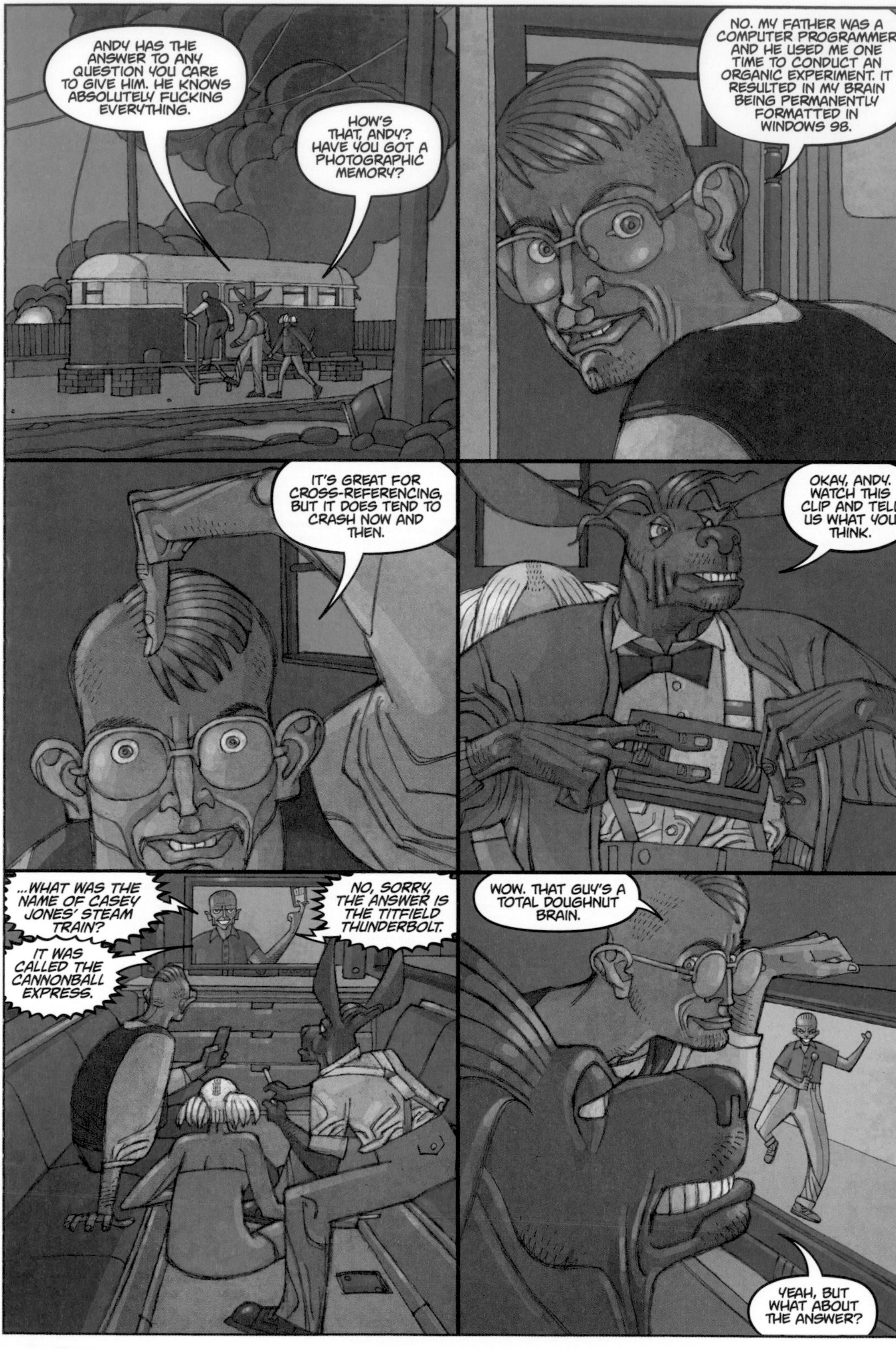
ANDY HAS THE ANSWER TO ANY QUESTION YOU CARE TO GIVE HIM. HE KNOWS ABSOLUTELY FUCKING EVERYTHING.
HOW'S THAT, ANDY? HAVE YOU GOT A PHOTOGRAPHIC MEMORY?
NO. MY FATHER WAS A COMPUTER PROGRAMMER AND HE USED ME ONE TIME TO CONDUCT AN ORGANIC EXPERIMENT. IT RESULTED IN MY BRAIN BEING PERMANENTLY FORMATTED IN WINDOWS 98.
IT'S GREAT FOR CROSS-REFERENCING, BUT IT DOES TEND TO CRASH NOW AND THEN.
OKAY, ANDY. WATCH THIS CLIP AND TELL US WHAT YOU THINK.
...WHAT WAS THE NAME OF CASEY JONES' STEAM TRAIN?
IT WAS CALLED THE CANNONBALL EXPRESS.
NO, SORRY, THE ANSWER IS THE TITFIELD THUNDERBOLT.
WOW. THAT GUY'S A TOTAL DOUGHNUT BRAIN.
YEAH, BUT WHAT ABOUT THE ANSWER?

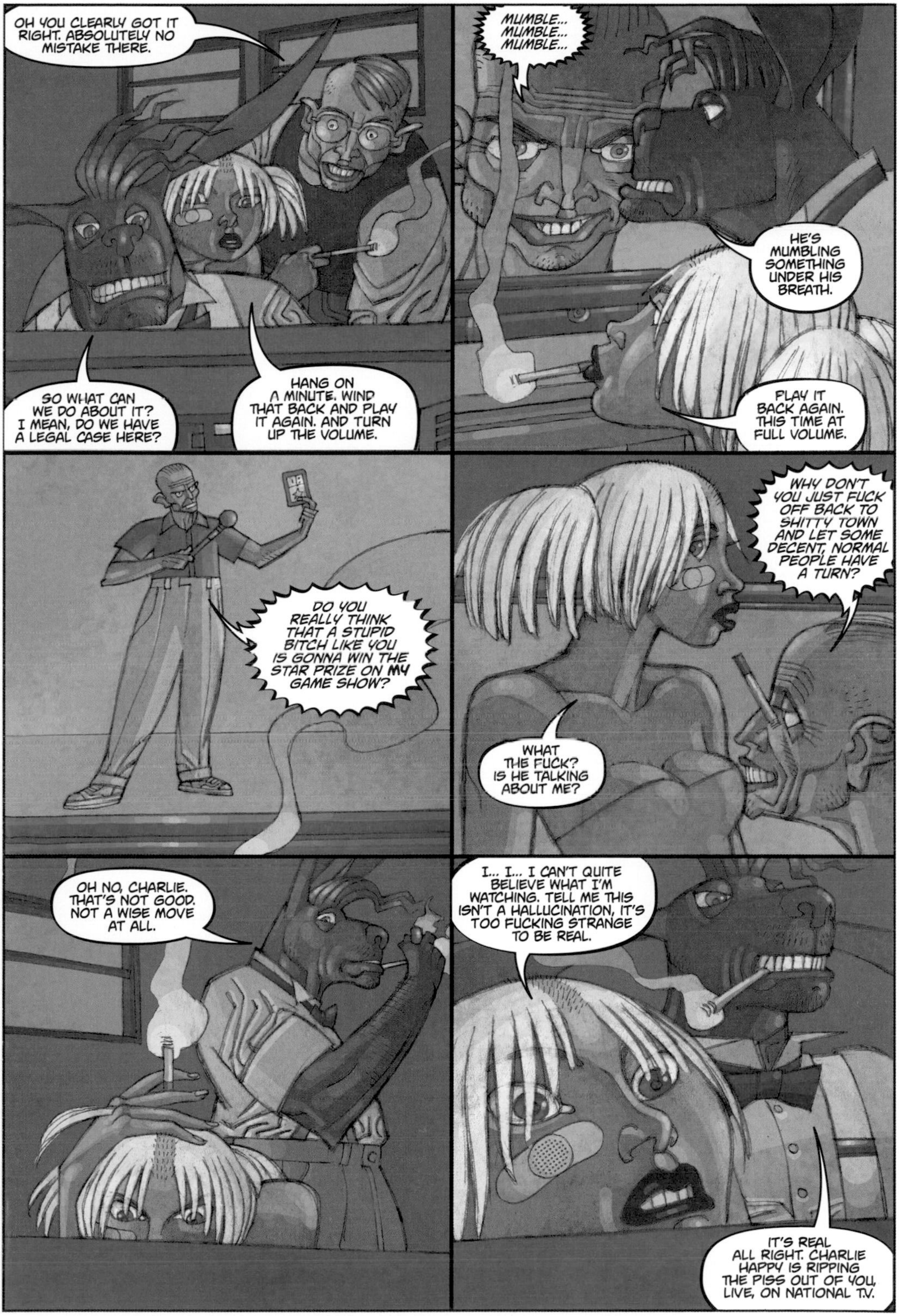
OH YOU CLEARLY GOT IT RIGHT. ABSOLUTELY NO MISTAKE THERE.
SO WHAT CAN WE DO ABOUT IT? I MEAN, DO WE HAVE A LEGAL CASE HERE?
HANG ON A MINUTE. WIND THAT BACK AND PLAY IT AGAIN. AND TURN UP THE VOLUME.
MUMBLE... MUMBLE... MUMBLE...
HE'S MUMBLING SOMETHING UNDER HIS BREATH.
PLAY IT BACK AGAIN. THIS TIME AT FULL VOLUME.
DO YOU REALLY THINK THAT A STUPID BITCH LIKE YOU IS GONNA WIN THE STAR PRIZE ON MY GAME SHOW?
WHY DON'T YOU JUST FUCK OFF BACK TO SHITTY TOWN AND LET SOME DECENT, NORMAL PEOPLE HAVE A TURN?
WHAT THE FUCK? IS HE TALKING ABOUT ME?
OH NO, CHARLIE. THAT'S NOT GOOD. NOT A WISE MOVE AT ALL.
I... I... I CAN'T QUITE BELIEVE WHAT I'M WATCHING. TELL ME THIS ISN'T A HALLUCINATION, IT'S TOO FUCKING STRANGE TO BE REAL.
IT'S REAL ALL RIGHT. CHARLIE HAPPY IS RIPPING THE PISS OUT OF YOU, LIVE, ON NATIONAL T.V.

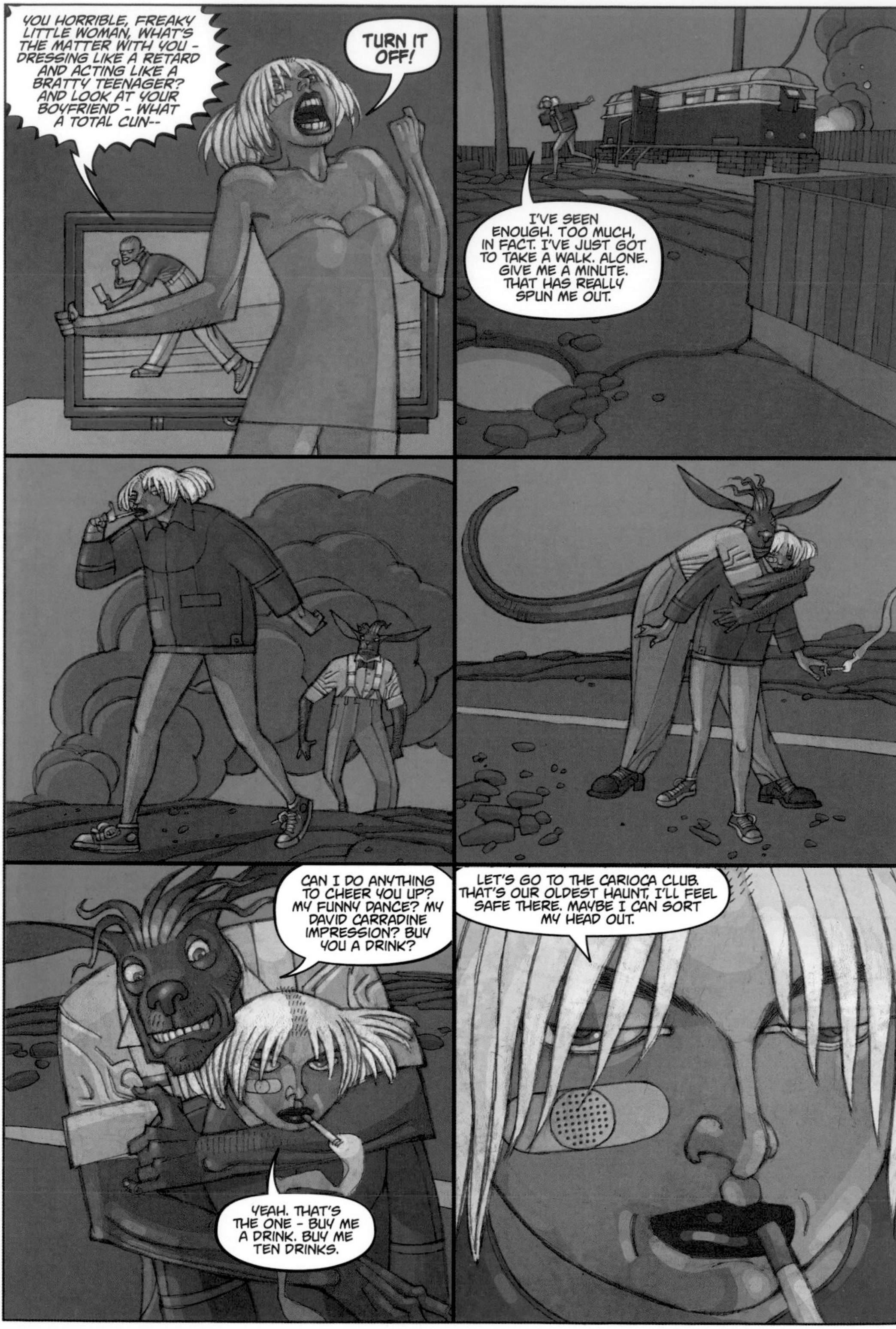
YOU HORRIBLE, FREAKY LITTLE WOMAN, WHAT'S THE MATTER WITH YOU - DRESSING LIKE A RETARD AND ACTING LIKE A BRATTY TEENAGER? AND LOOK AT YOUR BOYFRIEND - WHAT A TOTAL CUN--
TURN IT OFF!
I'VE SEEN ENOUGH. TOO MUCH, IN FACT. I'VE JUST GOT TO TAKE A WALK. ALONE. GIVE ME A MINUTE. THAT HAS REALLY SPUN ME OUT.
CAN I DO ANYTHING TO CHEER YOU UP? MY FUNNY DANCE? MY DAVID CARRADINE IMPRESSION? BUY YOU A DRINK?
YEAH. THAT'S THE ONE - BUY ME A DRINK. BUY ME TEN DRINKS.
LET'S GO TO THE CARIOCA CLUB. THAT'S OUR OLDEST HAUNT, I'LL FEEL SAFE THERE. MAYBE I CAN SORT MY HEAD OUT.

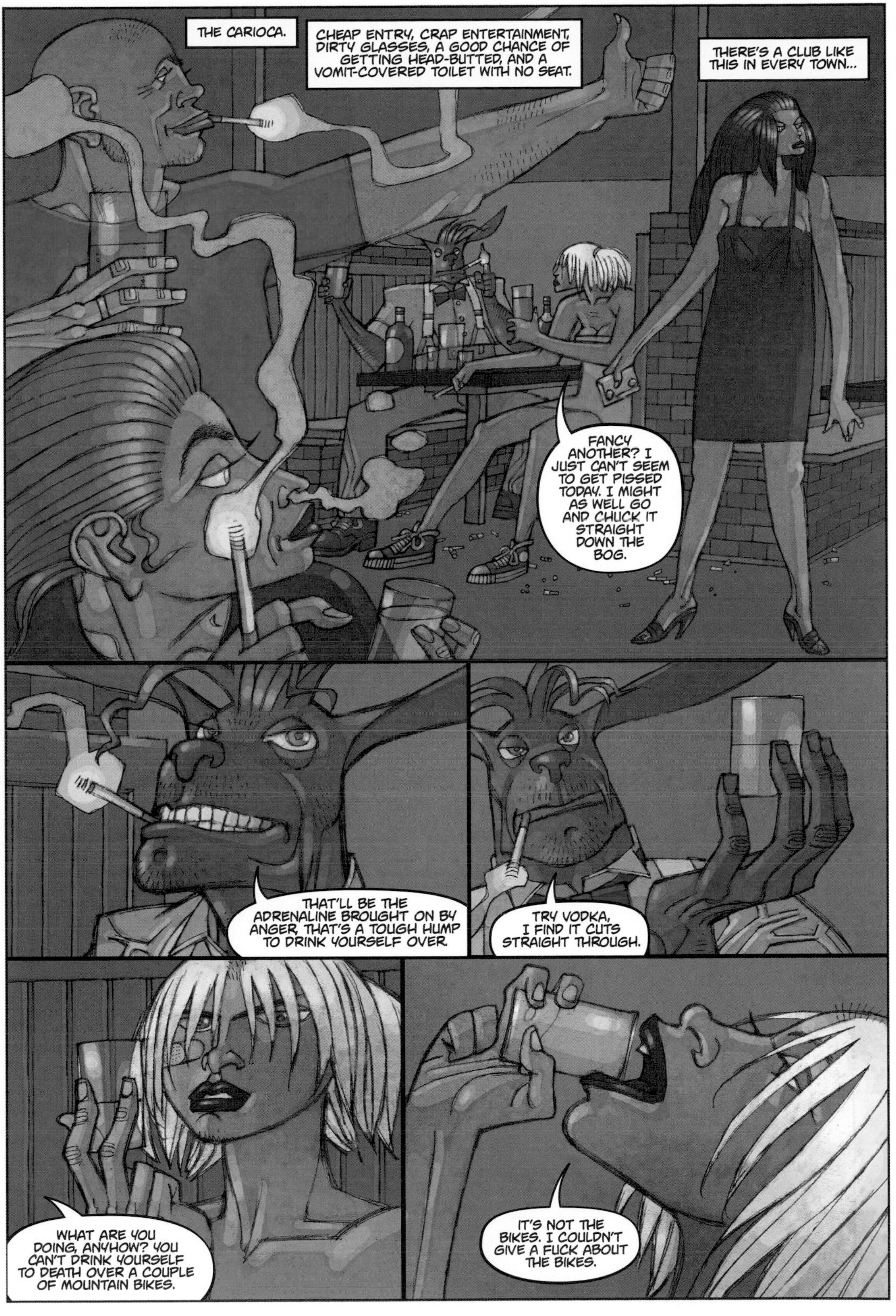
THE CARIOCA.
CHEAP ENTRY, CRAP ENTERTAINMENT, DIRTY GLASSES, A GOOD CHANCE OF GETTING HEAD-BUTTED, AND A VOMIT-COVERED TOILET WITH NO SEAT.
THERE'S A CLUB LIKE THIS IN EVERY TOWN...
FANCY ANOTHER? I JUST CAN'T SEEM TO GET PISSED TODAY. I MIGHT AS WELL GO AND CHUCK IT STRAIGHT DOWN THE BOG.
THAT'LL BE THE ADRENALINE BROUGHT ON BY ANGER, THAT'S A TOUGH HUMP TO DRINK YOURSELF OVER.
TRY VODKA, I FIND IT CUTS STRAIGHT THROUGH.
WHAT ARE YOU DOING, ANYHOW? YOU CAN'T DRINK YOURSELF TO DEATH OVER A COUPLE OF MOUNTAIN BIKES.
IT'S NOT THE BIKES. I COULDN'T GIVE A FUCK ABOUT THE BIKES.

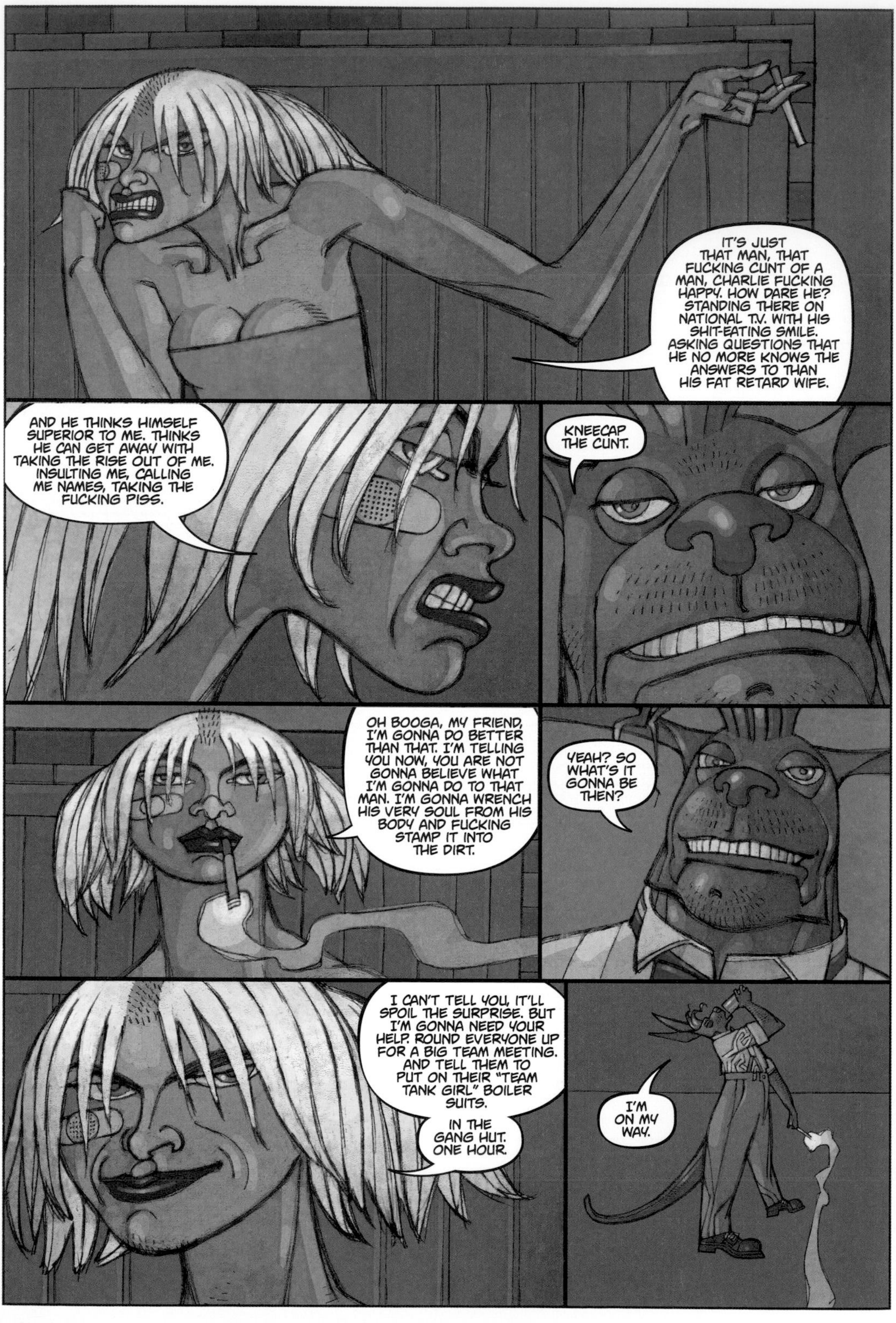
IT'S JUST THAT MAN, THAT FUCKING CUNT OF A MAN, CHARLIE FUCKING HAPPY. HOW DARE HE? STANDING THERE ON NATIONAL T.V. WITH HIS SHIT-EATING SMILE. ASKING QUESTIONS THAT HE NO MORE KNOWS THE ANSWERS TO THAN HIS FAT RETARD WIFE.
AND HE THINKS HIMSELF SUPERIOR TO ME. THINKS HE CAN GET AWAY WITH TAKING THE RISE OUT OF ME. INSULTING ME, CALLING ME NAMES, TAKING THE FUCKING PISS.
KNEECAP THE CUNT.
OH BOOGA, MY FRIEND, I'M GONNA DO BETTER THAN THAT. I'M TELLING YOU NOW, YOU ARE NOT GONNA BELIEVE WHAT I'M GONNA DO TO THAT MAN. I'M GONNA WRENCH HIS VERY SOUL FROM HIS BODY AND FUCKING STAMP IT INTO THE DIRT.
YEAH? SO WHAT'S IT GONNA BE THEN?
I CAN'T TELL YOU, IT'LL SPOIL THE SURPRISE. BUT I'M GONNA NEED YOUR HELP. ROUND EVERYONE UP FOR A BIG TEAM MEETING. AND TELL THEM TO PUT ON THEIR "TEAM TANK GIRL" BOILER SUITS.
IN THE GANG HUT. ONE HOUR.
I'M ON MY WAY.

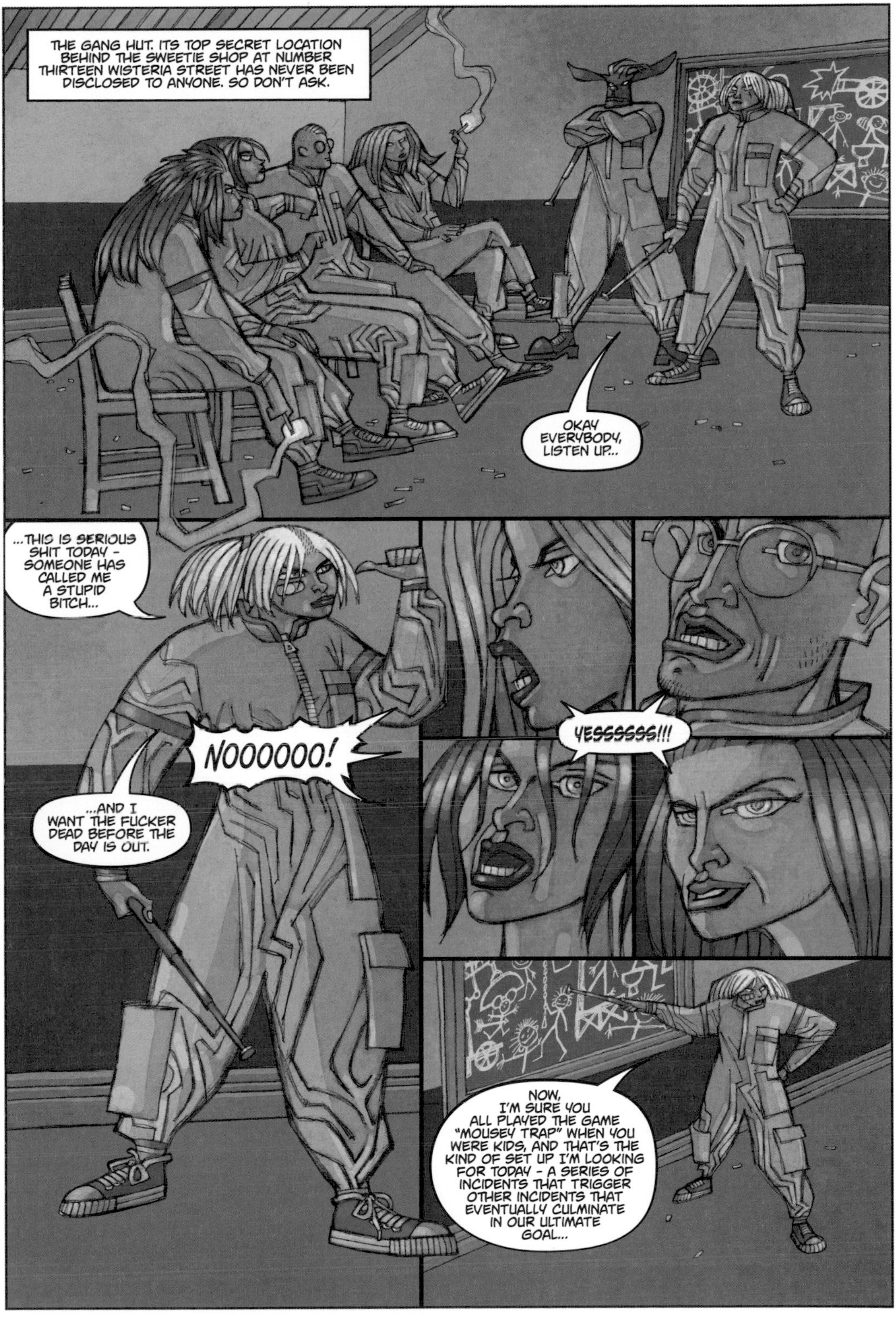
THE GANG HUT. ITS TOP SECRET LOCATION BEHIND THE SWEETIE SHOP AT NUMBER THIRTEEN WISTERIA STREET HAS NEVER BEEN DISCLOSED TO ANYONE. SO DON'T ASK.
OKAY EVERYBODY, LISTEN UP...
...THIS IS SERIOUS SHIT TODAY - SOMEONE HAS CALLED ME A STUPID BITCH...
NOOOOOO!
...AND I WANT THE FUCKER DEAD BEFORE THE DAY IS OUT.
YESSSSSS!!!
NOW, I'M SURE YOU ALL PLAYED THE GAME "MOUSEY TRAP" WHEN YOU WERE KIDS, AND THAT'S THE KIND OF SET UP I'M LOOKING FOR TODAY - A SERIES OF INCIDENTS THAT TRIGGER OTHER INCIDENTS THAT EVENTUALLY CULMINATE IN OUR ULTIMATE GOAL...

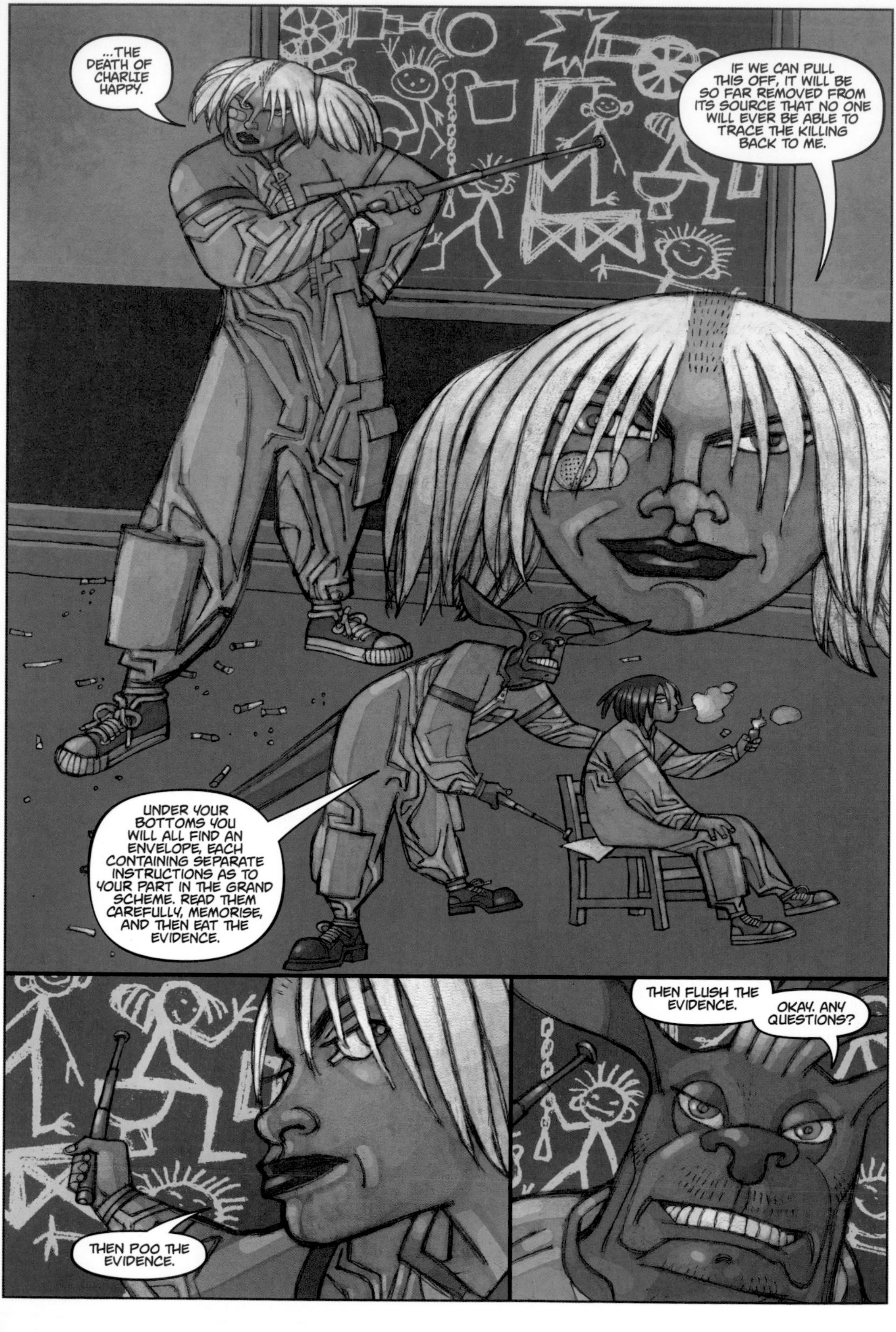
...THE DEATH OF CHARLIE HAPPY.
IF WE CAN PULL THIS OFF, IT WILL BE SO FAR REMOVED FROM ITS SOURCE THAT NO ONE WILL EVER BE ABLE TO TRACE THE KILLING BACK TO ME.
UNDER YOUR BOTTOMS YOU WILL ALL FIND AN ENVELOPE, EACH CONTAINING SEPARATE INSTRUCTIONS AS TO YOUR PART IN THE GRAND SCHEME. READ THEM CAREFULLY, MEMORISE, AND THEN EAT THE EVIDENCE.
THEN POO THE EVIDENCE.
THEN FLUSH THE EVIDENCE.
OKAY. ANY QUESTIONS?

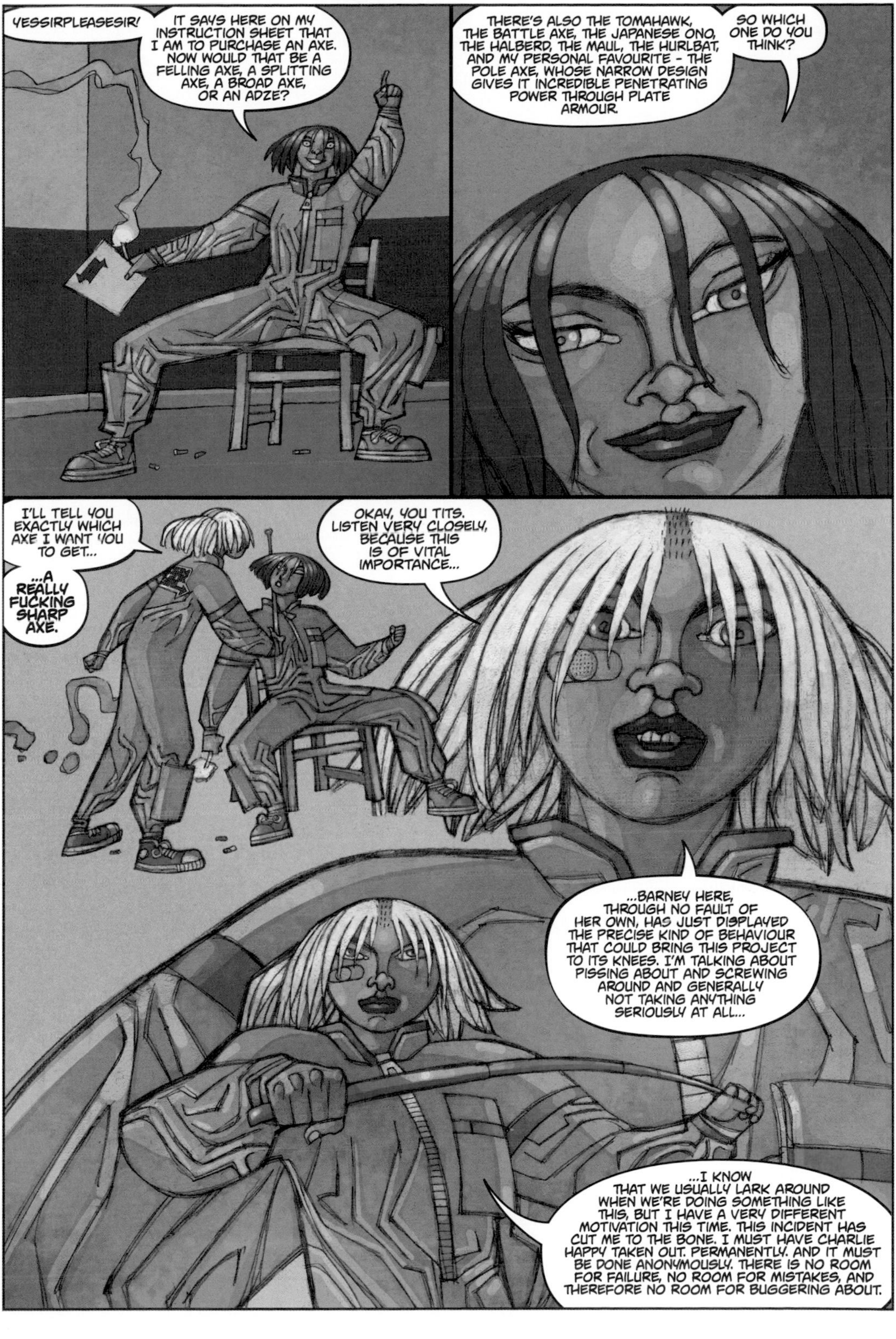

YESSIRPLEASESIR!
IT SAYS HERE ON MY INSTRUCTION SHEET THAT I AM TO PURCHASE AN AXE. NOW WOULD THAT BE A FELLING AXE, A SPLITTING AXE, A BROAD AXE, OR AN ADZE?
THERE'S ALSO THE TOMAHAWK, THE BATTLE AXE, THE JAPANESE ONO, THE HALBERD, THE MAUL, THE HURLBAT, AND MY PERSONAL FAVOURITE - THE POLE AXE, WHOSE NARROW DESIGN GIVES IT INCREDIBLE PENETRATING POWER THROUGH PLATE ARMOUR.
SO WHICH ONE DO YOU THINK?
I'LL TELL YOU EXACTLY WHICH AXE I WANT YOU TO GET...
...A REALLY FUCKING SHARP AXE.
OKAY, YOU TITS. LISTEN VERY CLOSELY, BECAUSE THIS IS OF VITAL IMPORTANCE...
...BARNEY HERE, THROUGH NO FAULT OF HER OWN, HAS JUST DISPLAYED THE PRECISE KIND OF BEHAVIOUR THAT COULD BRING THIS PROJECT TO ITS KNEES. I'M TALKING ABOUT PISSING ABOUT AND SCREWING AROUND AND GENERALLY NOT TAKING ANYTHING SERIOUSLY AT ALL...
...I KNOW THAT WE USUALLY LARK AROUND WHEN WE'RE DOING SOMETHING LIKE THIS, BUT I HAVE A VERY DIFFERENT MOTIVATION THIS TIME. THIS INCIDENT HAS CUT ME TO THE BONE. I MUST HAVE CHARLIE HAPPY TAKEN OUT. PERMANENTLY. AND IT MUST BE DONE ANONYMOUSLY. THERE IS NO ROOM FOR FAILURE, NO ROOM FOR MISTAKES, AND THEREFORE NO ROOM FOR BUGGERING ABOUT.

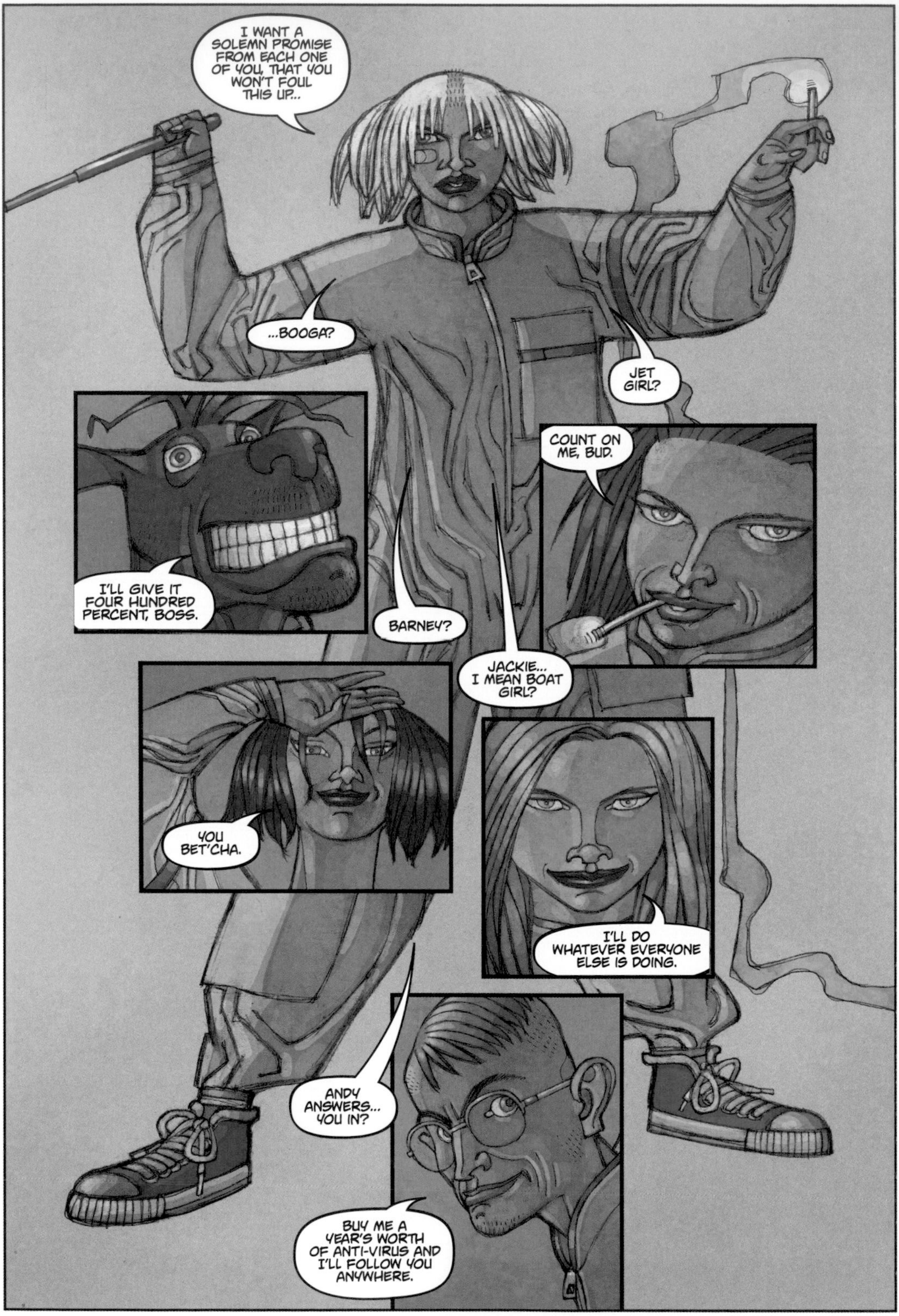
I WANT A SOLEMN PROMISE FROM EACH ONE OF YOU, THAT YOU WON'T FOUL THIS UP...
...BOOGA?
I'LL GIVE IT FOUR HUNDRED PERCENT, BOSS.
JET GIRL?
COUNT ON ME, BUD.
BARNEY?
YOU BET'CHA.
JACKIE... I MEAN BOAT GIRL?
I'LL DO WHATEVER EVERYONE ELSE IS DOING.
ANDY ANSWERS... YOU IN?
BUY ME A YEAR'S WORTH OF ANTI-VIRUS AND I'LL FOLLOW YOU ANYWHERE.

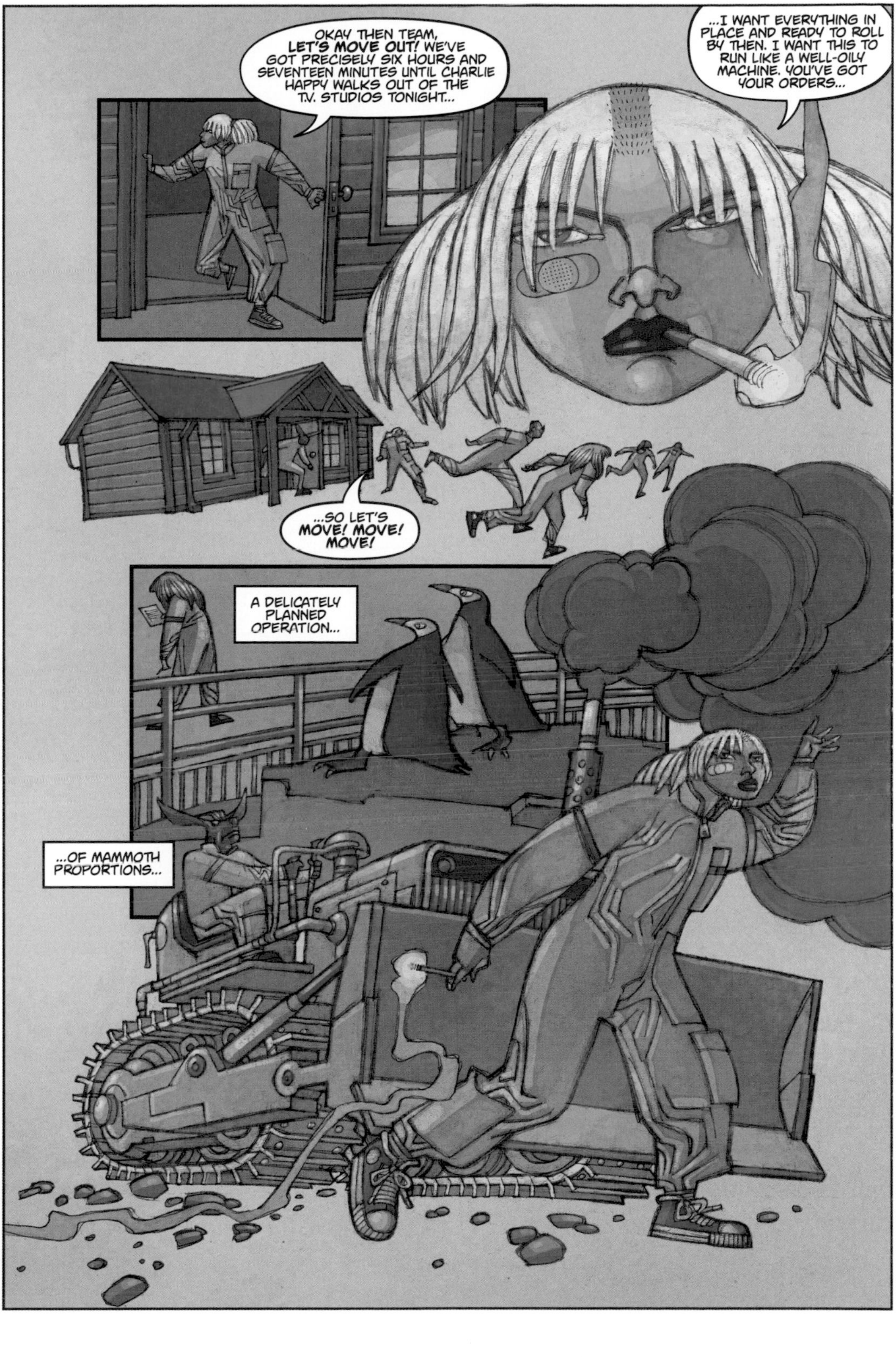
OKAY THEN TEAM, LET'S MOVE OUT! WE'VE GOT PRECISELY SIX HOURS AND SEVENTEEN MINUTES UNTIL CHARLIE HAPPY WALKS OUT OF THE T.V. STUDIOS TONIGHT...
...I WANT EVERYTHING IN PLACE AND READY TO ROLL BY THEN. I WANT THIS TO RUN LIKE A WELL-OILY MACHINE. YOU'VE GOT YOUR ORDERS...
...SO LET'S MOVE! MOVE! MOVE!
A DELICATELY PLANNED OPERATION...
...OF MAMMOTH PROPORTIONS...

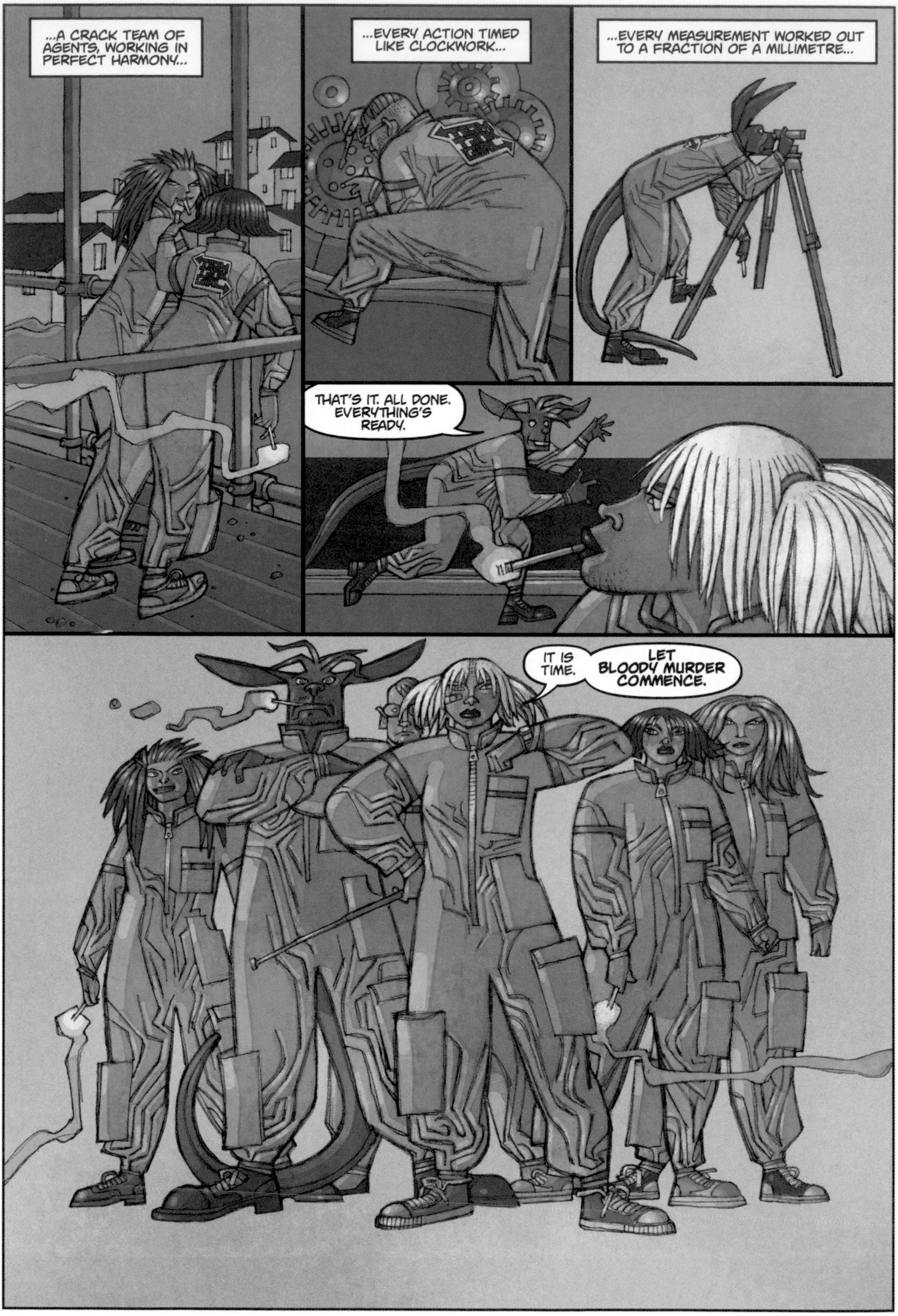
...A CRACK TEAM OF AGENTS, WORKING IN PERFECT HARMONY...
...EVERY ACTION TIMED LIKE CLOCKWORK...
...EVERY MEASUREMENT WORKED OUT TO A FRACTION OF A MILLIMETRE...
THAT'S IT. ALL DONE. EVERYTHING'S READY.
IT IS TIME.
LET BLOODY MURDER COMMENCE.

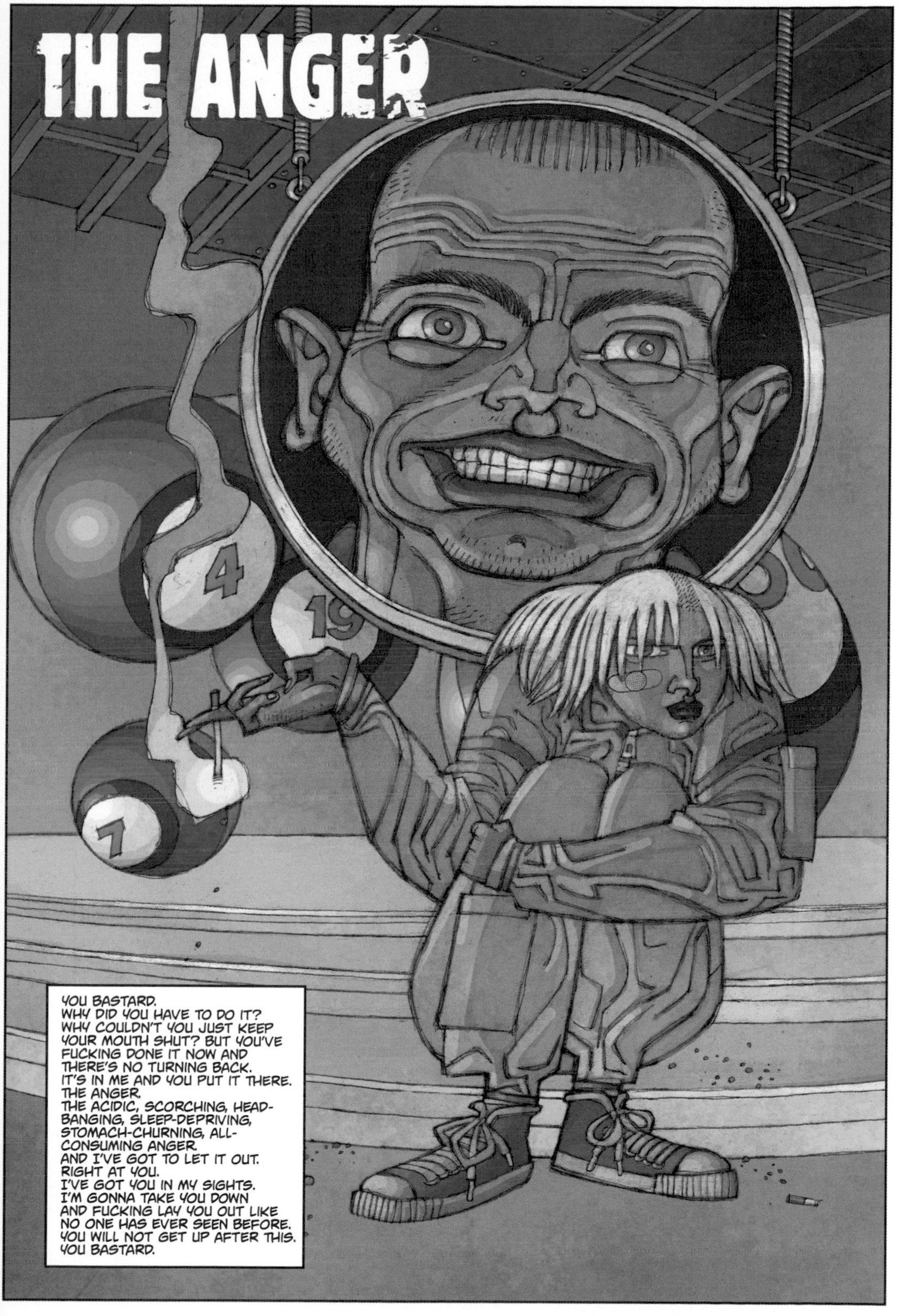
THE ANGER
4
19
7
YOU BASTARD.
WHY DID YOU HAVE TO DO IT?
WHY COULDN'T YOU JUST KEEP
YOUR MOUTH SHUT? BUT YOU'VE
FUCKING DONE IT NOW AND
THERE'S NO TURNING BACK.
IT'S IN ME AND YOU PUT IT THERE.
THE ANGER.
THE ACIDIC, SCORCHING, HEAD-
BANGING, SLEEP-DEPRIVING,
STOMACH-CHURNING, ALL-
CONSUMING ANGER.
AND I'VE GOT TO LET IT OUT.
RIGHT AT YOU.
I'VE GOT YOU IN MY SIGHTS.
I'M GONNA TAKE YOU DOWN
AND FUCKING LAY YOU OUT LIKE
NO ONE HAS EVER SEEN BEFORE.
YOU WILL NOT GET UP AFTER THIS.
YOU BASTARD.

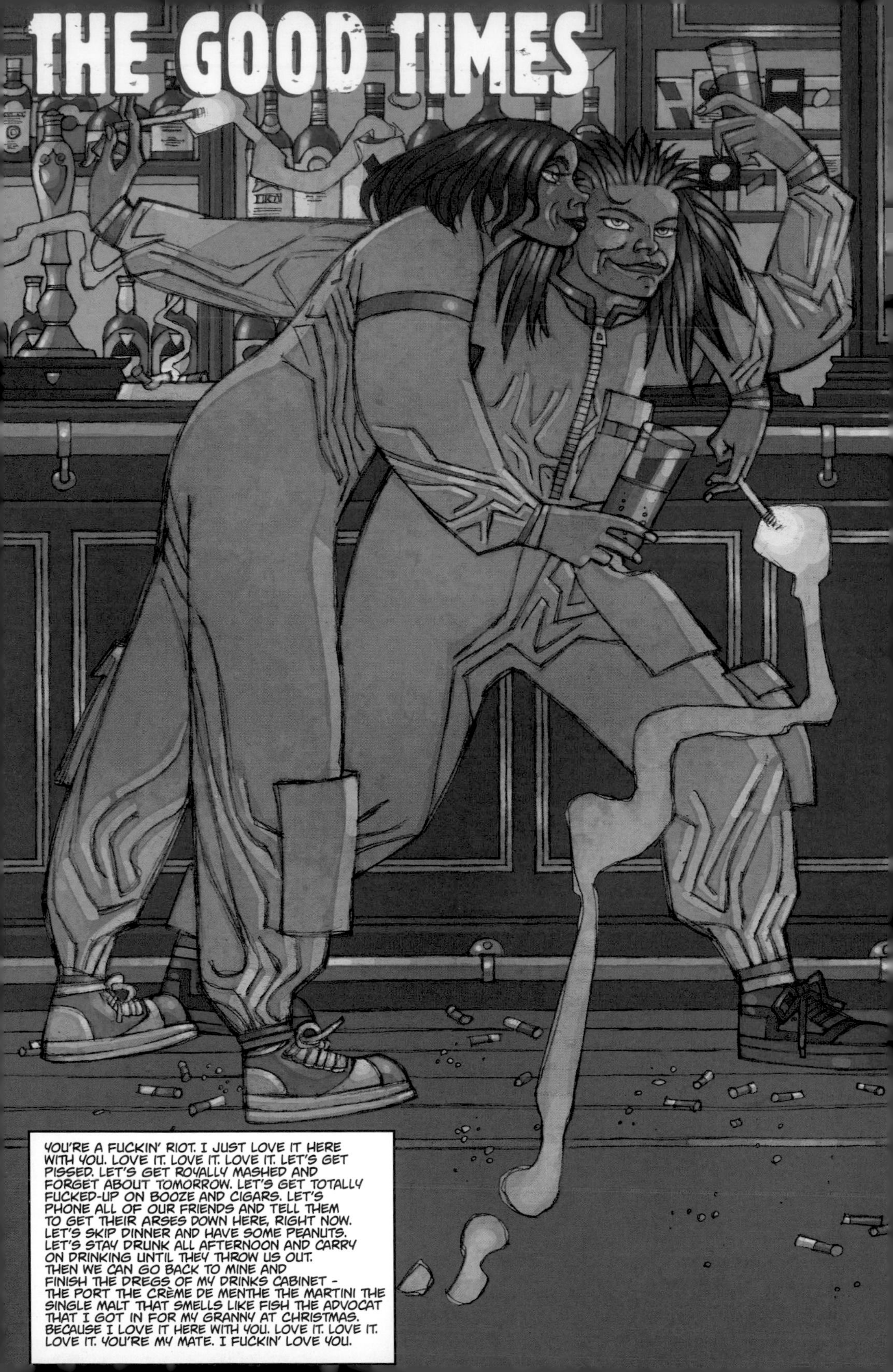
THE GOOD TIMES
YOU'RE A FUCKIN' RIOT. I JUST LOVE IT HERE WITH YOU. LOVE IT. LOVE IT. LOVE IT. LET'S GET PISSED. LET'S GET ROYALLY MASHED AND FORGET ABOUT TOMORROW. LET'S GET TOTALLY FUCKED-UP ON BOOZE AND CIGARS. LET'S PHONE ALL OF OUR FRIENDS AND TELL THEM TO GET THEIR ARSES DOWN HERE, RIGHT NOW. LET'S SKIP DINNER AND HAVE SOME PEANUTS. LET'S STAY DRUNK ALL AFTERNOON AND CARRY ON DRINKING UNTIL THEY THROW US OUT. THEN WE CAN GO BACK TO MINE AND FINISH THE DREGS OF MY DRINKS CABINET - THE PORT THE CRÈME DE MENTHE THE MARTINI THE SINGLE MALT THAT SMELLS LIKE FISH THE ADVOCAT THAT I GOT IN FOR MY GRANNY AT CHRISTMAS. BECAUSE I LOVE IT HERE WITH YOU. LOVE IT. LOVE IT. LOVE IT. YOU'RE MY MATE. I FUCKIN' LOVE YOU.

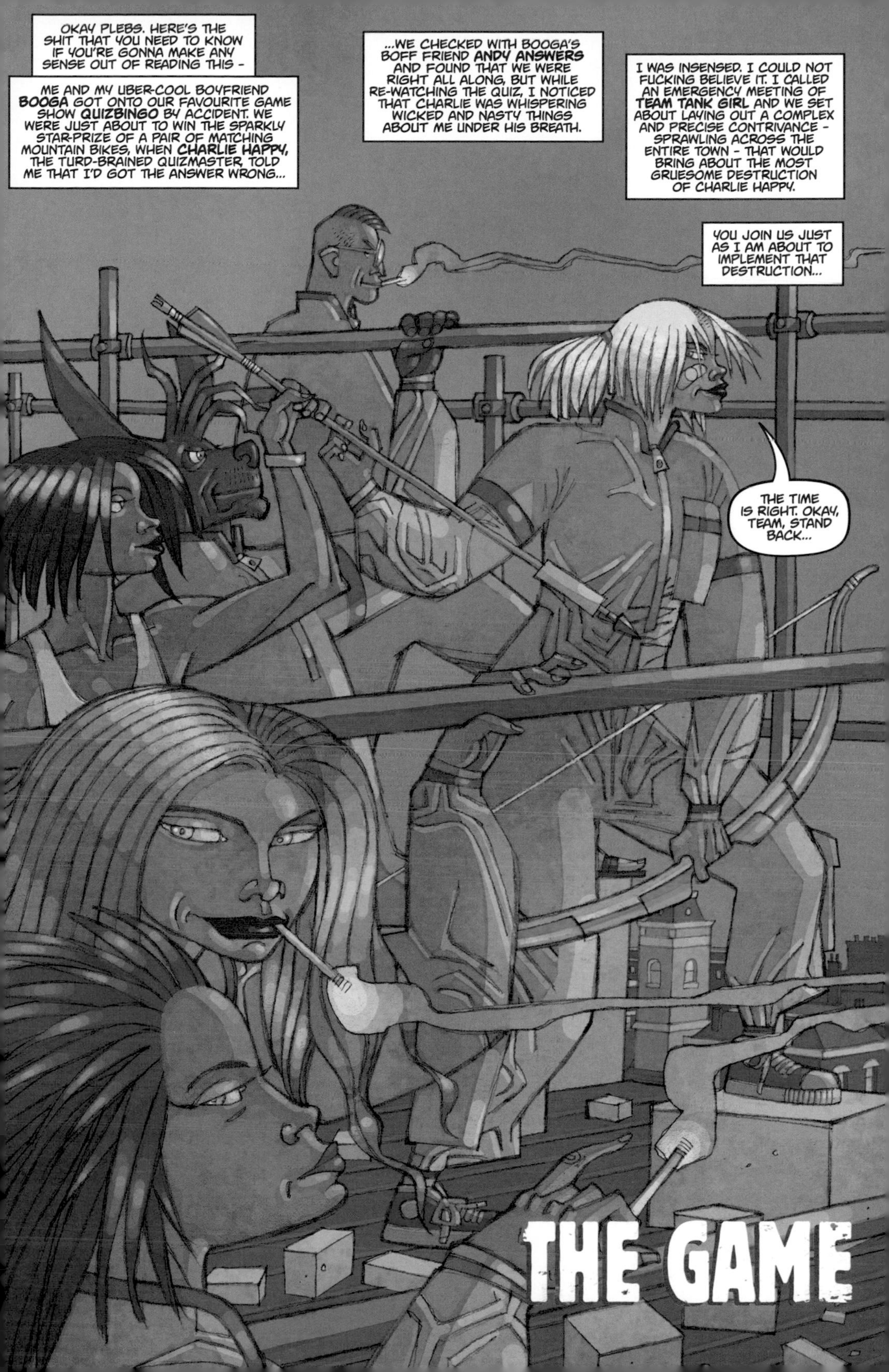
OKAY PLEBS. HERE'S THE SHIT THAT YOU NEED TO KNOW IF YOU'RE GONNA MAKE ANY SENSE OUT OF READING THIS -
ME AND MY UBER-COOL BOYFRIEND BOOGA GOT ONTO OUR FAVOURITE GAME SHOW QUIZBINGO BY ACCIDENT. WE WERE JUST ABOUT TO WIN THE SPARKLY STAR-PRIZE OF A PAIR OF MATCHING MOUNTAIN BIKES, WHEN CHARLIE HAPPY, THE TURD-BRAINED QUIZMASTER, TOLD ME THAT I'D GOT THE ANSWER WRONG...
...WE CHECKED WITH BOOGA'S BOFF FRIEND ANDY ANSWERS AND FOUND THAT WE WERE RIGHT ALL ALONG, BUT WHILE RE-WATCHING THE QUIZ, I NOTICED THAT CHARLIE WAS WHISPERING WICKED AND NASTY THINGS ABOUT ME UNDER HIS BREATH.
I WAS INSENSED. I COULD NOT FUCKING BELIEVE IT. I CALLED AN EMERGENCY MEETING OF TEAM TANK GIRL AND WE SET ABOUT LAYING OUT A COMPLEX AND PRECISE CONTRIVANCE - SPRAWLING ACROSS THE ENTIRE TOWN - THAT WOULD BRING ABOUT THE MOST GRUESOME DESTRUCTION OF CHARLIE HAPPY.
YOU JOIN US JUST AS I AM ABOUT TO IMPLEMENT THAT DESTRUCTION...
THE TIME IS RIGHT. OKAY, TEAM, STAND BACK...
THE GAME

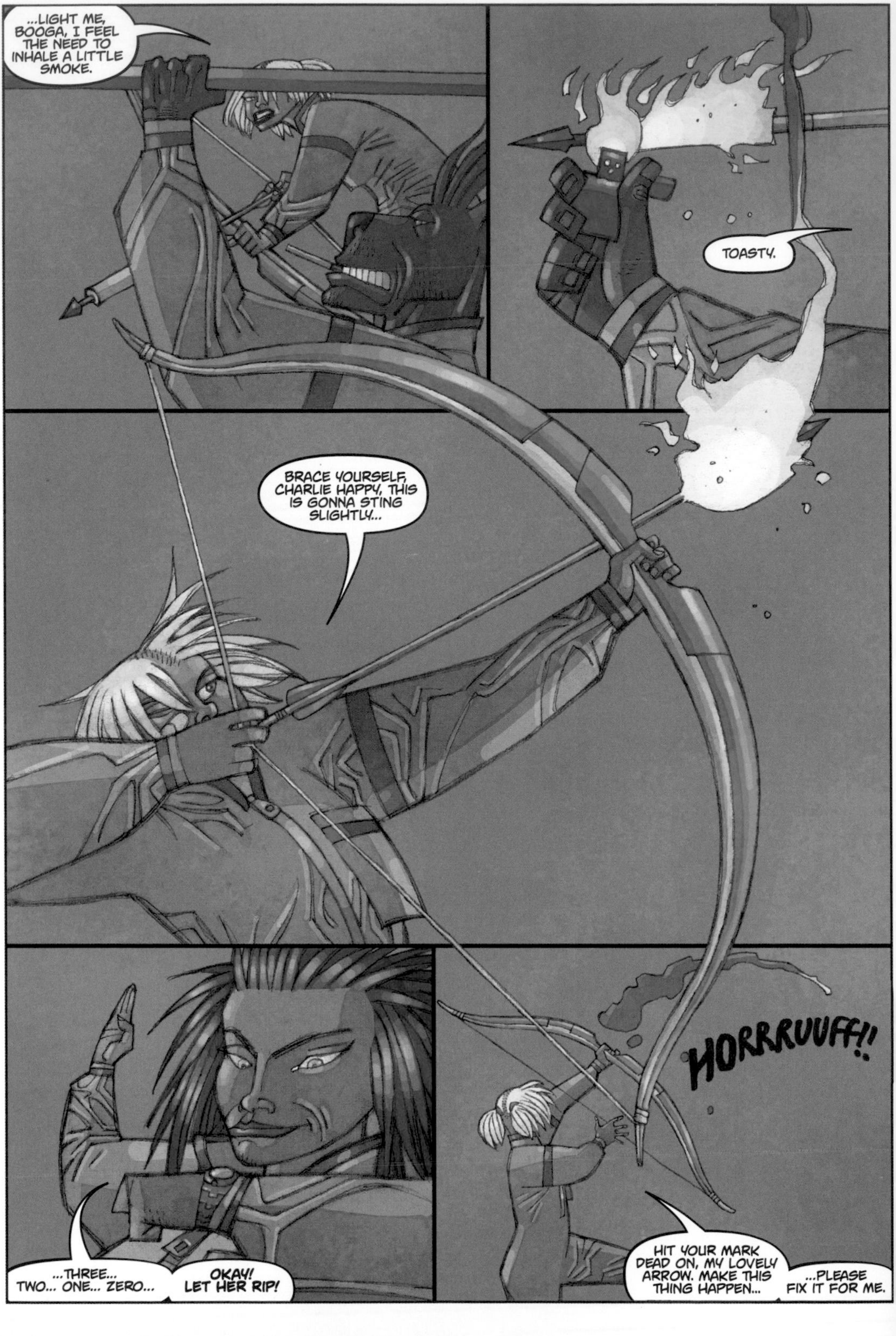
...LIGHT ME, BOOGA, I FEEL THE NEED TO INHALE A LITTLE SMOKE.
TOASTY.
BRACE YOURSELF, CHARLIE HAPPY, THIS IS GONNA STING SLIGHTLY...
...THREE... TWO... ONE... ZERO...
OKAY! LET HER RIP!
HORRRUUFF!!
HIT YOUR MARK DEAD ON, MY LOVELY ARROW. MAKE THIS THING HAPPEN...
...PLEASE FIX IT FOR ME.

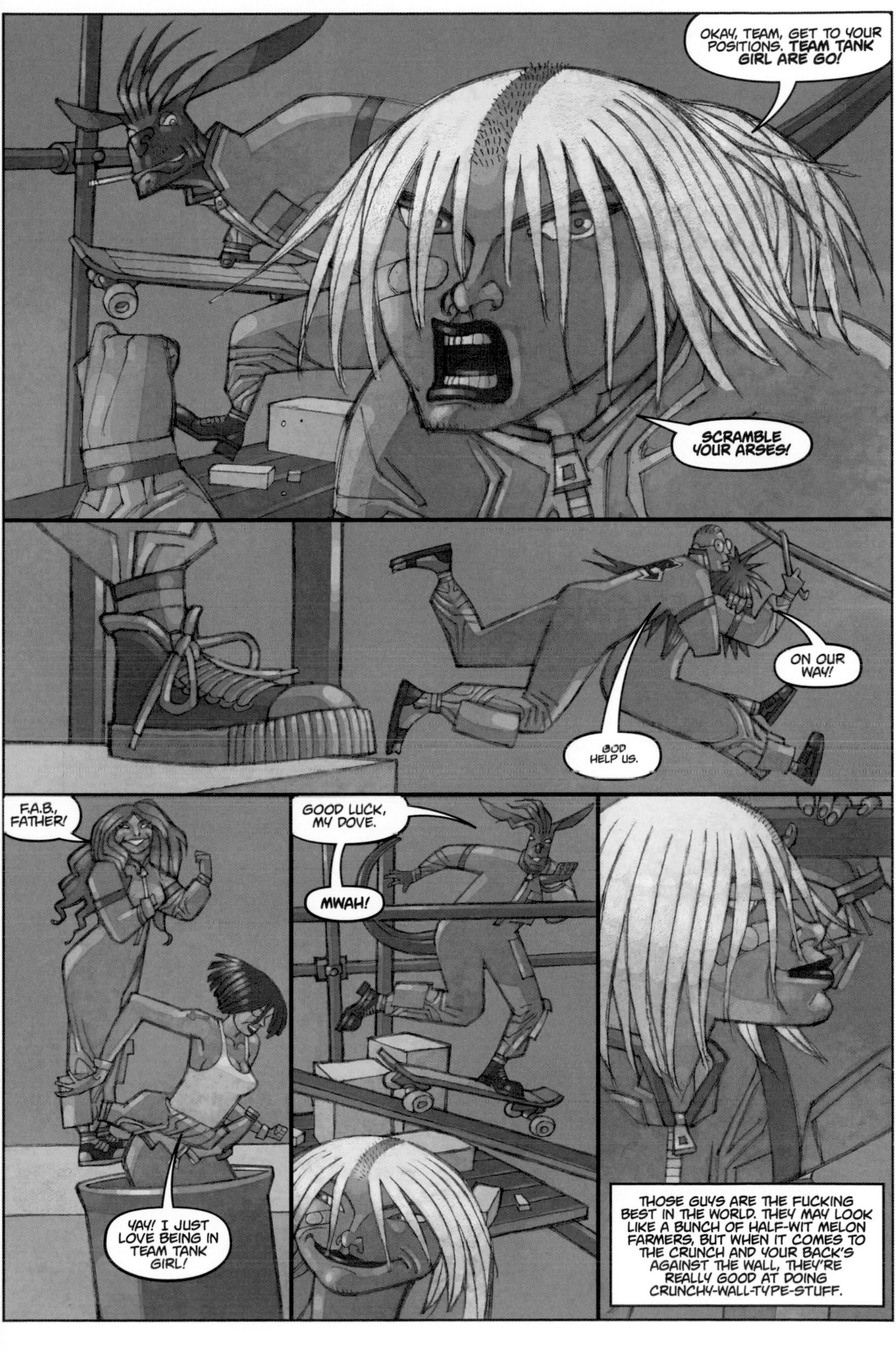
OKAY, TEAM, GET TO YOUR POSITIONS. TEAM TANK GIRL ARE GO!
SCRAMBLE YOUR ARSES!
ON OUR WAY!
GOD HELP US.
F.A.B., FATHER!
YAY! I JUST LOVE BEING IN TEAM TANK GIRL!
GOOD LUCK, MY DOVE.
MWAH!
THOSE GUYS ARE THE FUCKING BEST IN THE WORLD. THEY MAY LOOK LIKE A BUNCH OF HALF-WIT MELON FARMERS, BUT WHEN IT COMES TO THE CRUNCH AND YOUR BACK'S AGAINST THE WALL, THEY'RE REALLY GOOD AT DOING CRUNCHY-WALL-TYPE-STUFF.

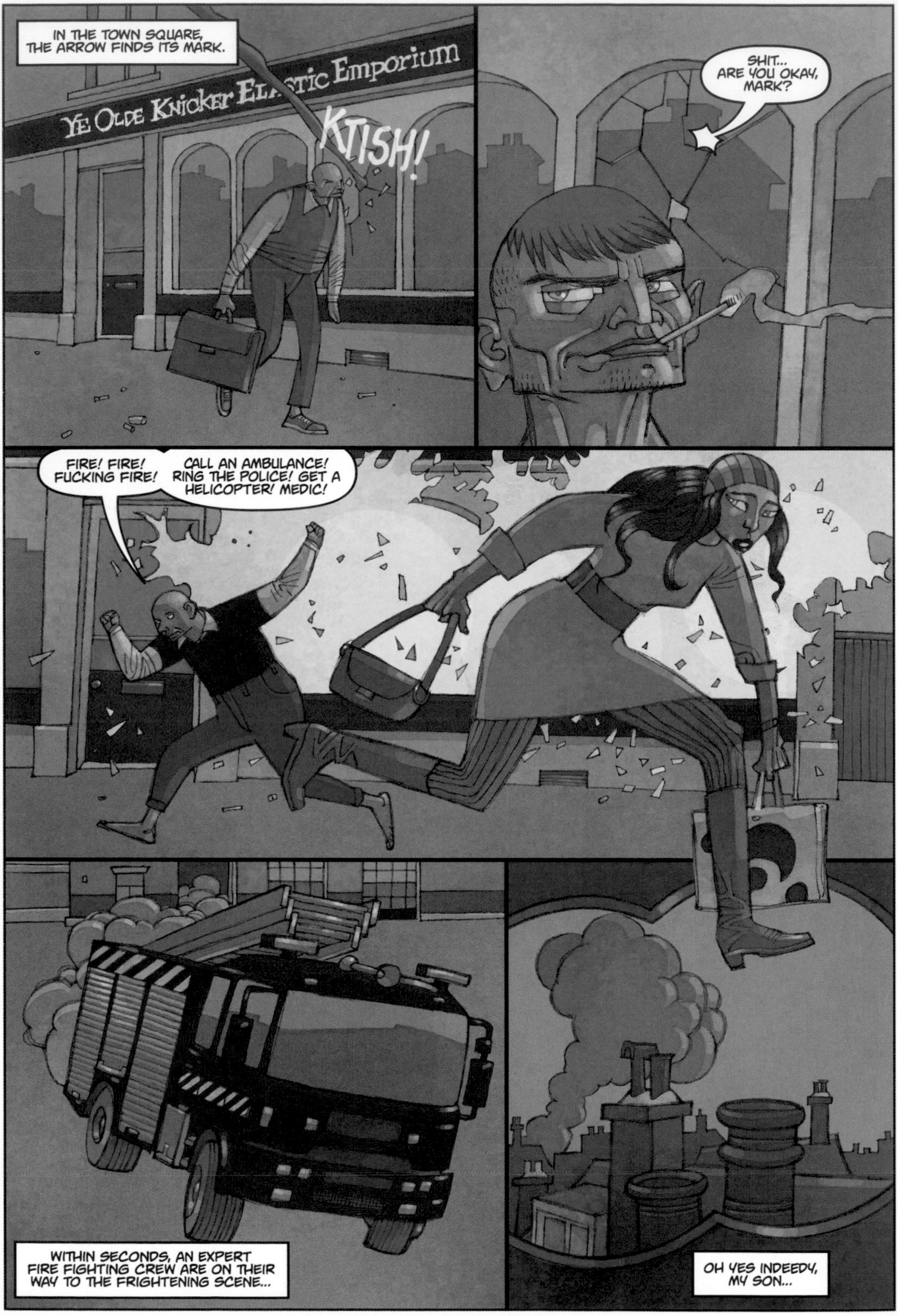
IN THE TOWN SQUARE, THE ARROW FINDS ITS MARK.
YE OLDE KNICKER ELASTIC EMPORIUM
KTISH!
SHIT... ARE YOU OKAY, MARK?
FIRE! FIRE! FUCKING FIRE!
CALL AN AMBULANCE! RING THE POLICE! GET A HELICOPTER! MEDIC!
WITHIN SECONDS, AN EXPERT FIRE FIGHTING CREW ARE ON THEIR WAY TO THE FRIGHTENING SCENE...
OH YES INDEEDY, MY SON...

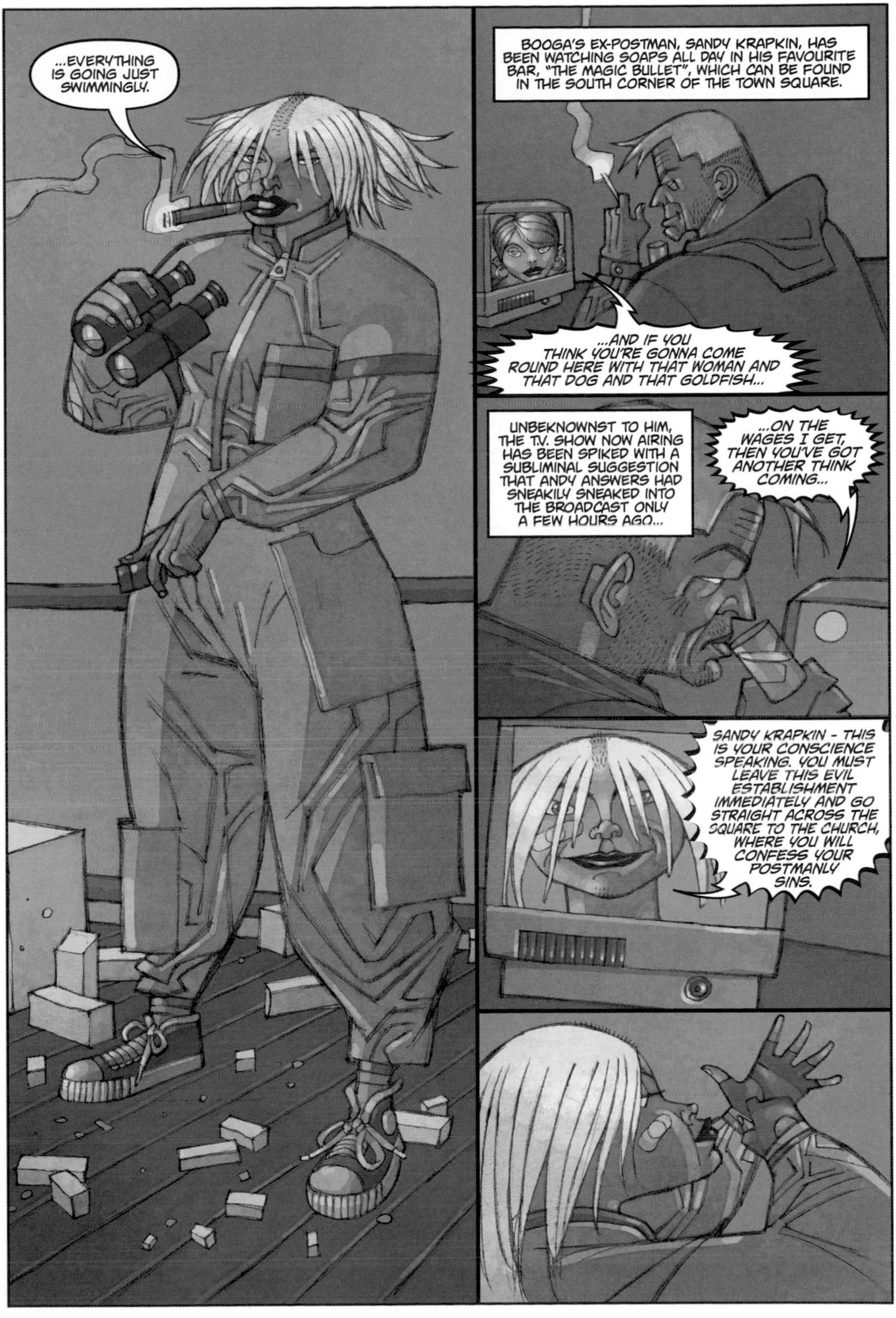
...EVERYTHING IS GOING JUST SWIMMINGLY.
BOOGA'S EX-POSTMAN, SANDY KRAPKIN, HAS BEEN WATCHING SOAPS ALL DAY IN HIS FAVOURITE BAR, "THE MAGIC BULLET", WHICH CAN BE FOUND IN THE SOUTH CORNER OF THE TOWN SQUARE.
...AND IF YOU THINK YOU'RE GONNA COME ROUND HERE WITH THAT WOMAN AND THAT DOG AND THAT GOLDFISH...
UNBEKNOWNST TO HIM, THE T.V. SHOW NOW AIRING HAS BEEN SPIKED WITH A SUBLIMINAL SUGGESTION THAT ANDY ANSWERS HAD SNEAKILY SNEAKED INTO THE BROADCAST ONLY A FEW HOURS AGO...
...ON THE WAGES I GET, THEN YOU'VE GOT ANOTHER THINK COMING...
SANDY KRAPKIN - THIS IS YOUR CONSCIENCE SPEAKING. YOU MUST LEAVE THIS EVIL ESTABLISHMENT IMMEDIATELY AND GO STRAIGHT ACROSS THE SQUARE TO THE CHURCH, WHERE YOU WILL CONFESS YOUR POSTMANLY SINS.

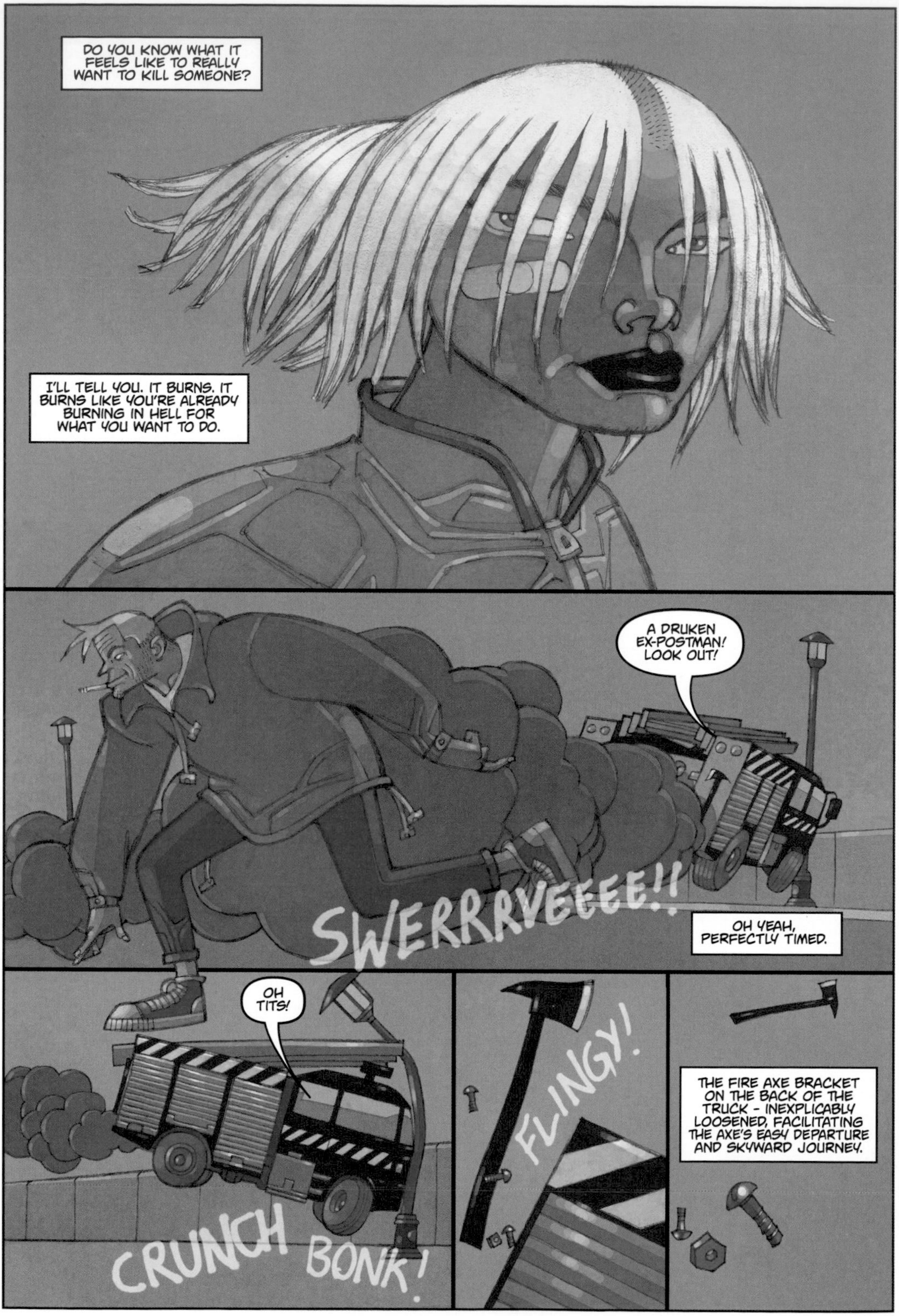
DO YOU KNOW WHAT IT FEELS LIKE TO REALLY WANT TO KILL SOMEONE?
I'LL TELL YOU. IT BURNS. IT BURNS LIKE YOU'RE ALREADY BURNING IN HELL FOR WHAT YOU WANT TO DO.
A DRUKEN EX-POSTMAN! LOOK OUT!
SWERRRVEEEE!!
OH YEAH, PERFECTLY TIMED.
OH TITS!
CRUNCH
BONK!
FLINGY!
THE FIRE AXE BRACKET ON THE BACK OF THE TRUCK - INEXPLICABLY LOOSENED, FACILITATING THE AXE'S EASY DEPARTURE AND SKYWARD JOURNEY.

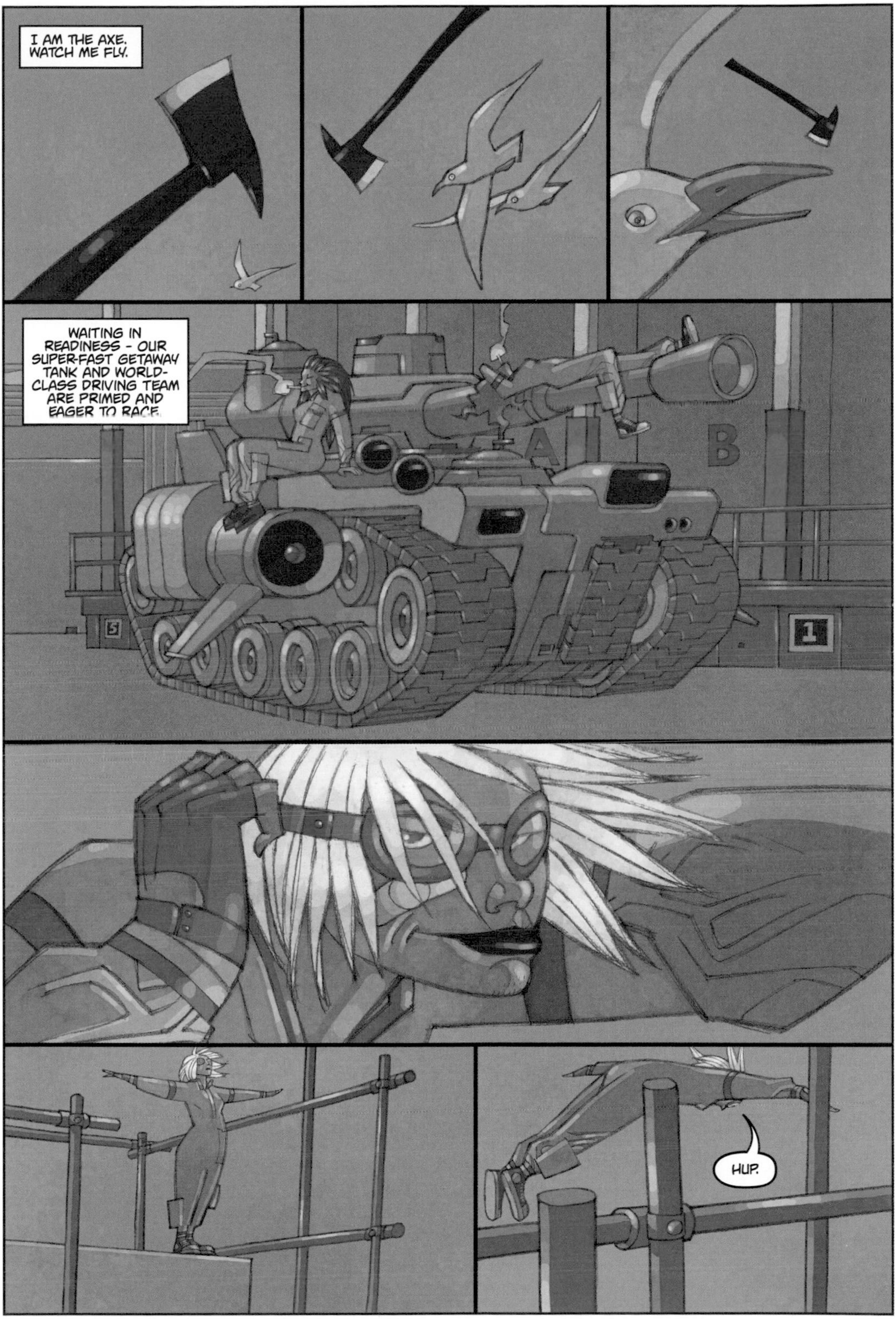
I AM THE AXE. WATCH ME FLY.
WAITING IN READINESS - OUR SUPER-FAST GETAWAY TANK AND WORLD-CLASS DRIVING TEAM ARE PRIMED AND EAGER TO RACE.
A
B
5
1
HUP.

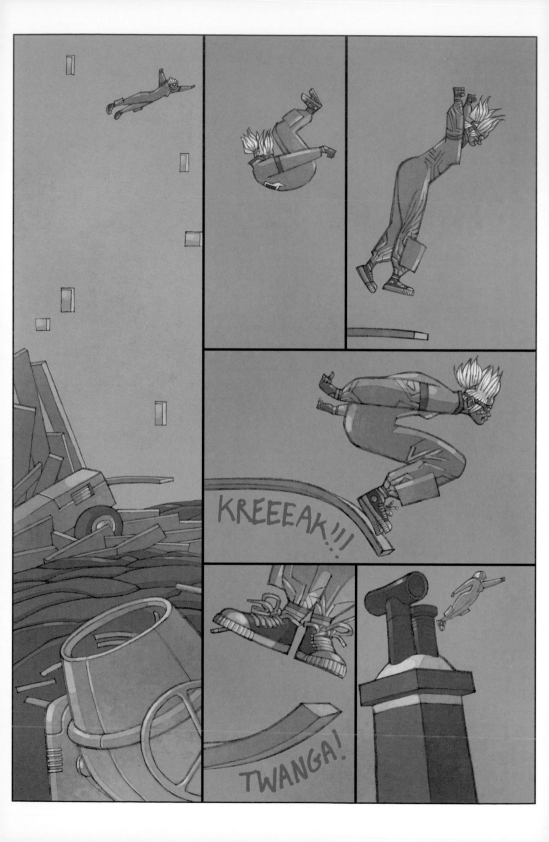

KREEEAK!!!

TWANGA!

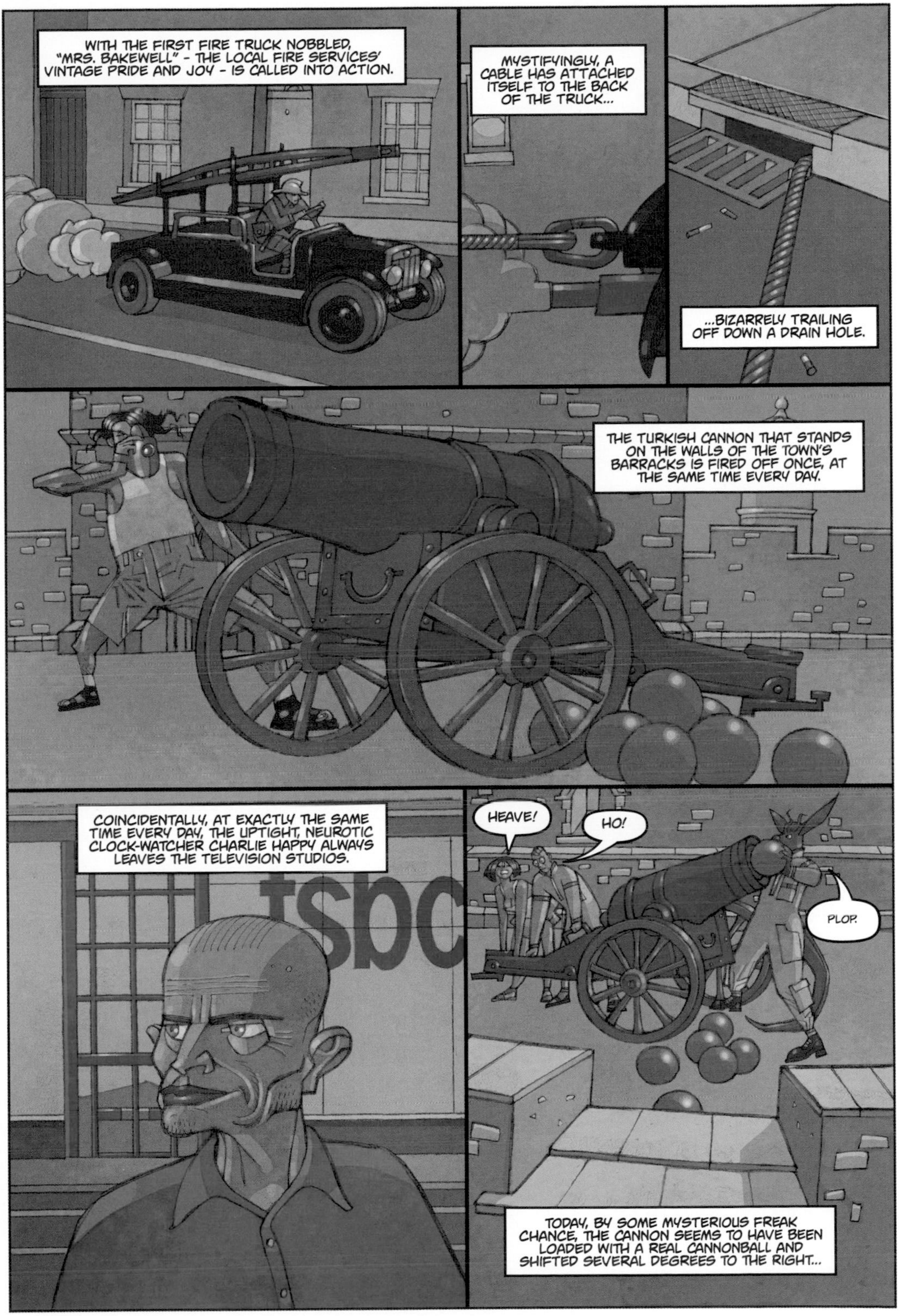

WITH THE FIRST FIRE TRUCK NOBBLED, "MRS. BAKEWELL" - THE LOCAL FIRE SERVICES' VINTAGE PRIDE AND JOY - IS CALLED INTO ACTION.
MYSTIFYINGLY, A CABLE HAS ATTACHED ITSELF TO THE BACK OF THE TRUCK...
...BIZARRELY TRAILING OFF DOWN A DRAIN HOLE.
THE TURKISH CANNON THAT STANDS ON THE WALLS OF THE TOWN'S BARRACKS IS FIRED OFF ONCE, AT THE SAME TIME EVERY DAY.
COINCIDENTALLY, AT EXACTLY THE SAME TIME EVERY DAY, THE UPTIGHT, NEUROTIC CLOCK-WATCHER CHARLIE HAPPY ALWAYS LEAVES THE TELEVISION STUDIOS.
tsbc
HEAVE!
HO!
PLOP.
TODAY, BY SOME MYSTERIOUS FREAK CHANCE, THE CANNON SEEMS TO HAVE BEEN LOADED WITH A REAL CANNONBALL AND SHIFTED SEVERAL DEGREES TO THE RIGHT...

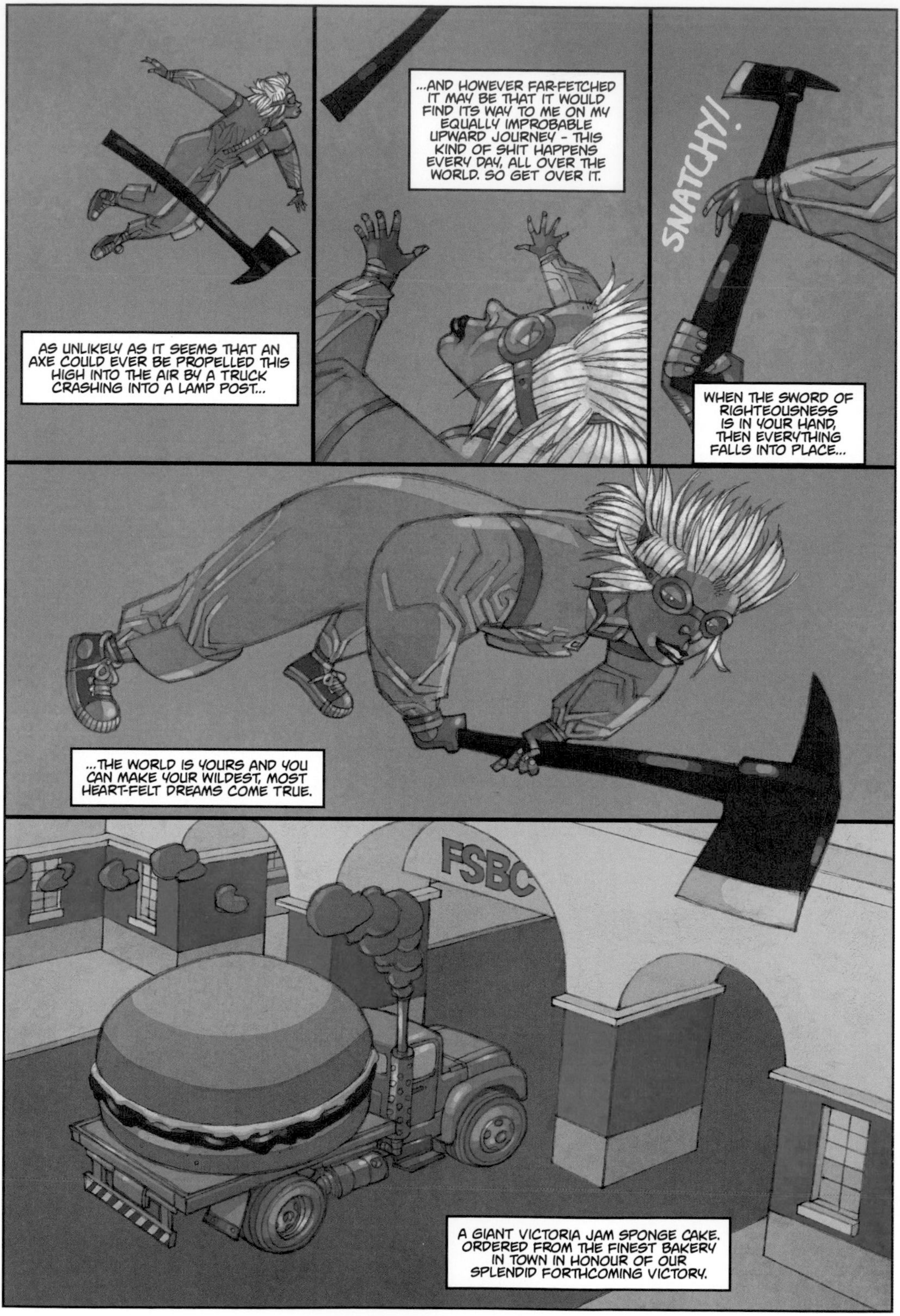

AS UNLIKELY AS IT SEEMS THAT AN AXE COULD EVER BE PROPELLED THIS HIGH INTO THE AIR BY A TRUCK CRASHING INTO A LAMP POST...
...AND HOWEVER FAR-FETCHED IT MAY BE THAT IT WOULD FIND ITS WAY TO ME ON MY EQUALLY IMPROBABLE UPWARD JOURNEY - THIS KIND OF SHIT HAPPENS EVERY DAY, ALL OVER THE WORLD. SO GET OVER IT.
SNATCHY!
WHEN THE SWORD OF RIGHTEOUSNESS IS IN YOUR HAND, THEN EVERYTHING FALLS INTO PLACE...
...THE WORLD IS YOURS AND YOU CAN MAKE YOUR WILDEST, MOST HEART-FELT DREAMS COME TRUE.
FSBC
A GIANT VICTORIA JAM SPONGE CAKE. ORDERED FROM THE FINEST BAKERY IN TOWN IN HONOUR OF OUR SPLENDID FORTHCOMING VICTORY.

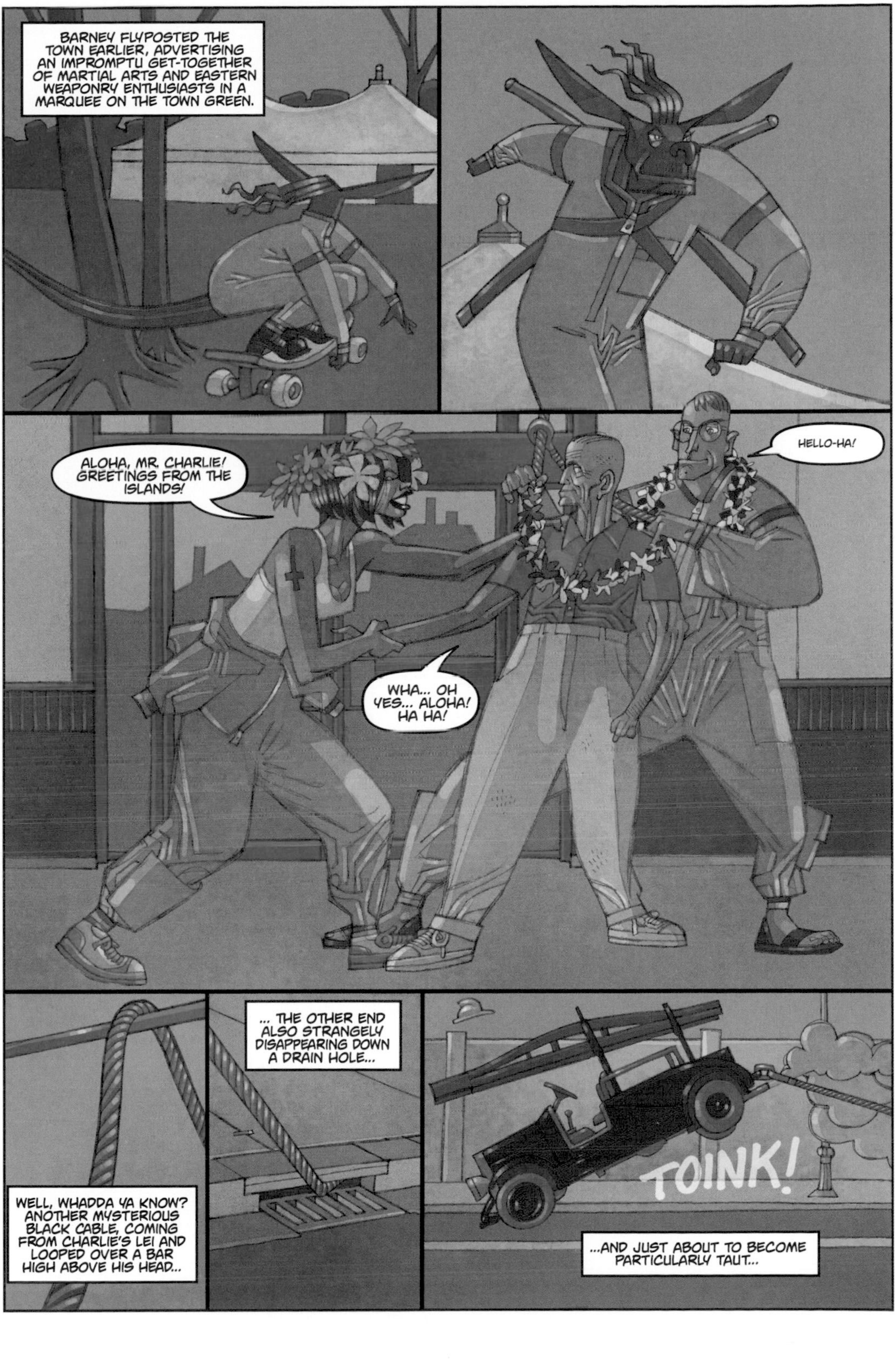
BARNEY FLYPOSTED THE TOWN EARLIER, ADVERTISING AN IMPROMPTU GET-TOGETHER OF MARTIAL ARTS AND EASTERN WEAPONRY ENTHUSIASTS IN A MARQUEE ON THE TOWN GREEN.
ALOHA, MR. CHARLIE! GREETINGS FROM THE ISLANDS!
HELLO-HA!
WHA... OH YES... ALOHA! HA HA!
WELL, WHADDA YA KNOW? ANOTHER MYSTERIOUS BLACK CABLE, COMING FROM CHARLIE'S LEI AND LOOPED OVER A BAR HIGH ABOVE HIS HEAD...
... THE OTHER END ALSO STRANGELY DISAPPEARING DOWN A DRAIN HOLE...
TOINK!
...AND JUST ABOUT TO BECOME PARTICULARLY TAUT...

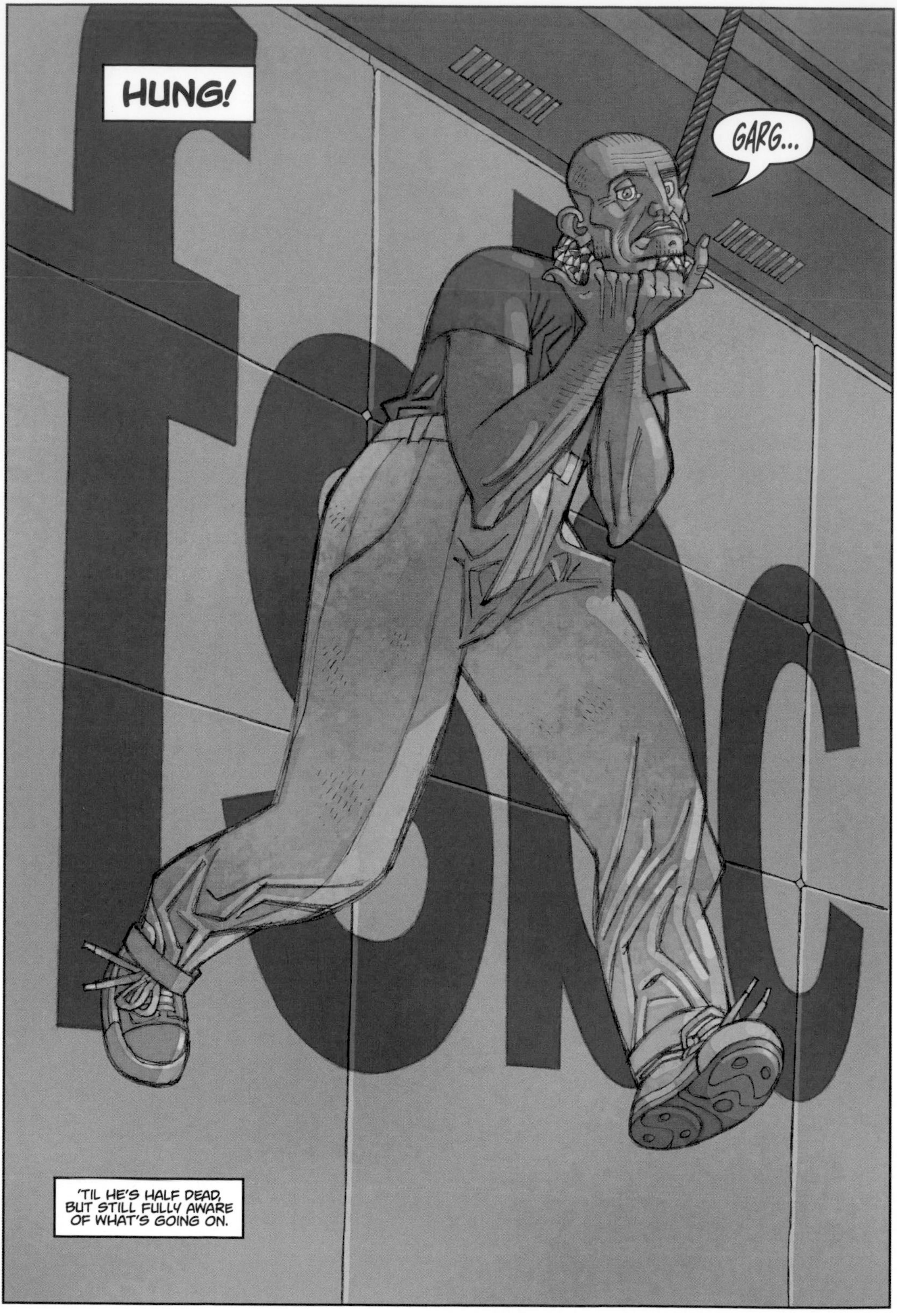
HUNG!
GARG...
'TIL HE'S HALF DEAD, BUT STILL FULLY AWARE OF WHAT'S GOING ON.

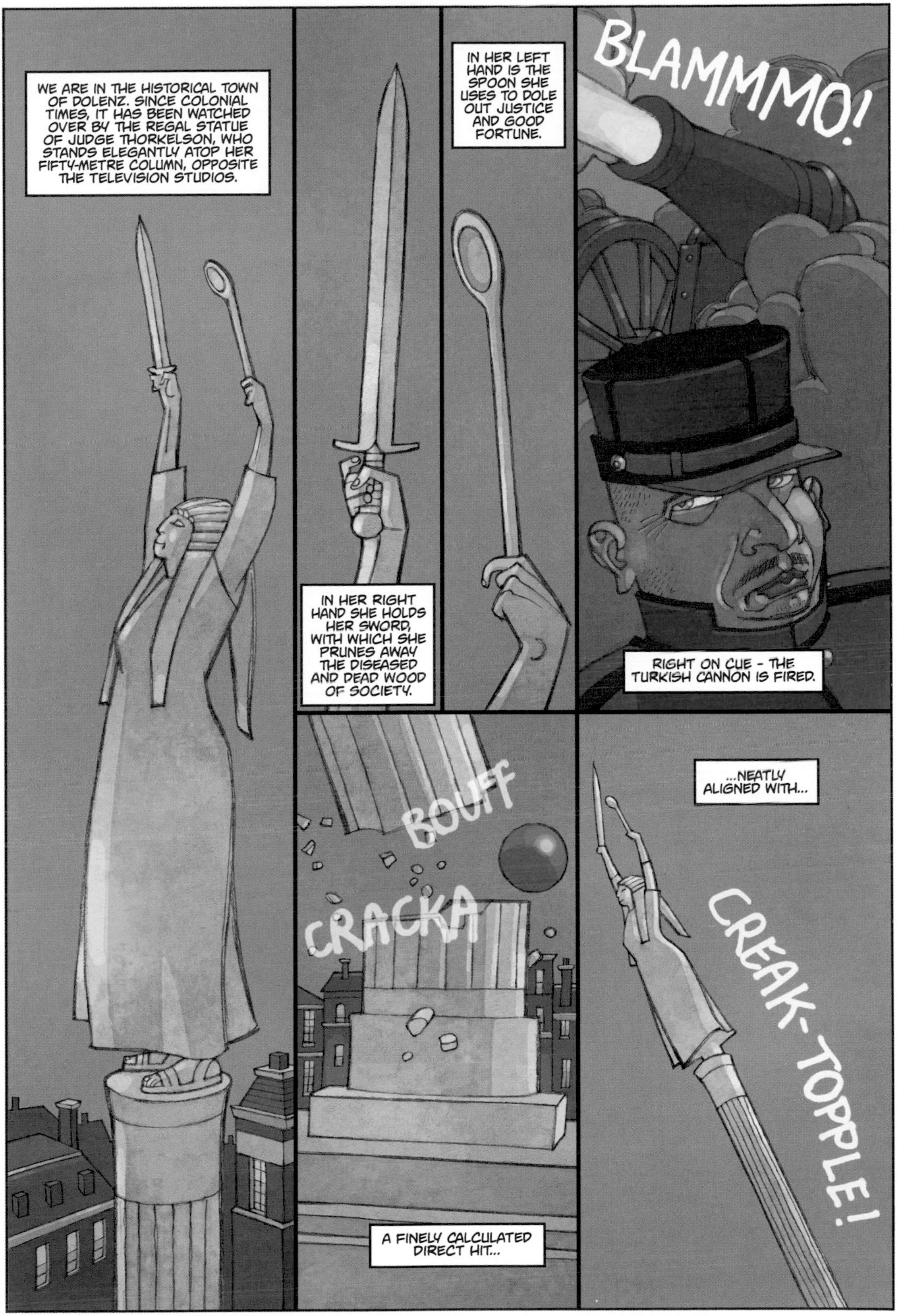
WE ARE IN THE HISTORICAL TOWN OF DOLENZ. SINCE COLONIAL TIMES, IT HAS BEEN WATCHED OVER BY THE REGAL STATUE OF JUDGE THORKELSON, WHO STANDS ELEGANTLY ATOP HER FIFTY-METRE COLUMN, OPPOSITE THE TELEVISION STUDIOS.
IN HER RIGHT HAND SHE HOLDS HER SWORD, WITH WHICH SHE PRUNES AWAY THE DISEASED AND DEAD WOOD OF SOCIETY.
IN HER LEFT HAND IS THE SPOON SHE USES TO DOLE OUT JUSTICE AND GOOD FORTUNE.
BLAMMMO!
RIGHT ON CUE - THE TURKISH CANNON IS FIRED.
BOUFF
CRACKA
A FINELY CALCULATED DIRECT HIT...
...NEATLY ALIGNED WITH...
CREAK-TOPPLE!

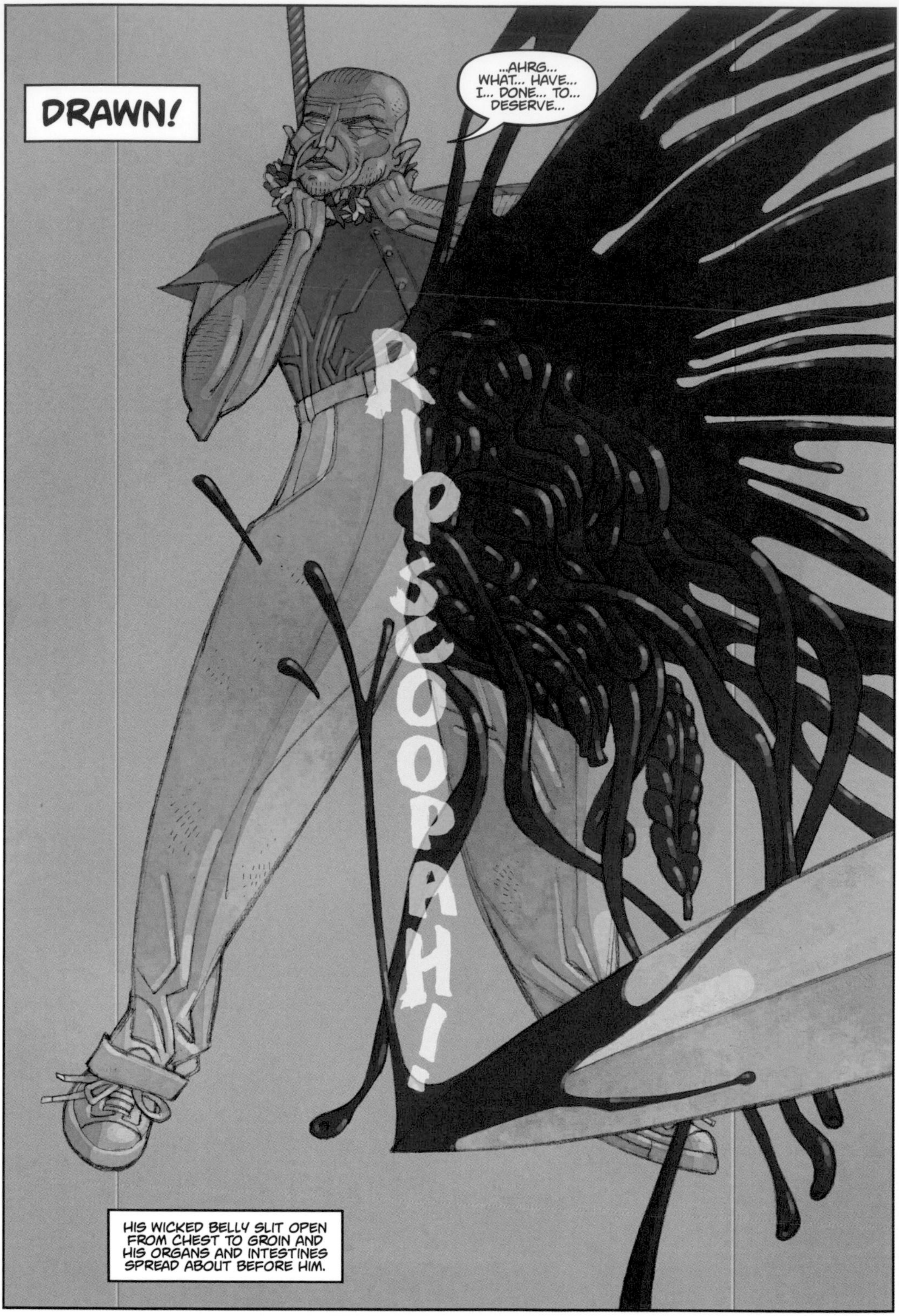
DRAWN!
...AHRG... WHAT... HAVE... I... DONE... TO... DESERVE...
RIPSCOOPAH!
HIS WICKED BELLY SLIT OPEN FROM CHEST TO GROIN AND HIS ORGANS AND INTESTINES SPREAD ABOUT BEFORE HIM.

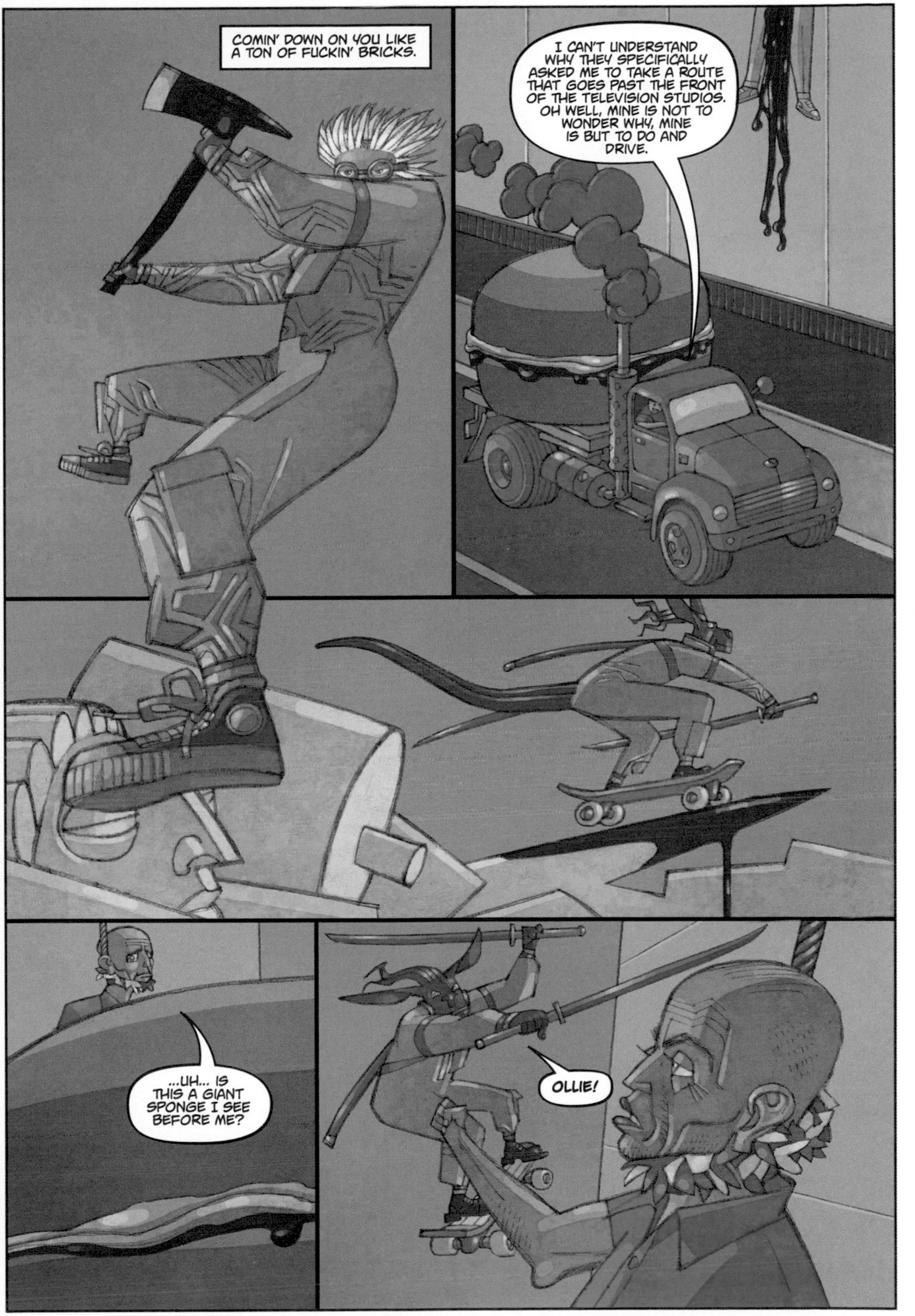
COMIN' DOWN ON YOU LIKE A TON OF FUCKIN' BRICKS.
I CAN'T UNDERSTAND WHY THEY SPECIFICALLY ASKED ME TO TAKE A ROUTE THAT GOES PAST THE FRONT OF THE TELEVISION STUDIOS. OH WELL, MINE IS NOT TO WONDER WHY, MINE IS BUT TO DO AND DRIVE.
...UH... IS THIS A GIANT SPONGE I SEE BEFORE ME?
OLLIE!

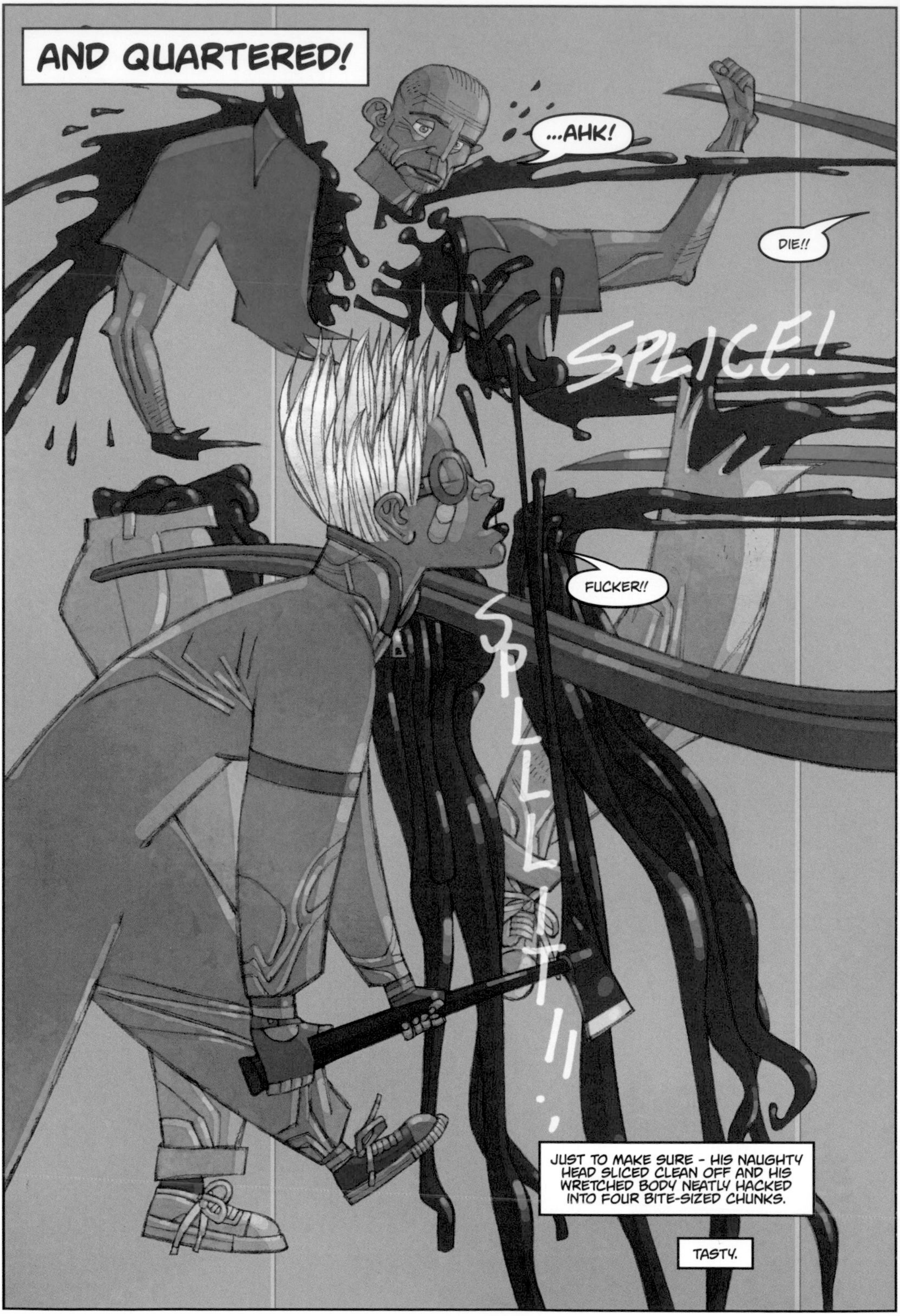
AND QUARTERED!
...AHK!
DIE!!
SPLICE!
FUCKER!!
SPLLLIT!!
JUST TO MAKE SURE - HIS NAUGHTY HEAD SLICED CLEAN OFF AND HIS WRETCHED BODY NEATLY HACKED INTO FOUR BITE-SIZED CHUNKS.
TASTY.

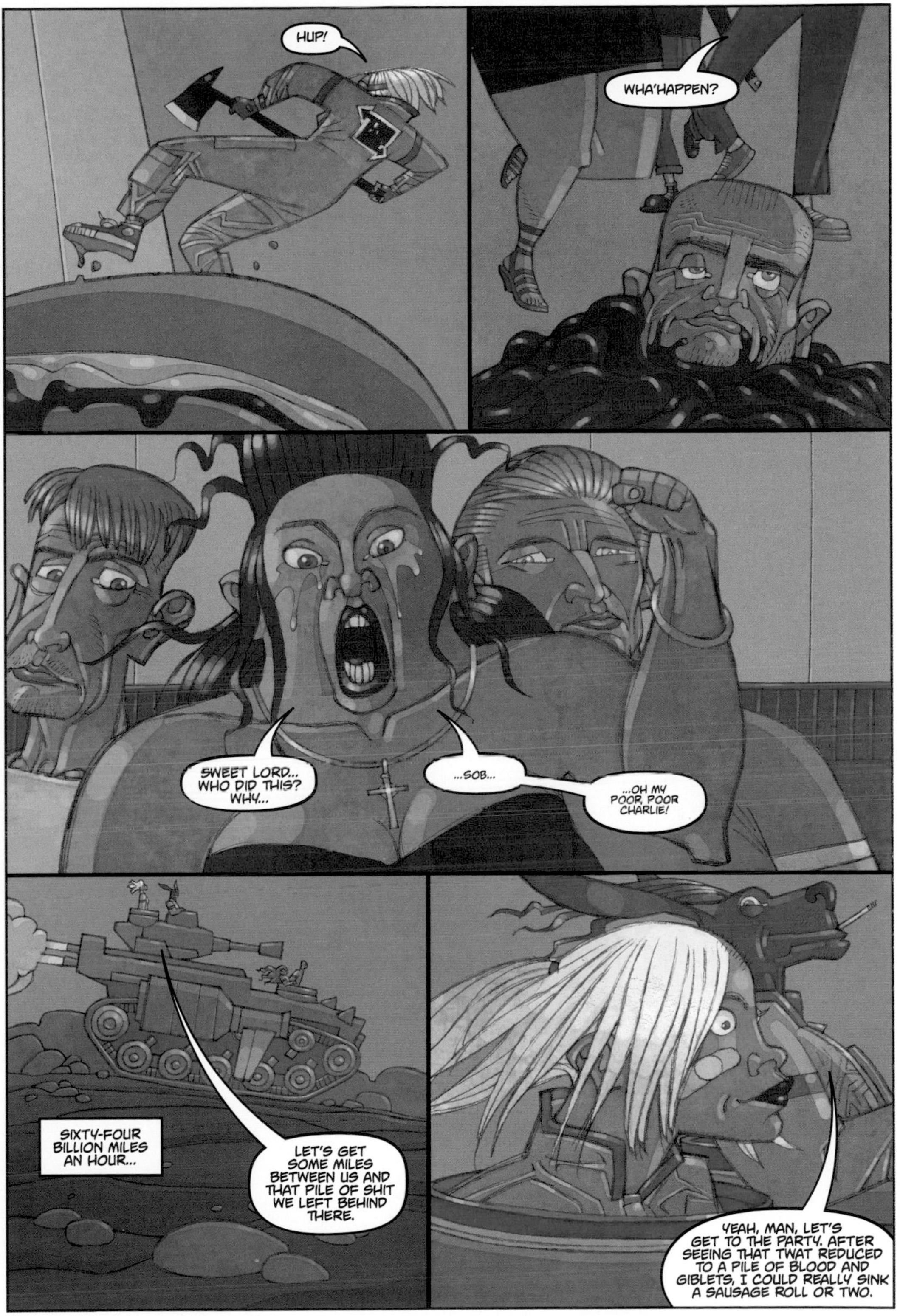
HUP!
WHA'HAPPEN?
SWEET LORD... WHO DID THIS? WHY...
...SOB...
...OH MY POOR, POOR CHARLIE!
SIXTY-FOUR BILLION MILES AN HOUR...
LET'S GET SOME MILES BETWEEN US AND THAT PILE OF SHIT WE LEFT BEHIND THERE.
YEAH, MAN, LET'S GET TO THE PARTY. AFTER SEEING THAT TWAT REDUCED TO A PILE OF BLOOD AND GIBLETS, I COULD REALLY SINK A SAUSAGE ROLL OR TWO.

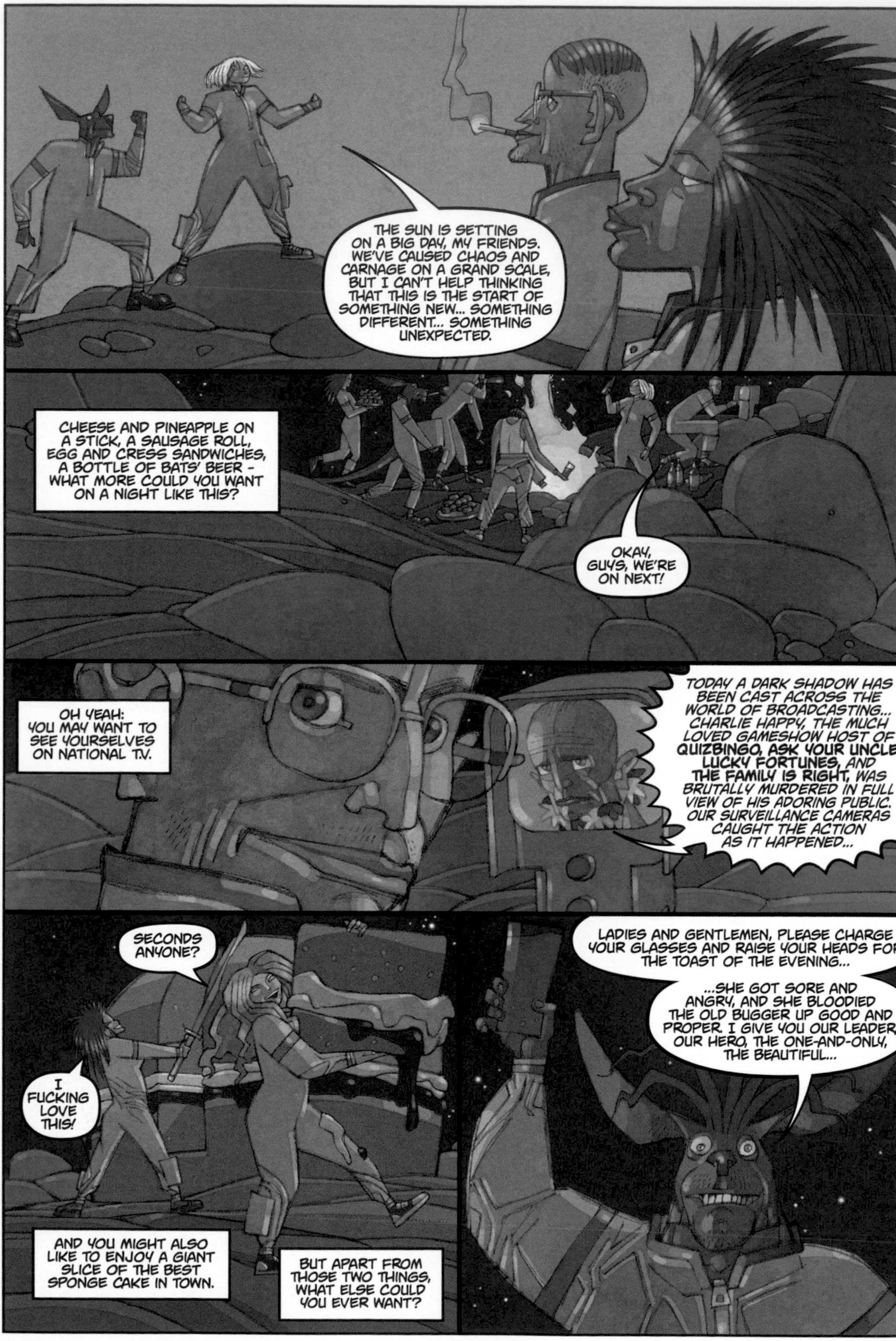
THE SUN IS SETTING ON A BIG DAY, MY FRIENDS. WE'VE CAUSED CHAOS AND CARNAGE ON A GRAND SCALE, BUT I CAN'T HELP THINKING THAT THIS IS THE START OF SOMETHING NEW... SOMETHING DIFFERENT... SOMETHING UNEXPECTED.
CHEESE AND PINEAPPLE ON A STICK, A SAUSAGE ROLL, EGG AND CRESS SANDWICHES, A BOTTLE OF BATS' BEER - WHAT MORE COULD YOU WANT ON A NIGHT LIKE THIS?
OKAY, GUYS, WE'RE ON NEXT!
OH YEAH: YOU MAY WANT TO SEE YOURSELVES ON NATIONAL T.V.
TODAY A DARK SHADOW HAS BEEN CAST ACROSS THE WORLD OF BROADCASTING... CHARLIE HAPPY, THE MUCH LOVED GAMESHOW HOST OF **QUIZBINGO, ASK YOUR UNCLE, LUCKY FORTUNES,** AND **THE FAMILY IS RIGHT,** WAS BRUTALLY MURDERED IN FULL VIEW OF HIS ADORING PUBLIC. OUR SURVEILLANCE CAMERAS CAUGHT THE ACTION AS IT HAPPENED...
SECONDS ANYONE?
I FUCKING LOVE THIS!
AND YOU MIGHT ALSO LIKE TO ENJOY A GIANT SLICE OF THE BEST SPONGE CAKE IN TOWN.
BUT APART FROM THOSE TWO THINGS, WHAT ELSE COULD YOU EVER WANT?
LADIES AND GENTLEMEN, PLEASE CHARGE YOUR GLASSES AND RAISE YOUR HEADS FOR THE TOAST OF THE EVENING...
...SHE GOT SORE AND ANGRY, AND SHE BLOODIED THE OLD BUGGER UP GOOD AND PROPER. I GIVE YOU OUR LEADER, OUR HERO, THE ONE-AND-ONLY, THE BEAUTIFUL...

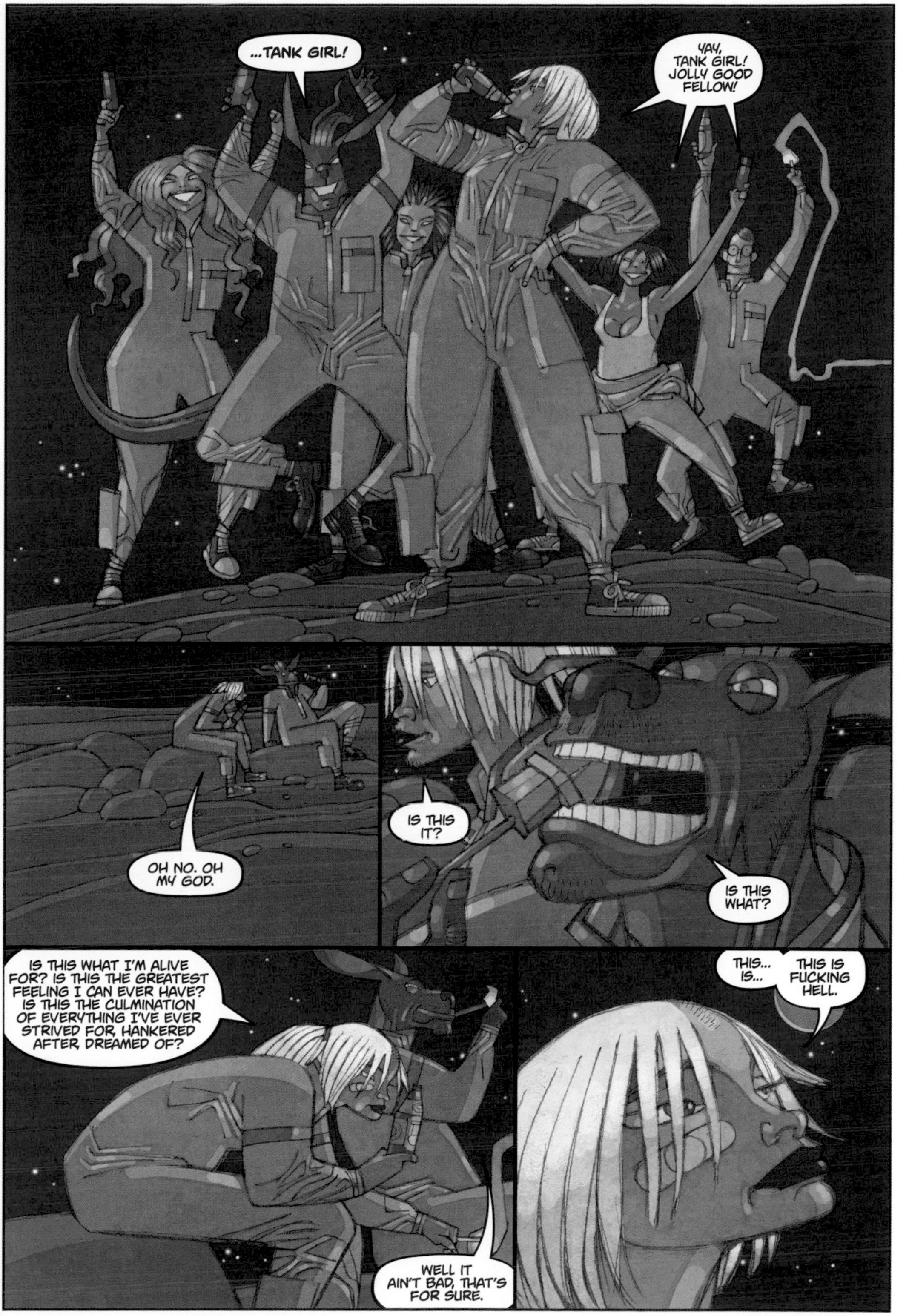
...TANK GIRL!
YAY, TANK GIRL! JOLLY GOOD FELLOW!
OH NO. OH MY GOD.
IS THIS IT?
IS THIS WHAT?
IS THIS WHAT I'M ALIVE FOR? IS THIS THE GREATEST FEELING I CAN EVER HAVE? IS THIS THE CULMINATION OF EVERYTHING I'VE EVER STRIVED FOR, HANKERED AFTER, DREAMED OF?
WELL IT AIN'T BAD, THAT'S FOR SURE.
THIS... IS...
THIS IS FUCKING HELL.

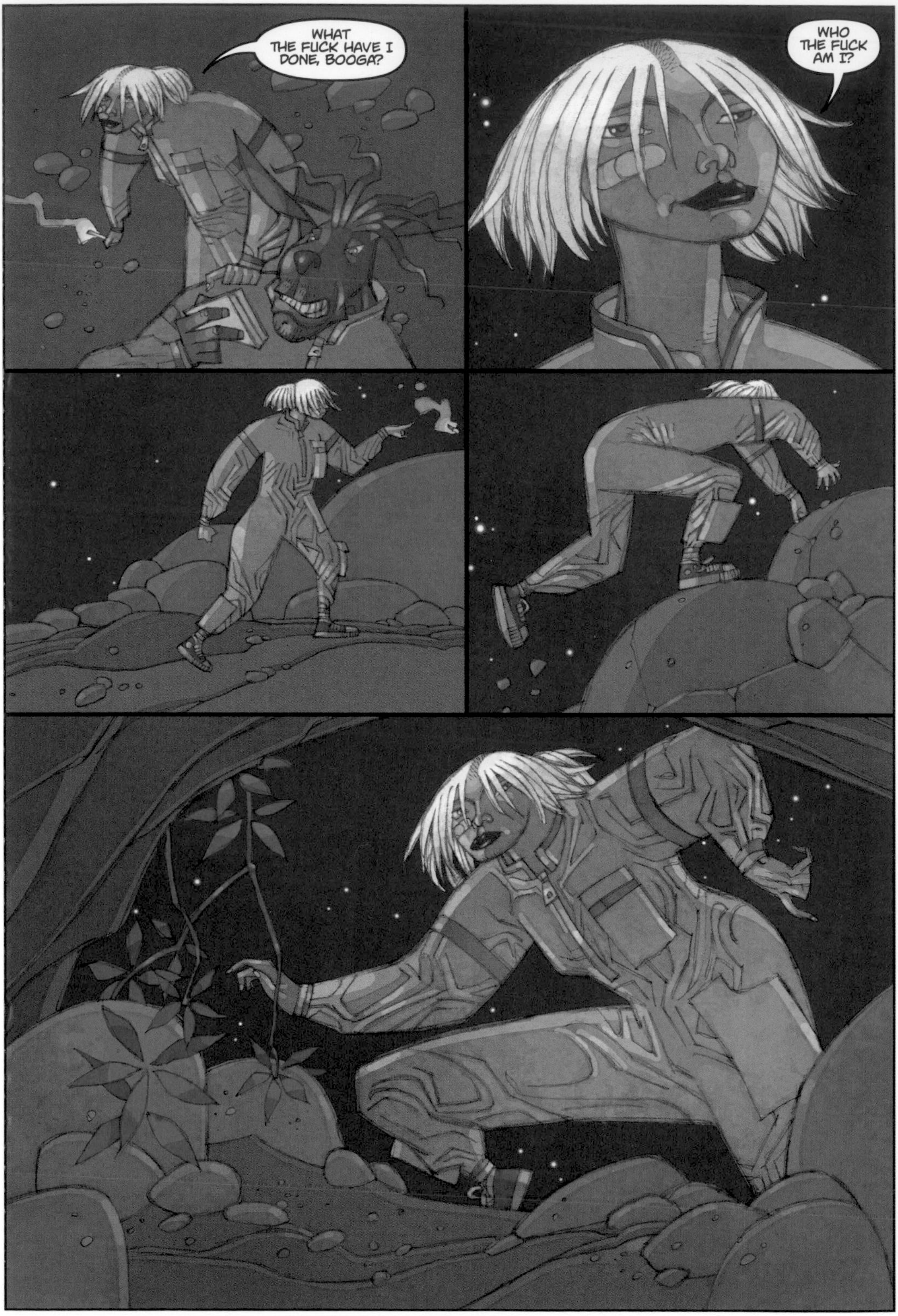
WHAT THE FUCK HAVE I DONE, BOOGA?
WHO THE FUCK AM I?

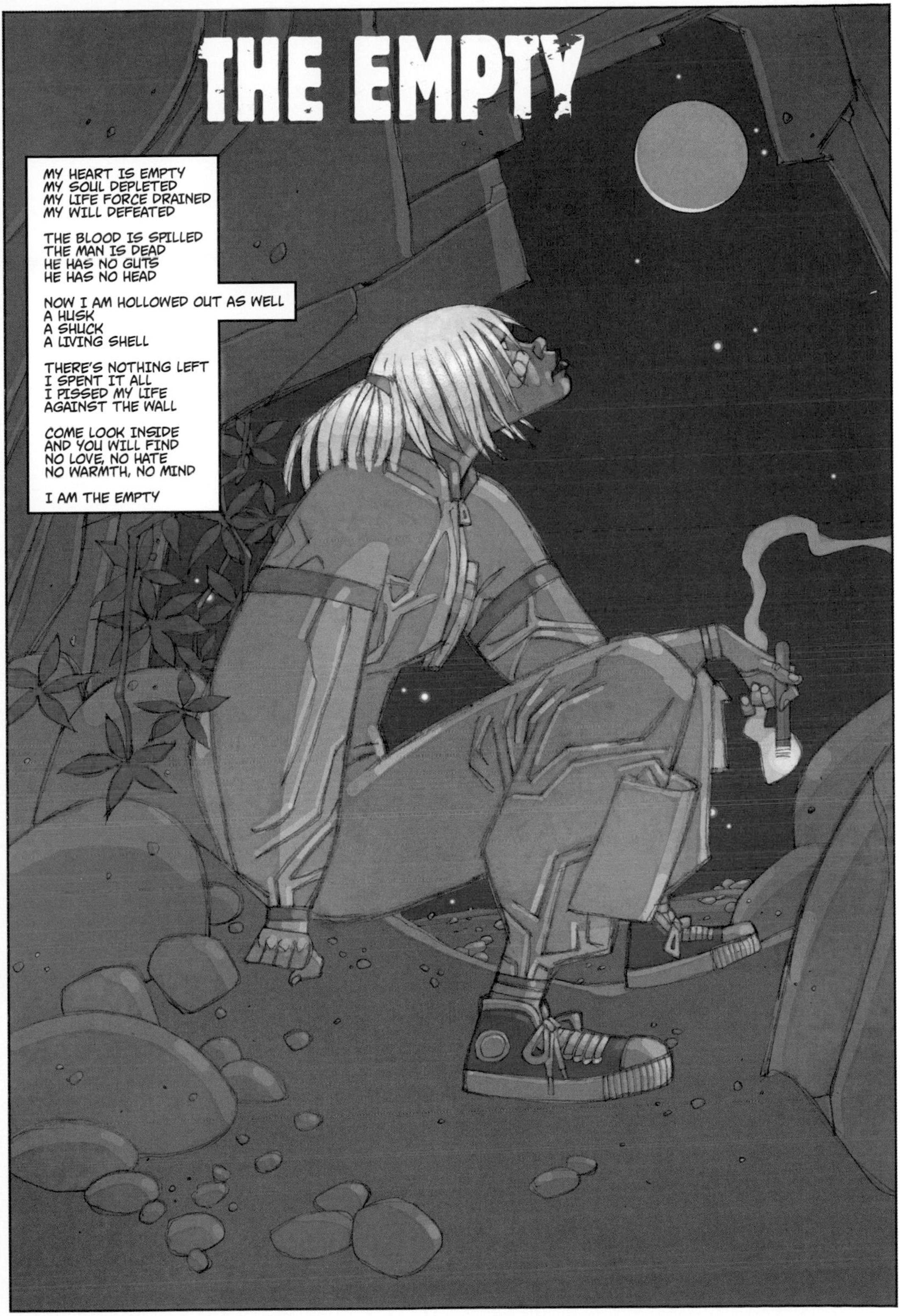
THE EMPTY
MY HEART IS EMPTY
MY SOUL DEPLETED
MY LIFE FORCE DRAINED
MY WILL DEFEATED
THE BLOOD IS SPILLED
THE MAN IS DEAD
HE HAS NO GUTS
HE HAS NO HEAD
NOW I AM HOLLOWED OUT AS WELL
A HUSK
A SHUCK
A LIVING SHELL
THERE'S NOTHING LEFT
I SPENT IT ALL
I PISSED MY LIFE
AGAINST THE WALL
COME LOOK INSIDE
AND YOU WILL FIND
NO LOVE, NO HATE
NO WARMTH, NO MIND
I AM THE EMPTY

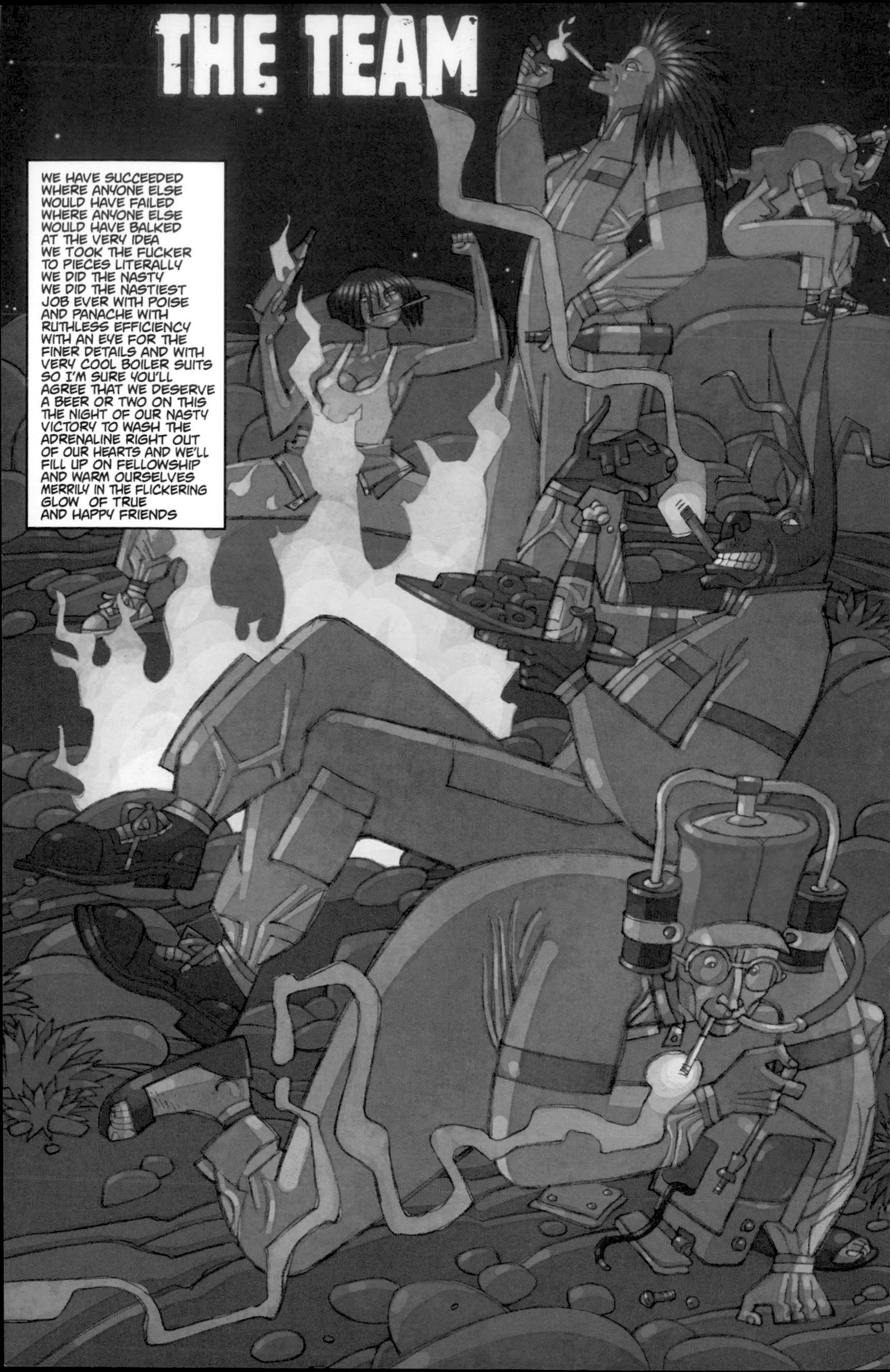
THE TEAM
WE HAVE SUCCEEDED WHERE ANYONE ELSE WOULD HAVE FAILED WHERE ANYONE ELSE WOULD HAVE BALKED AT THE VERY IDEA WE TOOK THE FUCKER TO PIECES LITERALLY WE DID THE NASTY WE DID THE NASTIEST JOB EVER WITH POISE AND PANACHE WITH RUTHLESS EFFICIENCY WITH AN EYE FOR THE FINER DETAILS AND WITH VERY COOL BOILER SUITS SO I'M SURE YOU'LL AGREE THAT WE DESERVE A BEER OR TWO ON THIS THE NIGHT OF OUR NASTY VICTORY TO WASH THE ADRENALINE RIGHT OUT OF OUR HEARTS AND WE'LL FILL UP ON FELLOWSHIP AND WARM OURSELVES MERRILY IN THE FLICKERING GLOW OF TRUE AND HAPPY FRIENDS

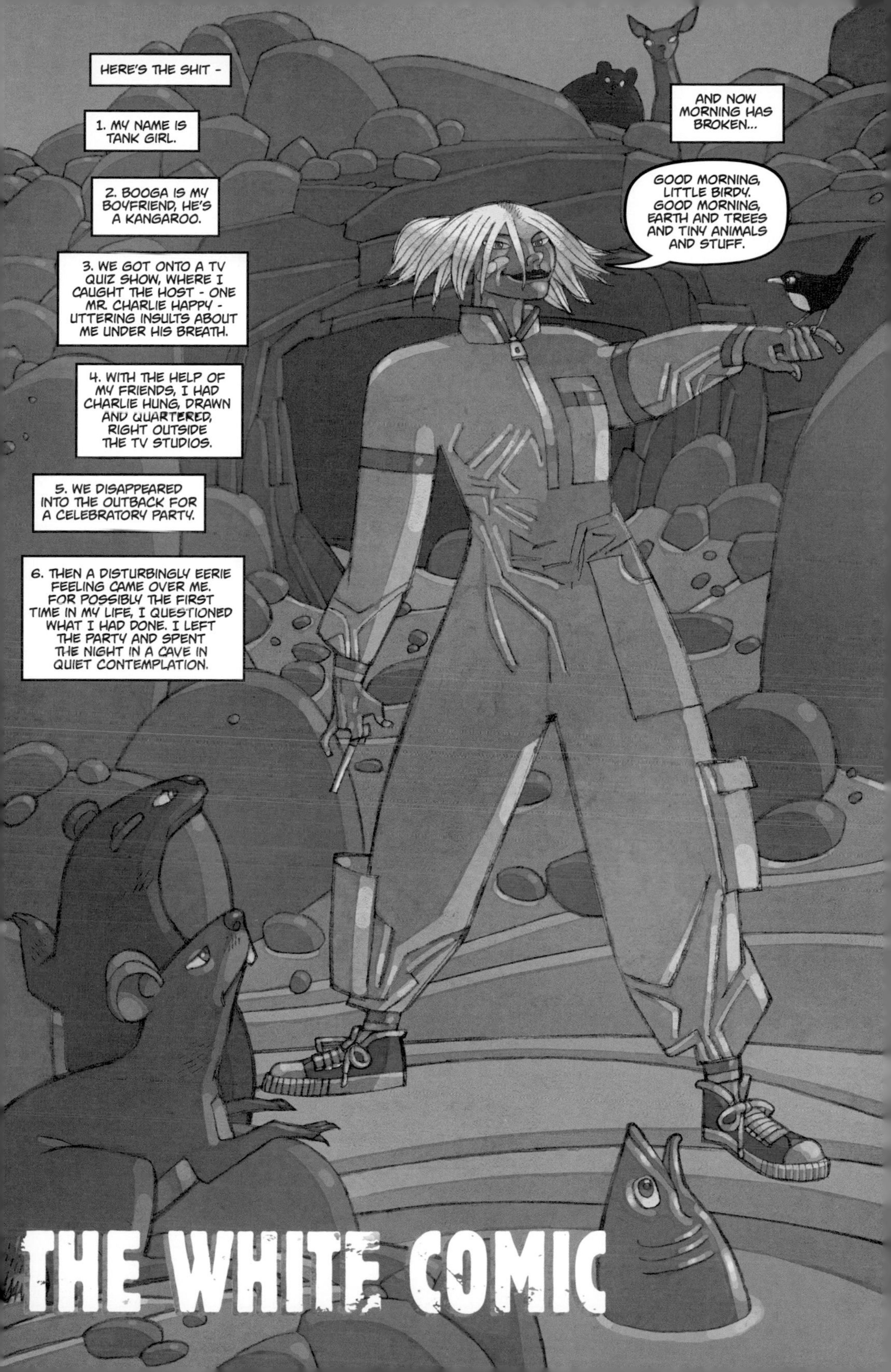
HERE'S THE SHIT -
1. MY NAME IS TANK GIRL.
2. BOOGA IS MY BOYFRIEND, HE'S A KANGAROO.
3. WE GOT ONTO A TV QUIZ SHOW, WHERE I CAUGHT THE HOST - ONE MR. CHARLIE HAPPY - UTTERING INSULTS ABOUT ME UNDER HIS BREATH.
4. WITH THE HELP OF MY FRIENDS, I HAD CHARLIE HUNG, DRAWN AND QUARTERED, RIGHT OUTSIDE THE TV STUDIOS.
5. WE DISAPPEARED INTO THE OUTBACK FOR A CELEBRATORY PARTY.
6. THEN A DISTURBINGLY EERIE FEELING CAME OVER ME. FOR POSSIBLY THE FIRST TIME IN MY LIFE, I QUESTIONED WHAT I HAD DONE. I LEFT THE PARTY AND SPENT THE NIGHT IN A CAVE IN QUIET CONTEMPLATION.
AND NOW MORNING HAS BROKEN...
GOOD MORNING, LITTLE BIRDY. GOOD MORNING, EARTH AND TREES AND TINY ANIMALS AND STUFF.
THE WHITE COMIC

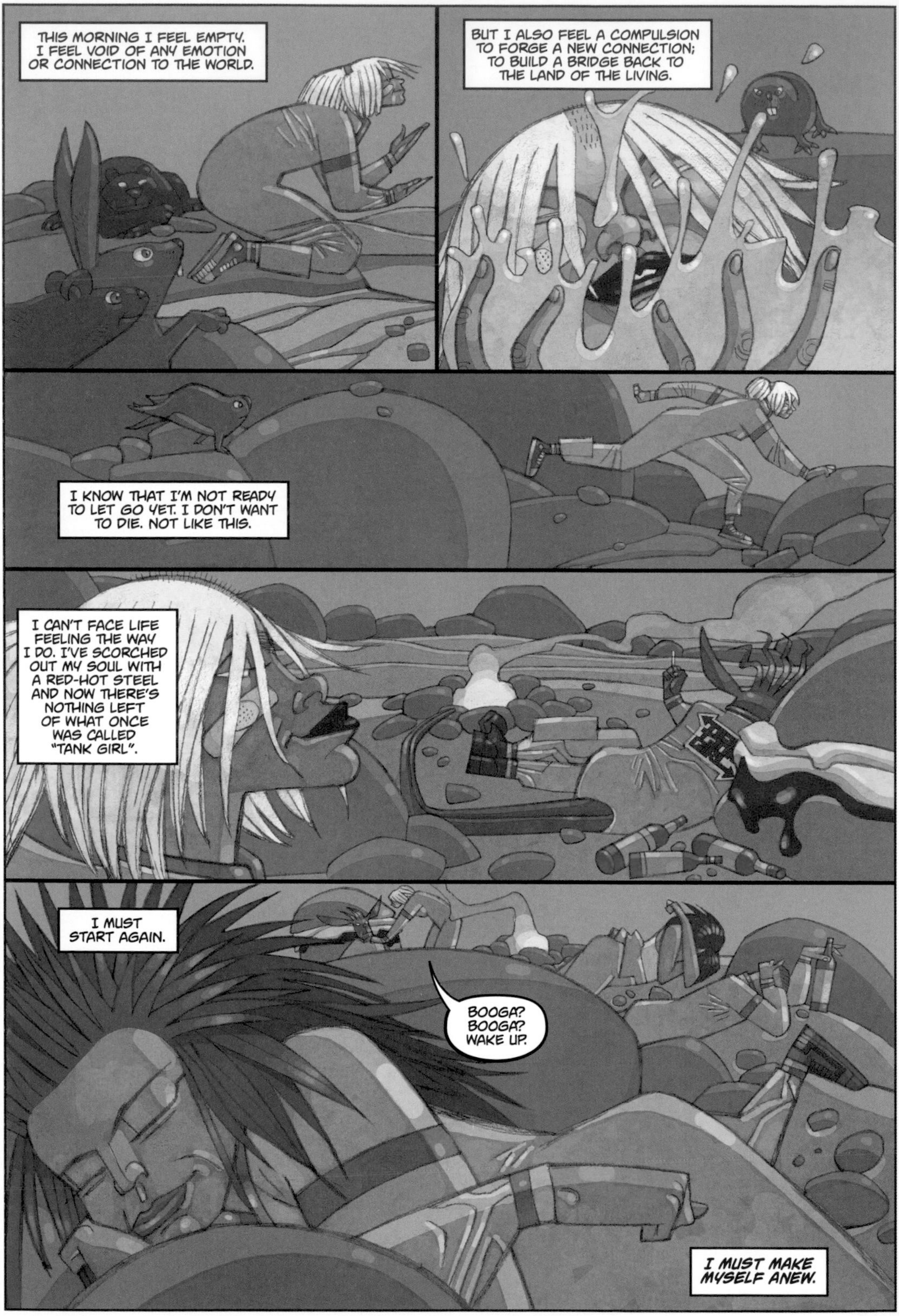

THIS MORNING I FEEL EMPTY. I FEEL VOID OF ANY EMOTION OR CONNECTION TO THE WORLD.
BUT I ALSO FEEL A COMPULSION TO FORGE A NEW CONNECTION; TO BUILD A BRIDGE BACK TO THE LAND OF THE LIVING.
I KNOW THAT I'M NOT READY TO LET GO YET. I DON'T WANT TO DIE. NOT LIKE THIS.
I CAN'T FACE LIFE FEELING THE WAY I DO. I'VE SCORCHED OUT MY SOUL WITH A RED-HOT STEEL AND NOW THERE'S NOTHING LEFT OF WHAT ONCE WAS CALLED "TANK GIRL".
I MUST START AGAIN.
BOOGA? BOOGA? WAKE UP.
I MUST MAKE MYSELF ANEW.

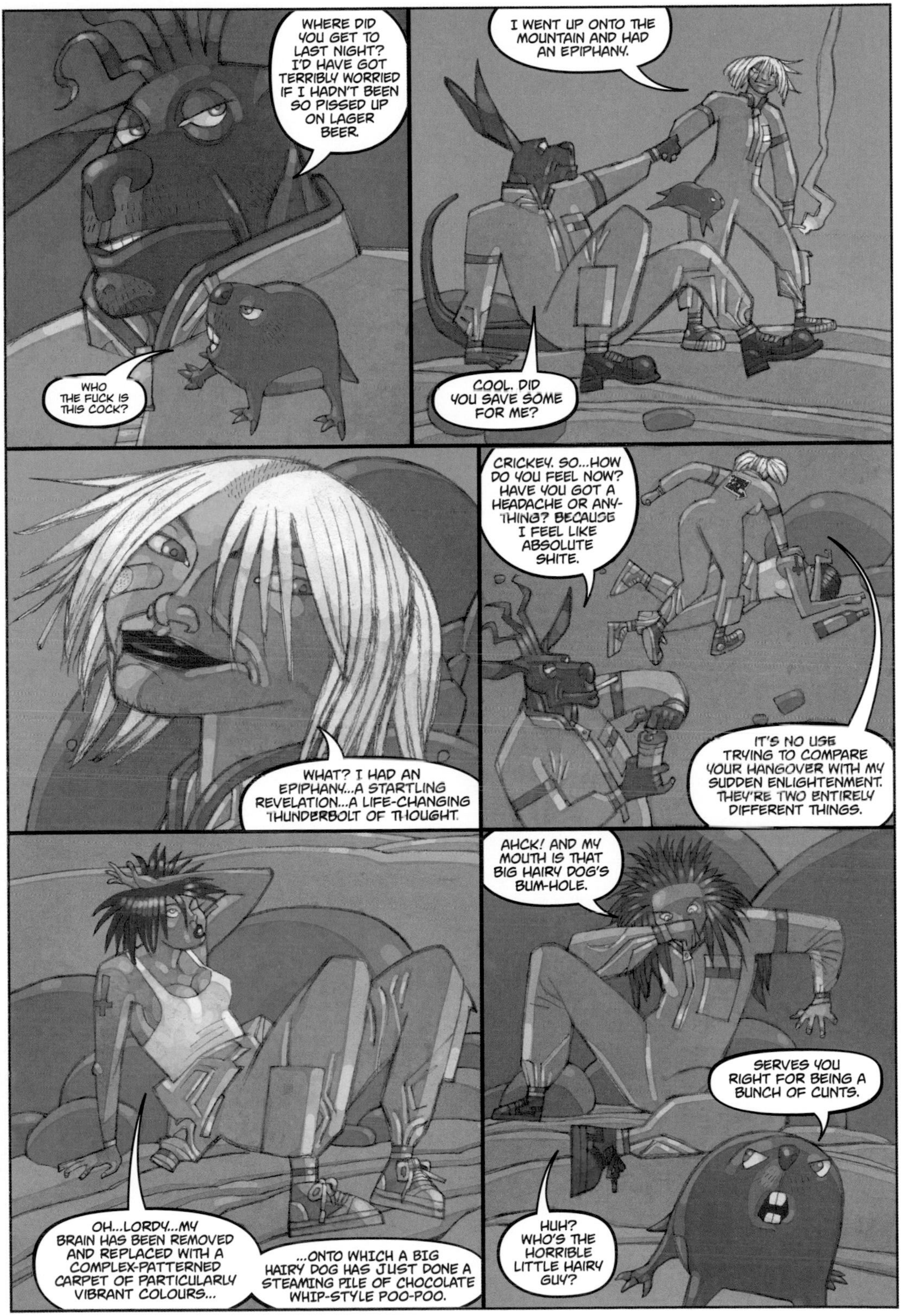
WHERE DID YOU GET TO LAST NIGHT? I'D HAVE GOT TERRIBLY WORRIED IF I HADN'T BEEN SO PISSED UP ON LAGER BEER.
WHO THE FUCK IS THIS COCK?
I WENT UP ONTO THE MOUNTAIN AND HAD AN EPIPHANY.
COOL. DID YOU SAVE SOME FOR ME?
WHAT? I HAD AN EPIPHANY...A STARTLING REVELATION...A LIFE-CHANGING THUNDERBOLT OF THOUGHT.
CRICKEY. SO...HOW DO YOU FEEL NOW? HAVE YOU GOT A HEADACHE OR ANY-THING? BECAUSE I FEEL LIKE ABSOLUTE SHITE.
IT'S NO USE TRYING TO COMPARE YOUR HANGOVER WITH MY SUDDEN ENLIGHTENMENT. THEY'RE TWO ENTIRELY DIFFERENT THINGS.
OH...LORDY...MY BRAIN HAS BEEN REMOVED AND REPLACED WITH A COMPLEX-PATTERNED CARPET OF PARTICULARLY VIBRANT COLOURS...
...ONTO WHICH A BIG HAIRY DOG HAS JUST DONE A STEAMING PILE OF CHOCOLATE WHIP-STYLE POO-POO.
AHCK! AND MY MOUTH IS THAT BIG HAIRY DOG'S BUM-HOLE.
SERVES YOU RIGHT FOR BEING A BUNCH OF CUNTS.
HUH? WHO'S THE HORRIBLE LITTLE HAIRY GUY?

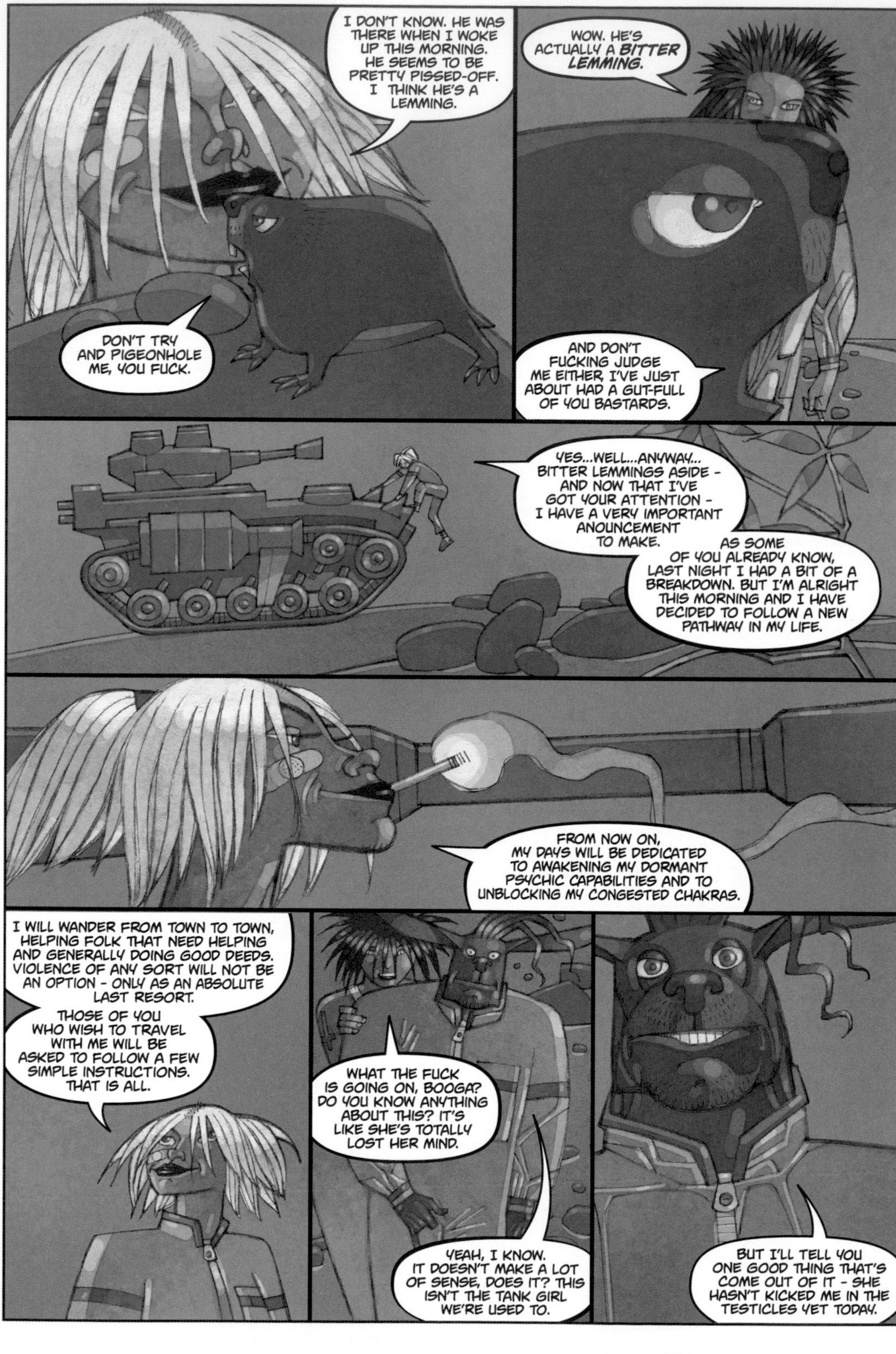
I DON'T KNOW. HE WAS THERE WHEN I WOKE UP THIS MORNING. HE SEEMS TO BE PRETTY PISSED-OFF. I THINK HE'S A LEMMING.
DON'T TRY AND PIGEONHOLE ME, YOU FUCK.
WOW. HE'S ACTUALLY A *BITTER LEMMING.*
AND DON'T FUCKING JUDGE ME EITHER, I'VE JUST ABOUT HAD A GUT-FULL OF YOU BASTARDS.
YES...WELL...ANYWAY... BITTER LEMMINGS ASIDE - AND NOW THAT I'VE GOT YOUR ATTENTION - I HAVE A VERY IMPORTANT ANOUNCEMENT TO MAKE.
AS SOME OF YOU ALREADY KNOW, LAST NIGHT I HAD A BIT OF A BREAKDOWN. BUT I'M ALRIGHT THIS MORNING AND I HAVE DECIDED TO FOLLOW A NEW PATHWAY IN MY LIFE.
FROM NOW ON, MY DAYS WILL BE DEDICATED TO AWAKENING MY DORMANT PSYCHIC CAPABILITIES AND TO UNBLOCKING MY CONGESTED CHAKRAS.
I WILL WANDER FROM TOWN TO TOWN, HELPING FOLK THAT NEED HELPING AND GENERALLY DOING GOOD DEEDS. VIOLENCE OF ANY SORT WILL NOT BE AN OPTION - ONLY AS AN ABSOLUTE LAST RESORT.
THOSE OF YOU WHO WISH TO TRAVEL WITH ME WILL BE ASKED TO FOLLOW A FEW SIMPLE INSTRUCTIONS. THAT IS ALL.
WHAT THE FUCK IS GOING ON, BOOGA? DO YOU KNOW ANYTHING ABOUT THIS? IT'S LIKE SHE'S TOTALLY LOST HER MIND.
YEAH, I KNOW. IT DOESN'T MAKE A LOT OF SENSE, DOES IT? THIS ISN'T THE TANK GIRL WE'RE USED TO.
BUT I'LL TELL YOU ONE GOOD THING THAT'S COME OUT OF IT - SHE HASN'T KICKED ME IN THE TESTICLES YET TODAY.

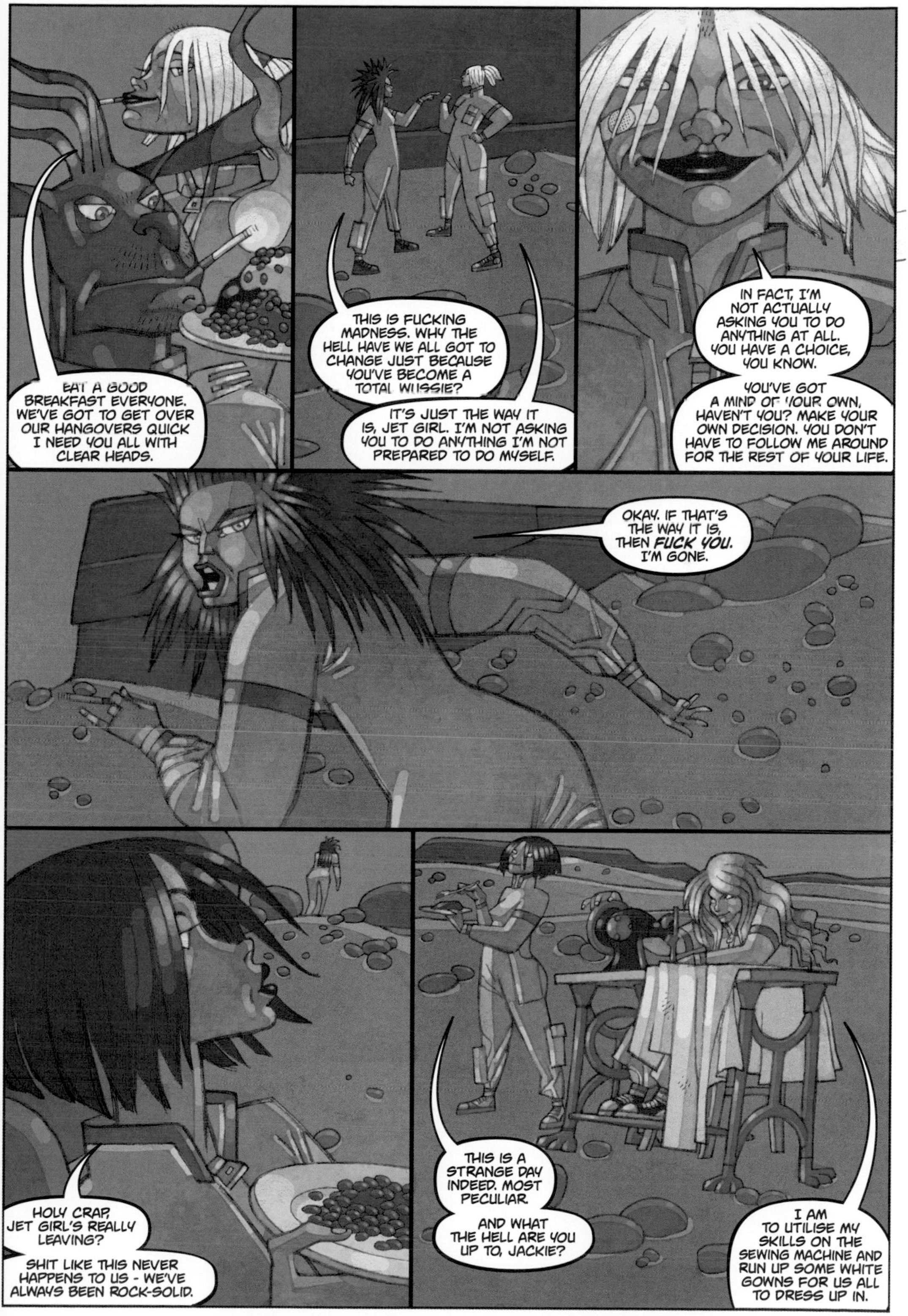
EAT A GOOD BREAKFAST EVERYONE. WE'VE GOT TO GET OVER OUR HANGOVERS QUICK I NEED YOU ALL WITH CLEAR HEADS.
THIS IS FUCKING MADNESS. WHY THE HELL HAVE WE ALL GOT TO CHANGE JUST BECAUSE YOU'VE BECOME A TOTAL WUSSIE?
IT'S JUST THE WAY IT IS, JET GIRL. I'M NOT ASKING YOU TO DO ANYTHING I'M NOT PREPARED TO DO MYSELF.
IN FACT, I'M NOT ACTUALLY ASKING YOU TO DO ANYTHING AT ALL. YOU HAVE A CHOICE, YOU KNOW.
YOU'VE GOT A MIND OF YOUR OWN, HAVEN'T YOU? MAKE YOUR OWN DECISION. YOU DON'T HAVE TO FOLLOW ME AROUND FOR THE REST OF YOUR LIFE.
OKAY. IF THAT'S THE WAY IT IS, THEN FUCK YOU. I'M GONE.
HOLY CRAP, JET GIRL'S REALLY LEAVING?
SHIT LIKE THIS NEVER HAPPENS TO US - WE'VE ALWAYS BEEN ROCK-SOLID.
THIS IS A STRANGE DAY INDEED. MOST PECULIAR.
AND WHAT THE HELL ARE YOU UP TO, JACKIE?
I AM TO UTILISE MY SKILLS ON THE SEWING MACHINE AND RUN UP SOME WHITE GOWNS FOR US ALL TO DRESS UP IN.

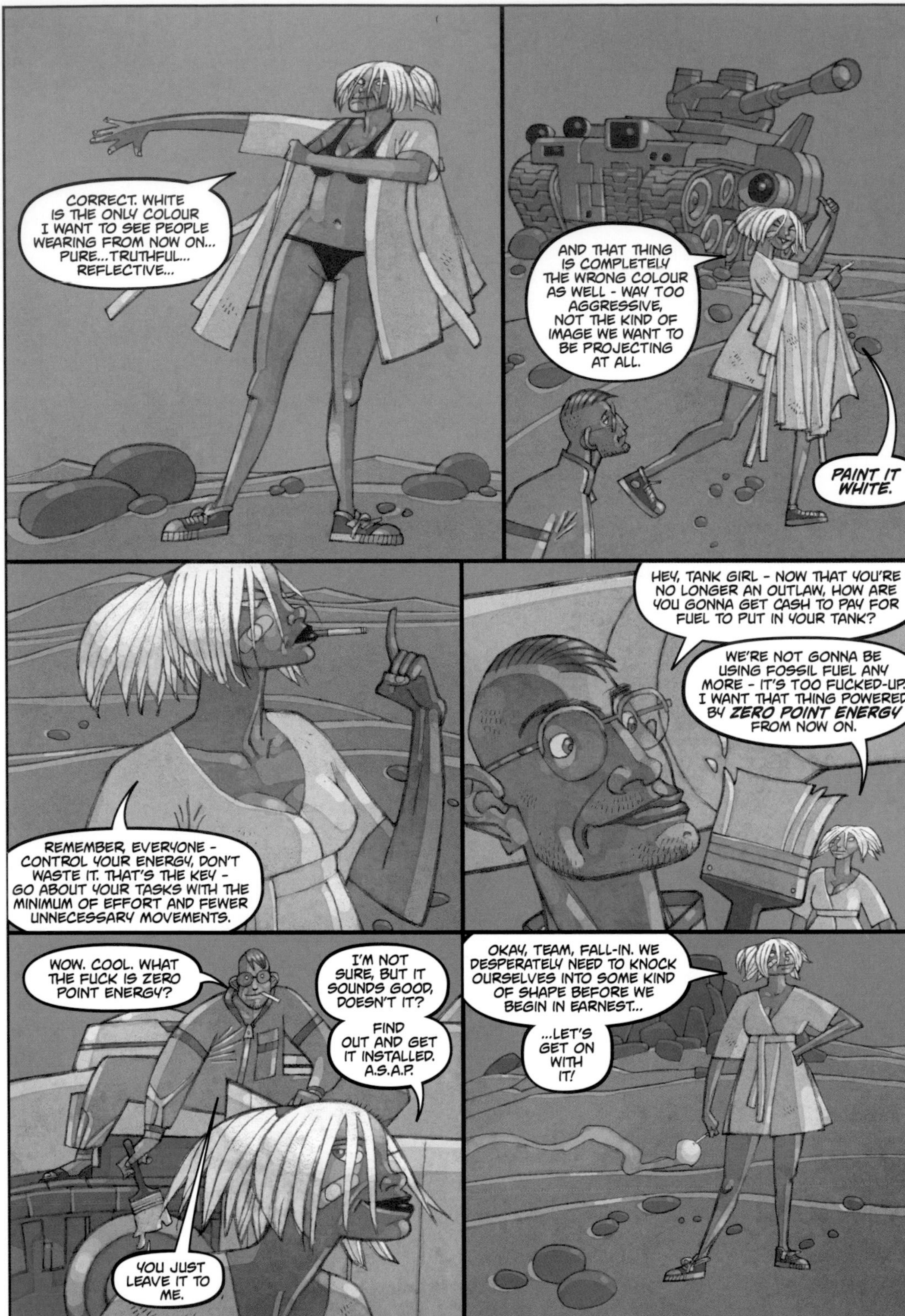
CORRECT. WHITE IS THE ONLY COLOUR I WANT TO SEE PEOPLE WEARING FROM NOW ON... PURE...TRUTHFUL... REFLECTIVE...
AND THAT THING IS COMPLETELY THE WRONG COLOUR AS WELL - WAY TOO AGGRESSIVE, NOT THE KIND OF IMAGE WE WANT TO BE PROJECTING AT ALL.
PAINT IT WHITE.
REMEMBER, EVERYONE - CONTROL YOUR ENERGY, DON'T WASTE IT. THAT'S THE KEY - GO ABOUT YOUR TASKS WITH THE MINIMUM OF EFFORT AND FEWER UNNECESSARY MOVEMENTS.
HEY, TANK GIRL - NOW THAT YOU'RE NO LONGER AN OUTLAW, HOW ARE YOU GONNA GET CASH TO PAY FOR FUEL TO PUT IN YOUR TANK?
WE'RE NOT GONNA BE USING FOSSIL FUEL ANY MORE - IT'S TOO FUCKED-UP. I WANT THAT THING POWERED BY ZERO POINT ENERGY FROM NOW ON.
WOW. COOL. WHAT THE FUCK IS ZERO POINT ENERGY?
I'M NOT SURE, BUT IT SOUNDS GOOD, DOESN'T IT?
FIND OUT AND GET IT INSTALLED. A.S.A.P.
YOU JUST LEAVE IT TO ME.
OKAY, TEAM, FALL-IN. WE DESPERATELY NEED TO KNOCK OURSELVES INTO SOME KIND OF SHAPE BEFORE WE BEGIN IN EARNEST...
...LET'S GET ON WITH IT!

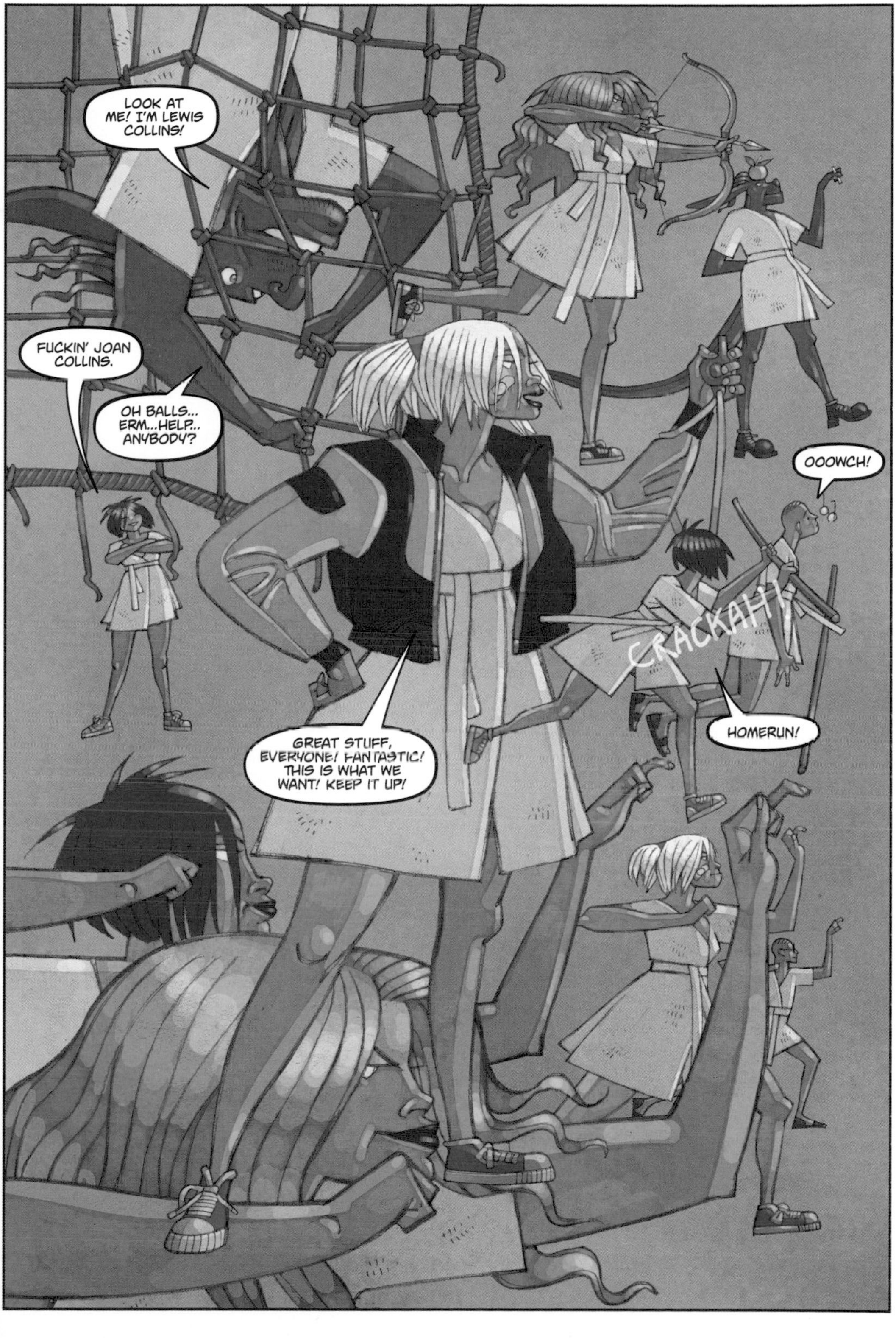
LOOK AT ME! I'M LEWIS COLLINS!
FUCKIN' JOAN COLLINS.
OH BALLS... ERM...HELP... ANYBODY?
OOOWCH!
CRACKAH!
HOMERUN!
GREAT STUFF, EVERYONE! FANTASTIC! THIS IS WHAT WE WANT! KEEP IT UP!

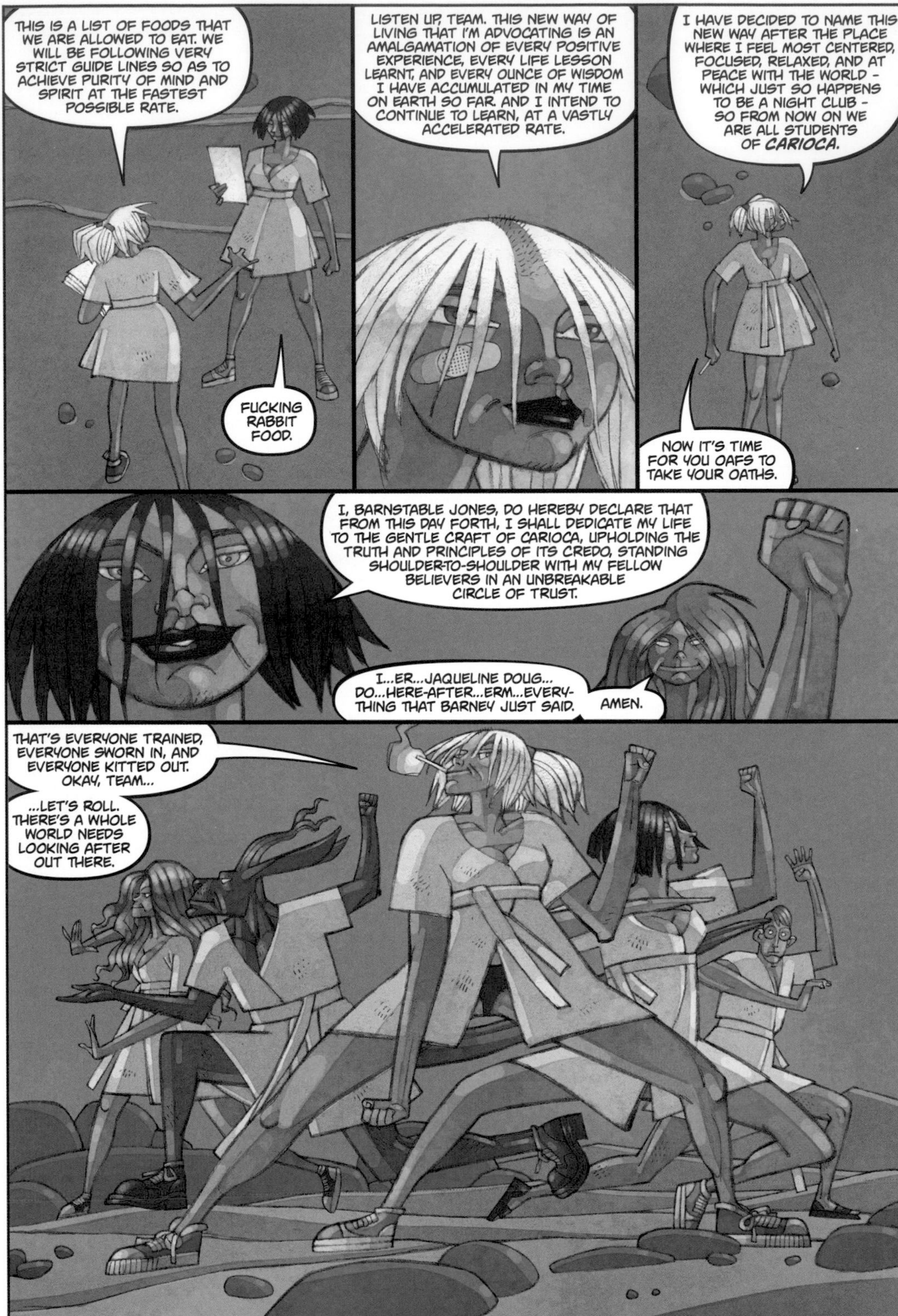
THIS IS A LIST OF FOODS THAT WE ARE ALLOWED TO EAT. WE WILL BE FOLLOWING VERY STRICT GUIDE LINES SO AS TO ACHIEVE PURITY OF MIND AND SPIRIT AT THE FASTEST POSSIBLE RATE.
FUCKING RABBIT FOOD.
LISTEN UP, TEAM. THIS NEW WAY OF LIVING THAT I'M ADVOCATING IS AN AMALGAMATION OF EVERY POSITIVE EXPERIENCE, EVERY LIFE LESSON LEARNT, AND EVERY OUNCE OF WISDOM I HAVE ACCUMULATED IN MY TIME ON EARTH SO FAR. AND I INTEND TO CONTINUE TO LEARN, AT A VASTLY ACCELERATED RATE.
I HAVE DECIDED TO NAME THIS NEW WAY AFTER THE PLACE WHERE I FEEL MOST CENTERED, FOCUSED, RELAXED, AND AT PEACE WITH THE WORLD - WHICH JUST SO HAPPENS TO BE A NIGHT CLUB - SO FROM NOW ON WE ARE ALL STUDENTS OF CARIOCA.
NOW IT'S TIME FOR YOU OAFS TO TAKE YOUR OATHS.
I, BARNSTABLE JONES, DO HEREBY DECLARE THAT FROM THIS DAY FORTH, I SHALL DEDICATE MY LIFE TO THE GENTLE CRAFT OF CARIOCA, UPHOLDING THE TRUTH AND PRINCIPLES OF ITS CREDO, STANDING SHOULDER-TO-SHOULDER WITH MY FELLOW BELIEVERS IN AN UNBREAKABLE CIRCLE OF TRUST.
I...ER...JAQUELINE DOUG... DO...HERE-AFTER...ERM...EVERY-THING THAT BARNEY JUST SAID.
AMEN.
THAT'S EVERYONE TRAINED, EVERYONE SWORN IN, AND EVERYONE KITTED OUT. OKAY, TEAM...
...LET'S ROLL. THERE'S A WHOLE WORLD NEEDS LOOKING AFTER OUT THERE.

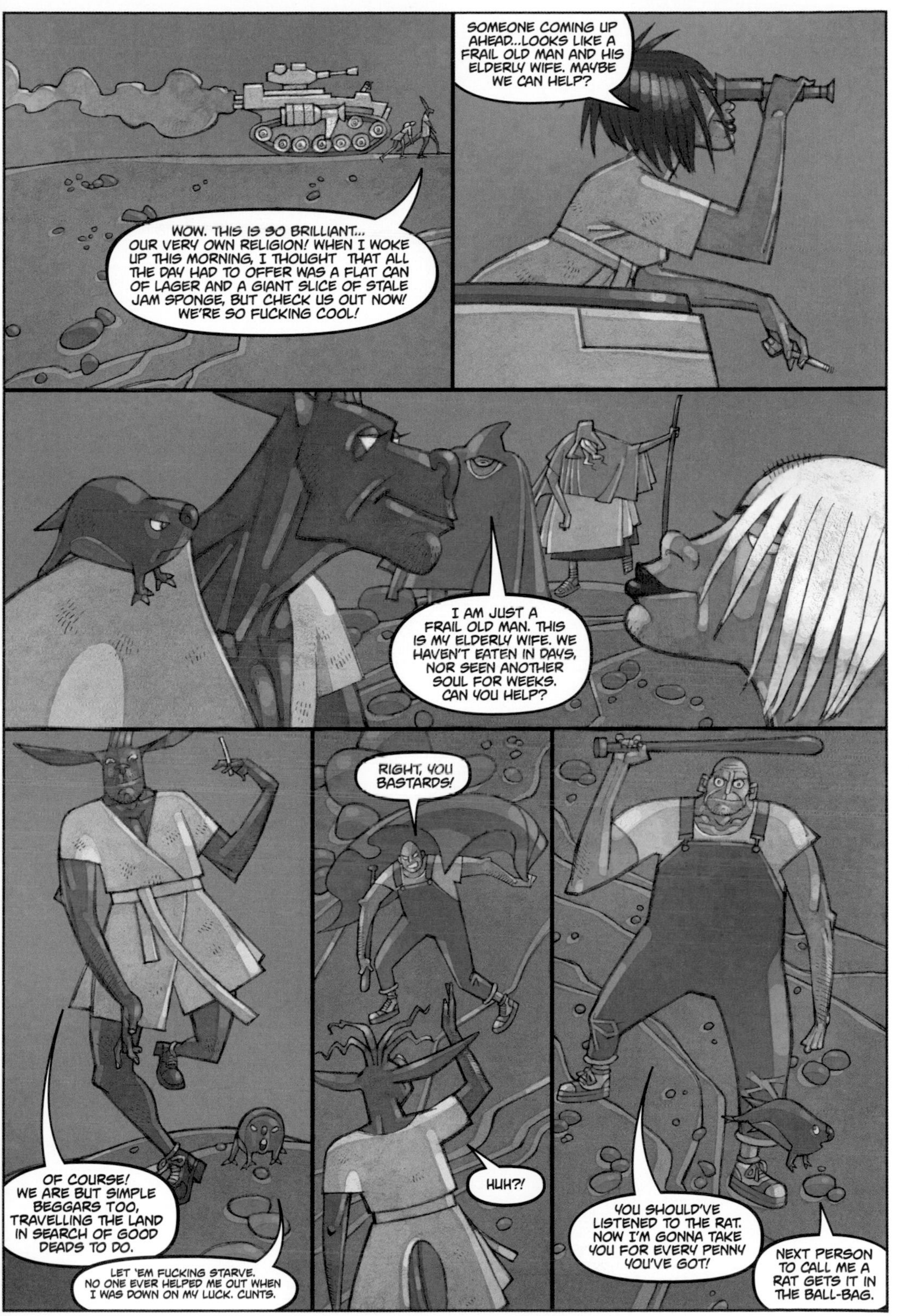
SOMEONE COMING UP AHEAD...LOOKS LIKE A FRAIL OLD MAN AND HIS ELDERLY WIFE. MAYBE WE CAN HELP?
WOW. THIS IS SO BRILLIANT... OUR VERY OWN RELIGION! WHEN I WOKE UP THIS MORNING, I THOUGHT THAT ALL THE DAY HAD TO OFFER WAS A FLAT CAN OF LAGER AND A GIANT SLICE OF STALE JAM SPONGE, BUT CHECK US OUT NOW! WE'RE SO FUCKING COOL!
I AM JUST A FRAIL OLD MAN. THIS IS MY ELDERLY WIFE. WE HAVEN'T EATEN IN DAYS, NOR SEEN ANOTHER SOUL FOR WEEKS. CAN YOU HELP?
OF COURSE! WE ARE BUT SIMPLE BEGGARS TOO, TRAVELLING THE LAND IN SEARCH OF GOOD DEADS TO DO.
LET 'EM FUCKING STARVE. NO ONE EVER HELPED ME OUT WHEN I WAS DOWN ON MY LUCK. CUNTS.
RIGHT, YOU BASTARDS!
HUH?!
YOU SHOULD'VE LISTENED TO THE RAT. NOW I'M GONNA TAKE YOU FOR EVERY PENNY YOU'VE GOT!
NEXT PERSON TO CALL ME A RAT GETS IT IN THE BALL-BAG.

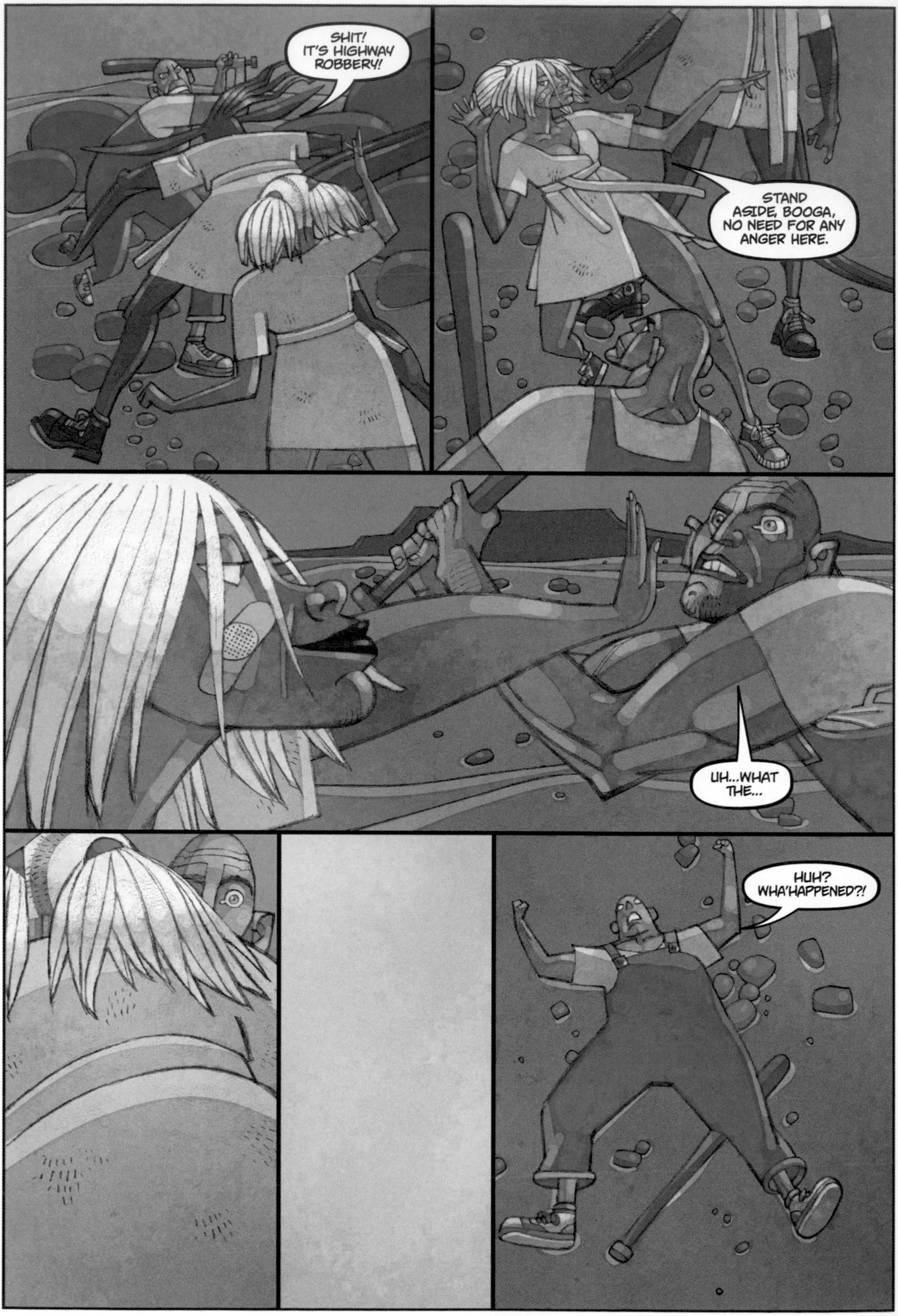
SHIT! IT'S HIGHWAY ROBBERY!
STAND ASIDE, BOOGA, NO NEED FOR ANY ANGER HERE.
UH...WHAT THE...
HUH? WHA'HAPPENED?!

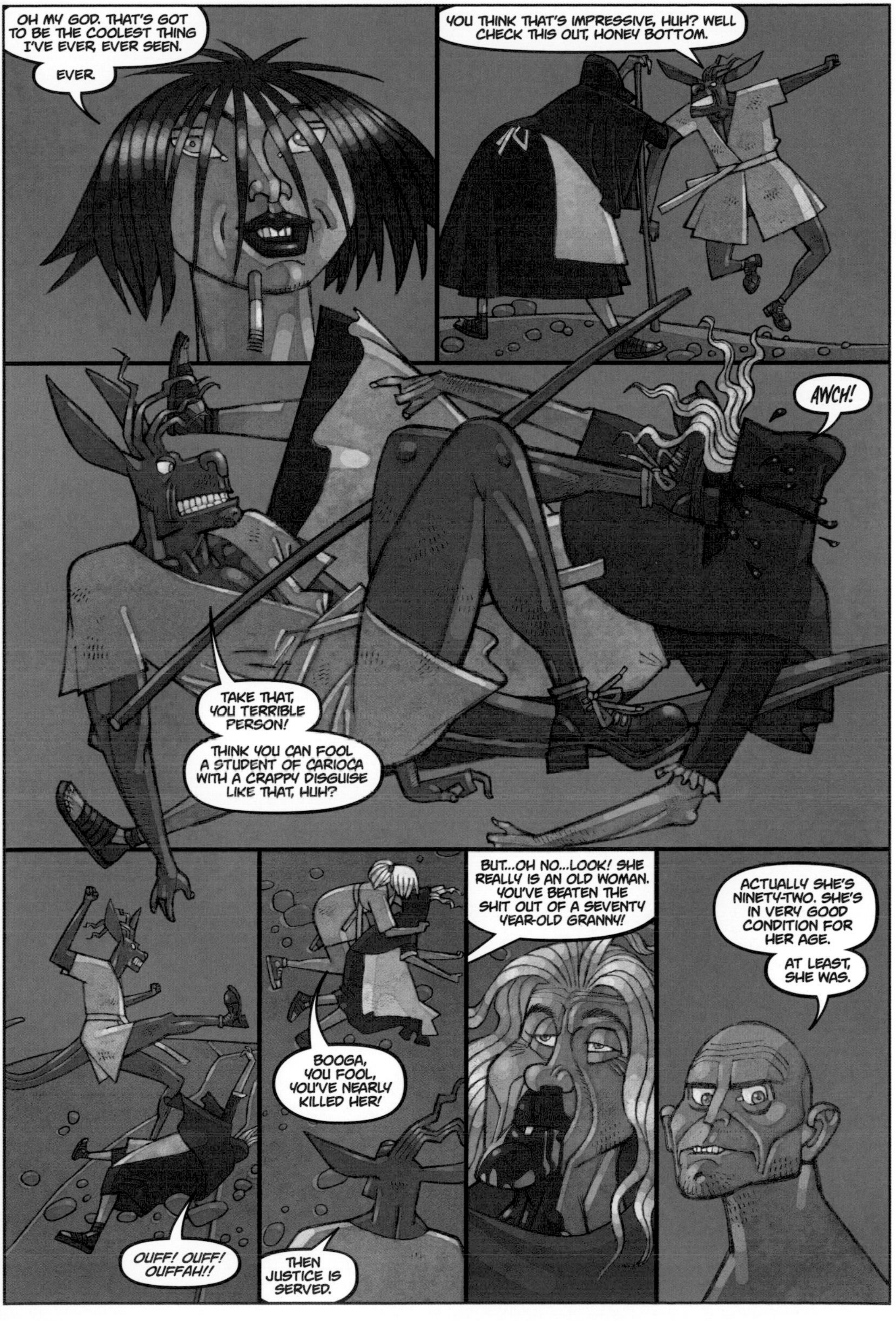
OH MY GOD. THAT'S GOT TO BE THE COOLEST THING I'VE EVER, EVER SEEN.
EVER.
YOU THINK THAT'S IMPRESSIVE, HUH? WELL CHECK THIS OUT, HONEY BOTTOM.
AWCH!
TAKE THAT, YOU TERRIBLE PERSON!
THINK YOU CAN FOOL A STUDENT OF CARIOCA WITH A CRAPPY DISGUISE LIKE THAT, HUH?
OUFF! OUFF! OUFFAH!!
BOOGA, YOU FOOL, YOU'VE NEARLY KILLED HER!
THEN JUSTICE IS SERVED.
BUT...OH NO...LOOK! SHE REALLY IS AN OLD WOMAN. YOU'VE BEATEN THE SHIT OUT OF A SEVENTY YEAR-OLD GRANNY!
ACTUALLY SHE'S NINETY-TWO. SHE'S IN VERY GOOD CONDITION FOR HER AGE.
AT LEAST, SHE WAS.

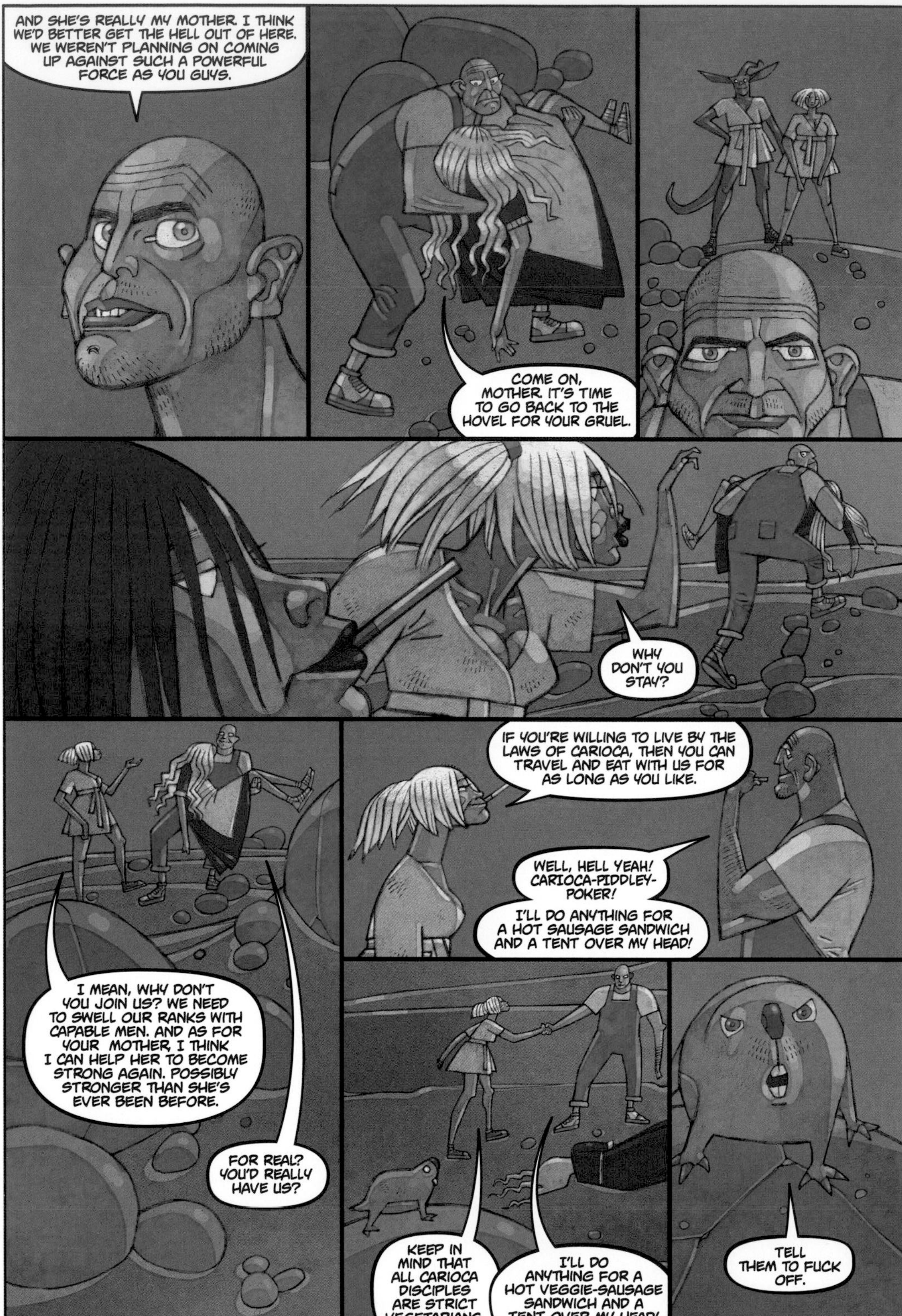
AND SHE'S REALLY MY MOTHER. I THINK WE'D BETTER GET THE HELL OUT OF HERE. WE WEREN'T PLANNING ON COMING UP AGAINST SUCH A POWERFUL FORCE AS YOU GUYS.
COME ON, MOTHER. IT'S TIME TO GO BACK TO THE HOVEL FOR YOUR GRUEL.
WHY DON'T YOU STAY?
I MEAN, WHY DON'T YOU JOIN US? WE NEED TO SWELL OUR RANKS WITH CAPABLE MEN. AND AS FOR YOUR MOTHER, I THINK I CAN HELP HER TO BECOME STRONG AGAIN. POSSIBLY STRONGER THAN SHE'S EVER BEEN BEFORE.
FOR REAL? YOU'D REALLY HAVE US?
IF YOU'RE WILLING TO LIVE BY THE LAWS OF CARIOCA, THEN YOU CAN TRAVEL AND EAT WITH US FOR AS LONG AS YOU LIKE.
WELL, HELL YEAH! CARIOCA-PIDDLEY-POKER!
I'LL DO ANYTHING FOR A HOT SAUSAGE SANDWICH AND A TENT OVER MY HEAD!
KEEP IN MIND THAT ALL CARIOCA DISCIPLES ARE STRICT VEGETARIANS.
I'LL DO ANYTHING FOR A HOT VEGGIE-SAUSAGE SANDWICH AND A TENT OVER MY HEAD!
TELL THEM TO FUCK OFF.

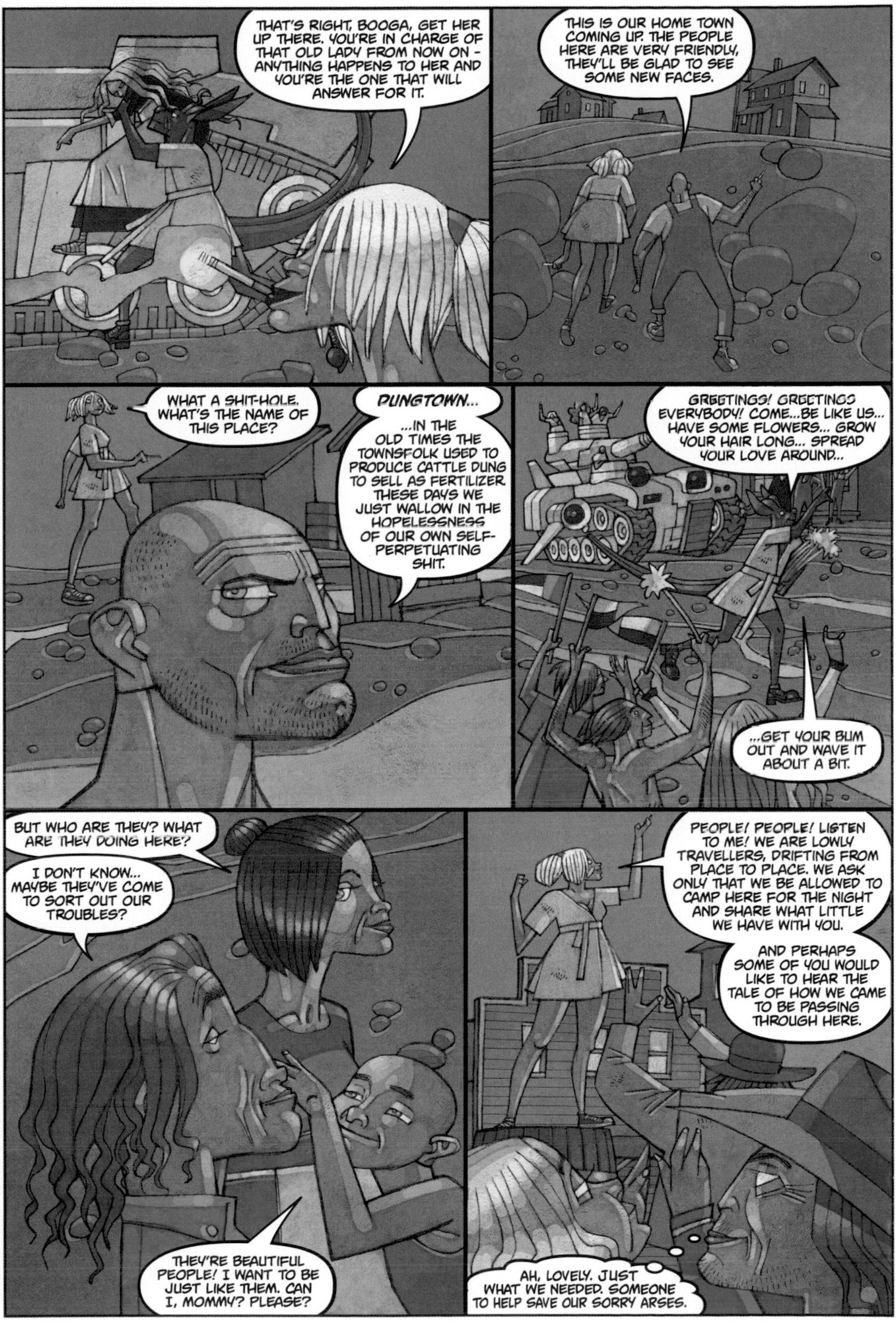
THAT'S RIGHT, BOOGA, GET HER UP THERE. YOU'RE IN CHARGE OF THAT OLD LADY FROM NOW ON - ANYTHING HAPPENS TO HER AND YOU'RE THE ONE THAT WILL ANSWER FOR IT.
THIS IS OUR HOME TOWN COMING UP. THE PEOPLE HERE ARE VERY FRIENDLY, THEY'LL BE GLAD TO SEE SOME NEW FACES.
WHAT A SHIT-HOLE. WHAT'S THE NAME OF THIS PLACE?
DUNGTOWN...
...IN THE OLD TIMES THE TOWNSFOLK USED TO PRODUCE CATTLE DUNG TO SELL AS FERTILIZER. THESE DAYS WE JUST WALLOW IN THE HOPELESSNESS OF OUR OWN SELF-PERPETUATING SHIT.
GREETINGS! GREETINGS EVERYBODY! COME...BE LIKE US... HAVE SOME FLOWERS... GROW YOUR HAIR LONG... SPREAD YOUR LOVE AROUND...
...GET YOUR BUM OUT AND WAVE IT ABOUT A BIT.
BUT WHO ARE THEY? WHAT ARE THEY DOING HERE?
I DON'T KNOW... MAYBE THEY'VE COME TO SORT OUT OUR TROUBLES?
THEY'RE BEAUTIFUL PEOPLE! I WANT TO BE JUST LIKE THEM. CAN I, MOMMY? PLEASE?
PEOPLE! PEOPLE! LISTEN TO ME! WE ARE LOWLY TRAVELLERS, DRIFTING FROM PLACE TO PLACE. WE ASK ONLY THAT WE BE ALLOWED TO CAMP HERE FOR THE NIGHT AND SHARE WHAT LITTLE WE HAVE WITH YOU.
AND PERHAPS SOME OF YOU WOULD LIKE TO HEAR THE TALE OF HOW WE CAME TO BE PASSING THROUGH HERE.
AH, LOVELY. JUST WHAT WE NEEDED. SOMEONE TO HELP SAVE OUR SORRY ARSES.

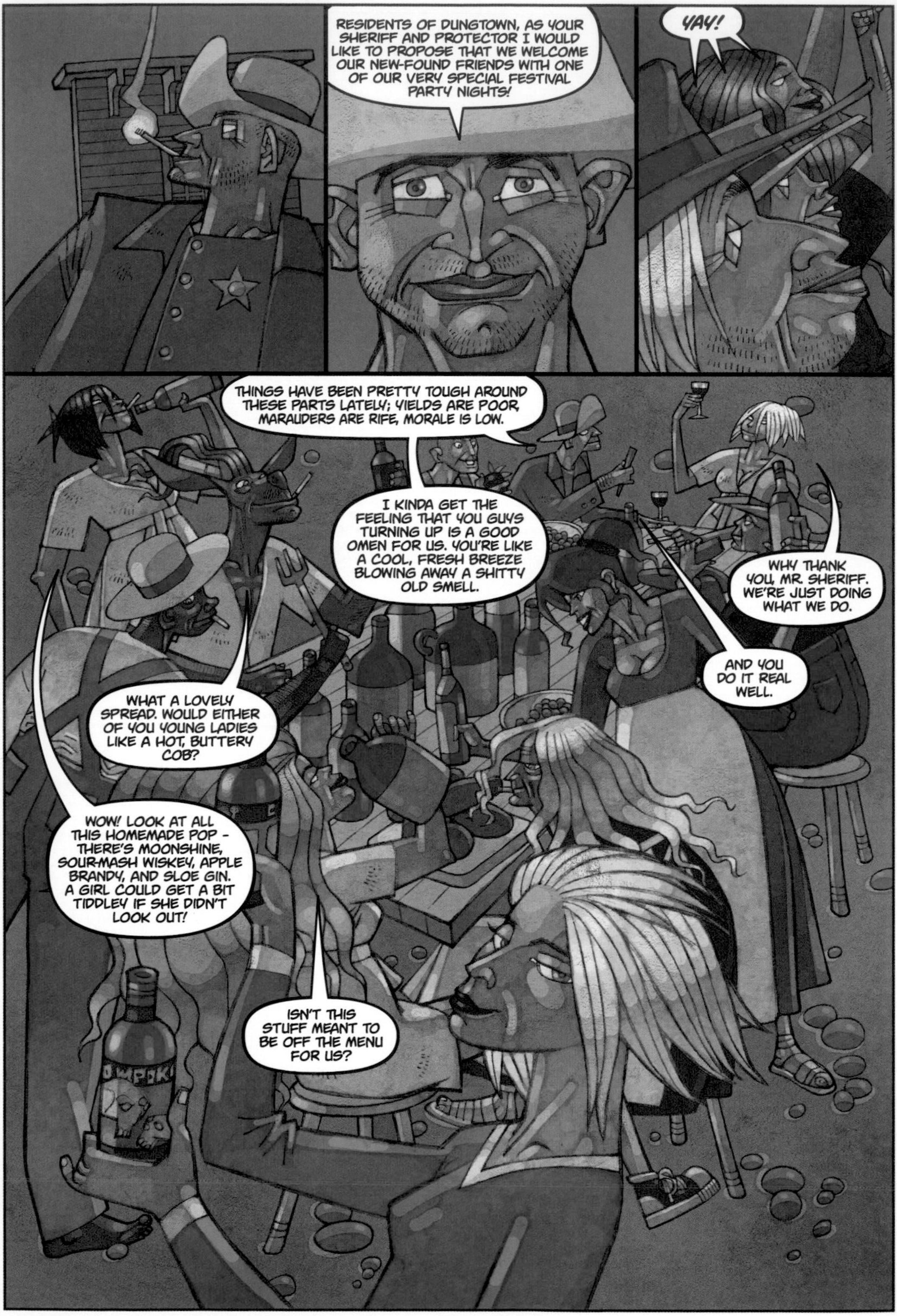
RESIDENTS OF DUNGTOWN, AS YOUR SHERIFF AND PROTECTOR I WOULD LIKE TO PROPOSE THAT WE WELCOME OUR NEW-FOUND FRIENDS WITH ONE OF OUR VERY SPECIAL FESTIVAL PARTY NIGHTS!
YAY!
THINGS HAVE BEEN PRETTY TOUGH AROUND THESE PARTS LATELY; YIELDS ARE POOR, MARAUDERS ARE RIFE, MORALE IS LOW.
I KINDA GET THE FEELING THAT YOU GUYS TURNING UP IS A GOOD OMEN FOR US. YOU'RE LIKE A COOL, FRESH BREEZE BLOWING AWAY A SHITTY OLD SMELL.
WHY THANK YOU, MR. SHERIFF. WE'RE JUST DOING WHAT WE DO.
AND YOU DO IT REAL WELL.
WHAT A LOVELY SPREAD. WOULD EITHER OF YOU YOUNG LADIES LIKE A HOT, BUTTERY COB?
WOW! LOOK AT ALL THIS HOMEMADE POP - THERE'S MOONSHINE, SOUR-MASH WISKEY, APPLE BRANDY, AND SLOE GIN. A GIRL COULD GET A BIT TIDDLEY IF SHE DIDN'T LOOK OUT!
ISN'T THIS STUFF MEANT TO BE OFF THE MENU FOR US?

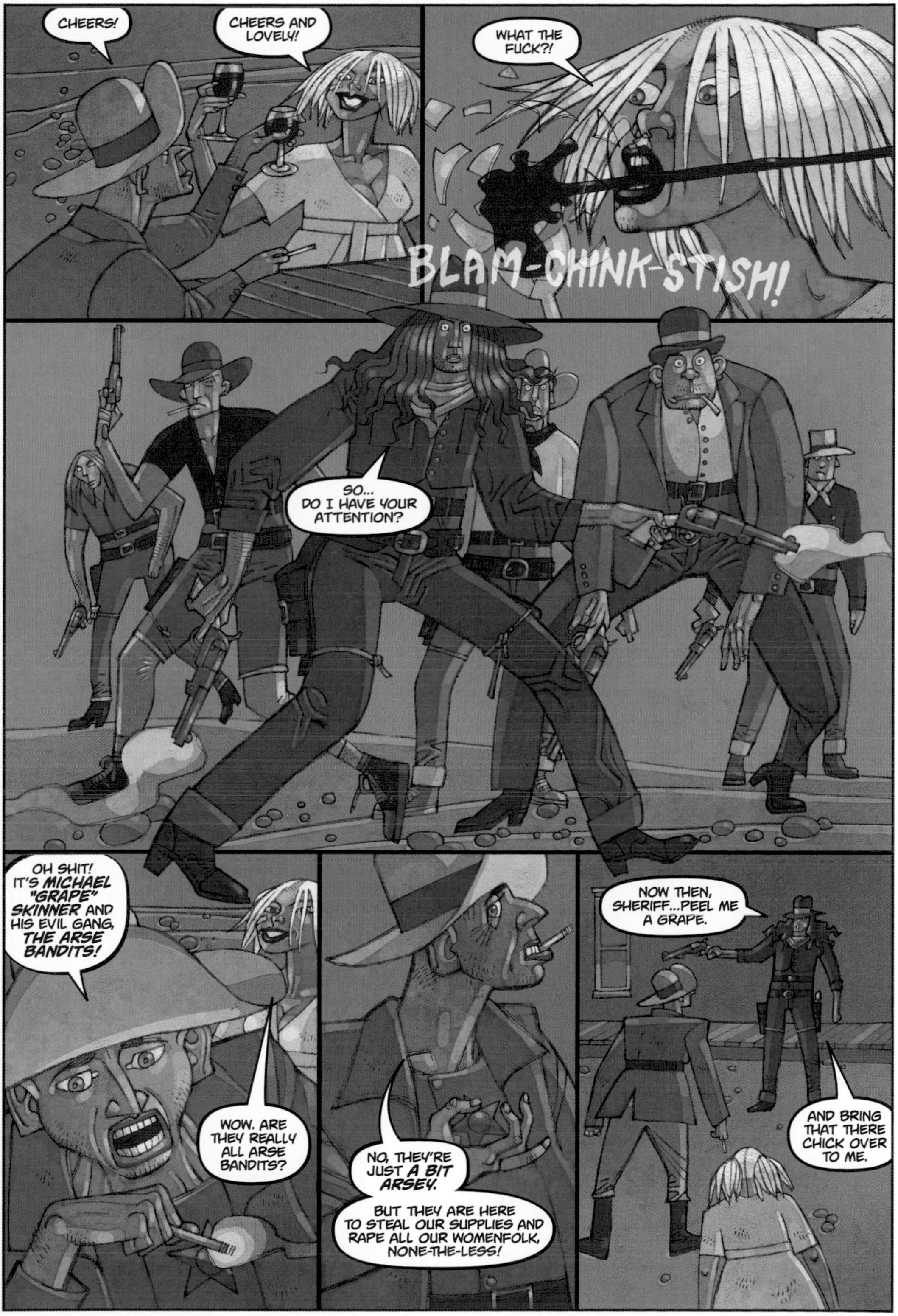

CHEERS!
CHEERS AND LOVELY!
WHAT THE FUCK?!
BLAM-CHINK-STISH!
SO... DO I HAVE YOUR ATTENTION?
OH SHIT! IT'S MICHAEL "GRAPE" SKINNER AND HIS EVIL GANG, THE ARSE BANDITS!
WOW. ARE THEY REALLY ALL ARSE BANDITS?
NO, THEY'RE JUST A BIT ARSEY.
BUT THEY ARE HERE TO STEAL OUR SUPPLIES AND RAPE ALL OUR WOMENFOLK, NONE-THE-LESS!
NOW THEN, SHERIFF...PEEL ME A GRAPE.
AND BRING THAT THERE CHICK OVER TO ME.

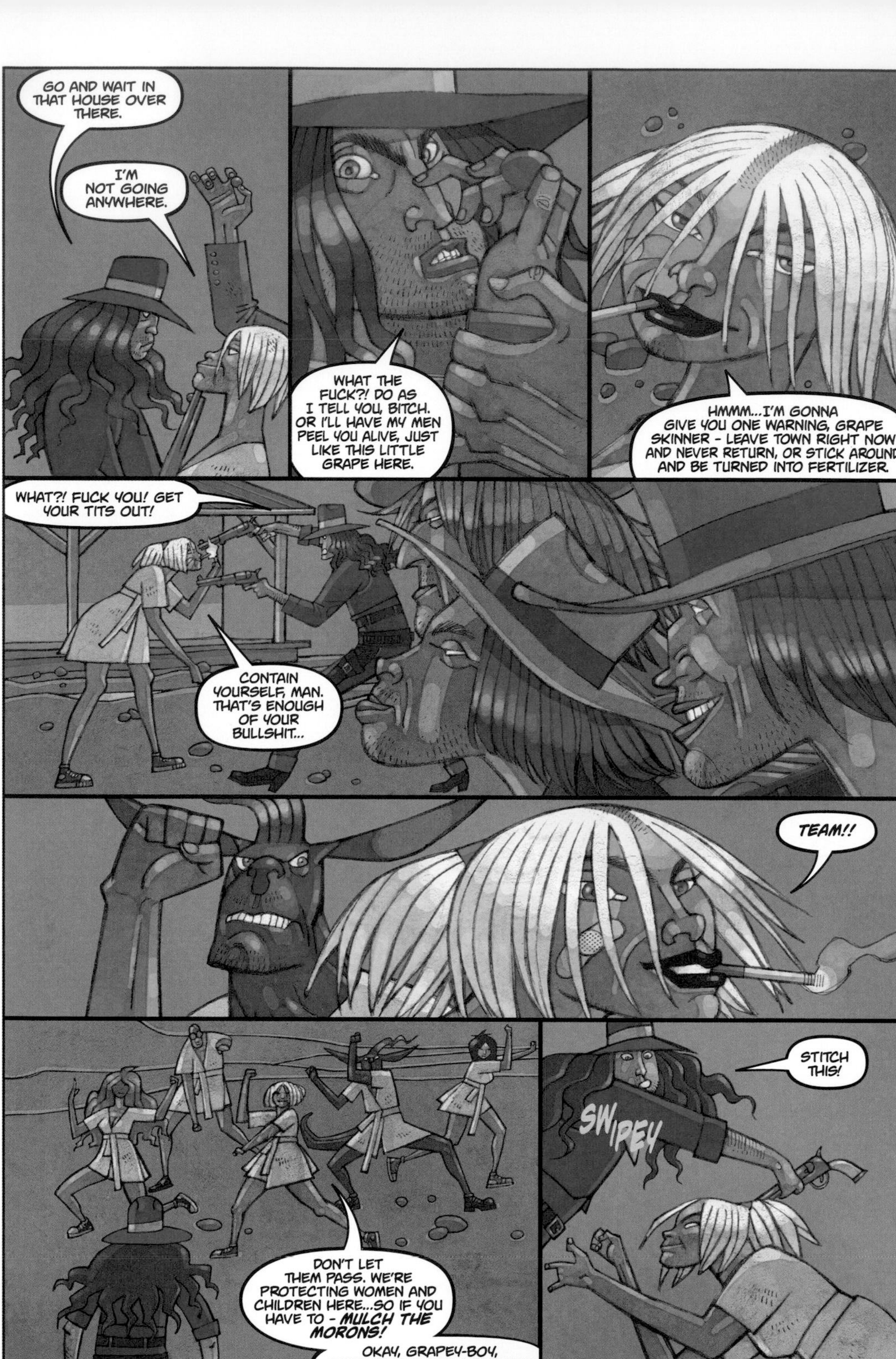
GO AND WAIT IN THAT HOUSE OVER THERE.
I'M NOT GOING ANYWHERE.
WHAT THE FUCK?! DO AS I TELL YOU, BITCH. OR I'LL HAVE MY MEN PEEL YOU ALIVE, JUST LIKE THIS LITTLE GRAPE HERE.
HMMM...I'M GONNA GIVE YOU ONE WARNING, GRAPE SKINNER - LEAVE TOWN RIGHT NOW AND NEVER RETURN, OR STICK AROUND AND BE TURNED INTO FERTILIZER.
WHAT?! FUCK YOU! GET YOUR TITS OUT!
CONTAIN YOURSELF, MAN. THAT'S ENOUGH OF YOUR BULLSHIT...
TEAM!!
DON'T LET THEM PASS. WE'RE PROTECTING WOMEN AND CHILDREN HERE...SO IF YOU HAVE TO - MULCH THE MORONS!
OKAY, GRAPEY-BOY, MAKE YOUR MOVE. AND DON'T SAY I DIDN'T WARN YOU.
STITCH THIS!
SWIPEY

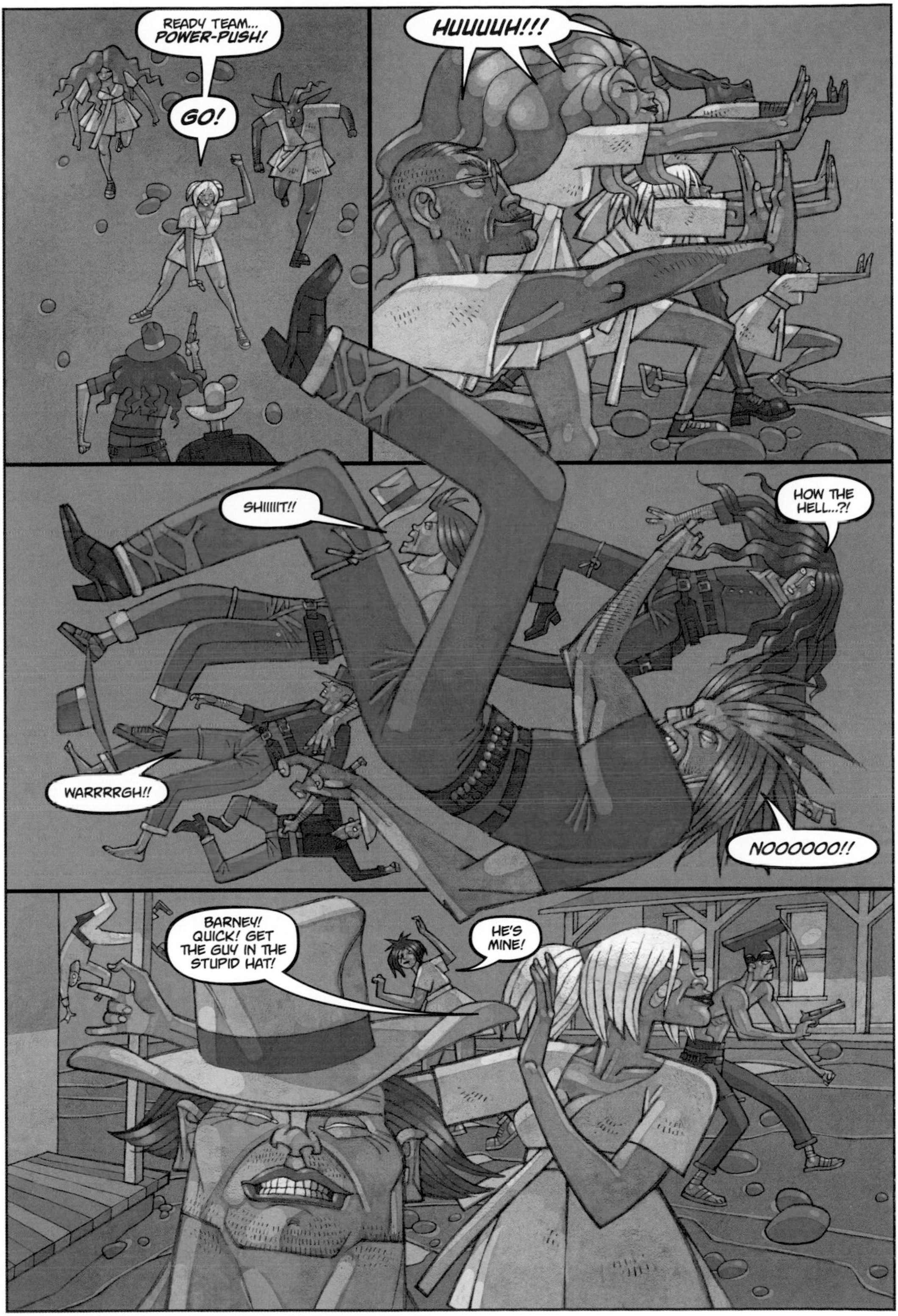
READY TEAM... POWER-PUSH!
GO!
HUUUUH!!!
SHIIIIIT!!
HOW THE HELL...?!
WARRRRGH!!
NOOOOOO!!
BARNEY! QUICK! GET THE GUY IN THE STUPID HAT!
HE'S MINE!

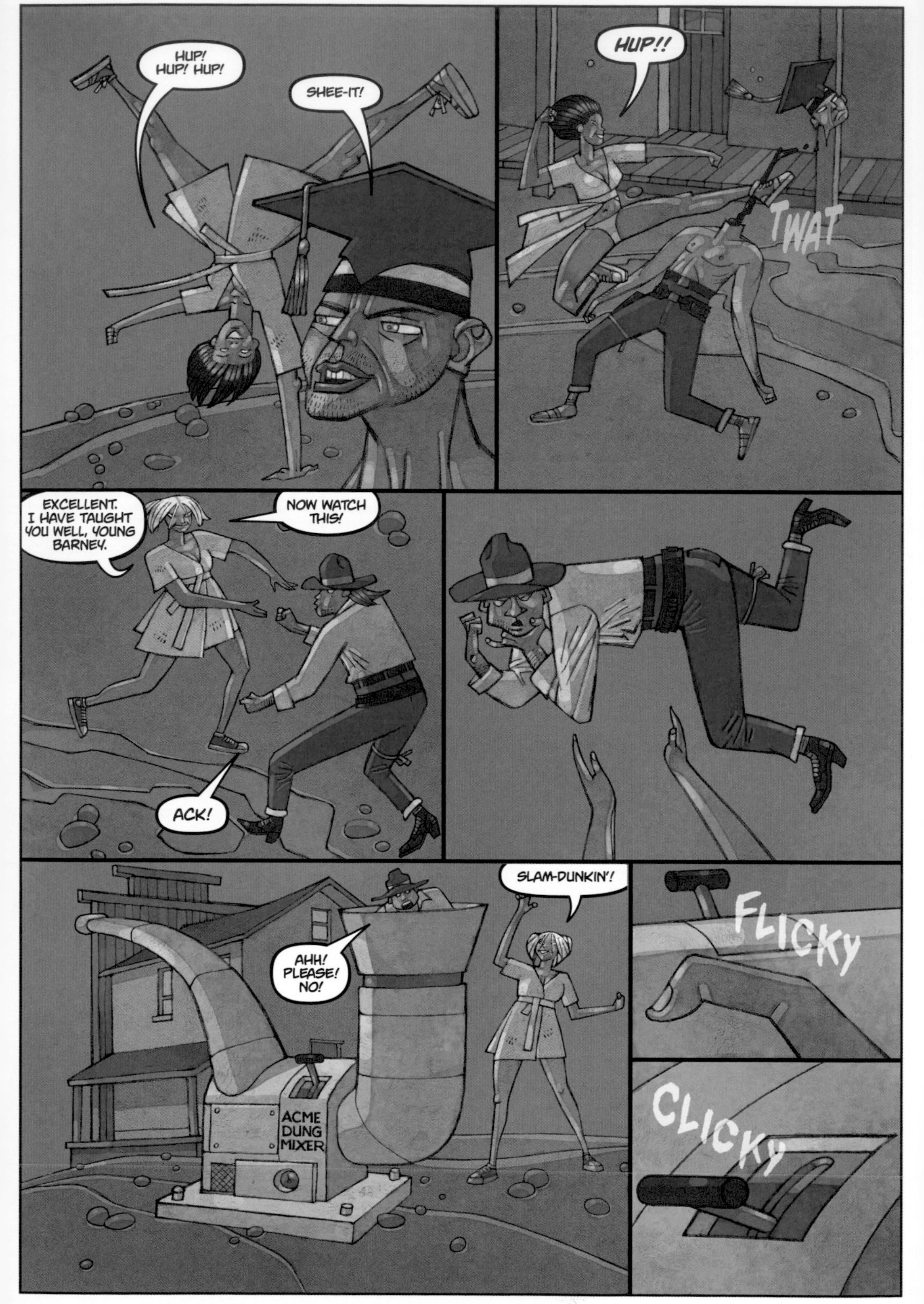
HUP! HUP! HUP!
SHEE-IT!
HUP!!
TWAT
EXCELLENT. I HAVE TAUGHT YOU WELL, YOUNG BARNEY.
NOW WATCH THIS!
ACK!
SLAM-DUNKIN'!
AHH! PLEASE! NO!
ACME DUNG MIXER
FLICKY
CLICKY

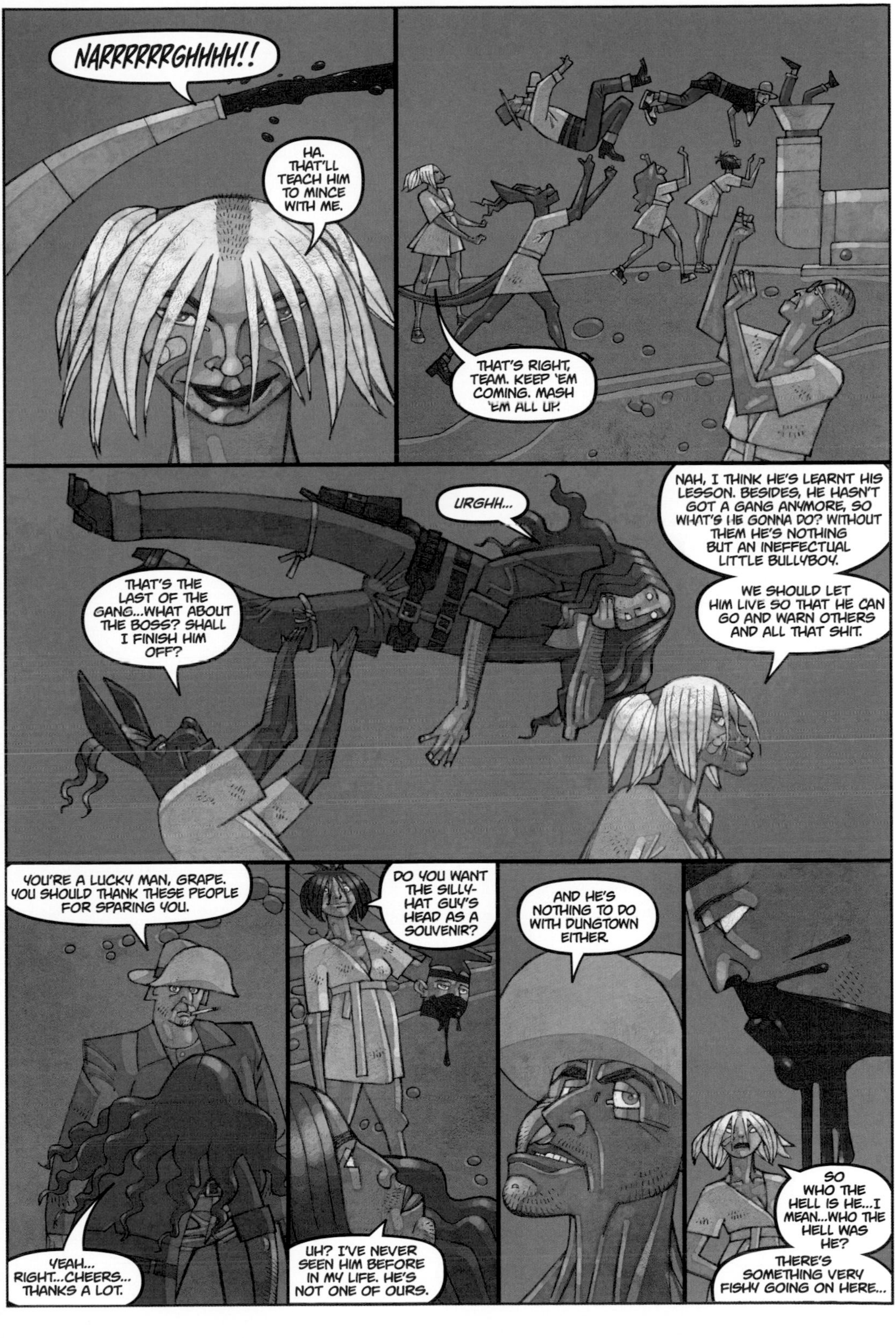
NARRRRRRGHHHH!!
HA. THAT'LL TEACH HIM TO MINCE WITH ME.
THAT'S RIGHT, TEAM. KEEP 'EM COMING. MASH 'EM ALL UP.
URGHH...
THAT'S THE LAST OF THE GANG...WHAT ABOUT THE BOSS? SHALL I FINISH HIM OFF?
NAH, I THINK HE'S LEARNT HIS LESSON. BESIDES, HE HASN'T GOT A GANG ANYMORE, SO WHAT'S HE GONNA DO? WITHOUT THEM HE'S NOTHING BUT AN INEFFECTUAL LITTLE BULLYBOY.
WE SHOULD LET HIM LIVE SO THAT HE CAN GO AND WARN OTHERS AND ALL THAT SHIT.
YOU'RE A LUCKY MAN, GRAPE. YOU SHOULD THANK THESE PEOPLE FOR SPARING YOU.
YEAH... RIGHT...CHEERS... THANKS A LOT.
DO YOU WANT THE SILLY-HAT GUY'S HEAD AS A SOUVENIR?
UH? I'VE NEVER SEEN HIM BEFORE IN MY LIFE. HE'S NOT ONE OF OURS.
AND HE'S NOTHING TO DO WITH DUNGTOWN EITHER.
SO WHO THE HELL IS HE...I MEAN...WHO THE HELL WAS HE?
THERE'S SOMETHING VERY FISHY GOING ON HERE...

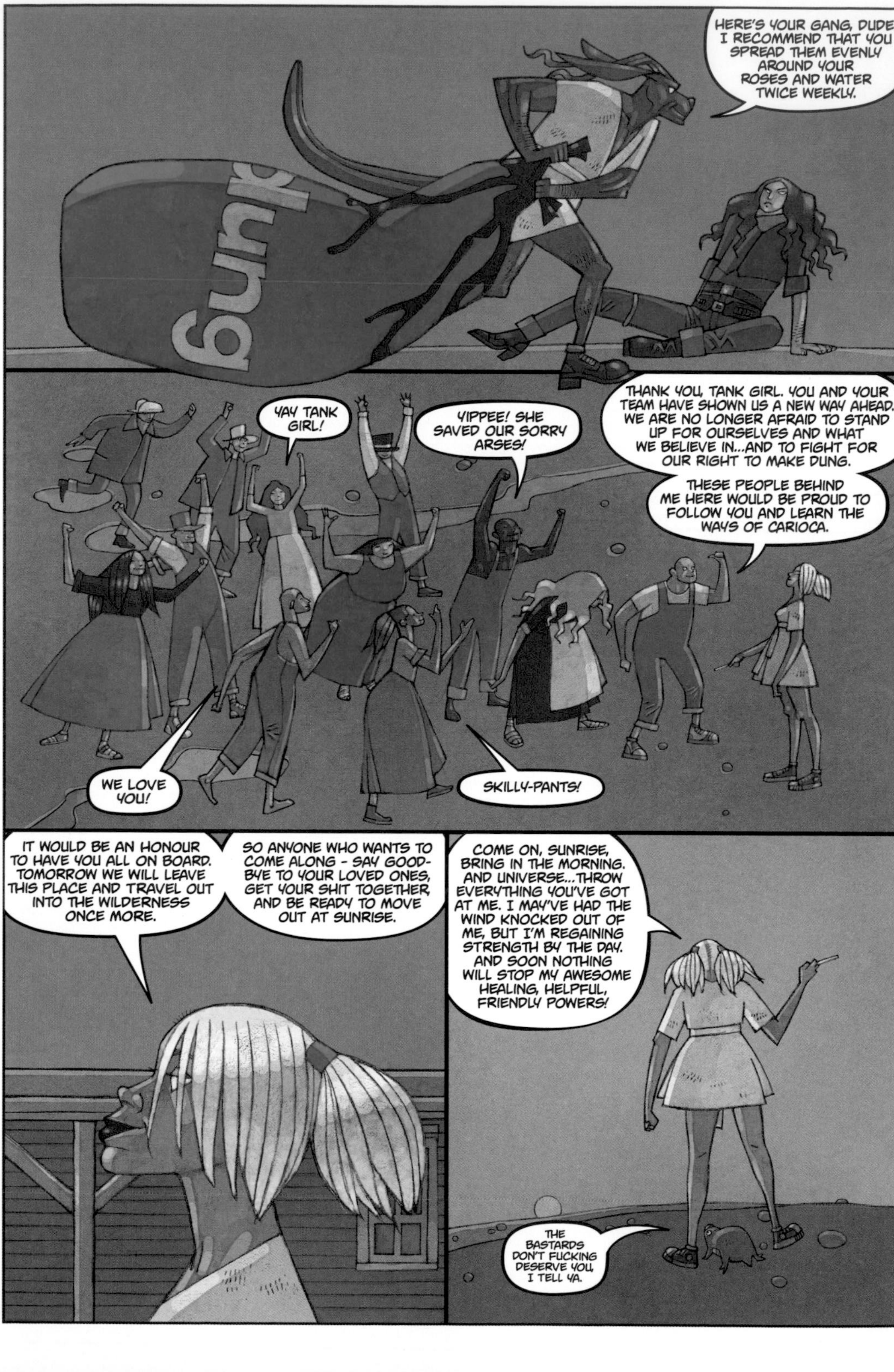
HERE'S YOUR GANG, DUDE. I RECOMMEND THAT YOU SPREAD THEM EVENLY AROUND YOUR ROSES AND WATER TWICE WEEKLY.
dung
YAY TANK GIRL!
YIPPEE! SHE SAVED OUR SORRY ARSES!
THANK YOU, TANK GIRL. YOU AND YOUR TEAM HAVE SHOWN US A NEW WAY AHEAD. WE ARE NO LONGER AFRAID TO STAND UP FOR OURSELVES AND WHAT WE BELIEVE IN...AND TO FIGHT FOR OUR RIGHT TO MAKE DUNG.
THESE PEOPLE BEHIND ME HERE WOULD BE PROUD TO FOLLOW YOU AND LEARN THE WAYS OF CARIOCA.
WE LOVE YOU!
SKILLY-PANTS!
IT WOULD BE AN HONOUR TO HAVE YOU ALL ON BOARD. TOMORROW WE WILL LEAVE THIS PLACE AND TRAVEL OUT INTO THE WILDERNESS ONCE MORE.
SO ANYONE WHO WANTS TO COME ALONG - SAY GOOD-BYE TO YOUR LOVED ONES, GET YOUR SHIT TOGETHER, AND BE READY TO MOVE OUT AT SUNRISE.
COME ON, SUNRISE, BRING IN THE MORNING. AND UNIVERSE...THROW EVERYTHING YOU'VE GOT AT ME. I MAY'VE HAD THE WIND KNOCKED OUT OF ME, BUT I'M REGAINING STRENGTH BY THE DAY. AND SOON NOTHING WILL STOP MY AWESOME HEALING, HELPFUL, FRIENDLY POWERS!
THE BASTARDS DON'T FUCKING DESERVE YOU, I TELL YA.

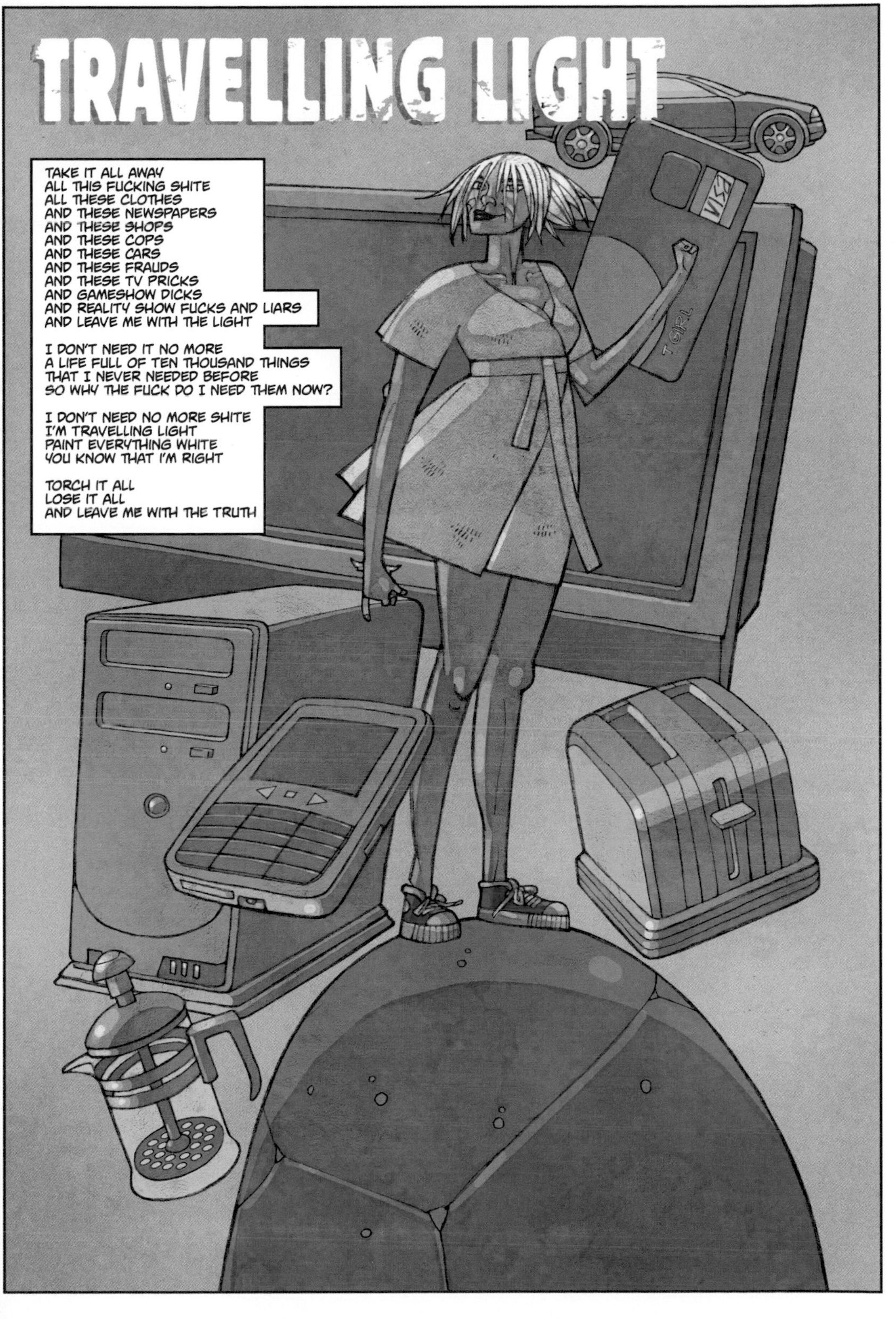
TRAVELLING LIGHT
TAKE IT ALL AWAY
ALL THIS FUCKING SHITE
ALL THESE CLOTHES
AND THESE NEWSPAPERS
AND THESE SHOPS
AND THESE COPS
AND THESE CARS
AND THESE FRAUDS
AND THESE TV PRICKS
AND GAMESHOW DICKS
AND REALITY SHOW FUCKS AND LIARS
AND LEAVE ME WITH THE LIGHT

I DON'T NEED IT NO MORE
A LIFE FULL OF TEN THOUSAND THINGS
THAT I NEVER NEEDED BEFORE
SO WHY THE FUCK DO I NEED THEM NOW?

I DON'T NEED NO MORE SHITE
I'M TRAVELLING LIGHT
PAINT EVERYTHING WHITE
YOU KNOW THAT I'M RIGHT

TORCH IT ALL
LOSE IT ALL
AND LEAVE ME WITH THE TRUTH
VISA
T GIRL

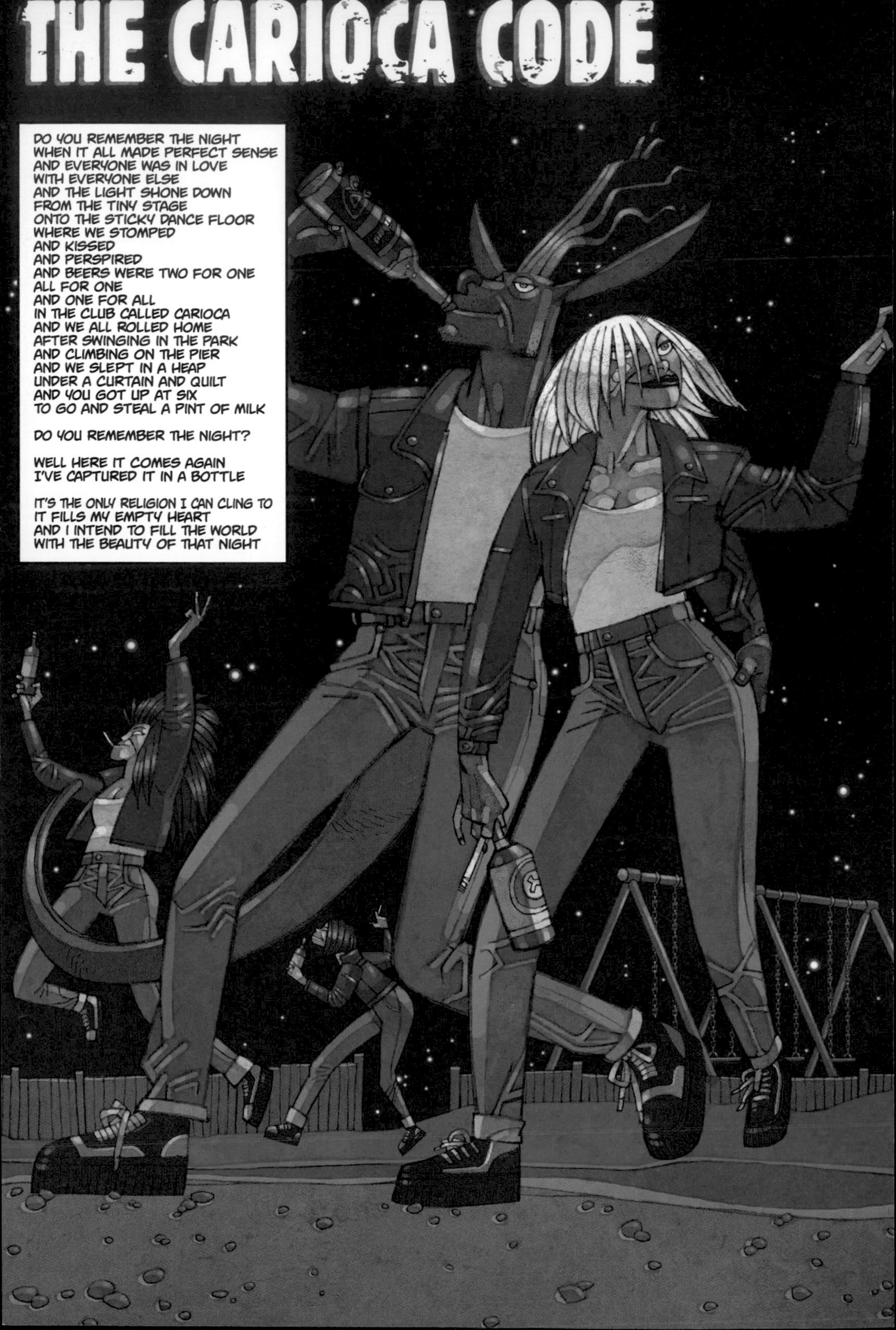
THE CARIOCA CODE
DO YOU REMEMBER THE NIGHT
WHEN IT ALL MADE PERFECT SENSE
AND EVERYONE WAS IN LOVE
WITH EVERYONE ELSE
AND THE LIGHT SHONE DOWN
FROM THE TINY STAGE
ONTO THE STICKY DANCE FLOOR
WHERE WE STOMPED
AND KISSED
AND PERSPIRED
AND BEERS WERE TWO FOR ONE
ALL FOR ONE
AND ONE FOR ALL
IN THE CLUB CALLED CARIOCA
AND WE ALL ROLLED HOME
AFTER SWINGING IN THE PARK
AND CLIMBING ON THE PIER
AND WE SLEPT IN A HEAP
UNDER A CURTAIN AND QUILT
AND YOU GOT UP AT SIX
TO GO AND STEAL A PINT OF MILK
DO YOU REMEMBER THE NIGHT?
WELL HERE IT COMES AGAIN
I'VE CAPTURED IT IN A BOTTLE
IT'S THE ONLY RELIGION I CAN CLING TO
IT FILLS MY EMPTY HEART
AND I INTEND TO FILL THE WORLD
WITH THE BEAUTY OF THAT NIGHT

THE GOLDEN HOUR

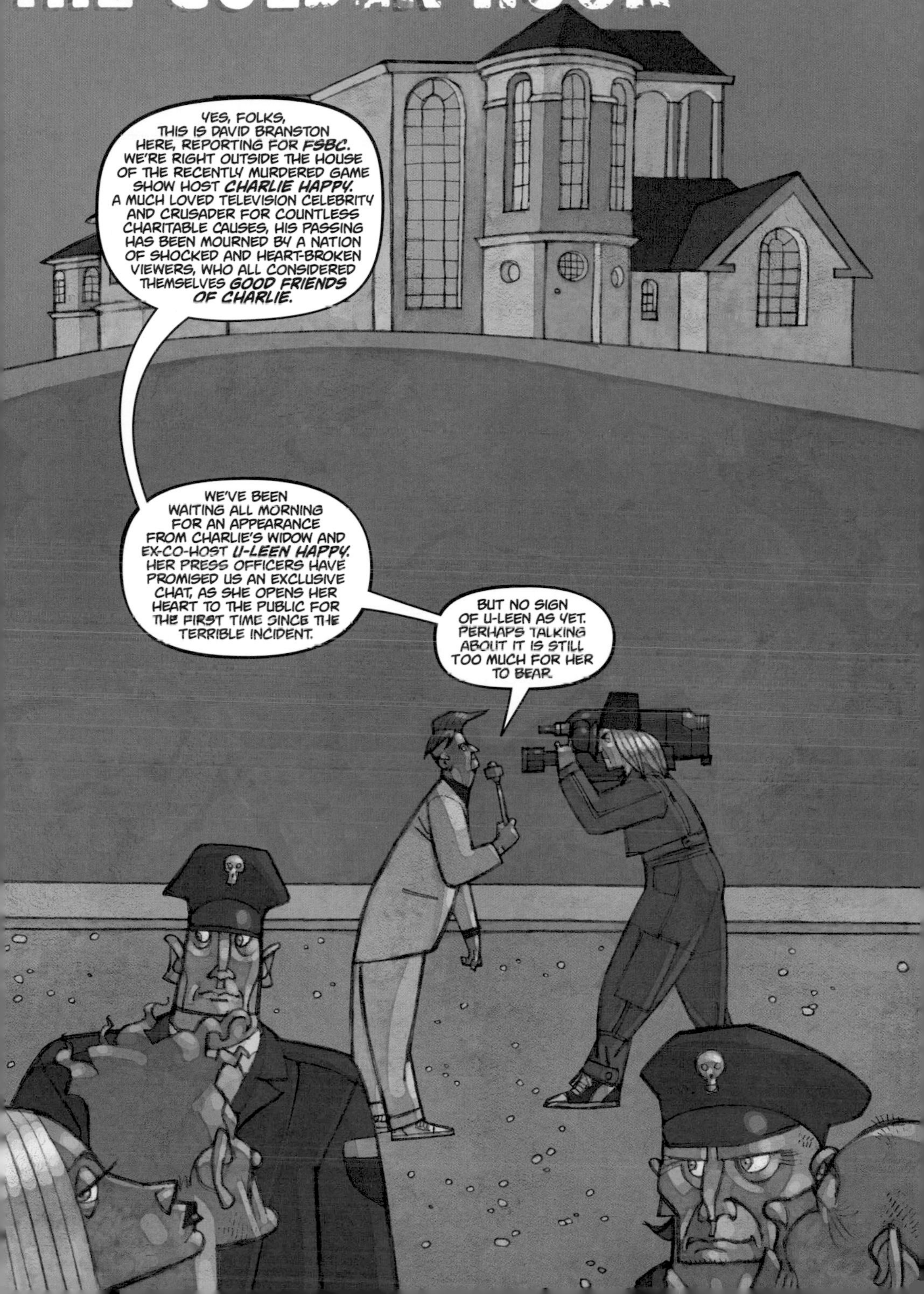

YES, FOLKS, THIS IS DAVID BRANSTON HERE, REPORTING FOR FSBC. WE'RE RIGHT OUTSIDE THE HOUSE OF THE RECENTLY MURDERED GAME SHOW HOST CHARLIE HAPPY. A MUCH LOVED TELEVISION CELEBRITY AND CRUSADER FOR COUNTLESS CHARITABLE CAUSES, HIS PASSING HAS BEEN MOURNED BY A NATION OF SHOCKED AND HEART-BROKEN VIEWERS, WHO ALL CONSIDERED THEMSELVES GOOD FRIENDS OF CHARLIE.
WE'VE BEEN WAITING ALL MORNING FOR AN APPEARANCE FROM CHARLIE'S WIDOW AND EX-CO-HOST U-LEEN HAPPY. HER PRESS OFFICERS HAVE PROMISED US AN EXCLUSIVE CHAT, AS SHE OPENS HER HEART TO THE PUBLIC FOR THE FIRST TIME SINCE THE TERRIBLE INCIDENT.
BUT NO SIGN OF U-LEEN AS YET. PERHAPS TALKING ABOUT IT IS STILL TOO MUCH FOR HER TO BEAR.

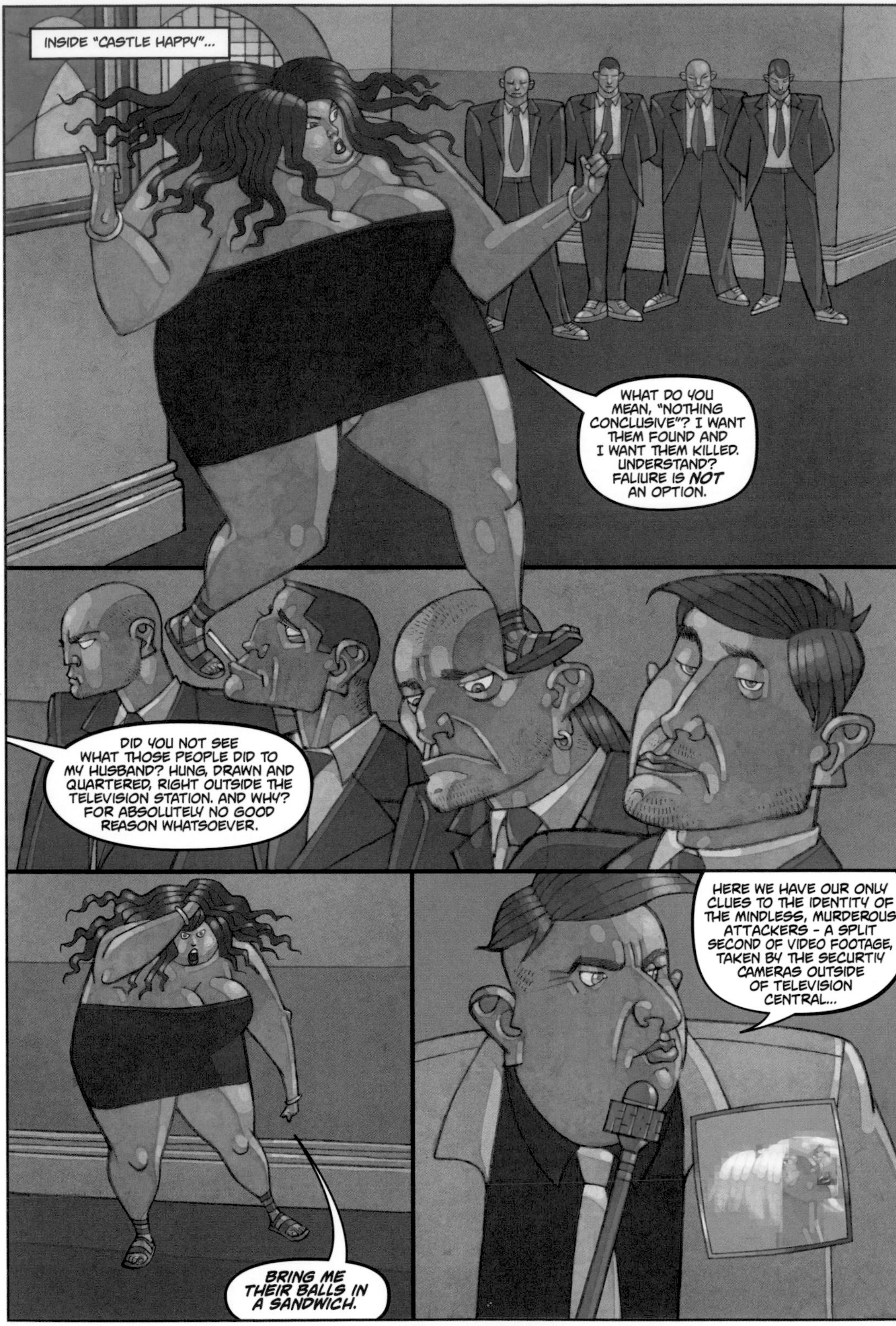
INSIDE "CASTLE HAPPY"...
WHAT DO YOU MEAN, "NOTHING CONCLUSIVE"? I WANT THEM FOUND AND I WANT THEM KILLED. UNDERSTAND? FALIURE IS NOT AN OPTION.
DID YOU NOT SEE WHAT THOSE PEOPLE DID TO MY HUSBAND? HUNG, DRAWN AND QUARTERED, RIGHT OUTSIDE THE TELEVISION STATION. AND WHY? FOR ABSOLUTELY NO GOOD REASON WHATSOEVER.
BRING ME THEIR BALLS IN A SANDWICH.
HERE WE HAVE OUR ONLY CLUES TO THE IDENTITY OF THE MINDLESS, MURDEROUS ATTACKERS - A SPLIT SECOND OF VIDEO FOOTAGE, TAKEN BY THE SECURTIY CAMERAS OUTSIDE OF TELEVISION CENTRAL...

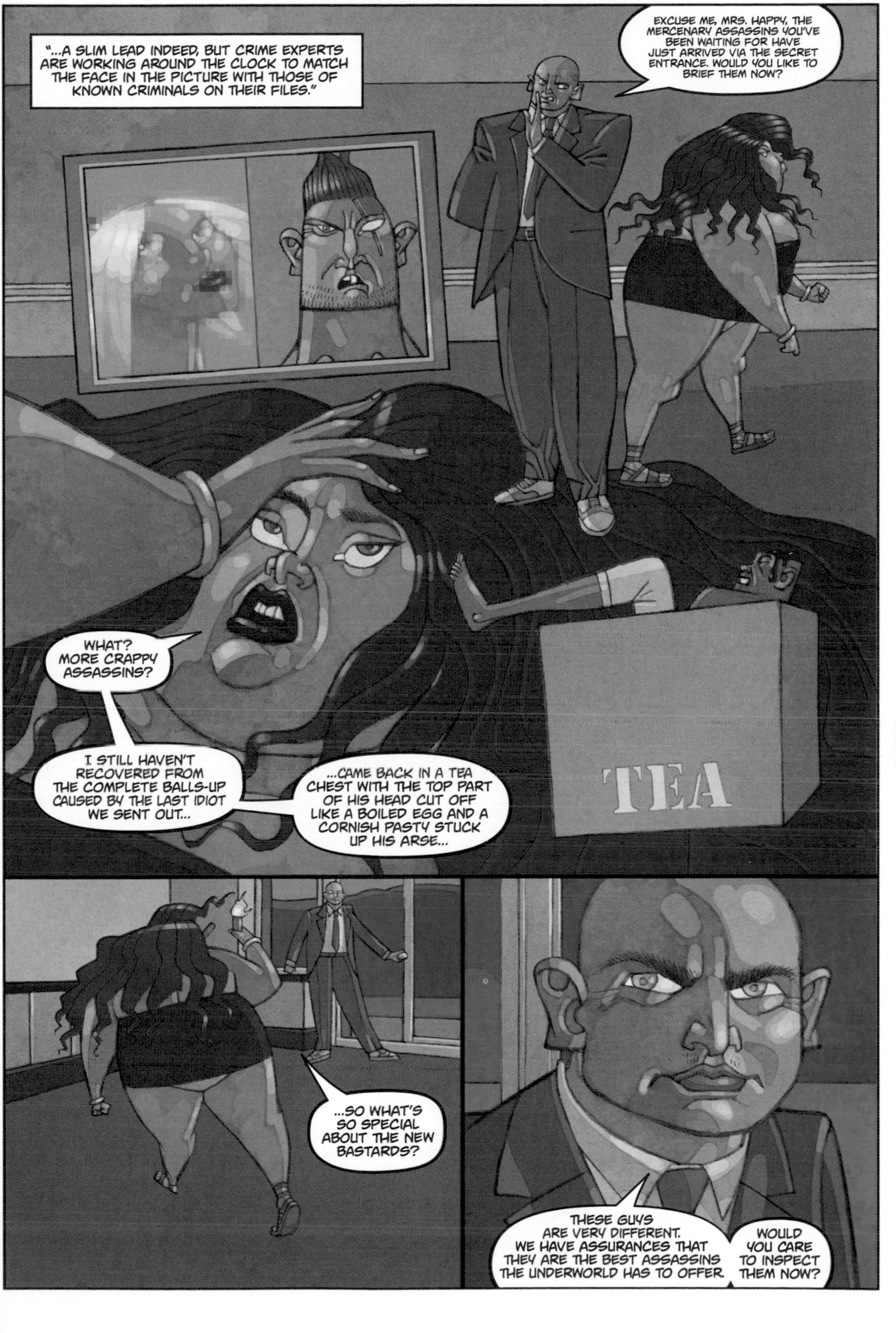
"...A SLIM LEAD INDEED, BUT CRIME EXPERTS ARE WORKING AROUND THE CLOCK TO MATCH THE FACE IN THE PICTURE WITH THOSE OF KNOWN CRIMINALS ON THEIR FILES."
EXCUSE ME, MRS. HAPPY, THE MERCENARY ASSASSINS YOU'VE BEEN WAITING FOR HAVE JUST ARRIVED VIA THE SECRET ENTRANCE. WOULD YOU LIKE TO BRIEF THEM NOW?
WHAT? MORE CRAPPY ASSASSINS?
I STILL HAVEN'T RECOVERED FROM THE COMPLETE BALLS-UP CAUSED BY THE LAST IDIOT WE SENT OUT...
...CAME BACK IN A TEA CHEST WITH THE TOP PART OF HIS HEAD CUT OFF LIKE A BOILED EGG AND A CORNISH PASTY STUCK UP HIS ARSE...
TEA
...SO WHAT'S SO SPECIAL ABOUT THE NEW BASTARDS?
THESE GUYS ARE VERY DIFFERENT. WE HAVE ASSURANCES THAT THEY ARE THE BEST ASSASSINS THE UNDERWORLD HAS TO OFFER.
WOULD YOU CARE TO INSPECT THEM NOW?

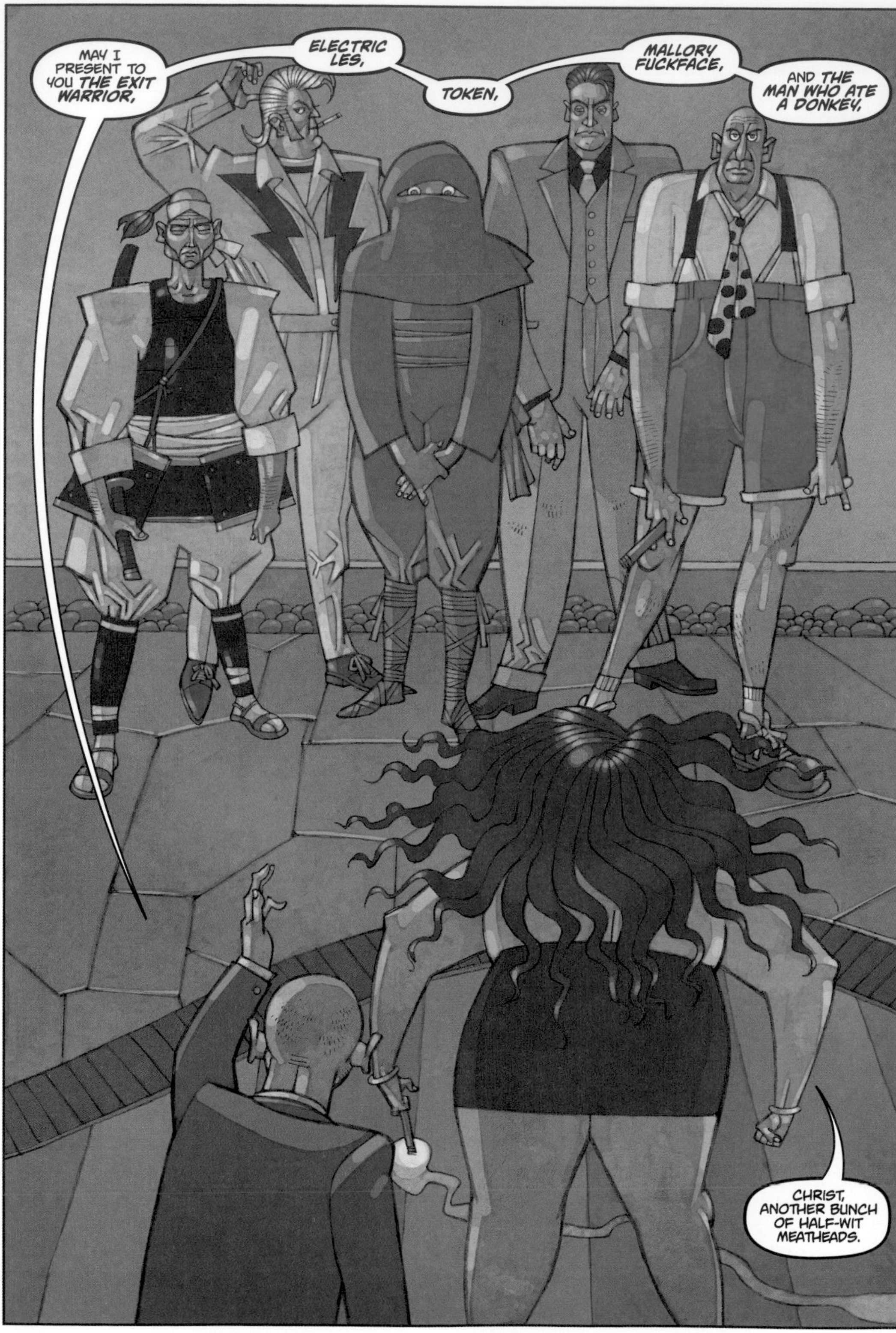
MAY I PRESENT TO YOU THE EXIT WARRIOR,
ELECTRIC LES,
TOKEN,
MALLORY FUCKFACE,
AND THE MAN WHO ATE A DONKEY,
CHRIST, ANOTHER BUNCH OF HALF-WIT MEATHEADS.

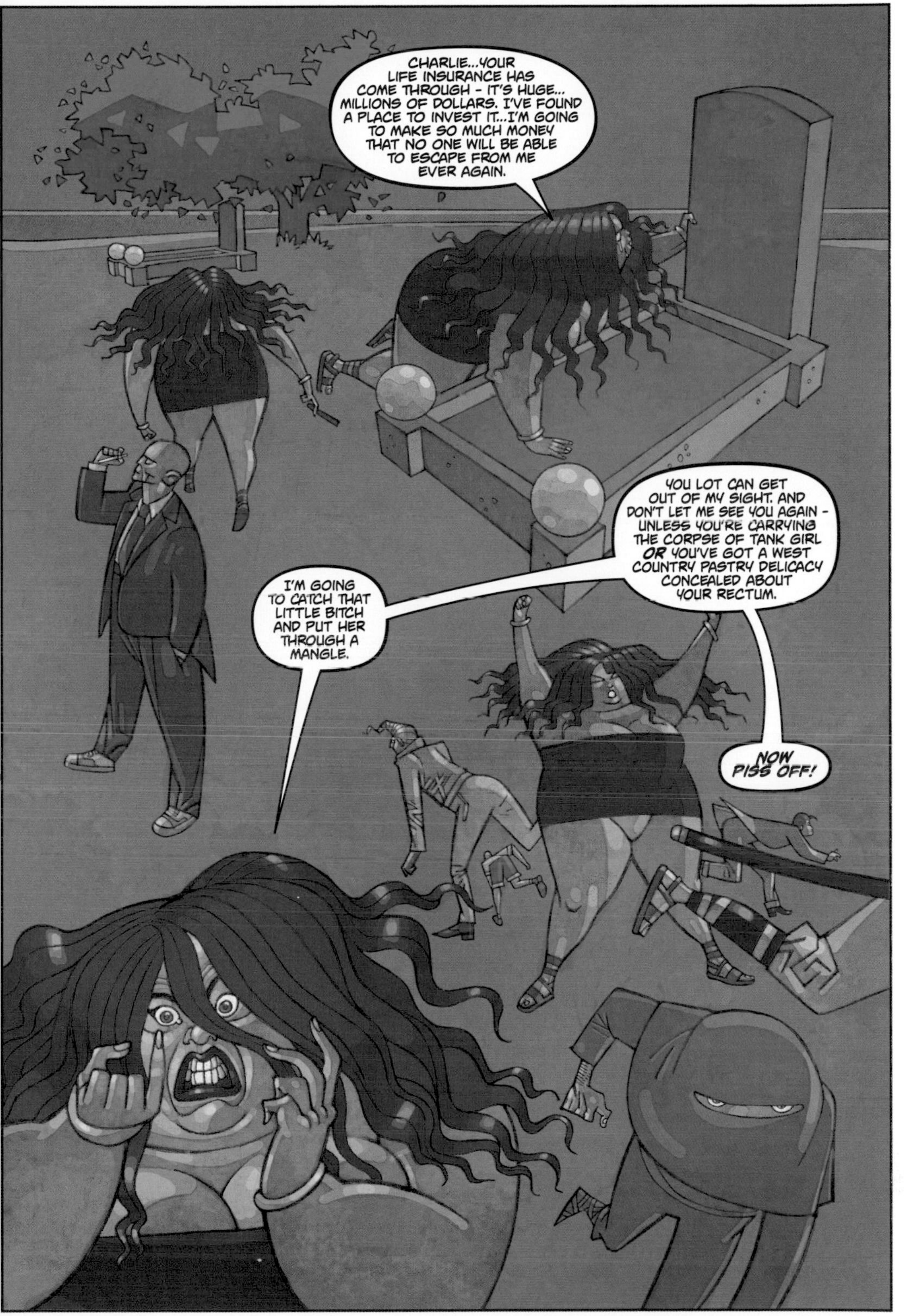
CHARLIE...YOUR LIFE INSURANCE HAS COME THROUGH - IT'S HUGE... MILLIONS OF DOLLARS. I'VE FOUND A PLACE TO INVEST IT...I'M GOING TO MAKE SO MUCH MONEY THAT NO ONE WILL BE ABLE TO ESCAPE FROM ME EVER AGAIN.
I'M GOING TO CATCH THAT LITTLE BITCH AND PUT HER THROUGH A MANGLE.
YOU LOT CAN GET OUT OF MY SIGHT. AND DON'T LET ME SEE YOU AGAIN - UNLESS YOU'RE CARRYING THE CORPSE OF TANK GIRL *OR* YOU'VE GOT A WEST COUNTRY PASTRY DELICACY CONCEALED ABOUT YOUR RECTUM.
NOW PISS OFF!

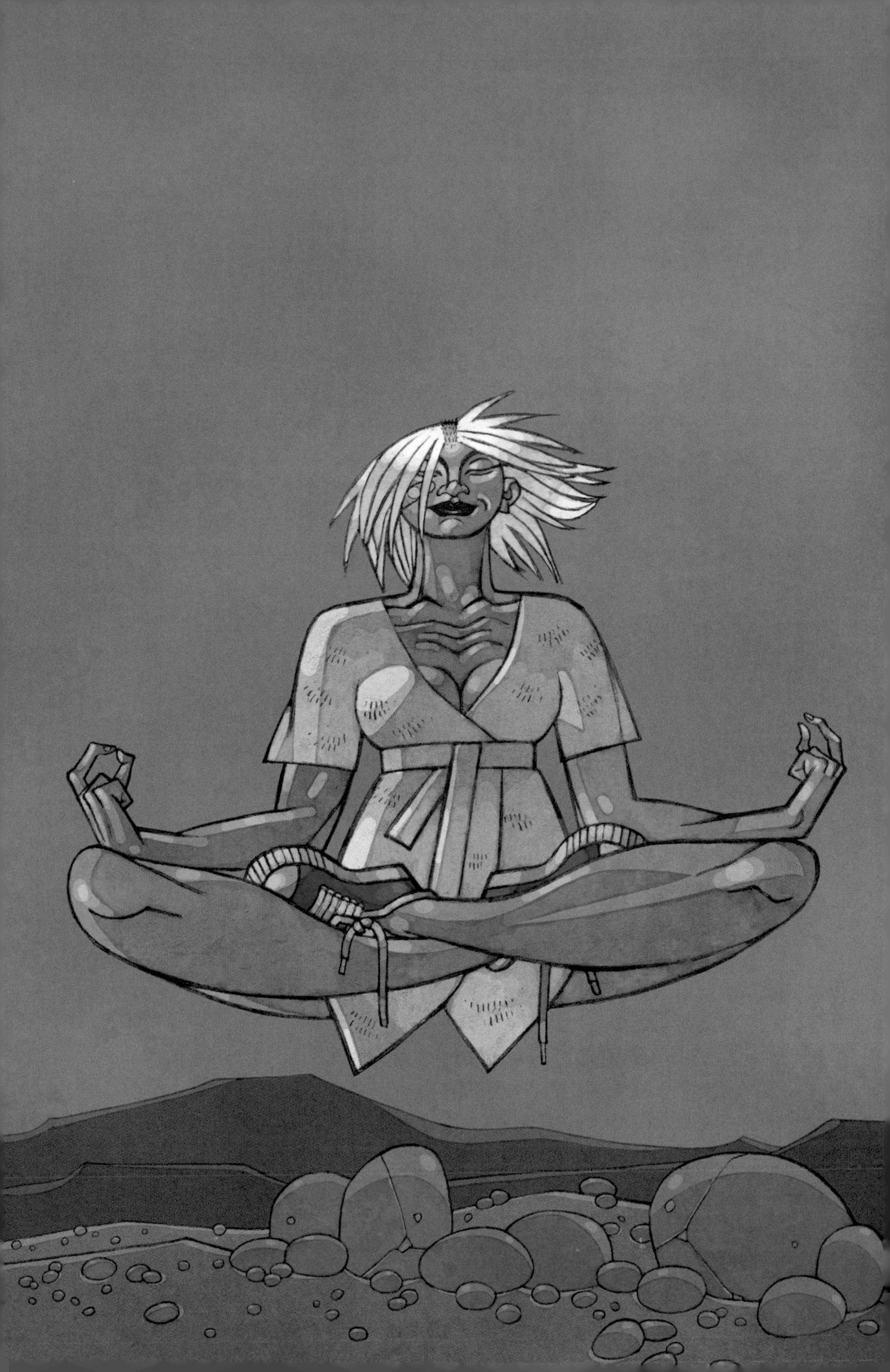

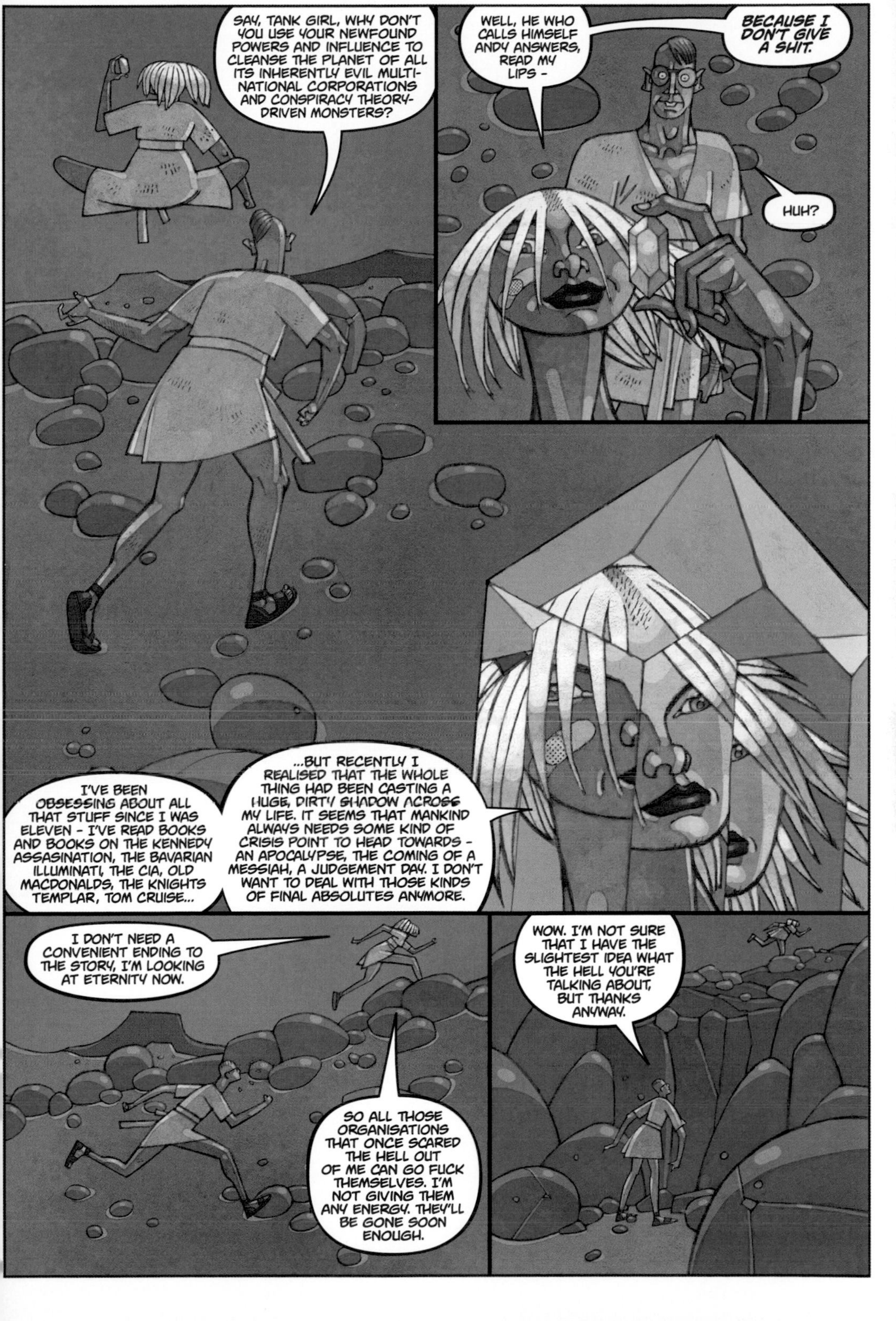
SAY, TANK GIRL, WHY DON'T YOU USE YOUR NEWFOUND POWERS AND INFLUENCE TO CLEANSE THE PLANET OF ALL ITS INHERENTLY EVIL MULTI-NATIONAL CORPORATIONS AND CONSPIRACY THEORY-DRIVEN MONSTERS?
WELL, HE WHO CALLS HIMSELF ANDY ANSWERS, READ MY LIPS -
BECAUSE I DON'T GIVE A SHIT.
HUH?
I'VE BEEN OBSESSING ABOUT ALL THAT STUFF SINCE I WAS ELEVEN - I'VE READ BOOKS AND BOOKS ON THE KENNEDY ASSASINATION, THE BAVARIAN ILLUMINATI, THE CIA, OLD MACDONALDS, THE KNIGHTS TEMPLAR, TOM CRUISE...
...BUT RECENTLY I REALISED THAT THE WHOLE THING HAD BEEN CASTING A HUGE, DIRTY SHADOW ACROSS MY LIFE. IT SEEMS THAT MANKIND ALWAYS NEEDS SOME KIND OF CRISIS POINT TO HEAD TOWARDS - AN APOCALYPSE, THE COMING OF A MESSIAH, A JUDGEMENT DAY. I DON'T WANT TO DEAL WITH THOSE KINDS OF FINAL ABSOLUTES ANYMORE.
I DON'T NEED A CONVENIENT ENDING TO THE STORY, I'M LOOKING AT ETERNITY NOW.
SO ALL THOSE ORGANISATIONS THAT ONCE SCARED THE HELL OUT OF ME CAN GO FUCK THEMSELVES. I'M NOT GIVING THEM ANY ENERGY. THEY'LL BE GONE SOON ENOUGH.
WOW. I'M NOT SURE THAT I HAVE THE SLIGHTEST IDEA WHAT THE HELL YOU'RE TALKING ABOUT, BUT THANKS ANYWAY.

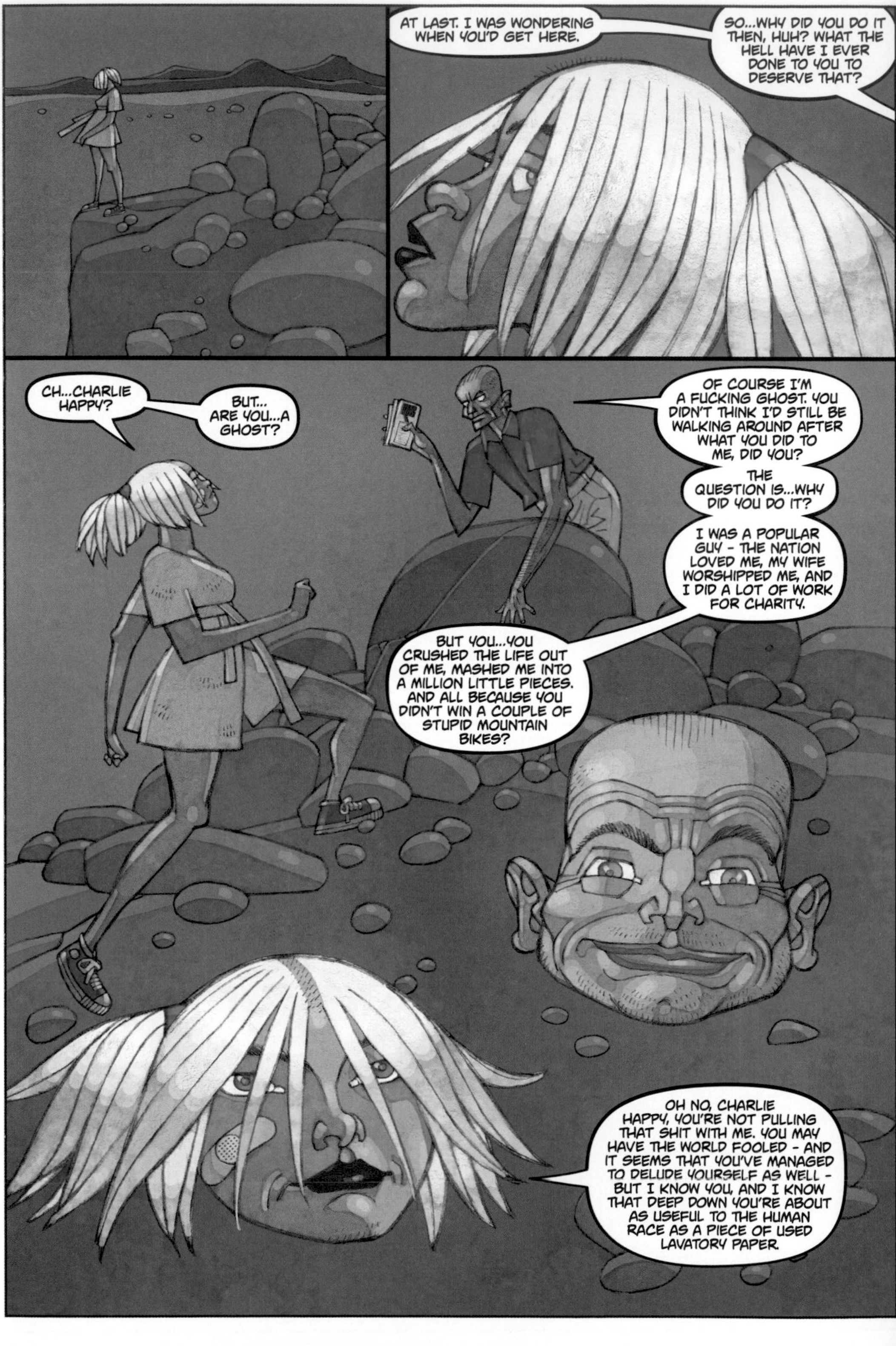
AT LAST. I WAS WONDERING WHEN YOU'D GET HERE.
SO...WHY DID YOU DO IT THEN, HUH? WHAT THE HELL HAVE I EVER DONE TO YOU TO DESERVE THAT?
CH...CHARLIE HAPPY?
BUT... ARE YOU...A GHOST?
OF COURSE I'M A FUCKING GHOST. YOU DIDN'T THINK I'D STILL BE WALKING AROUND AFTER WHAT YOU DID TO ME, DID YOU?
THE QUESTION IS...WHY DID YOU DO IT?
I WAS A POPULAR GUY - THE NATION LOVED ME, MY WIFE WORSHIPPED ME, AND I DID A LOT OF WORK FOR CHARITY.
BUT YOU...YOU CRUSHED THE LIFE OUT OF ME, MASHED ME INTO A MILLION LITTLE PIECES. AND ALL BECAUSE YOU DIDN'T WIN A COUPLE OF STUPID MOUNTAIN BIKES?
OH NO, CHARLIE HAPPY, YOU'RE NOT PULLING THAT SHIT WITH ME. YOU MAY HAVE THE WORLD FOOLED - AND IT SEEMS THAT YOU'VE MANAGED TO DELUDE YOURSELF AS WELL - BUT I KNOW YOU, AND I KNOW THAT DEEP DOWN YOU'RE ABOUT AS USEFUL TO THE HUMAN RACE AS A PIECE OF USED LAVATORY PAPER.

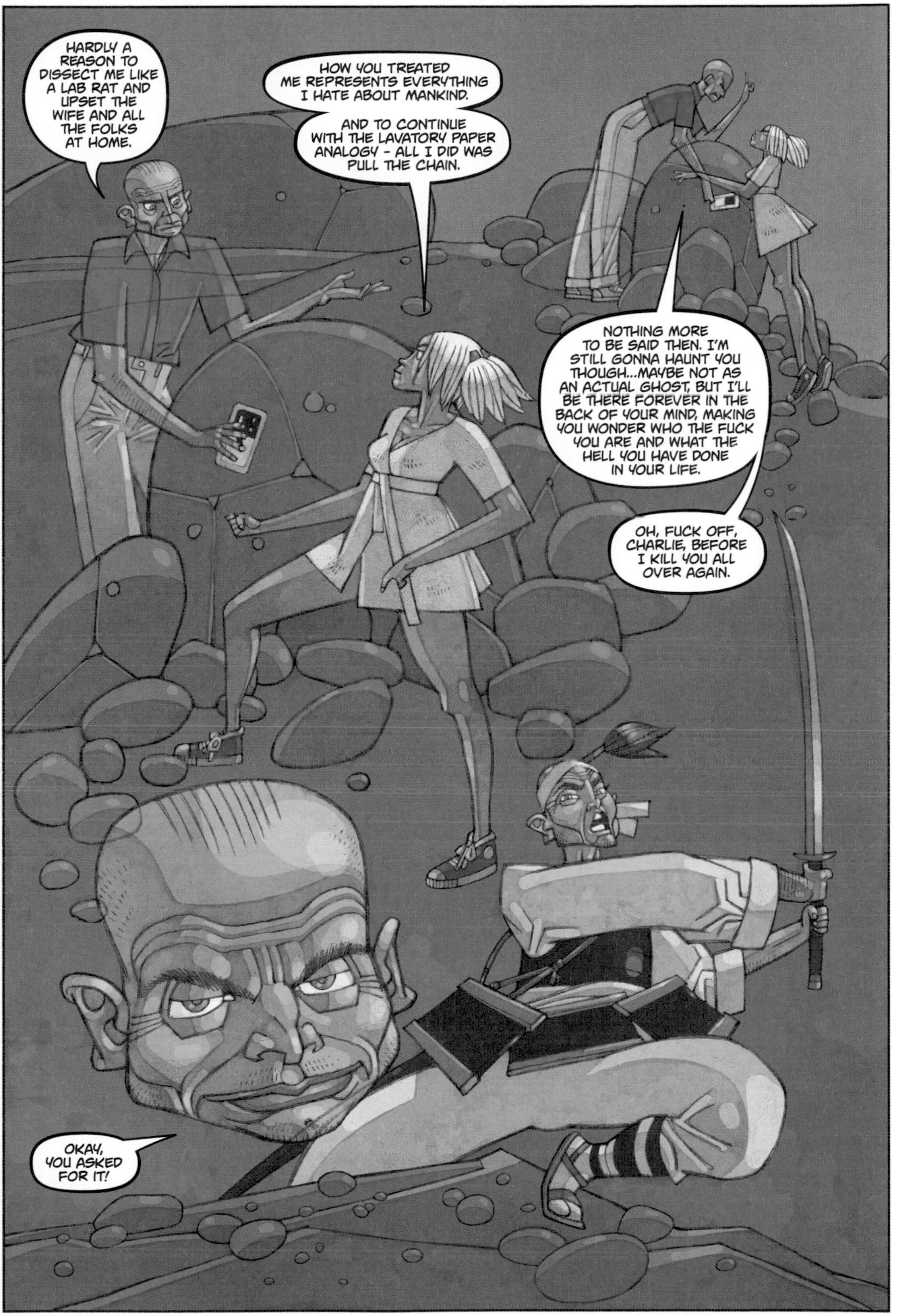
HARDLY A REASON TO DISSECT ME LIKE A LAB RAT AND UPSET THE WIFE AND ALL THE FOLKS AT HOME.
HOW YOU TREATED ME REPRESENTS EVERYTHING I HATE ABOUT MANKIND.
AND TO CONTINUE WITH THE LAVATORY PAPER ANALOGY - ALL I DID WAS PULL THE CHAIN.
NOTHING MORE TO BE SAID THEN. I'M STILL GONNA HAUNT YOU THOUGH...MAYBE NOT AS AN ACTUAL GHOST, BUT I'LL BE THERE FOREVER IN THE BACK OF YOUR MIND, MAKING YOU WONDER WHO THE FUCK YOU ARE AND WHAT THE HELL YOU HAVE DONE IN YOUR LIFE.
OH, FUCK OFF, CHARLIE, BEFORE I KILL YOU ALL OVER AGAIN.
OKAY, YOU ASKED FOR IT!

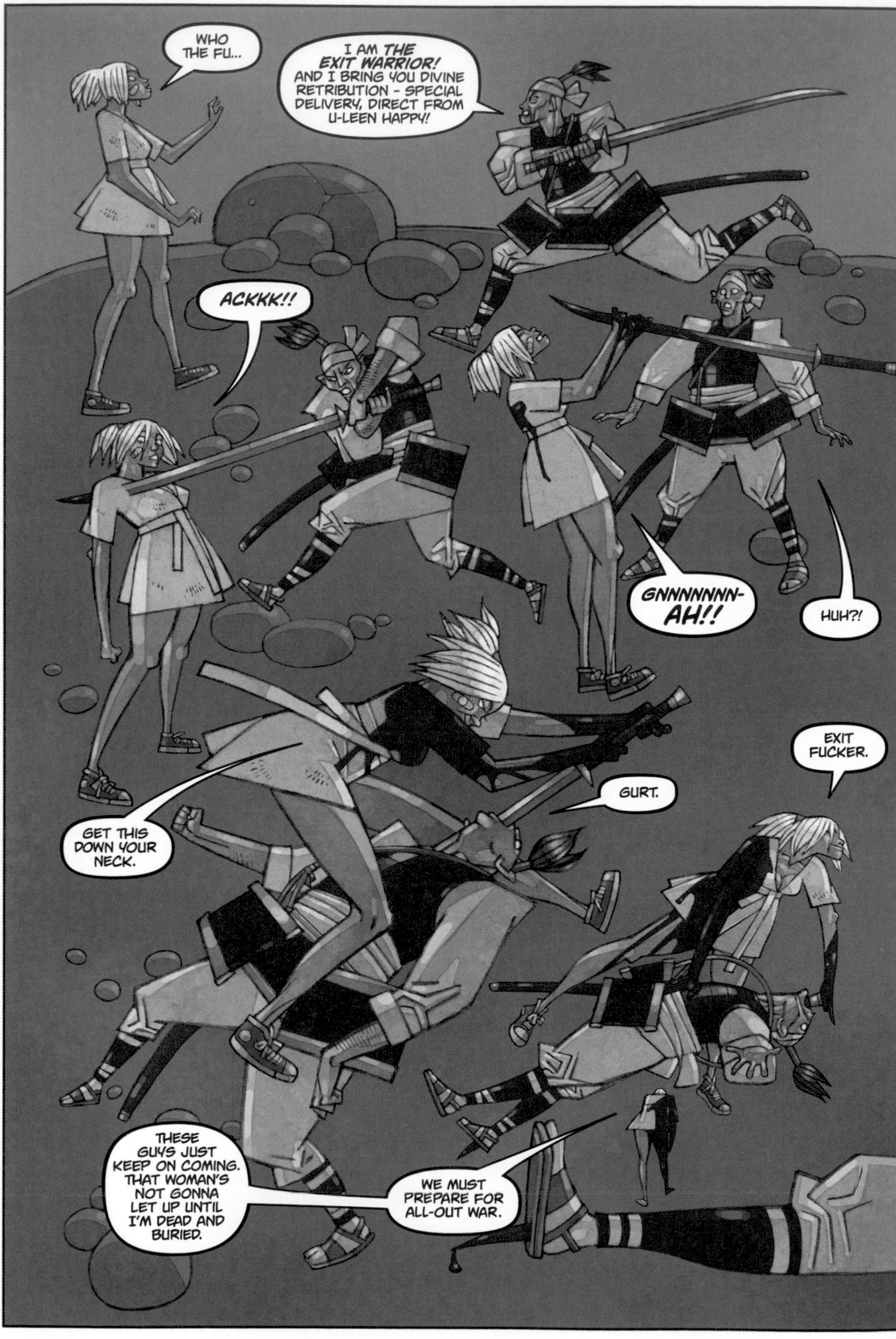
WHO THE FU...
I AM THE EXIT WARRIOR! AND I BRING YOU DIVINE RETRIBUTION - SPECIAL DELIVERY, DIRECT FROM U-LEEN HAPPY!
ACKKK!!
GNNNNNNN-AH!!
HUH?!
EXIT FUCKER.
GURT.
GET THIS DOWN YOUR NECK.
THESE GUYS JUST KEEP ON COMING. THAT WOMAN'S NOT GONNA LET UP UNTIL I'M DEAD AND BURIED.
WE MUST PREPARE FOR ALL-OUT WAR.

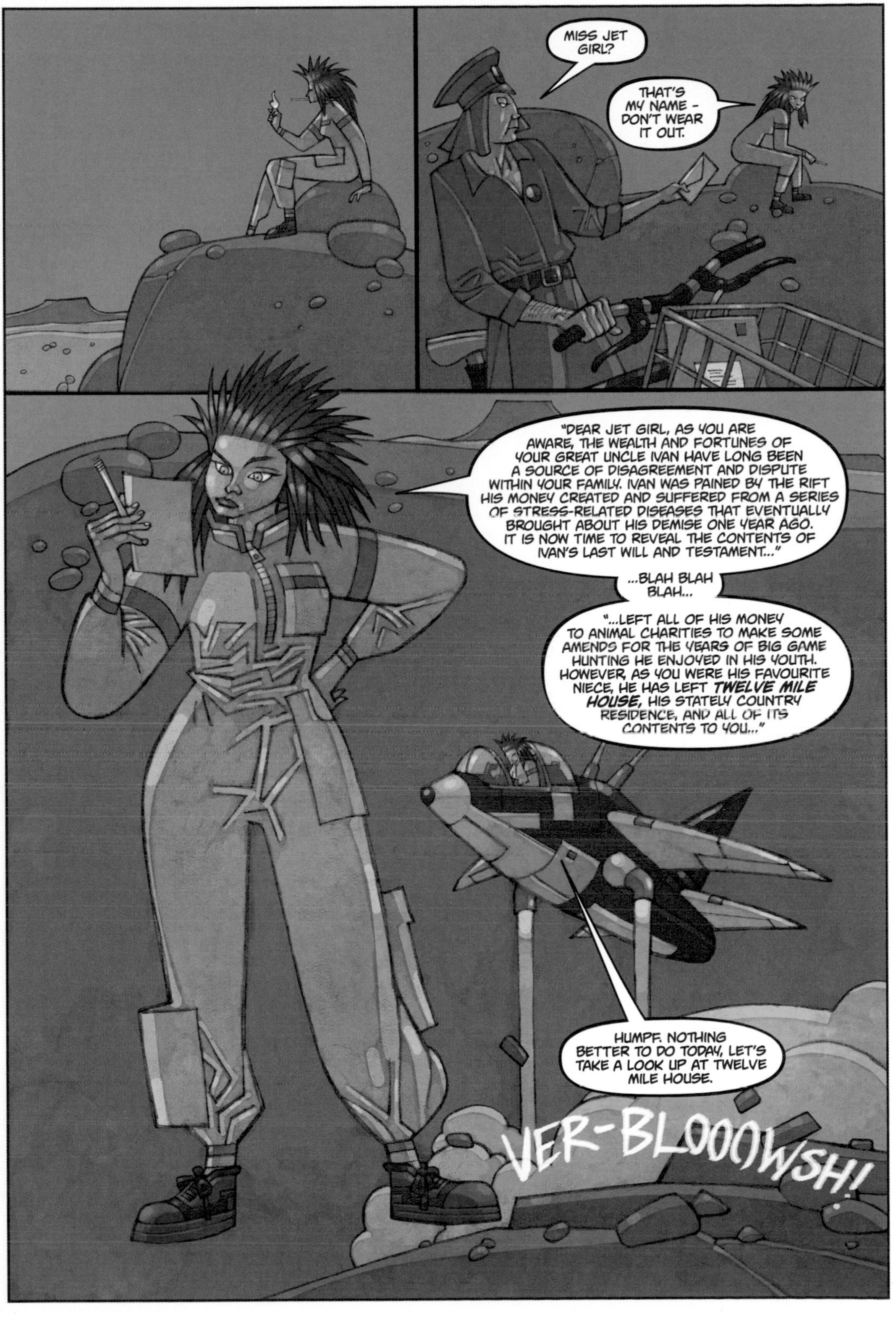
MISS JET GIRL?
THAT'S MY NAME - DON'T WEAR IT OUT.
"DEAR JET GIRL, AS YOU ARE AWARE, THE WEALTH AND FORTUNES OF YOUR GREAT UNCLE IVAN HAVE LONG BEEN A SOURCE OF DISAGREEMENT AND DISPUTE WITHIN YOUR FAMILY. IVAN WAS PAINED BY THE RIFT HIS MONEY CREATED AND SUFFERED FROM A SERIES OF STRESS-RELATED DISEASES THAT EVENTUALLY BROUGHT ABOUT HIS DEMISE ONE YEAR AGO. IT IS NOW TIME TO REVEAL THE CONTENTS OF IVAN'S LAST WILL AND TESTAMENT..."
...BLAH BLAH BLAH...
"...LEFT ALL OF HIS MONEY TO ANIMAL CHARITIES TO MAKE SOME AMENDS FOR THE YEARS OF BIG GAME HUNTING HE ENJOYED IN HIS YOUTH. HOWEVER, AS YOU WERE HIS FAVOURITE NIECE, HE HAS LEFT ***TWELVE MILE HOUSE,*** HIS STATELY COUNTRY RESIDENCE, AND ALL OF ITS CONTENTS TO YOU..."
HUMPF. NOTHING BETTER TO DO TODAY, LET'S TAKE A LOOK UP AT TWELVE MILE HOUSE.
VER-BLOOOWSH!

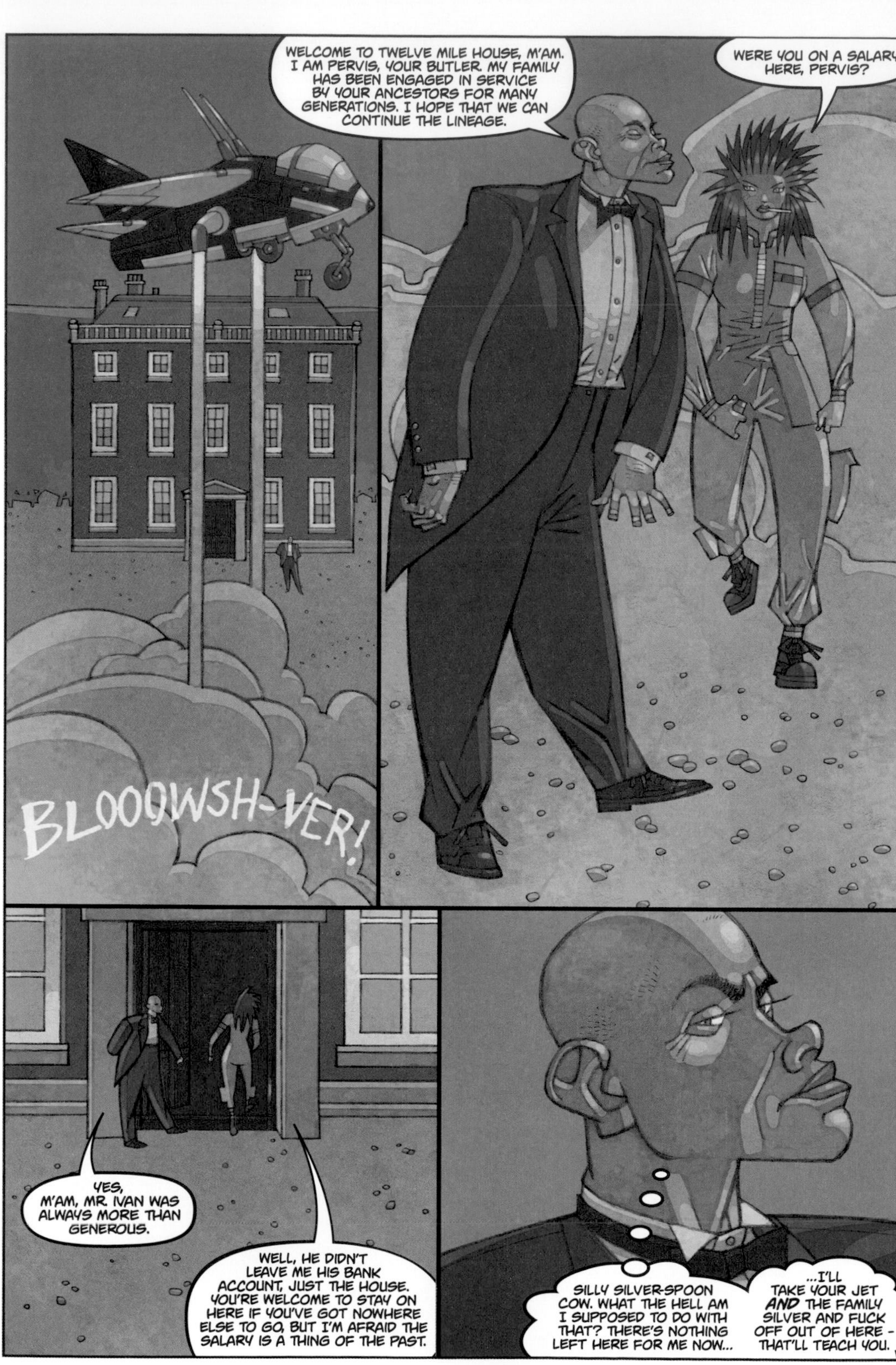
BLOOOWSH-VER!
WELCOME TO TWELVE MILE HOUSE, M'AM. I AM PERVIS, YOUR BUTLER. MY FAMILY HAS BEEN ENGAGED IN SERVICE BY YOUR ANCESTORS FOR MANY GENERATIONS. I HOPE THAT WE CAN CONTINUE THE LINEAGE.
WERE YOU ON A SALARY HERE, PERVIS?
YES, M'AM, MR. IVAN WAS ALWAYS MORE THAN GENEROUS.
WELL, HE DIDN'T LEAVE ME HIS BANK ACCOUNT, JUST THE HOUSE. YOU'RE WELCOME TO STAY ON HERE IF YOU'VE GOT NOWHERE ELSE TO GO, BUT I'M AFRAID THE SALARY IS A THING OF THE PAST.
SILLY SILVER-SPOON COW. WHAT THE HELL AM I SUPPOSED TO DO WITH THAT? THERE'S NOTHING LEFT HERE FOR ME NOW...
...I'LL TAKE YOUR JET **AND** THE FAMILY SILVER AND FUCK OFF OUT OF HERE - THAT'LL TEACH YOU.

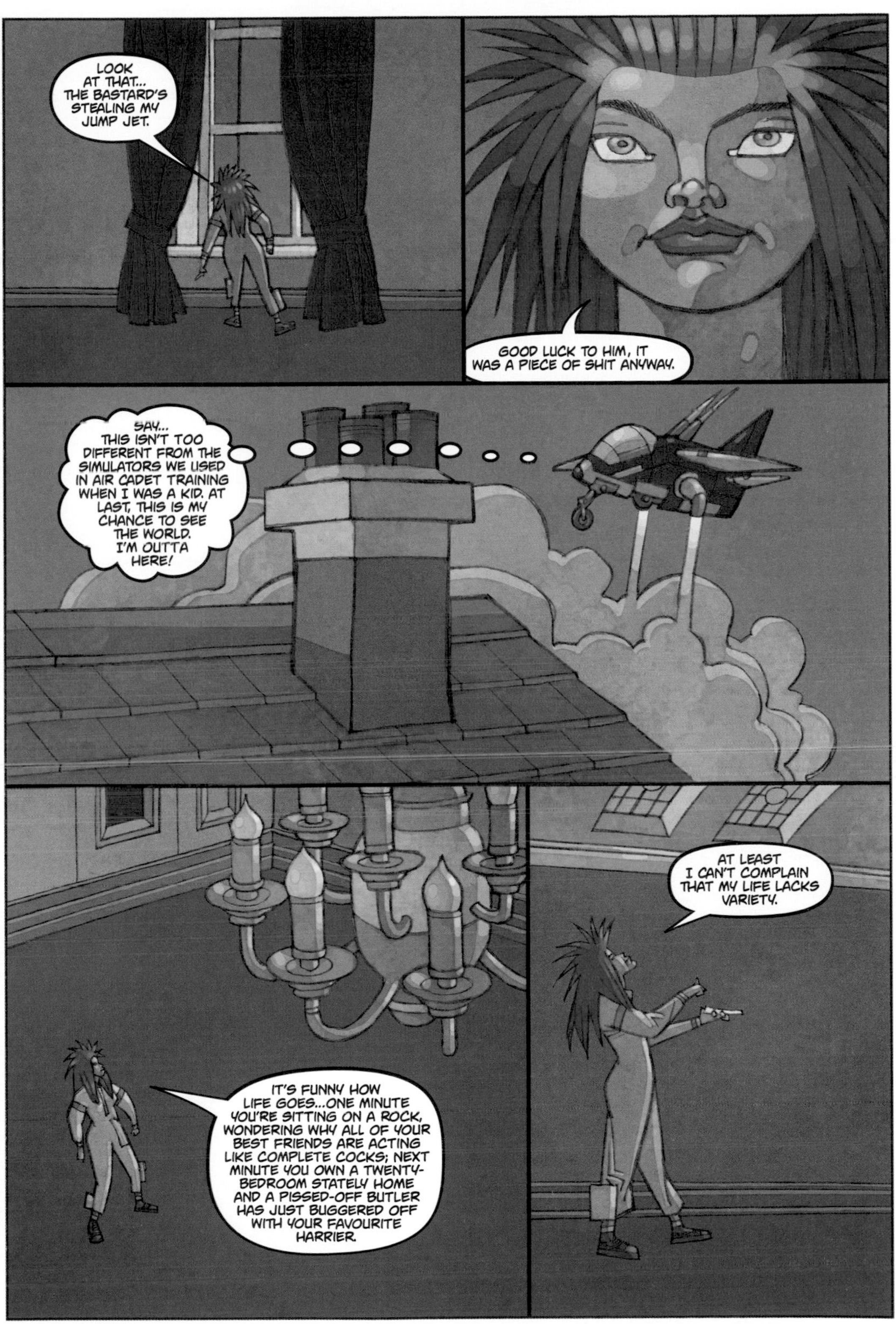
LOOK AT THAT... THE BASTARD'S STEALING MY JUMP JET.
GOOD LUCK TO HIM, IT WAS A PIECE OF SHIT ANYWAY.
SAY... THIS ISN'T TOO DIFFERENT FROM THE SIMULATORS WE USED IN AIR CADET TRAINING WHEN I WAS A KID. AT LAST, THIS IS MY CHANCE TO SEE THE WORLD. I'M OUTTA HERE!
IT'S FUNNY HOW LIFE GOES...ONE MINUTE YOU'RE SITTING ON A ROCK, WONDERING WHY ALL OF YOUR BEST FRIENDS ARE ACTING LIKE COMPLETE COCKS; NEXT MINUTE YOU OWN A TWENTY-BEDROOM STATELY HOME AND A PISSED-OFF BUTLER HAS JUST BUGGERED OFF WITH YOUR FAVOURITE HARRIER.
AT LEAST I CAN'T COMPLAIN THAT MY LIFE LACKS VARIETY.

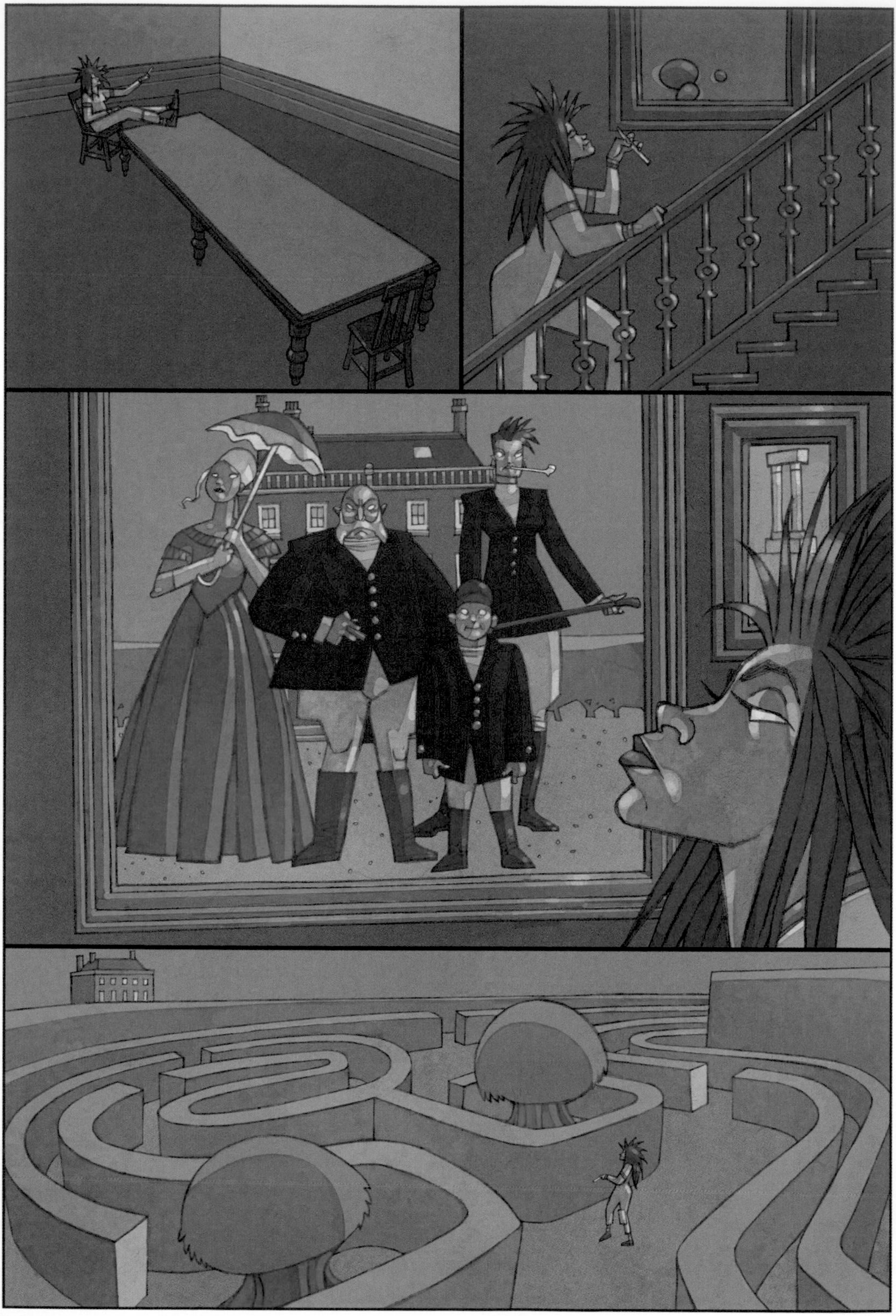

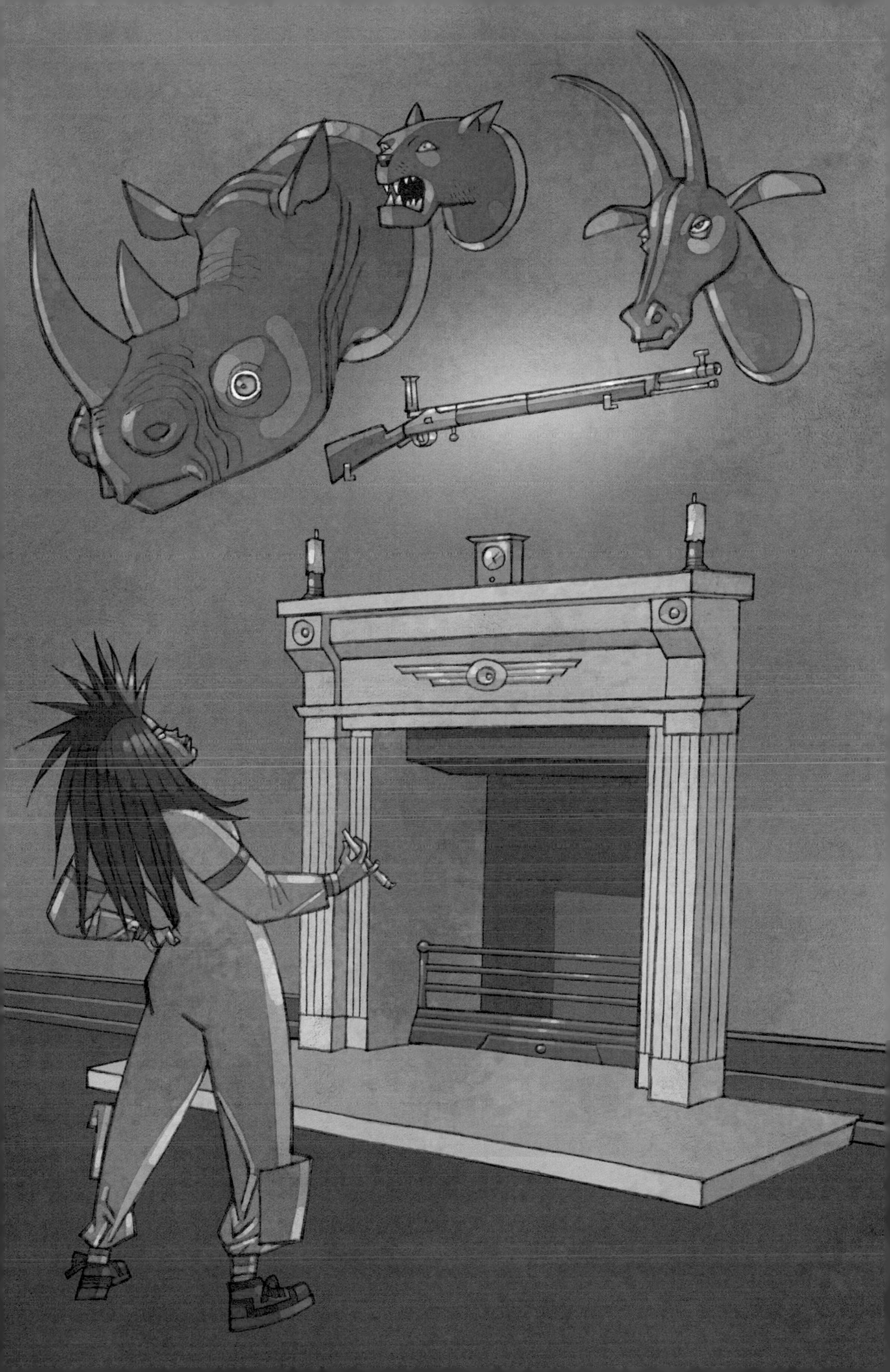

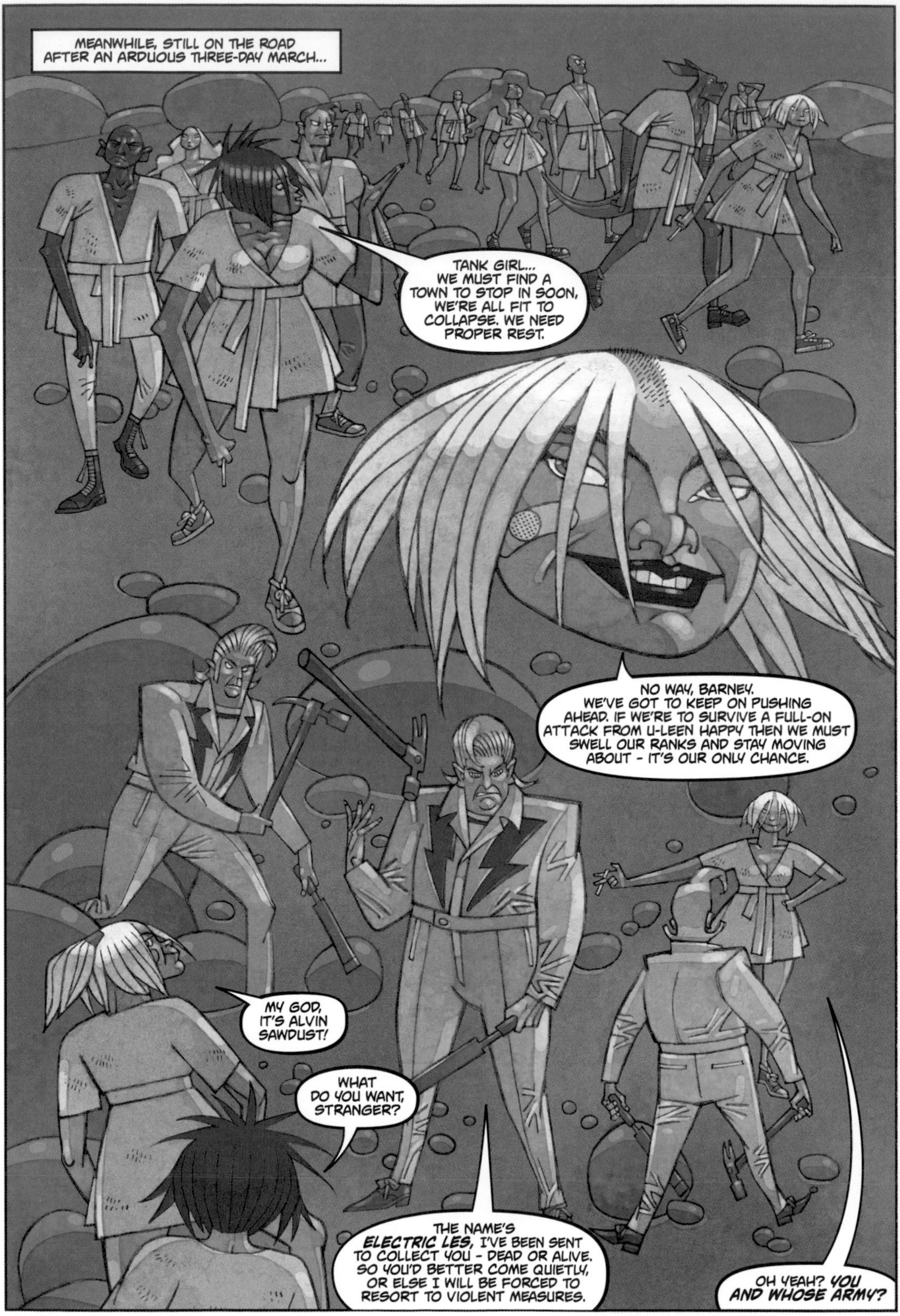
MEANWHILE, STILL ON THE ROAD AFTER AN ARDUOUS THREE-DAY MARCH...
TANK GIRL... WE MUST FIND A TOWN TO STOP IN SOON, WE'RE ALL FIT TO COLLAPSE. WE NEED PROPER REST.
NO WAY, BARNEY. WE'VE GOT TO KEEP ON PUSHING AHEAD. IF WE'RE TO SURVIVE A FULL-ON ATTACK FROM U-LEEN HAPPY THEN WE MUST SWELL OUR RANKS AND STAY MOVING ABOUT - IT'S OUR ONLY CHANCE.
MY GOD, IT'S ALVIN SAWDUST!
WHAT DO YOU WANT, STRANGER?
THE NAME'S ELECTRIC LES, I'VE BEEN SENT TO COLLECT YOU - DEAD OR ALIVE. SO YOU'D BETTER COME QUIETLY, OR ELSE I WILL BE FORCED TO RESORT TO VIOLENT MEASURES.
OH YEAH? YOU AND WHOSE ARMY?

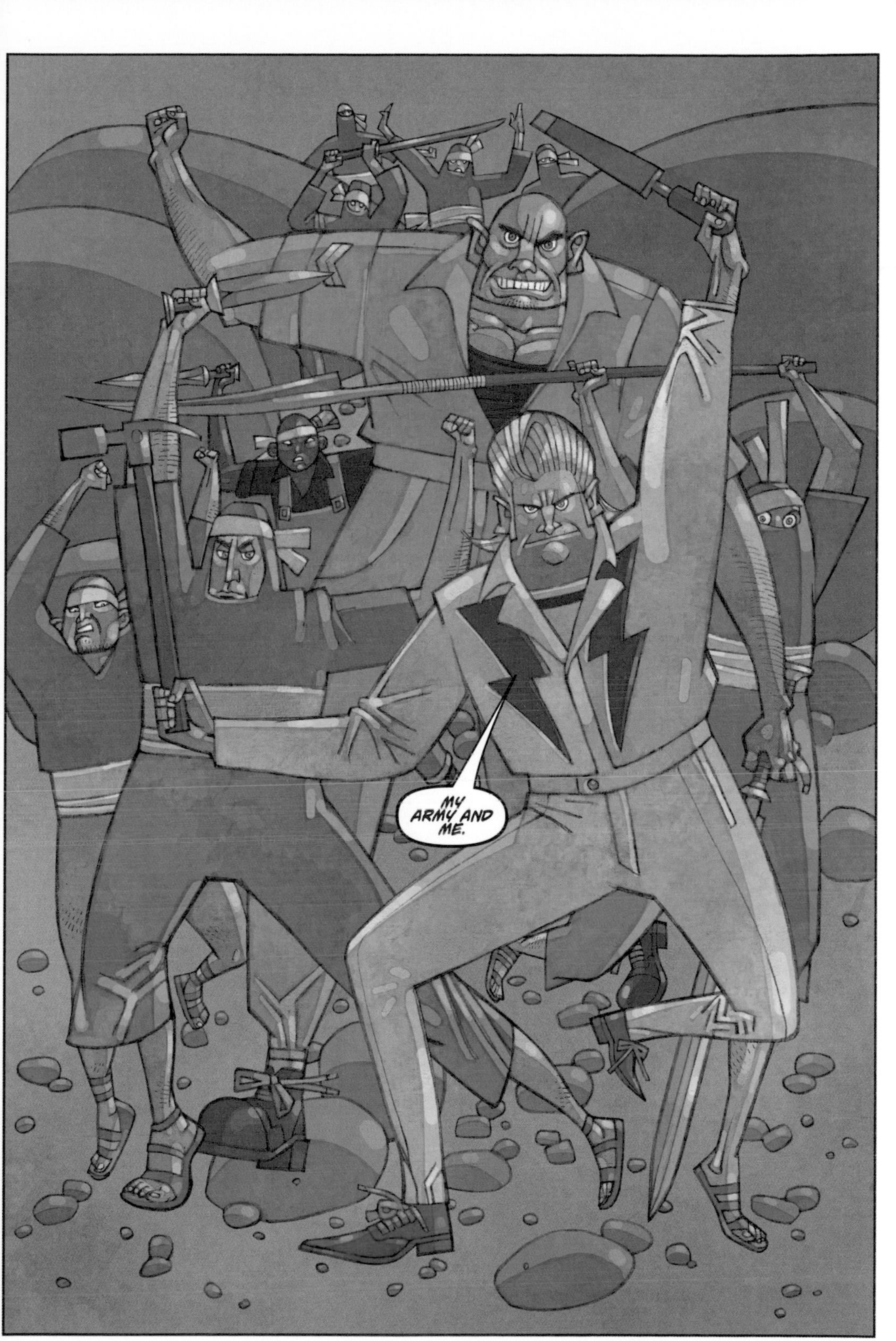
MY ARMY AND ME.

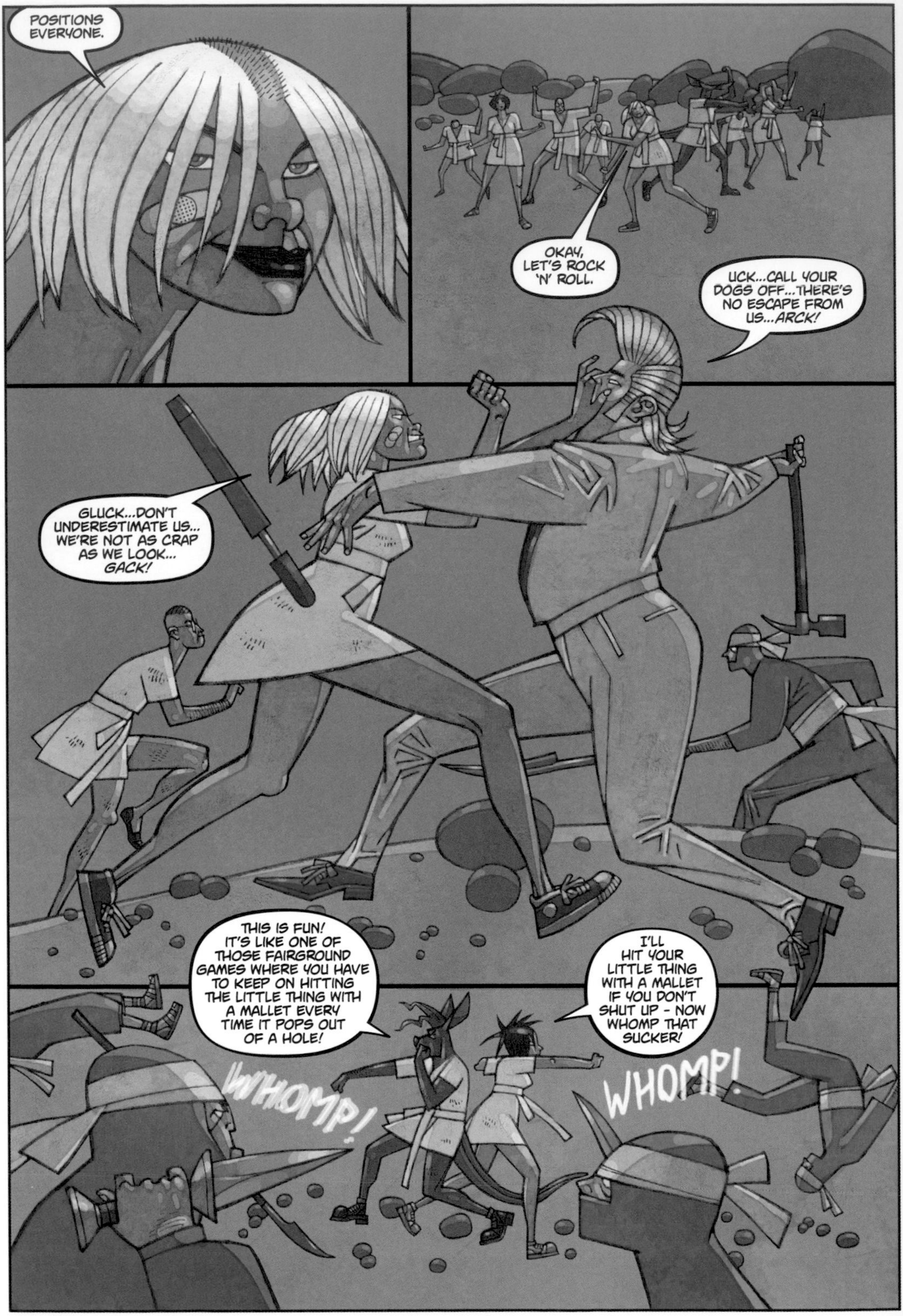
POSITIONS EVERYONE.
OKAY, LET'S ROCK 'N' ROLL.
UCK...CALL YOUR DOGS OFF...THERE'S NO ESCAPE FROM US...ARCK!
GLUCK...DON'T UNDERESTIMATE US... WE'RE NOT AS CRAP AS WE LOOK... GACK!
THIS IS FUN! IT'S LIKE ONE OF THOSE FAIRGROUND GAMES WHERE YOU HAVE TO KEEP ON HITTING THE LITTLE THING WITH A MALLET EVERY TIME IT POPS OUT OF A HOLE!
I'LL HIT YOUR LITTLE THING WITH A MALLET IF YOU DON'T SHUT UP - NOW WHOMP THAT SUCKER!
WHOMP!
WHOMP!

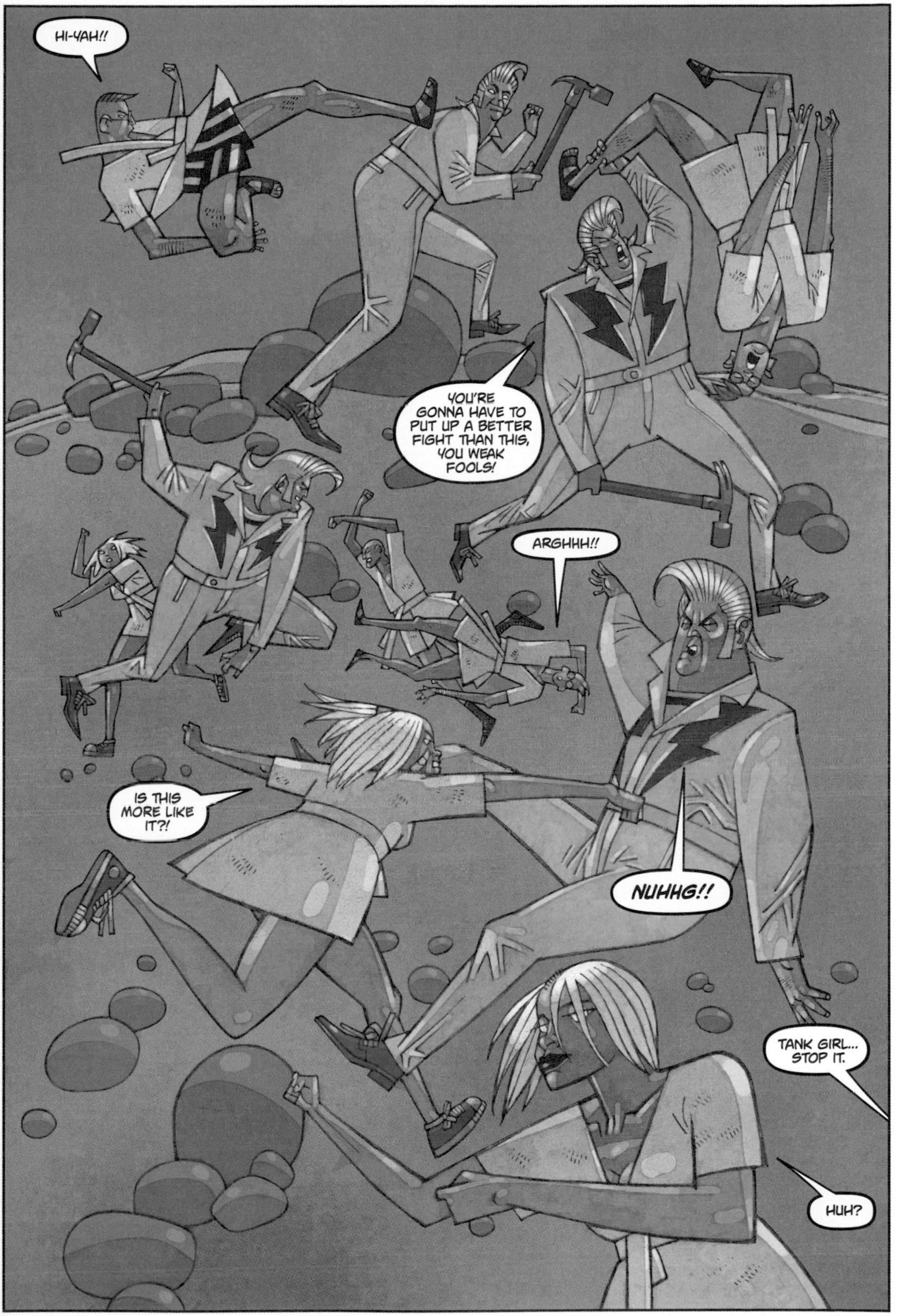
HI-YAH!!
YOU'RE GONNA HAVE TO PUT UP A BETTER FIGHT THAN THIS, YOU WEAK FOOLS!
ARGHHH!!
IS THIS MORE LIKE IT?!
NUHHG!!
TANK GIRL... STOP IT.
HUH?

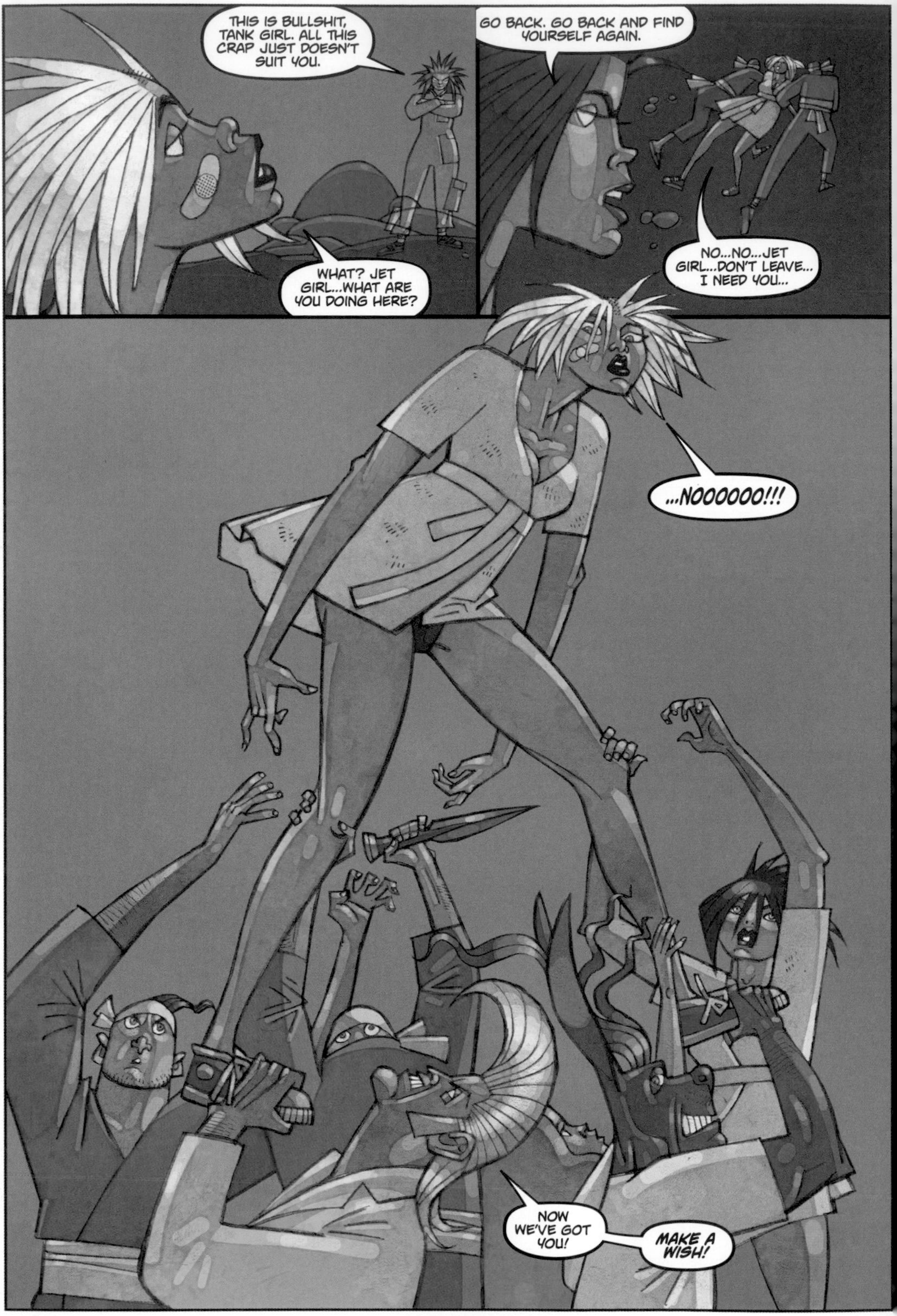
THIS IS BULLSHIT, TANK GIRL. ALL THIS CRAP JUST DOESN'T SUIT YOU.
WHAT? JET GIRL...WHAT ARE YOU DOING HERE?
GO BACK. GO BACK AND FIND YOURSELF AGAIN.
NO...NO...JET GIRL...DON'T LEAVE... I NEED YOU...
...NOOOOOO!!!
NOW WE'VE GOT YOU!
MAKE A WISH!

THE GOLDEN HOUR

ALL FLOWS
NOTHING LASTS –
THE RIVER OF THE FUTURE
THE OCEAN OF THE PAST
THE MORE YOU TRY TO NAIL IT
THE FASTER IT SLIPS AWAY
THE HARDER YOU HOLD ON
THE TOUGHER LIFE WILL GET
LOUIS THE SIXTEENTH AND MARIE ANTOINETTE
NOTHING IS FOR KEEPS
NONE OF THIS IS YOURS
CRIMEA, VIETNAM
NAPOLEONIC WARS
WIN A BIKE
WIN A CAR
WIN A HOLIDAY ON SATURN
SPOT THE BALL
WIN IT ALL
IT ALWAYS FOLLOWS THE SAME PATTERN –
EVERYTHING THAT YOU HOLD DEAR
AND THE ARMS WITH WHICH YOU HOLD
SHALL RETURN TO THE DUST
FROM WHENCE THEY CAME
BUT THIS HOUR
RIGHT NOW
IS GOLD

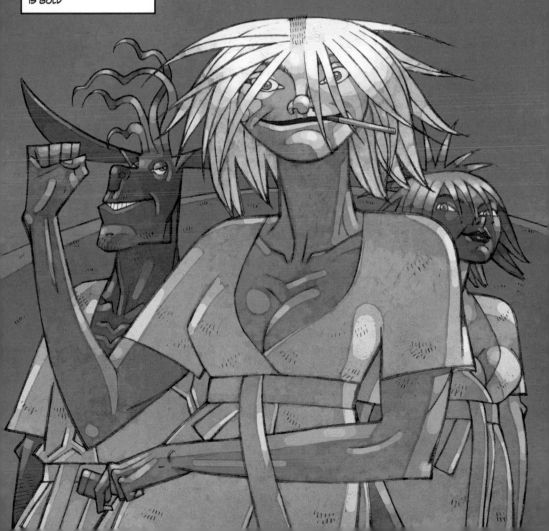

SONGWORDS

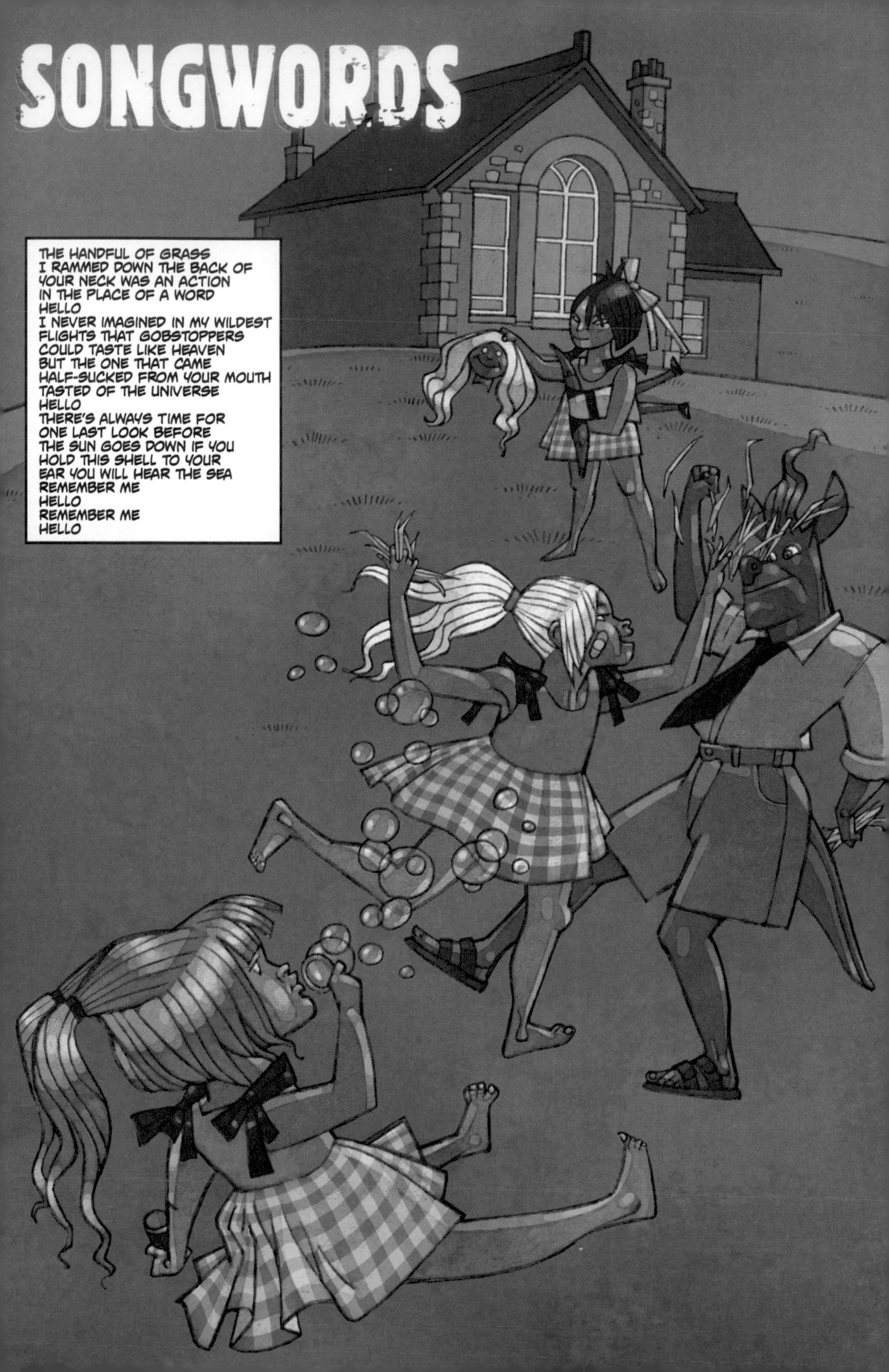
THE HANDFUL OF GRASS
I RAMMED DOWN THE BACK OF
YOUR NECK WAS AN ACTION
IN THE PLACE OF A WORD
HELLO
I NEVER IMAGINED IN MY WILDEST
FLIGHTS THAT GOBSTOPPERS
COULD TASTE LIKE HEAVEN
BUT THE ONE THAT CAME
HALF-SUCKED FROM YOUR MOUTH
TASTED OF THE UNIVERSE
HELLO
THERE'S ALWAYS TIME FOR
ONE LAST LOOK BEFORE
THE SUN GOES DOWN IF YOU
HOLD THIS SHELL TO YOUR
EAR YOU WILL HEAR THE SEA
REMEMBER ME
HELLO
REMEMBER ME
HELLO

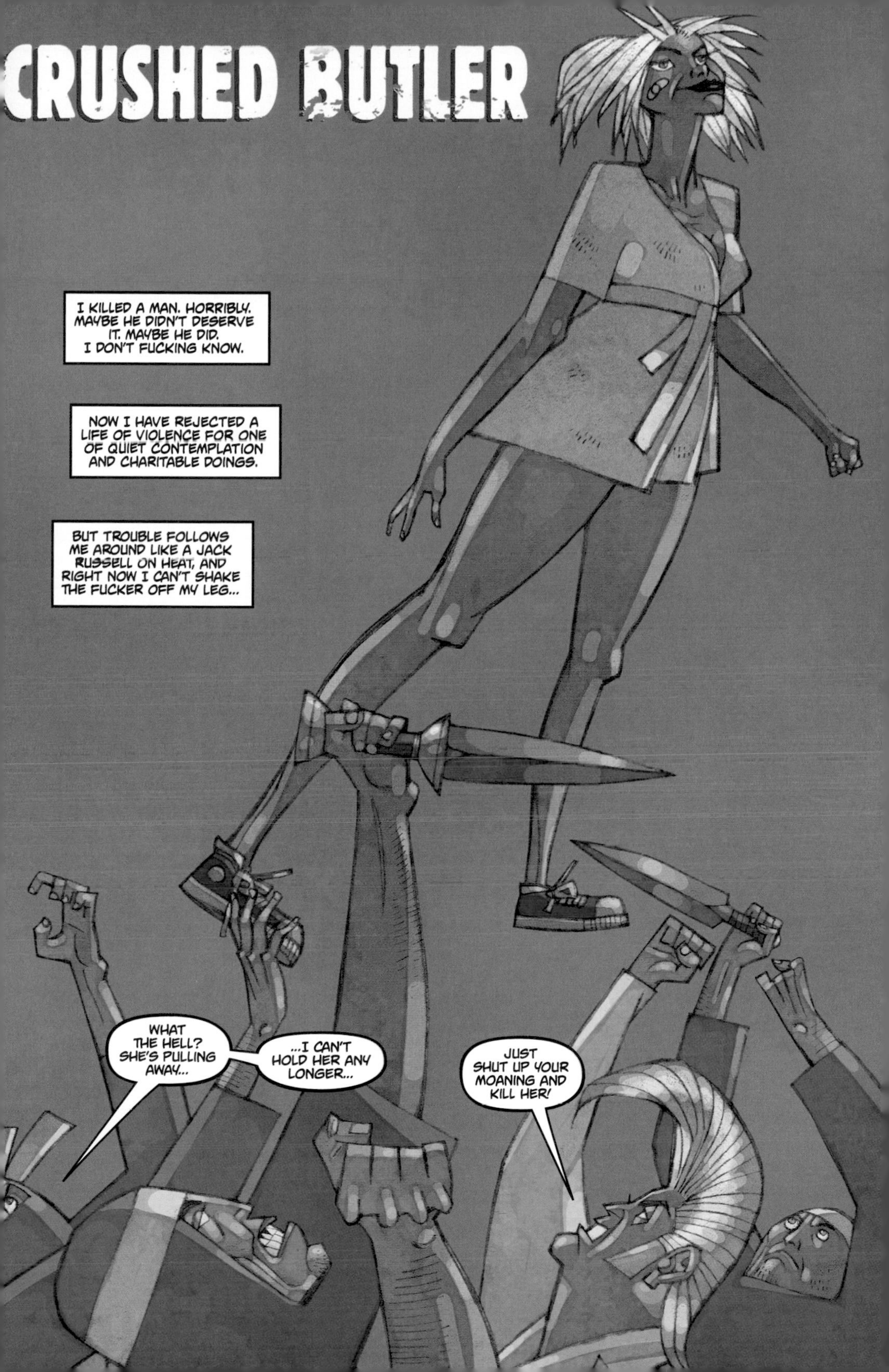
CRUSHED BUTLER
I KILLED A MAN. HORRIBLY. MAYBE HE DIDN'T DESERVE IT. MAYBE HE DID. I DON'T FUCKING KNOW.
NOW I HAVE REJECTED A LIFE OF VIOLENCE FOR ONE OF QUIET CONTEMPLATION AND CHARITABLE DOINGS.
BUT TROUBLE FOLLOWS ME AROUND LIKE A JACK RUSSELL ON HEAT, AND RIGHT NOW I CAN'T SHAKE THE FUCKER OFF MY LEG...
WHAT THE HELL? SHE'S PULLING AWAY...
...I CAN'T HOLD HER ANY LONGER...
JUST SHUT UP YOUR MOANING AND KILL HER!

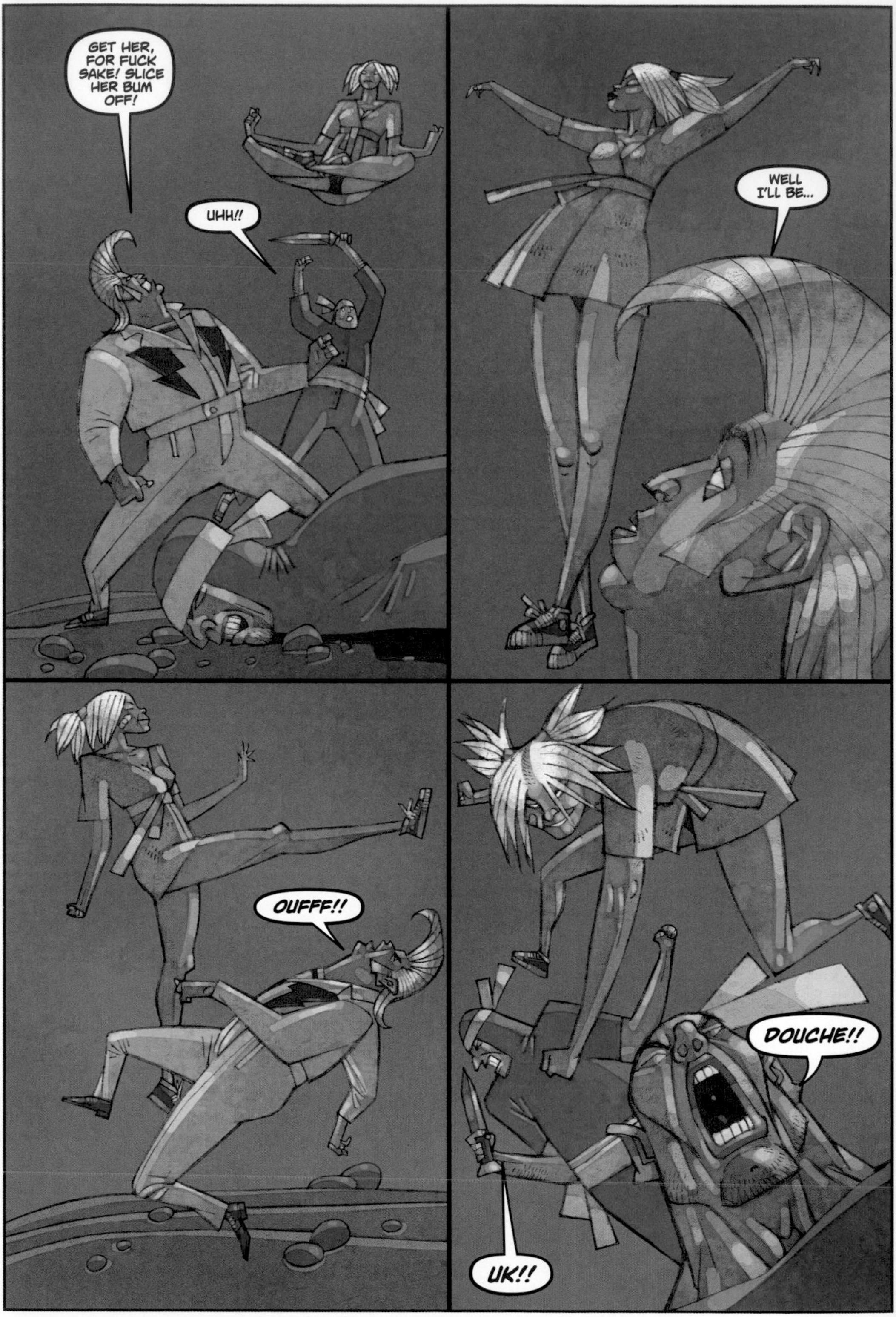
GET HER, FOR FUCK SAKE! SLICE HER BUM OFF!
UHH!!
WELL I'LL BE...
OUFFF!!
DOUCHE!!
UK!!

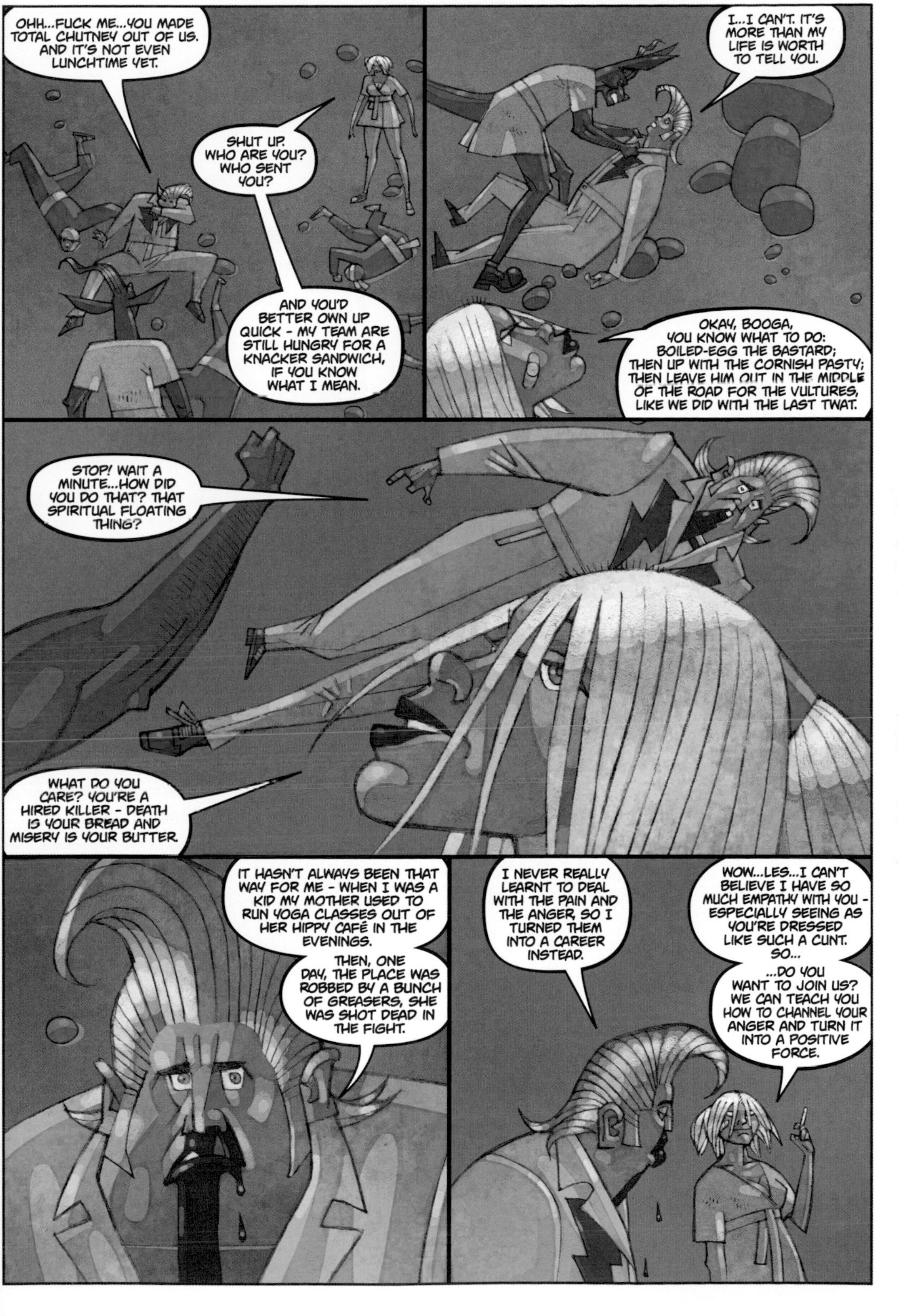
OHH...FUCK ME...YOU MADE TOTAL CHUTNEY OUT OF US. AND IT'S NOT EVEN LUNCHTIME YET.
SHUT UP. WHO ARE YOU? WHO SENT YOU?
AND YOU'D BETTER OWN UP QUICK - MY TEAM ARE STILL HUNGRY FOR A KNACKER SANDWICH, IF YOU KNOW WHAT I MEAN.
I...I CAN'T. IT'S MORE THAN MY LIFE IS WORTH TO TELL YOU.
OKAY, BOOGA, YOU KNOW WHAT TO DO: BOILED-EGG THE BASTARD; THEN UP WITH THE CORNISH PASTY; THEN LEAVE HIM OUT IN THE MIDDLE OF THE ROAD FOR THE VULTURES, LIKE WE DID WITH THE LAST TWAT.
STOP! WAIT A MINUTE...HOW DID YOU DO THAT? THAT SPIRITUAL FLOATING THING?
WHAT DO YOU CARE? YOU'RE A HIRED KILLER - DEATH IS YOUR BREAD AND MISERY IS YOUR BUTTER.
IT HASN'T ALWAYS BEEN THAT WAY FOR ME - WHEN I WAS A KID MY MOTHER USED TO RUN YOGA CLASSES OUT OF HER HIPPY CAFÉ IN THE EVENINGS.
THEN, ONE DAY, THE PLACE WAS ROBBED BY A BUNCH OF GREASERS, SHE WAS SHOT DEAD IN THE FIGHT.
I NEVER REALLY LEARNT TO DEAL WITH THE PAIN AND THE ANGER, SO I TURNED THEM INTO A CAREER INSTEAD.
WOW...LES...I CAN'T BELIEVE I HAVE SO MUCH EMPATHY WITH YOU - ESPECIALLY SEEING AS YOU'RE DRESSED LIKE SUCH A CUNT. SO...
...DO YOU WANT TO JOIN US? WE CAN TEACH YOU HOW TO CHANNEL YOUR ANGER AND TURN IT INTO A POSITIVE FORCE.

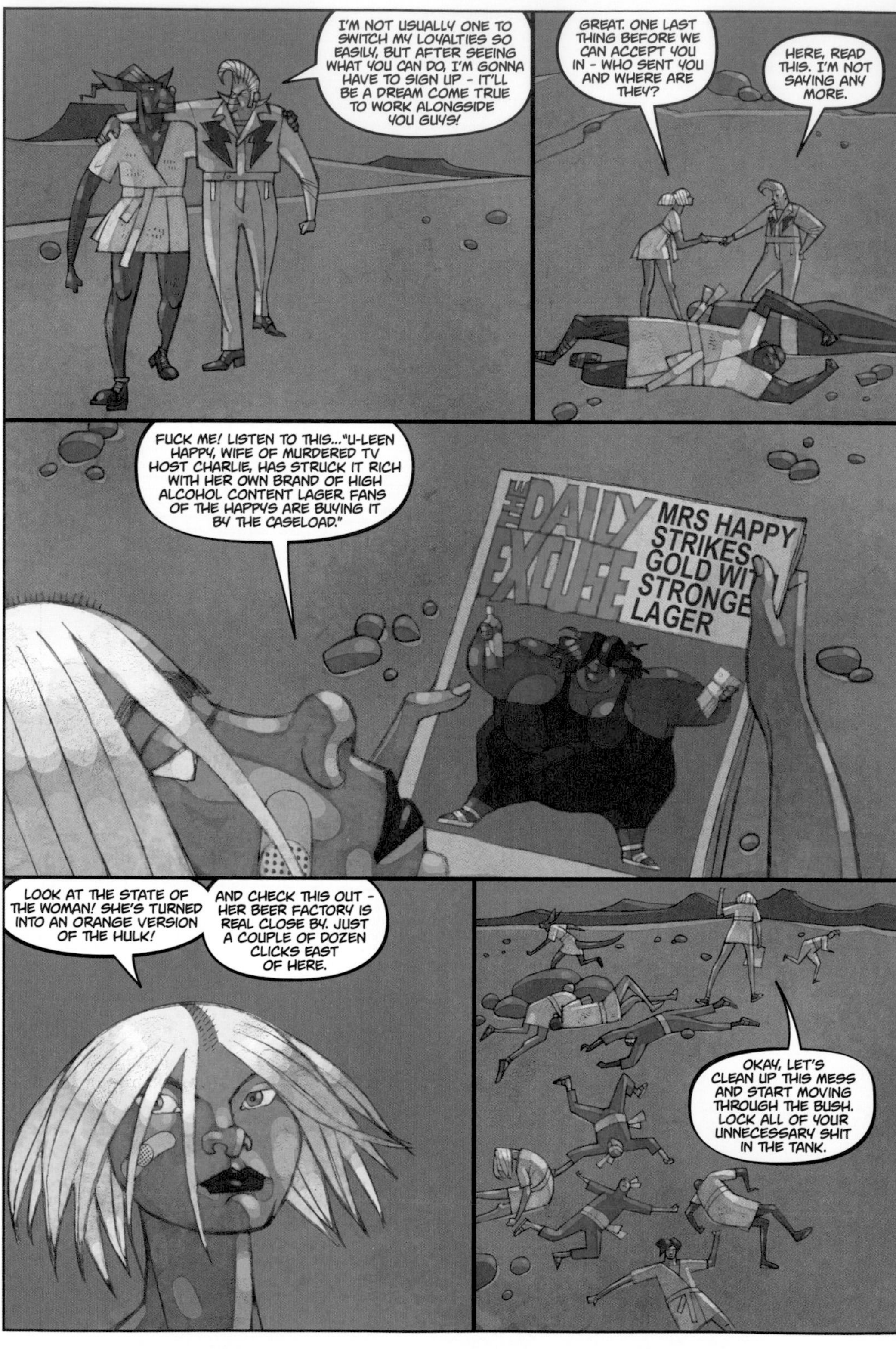
I'M NOT USUALLY ONE TO SWITCH MY LOYALTIES SO EASILY, BUT AFTER SEEING WHAT YOU CAN DO, I'M GONNA HAVE TO SIGN UP - IT'LL BE A DREAM COME TRUE TO WORK ALONGSIDE YOU GUYS!
GREAT. ONE LAST THING BEFORE WE CAN ACCEPT YOU IN - WHO SENT YOU AND WHERE ARE THEY?
HERE, READ THIS. I'M NOT SAYING ANY MORE.
FUCK ME! LISTEN TO THIS..."U-LEEN HAPPY, WIFE OF MURDERED TV HOST CHARLIE, HAS STRUCK IT RICH WITH HER OWN BRAND OF HIGH ALCOHOL CONTENT LAGER FANS OF THE HAPPYS ARE BUYING IT BY THE CASELOAD."
THE DAILY EXCUSE
MRS HAPPY STRIKES GOLD WIT STRONGE LAGER
LOOK AT THE STATE OF THE WOMAN! SHE'S TURNED INTO AN ORANGE VERSION OF THE HULK!
AND CHECK THIS OUT - HER BEER FACTORY IS REAL CLOSE BY. JUST A COUPLE OF DOZEN CLICKS EAST OF HERE.
OKAY, LET'S CLEAN UP THIS MESS AND START MOVING THROUGH THE BUSH. LOCK ALL OF YOUR UNNECESSARY SHIT IN THE TANK.

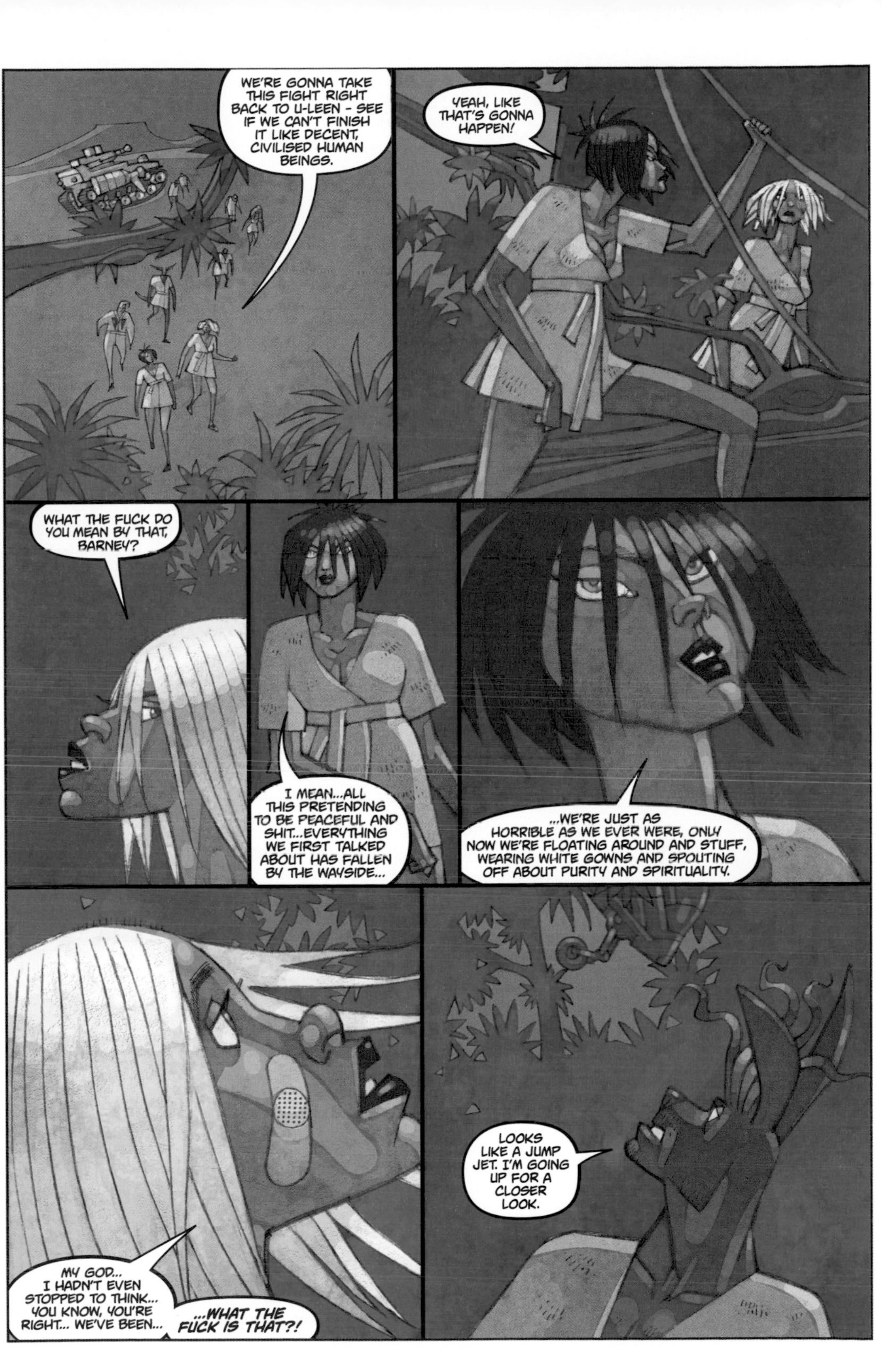
WE'RE GONNA TAKE THIS FIGHT RIGHT BACK TO U-LEEN - SEE IF WE CAN'T FINISH IT LIKE DECENT, CIVILISED HUMAN BEINGS.
YEAH, LIKE THAT'S GONNA HAPPEN!
WHAT THE FUCK DO YOU MEAN BY THAT, BARNEY?
I MEAN...ALL THIS PRETENDING TO BE PEACEFUL AND SHIT...EVERYTHING WE FIRST TALKED ABOUT HAS FALLEN BY THE WAYSIDE...
...WE'RE JUST AS HORRIBLE AS WE EVER WERE, ONLY NOW WE'RE FLOATING AROUND AND STUFF, WEARING WHITE GOWNS AND SPOUTING OFF ABOUT PURITY AND SPIRITUALITY.
MY GOD... I HADN'T EVEN STOPPED TO THINK... YOU KNOW, YOU'RE RIGHT... WE'VE BEEN...
...WHAT THE FUCK IS THAT?!
LOOKS LIKE A JUMP JET. I'M GOING UP FOR A CLOSER LOOK.

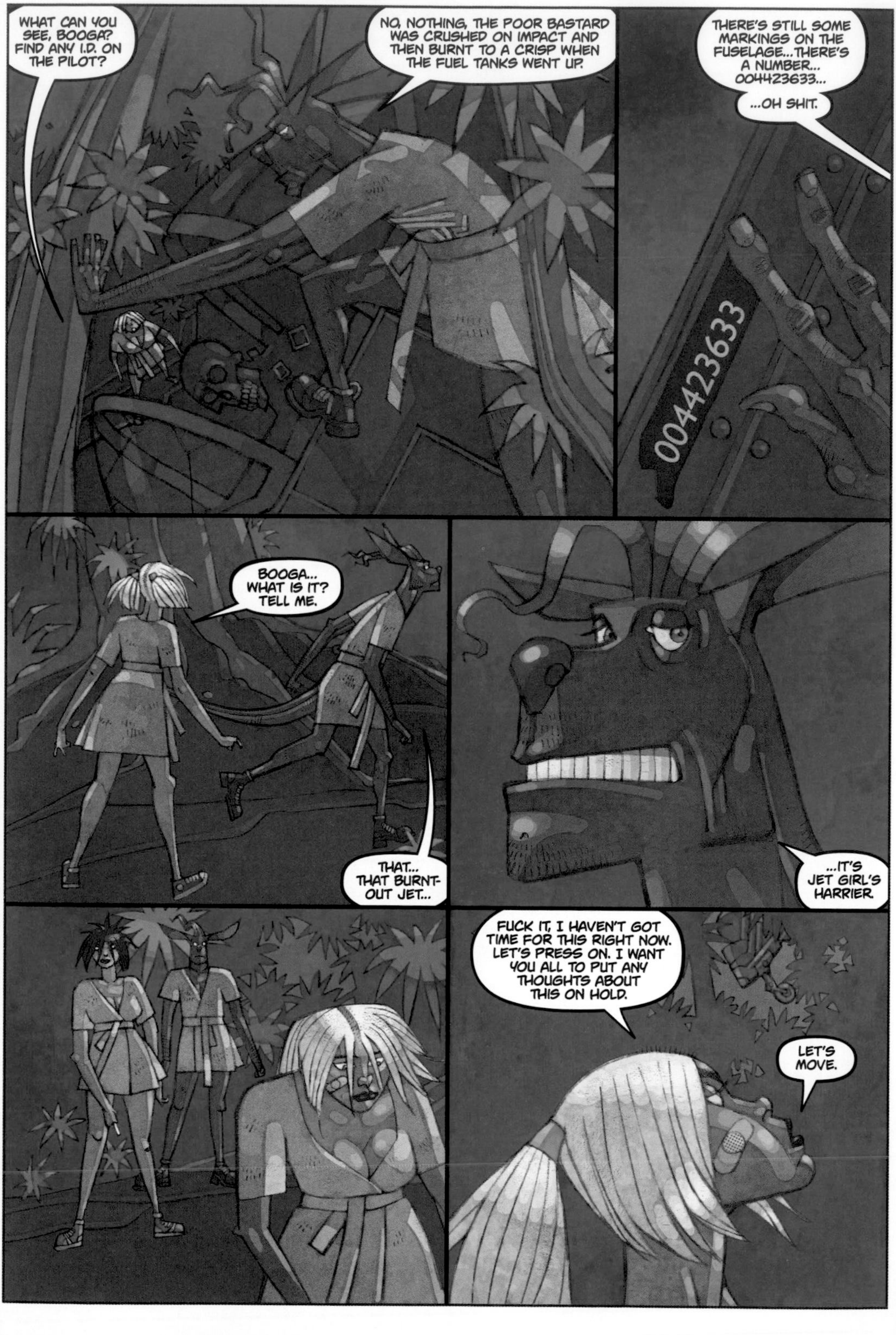
WHAT CAN YOU SEE, BOOGA? FIND ANY I.D. ON THE PILOT?
NO, NOTHING, THE POOR BASTARD WAS CRUSHED ON IMPACT AND THEN BURNT TO A CRISP WHEN THE FUEL TANKS WENT UP.
THERE'S STILL SOME MARKINGS ON THE FUSELAGE...THERE'S A NUMBER... 004423633...
...OH SHIT.
004423633
BOOGA... WHAT IS IT? TELL ME.
THAT... THAT BURNT-OUT JET...
...IT'S JET GIRL'S HARRIER.
FUCK IT, I HAVEN'T GOT TIME FOR THIS RIGHT NOW. LET'S PRESS ON. I WANT YOU ALL TO PUT ANY THOUGHTS ABOUT THIS ON HOLD.
LET'S MOVE.

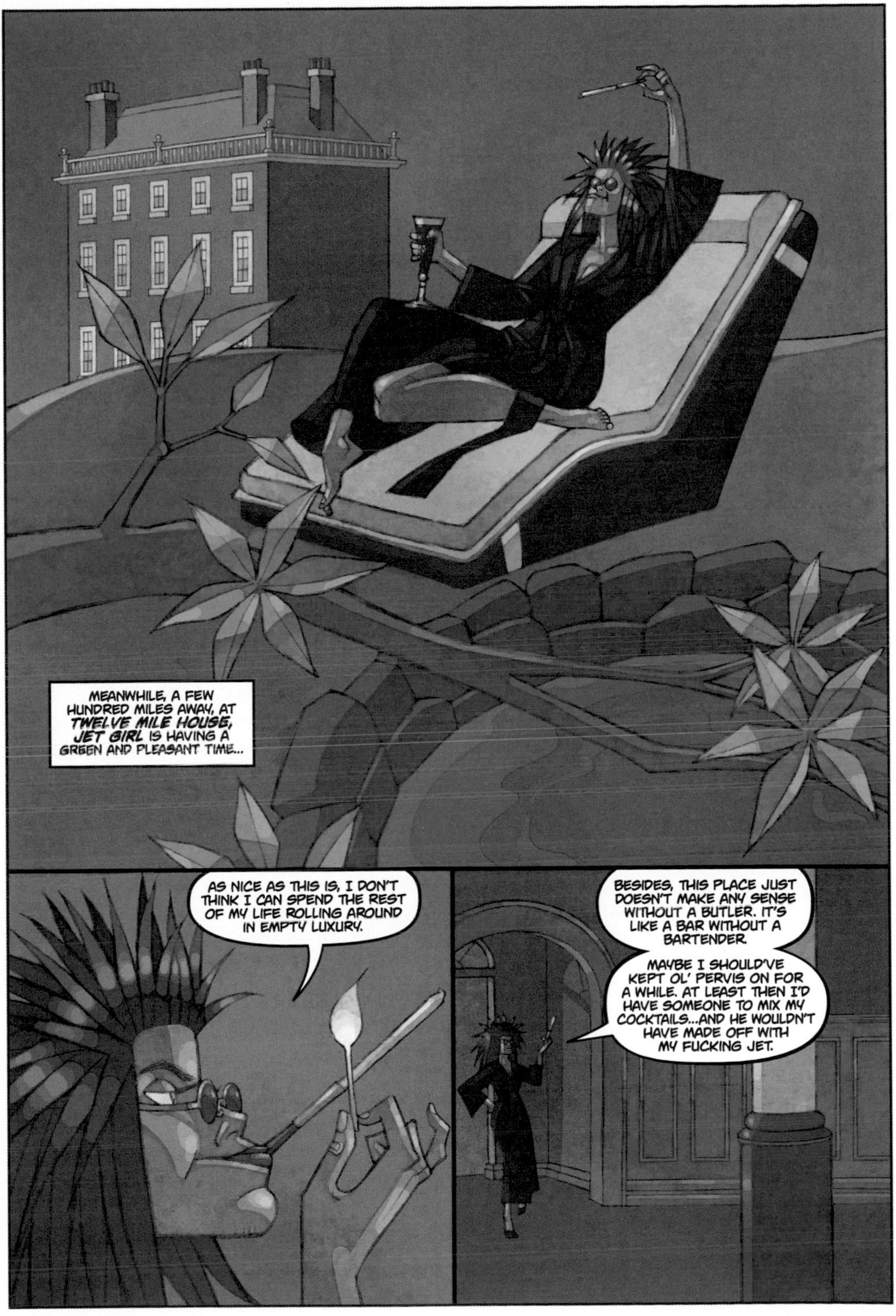
MEANWHILE, A FEW HUNDRED MILES AWAY, AT **TWELVE MILE HOUSE, JET GIRL** IS HAVING A GREEN AND PLEASANT TIME...
AS NICE AS THIS IS, I DON'T THINK I CAN SPEND THE REST OF MY LIFE ROLLING AROUND IN EMPTY LUXURY.
BESIDES, THIS PLACE JUST DOESN'T MAKE ANY SENSE WITHOUT A BUTLER. IT'S LIKE A BAR WITHOUT A BARTENDER.
MAYBE I SHOULD'VE KEPT OL' PERVIS ON FOR A WHILE. AT LEAST THEN I'D HAVE SOMEONE TO MIX MY COCKTAILS...AND HE WOULDN'T HAVE MADE OFF WITH MY FUCKING JET.

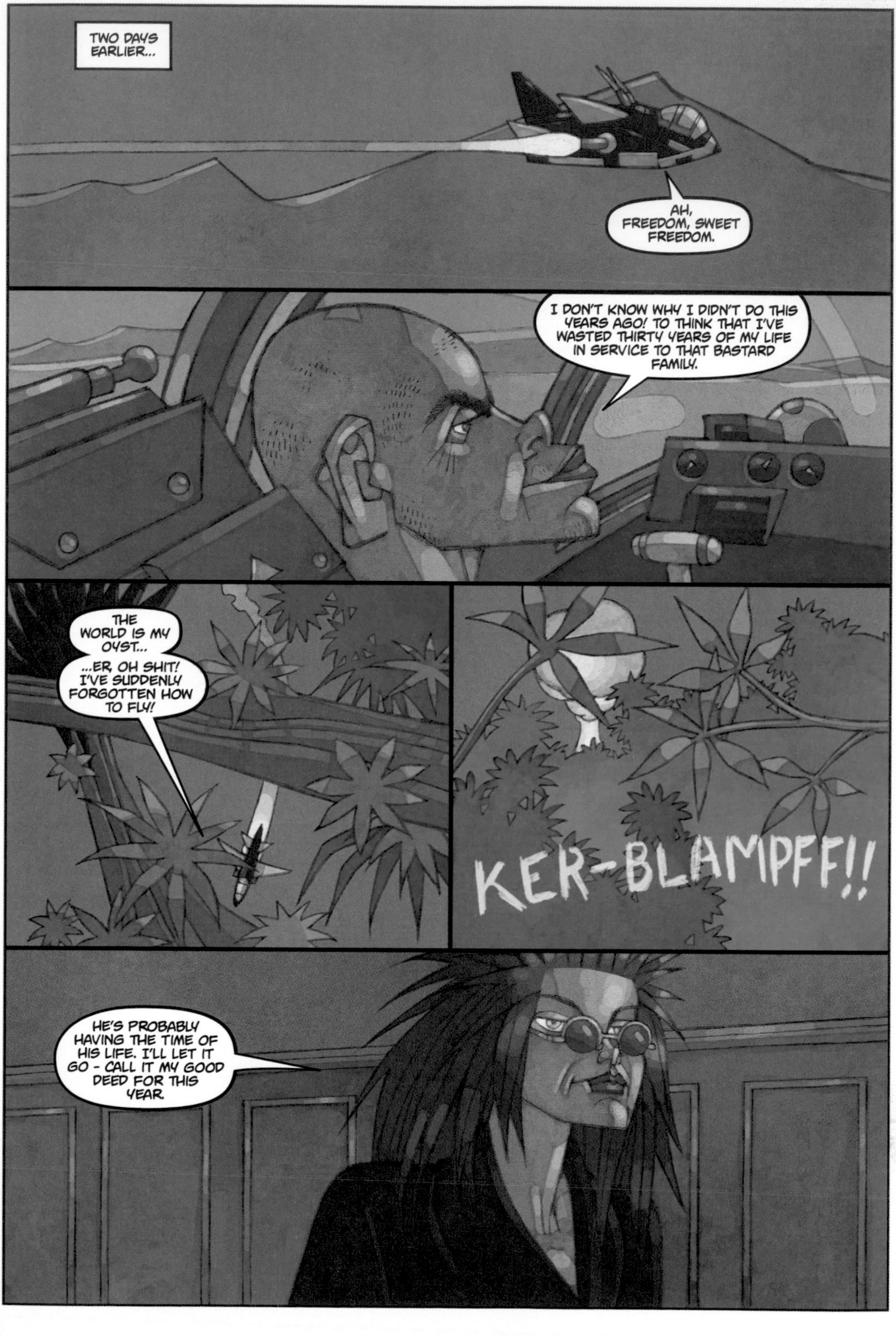
TWO DAYS EARLIER...
AH, FREEDOM, SWEET FREEDOM.
I DON'T KNOW WHY I DIDN'T DO THIS YEARS AGO! TO THINK THAT I'VE WASTED THIRTY YEARS OF MY LIFE IN SERVICE TO THAT BASTARD FAMILY.
THE WORLD IS MY OYST...
...ER, OH SHIT! I'VE SUDDENLY FORGOTTEN HOW TO FLY!
KER-BLAMPFF!!
HE'S PROBABLY HAVING THE TIME OF HIS LIFE. I'LL LET IT GO - CALL IT MY GOOD DEED FOR THIS YEAR.

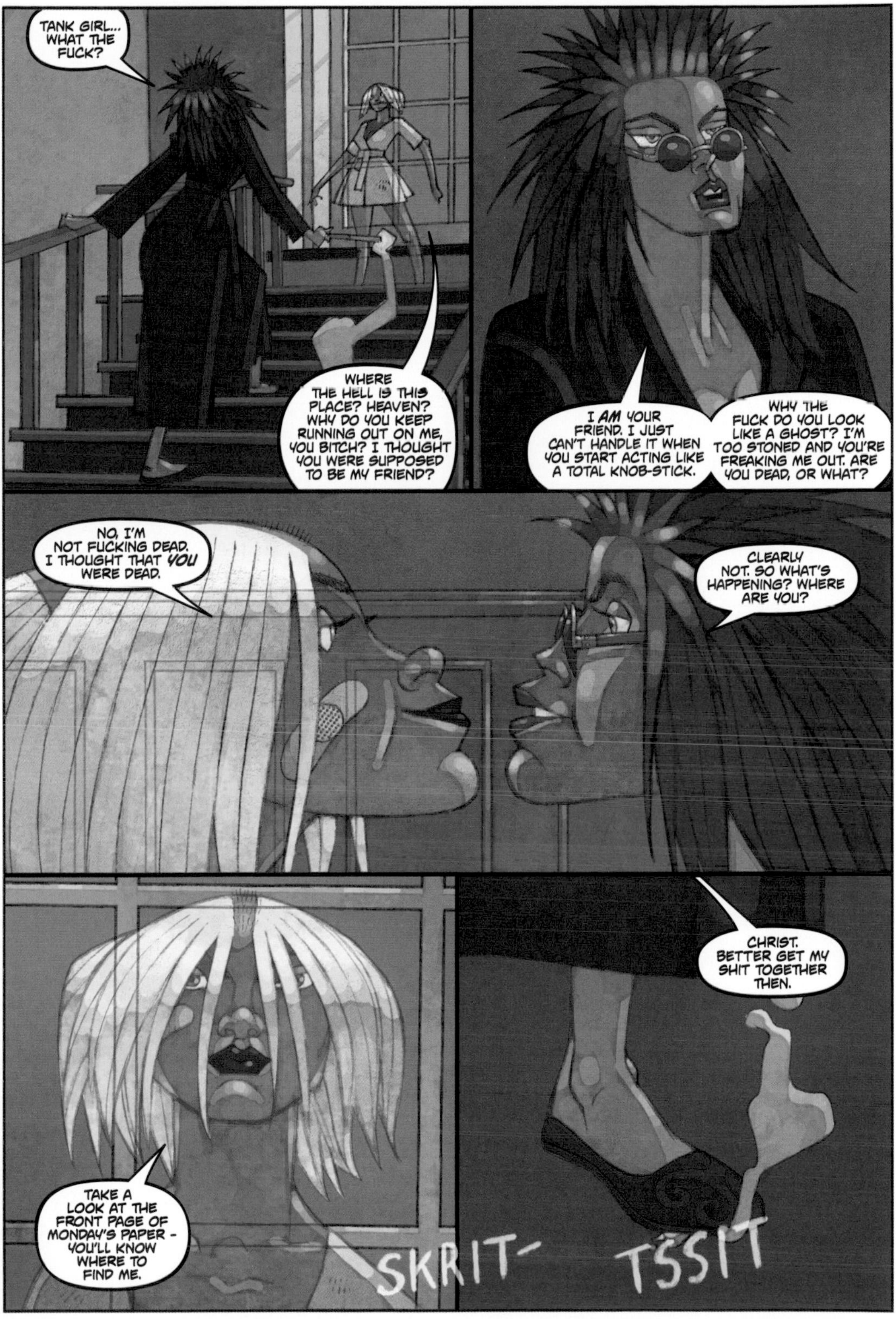
TANK GIRL... WHAT THE FUCK?
WHERE THE HELL IS THIS PLACE? HEAVEN? WHY DO YOU KEEP RUNNING OUT ON ME, YOU BITCH? I THOUGHT YOU WERE SUPPOSED TO BE MY FRIEND?
I AM YOUR FRIEND. I JUST CAN'T HANDLE IT WHEN YOU START ACTING LIKE A TOTAL KNOB-STICK.
WHY THE FUCK DO YOU LOOK LIKE A GHOST? I'M TOO STONED AND YOU'RE FREAKING ME OUT. ARE YOU DEAD, OR WHAT?
NO, I'M NOT FUCKING DEAD. I THOUGHT THAT YOU WERE DEAD.
CLEARLY NOT. SO WHAT'S HAPPENING? WHERE ARE YOU?
TAKE A LOOK AT THE FRONT PAGE OF MONDAY'S PAPER - YOU'LL KNOW WHERE TO FIND ME.
CHRIST. BETTER GET MY SHIT TOGETHER THEN.
SKRIT- TSSIT

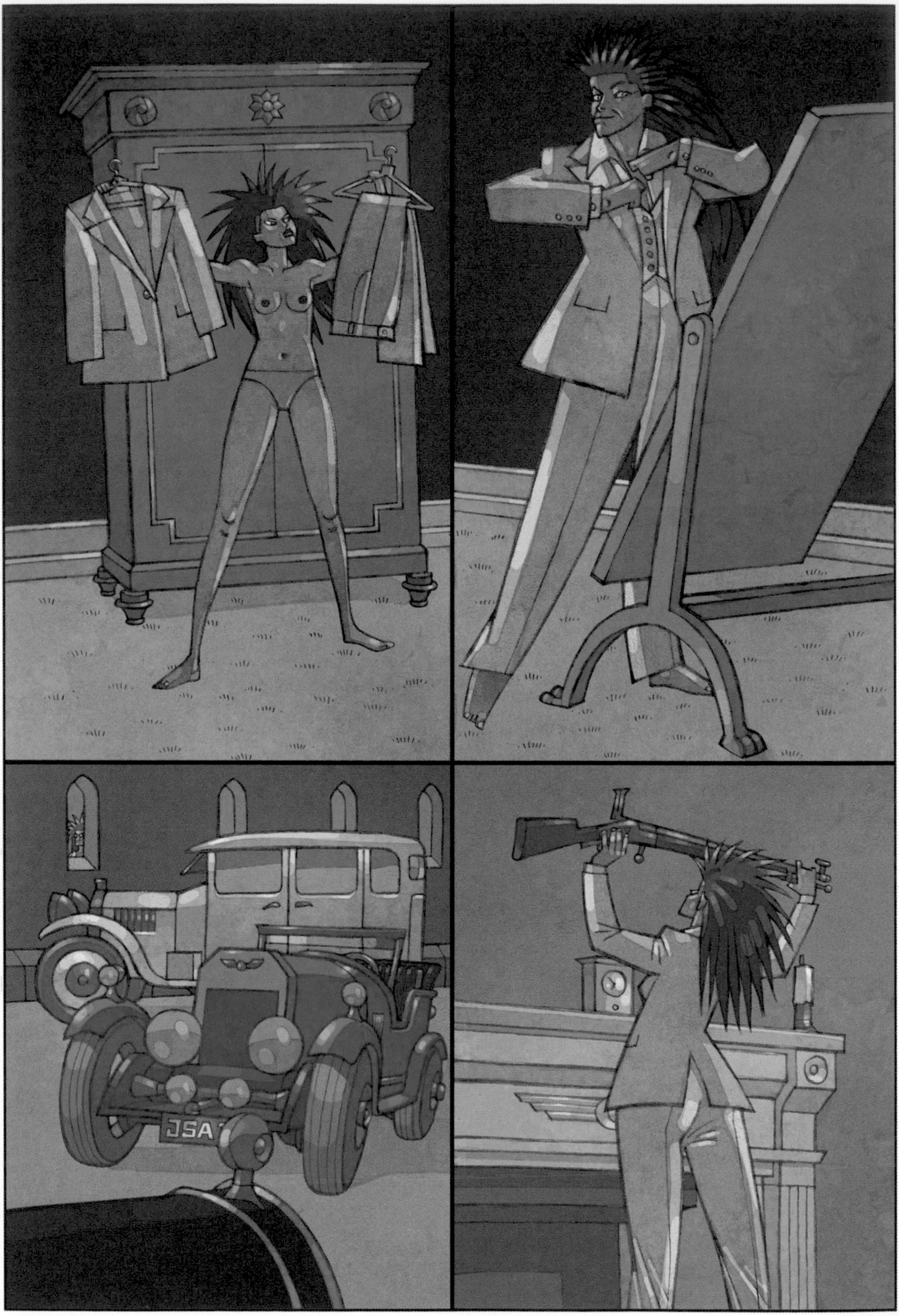
JSA

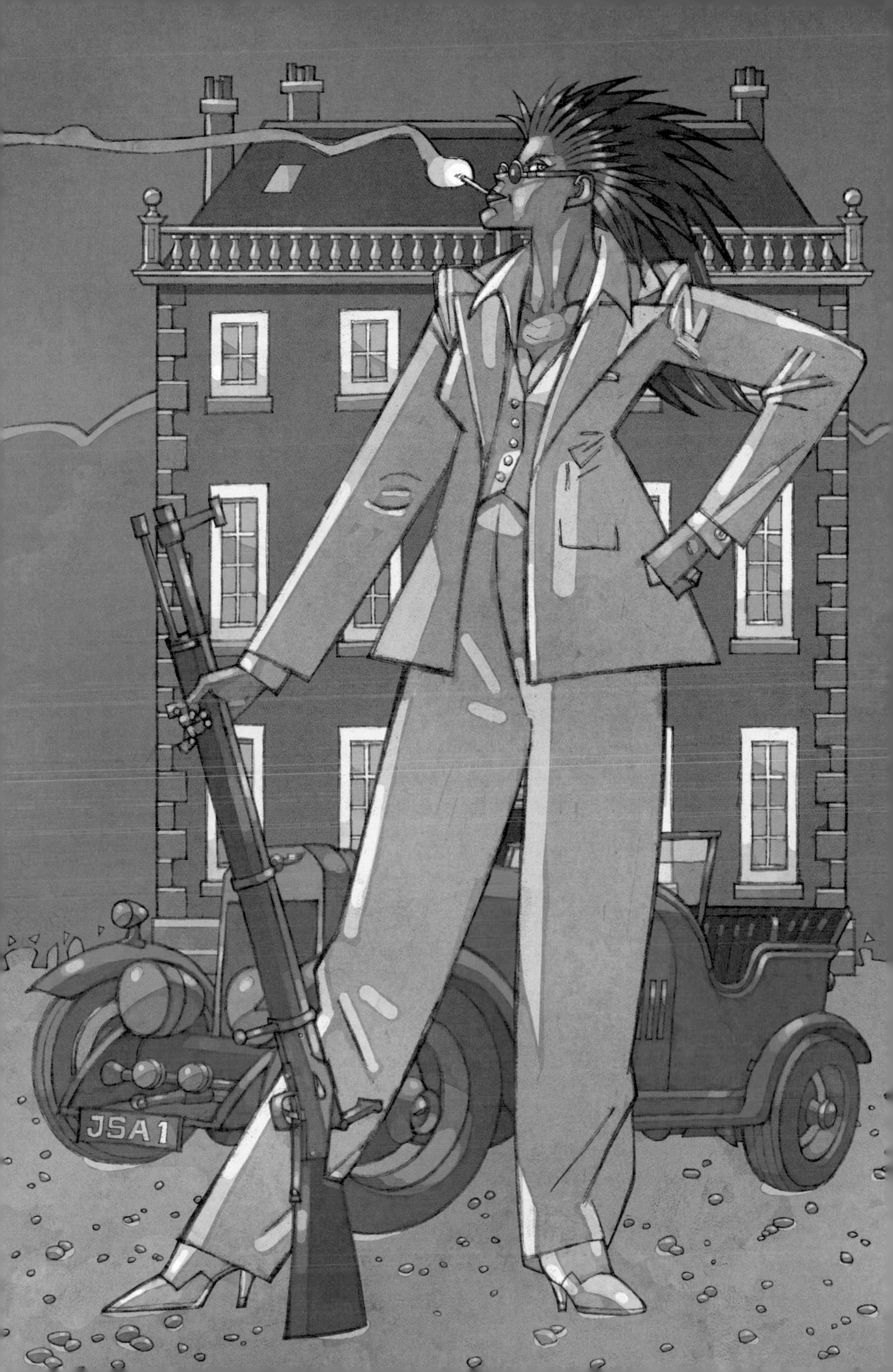
JSA 1

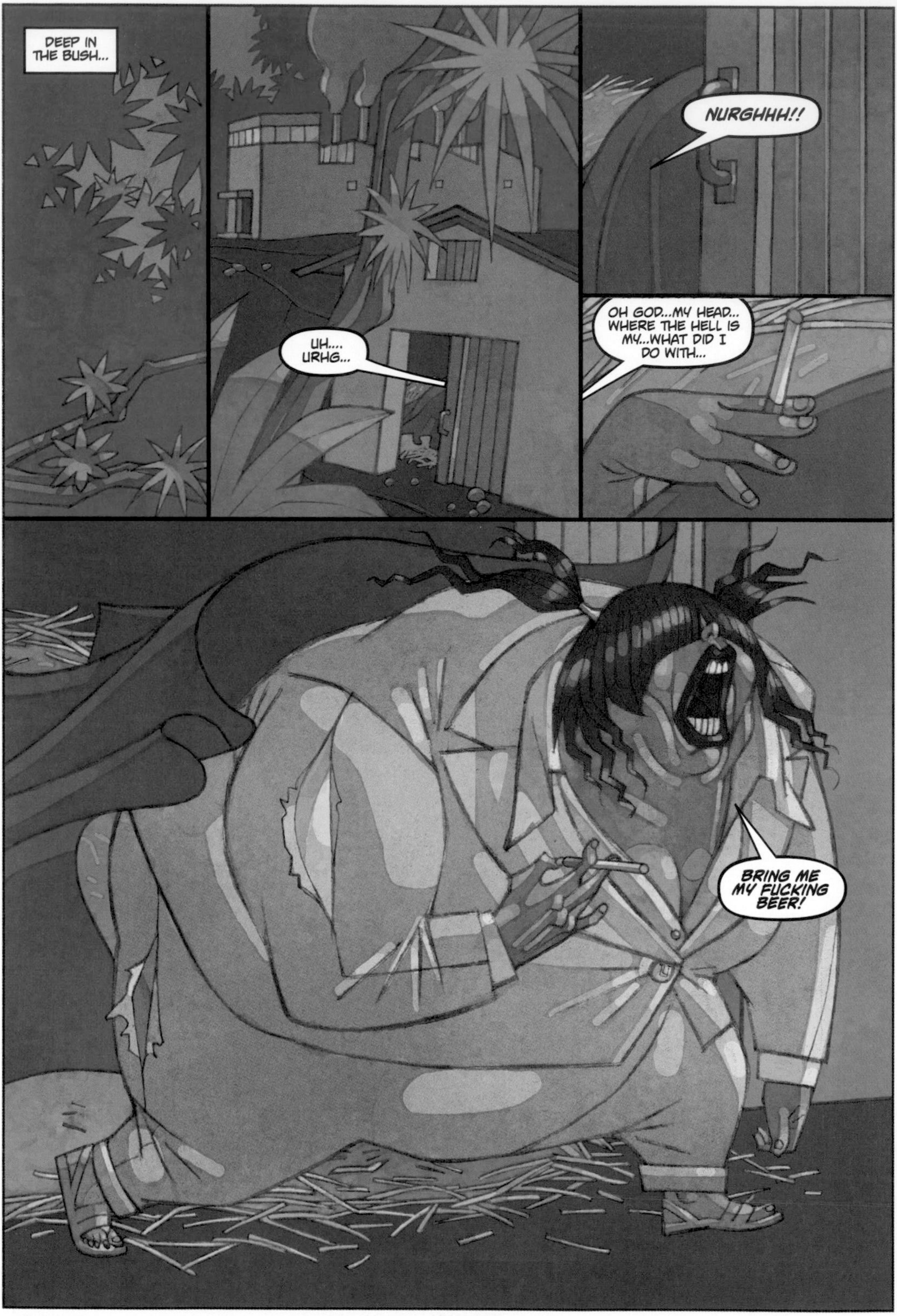
DEEP IN THE BUSH...
UH.... URHG...
NURGHHH!!
OH GOD...MY HEAD... WHERE THE HELL IS MY...WHAT DID I DO WITH...
BRING ME MY FUCKING BEER!

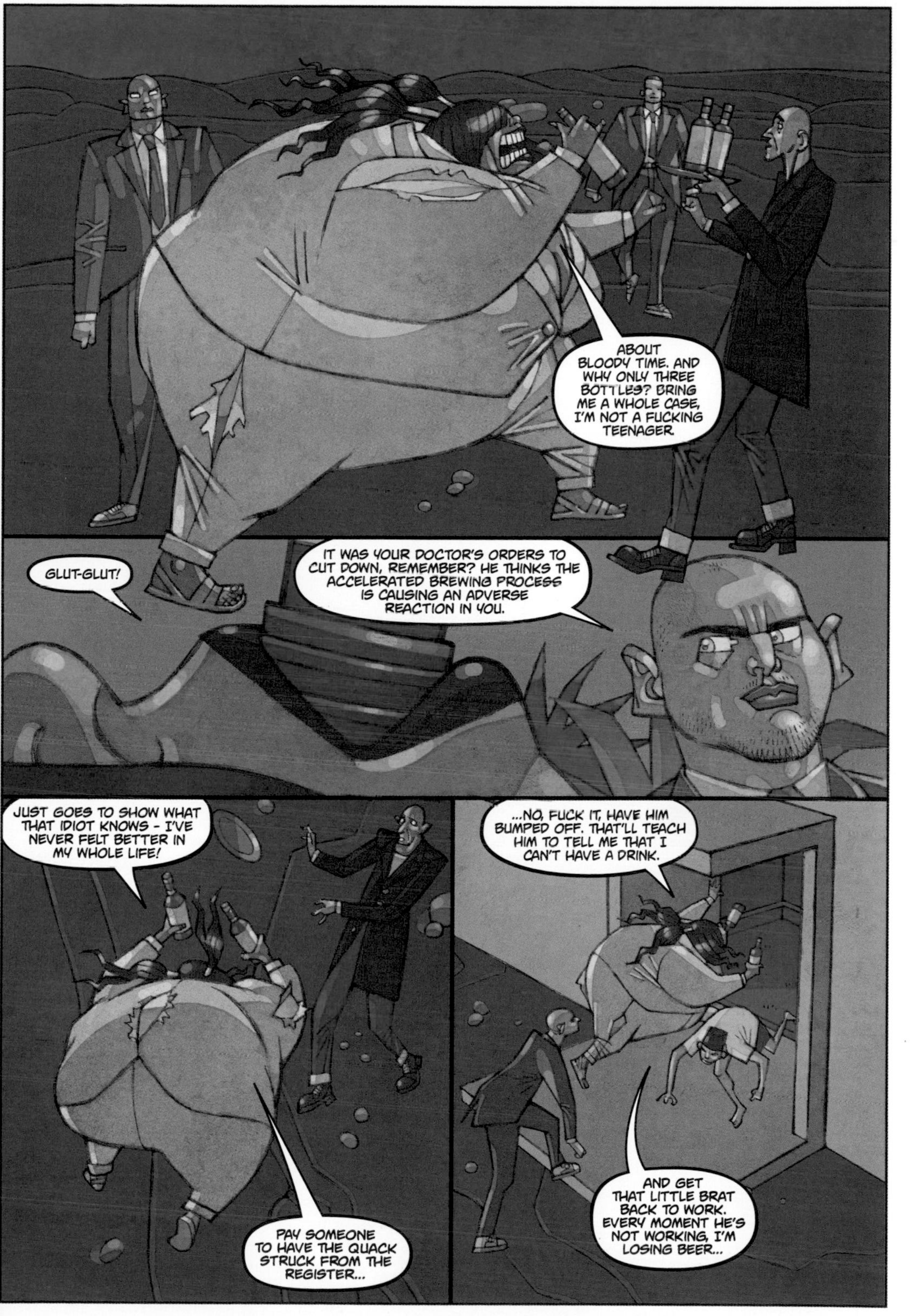
ABOUT BLOODY TIME. AND WHY ONLY THREE BOTTLES? BRING ME A WHOLE CASE, I'M NOT A FUCKING TEENAGER.
GLUT-GLUT!
IT WAS YOUR DOCTOR'S ORDERS TO CUT DOWN, REMEMBER? HE THINKS THE ACCELERATED BREWING PROCESS IS CAUSING AN ADVERSE REACTION IN YOU.
JUST GOES TO SHOW WHAT THAT IDIOT KNOWS - I'VE NEVER FELT BETTER IN MY WHOLE LIFE!
PAY SOMEONE TO HAVE THE QUACK STRUCK FROM THE REGISTER...
...NO, FUCK IT, HAVE HIM BUMPED OFF. THAT'LL TEACH HIM TO TELL ME THAT I CAN'T HAVE A DRINK.
AND GET THAT LITTLE BRAT BACK TO WORK. EVERY MOMENT HE'S NOT WORKING, I'M LOSING BEER...

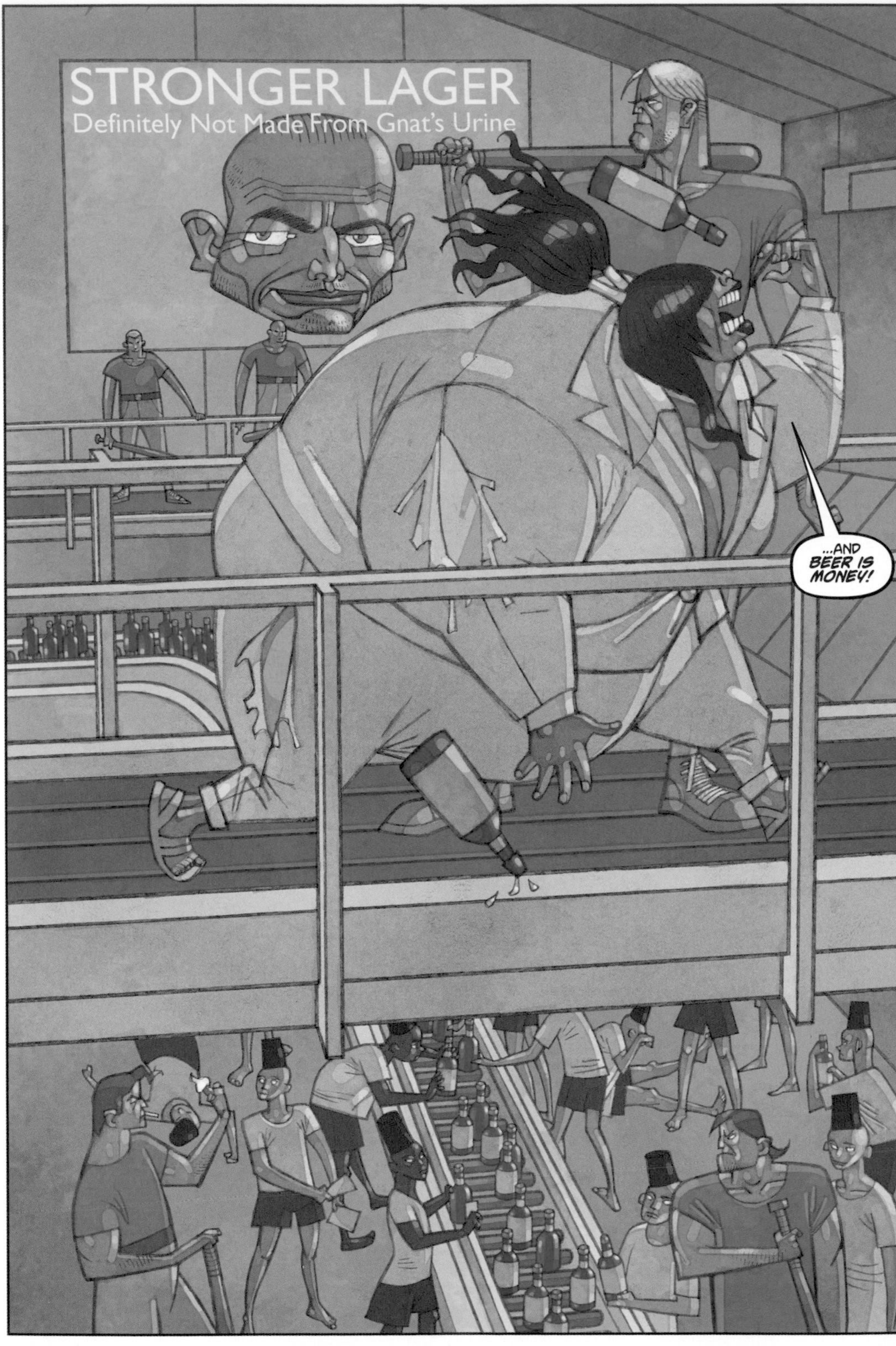
STRONGER LAGER
Definitely Not Made From Gnat's Urine
...AND BEER IS MONEY!

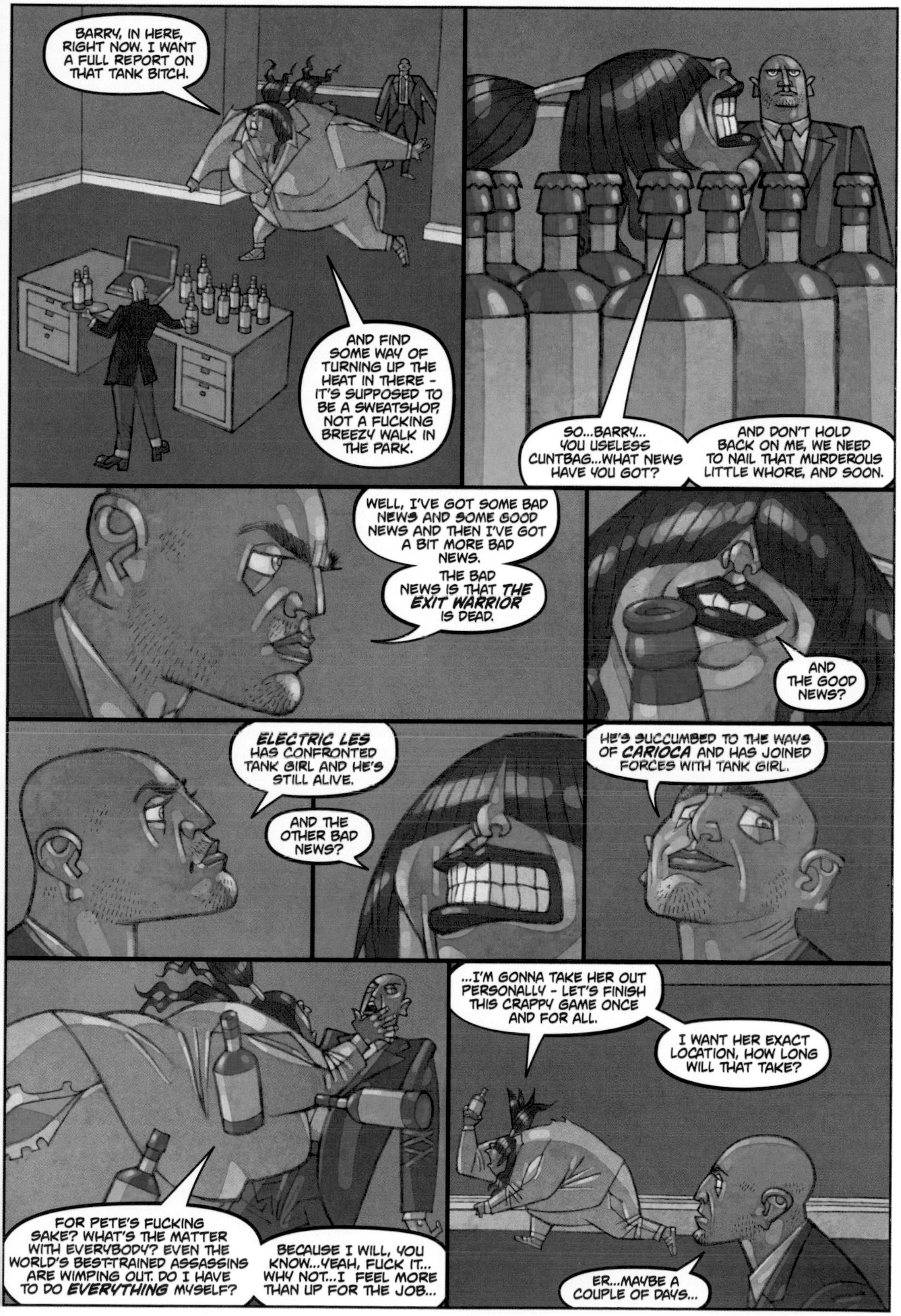
BARRY, IN HERE, RIGHT NOW. I WANT A FULL REPORT ON THAT TANK BITCH.
AND FIND SOME WAY OF TURNING UP THE HEAT IN THERE - IT'S SUPPOSED TO BE A SWEATSHOP, NOT A FUCKING BREEZY WALK IN THE PARK.
SO...BARRY... YOU USELESS CUNTBAG...WHAT NEWS HAVE YOU GOT?
AND DON'T HOLD BACK ON ME, WE NEED TO NAIL THAT MURDEROUS LITTLE WHORE, AND SOON.
WELL, I'VE GOT SOME BAD NEWS AND SOME GOOD NEWS AND THEN I'VE GOT A BIT MORE BAD NEWS.
THE BAD NEWS IS THAT THE EXIT WARRIOR IS DEAD.
AND THE GOOD NEWS?
ELECTRIC LES HAS CONFRONTED TANK GIRL AND HE'S STILL ALIVE.
AND THE OTHER BAD NEWS?
HE'S SUCCUMBED TO THE WAYS OF CARIOCA AND HAS JOINED FORCES WITH TANK GIRL.
FOR PETE'S FUCKING SAKE? WHAT'S THE MATTER WITH EVERYBODY? EVEN THE WORLD'S BEST-TRAINED ASSASSINS ARE WIMPING OUT. DO I HAVE TO DO EVERYTHING MYSELF?
BECAUSE I WILL, YOU KNOW...YEAH, FUCK IT... WHY NOT...I FEEL MORE THAN UP FOR THE JOB...
...I'M GONNA TAKE HER OUT PERSONALLY - LET'S FINISH THIS CRAPPY GAME ONCE AND FOR ALL.
I WANT HER EXACT LOCATION, HOW LONG WILL THAT TAKE?
ER...MAYBE A COUPLE OF DAYS...

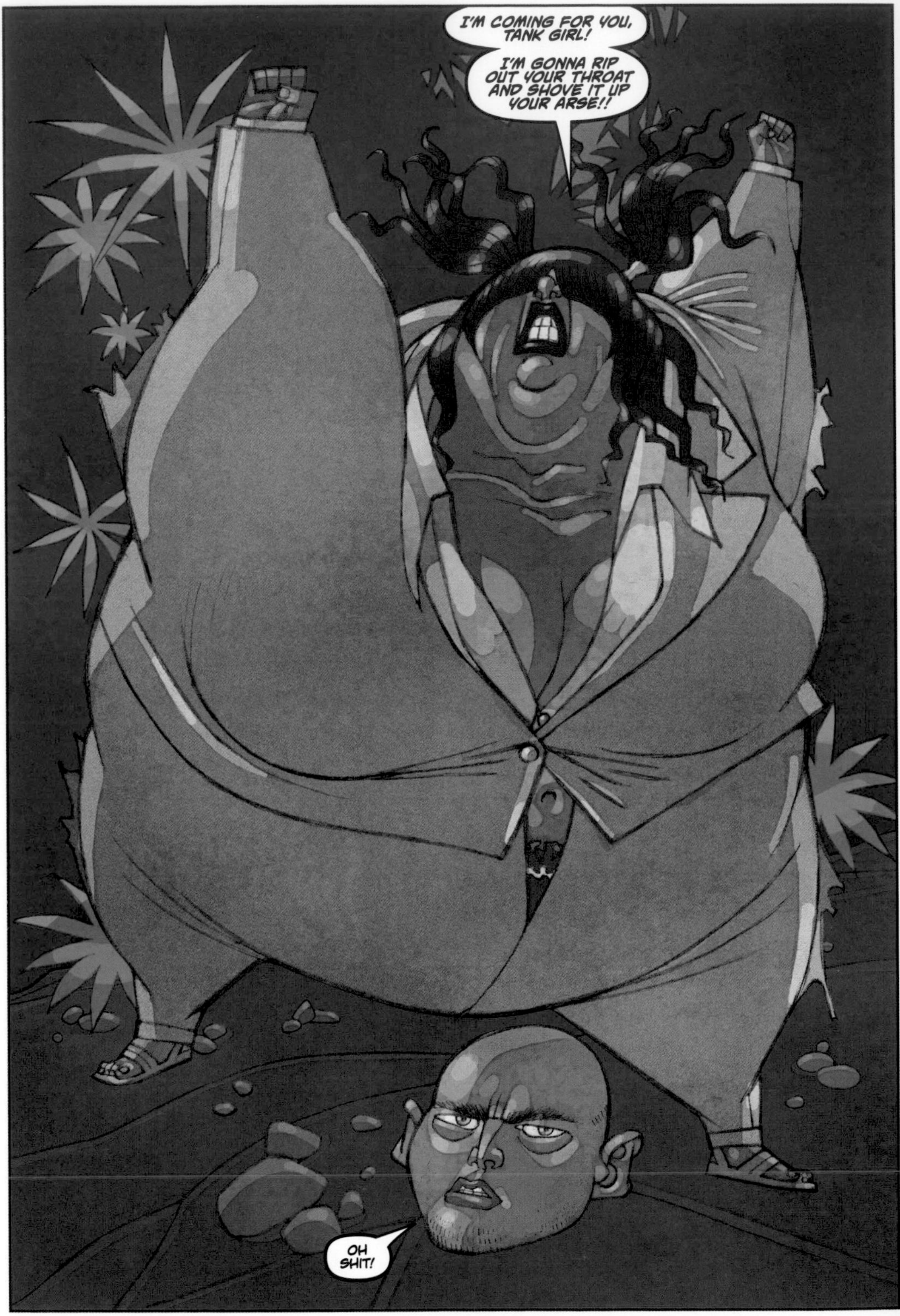
I'M COMING FOR YOU, TANK GIRL!
I'M GONNA RIP OUT YOUR THROAT AND SHOVE IT UP YOUR ARSE!!
OH SHIT!

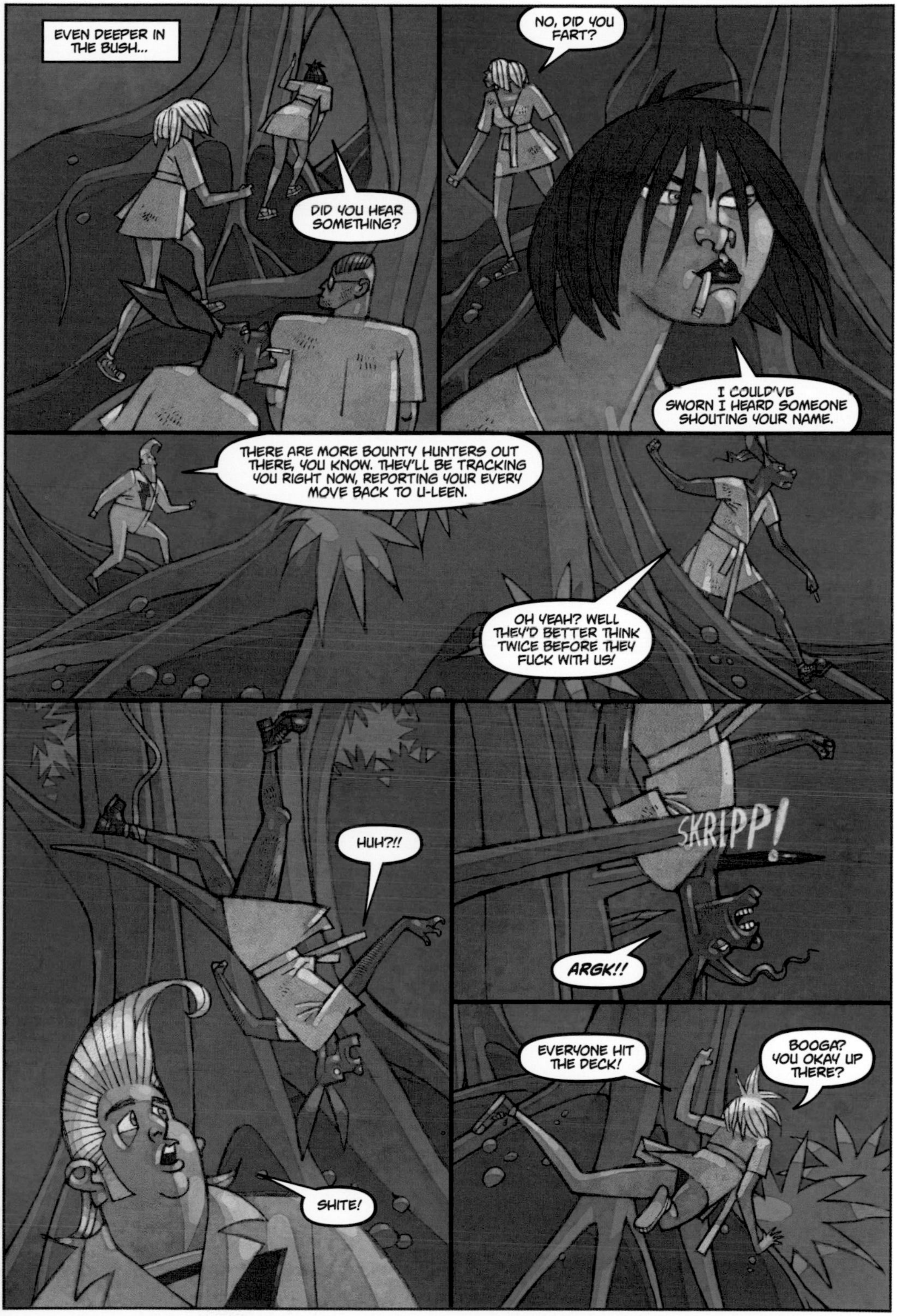
EVEN DEEPER IN THE BUSH...
DID YOU HEAR SOMETHING?
NO, DID YOU FART?
I COULD'VE SWORN I HEARD SOMEONE SHOUTING YOUR NAME.
THERE ARE MORE BOUNTY HUNTERS OUT THERE, YOU KNOW. THEY'LL BE TRACKING YOU RIGHT NOW, REPORTING YOUR EVERY MOVE BACK TO U-LEEN.
OH YEAH? WELL THEY'D BETTER THINK TWICE BEFORE THEY FUCK WITH US!
HUH?!!
SHITE!
SKRIPP!
ARGK!!
EVERYONE HIT THE DECK!
BOOGA? YOU OKAY UP THERE?

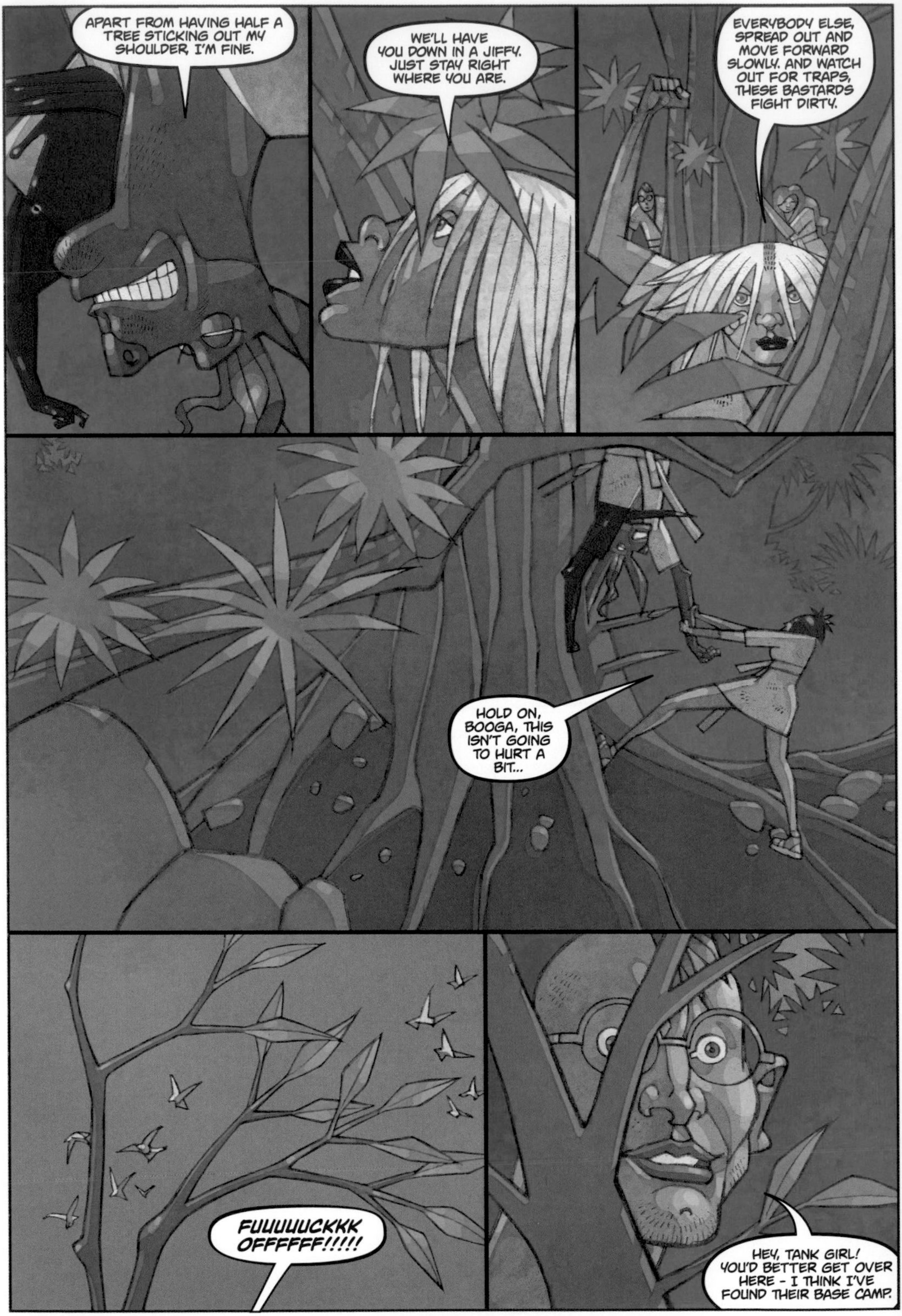
APART FROM HAVING HALF A TREE STICKING OUT MY SHOULDER, I'M FINE.
WE'LL HAVE YOU DOWN IN A JIFFY. JUST STAY RIGHT WHERE YOU ARE.
EVERYBODY ELSE, SPREAD OUT AND MOVE FORWARD SLOWLY. AND WATCH OUT FOR TRAPS, THESE BASTARDS FIGHT DIRTY.
HOLD ON, BOOGA, THIS ISN'T GOING TO HURT A BIT...
FUUUUUCKKK OFFFFFF!!!!!
HEY, TANK GIRL! YOU'D BETTER GET OVER HERE - I THINK I'VE FOUND THEIR BASE CAMP.

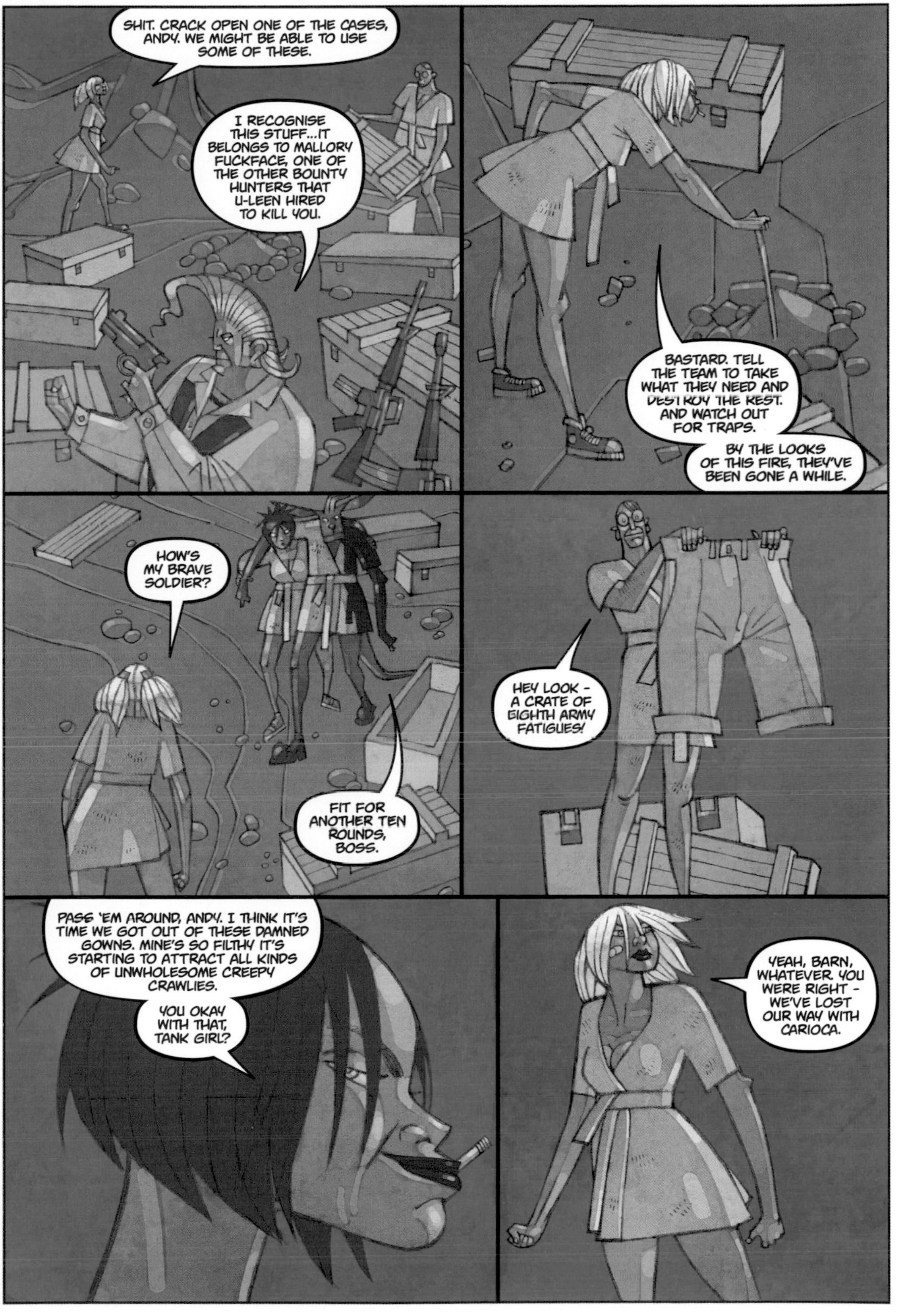
SHIT. CRACK OPEN ONE OF THE CASES, ANDY. WE MIGHT BE ABLE TO USE SOME OF THESE.
I RECOGNISE THIS STUFF...IT BELONGS TO MALLORY FUCKFACE, ONE OF THE OTHER BOUNTY HUNTERS THAT U-LEEN HIRED TO KILL YOU.
BASTARD. TELL THE TEAM TO TAKE WHAT THEY NEED AND DESTROY THE REST. AND WATCH OUT FOR TRAPS.
BY THE LOOKS OF THIS FIRE, THEY'VE BEEN GONE A WHILE.
HOW'S MY BRAVE SOLDIER?
FIT FOR ANOTHER TEN ROUNDS, BOSS.
HEY LOOK - A CRATE OF EIGHTH ARMY FATIGUES!
PASS 'EM AROUND, ANDY. I THINK IT'S TIME WE GOT OUT OF THESE DAMNED GOWNS. MINE'S SO FILTHY IT'S STARTING TO ATTRACT ALL KINDS OF UNWHOLESOME CREEPY CRAWLIES.
YOU OKAY WITH THAT, TANK GIRL?
YEAH, BARN, WHATEVER. YOU WERE RIGHT - WE'VE LOST OUR WAY WITH CARIOCA.

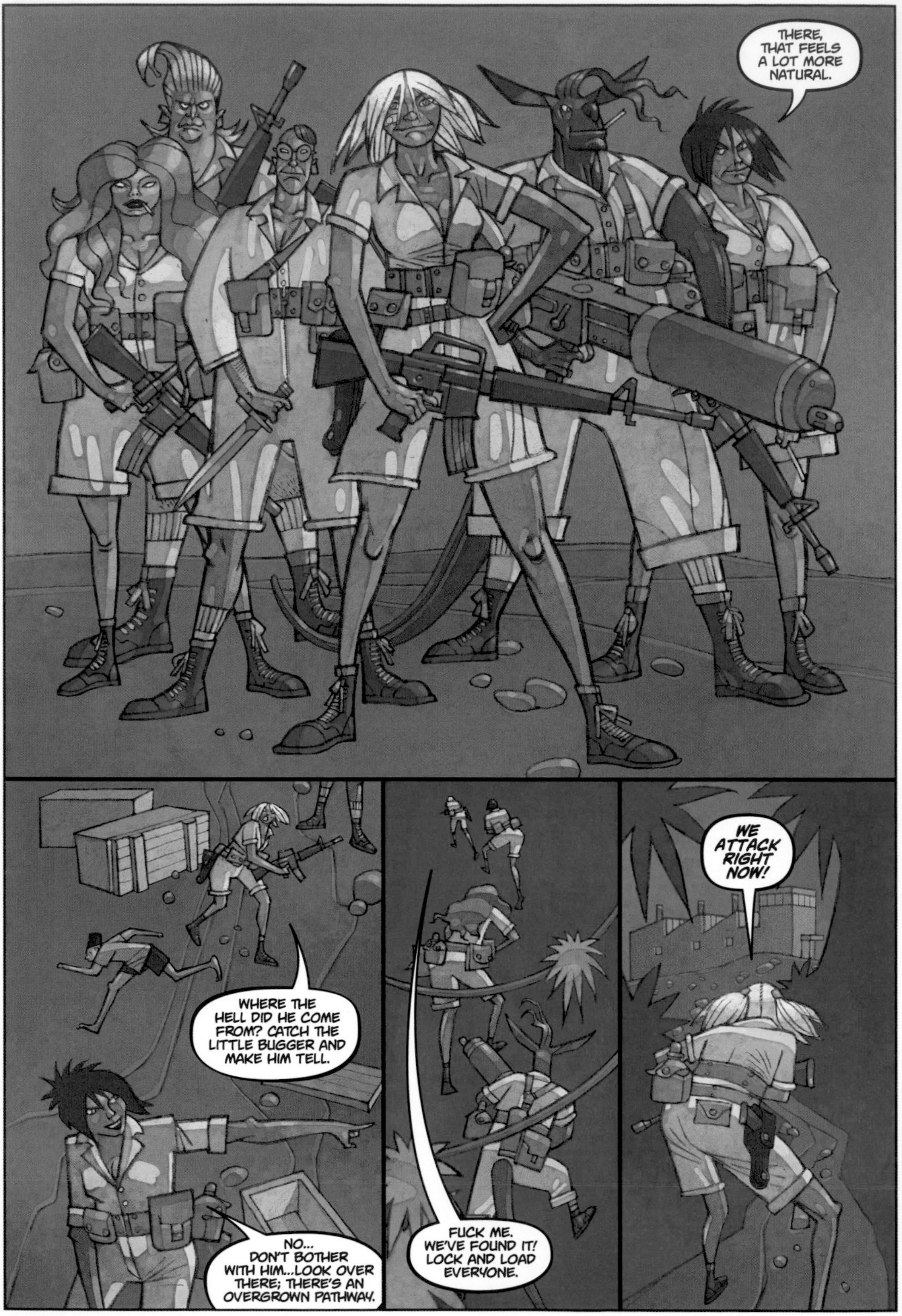
THERE, THAT FEELS A LOT MORE NATURAL.
WHERE THE HELL DID HE COME FROM? CATCH THE LITTLE BUGGER AND MAKE HIM TELL.
NO... DON'T BOTHER WITH HIM...LOOK OVER THERE; THERE'S AN OVERGROWN PATHWAY.
FUCK ME. WE'VE FOUND IT! LOCK AND LOAD EVERYONE.
WE ATTACK RIGHT NOW!

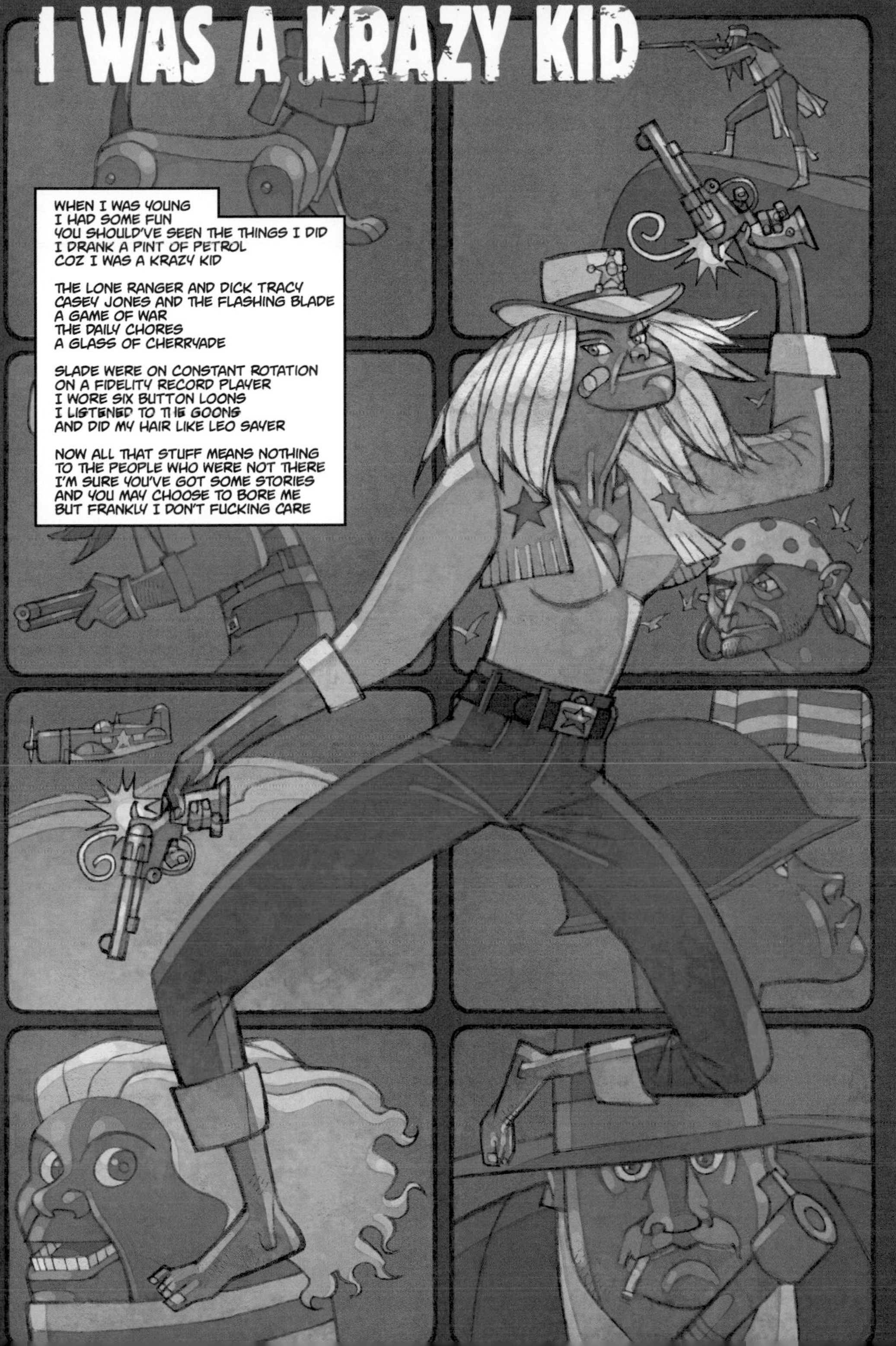
I WAS A KRAZY KID
WHEN I WAS YOUNG
I HAD SOME FUN
YOU SHOULD'VE SEEN THE THINGS I DID
I DRANK A PINT OF PETROL
COZ I WAS A KRAZY KID

THE LONE RANGER AND DICK TRACY
CASEY JONES AND THE FLASHING BLADE
A GAME OF WAR
THE DAILY CHORES
A GLASS OF CHERRYADE

SLADE WERE ON CONSTANT ROTATION
ON A FIDELITY RECORD PLAYER
I WORE SIX BUTTON LOONS
I LISTENED TO THE GOONS
AND DID MY HAIR LIKE LEO SAYER

NOW ALL THAT STUFF MEANS NOTHING
TO THE PEOPLE WHO WERE NOT THERE
I'M SURE YOU'VE GOT SOME STORIES
AND YOU MAY CHOOSE TO BORE ME
BUT FRANKLY I DON'T FUCKING CARE

THE MOONDOGS

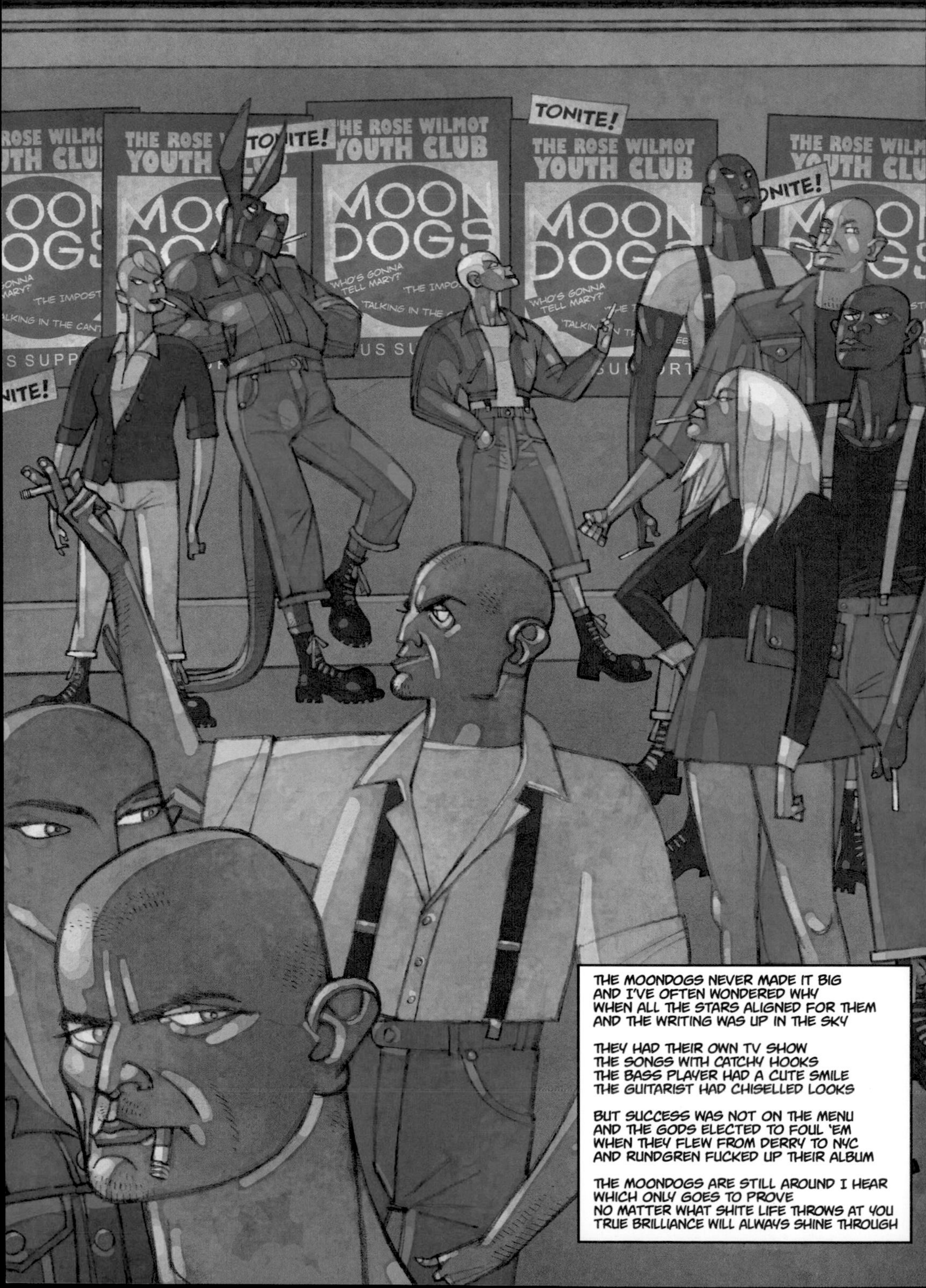
TONITE!
THE ROSE WILMOT YOUTH CLUB
MOON DOGS
'WHO'S GONNA TELL MARY?'
THE MOONDOGS NEVER MADE IT BIG
AND I'VE OFTEN WONDERED WHY
WHEN ALL THE STARS ALIGNED FOR THEM
AND THE WRITING WAS UP IN THE SKY
THEY HAD THEIR OWN TV SHOW
THE SONGS WITH CATCHY HOOKS
THE BASS PLAYER HAD A CUTE SMILE
THE GUITARIST HAD CHISELLED LOOKS
BUT SUCCESS WAS NOT ON THE MENU
AND THE GODS ELECTED TO FOUL 'EM
WHEN THEY FLEW FROM DERRY TO NYC
AND RUNDGREN FUCKED UP THEIR ALBUM
THE MOONDOGS ARE STILL AROUND I HEAR
WHICH ONLY GOES TO PROVE
NO MATTER WHAT SHITE LIFE THROWS AT YOU
TRUE BRILLIANCE WILL ALWAYS SHINE THROUGH

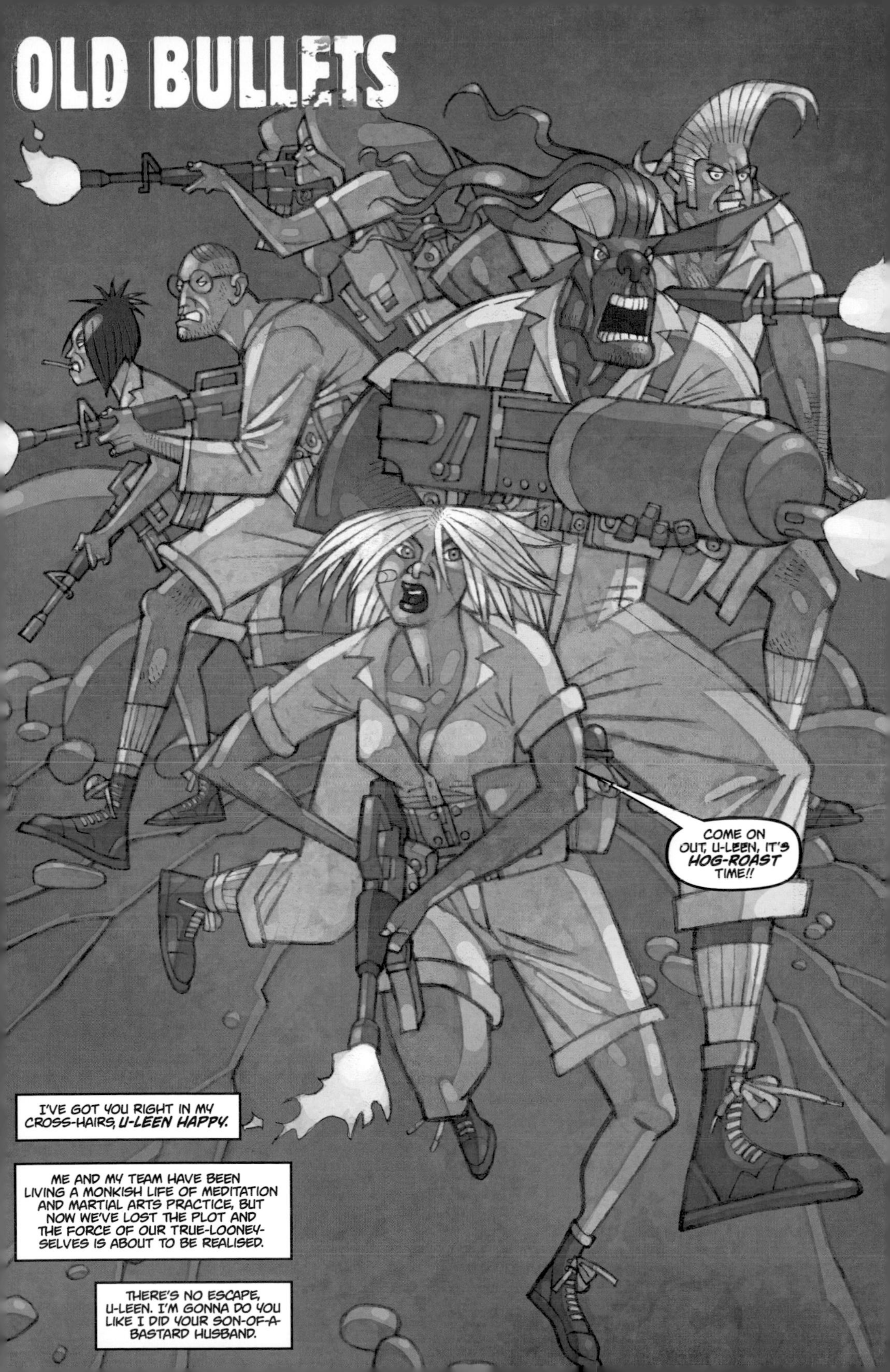
OLD BULLETS
COME ON OUT, U-LEEN, IT'S HOG-ROAST TIME!!
I'VE GOT YOU RIGHT IN MY CROSS-HAIRS, U-LEEN HAPPY.
ME AND MY TEAM HAVE BEEN LIVING A MONKISH LIFE OF MEDITATION AND MARTIAL ARTS PRACTICE, BUT NOW WE'VE LOST THE PLOT AND THE FORCE OF OUR TRUE-LOONEY-SELVES IS ABOUT TO BE REALISED.
THERE'S NO ESCAPE, U-LEEN. I'M GONNA DO YOU LIKE I DID YOUR SON-OF-A-BASTARD HUSBAND.

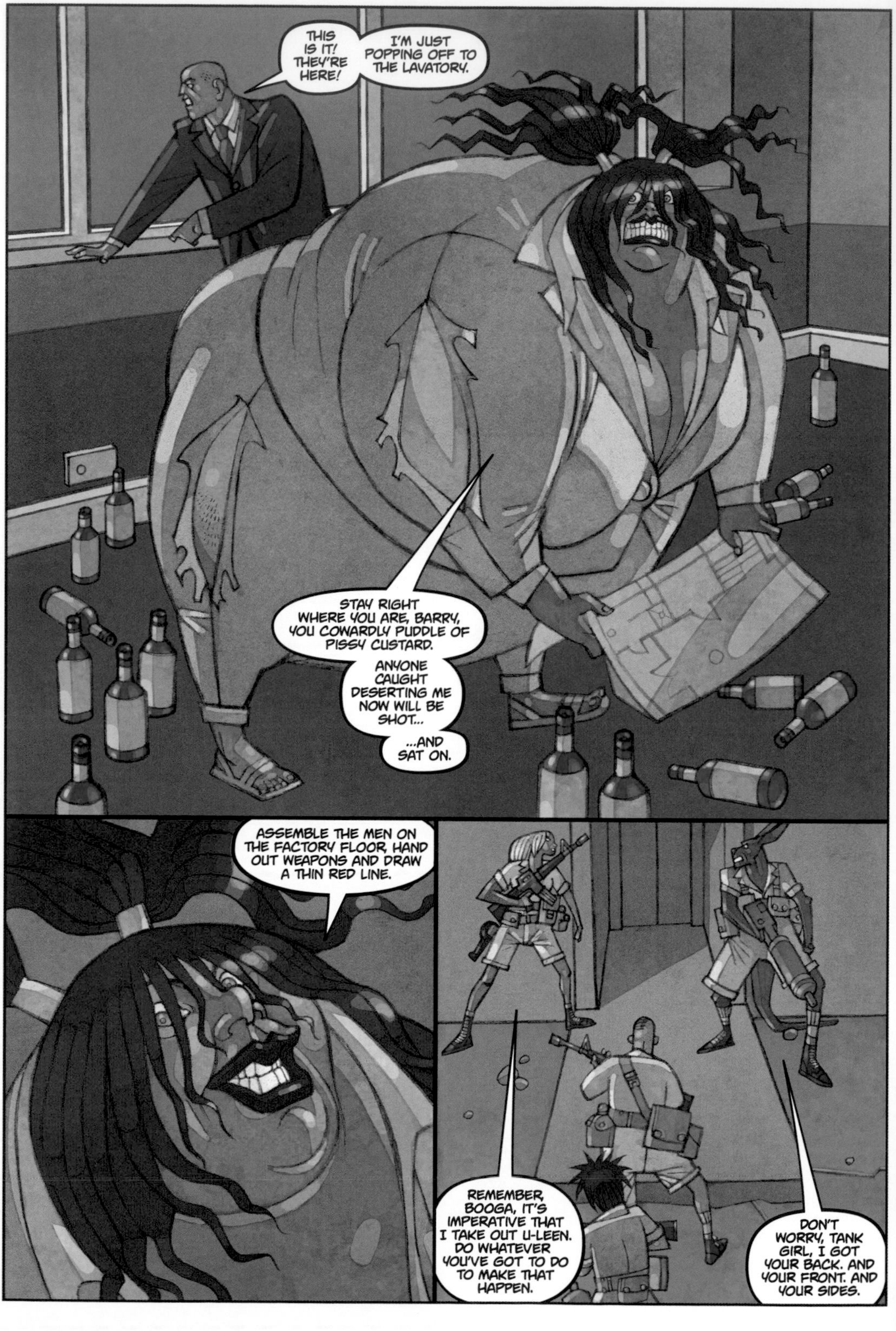
THIS IS IT! THEY'RE HERE!
I'M JUST POPPING OFF TO THE LAVATORY.
STAY RIGHT WHERE YOU ARE, BARRY, YOU COWARDLY PUDDLE OF PISSY CUSTARD.
ANYONE CAUGHT DESERTING ME NOW WILL BE SHOT...
...AND SAT ON.
ASSEMBLE THE MEN ON THE FACTORY FLOOR, HAND OUT WEAPONS AND DRAW A THIN RED LINE.
REMEMBER, BOOGA, IT'S IMPERATIVE THAT I TAKE OUT U-LEEN. DO WHATEVER YOU'VE GOT TO DO TO MAKE THAT HAPPEN.
DON'T WORRY, TANK GIRL, I GOT YOUR BACK. AND YOUR FRONT. AND YOUR SIDES.

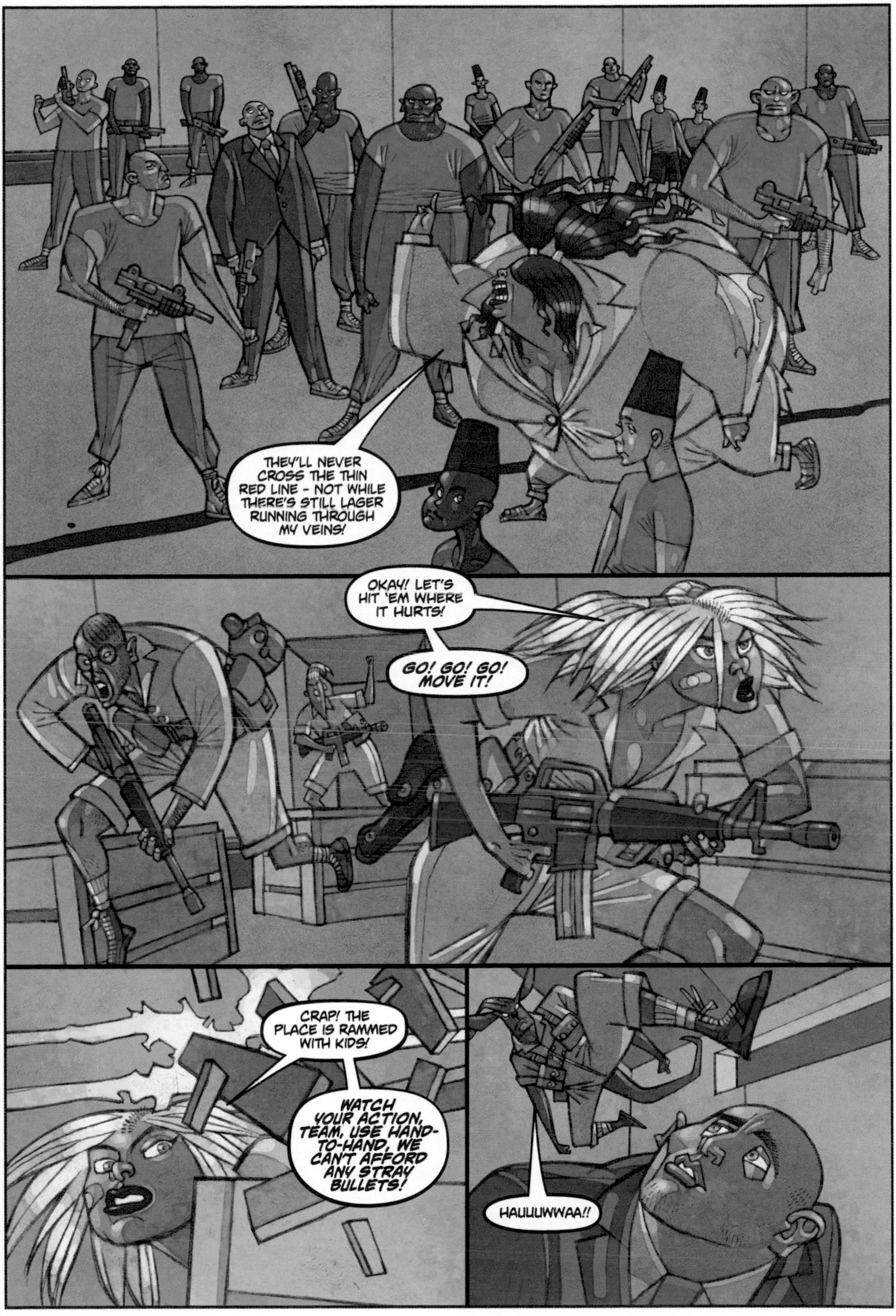
THEY'LL NEVER CROSS THE THIN RED LINE - NOT WHILE THERE'S STILL LAGER RUNNING THROUGH MY VEINS!
OKAY! LET'S HIT 'EM WHERE IT HURTS!
GO! GO! GO! MOVE IT!
CRAP! THE PLACE IS RAMMED WITH KIDS!
WATCH YOUR ACTION, TEAM, USE HAND-TO-HAND, WE CAN'T AFFORD ANY STRAY BULLETS!
HAUUUWWAA!!

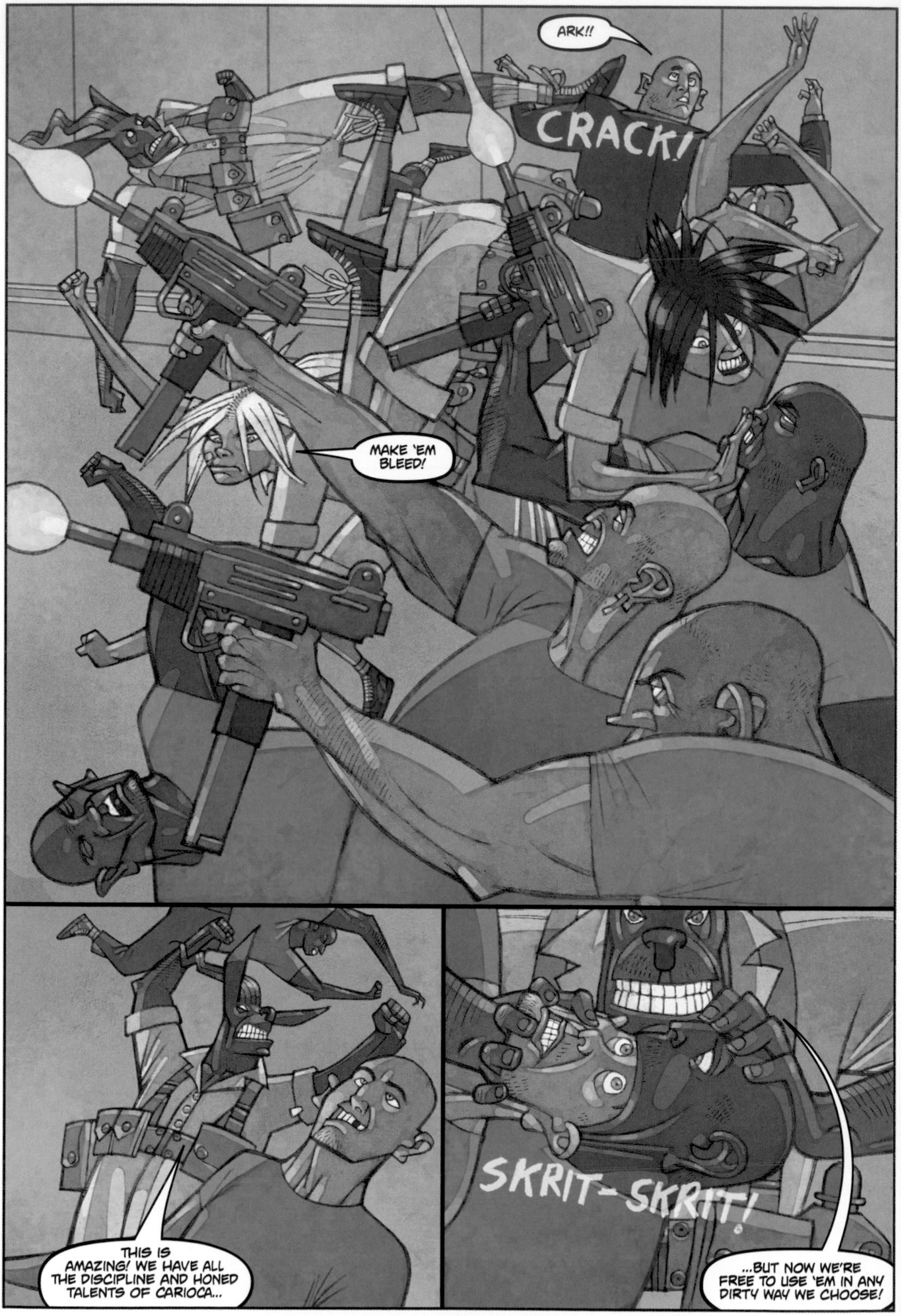
ARK!!
CRACK!
MAKE 'EM BLEED!
THIS IS AMAZING! WE HAVE ALL THE DISCIPLINE AND HONED TALENTS OF CARIOCA...
SKRIT-SKRIT!
...BUT NOW WE'RE FREE TO USE 'EM IN ANY DIRTY WAY WE CHOOSE!

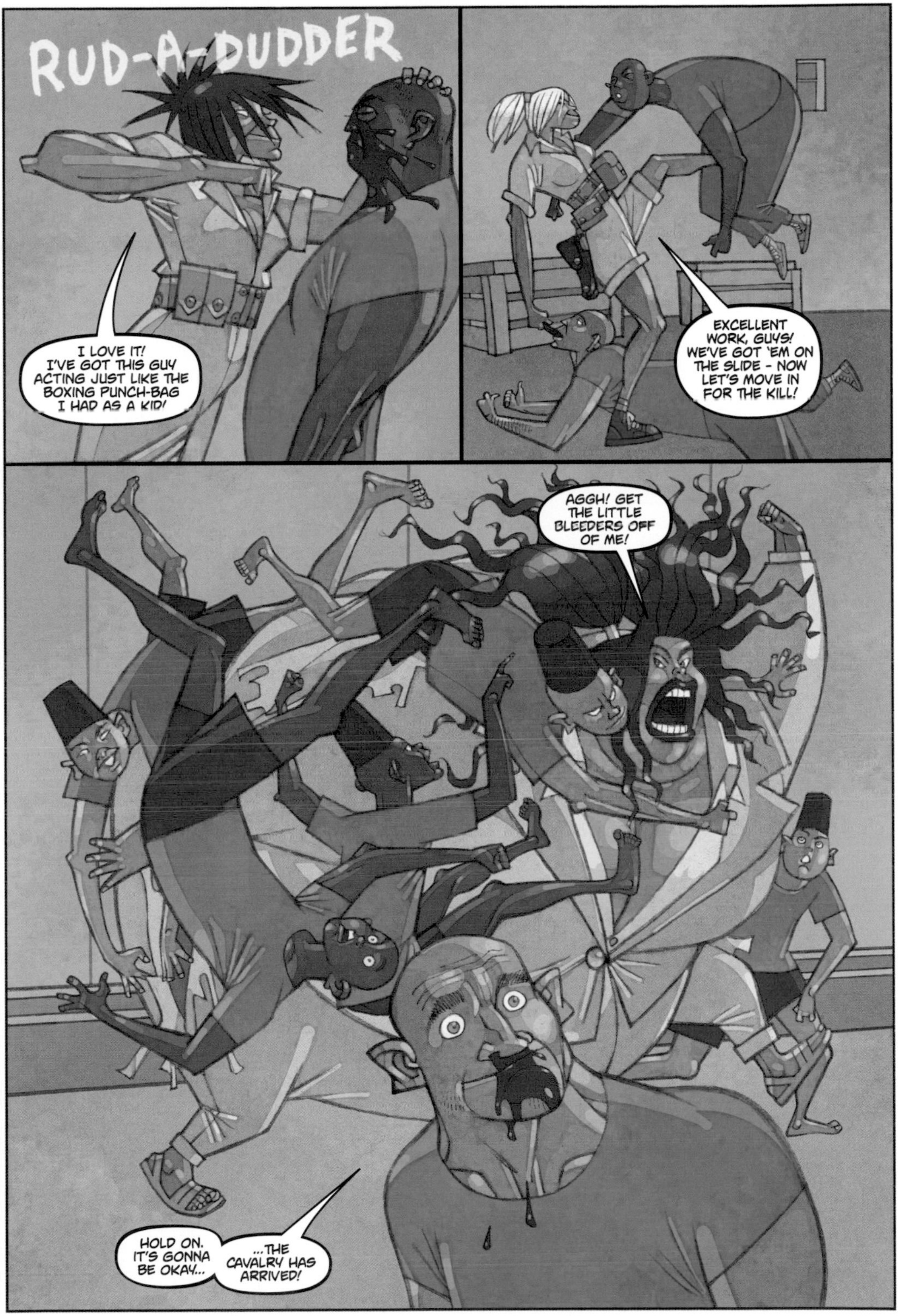
RUD-A-DUDDER
I LOVE IT! I'VE GOT THIS GUY ACTING JUST LIKE THE BOXING PUNCH-BAG I HAD AS A KID!
EXCELLENT WORK, GUYS! WE'VE GOT 'EM ON THE SLIDE - NOW LET'S MOVE IN FOR THE KILL!
AGGH! GET THE LITTLE BLEEDERS OFF OF ME!
HOLD ON. IT'S GONNA BE OKAY...
...THE CAVALRY HAS ARRIVED!

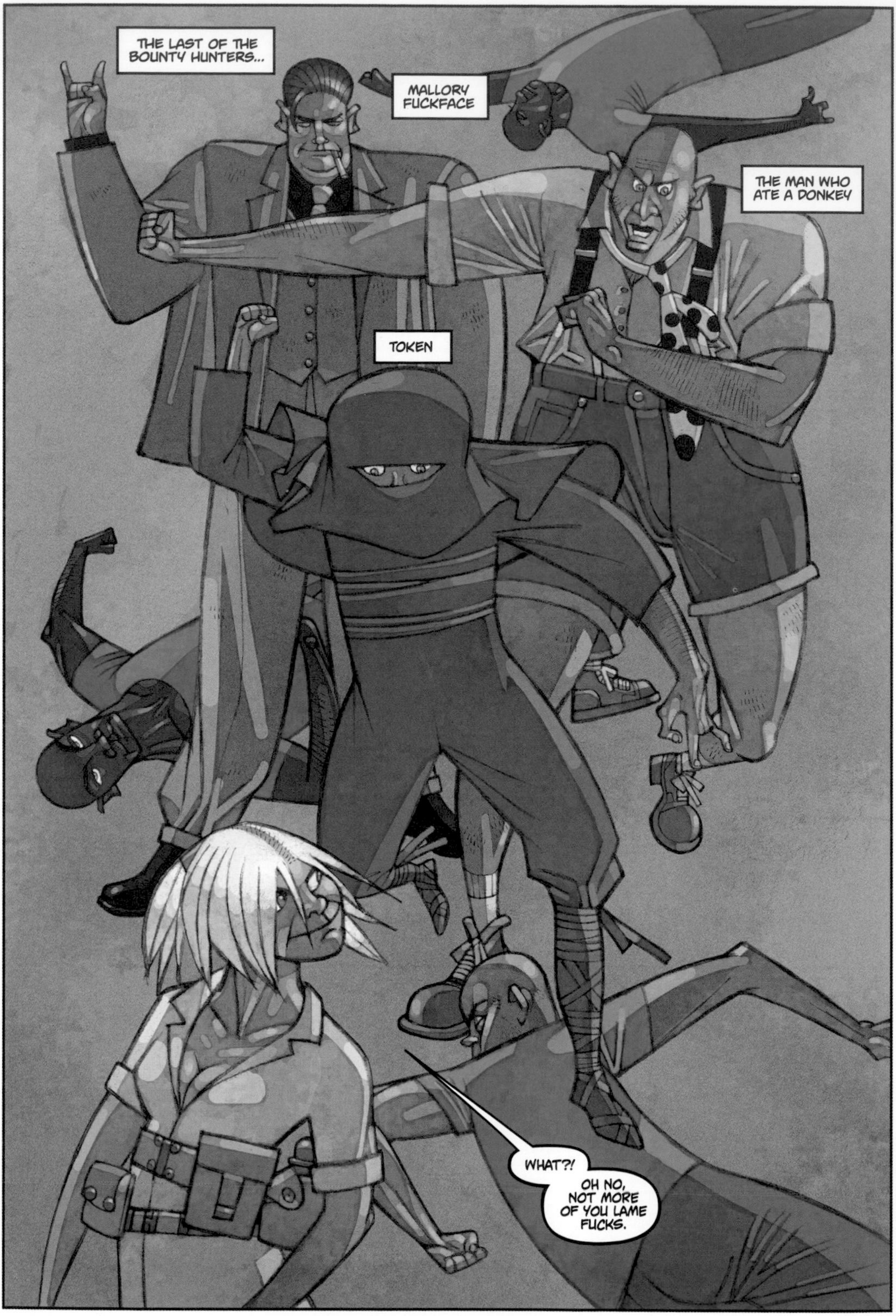
THE LAST OF THE BOUNTY HUNTERS...
MALLORY FUCKFACE
THE MAN WHO ATE A DONKEY
TOKEN
WHAT?!
OH NO, NOT MORE OF YOU LAME FUCKS.

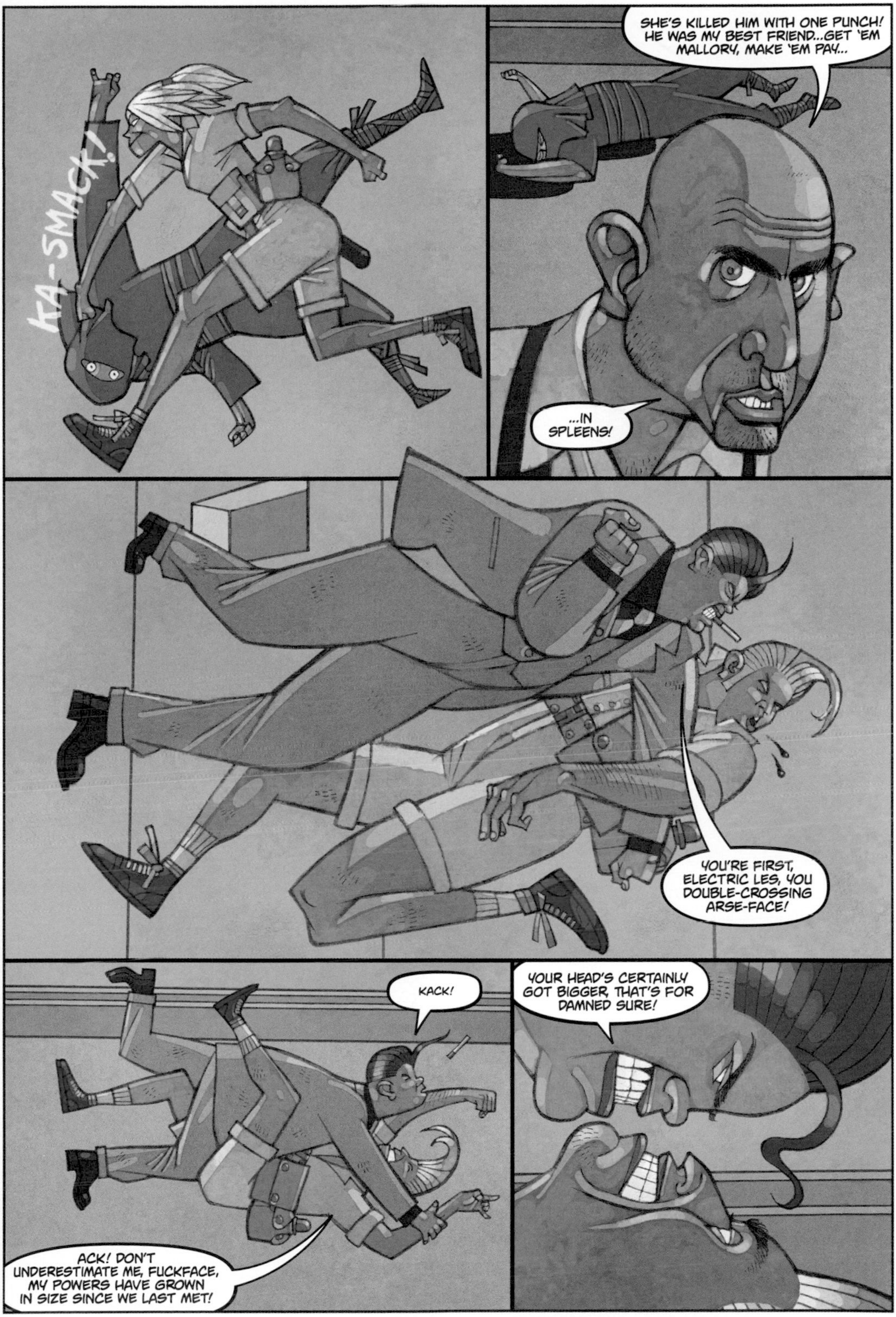
KA-SMACK!
SHE'S KILLED HIM WITH ONE PUNCH! HE WAS MY BEST FRIEND...GET 'EM MALLORY, MAKE 'EM PAY...
...IN SPLEENS!
YOU'RE FIRST, ELECTRIC LES, YOU DOUBLE-CROSSING ARSE-FACE!
KACK!
ACK! DON'T UNDERESTIMATE ME, FUCKFACE, MY POWERS HAVE GROWN IN SIZE SINCE WE LAST MET!
YOUR HEAD'S CERTAINLY GOT BIGGER, THAT'S FOR DAMNED SURE!

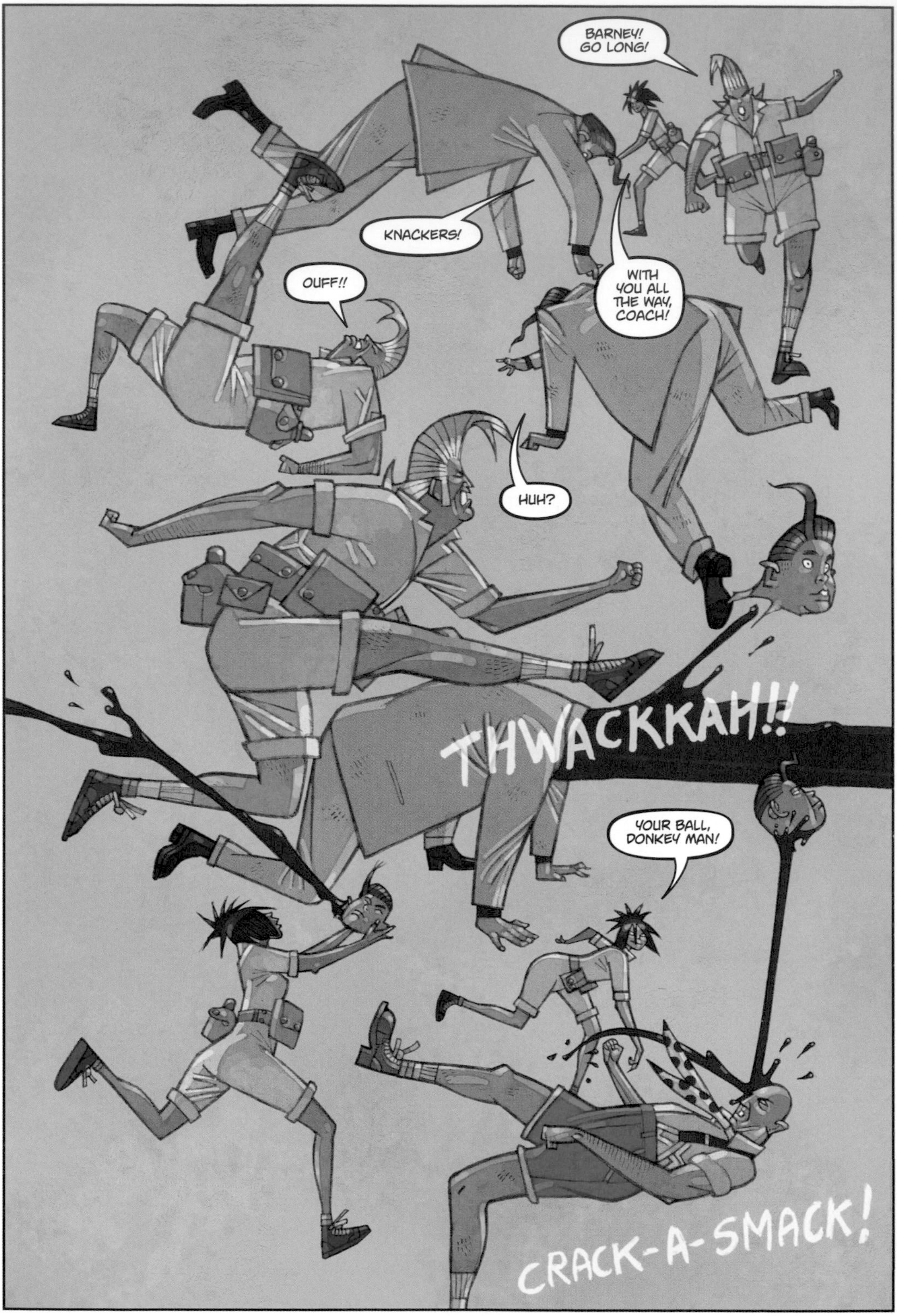
BARNEY! GO LONG!
KNACKERS!
WITH YOU ALL THE WAY, COACH!
OUFF!!
HUH?
THWACKKAH!!
YOUR BALL, DONKEY MAN!
CRACK-A-SMACK!

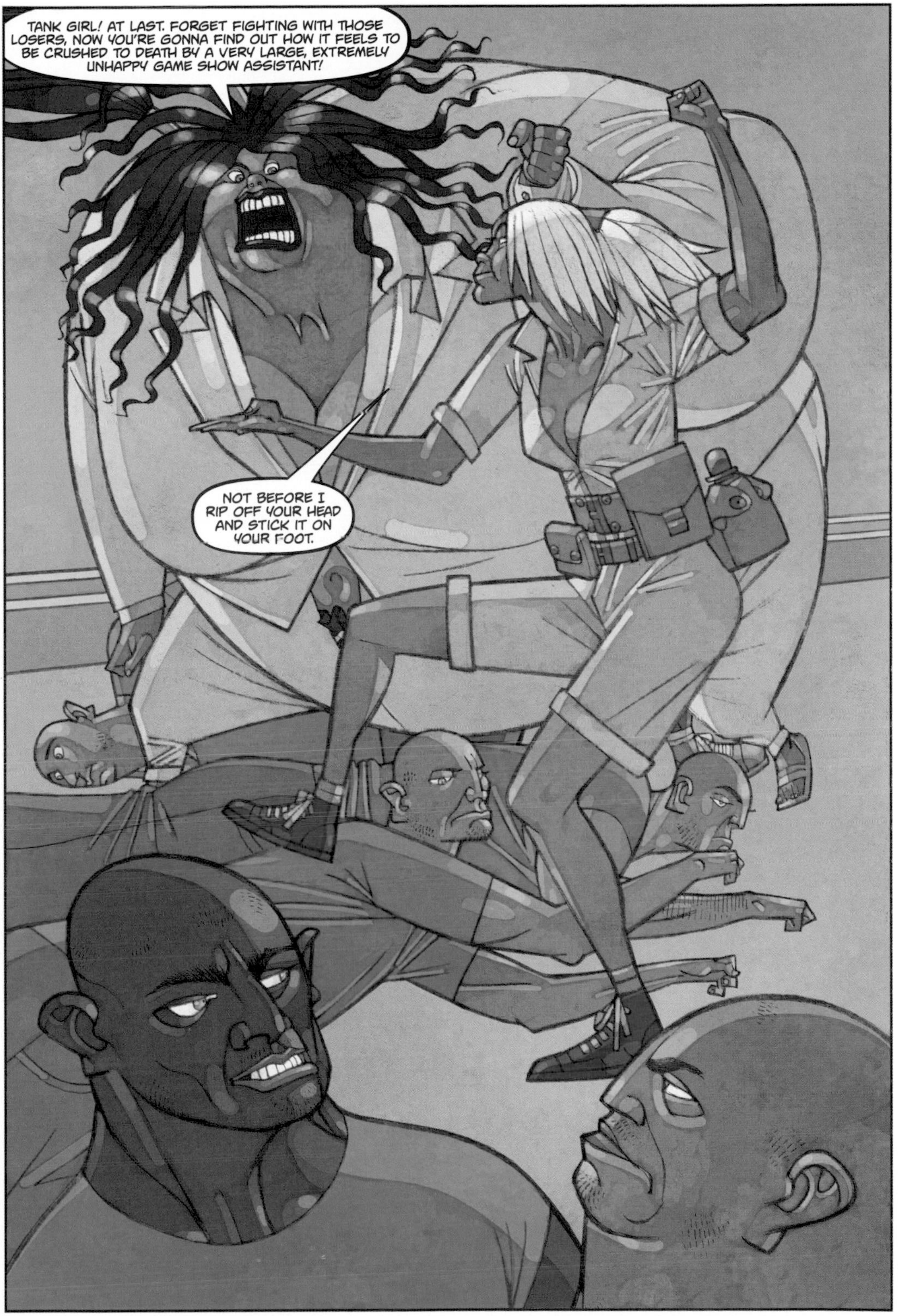
TANK GIRL! AT LAST. FORGET FIGHTING WITH THOSE LOSERS, NOW YOU'RE GONNA FIND OUT HOW IT FEELS TO BE CRUSHED TO DEATH BY A VERY LARGE, EXTREMELY UNHAPPY GAME SHOW ASSISTANT!
NOT BEFORE I RIP OFF YOUR HEAD AND STICK IT ON YOUR FOOT.

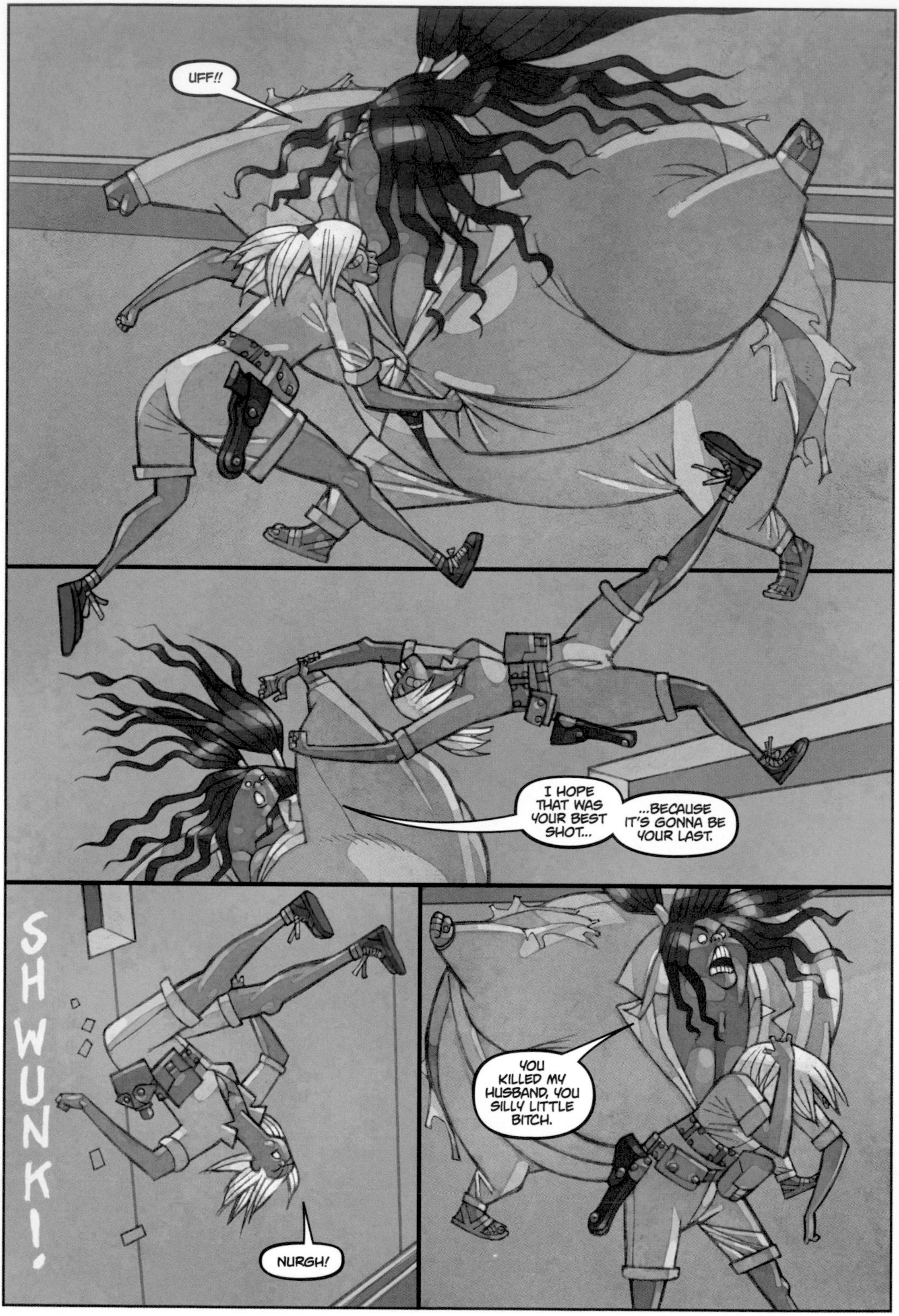
UFF!!
I HOPE THAT WAS YOUR BEST SHOT...
...BECAUSE IT'S GONNA BE YOUR LAST.
SHWUNK!
NURGH!
YOU KILLED MY HUSBAND, YOU SILLY LITTLE BITCH.

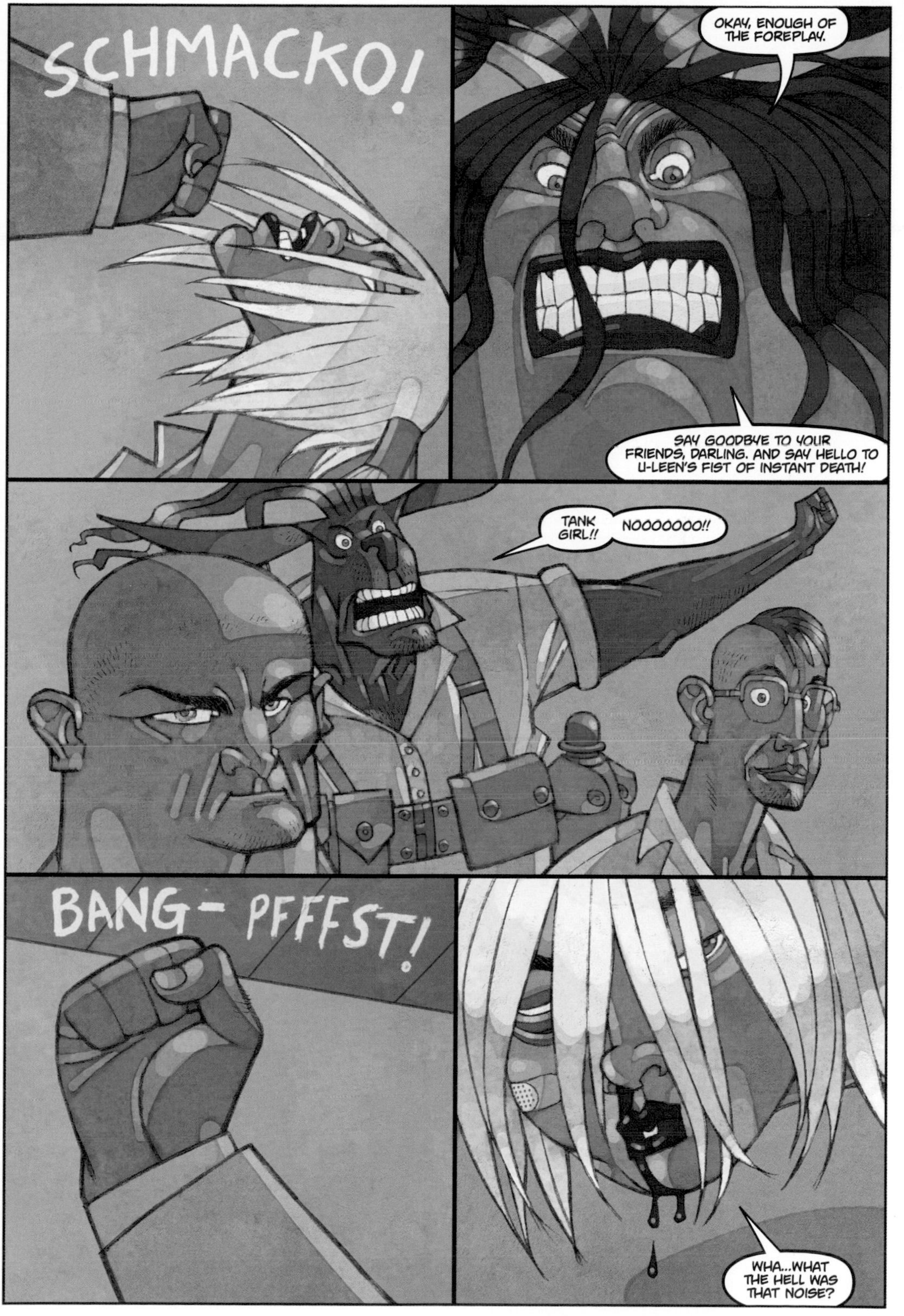
SCHMACKO!
OKAY, ENOUGH OF THE FOREPLAY.
SAY GOODBYE TO YOUR FRIENDS, DARLING. AND SAY HELLO TO U-LEEN'S FIST OF INSTANT DEATH!
TANK GIRL!!
NOOOOOOO!!
BANG- PFFFST!
WHA...WHAT THE HELL WAS THAT NOISE?

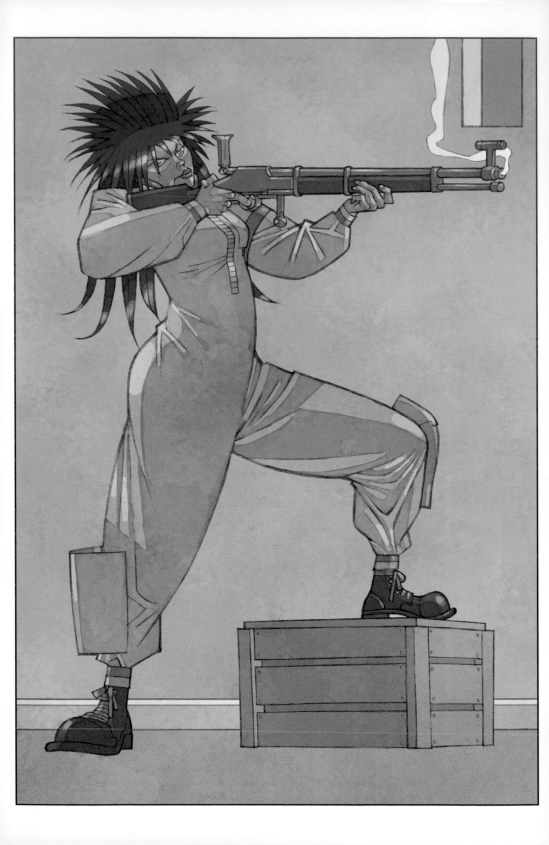

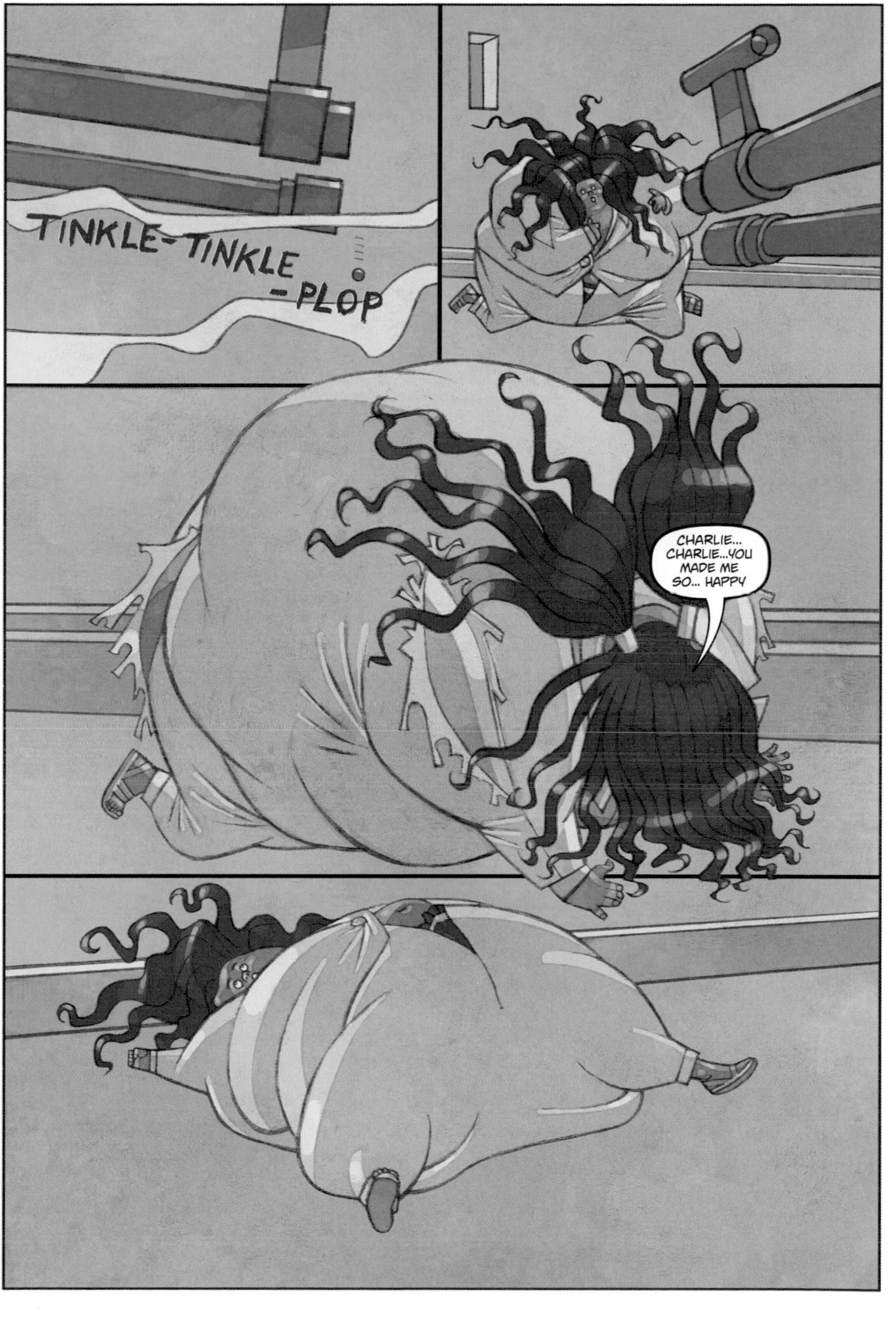
TINKLE-TINKLE
-PLOP
CHARLIE... CHARLIE...YOU MADE ME SO... HAPPY

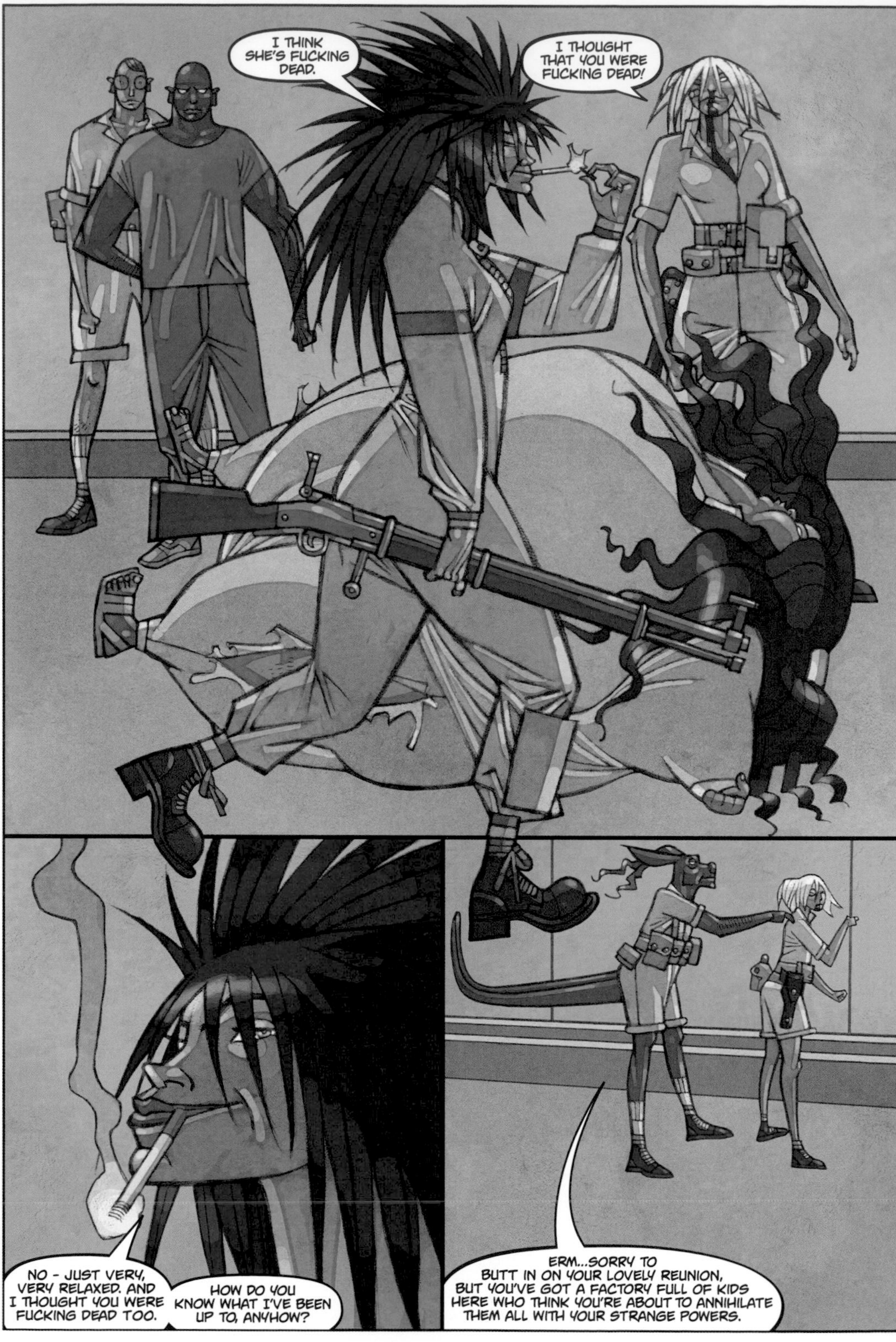
I THINK SHE'S FUCKING DEAD.
I THOUGHT THAT YOU WERE FUCKING DEAD!
NO - JUST VERY, VERY RELAXED. AND I THOUGHT YOU WERE FUCKING DEAD TOO.
HOW DO YOU KNOW WHAT I'VE BEEN UP TO, ANYHOW?
ERM...SORRY TO BUTT IN ON YOUR LOVELY REUNION, BUT YOU'VE GOT A FACTORY FULL OF KIDS HERE WHO THINK YOU'RE ABOUT TO ANNIHILATE THEM ALL WITH YOUR STRANGE POWERS.

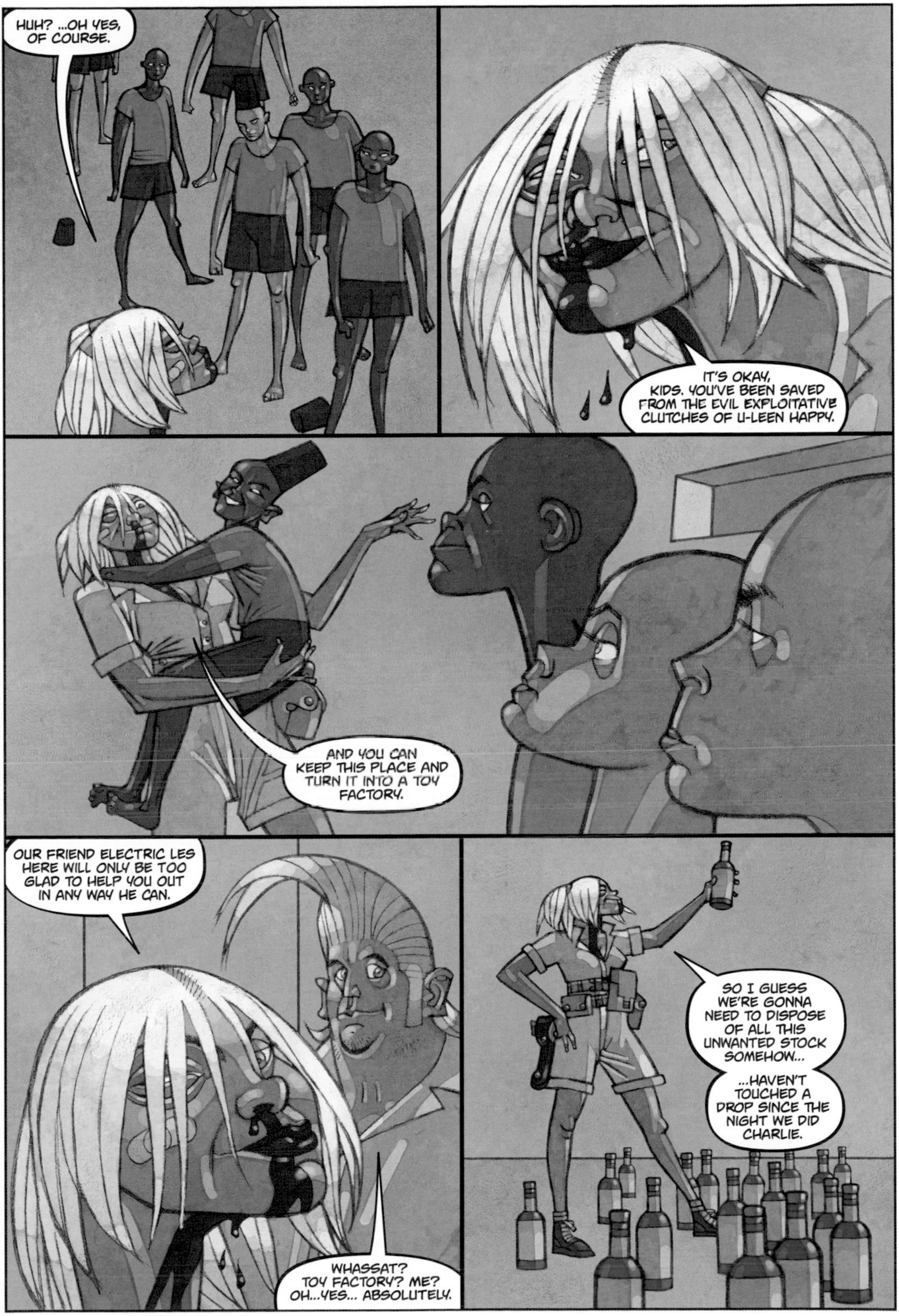
HUH? ...OH YES, OF COURSE.
IT'S OKAY, KIDS. YOU'VE BEEN SAVED FROM THE EVIL EXPLOITATIVE CLUTCHES OF U-LEEN HAPPY.
AND YOU CAN KEEP THIS PLACE AND TURN IT INTO A TOY FACTORY.
OUR FRIEND ELECTRIC LES HERE WILL ONLY BE TOO GLAD TO HELP YOU OUT IN ANY WAY HE CAN.
WHASSAT? TOY FACTORY? ME? OH...YES... ABSOLUTELY.
SO I GUESS WE'RE GONNA NEED TO DISPOSE OF ALL THIS UNWANTED STOCK SOMEHOW...
...HAVEN'T TOUCHED A DROP SINCE THE NIGHT WE DID CHARLIE.

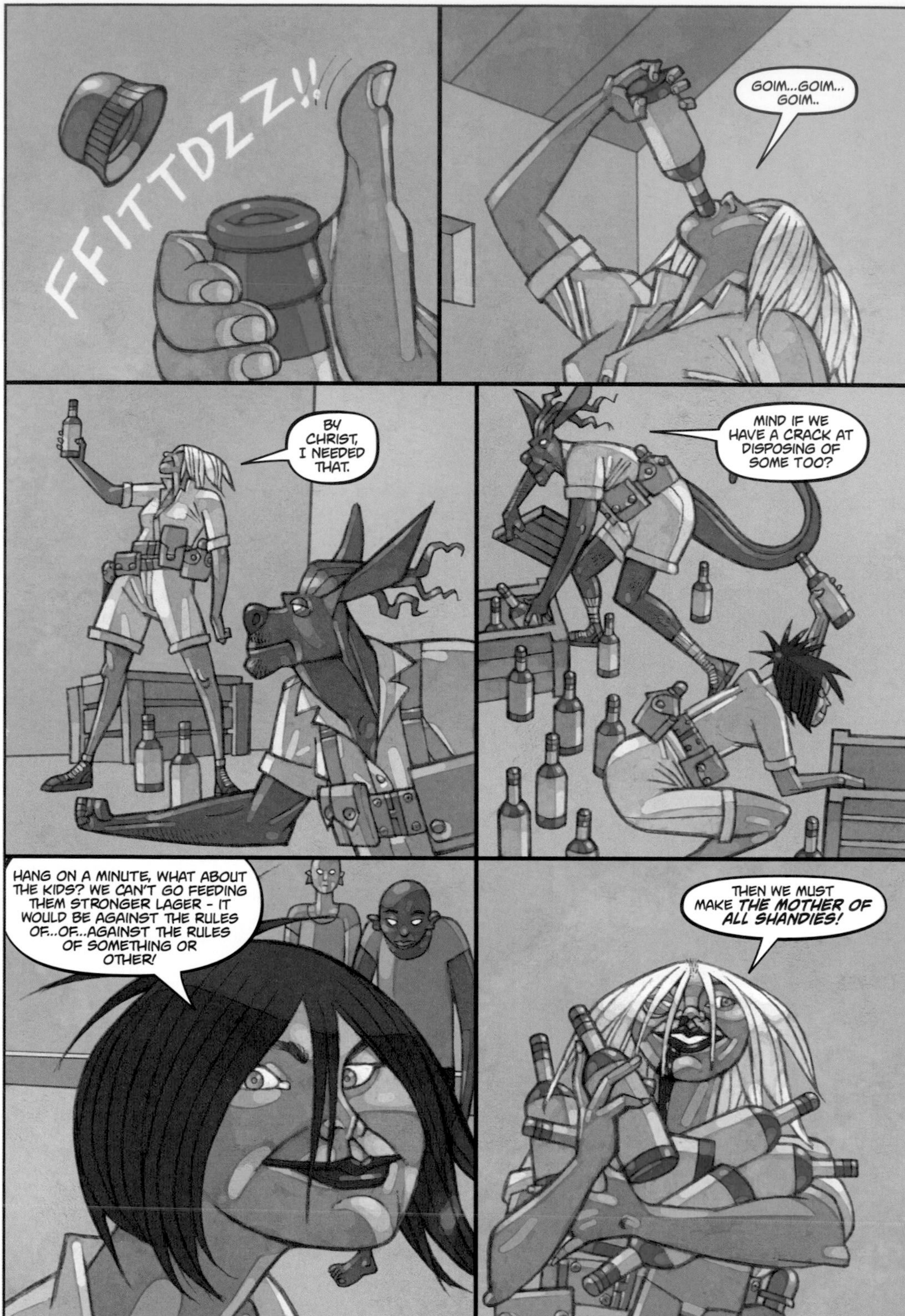

FFITTDZZ!!
GOIM...GOIM...
GOIM..
BY CHRIST, I NEEDED THAT.
MIND IF WE HAVE A CRACK AT DISPOSING OF SOME TOO?
HANG ON A MINUTE, WHAT ABOUT THE KIDS? WE CAN'T GO FEEDING THEM STRONGER LAGER - IT WOULD BE AGAINST THE RULES OF...OF...AGAINST THE RULES OF SOMETHING OR OTHER!
THEN WE MUST MAKE *THE MOTHER OF ALL SHANDIES!*

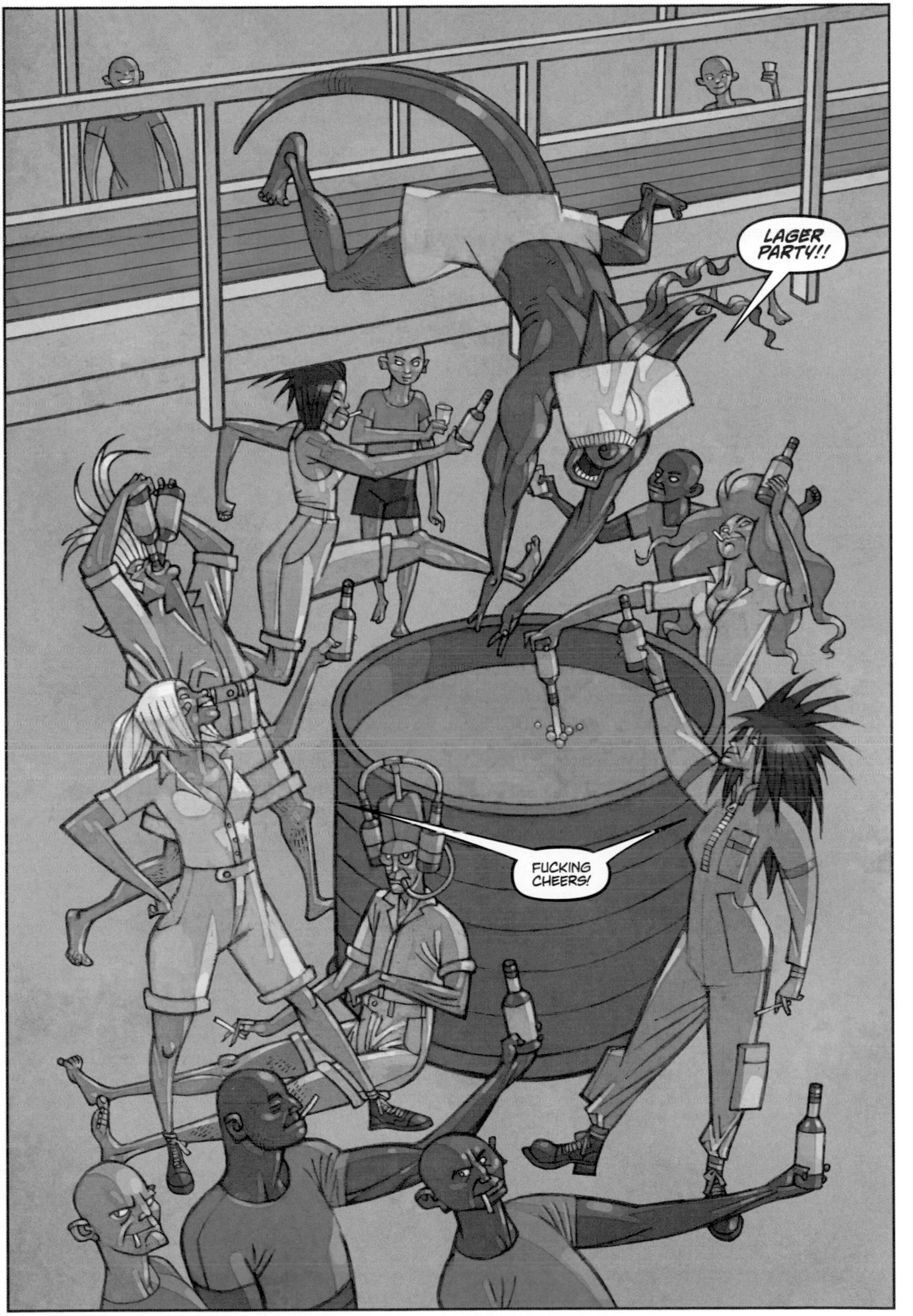
LAGER PARTY!!
FUCKING CHEERS!

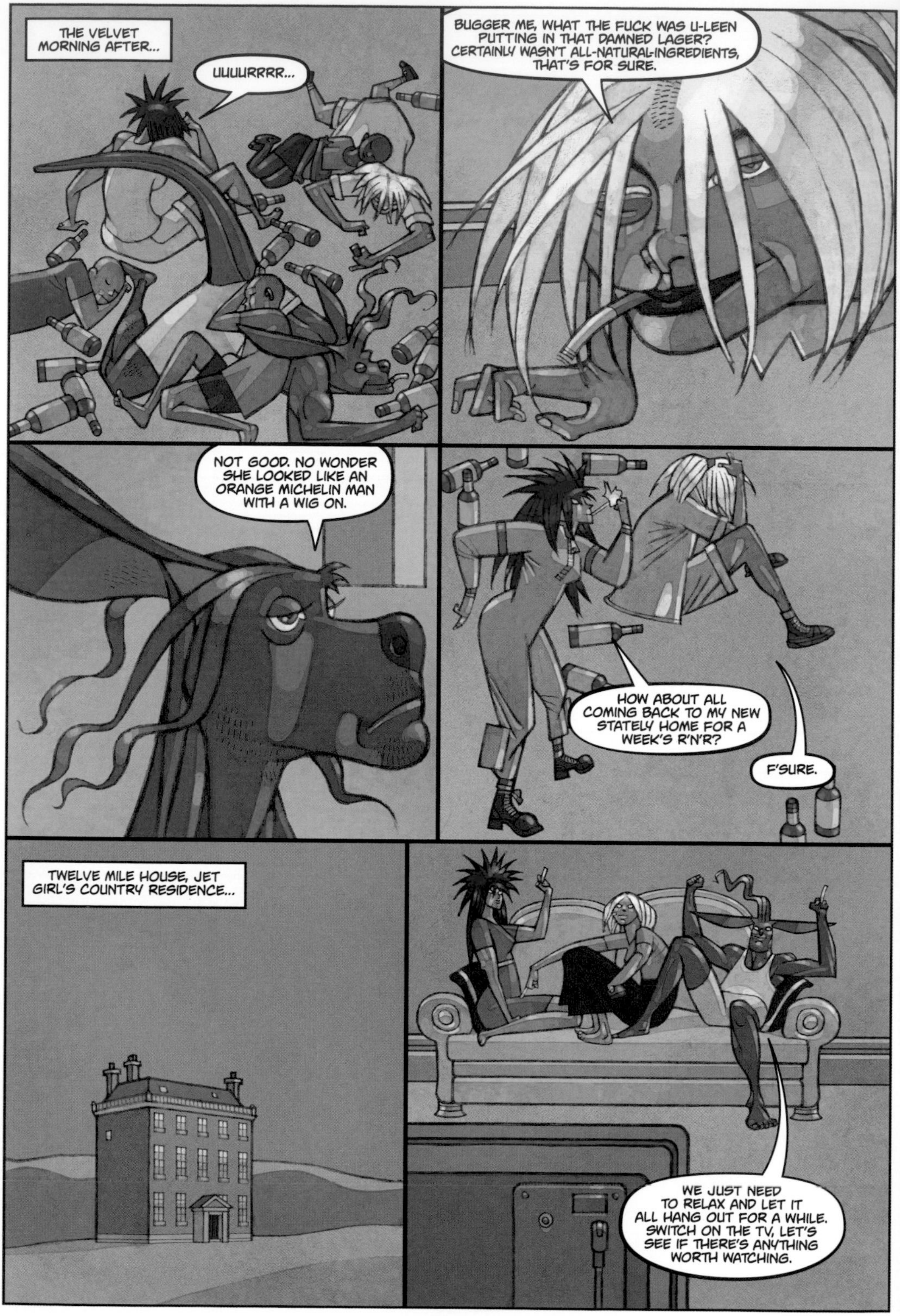
THE VELVET MORNING AFTER...
UUUURRRR...
BUGGER ME, WHAT THE FUCK WAS U-LEEN PUTTING IN THAT DAMNED LAGER? CERTAINLY WASN'T ALL-NATURAL-INGREDIENTS, THAT'S FOR SURE.
NOT GOOD. NO WONDER SHE LOOKED LIKE AN ORANGE MICHELIN MAN WITH A WIG ON.
HOW ABOUT ALL COMING BACK TO MY NEW STATELY HOME FOR A WEEK'S R'N'R?
F'SURE.
TWELVE MILE HOUSE, JET GIRL'S COUNTRY RESIDENCE...
WE JUST NEED TO RELAX AND LET IT ALL HANG OUT FOR A WHILE. SWITCH ON THE TV, LET'S SEE IF THERE'S ANYTHING WORTH WATCHING.

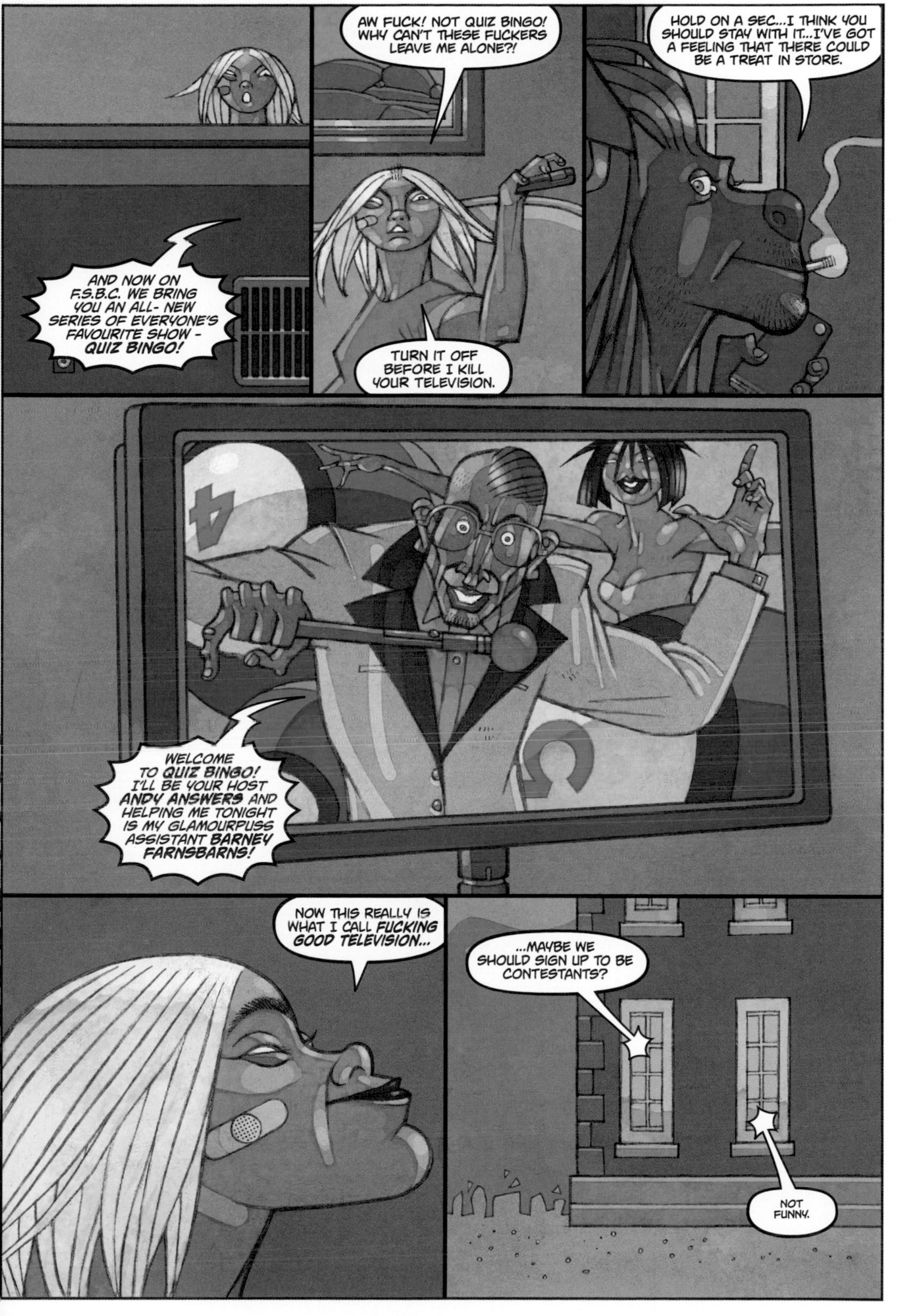
AND NOW ON F.S.B.C. WE BRING YOU AN ALL- NEW SERIES OF EVERYONE'S FAVOURITE SHOW - QUIZ BINGO!
AW FUCK! NOT QUIZ BINGO! WHY CAN'T THESE FUCKERS LEAVE ME ALONE?!
TURN IT OFF BEFORE I KILL YOUR TELEVISION.
HOLD ON A SEC...I THINK YOU SHOULD STAY WITH IT...I'VE GOT A FEELING THAT THERE COULD BE A TREAT IN STORE.
WELCOME TO QUIZ BINGO! I'LL BE YOUR HOST ANDY ANSWERS AND HELPING ME TONIGHT IS MY GLAMOURPUSS ASSISTANT BARNEY FARNSBARNS!
NOW THIS REALLY IS WHAT I CALL FUCKING GOOD TELEVISION...
...MAYBE WE SHOULD SIGN UP TO BE CONTESTANTS?
NOT FUNNY.

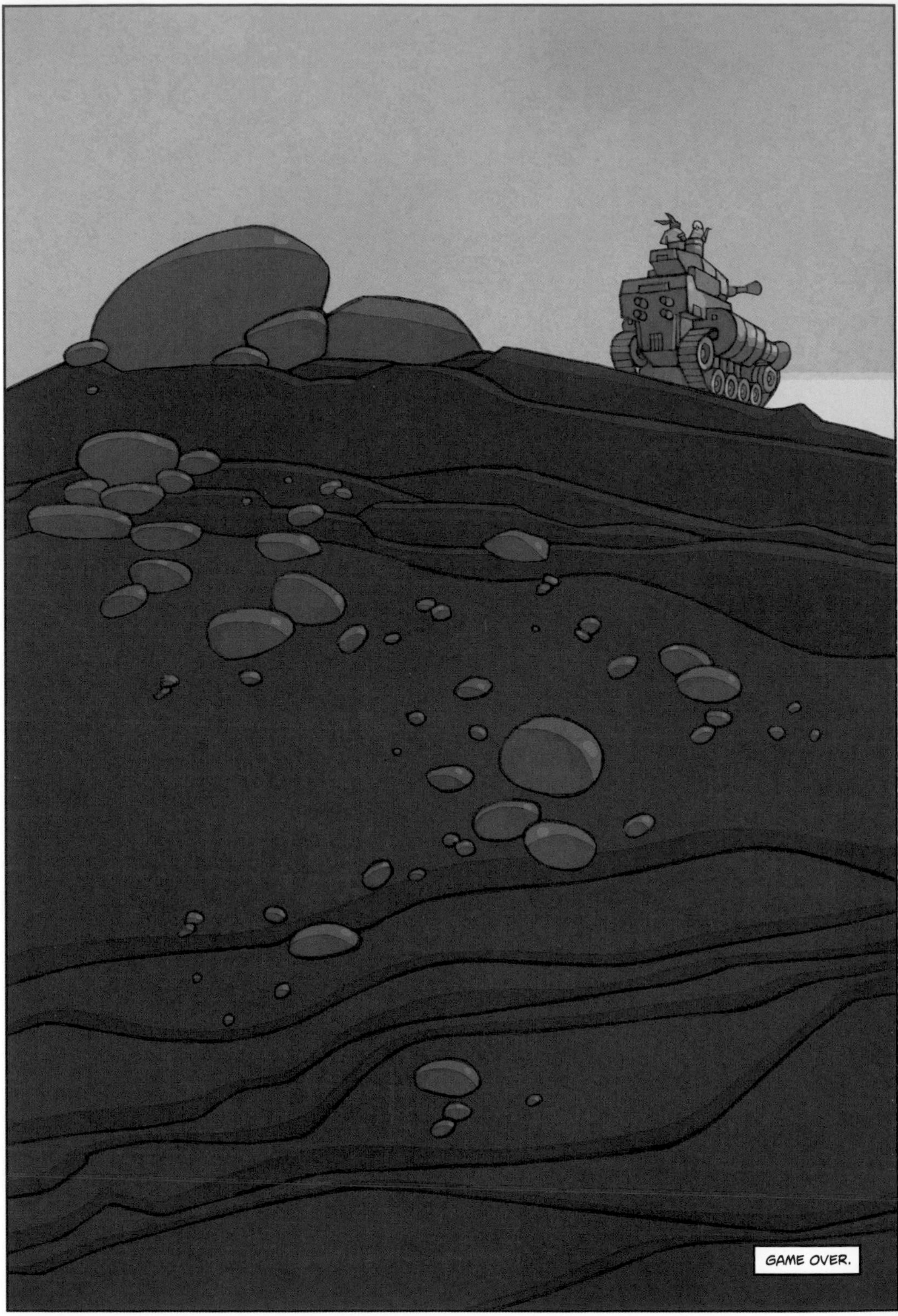
GAME OVER.

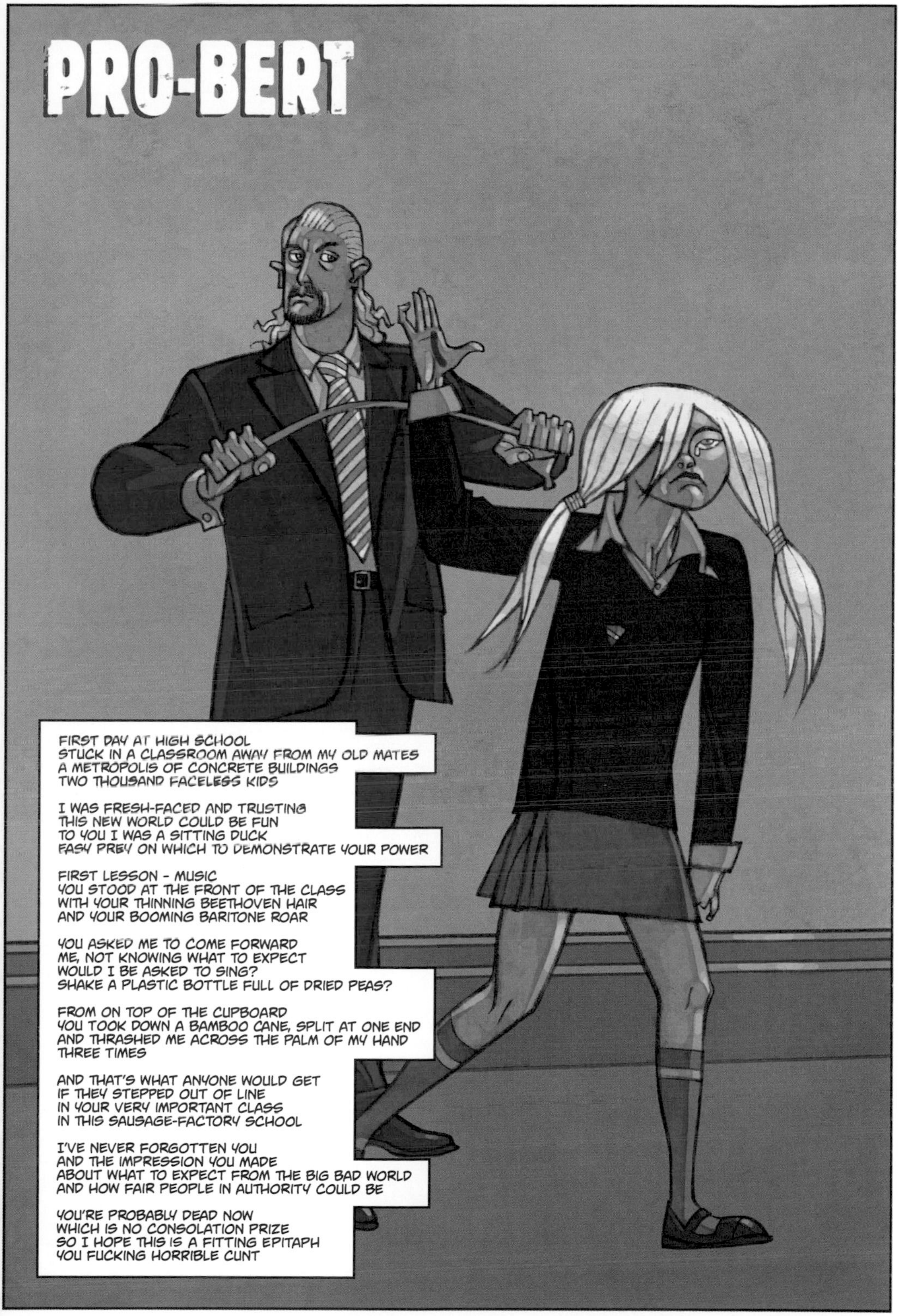
PRO-BERT
FIRST DAY AT HIGH SCHOOL
STUCK IN A CLASSROOM AWAY FROM MY OLD MATES
A METROPOLIS OF CONCRETE BUILDINGS
TWO THOUSAND FACELESS KIDS

I WAS FRESH-FACED AND TRUSTING
THIS NEW WORLD COULD BE FUN
TO YOU I WAS A SITTING DUCK
EASY PREY ON WHICH TO DEMONSTRATE YOUR POWER

FIRST LESSON - MUSIC
YOU STOOD AT THE FRONT OF THE CLASS
WITH YOUR THINNING BEETHOVEN HAIR
AND YOUR BOOMING BARITONE ROAR

YOU ASKED ME TO COME FORWARD
ME, NOT KNOWING WHAT TO EXPECT
WOULD I BE ASKED TO SING?
SHAKE A PLASTIC BOTTLE FULL OF DRIED PEAS?

FROM ON TOP OF THE CUPBOARD
YOU TOOK DOWN A BAMBOO CANE, SPLIT AT ONE END
AND THRASHED ME ACROSS THE PALM OF MY HAND
THREE TIMES

AND THAT'S WHAT ANYONE WOULD GET
IF THEY STEPPED OUT OF LINE
IN YOUR VERY IMPORTANT CLASS
IN THIS SAUSAGE-FACTORY SCHOOL

I'VE NEVER FORGOTTEN YOU
AND THE IMPRESSION YOU MADE
ABOUT WHAT TO EXPECT FROM THE BIG BAD WORLD
AND HOW FAIR PEOPLE IN AUTHORITY COULD BE

YOU'RE PROBABLY DEAD NOW
WHICH IS NO CONSOLATION PRIZE
SO I HOPE THIS IS A FITTING EPITAPH
YOU FUCKING HORRIBLE CUNT

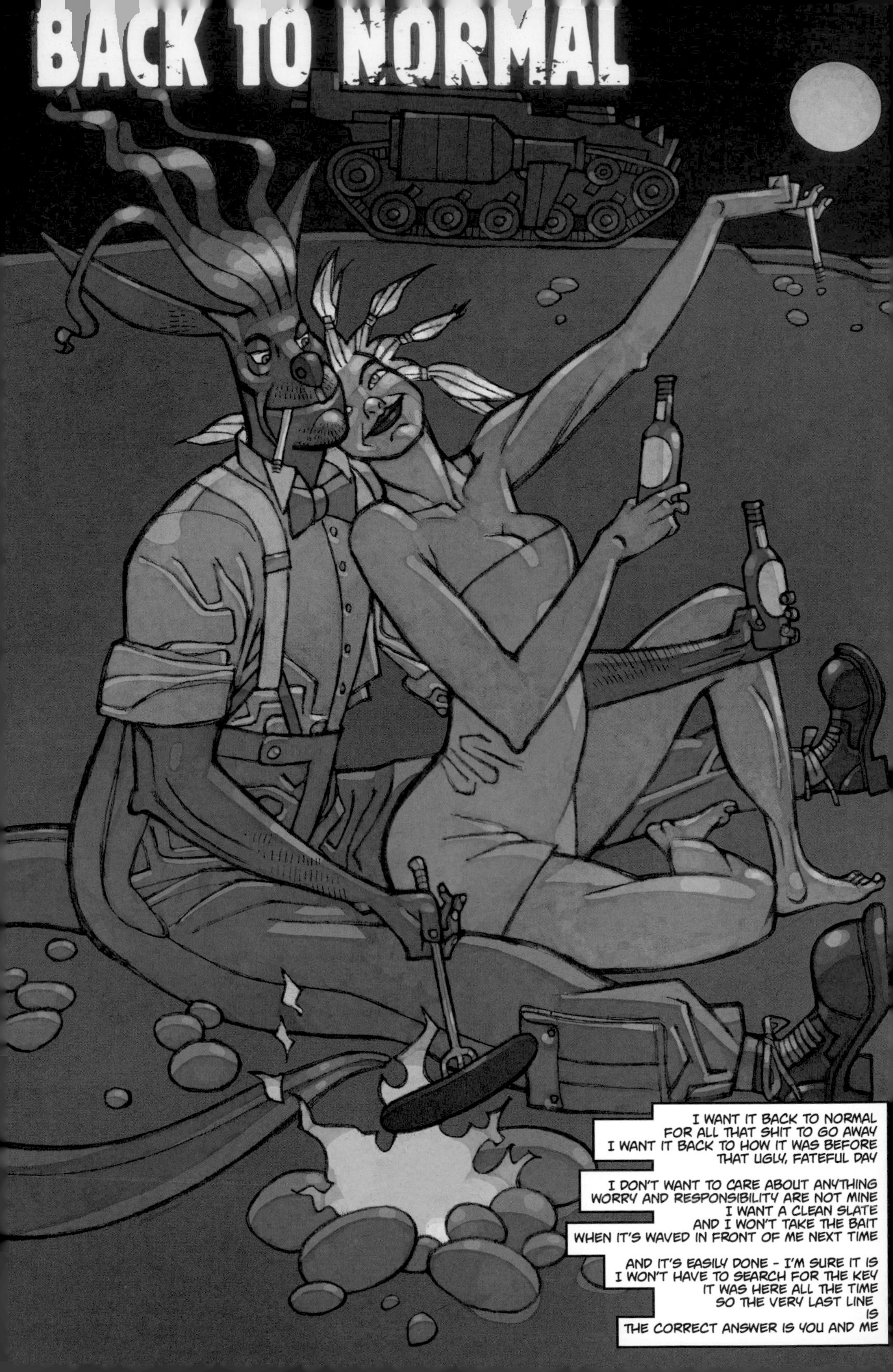
BACK TO NORMAL
I WANT IT BACK TO NORMAL
FOR ALL THAT SHIT TO GO AWAY
I WANT IT BACK TO HOW IT WAS BEFORE
THAT UGLY, FATEFUL DAY
I DON'T WANT TO CARE ABOUT ANYTHING
WORRY AND RESPONSIBILITY ARE NOT MINE
I WANT A CLEAN SLATE
AND I WON'T TAKE THE BAIT
WHEN IT'S WAVED IN FRONT OF ME NEXT TIME
AND IT'S EASILY DONE - I'M SURE IT IS
I WON'T HAVE TO SEARCH FOR THE KEY
IT WAS HERE ALL THE TIME
SO THE VERY LAST LINE
IS
THE CORRECT ANSWER IS YOU AND ME

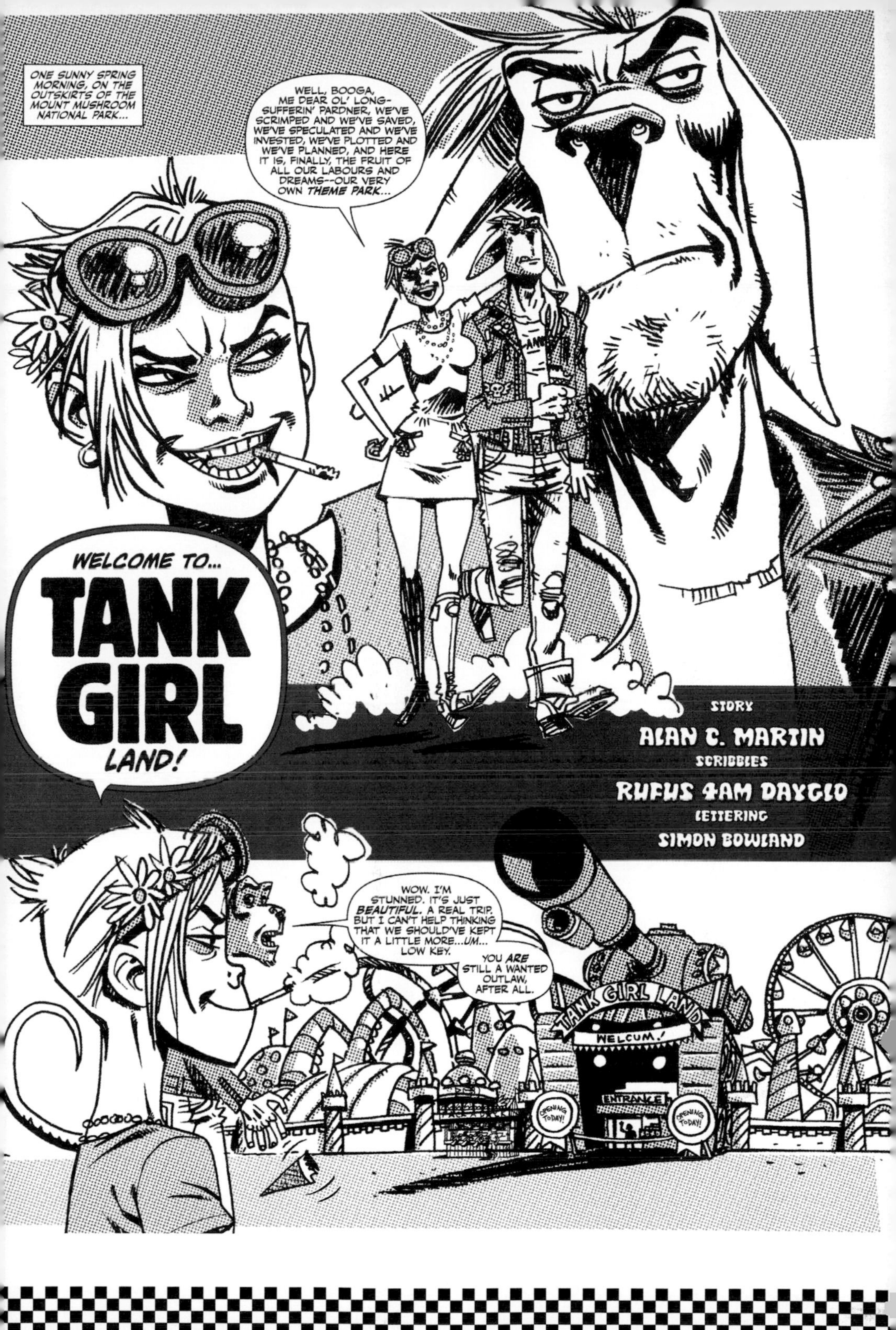

ONE SUNNY SPRING MORNING, ON THE OUTSKIRTS OF THE MOUNT MUSHROOM NATIONAL PARK...
WELL, BOOGA, ME DEAR OL' LONG-SUFFERIN' PARDNER, WE'VE SCRIMPED AND WE'VE SAVED, WE'VE SPECULATED AND WE'VE INVESTED, WE'VE PLOTTED AND WE'VE PLANNED, AND HERE IT IS, FINALLY, THE FRUIT OF ALL OUR LABOURS AND DREAMS--OUR VERY OWN THEME PARK...
WELCOME TO... TANK GIRL LAND!
STORY
ALAN C. MARTIN
SCRIBBLES
RUFUS 4AM DAYGLO
LETTERING
SIMON BOWLAND
WOW. I'M STUNNED. IT'S JUST BEAUTIFUL. A REAL TRIP. BUT I CAN'T HELP THINKING THAT WE SHOULD'VE KEPT IT A LITTLE MORE...UM... LOW KEY.
YOU ARE STILL A WANTED OUTLAW, AFTER ALL.
TANK GIRL LAND
WELCUM!
ENTRANCE
OPENING TODAY!
OPENING TODAY!

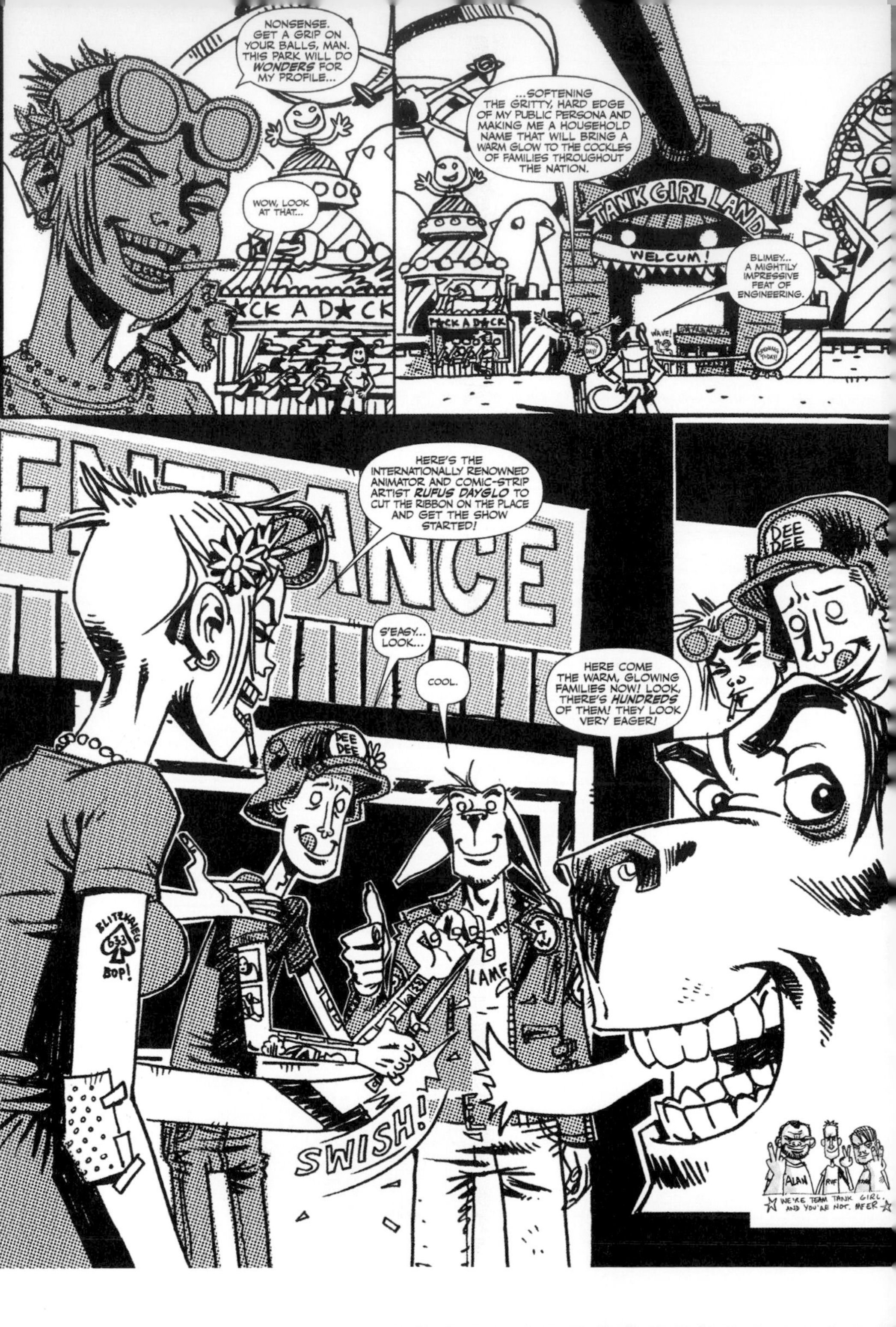
NONSENSE. GET A GRIP ON YOUR BALLS, MAN. THIS PARK WILL DO WONDERS FOR MY PROFILE...
WOW, LOOK AT THAT...
P★CK A D★CK
...SOFTENING THE GRITTY, HARD EDGE OF MY PUBLIC PERSONA AND MAKING ME A HOUSEHOLD NAME THAT WILL BRING A WARM GLOW TO THE COCKLES OF FAMILIES THROUGHOUT THE NATION.
TANK GIRL LAND
WELCUM!
BLIMEY... A MIGHTILY IMPRESSIVE FEAT OF ENGINEERING.
P★CK A D★CK
WAVE!
ENTRANCE
HERE'S THE INTERNATIONALLY RENOWNED ANIMATOR AND COMIC-STRIP ARTIST RUFUS DAYGLO TO CUT THE RIBBON ON THE PLACE AND GET THE SHOW STARTED!
DEE DEE
S'EASY... LOOK...
COOL.
HERE COME THE WARM, GLOWING FAMILIES NOW! LOOK, THERE'S HUNDREDS OF THEM! THEY LOOK VERY EAGER!
DEE DEE
BOP!
LAMF
SWISH!
ALAN
RUF
WE'RE TEAM TANK GIRL. AND YOU'RE NOT. MFER

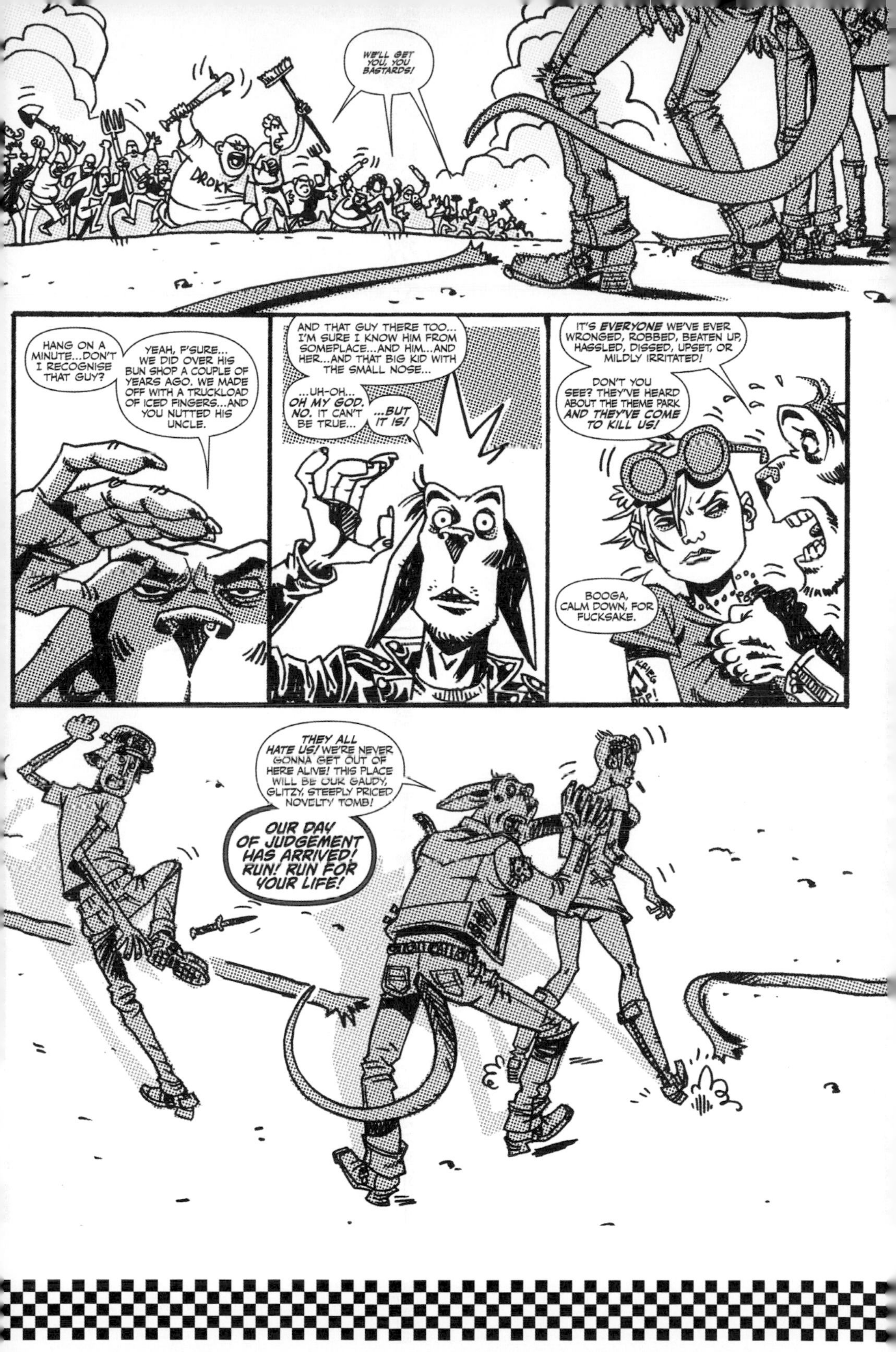
WE'LL GET YOU, YOU BASTARDS!
DROKK
HANG ON A MINUTE...DON'T I RECOGNISE THAT GUY?
YEAH, F'SURE... WE DID OVER HIS BUN SHOP A COUPLE OF YEARS AGO. WE MADE OFF WITH A TRUCKLOAD OF ICED FINGERS...AND YOU NUTTED HIS UNCLE.
AND THAT GUY THERE TOO... I'M SURE I KNOW HIM FROM SOMEPLACE...AND HIM...AND HER...AND THAT BIG KID WITH THE SMALL NOSE...
...UH-OH... OH MY GOD. NO. IT CAN'T BE TRUE...
...BUT IT IS!
IT'S EVERYONE WE'VE EVER WRONGED, ROBBED, BEATEN UP, HASSLED, DISSED, UPSET, OR MILDLY IRRITATED!
DON'T YOU SEE? THEY'VE HEARD ABOUT THE THEME PARK AND THEY'VE COME TO KILL US!
BOOGA, CALM DOWN, FOR FUCKSAKE.
THEY ALL HATE US! WE'RE NEVER GONNA GET OUT OF HERE ALIVE! THIS PLACE WILL BE OUR GAUDY, GLITZY, STEEPLY PRICED NOVELTY TOMB!
OUR DAY OF JUDGEMENT HAS ARRIVED! RUN! RUN FOR YOUR LIFE!

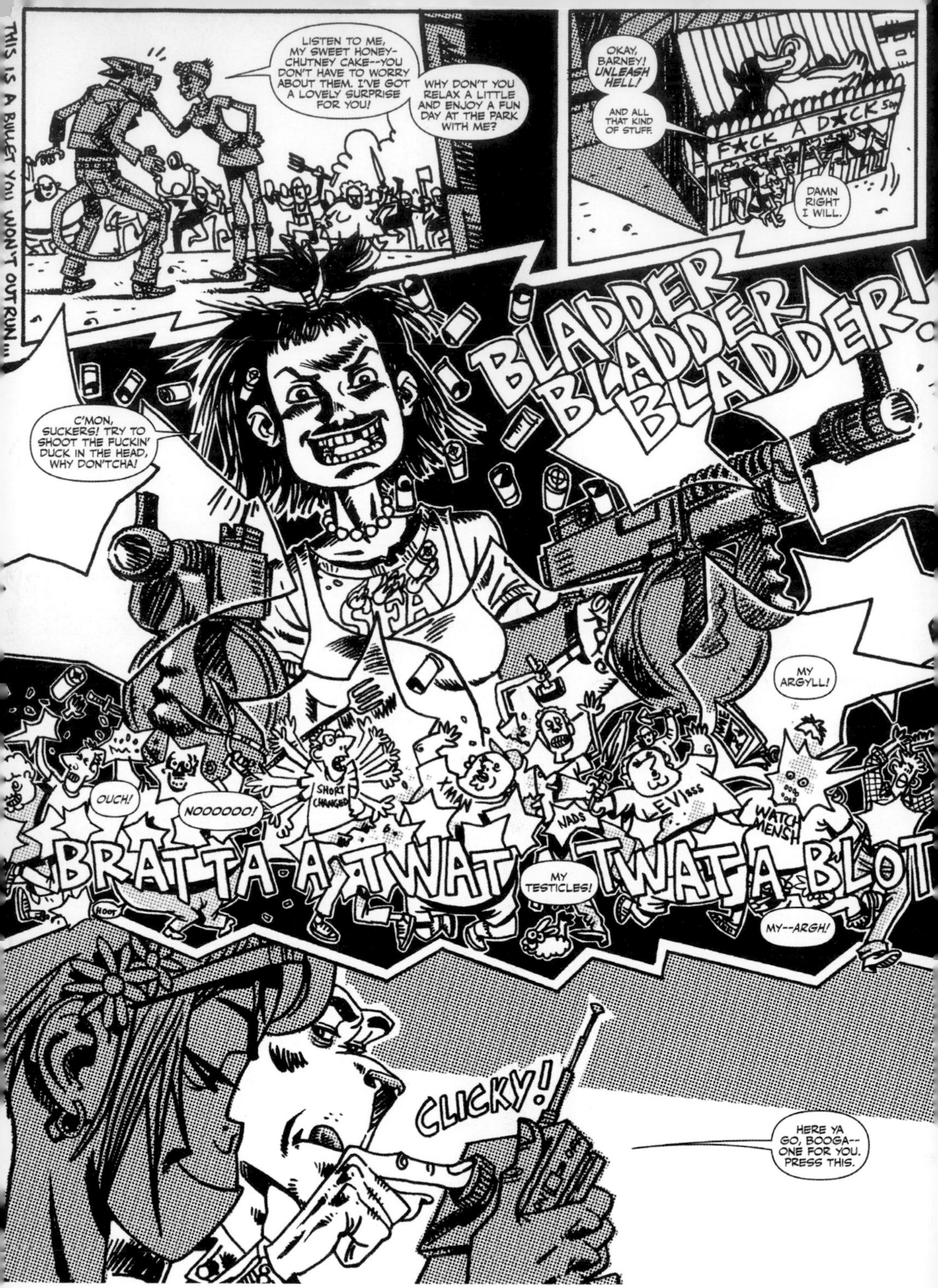
THIS IS A BULLET YOU WON'T OUTRUN...
LISTEN TO ME, MY SWEET HONEY-CHUTNEY CAKE--YOU DON'T HAVE TO WORRY ABOUT THEM. I'VE GOT A LOVELY SURPRISE FOR YOU!
WHY DON'T YOU RELAX A LITTLE AND ENJOY A FUN DAY AT THE PARK WITH ME?
OKAY, BARNEY! UNLEASH HELL!
AND ALL THAT KIND OF STUFF.
F★CK A D★CK
DAMN RIGHT I WILL.
BLADDER BLADDER BLADDER!
C'MON, SUCKERS! TRY TO SHOOT THE FUCKIN' DUCK IN THE HEAD, WHY DON'TCHA!
MY ARGYLL!
OUCH!
NOOOOOO!
SHORT CHANGED
XMAN
NADS
LEVIsss
WATCHMENSH
BRATTA A TWAT
MY TESTICLES!
TWAT A BLOT
MY--ARGH!
CLICKY!
HERE YA GO, BOOGA--ONE FOR YOU. PRESS THIS.

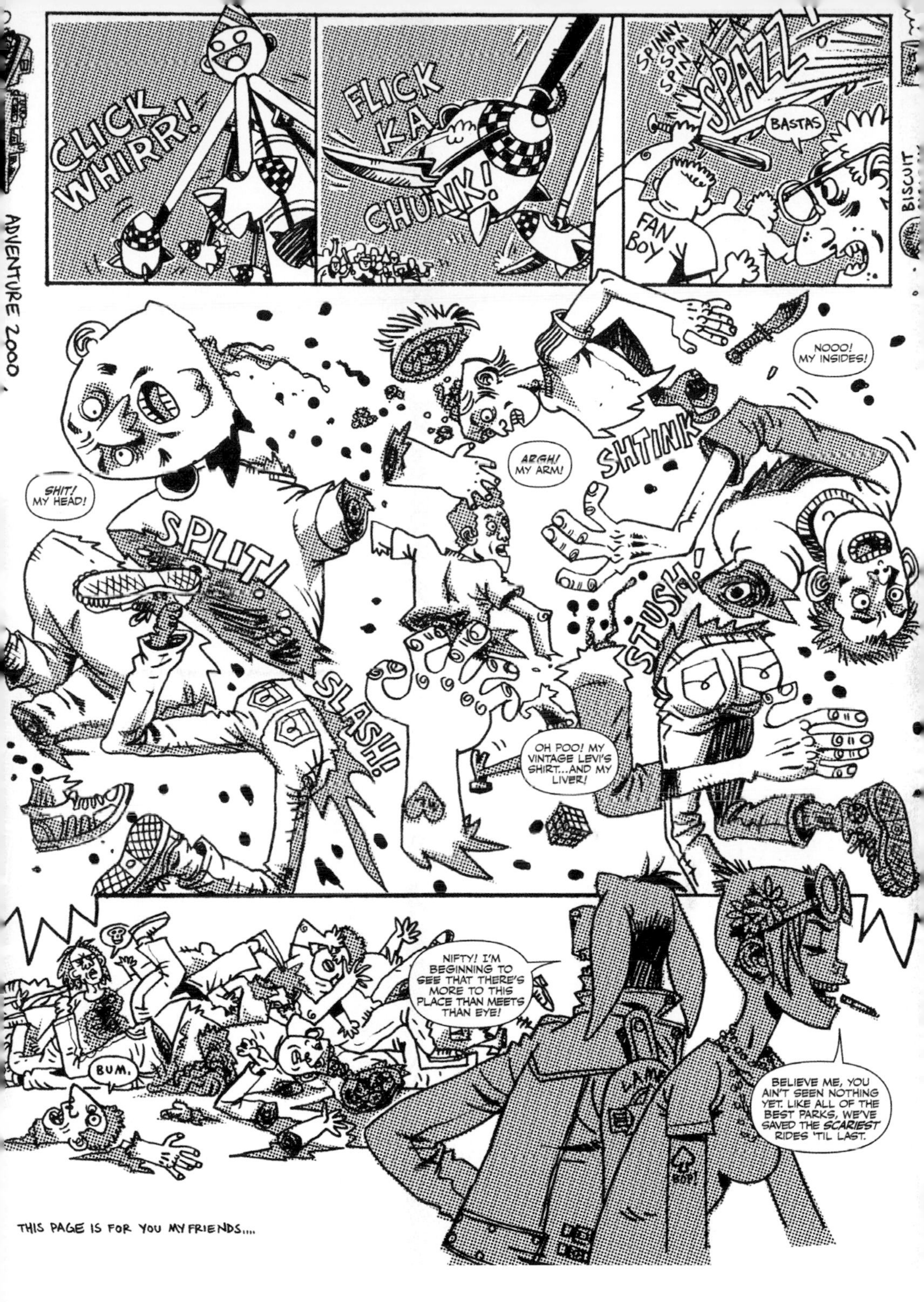
CLICK WHIRR!
FLICK KA
CHUNK!
SPINNY SPIN SPIN
SPAZZ!
BASTAS
FAN BOY
BISCUIT
ADVENTURE 2000
SHIT! MY HEAD!
SPLIT!
ARGH! MY ARM!
SHTINK
NOOO! MY INSIDES!
SLASH!
STUSH!
OH POO! MY VINTAGE LEVI'S SHIRT...AND MY LIVER!
NIFTY! I'M BEGINNING TO SEE THAT THERE'S MORE TO THIS PLACE THAN MEETS THAN EYE!
BUM.
BELIEVE ME, YOU AIN'T SEEN NOTHING YET. LIKE ALL OF THE BEST PARKS, WE'VE SAVED THE *SCARIEST* RIDES 'TIL LAST.
THIS PAGE IS FOR YOU MY FRIENDS....

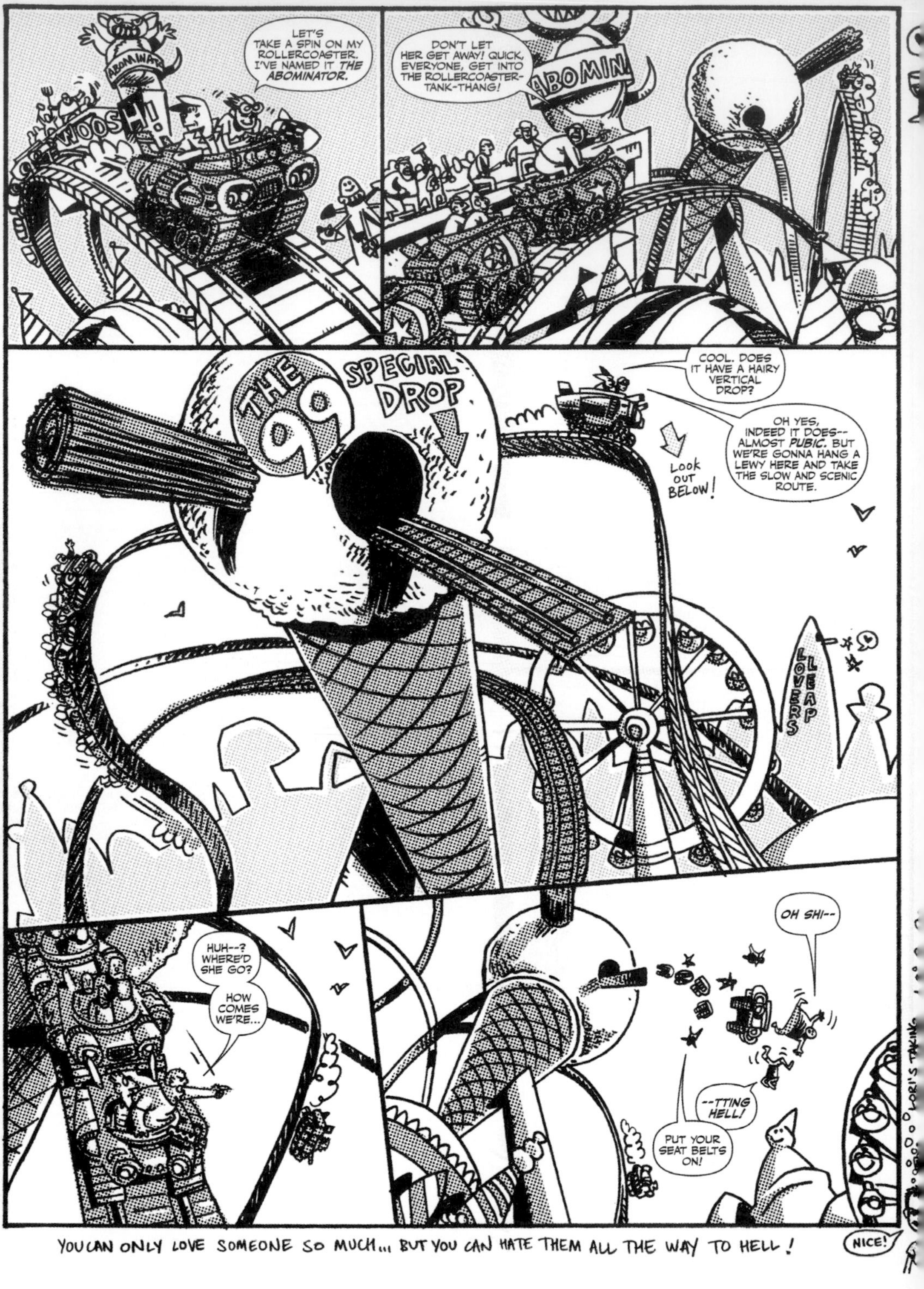
LET'S TAKE A SPIN ON MY ROLLERCOASTER. I'VE NAMED IT *THE ABOMINATOR.*
ABOMINATOR
WOOSH!
DON'T LET HER GET AWAY! QUICK, EVERYONE, GET INTO THE ROLLERCOASTER-TANK-THANG!
ABOMIN
THE SPECIAL DROP
COOL. DOES IT HAVE A HAIRY VERTICAL DROP?
OH YES, INDEED IT DOES-- ALMOST *PUBIC.* BUT WE'RE GONNA HANG A LEWY HERE AND TAKE THE SLOW AND SCENIC ROUTE.
LOOK OUT BELOW!
LOVERS LEAP
HUH--? WHERE'D SHE GO?
HOW COMES WE'RE...
OH SHI--
--TTING HELL!
PUT YOUR SEAT BELTS ON!
LORI'S TAKING

YOU CAN ONLY LOVE SOMEONE SO MUCH... BUT YOU CAN HATE THEM ALL THE WAY TO HELL!

NICE!

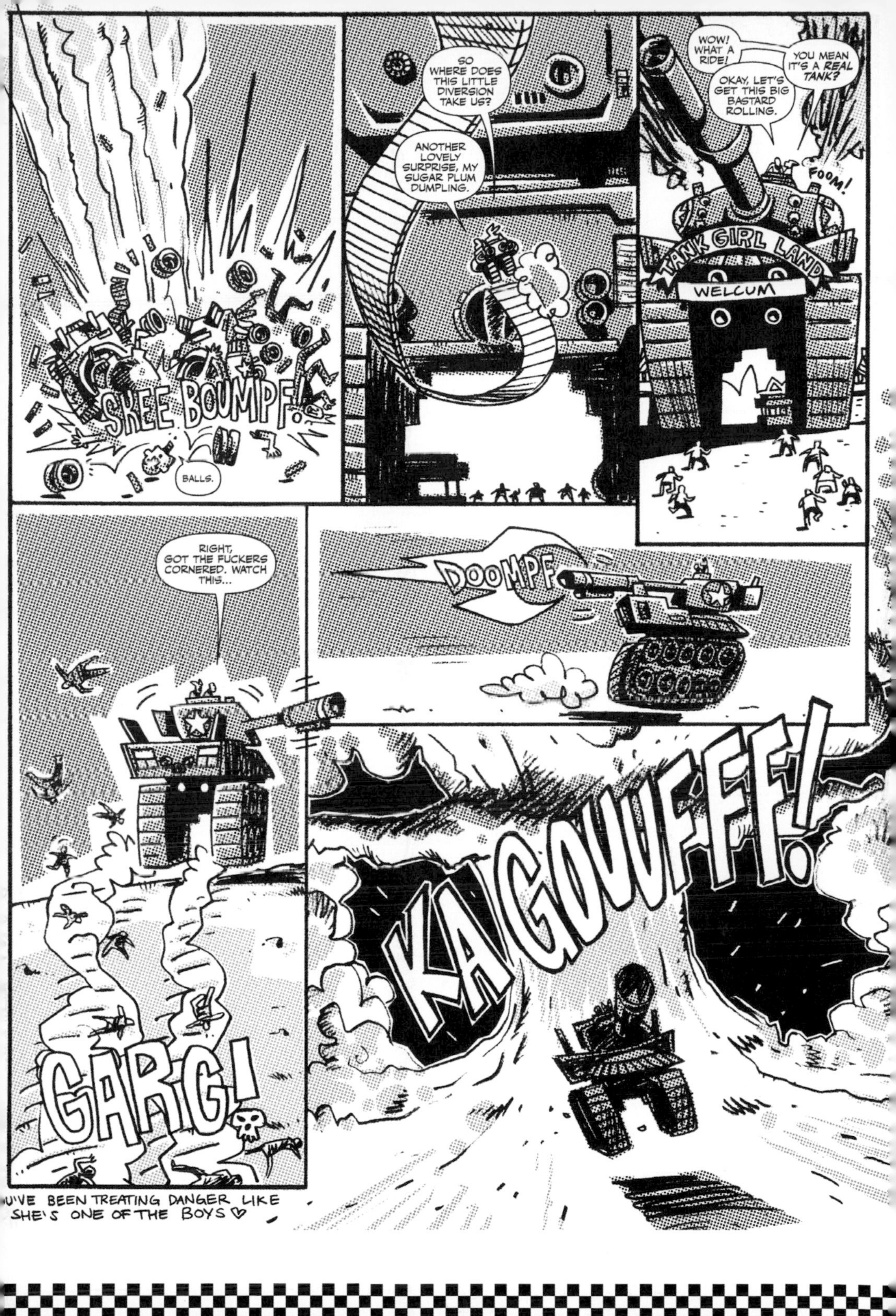
SHEE BOUMPF!
BALLS.
SO WHERE DOES THIS LITTLE DIVERSION TAKE US?
ANOTHER LOVELY SURPRISE, MY SUGAR PLUM DUMPLING.
WOW! WHAT A RIDE!
OKAY, LET'S GET THIS BIG BASTARD ROLLING.
YOU MEAN IT'S A REAL TANK?
FOOM!
TANK GIRL LAND
WELCUM
RIGHT, GOT THE FUCKERS CORNERED. WATCH THIS...
DOOMPF
KA GOUUFFF!
GARG!
U'VE BEEN TREATING DANGER LIKE SHE'S ONE OF THE BOYS ♡

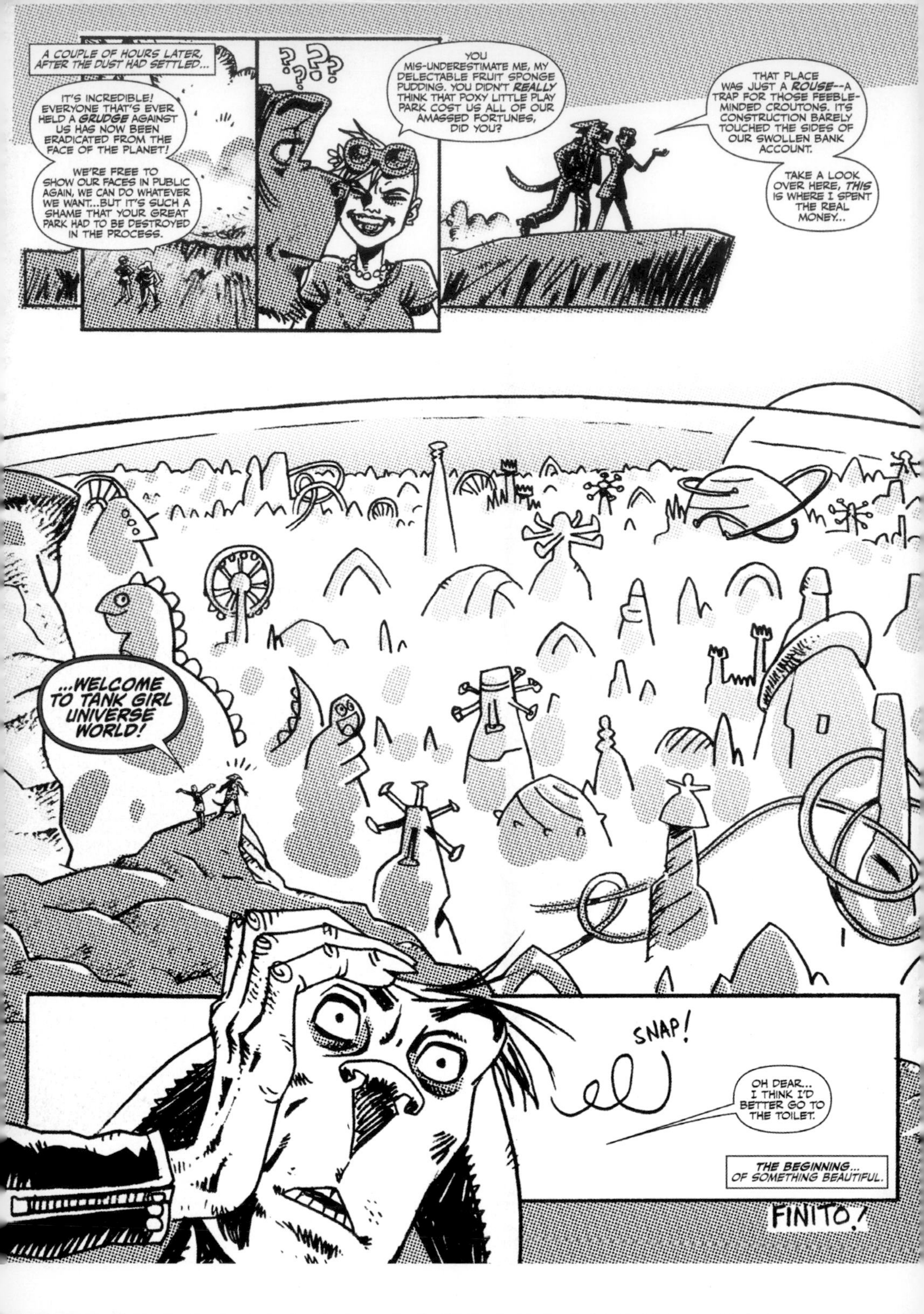

A COUPLE OF HOURS LATER, AFTER THE DUST HAD SETTLED...
IT'S INCREDIBLE! EVERYONE THAT'S EVER HELD A GRUDGE AGAINST US HAS NOW BEEN ERADICATED FROM THE FACE OF THE PLANET!
WE'RE FREE TO SHOW OUR FACES IN PUBLIC AGAIN, WE CAN DO WHATEVER WE WANT...BUT IT'S SUCH A SHAME THAT YOUR GREAT PARK HAD TO BE DESTROYED IN THE PROCESS.
???
YOU MIS-UNDERESTIMATE ME, MY DELECTABLE FRUIT SPONGE PUDDING. YOU DIDN'T REALLY THINK THAT POXY LITTLE PLAY PARK COST US ALL OF OUR AMASSED FORTUNES, DID YOU?
THAT PLACE WAS JUST A ROUSE--A TRAP FOR THOSE FEEBLE-MINDED CROUTONS. ITS CONSTRUCTION BARELY TOUCHED THE SIDES OF OUR SWOLLEN BANK ACCOUNT.
TAKE A LOOK OVER HERE, THIS IS WHERE I SPENT THE REAL MONEY...
...WELCOME TO TANK GIRL UNIVERSE WORLD!
SNAP!
OH DEAR... I THINK I'D BETTER GO TO THE TOILET.
THE BEGINNING... OF SOMETHING BEAUTIFUL.
FINITO!

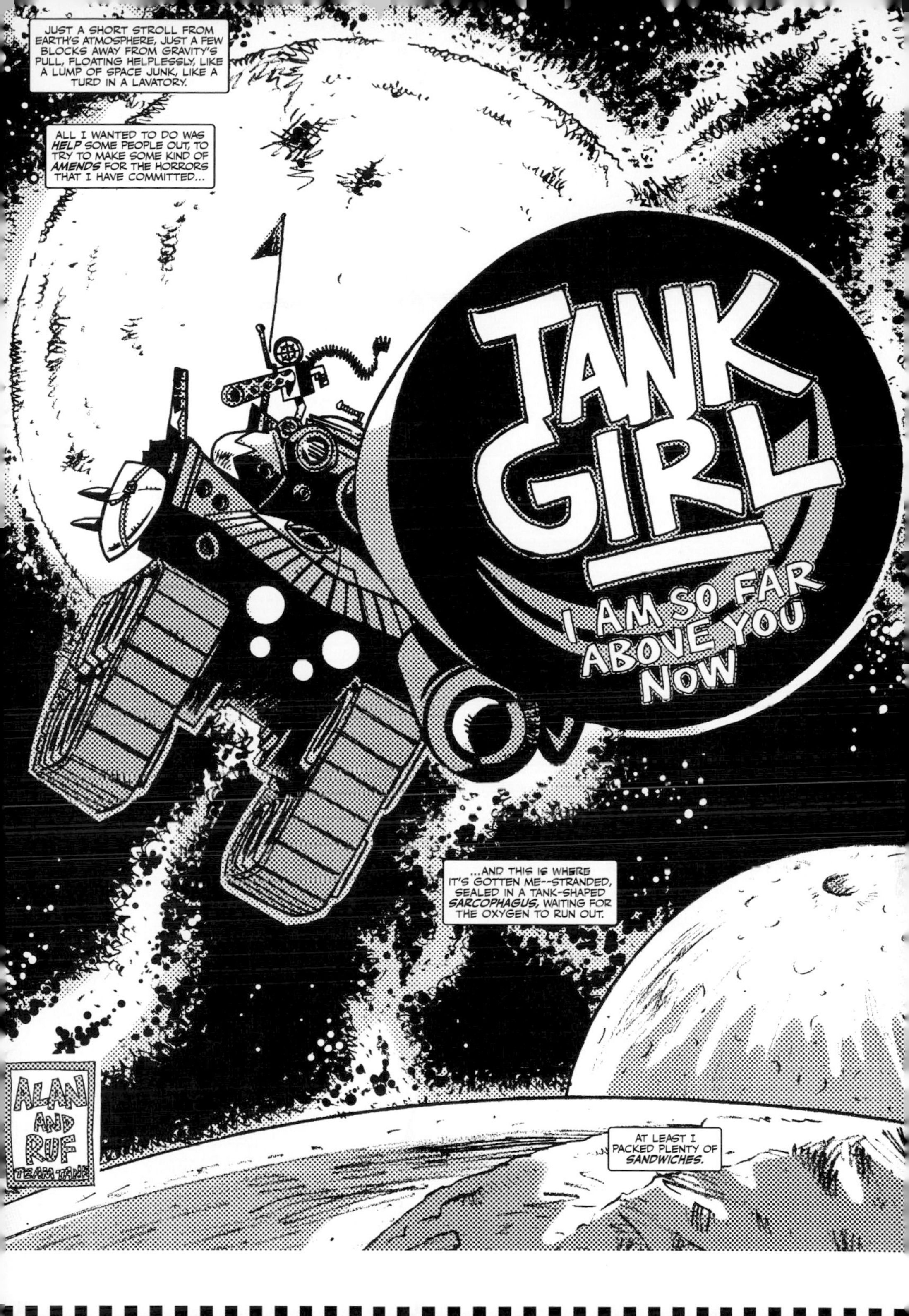

JUST A SHORT STROLL FROM EARTH'S ATMOSPHERE, JUST A FEW BLOCKS AWAY FROM GRAVITY'S PULL, FLOATING HELPLESSLY, LIKE A LUMP OF SPACE JUNK, LIKE A TURD IN A LAVATORY.
ALL I WANTED TO DO WAS *HELP* SOME PEOPLE OUT, TO TRY TO MAKE SOME KIND OF *AMENDS* FOR THE HORRORS THAT I HAVE COMMITTED...
TANK GIRL
I AM SO FAR ABOVE YOU NOW
...AND THIS IS WHERE IT'S GOTTEN ME--STRANDED, SEALED IN A TANK-SHAPED *SARCOPHAGUS,* WAITING FOR THE OXYGEN TO RUN OUT.
ALAN AND RUF
TEAM TANK
AT LEAST I PACKED PLENTY OF *SANDWICHES.*

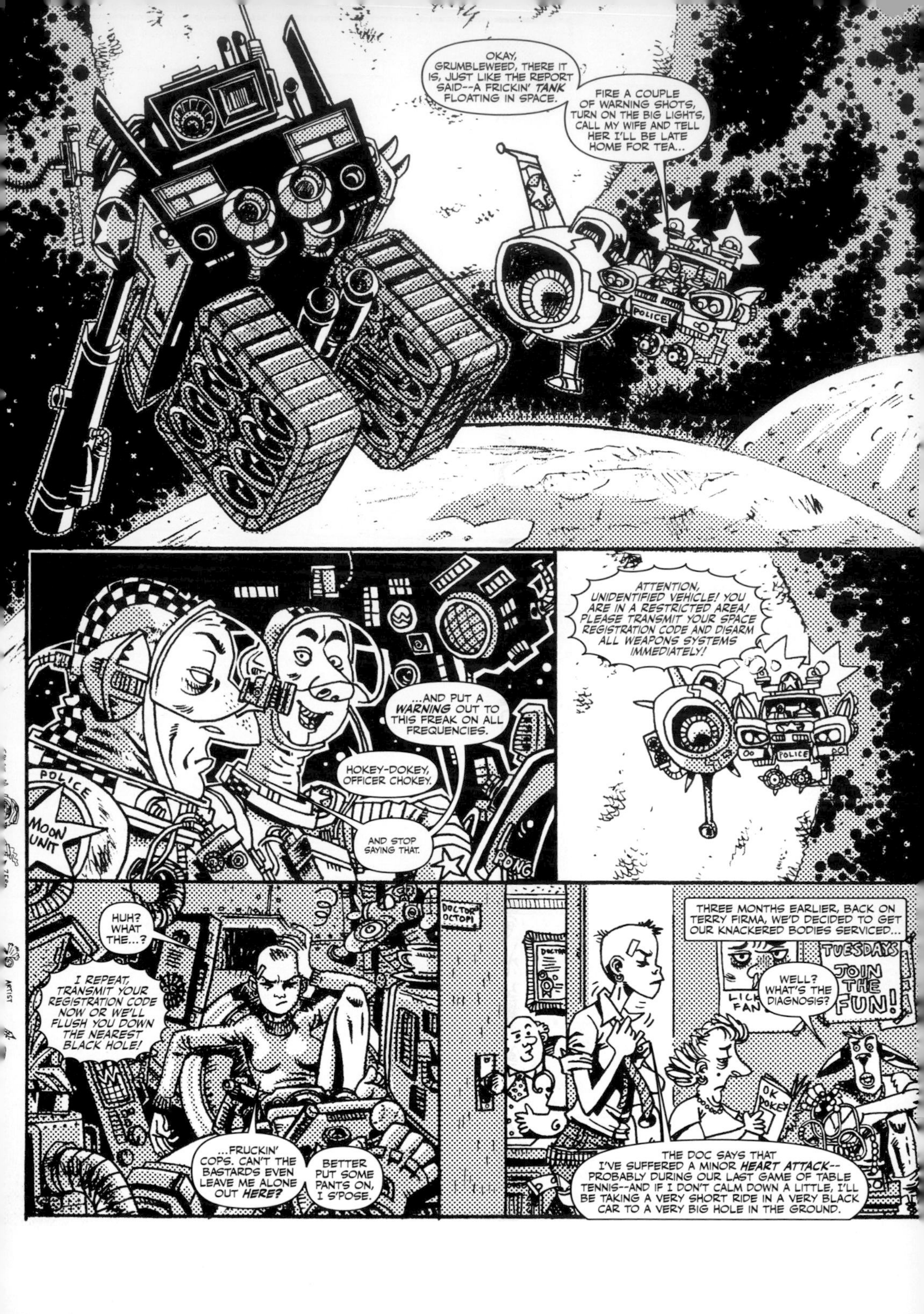
OKAY, GRUMBLEWEED, THERE IT IS, JUST LIKE THE REPORT SAID--A FRICKIN' TANK FLOATING IN SPACE.
FIRE A COUPLE OF WARNING SHOTS, TURN ON THE BIG LIGHTS, CALL MY WIFE AND TELL HER I'LL BE LATE HOME FOR TEA...
POLICE
...AND PUT A WARNING OUT TO THIS FREAK ON ALL FREQUENCIES.
HOKEY-DOKEY, OFFICER CHOKEY.
AND STOP SAYING THAT.
POLICE
MOON UNIT
PONG
ATTENTION, UNIDENTIFIED VEHICLE! YOU ARE IN A RESTRICTED AREA! PLEASE TRANSMIT YOUR SPACE REGISTRATION CODE AND DISARM ALL WEAPONS SYSTEMS IMMEDIATELY!
POLICE
HUH? WHAT THE...?
I REPEAT, TRANSMIT YOUR REGISTRATION CODE NOW OR WE'LL FLUSH YOU DOWN THE NEAREST BLACK HOLE!
...FRUCKIN' COPS. CAN'T THE BASTARDS EVEN LEAVE ME ALONE OUT HERE?
BETTER PUT SOME PANTS ON, I S'POSE.
DOCTOR OCTOPI
THREE MONTHS EARLIER, BACK ON TERRY FIRMA, WE'D DECIDED TO GET OUR KNACKERED BODIES SERVICED...
TUESDAYS JOIN THE FUN!
WELL? WHAT'S THE DIAGNOSIS?
OK POKEY
THE DOC SAYS THAT I'VE SUFFERED A MINOR HEART ATTACK--PROBABLY DURING OUR LAST GAME OF TABLE TENNIS--AND IF I DON'T CALM DOWN A LITTLE, I'LL BE TAKING A VERY SHORT RIDE IN A VERY BLACK CAR TO A VERY BIG HOLE IN THE GROUND.

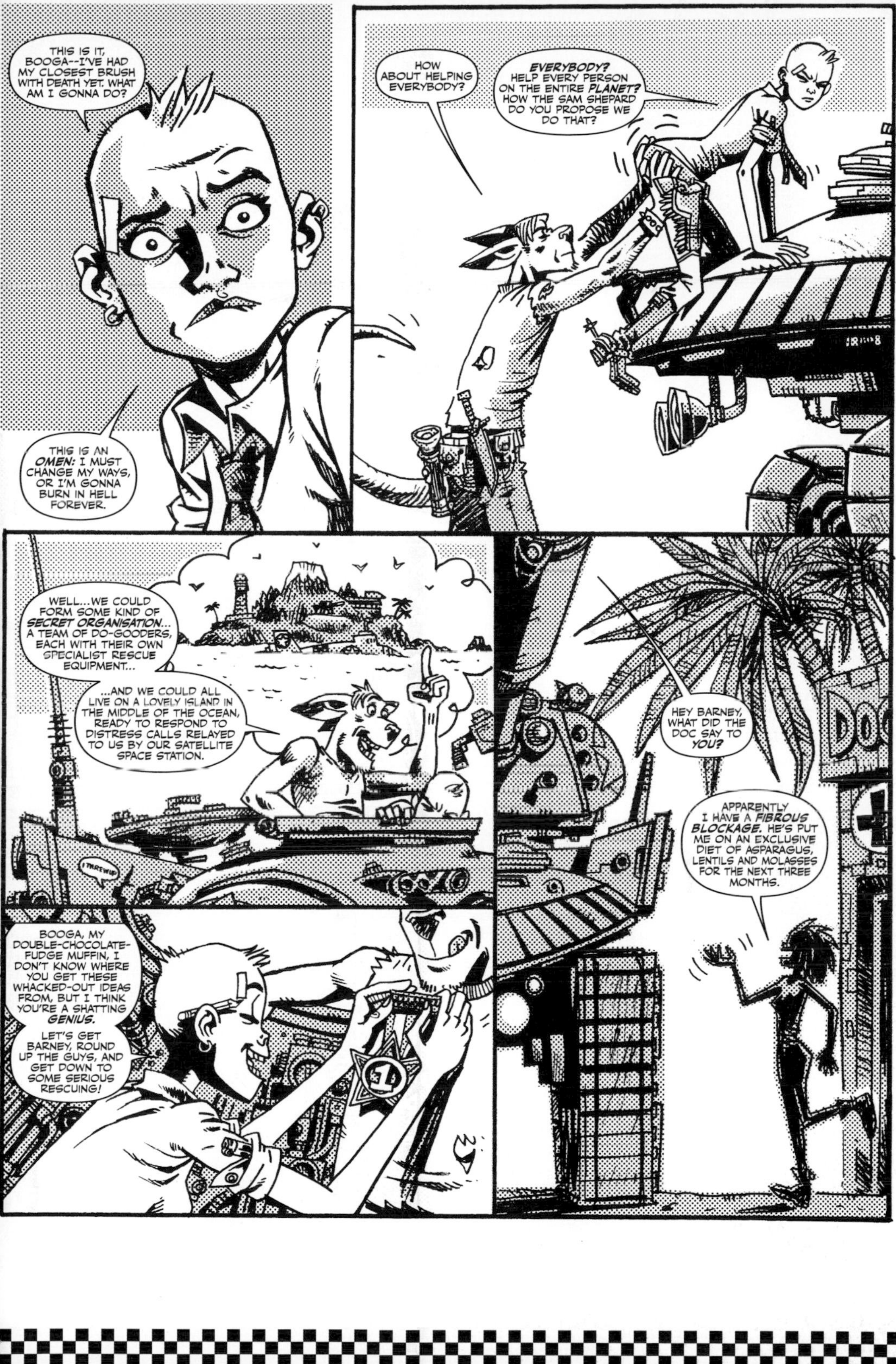
THIS IS IT, BOOGA--I'VE HAD MY CLOSEST BRUSH WITH DEATH YET. WHAT AM I GONNA DO?
THIS IS AN *OMEN:* I MUST CHANGE MY WAYS, OR I'M GONNA BURN IN HELL FOREVER.
HOW ABOUT HELPING EVERYBODY?
EVERYBODY? HELP EVERY PERSON ON THE ENTIRE *PLANET?* HOW THE SAM SHEPARD DO YOU PROPOSE WE DO THAT?
WELL...WE COULD FORM SOME KIND OF *SECRET ORGANISATION*... A TEAM OF DO-GOODERS, EACH WITH THEIR OWN SPECIALIST RESCUE EQUIPMENT...
...AND WE COULD ALL LIVE ON A LOVELY ISLAND IN THE MIDDLE OF THE OCEAN, READY TO RESPOND TO DISTRESS CALLS RELAYED TO US BY OUR SATELLITE SPACE STATION.
BOOGA, MY DOUBLE-CHOCOLATE-FUDGE MUFFIN, I DON'T KNOW WHERE YOU GET THESE WHACKED-OUT IDEAS FROM, BUT I THINK YOU'RE A SHATTING *GENIUS.*
LET'S GET BARNEY, ROUND UP THE GUYS, AND GET DOWN TO SOME SERIOUS RESCUING!
HEY BARNEY, WHAT DID THE DOC SAY TO *YOU?*
APPARENTLY I HAVE A *FIBROUS BLOCKAGE.* HE'S PUT ME ON AN EXCLUSIVE DIET OF ASPARAGUS, LENTILS AND MOLASSES FOR THE NEXT THREE MONTHS.

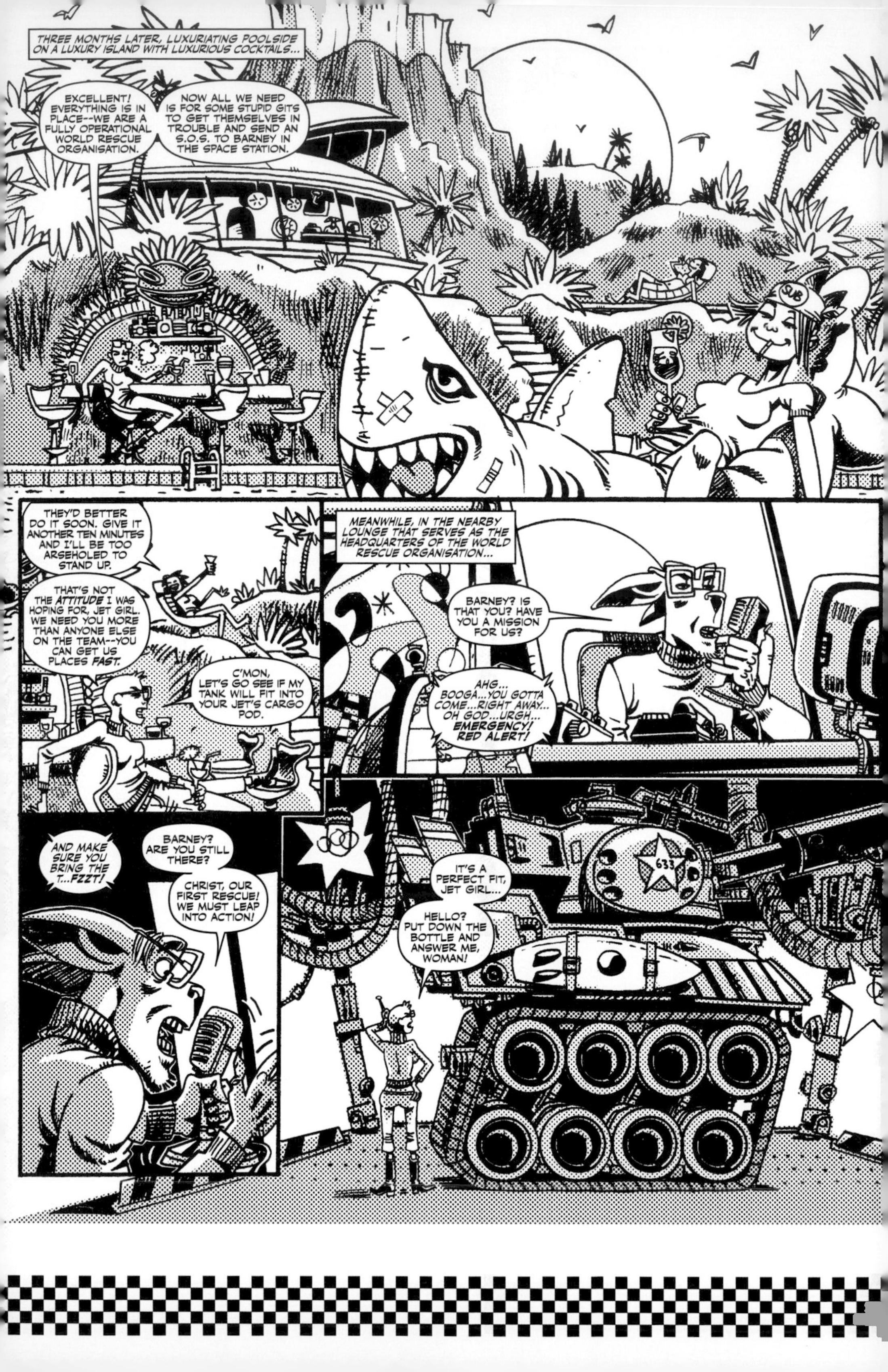

THREE MONTHS LATER, LUXURIATING POOLSIDE ON A LUXURY ISLAND WITH LUXURIOUS COCKTAILS...
EXCELLENT! EVERYTHING IS IN PLACE--WE ARE A FULLY OPERATIONAL WORLD RESCUE ORGANISATION.
NOW ALL WE NEED IS FOR SOME STUPID GITS TO GET THEMSELVES IN TROUBLE AND SEND AN S.O.S. TO BARNEY IN THE SPACE STATION.
SUB
THEY'D BETTER DO IT SOON. GIVE IT ANOTHER TEN MINUTES AND I'LL BE TOO ARSEHOLED TO STAND UP.
THAT'S NOT THE ATTITUDE I WAS HOPING FOR, JET GIRL. WE NEED YOU MORE THAN ANYONE ELSE ON THE TEAM--YOU CAN GET US PLACES FAST.
C'MON, LET'S GO SEE IF MY TANK WILL FIT INTO YOUR JET'S CARGO POD.
MEANWHILE, IN THE NEARBY LOUNGE THAT SERVES AS THE HEADQUARTERS OF THE WORLD RESCUE ORGANISATION...
BARNEY? IS THAT YOU? HAVE YOU A MISSION FOR US?
AHG... BOOGA...YOU GOTTA COME...RIGHT AWAY... OH GOD...URGH... EMERGENCY! RED ALERT!
AND MAKE SURE YOU BRING THE T...FZZT!
BARNEY? ARE YOU STILL THERE?
CHRIST, OUR FIRST RESCUE! WE MUST LEAP INTO ACTION!
IT'S A PERFECT FIT, JET GIRL...
HELLO? PUT DOWN THE BOTTLE AND ANSWER ME, WOMAN!
633

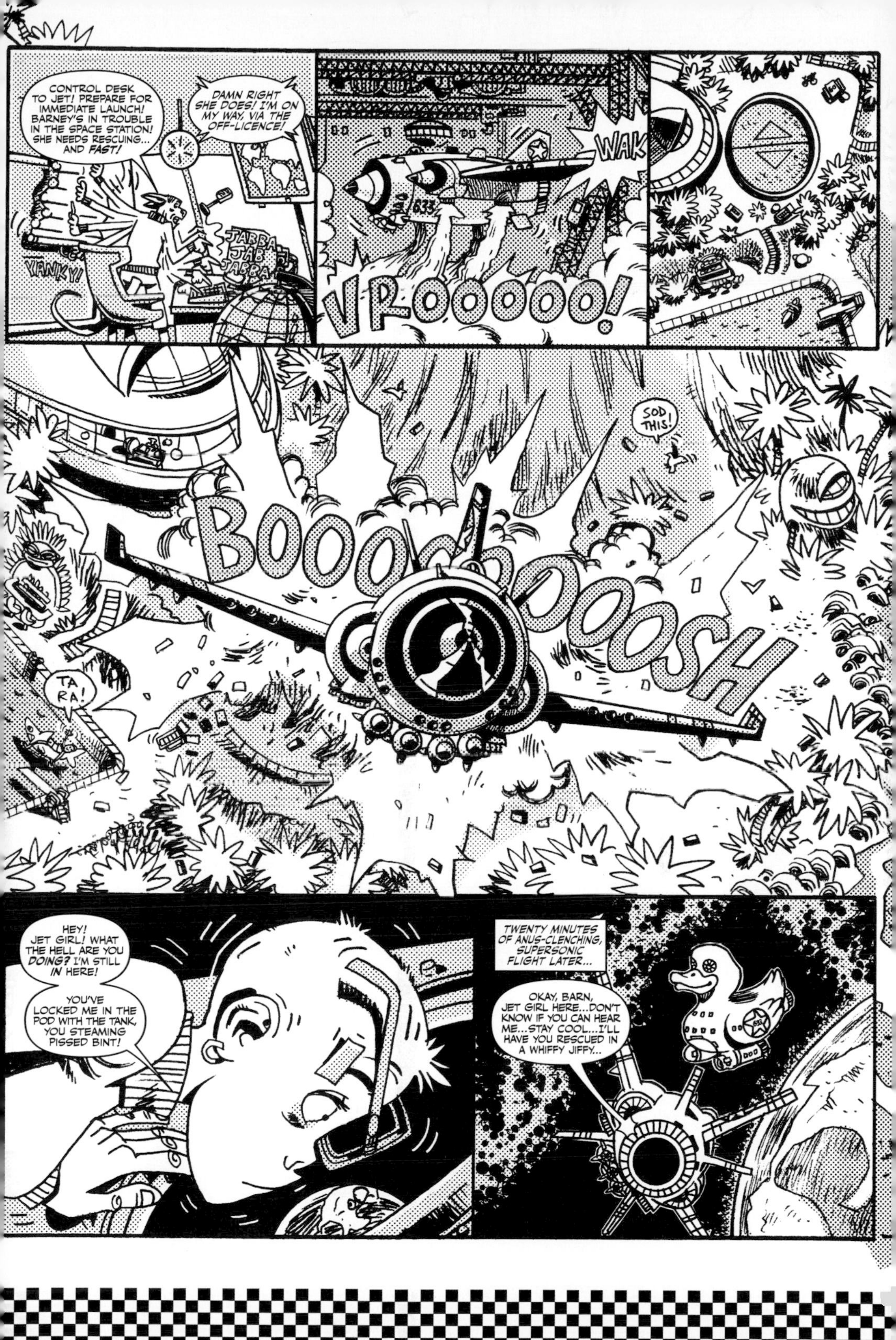
CONTROL DESK TO JET! PREPARE FOR IMMEDIATE LAUNCH! BARNEY'S IN TROUBLE IN THE SPACE STATION! SHE NEEDS RESCUING... AND FAST!
DAMN RIGHT SHE DOES! I'M ON MY WAY, VIA THE OFF-LICENCE!
YANKY!
JABBA JAB JABBA
WAK
VROOOOOO!
SOD THIS!
BOOOOOOOOOSH
TA RA!
HEY! JET GIRL! WHAT THE HELL ARE YOU DOING? I'M STILL IN HERE!
YOU'VE LOCKED ME IN THE POD WITH THE TANK, YOU STEAMING PISSED BINT!
TWENTY MINUTES OF ANUS-CLENCHING, SUPERSONIC FLIGHT LATER...
OKAY, BARN, JET GIRL HERE...DON'T KNOW IF YOU CAN HEAR ME...STAY COOL...I'LL HAVE YOU RESCUED IN A WHIFFY JIFFY...

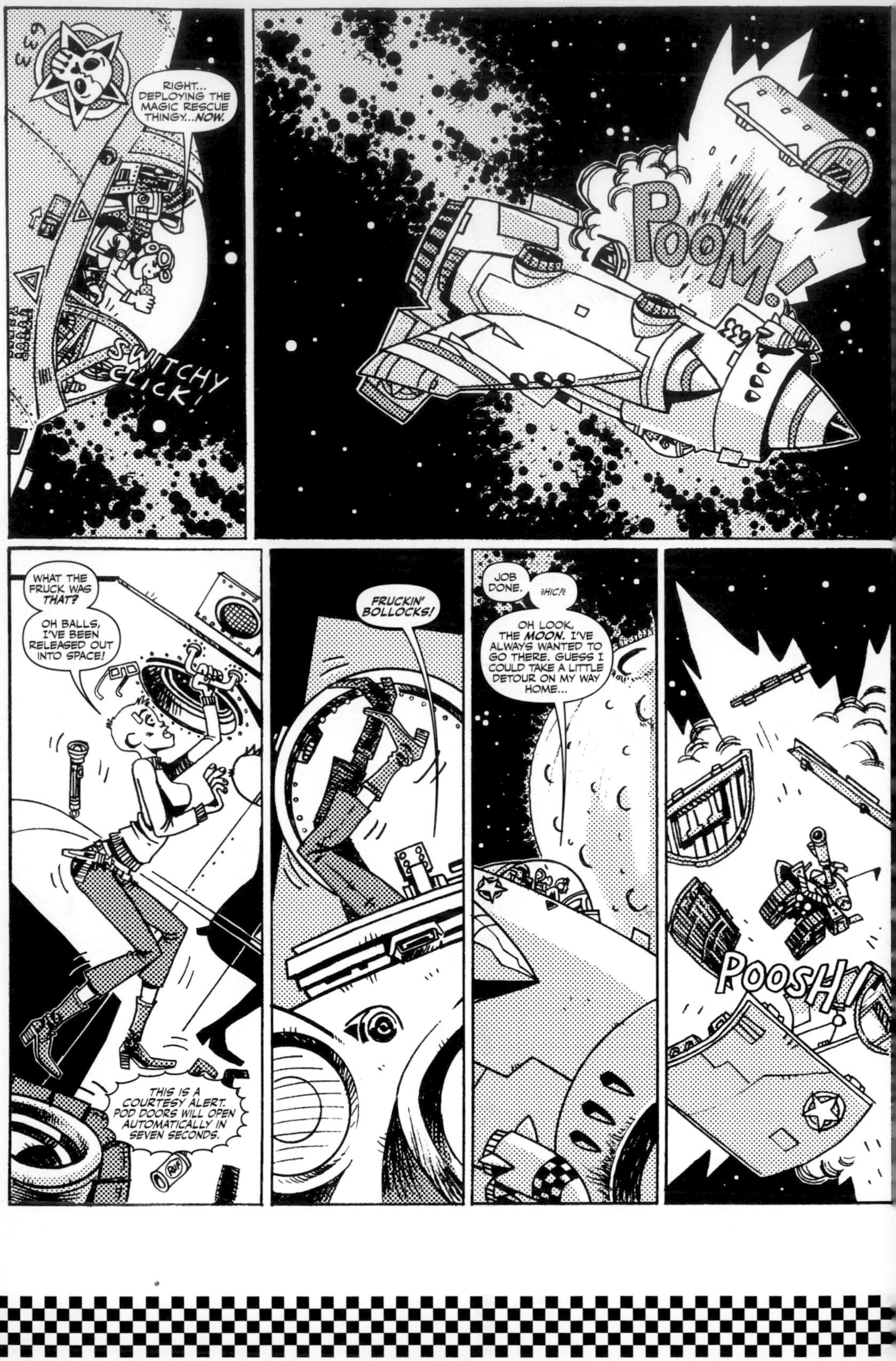
RIGHT... DEPLOYING THE MAGIC RESCUE THINGY... NOW.
SWITCHY CLICK!
POOM!
WHAT THE FRUCK WAS THAT?
OH BALLS, I'VE BEEN RELEASED OUT INTO SPACE!
THIS IS A COURTESY ALERT. POD DOORS WILL OPEN AUTOMATICALLY IN SEVEN SECONDS.
FRUCKIN' BOLLOCKS!
JOB DONE.
HIC!
OH LOOK, THE MOON. I'VE ALWAYS WANTED TO GO THERE. GUESS I COULD TAKE A LITTLE DETOUR ON MY WAY HOME...
POOSH!

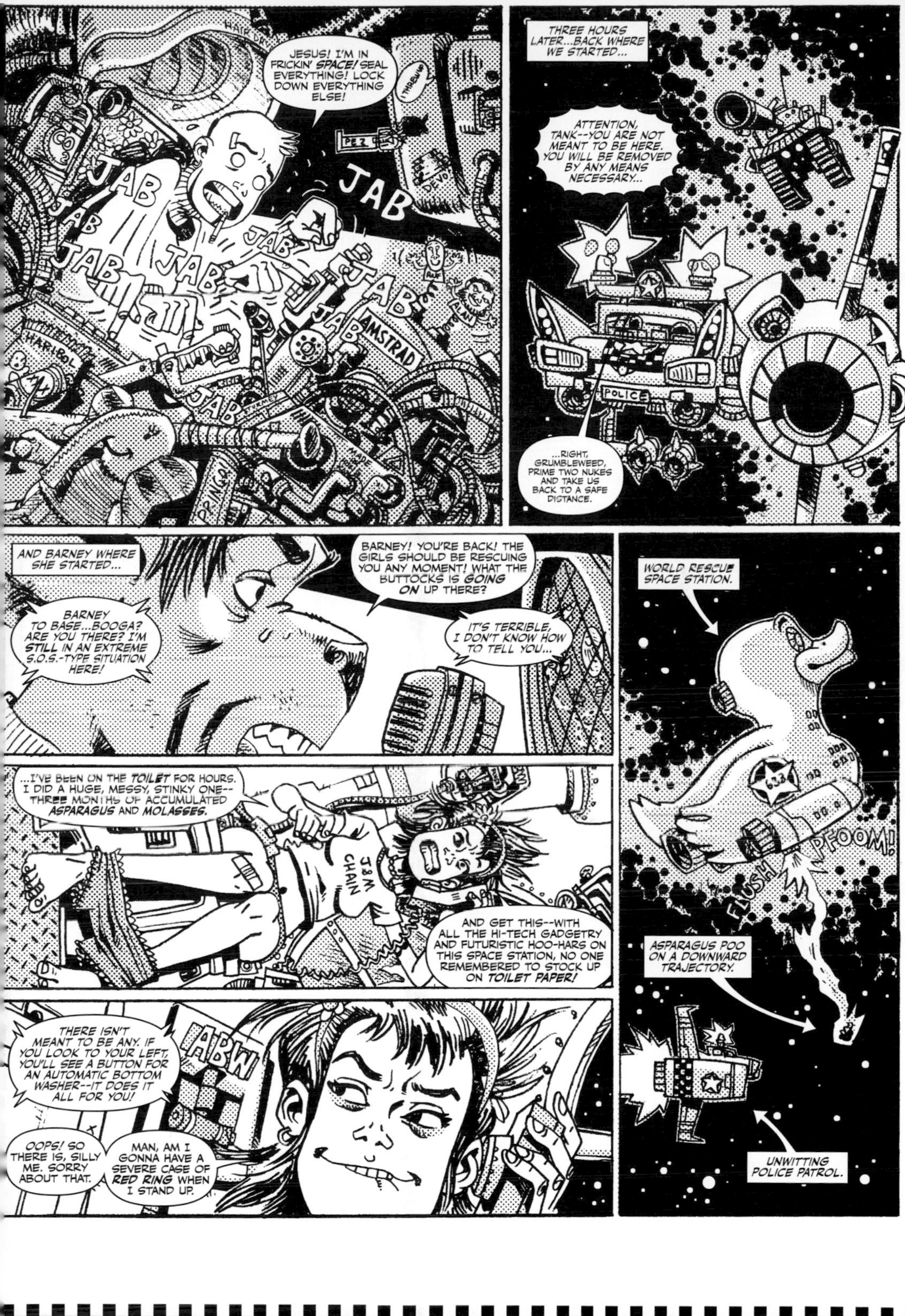
JESUS! I'M IN FRICKIN' *SPACE!* SEAL EVERYTHING! LOCK DOWN EVERYTHING ELSE!
JAB
JAB JAB JAB JAB JAB JAB JAB JAB JAB
AMSTRAD
HARIBO
DEVO
PEZ
THREE HOURS LATER...BACK WHERE WE STARTED...
ATTENTION, TANK--YOU ARE NOT MEANT TO BE HERE. YOU WILL BE REMOVED BY ANY MEANS NECESSARY...
POLICE
...RIGHT, GRUMBLEWEED, PRIME TWO NUKES AND TAKE US BACK TO A SAFE DISTANCE.
AND BARNEY WHERE SHE STARTED...
BARNEY TO BASE...BOOGA? ARE YOU THERE? I'M *STILL* IN AN EXTREME S.O.S.-TYPE SITUATION HERE!
BARNEY! YOU'RE BACK! THE GIRLS SHOULD BE RESCUING YOU ANY MOMENT! WHAT THE BUTTOCKS IS *GOING ON* UP THERE?
IT'S TERRIBLE, I DON'T KNOW HOW TO TELL YOU...
...I'VE BEEN ON THE *TOILET* FOR HOURS. I DID A HUGE, MESSY, STINKY ONE--THREE MONTHS OF ACCUMULATED *ASPARAGUS* AND *MOLASSES.*
J&M CHAIN
AND GET THIS--WITH ALL THE HI-TECH GADGETRY AND FUTURISTIC HOO-HARS ON THIS SPACE STATION, NO ONE REMEMBERED TO STOCK UP ON *TOILET PAPER!*
THERE ISN'T MEANT TO BE ANY. IF YOU LOOK TO YOUR LEFT, YOU'LL SEE A BUTTON FOR AN AUTOMATIC BOTTOM WASHER--IT DOES IT ALL FOR YOU!
ABW
OOPS! SO THERE IS, SILLY ME. SORRY ABOUT THAT.
MAN, AM I GONNA HAVE A SEVERE CASE OF *RED RING* WHEN I STAND UP.
WORLD RESCUE SPACE STATION.
FLUSH
PFOOM!
ASPARAGUS POO ON A DOWNWARD TRAJECTORY.
UNWITTING POLICE PATROL.

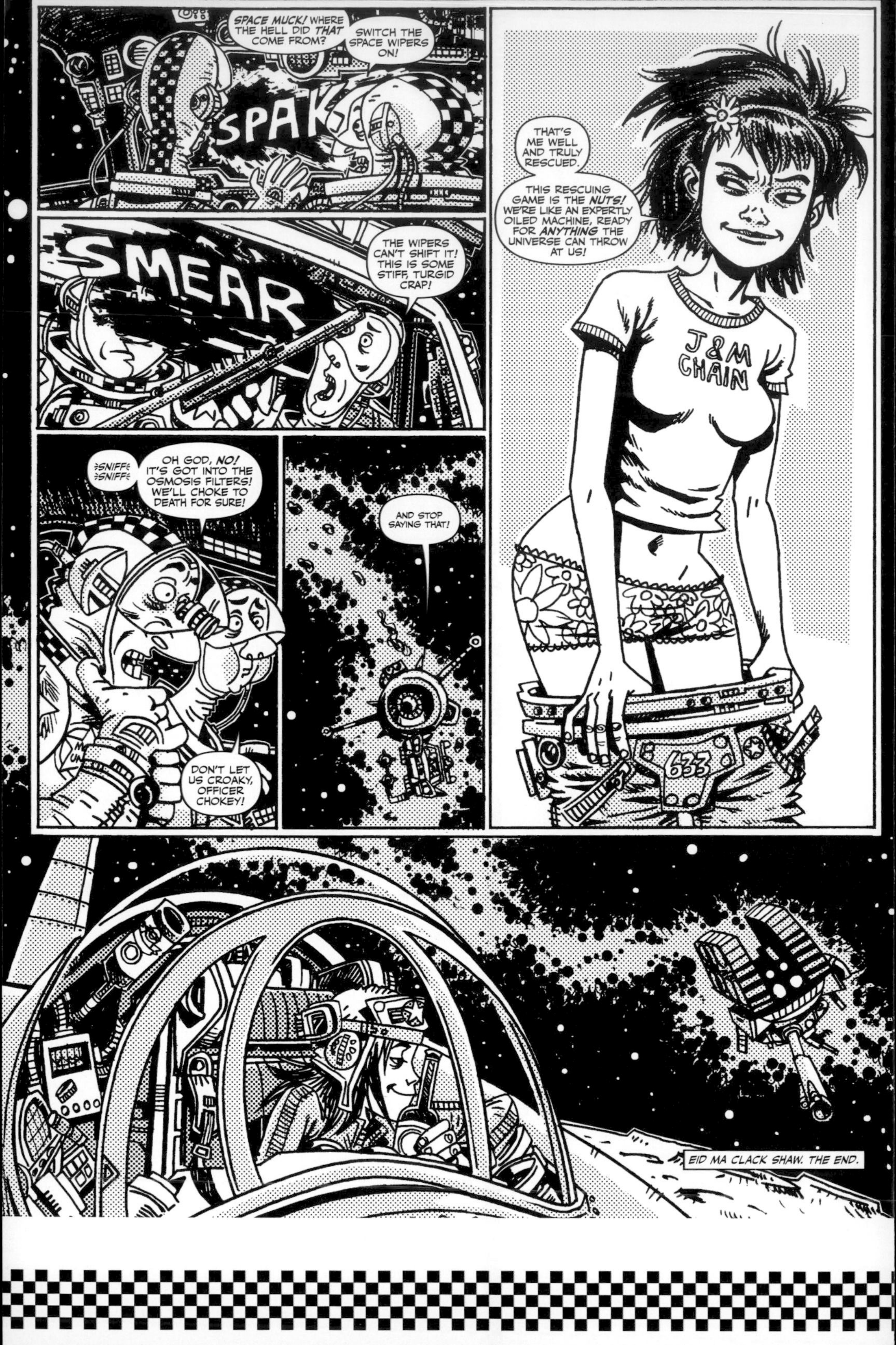
SPACE MUCK! WHERE THE HELL DID THAT COME FROM?
SWITCH THE SPACE WIPERS ON!
SPAK
SMEAR
THE WIPERS CAN'T SHIFT IT! THIS IS SOME STIFF, TURGID CRAP!
SNIFF SNIFF
OH GOD, NO! IT'S GOT INTO THE OSMOSIS FILTERS! WE'LL CHOKE TO DEATH FOR SURE!
DON'T LET US CROAKY, OFFICER CHOKEY!
AND STOP SAYING THAT!
THAT'S ME WELL AND TRULY RESCUED.
THIS RESCUING GAME IS THE NUTS! WE'RE LIKE AN EXPERTLY OILED MACHINE, READY FOR ANYTHING THE UNIVERSE CAN THROW AT US!
J&M CHAIN
EID MA CLACK SHAW. THE END.

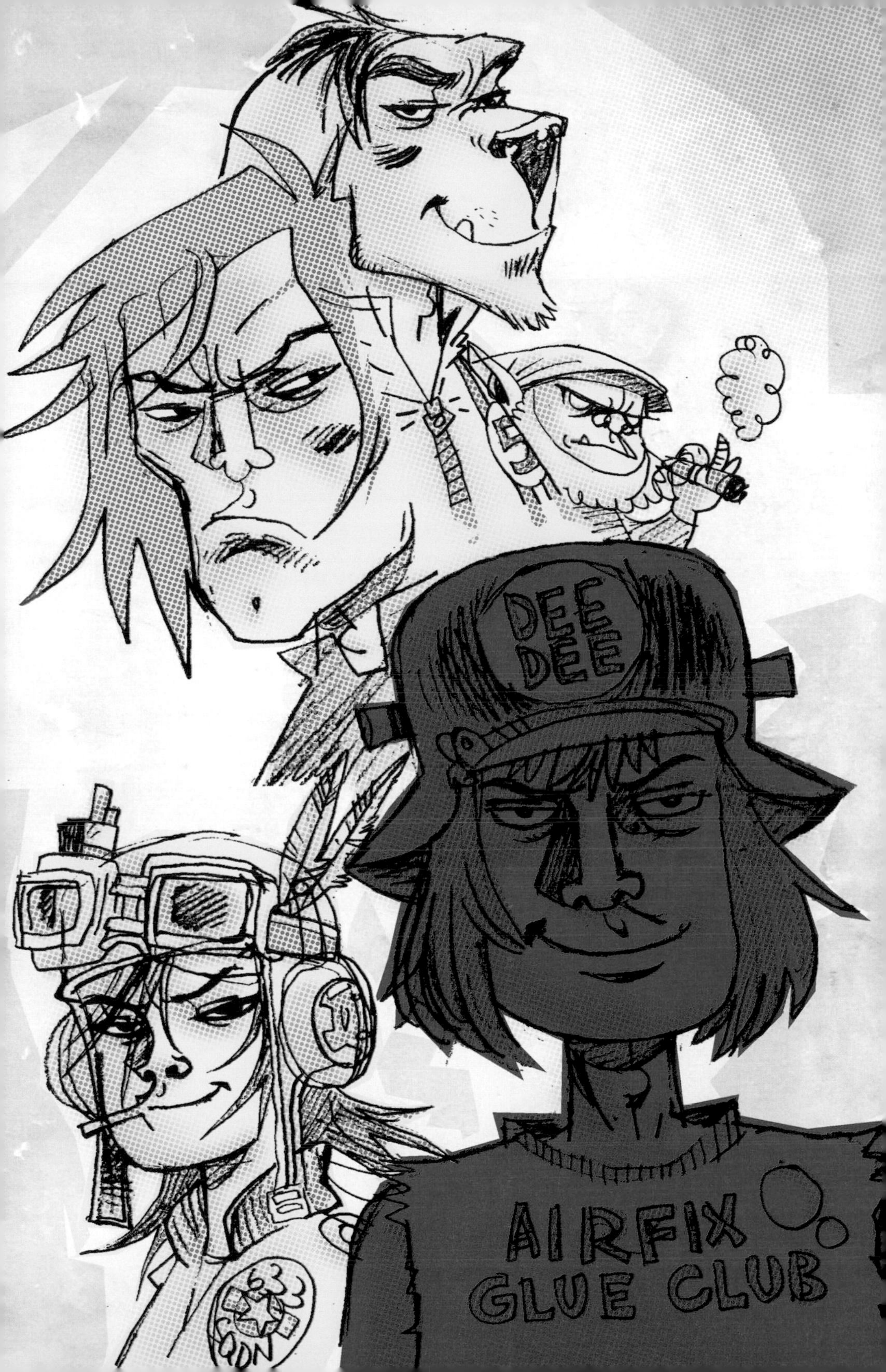
DEE DEE
AIRFIX
GLUE CLUB

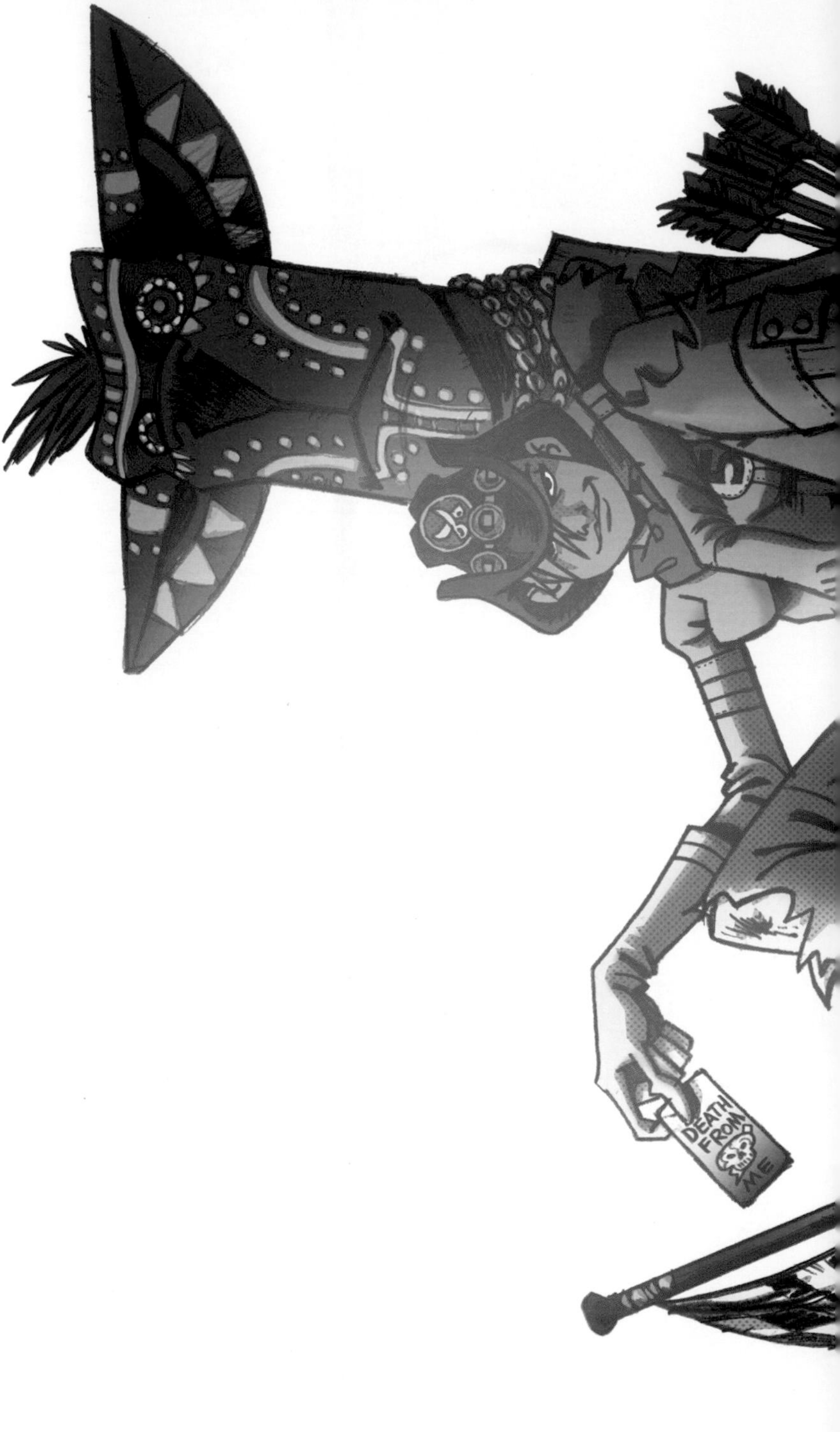
DEATH FROM ME

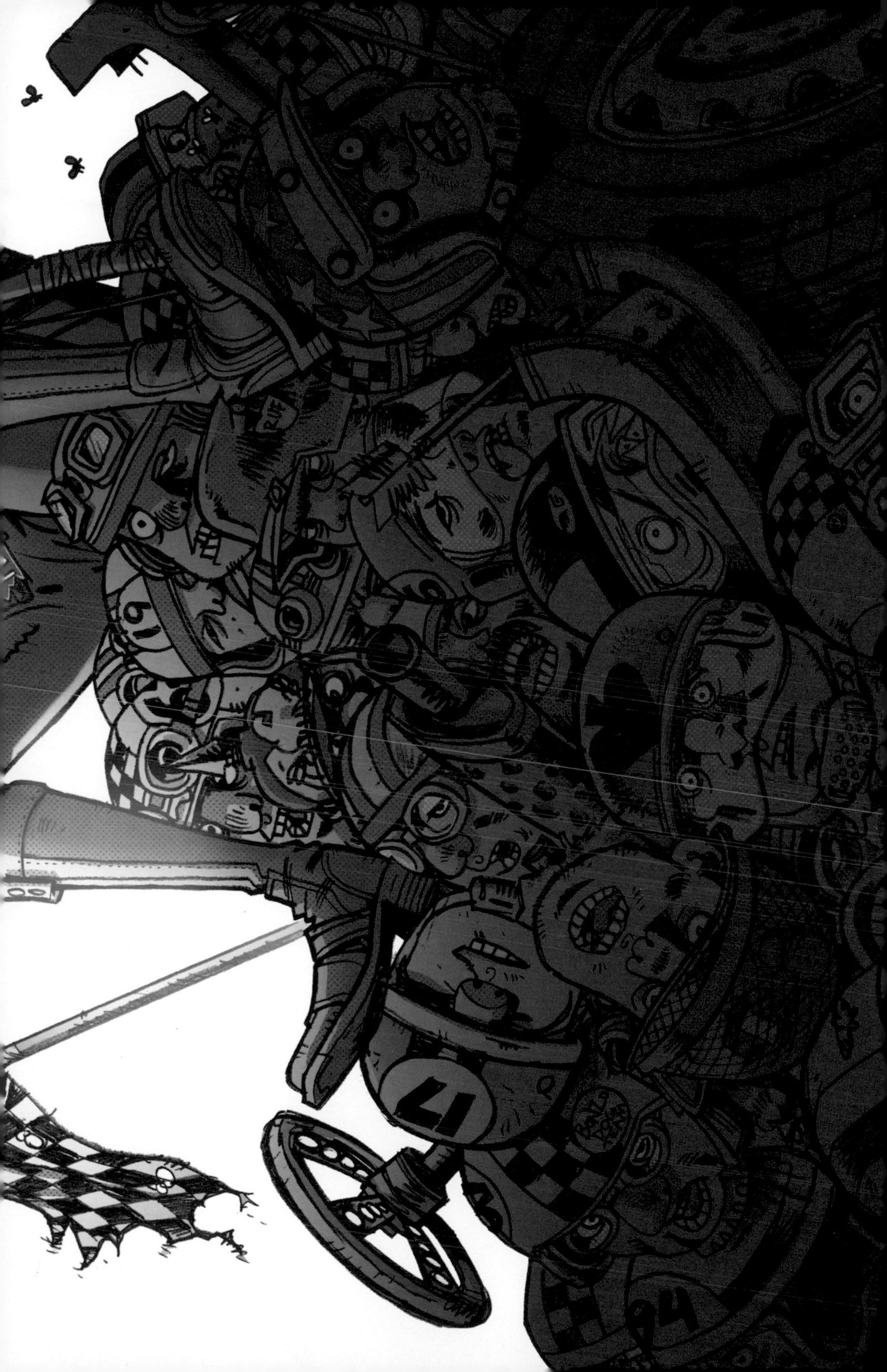

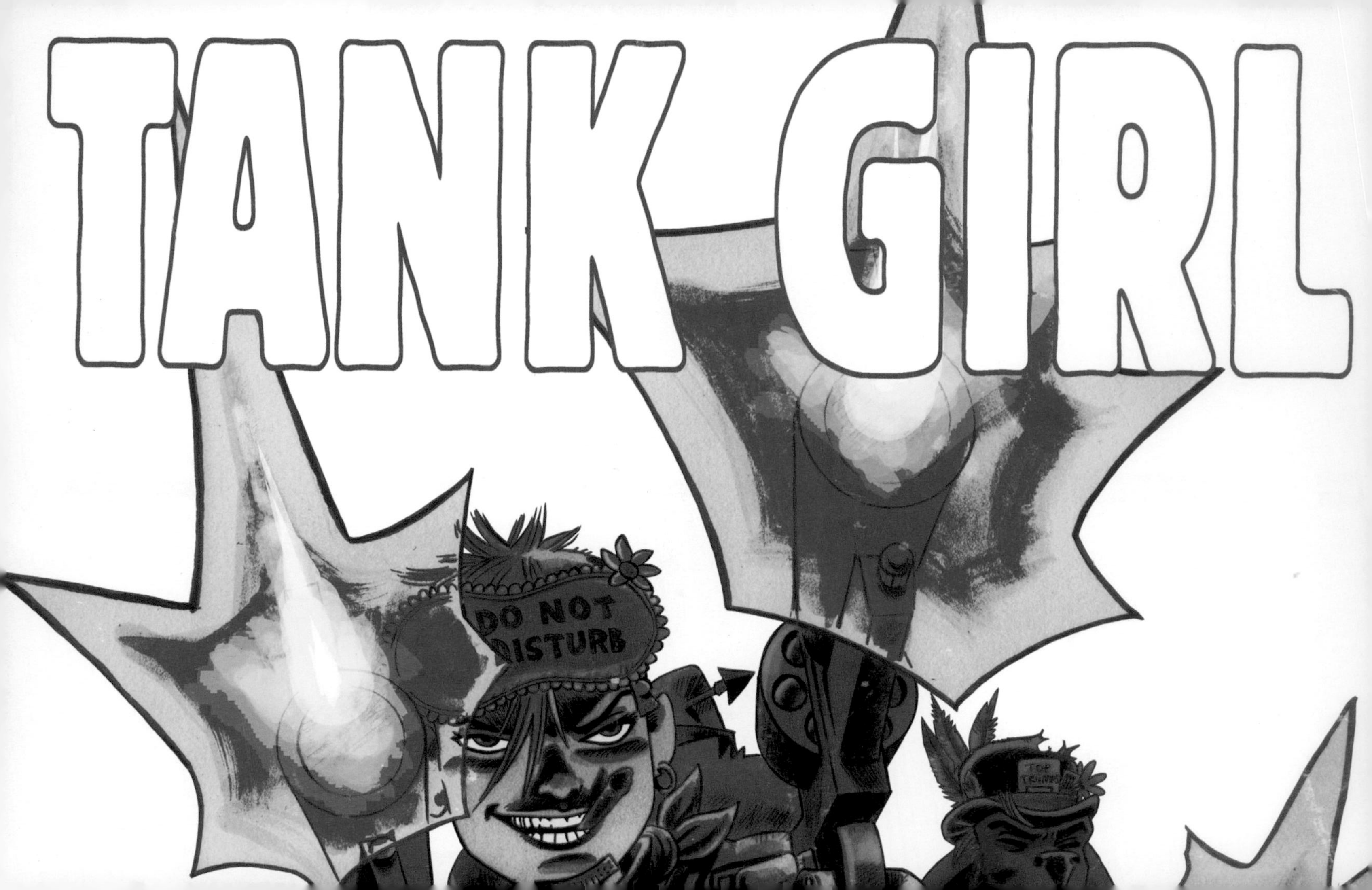
TANK GIRL
DO NOT DISTURB
TOP TRUMPS

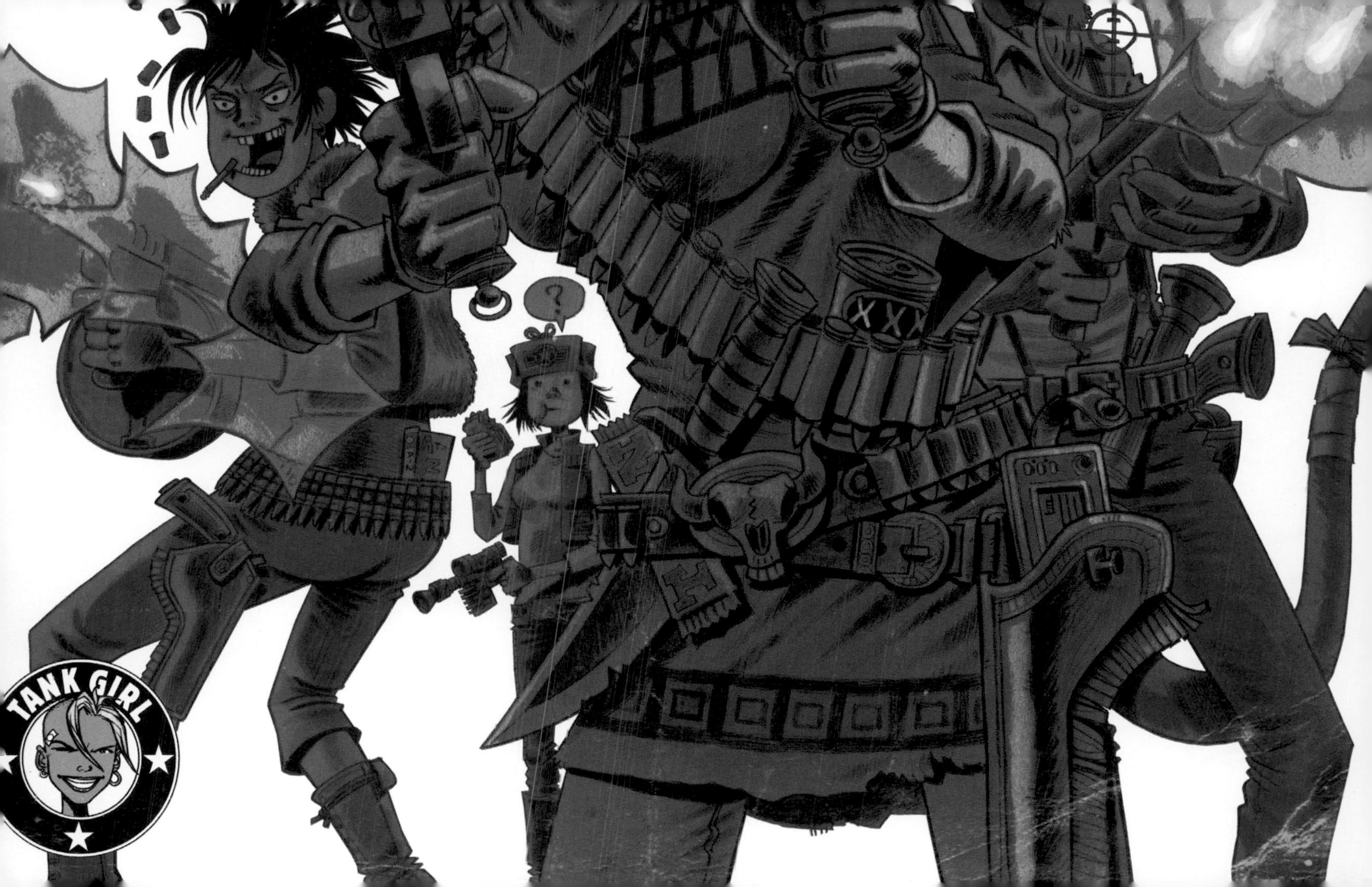
TANK GIRL

TANK★GIRL
COLLECTIONS

Martin and Parson present
The Wonderful World of Tank Girl

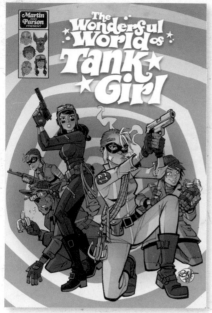

THE WONDERFUL WORLD OF TANK GIRL
ISBN: 9781785862076
Hardcover • $22.99

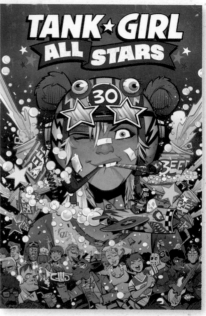

TANK★GIRL
ALL STARS
30

TANK GIRL ALL STARS
ISBN: 9781785864803
Hardcover • $29.99

TANK★GIRL
COLORING BOOK

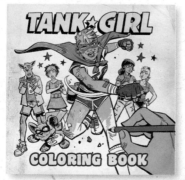

TANK GIRL COLOURING BOOK
ISBN: 9781785867514
Softcover • $14.99

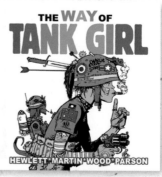

THE WAY OF
TANK GIRL
HEWLETT·MARTIN·WOOD·PARSON

THE WAY OF TANK GIRL
ISBN: 9781785864636
Hardcover • $14.99

AVAILABLE IN ALL GOOD COMIC AND BOOK STORES

FEATURING
**TWO GIRLS
ONE TANK,
GOLD, AND
WORLD WAR
TANK GIRL**

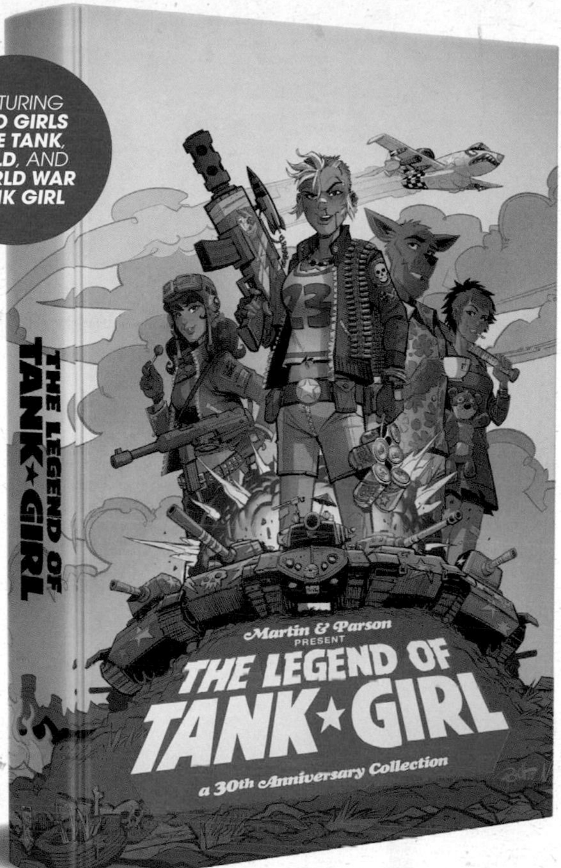
THE LEGEND OF TANK★GIRL
Martin & Parson
PRESENT
THE LEGEND OF
TANK★GIRL
a 30th Anniversary Collection

THE LEGEND OF TANK GIRL
ISBN: 9781785864643
Hardcover • $49.99

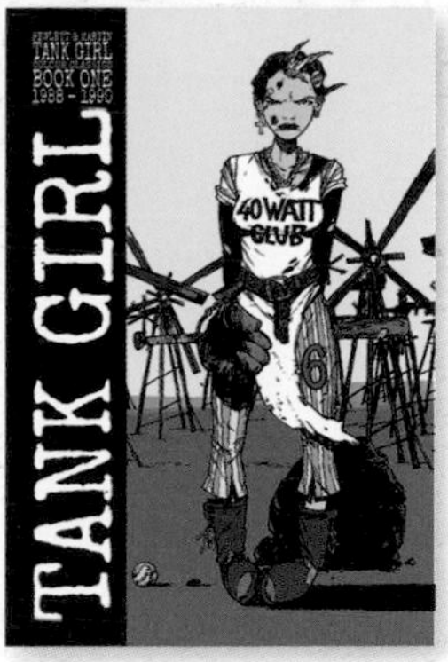
TANK GIRL
BOOK ONE
40 WATT CLUB

TANK GIRL COLOUR
CLASSICS VOL. 1
ISBN: 9781785866753
Hardcover • $24.99

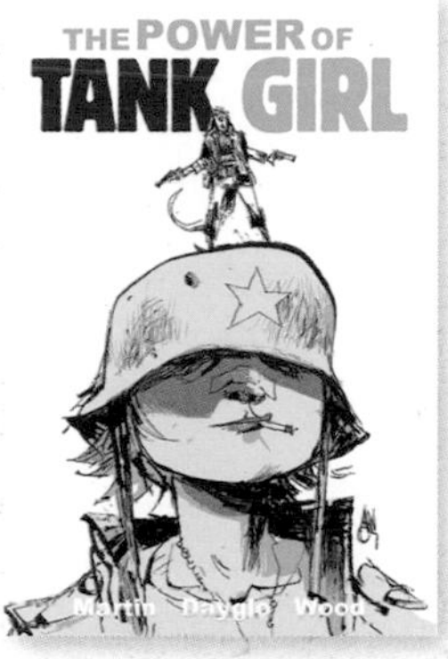
THE POWER OF
TANK GIRL
Martin Dayglo Wood

THE POWER OF
TANK GIRL OMNIBUS
ISBN: 9781782760641
Softcover • $24.99

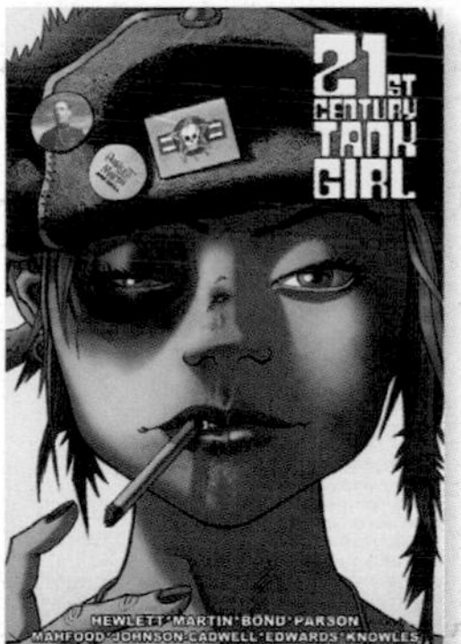
21ST CENTURY TANK GIRL
HEWLETT MARTIN BOND PARSON
MAHFOOD JOHNSON CADWELL EDWARDS KNOWLES

TANK GIRL:
21ST CENTURY TANK GIRL
ISBN: 9781782766612
Hardcover • $22.99

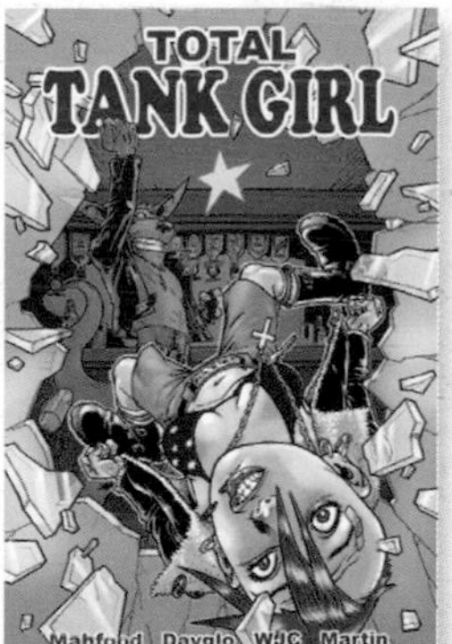
TOTAL
TANK GIRL
Mahfood Dayglo WJC Martin

TOTAL TANK GIRL
OMNIBUS
ISBN: 9781785863059
Softcover • $24.99

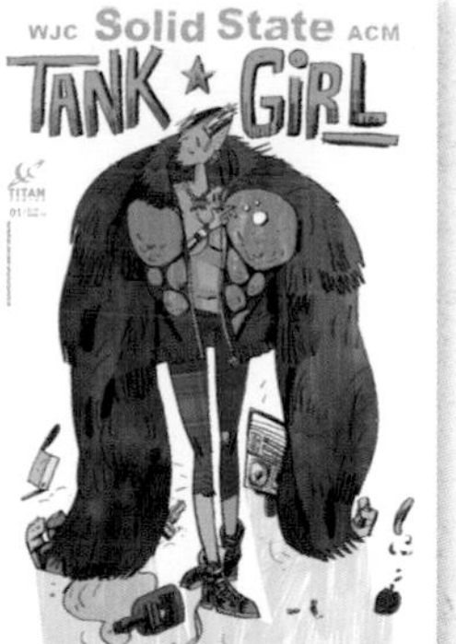
WJC Solid State ACM
TANK★GIRL
TITAN

TANK GIRL:
SOLID STATE TANK GIRL
ISBN: 9781782760030
Hardcover • $19.99

WWW.TITAN-COMICS.COM

TITAN COMICS

McMAHON & MARTIN

TANK GIRL

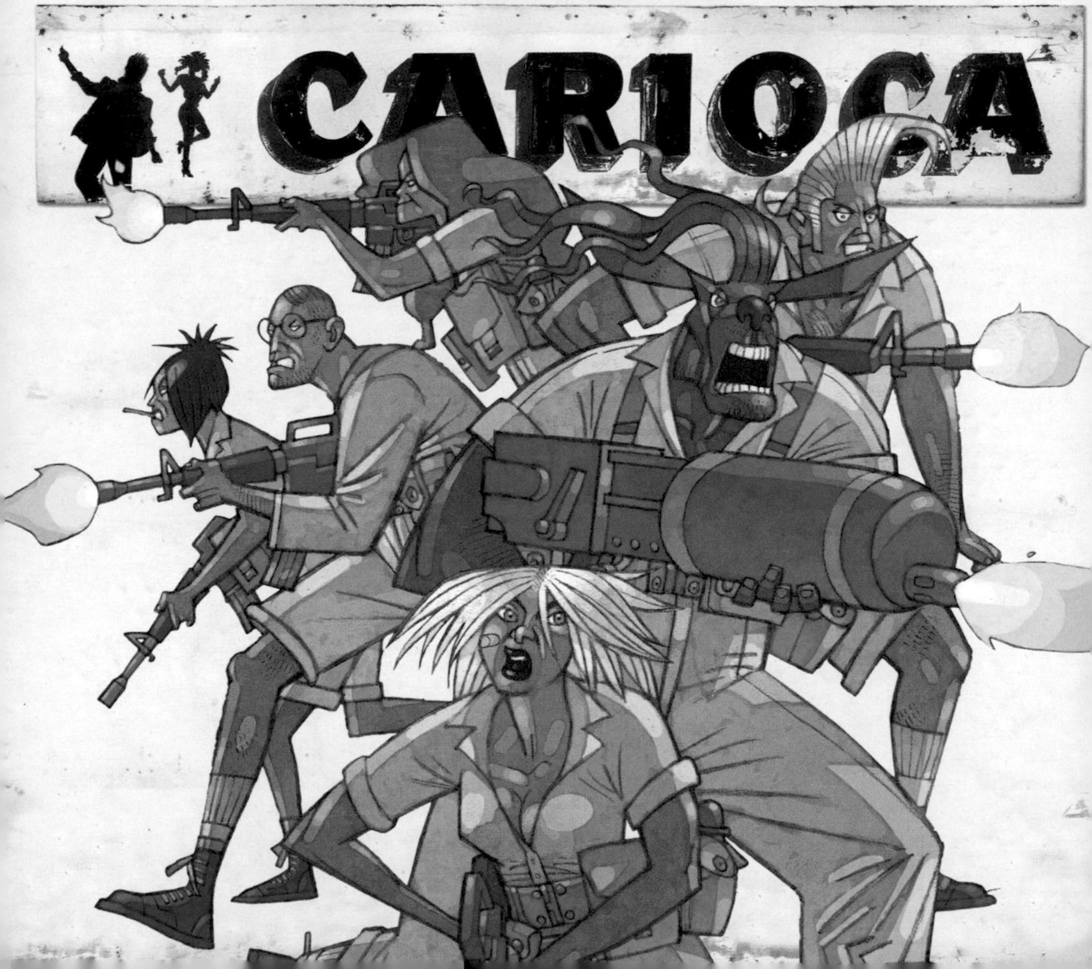
CARIOCA